WINE IN AMERICA

ASPEN SELECT SERIES

WINE IN AMERICA: LAW AND POLICY

Second Edition

Richard Mendelson
Director, Program on Wine Law and Policy
University of California at Berkeley

ASPEN PUBLISHING

To contact Customer Service, e-mail customer.service@aspenpublishing.com, call 1-800-950-5259, or mail correspondence to:

Aspen Publishing
Attn: Order Department
PO Box 990
Frederick, MD 21705

Printed in the United States of America.

1 2 3 4 5 6 7 8 9 0

ISBN 978-1-5438-5955-3

Front cover image: *La Vigne*, a steel sculpture by Richard Mendelson, 2000;
Photograph by Kurt-Inge Eklund, 2010.

SUSTAINABLE FORESTRY INITIATIVE Certified Sourcing
www.forests.org
SFI-00756

About Aspen Publishing

Aspen Publishing is a leading provider of educational content and digital learning solutions to law schools in the U.S. and around the world. Aspen provides best-in-class solutions for legal education through authoritative textbooks, written by renowned authors, and breakthrough products such as Connected eBooks, Connected Quizzing, and PracticePerfect.

The Aspen Casebook Series (famously known among law faculty and students as the "red and black" casebooks) encompasses hundreds of highly regarded textbooks in more than eighty disciplines, from large enrollment courses, such as Torts and Contracts to emerging electives such as Sustainability and the Law of Policing. Study aids such as the *Examples & Explanations* and the *Emanuel Law Outlines* series, both highly popular collections, help law students master complex subject matter.

Major products, programs, and initiatives include:

- **Connected eBooks** are enhanced digital textbooks and study aids that come with a suite of online content and learning tools designed to maximize student success. Designed in collaboration with hundreds of faculty and students, the Connected eBook is a significant leap forward in the legal education learning tools available to students.
- **Connected Quizzing** is an easy-to-use formative assessment tool that tests law students' understanding and provides timely feedback to improve learning outcomes. Delivered through CasebookConnect.com, the learning platform already used by students to access their Aspen casebooks, Connected Quizzing is simple to implement and integrates seamlessly with law school course curricula.
- **PracticePerfect** is a visually engaging, interactive study aid to explain commonly encountered legal doctrines through easy-to-understand animated videos, illustrative examples, and numerous practice questions. Developed by a team of experts, PracticePerfect is the ideal study companion for today's law students.
- The **Aspen Learning Library** enables law schools to provide their students with access to the most popular study aids on the market across all of their courses. Available through an annual subscription, the online library consists of study aids in e-book, audio, and video formats with full text search, note-taking, and highlighting capabilities.
- Aspen's **Digital Bookshelf** is an institutional-level online education bookshelf, consolidating everything students and professors need to ensure success. This program ensures that every student has access to affordable course materials from day one.
- **Leading Edge** is a community centered on thinking differently about legal education and putting those thoughts into actionable strategies. At the core of the program is the Leading Edge Conference, an annual gathering of legal education thought leaders looking to pool ideas and identify promising directions of exploration.

SUMMARY OF CONTENTS

CONTENTS

AUTHORS

Jason Barker is a partner in the Portland, Oregon office of Holland & Knight LLP. His multidisciplinary practice converges at the intersection of regulatory law and complex corporate transactions. In the beverage alcohol industry, he represents domestic and international brand owners (including distilleries, breweries, and wineries) and wholesalers on regulatory, corporate, and brand acquisition matters throughout the country. He also advises cannabis brand owners, including family office, private equity, and hedge fund investors, regarding threshold legalities and risks of cannabis investments, operations and strategic joint ventures within adult use, medical, and CBD markets. Mr. Barker is an adjunct professor at the University of Miami School of Law where he teaches upper-level law school courses regarding beverage alcohol and cannabis regulatory law. He is an associate member of the Oregon Brewer's Guild and the National Conference of State Liquor Administrators.

Carrie Bonnington, leader of Pillsbury's Wine, Beer & Spirits law practice and co-leader of the Restaurant, Food & Beverage Industry Team, is recognized in Chambers USA for her mastery of alcohol beverage laws and regulations. Highly regarded for her extensive alcohol beverage industry knowledge, Carrie represents wineries, breweries, distilleries, importers, distributors, retailers (on- and off-sale), and third-party providers in regulatory, transactional, and litigation matters. She advises on advertising, promotional, marketing, and other trade practice and tied-house issues. Carrie represents licensees in state alcohol beverage regulatory administrative proceedings and trials and structures multifaceted deals relating to production, distribution, acquisitions, sponsorships, marketing, and other similar matters.

Emily Harris Gant is a shareholder at Foster Garvey PC, where she is the chair of the firm's Commercial, IP, & Tech Transactions practice. She counsels wineries, breweries, distilleries, restaurants, hotels, and other retailers on liquor licensing, trade practice compliance, distribution issues, contracts, dispute resolution, and other liquor-related matters. She is also the chair of the Cannabis Practice, where she advises licensed producers, processors, retailers, and ancillary service providers. Like alcohol, cannabis is a highly regulated industry. Emily helps clients structure their business entities, contracts, and strategic partnerships to ensure compliance with each state's complex regulatory scheme.

Tracy Genesen is the vice president and general counsel of the Wine Institute, the public policy advocacy association representing over a thousand California wineries and affiliated businesses responsible for 85 percent of the nation's wine production and more than 90 percent of U.S. wine exports. Tracy is a seasoned beverage alcohol attorney who specializes in licensing, federal and state regulations, franchise laws, and distribution agreements. In addition, she has advised beverage alcohol companies on sales, marketing, and digital advertising platforms, including contests, promotions, and sweepstakes. Tracy has represented clients before federal agencies such as the Tax and Trade Bureau and the Federal Trade Commission and testified before the House Judiciary Committee on behalf of the wine industry. Prior to her appointment at Wine Institute, Tracy currently served as General Counsel to Edrington Americas, the North American arm of a Scotland-based distilled spirits manufacturer. Formerly a partner in two major law firms with a specialized wine, beer, and spirits practice, Genesen directed a variety of complex multi-district federal court litigations that focused on constitutional law matters and challenges to state alcohol regulatory statutes. She helped create and implement the American wine industry's litigation strategy for the landmark U.S. Supreme Court case of *Granholm v. Heald*, regarding direct-to-consumer shipping.

Scott Gerien is a director of Dickenson, Peatman & Fogarty in Napa, California, where he heads the firm's Intellectual Property department. Since his first case in 1996, *Kendall Jackson v. Gallo*, Scott has represented hundreds of wineries in intellectual property matters. Scott is very active with the International Trademark Association (INTA) and helped author the INTA Proposal for a Multilateral Register for Geographical Indications for Wines and Spirits. He is also a board member of the International Wine Law Association. In 2006, 2007, and 2009, Scott was identified by *Trademark Insider* as one of the top 50 trademark attorneys in the United States, and in 2009 *Wine Industry Business Journal* named him one of the top wine lawyers in Northern California and described him as "one of the most knowledgeable wine trademark-protection attorneys in the nation and the world." Trinity College, B.A., 1990; University of California Berkeley Law, J.D., 1996.

Katie Jackson is a second-generation proprietor and senior vice president of Corporate Social Responsibility at Jackson Family Wines, a position that is equal parts sustainability and advocacy. As the Jackson family's principal voice in promoting sustainable agriculture programs, Katie ensures that the family's vineyards throughout California and Oregon are certified sustainable. In 2016, Katie launched the U.S. wine industry's most comprehensive sustainability goals, which enabled the company to become the largest generator of onsite solar energy in the U.S. wine industry, reduce absolute greenhouse gas emissions by 17.8 percent, and help cofound International Wineries for Climate Action (IWCA) with Familia Torres of Spain in 2019. Today, Katie spearheads Rooted for Good: Roadmap to 2030, the most ambitious sustainability and environmental stewardship initiative in the company's 40-year history. Additionally, Katie co-manages the Government Relations and External Affairs Department, working on critical regulatory relations issues, and directs charitable donations for the company's community outreach program.

Erin Kelleher is a partner with Hinman & Carmichael LLP in San Francisco, where she specializes in licensing matters and transactions involving alcohol beverage licensees. Additionally, Ms. Kelleher has extensive knowledge of the laws related to the sale, distribution, and marketing of alcoholic beverages, the federal and state tied-house laws, and expertise with regulatory qualification requirements applicable to investors in alcohol beverage licensees. Ms. Kelleher has participated as a guest lecturer at Sonoma State University on wine regulatory topics and is an active member of numerous trade associations. Ms. Kelleher provides pro bono legal services to the industry and is licensed to practice in California and New York.

Carol Kingery Ritter is a partner with Dickenson, Peatman & Fogarty in Napa. She practices in the firm's business and real property practice groups. Carol specializes in complex vineyard, winery, and wine business sales and acquisitions, including the formation and restructuring of business entities to acquire assets or launch new businesses and the investigation of complicated real property and title issues. Carol's practice also includes general corporate formation, compliance and restructuring, and business contracts, with an emphasis on serving wine industry businesses. Carol has specific expertise in the preparation and negotiation of essential wine business contracts such as grape purchase agreements, vineyard leases, and vineyard redevelopment agreements. Carol also advises clients on the formation of American Viticultural Areas through TTB.

Erik Lawrence is a partner at GVM Law LLP in Napa. His practice focuses on business and real estate transactional law, specializing in servicing clients in all areas of the beverage alcohol industry. Prior to his legal career, he was an associate vice president in Wells Fargo's Commercial Banking Group. He received a Bachelor of Science degree in Managerial Economics from the University of California Davis in 1997 and a Juris Doctor degree from the University of California Davis School of Law in 2007, where he was managing editor of the *UC Davis Law Review* and a member of the Order of the Coif.

Justin McGuirk is senior counsel at Wine Institute, the premier public policy advocacy association of California wineries and the only U.S. organization advocating for wine at the state, federal, and international levels. Prior to joining Wine Institute, Justin was a senior associate at the law firm Reed Smith LLP, in its San Francisco office, where he represented and counseled wineries and other companies in a wide range of negotiations, litigation, and appeals. He has published articles on legal issues affecting the alcohol beverage industry and was a research assistant for Richard Mendelson on his book *Appellation Napa Valley: Building and Protecting an American Treasure*. Justin is a graduate of U.C. Berkeley Law (J.D.), where he has also lectured on wine and law, and Georgia State University (B.S., Public Policy).

Richard Mendelson is of counsel to the law firm of Dickenson, Peatman & Fogarty in Napa, California, where he has practiced wine law since 1986. He is past president and current director of the International Wine Law Association, headquartered in Paris. He also founded and directed the Program on Wine Law and Policy at the University of California, Berkeley, School of Law. He has taught wine law at numerous law and business schools at home and abroad. Mendelson is the author of *From Demon to Darling: A Legal History of Wine in America* (University of California Press 2009), which was awarded the Grand Prize in Economy and Law from the International Organization of Vine and Wine; *Spirit in Metal* (Val de Grâce 2011) on his work as a metal sculptor; and *Appellation Napa Valley: Building and Protecting an American Treasure* (Val de Grâce 2016), which was awarded the Grand Prize in Economy and Law from the International Organization of Vine and Wine and Best in the U.S. Award for Food and Wine Law from Gourmand International. He owns Premium Wine Properties, a real estate brokerage firm, and Mendelson Wines. Harvard College, B.A, 1975; Oxford University, Magdalen College, M.A., 1977; Stanford Law, J.D., 1982.

Viviann Stapp is executive vice president & general counsel at Jackson Family Wines. As the head of legal affairs and corporate secretary for Jackson Family Wines and its affiliated entities, Viviann is responsible for the management and oversight of all legal, corporate governance, and alcohol compliance matters for the Jackson family's wine- and vineyard-related companies. Prior to her tenure at Jackson Family Wines, Viviann was in private practice as a litigator in securities litigation, professional responsibility, and other complex commercial civil litigation matters. Viviann received her B.A. from Yale University in 2001 in Political Science and Studies in the Environment and her J.D. from the University of Chicago Law School in 2004.

James Terry was a director at Dickenson, Peatman & Fogarty since 1995 and is now retired. He represented buyers in numerous vineyard and winery acquisitions throughout California. His wine industry-related practice included alcoholic beverage law, business entity selection and formation, business planning, sales and acquisitions, grape purchase agreements, and vineyard leasing. Jim lectured extensively on wine law subjects in California. His publications include "Grapes to Wine: Business Models and the Regulation of Wine Production," published in the Organisation Internationale de La Vigne et Du Vin's *Le Bulletin de L'OIV* in 2006. University of California Berkeley, A.B., 1972; Santa Clara University School of Law, J.D., 1976; New York University School of Law, LL.M, 1978, where he was awarded the Donald L. Brown Fellowship in Trade Regulation.

Robert Tobiassen is president of the National Association of Beverage Importers (NABI), Washington, D.C., the only nation-wide trade association representing importers of wine, distilled spirits, and beer. Prior to joining NABI, he served as chief counsel of the Alcohol and Tobacco Tax and Trade Bureau, Department of the Treasury, and as associate chief counsel (Alcohol & Tobacco), Bureau of Alcohol, Tobacco, and Firearms. In his 34-year federal career, his portfolio covered alcohol and tobacco excise taxes and regulatory compliance and enforcement, litigation, unfair trade practices, administrative law, legislative drafting and congressional relations, and serving on USTR delegations to the World Trade Organization, World Wine Trade Group, and several wine and spirits negotiations with the European Commission. He was a delegate to the OIV between 1992 and 2000. He received the Presidential Rank Award for Meritorious Service (2003) from President G. W. Bush and the Treasury Secretary's Award for Distinguished Service from Secretary Tim Geithner (2012). He is a graduate of the University of California, Berkeley (B.A. 1975), Lewis and Clark Law School (J.D. 1978), and Georgetown University Law Center (LLM Taxation 1983). He is an active member of the District of Columbia Bar and an inactive member of the California and Oregon State Bars.

John Trinidad is a partner at Dickenson Peatman & Fogarty, where he is part of the firm's Wine Law, Business, Alcohol Beverage, and Geographical Indications practice groups. John advises wine and alcohol beverage industry clients on a broad range of legal issues, including licensing, business contracts, and the purchase and sale of winery brands and assets. John also advises clients on federal and state alcohol beverage regulations such as franchise laws, tied-house laws, labeling requirements, and the protection and promotion of American Viticultural Areas. He has been a lecturer on a variety of wine law issues at the University of California Davis School of Law, Sonoma State University's Executive MBA Program, and the University of California Davis Executive MBA Program. John joined DP&F after working harvest in Burgundy and California, bringing together his interest in the wine industry and his legal background. Prior to that, John worked as a litigator at leading law firms in Washington, D.C. and San Francisco, California. John is a graduate of Harvard College and the New York University School of Law.

FOREWORD

Mike Thompson

As the congressman from Northern California's premier wine growing region, I've been introduced to some of the world's top wine aficionados. They've talked extensively about how wine is more than just a beverage; it's a gateway to a better food experience, to a place's culture, to a vineyard's soil and climate, and to a winery's technique.

When they talk, I nod and smile. I'm truly appreciative of the passion they bring to wine. But when you were born and raised in the Napa Valley, when you are the third generation in the wine community, and when you have done every job in the industry from fixing tractors to washing out barrels to growing grapes, you *know* that wine is so much more.

In my congressional district, which includes the Napa Valley and Sonoma, Lake, Solano, and Contra Costa counties, wine is life. It's an economic backbone, spreading jobs beyond wineries and vineyards to restaurants, retail, and tourism. It's the taxes that pay for our schools and roads. It's the business name on the back of the little league uniforms and the patron of the new hospital wing. It's the farmer who religiously monitors the rain and temperature. It's the winery owner who grew an internationally recognized brand out of a few barrels in her cellar.

For us, great wines are more than just tasting notes. They are a testament to the hardworking people and incredible natural resources that make up our home. But they are also a product of the policies, laws, and regulations that govern how wine is made and sold.

When Richard Mendelson asked me to write the foreword to his comprehensive book on the policy and law behind wine, I saw it as an amazing opportunity to help tell the story of what I taste when I drink a wine from my congressional district—the people, the agriculture, as well as the tax policy, trade laws, and labeling regulations. A book like this goes beyond the wine in the bottle and back through the story of the economic, political, and legal factors that brought the wine into existence. And I believe that once you learn how these factors can be as complex and engaging as a 98 point Napa Valley cabernet, the wine on your palate will taste even better.

That is exactly what drove me to form the Congressional Wine Caucus when I first came to Congress in 1998. Most Members of Congress had no idea of the impact their policy decisions have on wine, but I soon found out they were eager to learn—and taste—more. The Wine Caucus, which today is one of the largest bipartisan and bicameral groups on Capitol Hill, meets regularly to discuss policies pertaining to wine, such as efforts to control agricultural pests, barriers to increasing American wine's presence in the global market, wine's impact on public health, and the implications of climate-related disasters on the wine community. But with those discussions, I also like to introduce my fellow representatives to the people behind the wine, whether it's the independent winemaker, the fifth-generation grape grower, or even the sommelier at a hip new restaurant. These are the people who bring the policies to life.

Over the years, I've seen congressional interest in wine grow as vineyards have taken root across our country. Now that wine is made in all 50 states, every representative and senator has reason to be invested in the success of American wine. And, like me, they are quickly learning that wine is more than a beverage or even an experience; it's an economic driver and community builder.

As a result, these Members of Congress have joined the people from my district, who know wine is not just a matter of what tastes good and what doesn't. They've seen how laws, policies, and court decisions such as the ones discussed in this book make a big difference in whether the wines from their congressional districts succeed or not. An issue they grappled with was a proposal in Congress to increase the federal excise tax on wine by a massive amount. Most people know intrinsically that an increase in the excise tax means higher prices on the wine shelves. But what members of the Congressional Wine Caucus discussed were the thousands of winery and vineyard jobs that would be lost as a result of the increase. We also talked about the vineyards that would be eaten up by development when the price of the excise tax eclipsed the value of the grapes. Fortunately, we were able to point out the consequences of the legislation for jobs and our agricultural lands, and the proposal was defeated.

But this example is exactly why the stories behind wine—the jobs, the land, and the communities—are so important to understand. Since Prohibition, an arcane and idiosyncratic maze of policies and laws has been erected around wine, to the point that most people who consider themselves oenophiles know very little about, and have been given few opportunities to understand, such critical elements of the wines they love to drink. The complex subject matters involved, such as constitutional law, intellectual property, taxation, international trade, and climate change, are often addressed by people far removed from the wineries and vineyards. Yet to someone like me or my neighbors at home, these subject matters are at the very center of American wine. And we know that the disconnect between people's understanding of wine and the policies and laws that govern it is a real threat to our way of life.

That is what makes this book—the first of its kind in America—such a critical read. Written by experienced wine law attorneys Richard Mendelson and colleagues, it provides valuable information and insights into the laws and policies that make American wine what it is. This book should be studied by any American student, scholar, government regulator, or policymaker who wants to truly understand wine.

Examples of why this book is so important are abundant. With complex policy decisions that are incredibly important to the future of American wine, there is a need for a deep understanding of wine policy and law, one that few have. Richard Mendelson's book is exactly the place to begin for those who want to quickly gain this understanding without having to immerse themselves in tens of thousands of pages of legal text.

As our wine community continues to recover from recent devastating wildfires and drought, our way of life in California and in districts across the country is threatened by the climate crisis. Lawmakers in Washington are at the table to set the climate policies that will protect America's proud tradition of world-class wine, and if we are to maintain that tradition, the moment demands action.

For most wine drinkers, taste is all that matters. And for those of us who are involved in making wine, that's fine by us. But anyone who wants to know the story behind the wine needs to look at the people, the land, the history, and the laws and policies that brought the wine to your table. This book is where to start.

Mike Thompson
Member of Congress and
Co-chair, Congressional Wine Caucus
November 2022

INTRODUCTION AND ACKNOWLEDGMENTS

What is wine law? Technically, it is a branch of administrative law concerning the regulation of wine, as a subset of alcoholic beverages. But this definition is altogether too narrow. In my wine law practice, spanning more than 35 years, I have handled a wide variety of legal matters of vital interest to the wine industry in areas such as land use, intellectual property, international trade, torts, specialized contracts (distributor agreements, grape purchase and sale agreements, vineyard leases), environmental law, tax law, constitutional law, and administrative law.

This being what I learned, this also is what I have taught. The Wine Law class at the University of California, Berkeley, School of Law ("Berkeley Law") is essentially a survey class covering diverse legal fields, all focused on wine. We also address important wine policy issues such as public health, climate change, agricultural preservation, and international trade policy. For embracing such a wide vision of wine law and allowing me to teach at their universities, I thank Berkeley Law and Pam Samuelson in particular, the University of Aix-Marseille Law Faculty (Jacques Audier), the University of Bordeaux Law Faculty (Dominique Denis, Antoine Vialard, and Jean-Marc Bahans), the University of Reims Law Faculty (Theodore Georgopoulos), and the University of California, Davis, School of Management (Bob Smiley).

Wine law is arcane and often counter-intuitive. Without an understanding of the history of temperance and Prohibition in our country, one cannot begin to comprehend the spirit or the letter of wine law. This is why I wrote my first book, *From Demon to Darling: A Legal History of Wine in America* (University of California Press 2009). As that book shows, our laws are deeply rooted in our history, and a firm grasp of that history is essential. For example, were it not for the saloons of the pre-Prohibition and Prohibition eras—those dens of iniquity that infuriated women temperance crusaders—we might not have special laws that prohibit trade practices such as tied-houses, free goods, and consignment sales, practices that are commonplace in other industries. And if we had not begun in the 1830s to devolve control over alcoholic beverages to local communities, we might not have local option elections on the sale and service of alcoholic beverages across the United States today.

Despite these deep historical roots, wine law is evolving rapidly as the wine industry expands at home and abroad. Nowhere is this more evident than in the area of Twenty-first Amendment jurisprudence, particularly in relation to direct-to-consumer interstate shipments of wine and intellectual property, where wine brands and appellations of origin are important focal points in the ongoing discussion at the World Trade Organization about geographical indications. I have long been fascinated by geographical indications, from my early days working for a Burgundy négociant, explaining the French appellation system to our customers, to my later work representing vintner-grower groups and the Napa Valley Vintners, the trade association of Napa Valley wineries, in establishing and protecting Napa Valley's appellations. I captured this history in *Appellation Napa Valley: Building and Protecting an American Treasure* (Val de Grâce 2016).

Wine law is idiosyncratic, as anyone who has dealt with the subject quickly realizes. It is a world unto itself, with its own constitutional provisions (intoxicating liquors are the subject of not just one, but two, constitutional amendments—the Eighteenth and the Twenty-first), its own language (tied-house, primary source, semi-generics, to name a few), and its own regulators at the state, federal, and sometimes local levels.

Finally, wine law is fun, in large part because wine itself is fun. My Berkeley Law students always look forward to our class wine tasting, which focuses on appellations of origin. Are appellations meaningful to consumers? Can consumers tell the difference between wines made from grapes grown in distinct appellations? The only way to know is to taste the product.

This book follows the general outline of my Wine Law class at Berkeley Law. We begin with an overview of the subject, followed by individual chapters on wine industry trade practices (Carrie Bonnington), wine labeling and advertising (John Trinidad), business models for grape growing and winemaking (Jim Terry and Erik Lawrence), Twenty-first Amendment jurisprudence (Tracy Genesen and Justin McGuirk), intellectual property involving wine brands and wine appellations (Scott Gerien and me), land use in the context of rural wineries and urban bars (Erin Kelleher and me), climate change effects and related mitigation, adaptation, and prevention (Katie Jackson, Carol Kingery Ritter, and Viviann Stapp), public health and social responsibility (Allyson Malecha and me), and international trade (Rob Tobiassen). I also have included in the second edition a new chapter by Jason Barker, Emily Gant, and me on the evolution of cannabis law, entitled Should We Regulate Cannabis Like Alcohol? My co-authors include my fellow teachers at Berkeley Law, Carrie Bonnington, Tracy Genesen, and John Trinidad, and other colleagues and friends. I have the utmost confidence in their abilities and their experience. I thank them all for their valuable contributions.

Finally, I thank my students, past and present, for their questions, opinions, and feedback; Berkeley Law student Allyson Malecha for her research and editorial assistance; the very capable Dean Rowan at the Berkeley Law Library; and my wife, Marilyn, for her patience and support and for sharing with me a love of wine and culture.

Richard Mendelson
Napa, California
November 2022

CHAPTER 1

U.S. WINE LAW: AN OVERVIEW

Richard Mendelson

The system of laws controlling the production, marketing, distribution, and sale of wine in the 50 states that comprise the United States is of recent origin compared to its foreign counterparts. This body of law has evolved rapidly from a set of liquor licensing and anti-drunkenness laws in colonial America to the present complex and interrelated set of local, state, and federal regulations that govern all aspects of the wine business.

Section A of this overview presents a brief history of American wine law. Section B discusses the modern-day federal and state wine laws and the regulatory authorities that enforce them. Section C focuses on the various operations and activities that are central to the wine business, beginning with viticulture, then wine production, and finally marketing, distribution, and sales. Many of these topics are addressed in greater detail in other chapters of the book, and those particular chapters are referenced where appropriate.

A. HISTORICAL OVERVIEW

While the first tax on wine in the United States did not appear until 1862,[1] evidence of grape growing and wine production can be traced back to the first European

---

1. In 1862 Congress imposed an internal revenue duty on domestic producers of wine made from grapes that was produced, sold, or removed for consumption in the U.S. Revenue Act of 1862, ch. 119, §75, 12 Stat. 432, 462, 465. No duty was imposed on artificial or imitation wines under that Act. In 1864 Congress expanded the coverage of the duties on internal and imported wine. Regarding imports, the statute imposed a duty on wines of all kinds based on the value of the product; the statute imposed special duty rates on champagne and sparkling wines. Act of June 30, 1864, ch. 171, §2, para. 1, 13 Stat. 202, 203 (increasing duties on imports). By a separate act on the same day, Congress expanded the coverage of the domestic duty on wine products. While the Act continued to impose the same domestic duty on wine made from grapes, it also provided for a duty "[o]n all other wines

settlers who established the American colonies. As civilization brought wine and winemaking to Europe, it did the same for America. Early settlers, however, were unsuccessful in producing quality wine from native grapes. Their efforts to cultivate European vines also failed because of the harsh climate on the east coast, with its excessively cold winters and its high humidity during the growing season.[2]

In the late 1700s, some progress was made in the utilization of native vines. However, it was not until the 1820s, after the introduction of American hybrids,[3] that decent domestic wines began to be produced that did not require fortification (the addition of spirits) or adulteration (the addition of extraneous substances). By the middle of the nineteenth century, winemaking had become an important but relatively small industry in the United States, with Ohio, Missouri, New York, and California leading the way. The consumption of wine was minuscule compared to that of beer and spirits; wine represented only 4 percent of the total volume of alcoholic beverages consumed in the United States in 1869.[4]

Wine could not escape the growing temperance movement in America,[5] despite the fact that temperance advocates targeted, at least initially, "ardent spirits."[6] Spirits, with their higher alcohol levels, were thought to be unhealthy by Dr. Benjamin Rush, a leading physician of the era. By contrast, Dr. Rush regarded

---

or liquors known or denominated as wine, not made from currants, rhubarb or berries produced by being rectified or mixed with other spirits, or into which any matter whatever may be infused to be sold as wine, or by any other name, and not otherwise provided for in this act." Revenue Act of 1864, ch. 173, §94, 13 Stat. 223, 264, 269.

2. Maynard A. Amerine, *American Wine Industry to 1960*, 145 Wine Production Technology in the United States 1, 1 (1981), describes the causes of these failures:

> Some plantings of the European grapes succeeded for a time but sooner or later most died. It was not for lack of care. Or interest. The problems were primarily climatic: excessively cold winters for cold-sensitive *V. vinifera* varieties and high humidity during the growing period. The periodic cold winters partially, and sometimes completely, killed the vines. The humid growing seasons fanned the growth of endemic cryptogamic diseases: downy and powdery mildew, anthracnose, black rot, etc. The death of the vine in the South Atlantic states may have been attributable to Pierce's disease, a bacterial disease that we will later find in California. Fungicides to control mildew, etc. were still far in the future. Finally, in many areas the native root louse, phylloxera, probably destroyed the susceptible *V. vinifera* varieties.

3. Hybrids are the offspring of two different grape species, occurring naturally by cross-pollination or induced by man "to combine in the progeny some of the desirable characteristics of the parents." Oxford Companion to Wine 499-500 (Jancis Robinson ed., Oxford University Press 1994). Many of today's commercial rootstocks are hybrids.

4. S. W. Shear & Gerald G. Pearce, Supply and Price Trends in the California Wine-Grape Industry, table 2 and figure 2 (Giannini Foundation of Agricultural Economics, Mimeographed Report No. 34, 1934). In 2016, wine accounted for 18.1 percent of the total domestic consumption of alcoholic beverages. Hannah Ritchie and Max Roser (2018), "Alcohol Consumption" published online at OurWorldInData.org, https://www.ourworldindata.org/alcohol-consumption (accessed July 11, 2022).

5. The genesis of the temperance movement in the United States is beyond the scope of this chapter. For further details, *see* Richard Mendelson, From Demon to Darling: A Legal History of Wine in America 6-49 (University of California Press 2009).

6. Ardent spirits, now an obsolete term, refers to the fiery taste of spirituous liquors. Liquor is used throughout this section to refer to any alcoholic beverage.

wine as a temperate beverage, reinforcing Minister Increase Mather's statement that "the wine is from God."[7] Gradually the temperance movement, like its members' pledges, became more severe, moving from opposition to spirits to a demand for teetotalism (complete abstinence from all alcoholic beverages).

The reasons for abstinence were numerous: religious dogma, moral concerns, cultural norms, social order, public health and safety, and worker efficiency, to name a few. Not surprisingly, there was and still is no consensus in the United States on what constitutes responsible use of alcohol and its opposite, harmful and hazardous use. The appropriate legal and policy prescriptions therefore have varied widely over time.[8] Thomas Jefferson, for example, envisioned an agrarian society in which domestic wine was cheap and plentiful, and spirits were heavily taxed to dampen demand for them. One hundred years later, Wayne Wheeler, as "boss" of the Anti-Saloon League, cleverly combined the forces of business and the church to pressure Congress to enact, and the states to ratify, National Prohibition. Wheeler's goal was to annihilate the "booze brothers" — beer, wine, and spirits.

During the colonial period, long before the nation's experiment with prohibition, Americans had made drunkenness a crime. The city of Baltimore, for example, defined drunkenness in 1638 as "drinking with excess to the noticable [sic] perturbation of any organ or sense or motion."[9] No arrest was more common than that for drunkenness. It also was a crime in many American colonies and later in early states to pay for labor with alcohol;[10] to sell alcoholic beverages on Sundays or during the hours of "divine service"; or to sell alcohol to a minor, an idler, a felon, a habitual drunkard, an actual drunkard, or a Native American, or to sell it within a given distance from a university or a church.

To regulate the lawful trade in alcoholic beverages, Americans relied on liquor licensing. The model was the English licensing system that applied, beginning in the sixteenth century, to public houses ("pubs"), alehouses (where beer was sold), dram shops (bars at which spirits could be sold in measured quantities (drams) of less than one gallon),[11] and other places where alcoholic beverages were sold. Sidney and Beatrice Webb, in *The History of Liquor Licensing in England Principally from 1700 to 1830*, summarized the purposes of liquor licensing in England:

> The device of licensing — that is, the requirement that any person desiring to pursue a particular occupation shall first obtain specific permission from a governing authority — may be used to attain many different ends. The licence

---

7. Increase Mather, Wo to Drunkards, Two Sermons Testifying against the Sin of Drunkenness: Wherein the Woefulness of that Evil, and the Misery of all that are addicted to it, is discovered from the Word of God 4 (Boston: Marmaduke Johnson 1673).

8. For more information on the legal and policy frameworks of alcohol use, refer to Chapter 9: Public Health and Social Responsibility.

9. Gallus Thomann, Colonial Liquor Laws, Part II: Liquor Laws of the United States; Their Spirit and Effect 71 (New York, U.S. Brewers' Ass'n 1887).

10. *Id.* at 11.

11. Ronald S. Beitman, Practitioner's Guide to Liquor Liability Litigation 3 n.2 (American Law Institute 1987).

> [sic] may be merely an occasion for extracting a fee or levying a tax. It may be an instrument for registering all those who are following a particular occupation, in order, for some reason or another, to ensure their being brought under public notice. It may be a device for limiting the numbers of those so engaged, or for selecting them according to their possession of certain qualifications. Finally, the act of licensing may be the means of imposing special rules upon the occupation, or of more easily enforcing the fulfillment either of these special rules or of the general law of the land.[12]

Liquor licenses in the young United States were granted by local officials at their sole discretion, sometimes with the requirement of letters of support from the immediate neighborhood or the local community. Unlicensed purveyors were subject to criminal prosecution. Licenses were conditioned on compliance with a host of measures. Pricing measures figured prominently. Price controls were used for various purposes, depending on the community's goals: to reduce consumption by raising prices, to eliminate price competition though fixed prices, or to encourage customers to drink wine and beer rather than spirits.[13] The licensing laws frequently specified which trade practices were allowed or banned. For example, there were restrictions on tippling (habitual drinking, sometimes referred to as soaking), free rounds, profanity, gambling, and other disreputable practices. Licensing had one other important benefit. From the government's perspective, licensing generated significant revenues from various fees, taxes, and other instruments, including license stamps, surety bonds, duties, and excise taxes.[14] Because the taxes and other sumptuary laws[15] were designed, in part, to curb excessive drinking, they became known as "sin" taxes.

Over time, the problem of drunkenness grew more severe, leading historian W. J. Rorabaugh to describe the United States of the early 1800s as "a nation of drunkards."[16] The apex of American drinking was between 1805 and 1830, when per capita consumption of absolute alcohol hovered around seven gallons.[17] In response, states and local communities adopted more stringent regulations. The number and locations of licensed premises were carefully controlled. Both civil

---

12. Sidney Webb & Beatrice Webb, The History of Liquor Licensing in England Principally from 1700 to 1830, at 4 (London, Longmans, Green and Co. 1903).

13. In the colony of Georgia, General James Oglethorpe, the colony's founder, proposed and the colony's trustees passed a law in 1735 that prohibited the importation and sale of rum, brandy, and other distilled spirits. Wine and beer were excluded. Phinizy Spalding, Oglethorpe in America 49 (Athens: University of Georgia Press 1984).

14. An excise is a tax on manufacture or sale or for a business license or charter. In the case of alcoholic beverages, the amount of the redundantly named "excise tax" depends on the alcoholic content of the particular beverage.

15. Sumptuary laws are defined in Black's Law Dictionary as "limit[ing] the expenditures that people can make for personal gratification or ostentatious display" or, "[m]ore broadly, any law whose purpose is to regulate conduct thought to be immoral, such as prostitution, gambling, or drug abuse." Black's Law Dictionary 1574 (9th ed. 2009).

16. W. J. Rorabaugh, The Alcoholic Republic 3-22 (Oxford University Press 1979).

17. *Id.* at 233, table A1.2. By contrast, average per capita alcohol consumption today is less than 10 liters. One gallon equals 3.785 liters.

and criminal nuisance actions against purveyors of liquor were authorized. Communities began to pass dram shop laws to circumvent the common law theory of tort liability, which held that the owner of a liquor establishment could not be held liable for any damages caused by a drunkard because the proximate cause of the damage was the intoxicated person, not the seller. Under the common law, even if the liquor store were to supply drinks to a minor or an obviously intoxicated person, the owner would not be liable.[18] The dram shop laws imposed statutory as opposed to common law liability on the owner for selling or serving alcohol to a minor, a habitual drunkard, or an intoxicated person who was subsequently involved in an accident. Some states required liquor purveyors to post a bond to pay for the actual damages sustained in such an accident, the support of injured parties and their families, and punitive damages.[19] Sometimes the recovery under the dram shop law was limited to the amount of the bond.

In the 1830s local jurisdictions began to hold "local option" elections at which the voters would decide whether beer, wine, or spirits could be sold within the jurisdiction's borders and, if so, at which types of establishments (for consumption on the premises with or without food or for takeout), on which days, and at what hours. In this way, the community would set its own drinking standards. Not surprisingly, the rise of the local option coincided with the growing politicization of the liquor issue in the United States.

In 1851 Neal Dow, the mayor of Portland, Maine, and an ardent prohibitionist, spearheaded the adoption of a state law that prohibited the manufacture and sale of intoxicating liquor in Maine, with only minor exceptions.[20] The Maine Law became the model for the first wave of prohibitory liquor laws in America. Now not only local jurisdictions but entire states were "dry." These laws, however, raised important constitutional questions regarding individual liberties,[21] private

---

18. The modern rule of common law liability on commercial servers of alcoholic beverages began with the decision of the New Jersey Supreme Court in *Rappaport v. Nichols*, 31 N.J. 188, 205 (1959). In its holding, the court stated,

> We are fully mindful that policy considerations and the balancing of the conflicting interests are the truly vital factors in the molding and application of the common law principles of negligence and proximate causation. But we are convinced that recognition of the plaintiff's claim will afford a fairer measure of justice to innocent third parties whose injuries are brought about by the unlawful and negligent sale of alcoholic beverages to minors and intoxicated persons, will strengthen and give greater force to the enlightened statutory and regulatory precautions against such sales and their frightening consequences, and will not place any unjustifiable burdens upon defendants who can always discharge their civil responsibilities by the exercise of due care.

19. Beitman, *supra* note 11, at 4.

20. The exceptions were for liquor used for mechanical and medicinal purposes, sold by an agent of the city or state government, and liquor "of foreign production . . . imported under the laws of the United States . . . contained in the original packages." 1851 Me. Acts 211 (repealed 1856).

21. John Stuart Mill believed that prohibition was an illegitimate interference with the rightful liberty of the individual. In *On Liberty* (1869), he acknowledged that prohibition was based on the doctrine of social rights and described the argument in its favor as follows:

> I claim, as a citizen, a right to legislate whenever my social rights are invaded by the social act of another . . . If anything invades my social rights, certainly the traffic in strong drink

property rights, and substantive and procedural due process. Prior to the adoption of the Fourteenth Amendment to the U.S. Constitution in 1868, state courts decided these cases based on the provisions of the particular state's constitution. After 1868, the Supreme Court established the law of the land with respect to whether prohibition violates the privileges or immunities of U.S. citizens; deprives any person of life, liberty, or property without due process of law; or denies any person the equal protection of the laws. In the key case of *Mugler v. Kansas*, 123 U.S. 623 (1887), the Supreme Court upheld Kansas's prohibitory law as a valid exercise of the state's police power under the Tenth Amendment[22] and found that it did not infringe on the Fourteenth Amendment.

Liquor commerce was another subject altogether. Article 1, §8 of the Constitution, known as the Commerce Clause, gives Congress the authority to regulate interstate and foreign commerce.[23] When the state of Maryland in 1827 imposed a license requirement and a licensing fee for the privilege of importing wine, among other goods, into that state from abroad, the Supreme Court by a vote of 6 to 1 invalidated the state law in light of Congress's express authorization of these imports.[24] According to Chief Justice John Marshall, who wrote the decision in *Brown v. Maryland*, only when the imported goods were "mixed up with the mass of property" in the state could Maryland exercise its police power. When an imported good "remain[ed] the property of the importer in his warehouse in the original form or package in which it was imported," the imported good was not subject to state interference.[25] This became known as the "original package" doctrine.

But Congress never explicitly authorized interstate commerce in liquor. Where Congress is silent, can the states legislate under their police power in matters affecting interstate commerce? In *The License Cases* of 1847, the Supreme Court

---

> does. It destroys my primary right of security, by constantly creating and stimulating social disorder. It invades my right of equality, by deriving a profit from the creation of a misery I am taxed to support. It impedes my right to free moral and intellectual development, by surrounding my path with dangers, and by weakening and demoralizing society, from which I have a right to claim mutual aid and intercourse.

But he quickly dismissed these arguments as well as prohibition, writing,

> So monstrous a principle is far more dangerous than any single interference with liberty; there is no violation of liberty which it would not justify; it acknowledges no right to any freedom whatever, except perhaps to that of holding opinions in secret, without ever disclosing them . . . The doctrine ascribes to all mankind a vested interest in each other's moral, intellectual, and even physical perfection, to be defined by each claimant according to his own standard.

John Stuart Mill, On Liberty 160-161 (London, Longman, Roberts & Green 1869).

22. The Tenth Amendment provides that "[t]he powers not delegated to the United States by the Constitution, nor prohibited by it to the States, are reserved to the States respectively, or to the people." U.S. Const. amend. X.

23. "The Congress shall have a Power … to regulate Commerce with foreign Nations, and among the several States, and with the Indian Tribes." U.S. Const. Article I, §8, cl. 3.

24. *Brown v. Maryland*, 25 U.S. 419 (1827).

25. *Id.* at 441-42.

in six separate opinions upheld a New Hampshire law requiring a license for the sale in that state of spirits in their original package imported from Massachusetts.[26] Because of the diversity of opinions, it was difficult to interpret the Court's Commerce Clause jurisprudence. Subsequently, the Court clarified its position and reversed its decision in *The License Cases*, holding that a state could neither prohibit the transportation of liquor from one state to another nor require a license for an importer of liquor from another state if the liquor remained in its original package.[27]

The original package doctrine opened a major hole in the states' prohibitory laws. Only Congress, through the exercise of its Commerce Clause authority, could change the situation. As prohibitionists grew more powerful, they exerted pressure on Congress to act.

Ultimately, Congress did so, not by setting specific standards for interstate and international trade in liquor but by deferring to state authority over the distribution and sale of alcohol within the state's borders. First, Congress passed the Wilson Act in 1890, which provided that

> All fermented, distilled, or other intoxicating liquors or liquids transported into any State or Territory or remaining therein for use, consumption, sale, or storage therein, shall upon arrival in such State or Territory be subject to the operation and effect of the laws of such State or Territory enacted in the exercise of its police powers, to the same extent and in the same manner as though such liquids or liquors had been produced in such State or Territory, and shall not be exempt therefrom by reason of being introduced therein in original packages or otherwise.[28]

When the Wilson Act failed to halt interstate liquor shipments into dry states for personal use rather than for resale,[29] Congress passed the Webb-Kenyon Act of 1913, which remains in effect today.[30] The Webb-Kenyon Act is subtitled "An Act divesting intoxicating liquors of their interstate character in certain cases." It provides that:

> The shipment or transportation, in any manner or by any means whatsoever, of any spirituous, vinous, malted, fermented, or other intoxicating liquor of any kind, from one State, Territory, or District of the United States, … into any other State,

---

26. *The License Cases*, 46 U.S. 504 (1847).

27. *Bowman v. Chicago Nw. Ry. Co.*, 125 U.S. 465 (1888) (states do not have the right to prevent the importation of liquor from another state); *Leisy v. Hardin*, 135 U.S. 100 (1890) (invalidating Iowa's ban on the sale of liquor imported from another state in its original package). The Court in *Leisy* stated clearly that liquor importers have the right to import beer from another state and to sell it, "by which act alone it would become mingled in the common mass of property within the state. Up to that point of time, we hold that, in the absence of congressional permission to do so, the state had no power to interfere by seizure, or any other action, in prohibition of importation and sale." 135 U.S. at 124.

28. Wilson Act, ch. 728, 26 Stat. 313 (1890) (codified at 27 U.S.C. §121 (2018).

29. *See Rhodes v. Iowa*, 170 U.S. 412 (1898).

30. Webb-Kenyon Act, ch. 90, 37 Stat. 699 (1913) (codified at 27 U.S.C. §122 (2018)).

> Territory, or District of the United States, … or from any foreign country into any State, Territory, or District of the United States, … which said spirituous, vinous, malted, fermented, or other intoxicating liquor is *intended*, by any person interested therein, *to be received, possessed, sold, or in any manner used, either in the original package or otherwise*, in violation of any law of such State, Territory, or District of the United States . . . is hereby prohibited.

(Emphasis added.)

Despite its extensive reach, the Webb-Kenyon Act did not halt the transportation of liquor through a state for delivery elsewhere.[31]

Historian Anne-Marie Szymanski has described the history of prohibition in America as a process of "local gradualism," essentially a step function from local to state to federal regulation of alcohol, growing stricter with each step.[32] But not all cities and states moved in the same direction at the same time. Jack Blocker concluded in *American Temperance Movements: Cycles of Reform* that there were three distinct cycles of prohibition: 1805-1840, 1851–1865, and 1907-1913.[33] Whether by step or cycle, prohibitionist sentiment in America advanced. With the Anti-Saloon League (ASL) at the helm, wary about future changes of people and policies in Congress and at the Supreme Court, prohibitionists pushed for a constitutional amendment to prohibit trade in liquor across America and make the country forever dry.

The perpetual symbol of the social evils surrounding alcohol and the rallying cry for the ASL was the saloon. The infamous Carrie Nation called attention to the sordid saloons through her hatchet attacks on them across the United States. Frances Willard was just as tireless a temperance reformer who spoke of "a war between the rum shops and religion."[34] However, she eschewed violence, telling the members of her Woman's Christian Temperance Union to be "wise as serpents

---

31. *See, e.g., Alcohol Div. of Dep't of Fin. & Taxation of Tenn. v. State ex rel. Strawbridge*, 63 So. 2d 358, 360 (Ala. 1953). The court reasoned as follows:

> Transportation of intoxicating liquors from one state through another state is within the protection of the commerce clause of the federal constitution and not subject to state interference. And this is true regardless of whether the state to which the liquor is being shipped prohibits the sale and traffic in such liquors. The Twenty-first Amendment to the Federal Constitution, together with the Webb-Kenyon Act, 27 U.S.C.A. §122, which prohibits the transportation or importation of intoxicating liquors into any state for delivery or use therein in violation of its laws, does not render such liquor contraband while passing through Alabama into another state for disposition in violation of the laws of the latter state, nor authorize seizure and condemnation of such liquors and the transporting vehicles under Alabama statutes.

32. Ann-Marie E. Szymanski, Pathways to Prohibition (Durham, NC: Duke University Press 2003).

33. Jack S. Blocker, Jr., American Temperance Movements: Cycles of Reform (Twayne Publishers 1989).

34. Let Something Good Be Said: Speeches and Writings of Frances E. Willard 4 (Carolyn DeSwarte Gifford & Amy R. Slagell eds., University of Illinois Press 2007).

and harmless as doves"[35] when they filed into saloons, Bibles in hand. All the while, the ASL, a single-issue, politically astute, well-funded organization, applied political pressure to advance the prohibitionist cause.

When the United States entered World War I, the country's enthusiasm for prohibition accelerated. The spirit of sacrifice and hostility to all things German were constant themes. Sacrifice meant the conservation of grain used to produce alcoholic beverages; beer and brewers were demonized because of their association with the Kaiser. In the midst of the national emergency, Congress adopted wartime prohibition and then, on December 18, 1917, passed a joint resolution proposing the Eighteenth Amendment to the Constitution, known as National Prohibition or simply Prohibition (with a capital *P*). That resolution was sent to the states for ratification. On January 16, 1920, the amendment went into effect. The Eighteenth Amendment reads in pertinent part as follows:

> §1. After one year from the ratification of this article the manufacture, sale, or transportation of intoxicating liquors within, the importation thereof into, or the exportation thereof from the United States and all territory subject to the jurisdiction thereof for beverage purposes is hereby prohibited.
>
> §2. The Congress and the several States shall have concurrent power to enforce this article by appropriate legislation.[36]

Intoxicating liquors were defined in the implementing legislation — titled the National Prohibition Act and popularly known as the Volstead Act after its author, Andrew Volstead, Chairman of the House Judiciary Committee — as those containing one-half of one percent or more alcohol by volume that were fit for use for beverage purposes.[37]

With Prohibition came the cessation of virtually all commercial winemaking in the country. For the next 14 years only limited winemaking was authorized, for the production of medicinal wine, wine for other non-beverage purposes, sacramental wine, and home winemaking for personal use.[38] Interestingly, the possession and consumption of alcoholic beverages were not unlawful during Prohibition. In colloquial terms, Prohibition America was not "bone dry." The Eighteenth Amendment killed the lawful liquor trade, but not drinking.

---

35. Mary C. Johnson, Our Method of Saloon-Visiting, in Hints and Helps in our Temperance Work 26 (Frances E. Willard ed., New York National Temperance Society and Publication House 1875).

36. U.S. Const. amend. XVIII, §§1-2 (repealed 1933).

37. National Prohibition (Volstead) Act, ch. 85, tit. 2, §1, 41 Stat. 305, 308 (1919) (repealed 1933).

38. *Id.* at tit. 2, §29, 41 Stat. 305, 316. After prescribing penalties for certain violations of the Act, including illegal manufacture and sale, the Volstead Act declares that "the penalties provided in this Act against the manufacture of liquor without a permit shall not apply to a person for manufacturing nonintoxicating cider and fruit juices exclusively for use in his home, but such cider and fruit juices shall not be sold or delivered except to persons having permits to manufacture vinegar."

The "iron law of prohibition" explains a great deal about alcohol consumption during Prohibition.[39] The theory states that, when a drug or alcohol is banned, particularly when it is part of a social or cultural custom (what Graham Sumner calls a "folkway"[40]), consumers turn to the stronger and more concealable form of it. Thus, spirits in flasks and hidden in boots, from which imagery is derived the term "bootlegger,"[41] gained popularity. Spirits consumption rose by 10 percent during Prohibition, while beer consumption fell by 70 percent. Surprisingly, wine consumption rose by 65 percent, largely because of the specific exemptions for home winemaking and sacramental wine.[42]

Despite the obvious failure of the prohibitionists to change the thinking and drinking habits of Americans, Prohibition continued because it was thought to be good for the country. Amending the federal Constitution was considered a dim prospect, which is why the ASL had pressed for its passage, even after the adoption of the Webb-Kenyon Act.

Prohibition, known widely today as "the noble experiment that failed," was costly for the country. The expense of enforcement at the federal and state levels was small to begin with and then skyrocketed; even then the prohibitory laws could not be effectively enforced. Bootlegging flourished, and criminal syndicates developed a large illegal liquor industry to service the demand of the public for alcohol. Public corruption was widespread, and many Americans ignored the Prohibition laws and, as a consequence, developed contempt for the law itself. Certain states passed anti-Prohibition referenda.

Repeal happened relatively swiftly. Just as World War I had accelerated National Prohibition, the Great Depression of 1929 led the government to search for new means of federal revenue and new sources of employment. The drys were unwilling to exempt beer and wine in order to save Prohibition. The election of 1932 was widely perceived as a Prohibition referendum. Franklin Roosevelt, who supported repeal, defeated Herbert Hoover, the incumbent, in a landslide. True to his word, President Roosevelt urged Congress to pass the repeal amendment and, even before that, requested modification of the Volstead Act to permit the sale of beer and wine with less than 3.2 percent alcohol by weight. Congress obliged on both counts.

National Prohibition ended on December 5, 1933, when three-quarters of the states ratified the Twenty-first Amendment to the U.S. Constitution, repealing Prohibition. The Amendment reads in pertinent part as follows:

---

39. Richard C. Cowan, *How the Narcs Created Crack*, Nat'l Rev., Dec. 5, 1986, at 30-31.

40. William Graham Sumner, Folkways: A Study of the Sociological Importance of Usages, Manners, Customs, Mores, and Morals 2-3 (Ginn and Co. 1906).

41. Although the term "bootlegger" explicitly refers to one who carries liquor in his bootleg, it has come to refer more generally to an illicit trader in liquor, and "bootlegging" to the illicit trade itself.

42. Mendelson, *supra* note 5, at 50-51.

> §1. The eighteenth article of amendment to the Constitution of the United States is hereby repealed.
>
> §2. The transportation or importation into any State, Territory, or possession of the United States for delivery or use therein of intoxicating liquors, in violation of the laws thereof, is hereby prohibited.[43]

The Twenty-first Amendment vests the states with broad power to regulate the importation and use of intoxicating liquor within their borders. This approach was not dictated by law or policy. The federal government, if it wished, could have controlled liquor production and commerce through the exercise of its Commerce Clause authority. But history has shown time and again that liquor is a politically divisive issue in the United States, and no politician wants to face the voter's scorn by setting national drinking standards. This explains the popularity of the local option — then and now. Let the voters decide! In addition, at the time of Repeal many states wanted to remain dry, which would have been impossible without the ability to close off their borders to alcohol through the exercise of their constitutionally delegated Commerce Clause authority.

Pursuant to the Twenty-first Amendment, each state adopted its own liquor laws and regulations and its own administrative machinery after Repeal, leading to the adage that the U.S. is not a single wine market but 50 separate markets. Some states remained dry entirely or partially. Other states reverted to liquor licensing or instituted government-run liquor monopolies.

Despite the diversity of approaches, which are described in detail in a later section, the states shared many goals. Foremost among them was the desire to promote temperance, defined as the moderate use of alcohol or, in the negative, the avoidance of excess. Equally significant, state governments looked to liquor as an important revenue source through excise and sales taxes and licensing fees. To accomplish both goals and ensure an orderly market for alcoholic beverages, the states established controls over alcoholic beverage trade and consumption.

The states realized that the social evils surrounding alcohol in the pre-Prohibition and Prohibition eras had numerous causes — economic, cultural, genetic, and otherwise. But a primary culprit in terms of market structure was the power wielded by the vertically and horizontally integrated liquor "trusts." Trusts were common in the spirits and beer sectors but less so in the wine business. Best known was the Whiskey Trust (the actual name of which was the Distillers' and Cattle Feeders' Trust), which in the late 1800s acquired numerous small-scale distilleries in an effort to control the price and quantity of whiskey on the market. Once a small distillery became part of the Trust, its production was carefully controlled, or the acquired plant was closed down entirely. The Trust also controlled its own distribution and sales outlets and insisted on "exclusive dealing" arrangements whereby the distributor or retailer could sell only the Trust's brands of liquor. The same held true for the large brewers who owned their own saloons. The goal was to maximize corporate profits, which meant more drinking.

---

43. U.S. Const., amend. XXI, §§1-2.

Rather than relying solely on "antitrust" laws to break up these monopolies (Congress had passed the Sherman Antitrust Act in 1890), the states took steps after Repeal to ensure that private liquor monopolies could not arise or, if they did, that they could not use their market power to ply consumers with alcohol in the quest for maximum profit. "Tied house" laws prohibited suppliers — including liquor producers, importers, and wholesalers — from owning or controlling the retail shops at which their own beverage brands would be sold. And "free goods" laws prohibited aggressive sales techniques, including commercial bribery, gifts of money, and other "things of value" that could lead to overconsumption of alcohol such as a "free lunch" strategically packed with salt to stimulate thirst. Tied-house and free goods laws are discussed in more detail by Carrie Bonnington in Chapter 2.

The states also sought to restore citizens' faith in the law and to banish criminals from the lawful liquor trade. The common theme was that there was no place for criminal syndicates and bootleggers in post-Prohibition America.

Finally, states took steps to stimulate their agricultural sector as a way to promote economic development. Wine, unlike beer and spirits, is tied directly to agriculture. Wine is made from grapes with little else, if anything, added. The finished wine is thought to reflect the *terroir* (site) where the grapes are grown; that distinctive taste is known as *goût de terroir* (taste of the site). Wine also contributes directly to agro-tourism. Beginning in the 1970s, many states adopted "farm winery" laws granting special privileges to local wineries that made wine from grapes grown in the state, including the privilege of direct sales to in-state consumers.

These and other measures favoring in-state liquor businesses over out-of-state businesses were upheld by state and federal courts in the first several decades following Repeal, despite the discriminatory effects of these laws on interstate trade. Judges relied on the Twenty-first Amendment, which gives states broad authority to regulate alcoholic beverages notwithstanding the constraints of the Commerce Clause.

Tracy Genesen and Justin McGuirk explain in Chapter 5 how the Supreme Court's Twenty-first Amendment jurisprudence has changed over time. Beginning in the 1980s, the Court explored the core purposes of the Twenty-first Amendment, such as temperance, establishment of an orderly market, and the avoidance of social evils. The Court then balanced the benefits of the state's preferential laws in serving those purposes against the harm to interstate commerce.

Around the same time, wine became a significant industry in the United States, with consumption growing steadily from 0.26 gallon (around one liter) per person in 1934 to 2.11 gallons (eight liters) per person in 1980.[44] Rising out of the ashes of Prohibition, this growth in wine consumption (see Table 1-1) along with the increasing sophistication of the American palate and the ever-improving quality of

---

44. The consumption statistics here and in Table 1-1 are from Wine Institute, www.wineinstitute.org/our-industry/statistics/us-wine-consumption (accessed July 21, 2022), and the U.S. Department of Commerce, Bureau of the Census, Current Population Reports, Series P-25.

domestic wines were astounding. Author Leon Adams, in his seminal book *The Wines of America*, first published in 1973, aptly called it the Wine Revolution.[45]

Table 1-1 U.S. Per Capita Wine Consumption Since 1934

Year	U.S. Population, in Millions	Wine Consumption, in Millions of Gallons	All Ages Per Capita Consumption, in Millions of Gallons
1934	126	33	0.26
1940	132	90	0.68
1950	152	141	0.92
1960	181	163	0.90
1970	205	267	1.30
1980	227	480	2.11
1990	249	506	2.03
2000	282	565	2.00
2010	309	798	2.58
2020	327	1,000	3.07
2021	336	1,100	3.18

With the development of the Internet in the 1990s, coupled with the expanding number of wineries (1,800 in 1995 and over 5,000 in 2008) and the consolidation of wholesalers (3,000 wholesalers in 1995 and only 700 in 2008), wineries — particularly smaller ones that could find no wholesaler to carry their wines — began to ship more wine directly to consumers in interstate commerce, bypassing wholesalers and retailers.[46] Certain states allowed direct-to-consumer sales and shipments, some only if the producer's state granted reciprocal shipping rights to wineries located in the destination state.

New York and Michigan, along with many other states, adopted a different approach. They allowed in-state wineries to sell and ship their wines directly to in-state consumers but prohibited out-of-state wineries from doing so. The out-of-state wineries had two options: in New York, they could establish a physical presence as a licensed New York branch winery and sell their out-of-state wines to consumers from that location; or, in either state, they could sell their wines to an in-state wholesaler who, in turn, would sell the wines to an in-state retailer who would sell them to in-state consumers. With a mark-up at each step of the so-called three-tier distribution system, the out-of-state producer received less money for its wines, and the consumer paid directly or indirectly for the higher cost of

45. Leon D. Adams, The Wines of America 38 (4th ed., McGraw-Hill 1990).

46. Jack Heeger, Industry Trends Discussed at Wine & Grape Symposium, Napa Valley Reg., February 8, 2008, available at http://napavalleyregister.com/wine/industry-trends-discussed-at-wine-grape-symposium/article_ 5e8eb15a-3185-5a37-bf4f-94677eedc366.html.

fulfillment. Finally, a few states prohibited direct-to-consumer shipping from in-state or out-of-state wineries; all wine shipments in those states had to pass through the three-tier distribution system.

Ultimately, these distribution schemes were challenged on Commerce Clause grounds. Different circuits reached different conclusions, making the issue ripe for resolution by the U.S. Supreme Court. In the seminal 2005 case of *Granholm v. Heald*,[47] the Court decided in a 5-4 decision that the Twenty-first Amendment does not authorize a state to allow in-state wineries to sell and ship directly to in-state consumers while withholding that same privilege from an out-of-state winery. Such facial discrimination, said the Court, cannot be sanctioned under the Commerce Clause.

Granholm did not require any state to provide wineries with the right of direct-to-consumer sale and shipment; indeed, the Court fashioned no remedy in the case. The Court's mandate was to end discrimination and level the playing field between in-state and out-of-state wineries with respect to direct shipments. Following *Granholm*, some states "leveled down" by prohibiting any winery, in-state or out-of-state, from shipping wine directly to in-state consumers; most states "leveled up," allowing all wineries to ship their wines to in-state consumers. The significance of *Granholm* cannot be underestimated, both for its holding and for the simple fact that, unlike the earlier liquor law cases decided by the Supreme Court, this case concerned wine, not beer or spirits. Wine had come of age.

B. REGULATORY STRUCTURE AND APPROACHES

Because the Twenty-first Amendment explicitly authorizes the states to control the delivery and use of alcoholic beverages within their borders (that is, intrastate commerce), each state had to develop its own alcoholic beverage regulatory scheme after Repeal. Some states, in turn, ceded this control to local jurisdictions through the local option. The federal government retained jurisdiction over interstate commerce in alcoholic beverages and developed a separate and independent regulatory regime. Only in the sphere of intrastate retail sales did the states have exclusive jurisdiction. As a result, three levels of government — local, state, and federal — are intimately involved in regulating the wine business in the United States. This concurrent authority is a hallmark of U.S. wine law.

1. LOCAL OPTION

After Prohibition, many states reestablished the local option, a practice that had begun in the early 1800s. Under the local option, local jurisdictions (counties, cities, even voting precincts) vote on whether, when, and where beer, wine, or

47. 544 U.S. 460 (2005).

spirits can be sold within their respective boundaries. Typical local option ballots include one or more of the following questions:

(a) Shall the sale of [beer, wine, or spirits] be prohibited within this [local voting unit]?
(b) Shall the sale of [beer, wine, or spirits] be prohibited within this [local voting unit] on any Sunday?
(c) Shall the sale of [beer, wine, or spirits] be prohibited within this [local voting unit] for consumption on the premises where sold?
(d) Shall the sale of [beer, wine, or spirits] be prohibited within this [local voting unit] between the hours hereafter specified?

Sometimes the local option questions are more specific. For example, Kentucky in 2000 authorized local option elections for the service of alcoholic beverages at golf courses. The Kentucky local option law provides:

> (1) To promote economic development and tourism in a county containing a city that has, in whole or in part, voted to discontinue prohibition, with the exception of a territory that has discontinued prohibition in accordance with KRS 242.1292, a local option election for the limited sale of alcoholic beverages may be held in any precinct containing a nine (9) or an eighteen (18) hole golf course that meets United States Golf Association criteria as a regulation golf course, notwithstanding any other provisions of the Kentucky Revised Statutes.
> (2) A local option election for the limited sale of alcoholic beverages held under subsection (1) of this section shall be conducted in the same manner specified in KRS 242.020 to 242.120, except that the form of the proposition to be voted upon shall be "Are you in favor of the sale of alcoholic beverages by the drink at (name of golf course) in the (name of precinct)?"
> (3) Upon approval of the proposition, the Department of Alcoholic Beverage Control may issue a license to the golf course for the sale of alcoholic beverages by the drink as provided in KRS 243.030 and KRS 243.040.
> (4) No alcoholic beverage license shall be issued to any applicant within the precinct except the nine (9) or the eighteen (18) hole regulation golf course named in the proposition.[48]

Jurisdictions that have wet establishments inside dry territory often are referred to as "damp" or "moist."[49] There is no common term to describe dry cities within wet counties. Suffice it to say that the local option is still prevalent across the United States, in both control and license states.

---

48. Kentucky Revised Statutes §242.123 (2021).

49. In Connecticut "damp" towns, although not defined by state statute, are municipalities that allow some liquor to be sold within an otherwise dry city. The Town of Wilton is an example of a damp town. In 1992 residents repealed the town's prohibition law to allow restaurants to obtain permits to serve alcohol in the town but did not extend that right to grocery stores or package stores. *See* Meghan Reilly, Connecticut General Assembly Office of Legislative Research, "Damp" Towns (Feb. 5, 2009), http://www.cga.ct.gov/2009/rpt/2009-R-0101.htm (accessed June 11, 2022).

2. THE STATES

The states employed two basic methods to regulate the wine industry and protect the public health, safety, and welfare: licensing private individuals to distribute and sell alcoholic beverages in the 32 "open" or license states and the District of Columbia, and establishing state monopolies in the wholesale and/or retail distribution of alcoholic beverages in the 18 "control" states. The control states, in alphabetical order, are Alabama, Idaho, Iowa, Maine, Michigan, Mississippi, Montana, New Hampshire, North Carolina, Ohio, Oregon, Pennsylvania, Utah, Vermont, Virginia, Washington, West Virginia, and Wyoming.

a. License States

In an open or license state, the chief function of the state alcoholic beverage control agency, often referred to as ABC,[50] is the issuance of licenses to all individuals and business entities in the distribution channel — manufacturers, importers, wholesalers, and retailers. This authority is granted by the state constitution[51] and/or the state legislature.

Generally speaking, each owner of an alcoholic beverage business and each place of business in the state must be qualified by the state before the business commences and must post a bond to assure the state that all taxes, fines, and penalties will be paid. The applicants for a liquor license must be of good moral character and without a criminal record.[52] And the prospective licensee cannot hold a prohibited tied-house ownership interest in another tier of the distribution channel. Tied-house laws vary considerably from state to state in terms of their proscriptions and their exceptions.

Sometimes the tied-house rules and exceptions seem to defy logic. For example, in California, a wine wholesaler or importer cannot own an interest in an on-sale retail license of any type. An on-sale license allows the sale of beer, wine, and/or spirits (depending on the license type) with or without food (again, depending on the license type) to members of the public for consumption on the licensed premise. By contrast, a winery, known as a winegrower in California licensing lexicon,[53] can hold one or more on-sale retail licenses for a bona fide eating place (restaurant) so long as the winery's brands are not sold at more than two restaurants owned by the winery, and even then, the winery's brands cannot

---

50. Thus, the California Department of Alcoholic Beverage Control is the California ABC. Other abbreviations are used in other states (e.g., the SLA for the State Liquor Authority of New York).

51. *See, e.g.*, Cal. Const. art. XX, §22.

52. Criminal convictions for misdemeanors and even certain felonies may not be disqualifying. Even with a disqualifying conviction, a person may be awarded a liquor license upon proof of rehabilitation or expungement of the conviction, depending on the laws of the particular state.

53. Jefferson E. Peyser, longtime counsel of Wine Institute, the trade association of California wineries, coined the term "winegrower" to underscore the agricultural roots of the wine industry.

constitute more than 15 percent of all wine brands offered for sale at those restaurants.[54]

Many states limit the maximum number of retail establishments in a given area (based on population or reported crimes) or restrict the number of licenses issued to a particular person. In California, retail licenses cannot be issued in areas of "undue concentration of licenses" unless the applicant can show that public convenience or necessity requires issuance of the license.[55] "Undue concentration" includes areas of high crime and census areas where the density of licenses is greater than the county average. This concept is discussed in more detail in Chapter 7.

Typically, the proposed alcoholic beverage premise must be posted with a notice prior to commencing business so that there is an opportunity for interested persons to object to the issuance of the license. Special consideration often is given to residences, churches, and schools that are near a proposed licensed premise to ensure that the business operations do not interfere with those existing uses.

Licenses generally are not freely alienable. They are not subject to attachment or execution, and they do not follow the laws of descent or distribution upon the death of the licensee. In fact, the state, subject to the legitimate exercise of its police power and the constitutional mandates of due process, may grant or withhold alcoholic beverage licenses at will. Often the state seeks the input of the local jurisdiction in which the licensed premise will be located before it will issue an alcoholic beverage license. Sometimes the state delegates its licensing authority to the local jurisdiction. If a license is refused, the applicant generally has the right to a public hearing on the merits of the particular case. Such administrative hearings generally do not follow common law or statutory rules of evidence. Most states, however, do provide for a review of administrative proceedings by an administrative appeals board or by a court of competent jurisdiction.[56] A similar process is followed for license revocation. Common grounds for revocation are violation of the alcoholic beverage laws, misrepresentation of material facts in the licensing applications, the conviction of any offense involving moral turpitude, and bankruptcy.

To conduct an interstate business in the open states, the out-of-state manufacturer or the manufacturer's national distributor generally must obtain a permit as an out-of-state shipper or nonresident seller that allows it to sell alcoholic beverages directly to wholesalers in the particular state. The manufacturer or distributor may be required to register its brands in that state, obtain a bond to secure payment of the state's excise tax, designate its wholesalers there, post its wholesale prices, and submit to the state liquor control authorities monthly reports

54. Cal. Bus. & Prof. Code §25503.15(b) (2021).

55. *Id.* §§23958, 23958.4 (2021).

56. In California, a three-person ABC Appeals Board, the members of which are appointed by the governor and confirmed by the state senate, hears administrative appeals "from a decision of the department ordering any penalty assessment, issuing, denying, transferring, suspending or revoking any license for the manufacture, importation or sale of alcoholic beverages." Cal. Const. art. XX, §22(d).

of wines shipped into the state. This information allows the state to track the whereabouts of all alcoholic beverages in the state and to prevent unlawful production (moonshining) and unlawful sales (bootlegging). This is part and parcel of ensuring an orderly market for alcoholic beverages. The information also is used by the state to enforce state franchise laws (discussed below) and, in those states with "primary source" laws (also discussed below), to ensure that state wholesalers are importing only those brands for which the manufacturer has designated them as authorized agents.

The state ABC, or in some states a separate Department of Revenue or Board of Equalization, is responsible for collecting excise taxes and enforcing the state's laws, regulations, and rules concerning industry business practices (also known as trade practices). This agency also is often involved with maintaining public health and safety surrounding alcohol, a subject discussed in Chapter 9. One area that receives considerable attention is responsible beverage service at licensed establishments, including the prevention of liquor sales to minors. ABC officials typically work closely with local law enforcement officials.

b. Control States

In the 18 control or monopoly states, the state government (or, in certain counties of Maryland, the county government[57]) participates directly as a wholesaler and/or retailer of alcoholic beverages. This system, based on research funded by John D. Rockefeller Jr. and modeled after the state liquor monopolies of Finland, Norway, and Sweden (among other nations), eliminates the role of private enterprise in the liquor market in whole or in part.[58] Only in this way, monopoly states contend, can the states protect the public health, safety, and welfare with respect to the sale and consumption of alcoholic beverages.

The extent of the government monopoly varies from jurisdiction to jurisdiction. Today, in fact, most control states are hybrids — part monopoly, part open — rather than pure monopolies. For example, some state monopolies extend only to beverages with higher levels of alcohol such as spirits, fortified wines, and malt liquor (sometimes referred to as "heavy beer" or "strong beer"), leaving other wines and beers to be sold by private individuals, who obtain licenses from the state's liquor authority. As Harold Holder and Kathleen Janes write:

> One of the legacies from the end of Prohibition in the U.S. has been to target distilled spirits for monopoly control. The beverage next most controlled is wine. Beer is rarely a part of the monopoly control or involvement of the state.

---

57. Montgomery County, Maryland, is an example of such a local control jurisdiction.

58. No state engages directly in the manufacture of alcoholic beverages, although the regulations of some states would allow it.

> This beverage distinction in the U.S. reflects which beverages are viewed as the most subject to abuse in the eyes of elected officials, i.e., which beverages are considered the "most dangerous." These distinctions reflect the amount of ethanol per liquid ounce rather than the amount of ethanol typically consumed per drinking occasion by type of beverage.[59]

Other states operate a retail monopoly but leave the wholesale tier open to private enterprise. The control states also differentiate between on-premises sales (for consumption on the seller's premises, such as a restaurant or bar) and off-premises sales (for take away, such as a liquor store), with the state monopoly often covering the latter but not the former. In that situation, privately licensed hoteliers, restaurateurs, and bar owners sell alcoholic beverages to their customers.

As mentioned previously, the role of the state may vary depending on the particular beverage, but the states, not surprisingly, do not maintain uniform definitions of the beverage types. An example is the different definitions of wine and fortified wine. In Montana, a table wine can contain no more than 16 percent alcohol by volume, and fortified wine can contain more than 16 percent up to 24 percent alcohol. Washington uses a cutoff of 14 percent to distinguish a table wine from a fortified wine, but in this era of high-alcohol wines, the state exempts from the category of fortified wines those wines over 14 percent that have a cork closure and have been aged for at least two years or that are produced solely as the result of natural fermentation without any added spirits, brandy, or alcohol.

Over the past several decades, there has been a marked trend to privatize wine sales in the control states, allowing wines to be sold at retail in a variety of licensed premises such as bottle shops, grocery stores, convenience stores, drive-through establishments, and sometimes even shops attached to gas stations. A similar expansion of available retail sales outlets has occurred in the license states. Some control states decided to privatize at the wholesale level but to maintain "state stores," sometimes referred to as state-operated "package stores," where wine and other liquors are sold at retail for off-premises consumption. Some control states established "agency stores" operated by third parties under contract to the state that follow the state's rules regarding beverages sold, pricing, hours of operation, etc. And sometimes state stores and private retailers sell the same alcoholic beverages. The variations are seemingly endless.

---

59. Harold D. Holder & Kathleen Janes, Control of Alcoholic Beverage Availability: State Alcoholic Beverage Control Systems Having Monopoly Functions in the United States, in State Monopolies and Alcoholic Prevention 355, 361 (Timo Kortteinen ed., Report from the Soc. Research Inst. of Alcohol Studies No. 181, 1989).

To conduct interstate commerce with a control state, the out-of-state manufacturer or the out-of-state wholesaler must obtain a wine shipper's or seller's permit to sell their wines to the state monopoly (often through an agent) or, in some states, to a licensed wholesaler, and the products must be listed with the state control boards prior to their importation.

Control states have the legally prescribed mission to protect and benefit the public. Their primary means of accomplishing this goal is to control the availability and price of alcoholic beverages. Because many, if not most, retail outlets are state owned, the state is able to control directly their number and location. Generally, there are fewer retail outlets in a control state, although some control states establish state stores or agency stores in rural areas where alcohol otherwise would be unavailable. In terms of pricing, the control states impose fixed prices, mandatory price markups, and/or taxes that generally result in higher retail prices than one finds for the same products in the license states.[60] This is why the popular Charles Shaw wine, known commonly as "Two Buck Chuck," may be "Four Buck Chuck" in a control state. As with every other maxim in the field of wine law, there are exceptions. New Hampshire, for example, keeps its markups and taxes low and its range of offerings high to encourage wine sales, leading consumers from nearby states to travel there for the sole purpose of purchasing wine.

The credo of most control states is that less availability and higher prices for alcoholic beverages translate into a lower average alcohol consumption rate among the states' consumers. This, in turn, is said to be associated with fewer injuries, less risk of certain diseases such as cirrhosis and fetal alcohol syndrome, less crime, and increased worker productivity. Chapter 9 reviews the evidence in support of this argument, as well as various alternative means of liquor control.

3. THE FEDERAL GOVERNMENT

When the Twenty-first Amendment took effect and the states adopted their own laws and regulations governing the delivery and use of alcoholic beverages within their jurisdictions, many observers thought that there would be no place for federal liquor law. But the Twenty-first Amendment did not grant the states complete and exclusive control over commerce in intoxicating liquors.[61] Congress believed that federal involvement was necessary to eradicate criminal operations like bootlegging and racketeering that crossed state lines. Just as important, the federal government had grown accustomed to its liquor tax revenue and did not want to

---

60. The control states' pricing measures vary but generally include fixed wholesale or retail prices (with price changes allowed up to four times a year on advance notice ranging from 45 to 75 days, unless the state control board rejects the change) and minimum or percentage markups. State excise taxes on table wine in the control states range from $0.30 per gallon in Ohio to $1.75 per gallon in Iowa. *See* Federation of Tax Administrators, State Tax Rates on Wine (Jan. 1, 2022), http://ww.taxadmin.org/fta/assets/docs/Research/Rates/wine.prd (accessed June 11, 2022), for a list of all the states' excise tax rates on wine).

61. *William Jameson & Co. v. Morgenthau*, 307 U.S. 171, 172-73 (1939).

relinquish its excise taxes on wine,[62] beer, and spirits. In fact, the federal government had begun taxing spirits in 1794 to help pay the debts of the Revolutionary War and for a related social purpose — to restrain consumption of spirits.[63]

The U.S. Treasury Department, through the monitoring and oversight activities related to the exercise of its tax authority, has a long and intimate involvement with the alcoholic beverage industry in America. This explains why the Treasury rather than the Department of Agriculture or the Food and Drug Administration has the primary responsibility for regulating the alcoholic beverage industry. Today that responsibility resides in the Department's Alcohol and Tobacco Tax and Trade Bureau (TTB).[64]

---

62. An excise tax applicable to all still and sparkling wines was levied by the U.S. Congress in 1914. Wine Tax Law of 1914, ch. 331, §2, 38 Stat. 745, 746. The 1914 Act taxed still wines at the rate of 1 cent per pint, 2 cents per quart, and 8 cents per gallon. Sparkling wines were taxed at 10 cents per pint and 20 cents per quart. In 1916 the present system of classifying still wines for tax purposes by alcoholic content was adopted. Revenue Act of 1916, ch. 463, 39 Stat. 7546, 783-787. Since that time, the tax rates for various wines have been changed; the last rate change for wines occurred in 1991, when the excise tax on wine was increased by $0.90 per gallon with the exception of sparkling wine. Revenue Reconciliation Act of 1990, 104 Stat. 1388-415, §11201 (1990). That law also provided for a tax credit of up to $0.90 per gallon for small domestic producers of wine, other than sparkling. 26 U.S.C. §5041(c) (2020). In 2017, Congress passed the Tax Cuts and Jobs Act that included a Craft Beverage Modernization (CBM) provision that established a tiered tax credit system for domestic and imported wine, with different tax credits depending on the amount of wine production and the tax class of the wine. The credits included a $1 per gallon credit on the first 30,000 wine gallons, $0.90 for the next 100,000 wine gallons, and $0.535 for the next 620,000 wine gallons. The CBM provisions also adjusted the alcohol content for certain wine tax classes from 14 percent to 16 percent alcohol by volume. An Act to provide for reconciliation pursuant to titles II and V of the concurrent resolution on the budget for fiscal year 2018, 115th Cong. Pub. L. 97 §2054 (2017). The Taxpayer Certainty and Disaster Tax Act of 2020, included in the Consolidated Appropriations Act, made permanent most of the CBM provisions. Consolidated Appropriations Act, 2021, 116th Cong. Pub. L. 134, §1184.

63. The distilled spirits tax did not sit well with the farmers of southwestern Pennsylvania, who opposed it by spearheading the Whiskey Rebellion. President Washington responded by sending in federal troops to quell the uprising. *See* William Hogeland, The Whiskey Rebellion: George Washington, Alexander Hamilton, and the Frontier Rebels Who Challenged America's Newfound Sovereignty (New York: Simon & Schuster 2006).

64. The TTB was created by the Homeland Security Act of 2002, Pub. L. No. 107-296, §111(d), 116 Stat. 2135 (2002) (codified at 6 U.S.C. §531(d) (2020)). Its predecessor agency, the Bureau of Alcohol, Tobacco, and Firearms, commonly known as ATF, had broader authority than the TTB. Essentially, ATF's functions dealing with firearms, explosives, and arson, as well as the smuggling of tobacco and alcohol, were kept in ATF, which was transferred to the Justice Department and renamed the Bureau of Alcohol, Tobacco, Firearms, and Explosives. The TTB assumed regulatory and tax oversight of the wine industry.

TTB administers two principal laws related to alcoholic beverages — the Internal Revenue Code (IRC)[65] and the Federal Alcohol Administration (FAA) Act.[66] The IRC governs the taxation and production of wine. The internal revenue laws are designed primarily to protect and secure the government's tax revenue. The IRC regulations are designed to ensure that no alcoholic beverage subject to tax escapes taxation.

In addition to the extensive system of control over the production and treatment of wine that exists under the IRC, the FAA Act established a system of controls designed to protect the wine consumer from fraud and deception and to foster fair marketing practices. The focal points of the FAA Act are the permit requirements for producers, wholesalers, and importers (but not retailers) of alcoholic beverages; the trade practice provisions that regulate unlawful economic practices in restraint of trade; and labeling, advertising, and marketing practices.[67]

The IRC and the FAA Act are the principal pillars of federal supervision and oversight of the wine industry.[68] Under each act, TTB is vested with the authority to promulgate additional rules in the form of regulations. The issuance of these regulations is controlled by the Administrative Procedures Act,[69] which requires that rules be issued through a procedure called informal rulemaking, commonly referred to as Notice and Comment Rulemaking. TTB first publishes rules as proposals and then solicits public participation through public hearings or the submission of written comments. Only after this process is completed will TTB issue new regulations. This openness in the rulemaking process enables TTB to acquire the widest possible range of views, which is critical to informed decision-making and protects the public against closed-door decision-making.

In terms of its operations and internal structure, TTB is headed by an Administrator and divided into several divisions. The Trade Investigations Division, Tax Audit Division, and Trade Analysis and Enforcement Division, collectively known as Field Operations, ensure that the members of the regulated industry comply with federal laws and regulations. These divisions conduct audits, investigations, and product analyses in an effort to eliminate tax diversion, fraud, and evasion and to prevent unfair competition in the industry. The Regulations and Rulings Division develops regulations, rulings, and internal regulatory interpretations. The Advertising, Labeling and Formulation Division reviews the labels of all alcoholic beverages offered for sale in the United States, both foreign and domestic; issues certificates of label approval (COLAs) for those beverages; and monitors alcoholic beverage advertising for deceptive practices. John Trinidad discusses wine labeling and advertising in Chapter 3.

---

65. 26 U.S.C. §§5001-5691 (2020).

66. 27 U.S.C. §§201-219(A) (2020).

67. The federal regulatory requirements to establish a winery are discussed in more detail below and in Chapter 4.

68. TTB also enforces the previously mentioned Webb-Kenyon Act, 27 U.S.C. §122 (2020), and the Alcoholic Beverage Labeling Act, 27 U.S.C. §§213-219(a) (2020), which prescribes a "Government Warning" on all alcoholic beverage labels (27 U.S.C. §215(a)).

69. 5 U.S.C. §§551-559 (2020).

TTB also has an International Trade Division that facilitates worldwide trade in wine by educating foreign governments about U.S. alcoholic beverage laws and regulations and by offering technical assistance to domestic producers wishing to export their products to other countries. This division also works with the Office of the United States Trade Representative and represents the interests of domestic alcoholic beverage producers in international negotiations, such as the Wine Accords between the United States and the European Union, discussed by Rob Tobiassen in Chapter 10.

The TTB's statutory mandate often overlaps with that of other federal agencies. Customs and Border Protection aids TTB by ensuring that importers of alcoholic beverages have a valid basic permit, that excise taxes are paid, and that alcoholic beverage products carry labels that TTB has approved prior to release of the products into interstate commerce. TTB also consults with the Food and Drug Administration (FDA) for expert advice on health and safety issues related to alcoholic beverages. As an example, TTB incorporates in its regulations on winemaking processes and materials the FDA's "Generally Recognized as Safe" (GRAS) standards,[70] and TTB has worked closely in recent years with the FDA on rulemaking for allergen labeling on alcoholic beverages. TTB and FDA occasionally have sparred (for example, over ingredient labeling for alcoholic beverages), and the two agencies have entered into several agreements outlining their respective areas of authority over alcoholic beverages.[71] TTB and the U.S. Department of Agriculture exercise concurrent jurisdiction over alcoholic beverage labels that bear an organic claim. The jurisdictions of TTB and the U.S. Patent and Trademark Office intersect in matters of brand names (trademarks) and appellations (certification marks), as explained further in Chapter 6. Finally, TTB and the Federal Trade Commission each enforce their own regulations concerning alcoholic beverage advertising.

C. REGULATING THE WINE INDUSTRY, FROM GRAPES TO WINE TO THE CONSUMER

The combination of federal and state wine laws makes for a complicated regulatory environment. To better understand the interaction of these laws, in this section I focus on the state and federal legal provisions governing each aspect of the wine business, from grape growing to winemaking to wine distribution and sales. First, I examine the laws governing viticultural practices, that is, the cultivation of vines and the growing of grapes. Second, I discuss the laws and regulations pertaining

70. 27 C.F.R. §24.246 (2021).

71. *See, e.g.*, Alcohol and Tobacco Tax and Trade Bureau, U.S. Department of the Treasury, *Alcohol Beverages Containing Added Caffeine, Industry Circular* 2010-8 (2010); Major Food Allergen Labeling for Wines, Distilled Spirits and Malt Beverages, 71 Fed. Reg. 42329, 42331 (2006); Memorandum of Understanding, 52 Fed. Reg. 45502, 45503-04 (1987); Food and Drug Administration, Trade Correspondence No. 224 (1940); *see also* Mendelson, *supra* note 5, at 132, 167-172.

to wine production. Third, I address the laws relating to the distribution and marketing of wines. With respect to state law, I focus in this section on California, where 90 percent of all domestic wines are produced.

1. VITICULTURAL PRACTICES

The federal and state governments exercise limited control over viticultural practices. Unlike many other countries, the United States does not regulate the acreage used for grape growing or the harvesting practices adhered to by grape growers. However, information on wine labels regarding the designation of a geographic area where grapes are grown (appellations of origin) and representations of varietal content and vintage dates are regulated by the federal government. At least two states, California and Oregon, supplement the federal labeling laws with their own stricter standards on grape origin; Oregon also has a stricter rule on varietal content.[72]

In California, the Department of Food and Agriculture (CDFA) seeks to ensure the orderly marketing and distribution of farm products, including grapes, by licensing all processors of those products (wineries) as well as produce dealers (resellers of grapes or must). The California Food and Agriculture Code spells out the payment obligations of processors and dealers and provides the grower a lien on grapes and the resulting wine until the grower receives payment for its fruit.[73] CDFA, assisted by its Wine Grape Inspection Advisory Committee, also establishes "objective criteria and inspection procedures for all quality conditions that have an effect on the acceptance of, or on the amount of the purchase price of, fresh grapes for wine and byproduct purposes."[74]

California permits growers to have wines made from their own grapes by qualified wineries. The growers, after obtaining the proper licenses, can sell those wines in intrastate or interstate commerce. These are referred to as "custom crush" operations, which are discussed in more detail in Chapter 4.

At the state and local levels, there also are extensive environmental, resource conservation, and land use laws governing vineyard development and operations. For example, local zoning laws may prohibit grape growing in industrial or commercial zones or, conversely, may limit commercial and industrial operations in exclusively agricultural zones. Land use laws are discussed in more detail in Chapter 7. States may promote grape growing through various tax benefits. Grading permits, erosion control plans, and other local, state, and federal approvals also may be required in order to plant a vineyard. In California local permits, if discretionary, require compliance with the California Environmental Quality Act,

---

72. *See, e.g.*, Cal. Code Regs., tit. 17, §§17010(a)(3), 17015 (2022); Or. Admin. R. 845-010-0915 (varietal content), 845-010-0920 (origin) (2022).

73. Cal. Food & Agric. Code §§55631-55653 (2021).

74. *Id.* at §41207.5(b).

which considers the environmental impacts of the particular development proposal.[75]

2. WINE PRODUCTION

The two major federal laws administered by TTB, the Internal Revenue Code (IRC), and the Federal Alcohol Administration (FAA) Act, control the production and labeling of wine. The IRC governs the taxation and production of wine. The FAA Act regulates the distribution, labeling, and advertising of wine.

The internal revenue statute is the oldest and most extensive law in the United States regulating the wine industry. Although the present law was enacted in 1954, with significant amendments in 1958, this statute actually dates from 1862, when Congress first imposed an internal revenue tax on domestic producers of "wine, made of grapes."

Over the years, Congress has expanded the coverage of other products taxed as wine, and today the wine tax is imposed on "all wines (including imitation, substandard, or artificial wine, and compounds sold as wine)."[76] However, when a wine product is in excess of 24 percent alcohol by volume, it is classified as a distilled spirit and taxed accordingly.[77] By using such terms as "imitation," "substandard," "artificial," and "compounds sold as wine," Congress intended, for tax purposes, that the term "wine" would apply to a broad category of products.[78]

The rate of taxation, which is the same whether the wine is imported or domestically produced, is determined by the alcoholic content of the product and the quantity and source of its effervescence, if any. But the tax rates do not vary in direct proportion to alcoholic content. This is true not only within the wine category but across all alcoholic beverages. Distilled spirits are taxed at the highest rate and beer at the lowest.[79] For wine, the excise tax rates range from a low of \$0.17 per gallon on still wine having not more than 16 percent alcohol by volume to a high of \$3.40 per gallon for sparkling wines that are naturally effervescent (that is, wine containing more than 0.392 gram of carbon dioxide per hundred milliliters of wine).[80]

75. Cal. Pub. Res. Code §§21000-21177 (2022).

76. 26 U.S.C. §5041(a) (2018).

77. *Id.*

78. Some of these classifications, such as "substandard," are rarely seen or used.

79. For the current federal excise tax rates for distilled spirits and beer, *see* https://www.ttb.gov/tax-audit/tax-and-fee-rates.

80. 26 U.S.C. §5041(a)-(c) (2018).

Table 1-2 Federal Excise Tax Rates for Wine

WINE — Tax Rates and Tax Credits on Domestic Removals or Imports (2018 to 2022)

Tax Class	Tax Rate per Wine Gallon[81]	Tax Credits per Calendar Year (and Effective Tax Rates per Wine Gallon After Applicable Credits)		
		• Domestic wine producers are entitled to tax credits on wine they produce and may transfer their tax credits to other wineries or to bonded wine cellars that receive their wine in bond • Electing U.S. importers may take advantage of tax credits appropriately assigned to them by a foreign winery		
		First 30,000 Wine Gallons	**Over 30,000 up to 130,000 Wine Gallons**	**Over 130,000 up to 750,000 Wine Gallons**
		Still Wine		
16% and under alcohol by volume (0.392g CO2/100mL or less)	$1.07	$1 credit ($0.07)	90¢ credit ($0.17)	53.5¢ credit ($0.535)
Over 16 - 21% alcohol by volume (0.392g CO2/100mL or less	$1.57	$1 credit ($0.57)	90¢ credit ($0.67)	53.5¢ credit ($1.035)
Over 21 - 24% alcohol by volume (0.392g CO2/100mL or less)	$3.15	$1 credit ($2.15)	90¢ credit ($2.25)	53.5¢ credit ($2.615)

81. A "wine gallon" means a U.S. gallon of liquid measure equivalent to a volume of 231 cubic inches. Id. §5041(d).

Low alcohol by volume wine No more than 0.64g CO2/100mL; derived primarily from grapes or from grape juice concentrate and water; containing no fruit product or fruit flavoring other than grape; and containing less than (not equal to) 8.5% alcohol by volume	$1.07	$1 credit ($0.07)	90¢ credit ($0.17)	53.5¢ credit ($0.535)
Artificially Carbonated Wine				
Over 0.392g CO2/100mL — injected or otherwise added	$3.30	$1 credit ($2.30)	90¢ credit ($2.40)	53.5¢ credit ($2.765)
Sparkling Wine				
Over 0.392g CO2/100mL — naturally occurring	$3.40	$1 credit ($2.40)	90¢ credit ($2.50)	53.5¢ credit ($2.865)

In order to protect the government's source of revenue, the internal revenue law authorizes the federal government to impose various requirements on producers of wine. Since the tax on wine is paid by the producer on the final wine product at the time of its removal from the winery, most controls are focused there.[82]

Every person desiring to establish premises for the production, blending, cellar treatment, storage, bottling, packaging, or repackaging of non-tax-paid wine must qualify at the federal level as a bonded winery or bonded wine cellar.[83] The applicant must file the permit application with the TTB prior to commencing operations. In that application, he or she provides the location of the wine premises and describes the land, buildings, and equipment. If the premises consist of one or more entire buildings, the applicant must describe the size of each building, the material of which it is constructed, and the purpose for which it will be used.[84] The details can seem picayune, such as the need to describe all windows, doors, and other means of ingress and egress, as well as the means of securing them. This is necessary to allow TTB to "secure the revenue," that is, to ensure that its excess

82. Historically, occupational taxes were imposed on sellers of wine, including wine producers, wholesalers, and retailers. 26 U.S.C. §§5081 (producers), 5111 (wholesale dealers), 5121 (retail dealers). Although these taxes were recently repealed, occupational tax registration still is required.

83. 26 U.S.C. §5351 (2018). Any premises engaged in the production operation may be designated as a bonded winery as opposed to a bonded wine cellar. The latter may be involved only in non-production operations such as blending and bottling.

84. 27 C.F.R. §24.166 (2021).

tax revenue is protected by preventing theft of the underlying wine. Generally, the applicant attaches a drawing illustrating the layout of the bonded premises and all equipment there.

The federal government also protects its tax revenue through a "bond" requirement.[85] A bond is a guarantee, usually given by an insurance company, that covers the potential tax liability on the wines stored on the bonded premises, should the winery fail to pay its taxes. Taxes are paid by filing a tax return with an accompanying tax payment after the wine has been removed from the bonded premises. Returns are filed and payments are made twice each month, unless the tax is prepaid or no tax is due.[86]

Many of these same qualification requirements reappear under state and local law. A prospective winery must contact various local (city or county) and state agencies as well as TTB and abide by their respective regulations. Only after the applicant has qualified with TTB and obtained any required state and local licenses and permits may operations commence.

The IRC also imposes an extensive system of controls over production practices, cellar treatment, and classification of wine. These controls date back well into the nineteenth century. Federal law defines proper cellar treatment as those practices and procedures in the United States, whether historical or newly developed, that employ various methods and materials to correct or stabilize wine in order to produce a finished product acceptable in good commercial practice.[87] This law specifically identifies particular winemaking methods and materials used in customary commercial practice as lawful cellar treatment in the absence of regulations finding them to be improper.[88] These provisions are designed to ensure that all wines sold in the United States are safe to consume and, by extension, that the federal government will receive its tax revenue when the wine is "removed from bond." Were it never removed from bond, no taxes would be due.

TTB imposes extensive recordkeeping requirements on wineries and has authority to enter the business premises of a winery during all business hours. The producer must be able to account for all wine on the bonded premise and to prove the veracity of every label claim by reference to detailed production, processing, and storage records. Inspections are conducted on a regular basis, at which time TTB inspectors ensure that the proper taxes have been paid and that proper cellar treatment and production practices are being followed. Generally speaking, TTB audits are of three types: a product integrity audit, a tax audit, or a trade practices audit.

---

85. *See, e.g.*, 27 C.F.R. §24.146(a) (2021).

86. *Id.* §24.271.

87. 26 U.S.C. §5382(a) (2018); 27 C.F.R. §§24.175-218 (2021).

88. In the case of imported wines, 26 U.S.C. §5382(a) (2020) requires certification by the government of the producer's country that the wine has been produced in accordance with practices and procedures approved in the United States or that it is covered by an international agreement. The content, validity and use of such certifications are described in Treasury Decision Labeling and Advertising of Wine, 27 C.F.R. §§4.1-4.101 (2021); Wine, *Id.* §§27.1-27.221.

Present federal law contains specific provisions governing the cellar treatment, amelioration, and sweetening of wines. These requirements are very technical in nature. The standards on amelioration and sweetening are based on the classification of the wine involved. Classifications of wine include "natural wine"[89] made from grapes or fruit; "specially sweetened natural wine,"[90] which is wine produced by adding sugar; "special natural wine,"[91] which is wine flavored by herbs, spices, or other natural essences; "agricultural wine,"[92] which is wine made from agricultural products other than grapes; and "effervescent wines," which include natural sparkling wines and artificially carbonated wines.

California and certain other states supplement TTB's list of authorized winemaking practices. For example, California prohibits the addition of sugar to wine, although the addition of concentrated grape must is allowed.[93]

Together, these state and federal laws are designed to prevent fraudulent winemaking which, along with label fraud, is the primary means of counterfeiting wine.

In addition to the extensive system of control over the production and treatment of wine that exists under the IRC, the FAA Act introduces into the marketplace a system of controls designed to protect the wine consumer from fraud and deception and to eliminate unfair competition. The focal point of the statute is its permit requirements for producers, wholesalers, and importers of wines and spirits, but not beer, and its trade practice provisions.

The FAA Act, enacted in 1935, is the other primary pillar of federal wine authority.[94] This statute requires the approval of the United States Treasury Department before anyone can engage in the business of importing, producing, or blending wine, or purchasing wine at wholesale for resale to a trade buyer. This approval, in the form of a basic permit issued by TTB,[95] is given only if an extensive background investigation by TTB indicates that the applicant is likely to maintain business operations in conformity with federal and state laws. Once the permit is issued, it remains in force unless and until it is revoked, voluntarily surrendered, or automatically terminated.[96] Since the permit cannot be sold or transferred, it automatically terminates if there is a change in control of the entity

---

89. 26 U.S.C. §5381 (2006).

90. *Id.*§5385.

91. *Id.*§5386.

92. *Id.*§5387.

93. Cal. Code Regs. Tit. 17, §17010(a) (2021.)

94. Before the passage of the FAA Act, President Franklin Roosevelt established by executive order the Federal Alcohol Control Administration (FACA) to guide the post-Prohibition wines and spirits industries through the development of voluntary industry codes. The National Industrial Recovery Act, ch. 90, 48 Stat 195 (1933), *amended by* Act of June 14, 1935, ch. 246, 49 Stat. 375, under which authority Roosevelt established the FACA, was ruled unconstitutional in *A.L.A. Schechter Poultry Corp. v. United States*, 295 U.S. 495 (1935). Subsequently, Congress adopted the FAA Act, ch. 814, 49 Stat. 977 (1935) (codified as amended at 27 U.S.C. §§201-219(a) (2020).

95. 27 U.S.C. §203 (2018).

96. 27 U.S.C. §204(g) (2018).

holding it.[97] However, in the case of a winery sale, operations are allowed to continue under the seller's basic permit until a new permit is issued to the buyer.[98]

In California, a license to engage in the wine business is required in addition to a federal basic permit.[99] However, unlike the federal permit system, the responsible state agency — here, the California ABC — issues licenses to wine retailers as well as wine producers, importers, and wholesalers. California ABC licenses are particular to a person, premise, and type of beverage.[100] For example, a winegrower (winery) licensee cannot brew beer under that license, although a separate beer manufacturer's license can be obtained; a beer and wine wholesaler cannot sell distilled spirits; and an off-sale beer and wine retailer cannot allow wine to be consumed on the premise without a separate on-sale beer and wine license. That being said, California affords winegrowers perhaps the broadest privileges of any licensee. Along with the right to produce and blend wine, winegrowers can offer wine tastings, sell their wine for on-premises consumption, and even operate a restaurant at the winery where any producer's wine, beer, or brandy may be served.[101] A winegrower's license application, like the application for any other ABC license, must include detailed personal and financial information, which is thoroughly examined by ABC prior to license issuance.

The trade practice provisions of the FAA Act and the California ABC Act prohibit all producers, importers, and wholesalers of alcoholic beverages from engaging in specified practices that tend to produce monopolistic control over retailers. Federal and state tied-house and free goods laws are discussed in more detail in Chapter 2.

The FAA Act is also a consumer protection law, as is evident from a reading of §5(e) of the Act, controlling the labeling of wines.[102] This section makes it unlawful to sell, ship, receive in interstate or foreign commerce, or remove from customs custody any wine,

> unless such products are bottled, packaged, and labeled in conformity with such regulations, to be prescribed by the Secretary of the Treasury, with respect to packaging, marking, branding, and labeling and size and fill of container (1) as will prohibit deception of the consumer with respect to such products or the quantity thereof and as will prohibit, irrespective of falsity, such statements relating to age, manufacturing processes, analyses, guarantees, and scientific or irrelevant matters as the Secretary of the Treasury finds to be likely to mislead the consumer; (2) as will provide the consumer with adequate information as to the identity and quality of the products, the alcoholic content thereof . . . ; (4) as will prohibit statements on the label that are disparaging of a competitor's products or are false, misleading, obscene, or indecent; and (5) as will prevent deception of the consumer by use of a trade or brand name that is the name of any living

97. *Id.*
98. 27 C.F.R.§1.44 (2021).
99. Cal. Bus. & Prof. Code §23300 (2021).
100. *See, e.g., id.* §23320.
101. *Id.* §§23356.1, 23358.
102. 27 U.S.C. §205(e) (2018).

> individual of public prominence, or existing private or public organization, or is a name that is in simulation or is an abbreviation thereof, and as will prevent the use of a graphic, pictorial, or emblematic representation of any such individual or organization, if the use of such name or representation is likely falsely to lead the consumer to believe that the product has been endorsed, made, or used by, or produced for, or under the supervision of, or in accordance with the specifications of, such individual or organization.

At the hearings before the House Ways and Means Committee on the bill proposing the FAA Act, Mr. Choate, Administrator of the Federal Alcohol Control Administration, made the following statement concerning the objectives of §5(e):

> The purpose was to provide such regulations, not laid down in statute, so as to be inflexible, but laid down under the guidance of Congress, under general principles, by a body which could change them as changes were found necessary.
>
> Those regulations were intended to insure that the purchaser should get what he thought he was getting, that representations both in labels and in advertising should be honest and straight-forward and truthful. They should not be confined, as the pure food regulations have been confined, to prohibitions of falsity, but they should also provide for the information of the consumer, that he should be told what was in the bottle, and all the important factors which were of interest to him about what was in the bottle.[103]

The TTB enforces §5(e) through a label approval process that must be completed prior to the product's sale by the winery or, in the case of imported wine, prior to its removal from customs custody.[104] The label approval is known as a COLA (its full title is Application for and Certification/Exemption of Label/Bottle Approval). States can and do supplement the federal labeling regulations with rules of their own. Oregon, for example, has perhaps the most rigorous labeling standards in the country for appellation grape source content[105] and varietal content.[106]

Although TTB has regulations similar to those for labeling that apply to the advertising of wines,[107] the FAA Act does not mandate prior approval of wine advertisements. However, the law does prohibit any advertisement that is inconsistent with any statement on the wine label.[108] The labeling and advertising regulations for wine are covered in Chapter 3.

---

103. Federal Alcohol Control Act: Hearing on H.R. 8539 Before the H. Comm. on Ways and Means, 74th Cong. 10 (1935) (statement of Joseph H. Choate Jr., Chairman and Director, Federal Alcohol Control Administration).

104. 27 C.F.R. §4.50(a) (2021).

105. Or. Admin. R. 845-010-0920 (2020).

106. *Id.* 845-010-0915.

107. 27 U.S.C. §205(f) (2020).

108. 27 C.F.R. §4.64(b) (2021).

3. DISTRIBUTION AND MARKETING

I previously described the three-tier distribution system, involving separate and distinct manufacturers, wholesalers, and retailers, with alcoholic beverages passing from one level to the next and ultimately to the consumer. This system is enforced by state licensing laws that grant specific sales privileges to specific licensees and by so-called at-rest laws. The latter laws, which exist in around 30 states, require that wine shipped from out of state physically arrive and remain at the premises of an in-state wholesaler before it is transferred to a retailer. The retailer in turn must take physical possession of the wine before shipping it to a consumer.

The three-tier system is not mandated by TTB, and it is not the only way to sell wine in the United States. Depending on the laws of the particular state, manufacturers might be authorized to sell their wines directly to retailers, with or without the assistance of a broker,[109] or to consumers. This is the case in California. Winery sales to retailers are known as self-distribution; winery sales to consumers are called direct-to-consumer sales.

As mentioned above, tied-house laws at the federal and state levels prohibit the vertical integration commonly found in the pre-Prohibition era. Whereas many state tied-house laws present "bright-line" standards — such as the California provisions that prohibit an alcoholic beverage manufacturer, importer, or wholesaler from having "any interest, direct or indirect," [110]in a retailer and vice versa (subject to enumerated exceptions that have expanded greatly in recent years) — the FAA Act prohibits any supplier from *inducing* a retailer to purchase his products to the *exclusion* of other products in interstate commerce.[111] The federal Act specifically prohibits suppliers from obtaining preferred treatment from retailers by acquiring an interest in the retailers' license or property; by giving those retailers money, equipment, or services;[112] by guaranteeing the retailers' financial obligations; by extending excessive credit to them; or by giving the retailers any "other thing of value."[113] Federal law also prohibits a variety of other unfair trade or marketing practices by suppliers that can restrict interstate commerce, deceive consumers, or jeopardize government revenue. These practices

---

109. *See, e.g.*, Cal. Bus. & Prof. Code §23377 (2009) (licensed wine brokers). The main distinction between a broker and a wholesaler is that the former does not take title to the goods but typically solicits an order and forwards it to the winery. By contrast, a wholesaler buys wine from a winery for purposes of resale, typically to other wholesalers and retailers.

110. *See, e.g., id.* §25500. Such interests include corporate control over, or financial interests in, the alcoholic beverage business, business property, or alcoholic beverage license. Depending on the state's attribution rules, the tied-house prohibition may extend to spouses, affiliates, agents, subsidiaries, or others.

111. 27 U.S.C. §205(b) (2018).

112. An important exception to the general prohibition of payments to retailers is for consumer-related activities such as wine tastings and coupons. For other exceptions, *see* 27 C.F.R. §§6.81-6.102 (2021).

113. 27 U.S.C. §205(b) (2020).

include consignment sales, exclusive outlets,[114] and commercial bribery.[115] In each instance (other than consignment sales), federal law is violated only if the practice occurs in interstate commerce and there is evidence of exclusion of competitors' wines in the marketplace. As a practical matter, the exclusion requirement makes federal enforcement of trade practices laws substantially more difficult than similar state laws that do not require exclusion.

States have their own trade practice provisions relating to alcoholic beverage sales that may or may not mirror those of federal law. Most states, for example, have regulatory controls over sales promotion devices that might stimulate alcohol consumption. California, for example, prohibits any licensee from giving "directly or indirectly, any premium, gift, or free goods in connection with the sale or distribution of any alcoholic beverage," except as specifically authorized by the California ABC. Authorized exceptions include retailer advertising specialties (such as coasters, menu cards, calendars, and napkins) and consumer advertising specialties (such as ashtrays, corkscrews, posters, and bottle stoppers).[116] These specialty items are limited in unit cost and in the total dollar amount of the giveaway to any single retailer. While most exceptions like these are established administratively by the alcoholic beverage regulatory agency itself, through rulemaking or interpretations of existing laws, sometimes a special law is required. As an example, the California legislature passed a law to permit manufacturers to give to on-premise retailers "paper beverage coasters less than 25 square inches in size and having a value of less than five cents ($0.05) per coaster."[117]

Some states ban credit sales altogether. And most states control advertising in some fashion, effectively limiting standardized national advertising content. Other states control the methods of contacting purchasers (solicitations, phone and mail orders, auctions, etc.).

Separate and apart from specific state and federal alcoholic beverage laws, relations among manufacturers and wholesalers often are regulated by specific state alcoholic beverage franchise laws.[118] The original purpose of these franchise laws was to protect the in-state wholesaler from what were perceived to be unfair requirements imposed by the typically larger out-of-state producer.[119] Recently,

---

114. An exclusive outlet is created when a retailer agrees to purchase and sell only the products of one supplier. *Id.* §205(a).

115. Commercial bribery occurs when a supplier induces the employees of a retailer through various means, including gifts and payments, to purchase the supplier's products to the exclusion of products sold by other suppliers. *Id.* §205(c).

116. Cal. Bus. & Prof. Code §25600(a)(1) (2020;) Cal. Code Regs., tit. 4, §106(e)(1)-(2) (2020).

117. Cal. Bus. & Prof. Code §25501(a).

118. As background reading on alcoholic beverage franchise laws, *see* Douglas Glen Whitman, Strange Brew: Alcohol and Government Monopoly (Oakland: Independent Institute 2003) and Susan C. Cagann, Contents Under Pressure: Regulating the Sales and Marketing of Alcoholic Beverages, in Social and Economic Control of Alcohol 57, 67-69 (Carole L. Jurkiewicz & Murphy J. Painter eds., Public Administration and Public Policy No. 135 (2008)).

119. The concerns are essentially about adhesion contracts imposed by the out-of-state franchisor with greater economic might and a superior bargaining position. Today, however, many wineries are dwarfed in size and muscle by the out-of-state wholesalers. Assuming a small winery

the wholesale tier has contracted and consolidated; many wholesalers are now far larger than the producers whose products they carry.

California has no alcoholic beverage franchise law, but among the states that do, wine is not always a covered product. Some franchise laws cover beer and/or distilled spirits but not wine; other, broader franchise laws cover both alcoholic and non-alcoholic products. Presently, 21 states have some type of franchise law provision concerning wine. Most franchise laws regulate the territories in which wholesalers and manufacturers may conduct business. Some states require exclusive territories, that is, the appointment of one wholesaler per manufacturer in a given area. Other states permit multiple, non-exclusive territorial appointments, referred to as dualing. Oklahoma requires manufacturers to sell wines to all licensed wholesalers in that state.

State franchise laws also regulate the business relationship between a manufacturer and wholesaler. Many state laws require a showing of "good cause," as defined under local law, to make any change in a distribution relationship, including the termination, replacement, or addition of wholesalers. Good cause may include a wholesaler's bankruptcy, the sale of substantial assets of the wholesaler's business, repeated violations of state or federal law, or the wholesaler's failure to meet reasonable performance standards following notice of non-performance and an opportunity to cure. The practical effect of these laws is to make it difficult, if not impossible, for a winery to terminate an out-of-state wholesaler. In states where there are no specific statutory termination provisions, as in California, general legal principles apply, including the covenant of good faith and fair dealing, which is implied in all California contracts and related unfair competition and antitrust laws.

Many states have adopted another mechanism to eliminate tax evasion and ensure product integrity. These are known as "primary source" laws that require an out-of-state winery or wholesaler that wishes to sell its wine in that state to establish that it lawfully produced the wine (in the case of a winery) or purchased the wine (in the case of the importer or wholesaler) and by written contract has the sole right to distribute the wine in the United States. This applies to both domestic and foreign wines. Florida's primary source law is typical; wine shipments into the state must come from "a licensed primary American source of supply," which must be the manufacturer or the primary importer.[120] Primary source laws effectively close off the "secondary market," also known as the gray market, to wines and other alcoholic beverages that otherwise could enter the market lawfully — for example, from a wholesaler in another state or from abroad.

Antitrust laws, which date from the period of massive industrialization following the Civil War, apply to the alcoholic beverage industry as they do to other sectors of the economy. The Sherman Act of 1890[121] prohibits all contracts, combinations, and conspiracies that unreasonably restrain trade. This Act has been

---

can even find a wholesaler to represent its brand in a particular state, it rarely can dictate the terms of the producer-wholesaler relationship.

120. Fla. Stat. §564.045(1), (4) (2020).

121. Sherman Anti-Trust Act, ch. 647, 26 Stat. 209 (1890) (codified at 15 U.S.C. §§1-7 (2020)).

the basis of lawsuits involving price fixing, allocation of customers and territories, and refusals to deal. The Clayton Act[122] and particularly the Robinson-Patman Act[123] prohibit, *inter alia*, price discrimination, exclusive dealing, and tie-ins. Violations of both federal laws are punishable as felonies, with the violator also subject to civil actions for treble damages and attorney's fees. Several states have enacted ancillary or parallel laws.

Under federal and state antitrust laws, a few actions automatically are presumed to be anticompetitive and hence are per se illegal. Other business conduct is judged case by case, based on the "rule of reason." The choice between these methods of analysis depends largely on the nature of the restraint and whether the agreement or conduct in question is "horizontal" or "vertical." Horizontal agreements are made between parties on the same level of distribution. For example, an agreement between two wineries to fix the prices they charge wholesalers would be classified as a horizontal price restraint, which is per se unlawful under the Sherman Act. Vertical agreements, by contrast, involve parties on different levels of the distribution system. For example, an agreement between a winery and a wholesaler to allocate customers, products, or territories in a given market is a vertical non-price restriction, subject to the rule of reason.[124] Resale price management, in which a manufacturer requires a reseller (e.g., a wholesaler or a retailer) to sell the manufacturer's product at a specific price, used to be classified as per se illegal but, following the Supreme Court's decision in *Leegin Creative Leather Products, Inc. v. PSKS, Inc.*, 127 S. Ct. 2705 (2007), is now judged by the rule of reason.

Under the Robinson-Patman Act, a manufacturer may not sell the same product to two different customers in the same tier of distribution at different prices unless there is a commercially justifiable reason. Valid reasons include a cost justification (such as volume discounts or variable sales costs) and the need to meet the competition. Additionally, tying arrangements, whereby a customer must purchase an undesired product to obtain a desired product, and full-line forcing, whereby a customer must handle all product lines even if he or she desires only one product, are subject to close antitrust scrutiny concerning their commercial impact and the manufacturer's economic power.

Antitrust laws and principles often conflict with state franchise laws. For example, many franchise laws mandate contract terms in an alcoholic beverage distribution relationship that entrench incumbent wholesalers appointed on an exclusive basis in given market areas and that restrict market entry by new and possibly more efficient wholesalers. As such, these laws have a potentially anticompetitive effect, which permits the survival of inefficient distributional arrangements. State franchise laws and many state pricing schemes for alcoholic beverages have been protected from antitrust attack because, under common law,

---

122. Clayton Anti-Trust Act, Pub. L. No. 63-212, 38 Stat. 730 (1914) (codified at 15 U.S.C. §§12–27; 29 U.S.C. §§52-53 (2020).

123. Robinson-Patman Price Discrimination Act, Pub. L. No. 74-692, 49 Stat. 1526 (1936) (codified at 15 U.S.C. §§13-13b, 21a (2020)).

124. Today almost all vertical non-price restraints are judged by the rule of reason.

state action for specific state purposes is immune from antitrust attack.[125] This is known as the *Parker* immunity doctrine, established by the Supreme Court in *Parker v. Brown.*[126]

D. CONCLUSION

Wine law in the United States is not a single body of law administered by a single governmental agency. It exists at the local, state, and federal levels in the form of specific alcoholic beverage laws and regulations, as well as in countless related fields of law. This complexity is the result of our nation's complicated history of regulating alcoholic beverages and our state and federal governments' efforts to protect their revenues and the public at large. Like our country's wines, wine law is organic, diverse, sophisticated, and always exciting.

125. *Parker v. Brown*, 317 U.S. 341, 352 (1943).
126. *Id.*

CHAPTER 2

TIED HOUSE AND TRADE PRACTICES

Carrie L. Bonnington

Tied house laws limit relationships between manufacturers and wholesalers on the one hand and retailers on the other (and sometimes between manufacturers and wholesalers). Tied house laws generally address two types of relationships: (1) ownership interest between the tiers, and (2) things of value passing between the tiers, often referred to as "trade practices."

Trade practice laws in the wine, beer, and spirits industries regulate relationships among industry members. Nearly every state and the federal government have enacted trade practices laws. The laws are designed to prevent domination of retailers by suppliers (generally, producers, importers, and wholesalers[1]) ("tied house laws") and to prohibit commercial bribery and other unlawful inducements designed to promote the aggressive sale of alcohol beverages[2] ("free goods laws"). The laws are arcane, complicated, sometimes contradictory, often frustrating, and, in many jurisdictions but especially in California, riddled with exceptions. They are subject to varying regulatory interpretations and have, not surprisingly, engendered their own jurisprudence. Because these laws regulate practices involving the sale and distribution of alcohol beverages, wine lawyers must understand them to advise their clients. This is often a challenging task as most tied house laws were enacted long ago and could not have contemplated today's modern business practices and relationships.

In this chapter, we address federal and state tied house and trade practice laws. In the state section, we focus on four states, all of which are leaders in the production, distribution, sale, and/or marketing of wine: California, New York,

1. In the alcohol beverage industry, the terms "wholesaler" and "distributor" are synonymous.

2. The term "alcoholic beverages" is generally disfavored in the industry as it has the tendency to suggest misuse or excessive consumption. Some industry members have adopted the term "alcohol beverages" as an alternative.

Texas, and Washington. California is our primary focus, as it produces an average of 81 percent of total U.S. wine productions.

A. HISTORICAL BACKGROUND

The Twenty-first Amendment to the Constitution allows states greater latitude to regulate the sale and distribution of wine and other alcohol beverages than any other consumer product.[3] Each state has enacted laws governing the sale and distribution of alcohol beverages.[4] However, in 1935, when the states turned their attention to such regulation after Repeal, there was widespread agreement that they should adopt laws to curtail the excesses that led to Prohibition in the first place.

The "drys" blamed aggressive marketing of alcohol beverages for many of these excesses. Breweries controlled bars in their local markets and worked hard to encourage consumption of their products.[5] As a first step in curbing such alleged abuses, most states adopted a three-tier system of distribution, with the intent of separating the three tiers from each other: "Manufacturing interests were to be separated from wholesale interests; wholesale interests were to be segregated from retail interests."[6] In most states, however, the separation is between "suppliers" (producers, importers, and distributors) on the one hand and retailers on the other. The three-tier system exists in some form in every state, although it looks a bit different in the 17 states and one county[7] known as "control" or "monopoly" states, where the state itself participates in some aspect of the sale or distribution of alcohol beverages.[8]

Having separated the three tiers, the states sought to strengthen and protect each tier from the others. Tied house laws are the most notable example of this protection.[9]

---

3. Indeed, alcohol beverages are the only presently traded commodities the Constitution specifically addresses; and not only once, but twice. The Eighteenth Amendment enacted Prohibition and the Twenty-first Amendment repealed it.

4. Such diversity of treatment is otherwise prohibited by the Commerce Clause of the Constitution, which has become an uneasy but strengthening counterweight to the Twenty-first Amendment in the jurisprudence of the Supreme Court. *Compare, e.g., State Bd. of Equalization of the State of Cal. v. Young's Mkt. Co.*, 299 U.S. 59 (1936), with *Granholm v. Heald*, 544 U.S. 460 (2005).

5. A Review of Tied-House Laws That Impinge on the State's Wine Industry and the Status of Direct Shipment Regulations Nationwide: Joint Hearing Before the S.Comm on Governmental Affairs and the S. Select Comm. on California's Wine Industry, 1999 Leg., App. B, "Tied-House Law" History (Cal. 1999) (testimony of John Peirce, Staff Counsel of the California Department of Alcoholic Beverage Control).

6. Cal Beer Wholesalers Ass'n v. Alcoholic Beverage Control Appeals Board, 5 Cal. 3d 402, 407 (1971).

7. Alabama, Idaho, Iowa, Maine, Michigan, Mississippi, Montana, New Hampshire, North Carolina, Ohio, Oregon, Pennsylvania, Utah, Vermont, Virginia, West Virginia, Wyoming, and Montgomery County, Maryland.

8. Some control states occupy one or more of the three distribution tiers, while others are only control states for distilled spirits.

9. But see note 93, infra.

One of the most notorious practices that led to the enactment of Prohibition was the so-called tied house evil. Bars and restaurants, tied by ownership to their parent breweries, often offered free meals provided the patron ordered a drink.[10] The temperance movement attributed numerous social evils to tied houses, including "political corruption, proliferation of saloons, increase in alcohol consumption, and irresponsible ownership of retail outlets."[11] The tied house laws were "aimed to prevent two particular dangers: the ability and potentiality of large firms to dominate local markets through vertical and horizontal integration and the excessive sales of alcoholic beverages produced by the overly aggressive marketing techniques of larger alcoholic beverage concerns."[12]

Most states saw the principal tied house evil as *control* of retailers by suppliers. Tied house statutes normally prohibit such control. Some states, however, such as California, adopted even more stringent laws designed to prohibit control. In general, California's tied house laws prohibit the *direct* or *indirect* ownership of *any interest* by a supplier in a retail license and the business or equipment used in the retail business.[13] These laws generally regulate two major categories: the ownership of interests the supplier may have in a retailer and the benefits a supplier may provide to a retailer.

California's tied house scheme was so aggressive, it is now riddled with statutory exceptions. These exceptions (examined below) are often difficult to secure and fiercely opposed, most often from wholesalers eager to maintain a distribution monopoly.

Before examining California's tied house scheme, we will first outline federal tied house laws.

B. FEDERAL TIED HOUSE REGULATION

As the nation emerged from Prohibition, the federal government sought to safeguard the newly legal alcohol industry from the corruption that became rampant during the ban.[14] As part of the New Deal, the Roosevelt administration established the Federal Alcohol Control Administration under the National Industrial Recovery Act (NIRA).[15] When the Supreme Court declared the NIRA unconstitutional in 1935, alcohol was again left unregulated. In the words of one court, the industry was "infested with bootleggers and racketeers anxious to continue their trade and willing to thwart tax and health laws."[16] Congress, which

10. Hence the admonition, still in use today, "There is no such thing as a free lunch!"

11. *National Distrib. Co., Inc. v. U.S. Treasury Dep't, Bureau of Alcohol, Tobacco and Firearms*, 626 F.2d 997, 1010 (D.C. Cir. 1980).

12. *Cal Beer Wholesalers Ass'n*, 5 Cal. 3d at 407.

13. Cal. Bus. & Prof. Code §§25500 (on-sale licensees), 25502 (off-sale licensees).

14. *Fedway Assocs., Inc. v. U.S. Treasury, Bureau of Alcohol, Tobacco and Firearms*, 976 F.2d 1416 (D.C. Cir. 1992).

15. *National Distrib.*, 626 F.2d at 1005.

16. *Id.*

sought to rely on the existing antitrust laws to regulate alcohol after the demise of the NIRA, acted quickly to adopt the Federal Alcohol Administration (FAA) Act of 1935.[17]

1. FEDERAL ALCOHOL ADMINISTRATION ACT

Now codified at 27 U.S.C. Section 201 *et seq.*, the FAA Act contains the federal tied house restriction at Section 205(b). The tied house provision of the FAA Act prohibits a supplier[18] from inducing a retailer to purchase its products to the "exclusion in whole or in part" of products from other suppliers[19] in a transaction that implicates interstate commerce.

Of the three necessary jurisdictional elements — (1) a sale in interstate or foreign commerce, (2) an unlawful inducement, and (3) exclusion of competitors' products — the first two are usually easiest to prove.

With respect to the second element, unlawful inducement, the regulation lists as means of inducement: owning any interest in the business, real, or personal property of a retailer; giving, selling, or renting any fixture or thing of value to a retailer (subject to exceptions); paying a retailer for advertising; guaranteeing a loan for a retailer or extending more than customary credit; requiring a retailer to buy a quota of products (including tie-in sales); and commercial bribery.[20]

The third element, exclusion, is more difficult to evaluate. The courts have read the exclusion requirement narrowly, so that it prevents the application of the federal tied house laws in the majority of cases. The D.C. Circuit examined the exclusion criterion at great length in the leading case, *Fedway Associates, Inc. v. United States Treasury Department Bureau of Alcohol, Tobacco and Firearms.*[21]

Circuit Judge Ruth Bader Ginsberg provided the following summary of the case in her decision:

> Fedway's promotional campaign lasted for three months, during which retailers were offered — on a non-discriminatory basis — certain consumer electronic goods if they agreed to purchase designated quantities of Finlandia vodka or Captain Morgan spiced rum. As described by the Bureau, retailers would get a microwave oven for purchasing five cases of liquor from Fedway; a thirteen-inch color television for ten cases; a compact disc player for fifteen cases; and a VCR for twenty-five cases. The wholesale value of these items ranged from $104 to $280. The retailers were under no obligation to participate. If they chose to participate, they would not be bound by contract to buy less vodka or rum from Fedway's rivals. The promotion placed no restrictions on how or where retailers

---

17. *Fedway*, 976 F.2d at 1418.

18. "[A]ny person engaged in business as a distiller, brewer, rectifier, blender, or other producer, or as an importer or wholesaler, of distilled spirits, wine, or malt beverages, or as a bottler, or warehouseman and bottler, of distilled spirits, directly or indirectly or through an affiliate." 27 U.S.C. §205 (2006).

19. 27 U.S.C. §205(b) (2022).

20. *Id.*

21. *Fedway*, 976 F.2d n.14.

> used the incentive equipment; a TV or VCR could be used on the retailer's premises (a popular choice for bar owners) or given to an employee for use at home. The case against Fedway rests solely on this single campaign. No prior or subsequent Fedway promotion figures in the record we are called upon to review.
>
> The three-month promotion successfully boosted Fedway's sales of Finlandia vodka and Captain Morgan spiced rum. Several retailers testified that the promotion led them to buy more cases of Fedway's liquor than they otherwise would have; a few even bought enough cases to qualify for more than one electronic gadget. Most important, many of these same retailers also testified that their increased purchases of Fedway liquor in turn led them to purchase less vodka and rum distributed by rival wholesalers.[22]

The court in *Fedway* determined that "Congress intended the 'exclusion' criterion to direct the regulator to determine something more" than merely leading a retailer to purchase less of a product than it would have otherwise.[23] Instead, "Congress used 'exclusion' to indicate placement of retailer independence at risk by means of a 'tie' or 'link' between the wholesaler and the retailer or by any other means of wholesaler control."[24]

Accordingly, an unlawful inducement in and of itself does not necessarily violate the FAA Act. The general rule is "that transactions between suppliers and retailers do not induce the 'exclusion in whole or in part' of competing suppliers unless their purpose or potential effect is to lead to supplier control over ostensibly independent purchasers."[25] Exclusion therefore requires more than the face of the statute suggests and is thus quite difficult to prove.

In fact, the courts have been reluctant to hold that a practice violates the FAA Act, short of "egregious violations" by a supplier that so dominate a retailer that the retailer is compelled to purchase substantially all of its beverage products from that wholesaler.[26]

2. CODE OF FEDERAL REGULATIONS

The Alcohol and Tobacco Tax and Trade Bureau (TTB) of the U.S. Department of the Treasury (formerly that portion of the Bureau of Alcohol, Tobacco, and Firearms that regulated alcohol beverages[27]) is the agency charged with enforcing the federal tied house laws and issuing the operative administrative regulations.[28] TTB regulations not only clarify the meaning of the statutory

---

22. *Id.* at 1418.

23. *Id.* at 1420.

24. *Id.* Although *Fedway* addressed a relationship between a wholesaler and a retailer, a similar analysis applies to relationships between other suppliers (a winery, distillery, or importer) and a retailer.

25. *Foremost Sales Promotions v. Dir., Bureau of Alcohol, Tobacco and Firearms*, 860 F.2d 229, 237 (7th Cir. 1998).

26. *Id.* at 238.

27. ATF is now the Bureau of Alcohol, Tobacco, Firearms, and Explosives and is part of the Department of Justice.

28. 27 C.F.R. §§6.1-6.153 (2022).

language but also provide exceptions to the general prohibitions contained in the FAA Act.[29] (Interestingly, the regulations do not apply to any transaction between an industry member and a retailer wholly owned by the industry member.[30])

Federal regulations specifically identify certain acts that are violations (i.e., "red light" acts), certain acts that are not violations (i.e., "green light" acts), and certain acts that "put retailer independence at risk" and therefore may be deemed an unlawful inducement (i.e., "yellow light" acts).

Red light acts include, but are not limited to, an industry member renting display space at a retail establishment (Section 6.35); an industry member furnishing, giving, renting, lending, or selling any equipment, fixtures, signs, supplies, money, services, or other things of value to a retailer (Section 6.41); furnishing free warehousing by delaying delivery of distilled spirits, wine, or malt beverages beyond the time that payment for the product is received (Section 6.44); paying or crediting a retailer for any advertising, display, or distribution service (Section 6.51); an arrangement in which an industry member participates with a retailer in paying for an advertisement placed by the retailer (i.e. cooperative advertising) (Section 6.52); purchase, by an industry member, of advertising on signs, scoreboards, programs, scorecards, and the like at ballparks, racetracks, or stadiums from the retail concessionaire (Section 6.53); rental by an industry member of display space at a retail establishment (Section 6.56); and requiring a retailer to take and dispose of any quota of distilled spirits, wine, or malt beverages (i.e. quota sales) (Section 6.71).

Green light acts include, but are not limited to, giving or selling product displays provided the total value of all product displays does not exceed $300 per brand in any one retail establishment at one time, and the displays contain conspicuous and substantial advertising matter on the product (Section 6.83); point-of-sale advertising materials such as posters, placards, designs, inside signs (electric, mechanical, or otherwise), window decorations, trays, coasters, mats, menu cards, meal checks, paper napkins, foam scrapers, back bar mats, thermometers, clocks, calendars, and alcoholic beverage lists or menus (Section 6.84(1)); consumer advertising specialties such as trading stamps, non-alcoholic mixers, pouring racks, ashtrays, bottle or can openers, corkscrews, shopping bags, matches, printed recipes, pamphlets, cards, leaflets, blotters, postcards, pencils, shirts, caps, and visors (Section 6.84(2)); giving a sample of distilled spirits, wine, or malt beverages to a retailer who has not purchased the brand from that industry member within the last 12 months (Section 6.91);[31] packaging and distributing distilled spirits, wine, or malt beverages in combination with other, non-alcoholic items for sale to consumers (i.e. combination packaging) (Section 6.93); and

---

29. *Id.* §6.81.

30. *Id.* §6.3(a).

31. For each retail establishment the industry member may not give more than 3 gallons of any brand of malt beverage, 3 liters of any brand of wine, and 3 liters of distilled spirits. If a particular product is not available in a size within the prescribed quantity limitations, the industry member may furnish the next larger size to a retailer.

providing coupons and other direct offerings subject to certain limitations (Section 6.96).[32]

Yellow light acts, those that put retailer independence at risk, include, but are not limited to, an industry member resetting stock (other than the industry member's product) for a retailer; purchasing or renting display, shelf, storage, or warehouse space (i.e., slotting allowance); less than 100 percent ownership of an industry member in a retailer, where such ownership influences the purchases of the retailer; and requiring a retailer to purchase one product in order to purchase a different product at the same time (Section 6.152). Engaging in any yellow light acts comes with some risk and should be evaluated on a case-by-case basis.

3. TTB ENFORCEMENT

While TTB's enforcement focus changes from time to time to address current industry trends, pay to play schemes (*e.g.*, slotting fees) have remained an enforcement priority for the last decade. TTB has brought dozens of actions against suppliers allegedly providing a retailer a thing of value in exchange for favorable product placement. TTB concluded a significant trade practice investigation in 2011 that resulted in TTB collecting offers in compromise (OIC) totaling $1.9 million from six industry members who participated in a nationwide beverage program implemented by Harrah's Hotels and Casinos.[33]

TTB's investigation largely focused on activities in the Las Vegas area and alleged that the industry members furnished, through a third party, nearly $2 million in inducements and subsidiaries during the program's two-year period. TTB claimed the inducements were used to obtain preferential product display and shelf space at Harrah's Hotels and Casinos in Nevada. After the matter was resolved by settlement, TTB published an Industry Circular, "Guidance Regarding Industry Member's Participation in Retail Programs."[34]

Another recent enforcement priority for TTB relates to alleged consignment sale violations. In and around 2019, TTB accepted offers in compromise from dozens of small wineries for allegedly violating the consignment sale provisions of the FAA which, among other things, prohibit conditional sales and giving the right of return.[35] The wineries and distributor claimed, among other things, that their arrangements were merely for extended credit terms.[36] Most industry

32. With respect to coupons, all retailers within the market where the coupon offer is made may redeem such coupons, and an industry member may not reimburse a retailer for more than the face value of all coupons redeemed, plus a usual and customary handling fee for the redemption of coupons. Industry members may make direct offerings to consumers. Officers, employees, and representatives of wholesalers or retailers are prohibited from participating.

33. *See* https://www.winebusiness.com/content/file/press_release_fy-11-4_faa_oic.pdf.

34. *See* https://www.ttb.gov/images/industry_circulars/archives/2012/12-01.html.

35. 27 CFR Part 11.

36. TTBGov - Administrative Cases.

members ultimately settled by agreeing to short suspensions.[37] TTB issued a new advisory setting forth its position on consignment sales in March 2022.[38]

4. PREEMPTION

The Twenty-first Amendment gives states broad powers to regulate the importation and use of alcohol beverages within their borders.[39] The Supreme Court has noted, "a state has virtually complete control only over interests that engage the core powers reserved to the states by the Twenty-first Amendment — that of exercising control over whether to permit importation or sale of liquor or how to structure the liquor distribution system."[40] The federal government, however, retains Commerce Clause authority to regulate alcohol beverages as they affect interstate commerce.[41] Accordingly, activities relating to the sale and distribution of alcohol beverages must be considered with both the state and federal rules in mind.

The issue of preemption and the relationship between federal and state laws was thoroughly analyzed by the Ninth Circuit in *Stein Distributing Company, Inc. v. Department of the Treasury Bureau of Alcohol, Tobacco & Firearms.*[42] In 1986 Stein Distributing was the largest beer and wine wholesaler in Boise, Idaho. Consistent with industry practice, Stein routinely prepared schematic diagrams depicting proposed product arrangements for its customers. In addition, Stein provided people to arrange or "reset" the beer and wine sections to conform to the schematics, which often included moving its competitors' products.[43] Stein argued that its actions were authorized by state law[44] and, therefore, could not violate federal tied house laws.

After a complete hearing and ruling by an administrative law judge, the director of the Bureau (on a petition for review) determined that Stein's wine wholesaling activities violated federal tied house prohibitions.[45] The Ninth Circuit upheld the director's ruling, finding that the state statute "permitting wholesalers to reset retailers' wine sections involves neither the state interest in controlling the importation of liquor into the state nor the state interest in structuring the liquor distribution system."[46] Moreover, the state and federal statutes were not in conflict

---

37. https://www.ttb.gov/images/pdfs/fo-compromise/2020/angels-share-suspension-signed.pdf.

38. https://www.ttb.gov/industry-circulars/ttb-industry-circular-2022-1.

39. *Stein Distrib. Co. v. Dep't of the Treasury Bureau of Alcohol, Tobacco & Firearms*, 779 F.2d 1407, 1410 (9th Cir. 1986).

40. *Id.* (citing *Capital Cities, Inc. v. Crisp*, 467 U.S. 691 (1984)) (internal quotes omitted).

41. *Stein Distrib. Co.*, 779 F.2d at 1410.

42. *Id.*

43. *Id.* at 1409.

44. Idaho law allows "wholesalers, with the permission of the retailer, to reset all wine upon the retailers' shelves." *Id.* at 1410.

45. *Id.* at 1409. Notably, the director found that Stein Distributing's actions with respect to beer did not violate federal tied house laws because there was no state law imposing a similar restriction, an enforcement requirement brewers inserted in the FAA Act's "penultimate clause" at the statute's adoption.

46. *Id.* at 1410.

and, therefore, the Twenty-first Amendment was not implicated. As the Ninth Circuit noted: "This is not, therefore, a case where state law compels conduct prohibited by federal law."[47]

As *Stein Distributing* clearly demonstrates, licensees must consider both state and federal rules when analyzing the legality of their actions with respect to the sale and distribution of alcohol beverages.

C. CALIFORNIA TIED HOUSE REGULATION

The California Constitution instructs the legislature to regulate the licensed beverage trade.[48] The Constitution authorizes the California Department of Alcoholic Beverage Control (ABC) to suspend or revoke any alcoholic beverage license inconsistent with the "public welfare and morals."[49] The California ABC Act,[50] including the tied house laws,[51] is codified in the Business and Professions Code. The accompanying administrative regulations are in Title 4 of the California Code of Regulations.[52]

The California tied house laws are both more comprehensive and more exception-filled than their federal counterparts, but still represent one of the strictest tied house regulatory schemes in the country. Most significantly, while the federal laws require exclusion of a competitor's product to find a violation, the California law requires *only an unlawful interest or inducement leading to an unlawful act.* California ABC enforcement is therefore much easier and more vigorous than TTB activities against similar alleged abuses.

The California tied house restrictions, unlike the federal ones, act against both suppliers (producers, importers, and wholesalers) and retailers. As noted, the laws address two major categories: the ownership interests a supplier may have in a retailer and the benefits a supplier may provide to a retailer.

1. RESTRICTED OWNERSHIP LAWS AND EXCEPTIONS

The most fundamental of the tied house restrictions are those dealing with ownership. True to the historical purpose of the laws, California's tied house regime begins by prohibiting a supplier from owning any interest in a retailer. Note how much further this restriction goes than simple prohibition of a brewer owning pubs in its local market. The formula appears to be all-inclusive: complete prohibition of a supplier[53] from holding "the ownership, directly or indirectly, of

47. *Id.* at 1411.

48. Cal. Const. art. XX, §22.

49. *Id.*

50. Cal. Bus. & Prof. Code §§23000 *et. seq.* (2022).

51. Cal. Bus. & Prof. Code §§23771-72, 25500-25512 (2022).

52. Cal. Code Regs., Tit. 4, §§1-150 (2022).

53. A manufacturer, winegrower, manufacturer's or winegrower's agent, rectifier, distiller, bottler, importer, wholesaler, or officer or director or agent of one of the above. The California

any interest in any" retailer, be it an on-sale[54] or off-sale[55] licensee.[56] The ban operates both ways, and retailers (both on- and off-sale) are similarly prohibited from owning any interests in suppliers.[57] California tied house restrictions therefore do not prohibit just the traditional tied house but *any* cross-ownership interest whatsoever between the supplier tiers and retail tier, no matter how small or attenuated, whether or not it might lead to actual control of a retailer.[58] For example, the California ABC takes the position that if an investment group that owned a California retailer purchased a foreign winery, it would be a prohibited tied house interest even if the investment group signed an undertaking that not one drop of the winery's products would be imported into the United States. Even when California created an exception for private equity funds in 2016, that exception merely excused certain passive investors from being subject to pre-licensing qualification investigations but still required the funds to declare that none of its investors had any prohibited tied house interests.[59]

The breadth of the tied house restrictions, combined with evolving economic realities and the acquisition of ever more retail licenses by persons with an interest, however slight, in a supplier, has given rise to an almost equally broad patchwork of exceptions.[60]

Nearly every modern exception is carefully tailored to apply only to the person who requested it, a political necessity to secure wholesaler neutrality or support. The exceptions include the ability of a supplier to lease space to a retailer at fair market value (with ABC approval);[61] to own a diminutive amount of stock and serve on the board of a publicly traded retailer (enacted to permit the president of Joseph E. Seagram, then a major spirits supplier, to serve on the board of Safeway

---

legislature adopted the term "winegrower" at the request of the California Wine Institute to emphasize wine's agricultural roots and to attempt to move it, at least to some degree, away from a manufactured product.

54. An entity, such as a bar or restaurant, that sells alcohol for consumption on the premises.

55. An entity, such as a grocery or liquor store, that sells alcohol for consumption off the premises.

56. Cal. Bus. & Prof. Code §§25500 (wine and spirits suppliers prohibited from owning on-sale licenses), 25501 (similar prohibitions for beer suppliers), 25502 (similar prohibitions for off-sale licenses) (2022).

57. *Id.* §§25505 (prohibiting on-sale licensees from owning any interest in a wine supplier), 25506 (prohibiting off-sale licensees from owning any interest in a spirits supplier); *see also Cal. Beer Wholesalers Ass'n, 5 Cal. 3d 402.*

58. Even stricter prohibitions apply to manufacturers of distilled spirits. The statute prohibits any person who manufactures distilled spirits anywhere (including locations outside California) from holding any distilled spirits license other than a manufacturing license. Cal. Bus. & Prof. Code §§23771-72 (2022). Specifically, manufacturers of distilled spirits are prohibited from holding any interest whatsoever in a wholesaler's, rectifier's, or retailer's license. *Id.* §23772.

59. *Id.* §23405.4.

60. These include permitting suppliers to own a single on-sale license provided it is for a club or on a vehicle such as a boat, train, or airplane, *id.* §25500(c); and to own a single on-sale license in a county with a population of less than 15,000, *id.* §25500(b), and an off-sale license in a county of similar size, if the license was held before September 19, 1947. *Id.* §25502(b). Winegrowers are allowed to hold off-sale licenses directly. *Id.* §25507.

61. *Id.* §25503.10.

Stores);[62] and to own hotels of a certain size (enacted to permit Grand Metropolitan, a British alcoholic beverage supplier, to own the Intercontinental Hotel group, which in turn owned and operated the Mark Hopkins Hotel). The section was later amended to lower the number of required hotel rooms from 150 to 100 (to permit Bass Ale to own Holiday Inns)[63] and to allow a supplier to own marine parks (enacted to permit Anheuser-Busch (which it later sold) to own SeaWorld in San Diego; the rooms threshold was later lowered to 25 to permit an international spirits manufacturer to acquire a high-end boutique hotel;[64] to own the premises of an on-sale[65] or off-sale[66] licensed cooking school (these sections permitted McKesson Corp., then an alcoholic beverage wholesaler, to own the California Culinary Academy in San Francisco); to own, serve on the board of, and promote a cooking school in Napa County (to permit vintners to participate in the Culinary Institute of America in St. Helena);[67] to own cruise ships (added at the request of a major brewer that was considering the purchase of a cruise line but later opted against it);[68] to own movie production theme parks (added at the request of Joseph E. Seagram when it purchased Universal Studios; Universal is now an asset of NBC Universal, in turn now owned 51 percent by Comcast and 49 percent by General Electric);[69] and to own an interactive entertainment facility.[70] A special section of the ABC Act was adopted to permit COPIA, a wine, food, and art cultural museum in Napa, to hold a special license that includes on- and off-sale privileges and also permits suppliers to own, serve on the board of, and promote the organization.[71]

Another special section permits winegrowers to own on-sale licenses if none of its products are sold by such licensees,[72] but this provides very limited help to winegrowers who want to actively participate in restaurant ownership. The legislature partially cured the problem first by permitting small winegrowers to own up to two on-sale licenses under highly restrictive conditions,[73] and then by permitting winegrowers of any size to own interests in any number of on-sale licenses, provided they sell their own wines in no more than two such licensed premises and that the number of wine items produced by the winegrower does not exceed 15 percent of the wines offered for sale by the retailer by brand.[74] (Microbreweries, on the other hand, can hold up to six on-sale licenses.[75]) Note

62. *Id.* §25503.11. A parallel section, §25503.12, permits a retailer to own a diminutive amount of stock in a supplier.
63. *Id.* §25503.16.
64. *Id.*
65. *Id.* §25503.17.
66. *Id.* §25503.18.
67. *Id.* §25503.20.
68. *Id.* §25503.19.
69. *Id.* §25503.29.
70. *Id.* §25503.37.
71. *Id.* §23396.2(g). Unfortunately, COPIA has ceased operations.
72. *Id.* §25503.15(a).
73. *Id.* §25503.15(b).
74. *Id.* §25503.30.
75. *Id.* §25503.28.

that the tied house laws do not apply to restaurants at winery premises that operate pursuant to the winegrower's production license, although distilled spirits may not be served.[76]

2. PROHIBITED TRADE PRACTICES AND EXCEPTIONS

The second branch of California tied house regulations are those restricting the benefits a supplier may provide to a retailer. At the outset, the statute dictates that no supplier shall "furnish, give, or lend any money or other thing of value, directly or indirectly, to, or guarantee the repayment of any loan or the fulfillment of any financial obligation of, any [retailer]."[77] Further, suppliers are prohibited from engaging in consignment sales of alcohol beverages to retailers, giving secret rebates or making secret concessions as part of a sale, engaging in price discrimination, paying a retailer for advertising space, or, subject to exceptions at Section 25611.1, giving signs and displays to retailers.[78] Finally, commercial bribery — giving anything of value to a retailer's employee in the hope of gaining customers — is prohibited.[79] This prohibition not only acts against suppliers, but also makes it a misdemeanor for retail employees to accept such a bribe.[80]

The tied house restrictions on benefits are equally challenging in today's business environment. Like the restrictions on ownership, these are well tempered by exceptions, many of which are critical for the industry to function efficiently. Thus, suppliers can provide retailers with certain signs, displays, and promotional material,[81] and a wholesaler can sell or rent any lawful product to a retailer at the market price.[82] Brewers can provide wholesalers and retailers with specified tapping equipment.[83] Suppliers can provide shelf stocking services (but are permitted to touch only their own goods)[84] and free food, drink, and entertainment at meetings at the supplier's premises,[85] at retailers' conventions,[86] and to retailers and certain retailer employees at business meetings, along with surface transportation to and from the meetings and tickets for entertainment events, including food, beverages, and transportation.[87] However, the law does not permit winegrowers to fly retailers to the winery or provide lodging for them at winery guest houses. Certain suppliers can provide consumers with free entertainment,

---

76. *See id.* §23358.

77. *Id.* §25500 (wine and spirits at on-sale premises). Similar prohibitions for beer suppliers are found at §25501 (with the exception of coasters and table tents) and for off-sale licenses at §25502.

78. *Id.* §25503.

79. *Id.* §25503(d).

80. *Id.*

81. *Id.* §25503.1.

82. *Id.*

83. *Id.* §25510.

84. *Id.* §25503.2.

85. *Id.* §25503.7.

86. *Id.* §25503.3.

87. *Id.* §25503.27.

wine, and spirits (but not beer) at private parties under highly restricted conditions.[88]

An important and well-used exception permits suppliers to provide courses of instruction for licensees and, as part of those courses, to supply the products they are discussing.[89] Beer producers and wholesalers can provide similar instruction (with small tastes of beer) to consumers on or off retail premises.[90] Winemakers' dinners can occur at a retailer's premises and include small free tastes of wine.[91] Like all tied house exceptions, such events are subject to numerous restrictions.

Suppliers can pay retailers for market research data[92] and provide consumers, under certain conditions, with addresses of on-sale[93] and off-sale[94] retailers who sell their goods. Numerous exceptions permit suppliers to pay retailers for advertising space in specified venues, including stadiums and arenas,[95] zoos and aquariums,[96] horse racetracks,[97] even water-skiing arenas that meet certain specifications,[98] and a mixed-use office, residential, retail, dining, and entertainment district of 90 acres or more in Orange County.[99]

Many other tied house exceptions exist. And while the legislature has shown some willingness to create more as the need arises, it is now much harder, as previously noted, to obtain such exceptions than in the past, primarily due to wholesalers' concern that each exception further attenuates their statutory monopoly.

3. TIED HOUSE AND TRADE PRACTICE CASE LAW

The California tied house restrictions have been heavily litigated, in part because they prohibit practices commonplace in other industries. While the meaning of the law on its face seems relatively clear, the courts have added their own gloss to the statutory language. The tied house jurisprudence provides useful examples of how the restrictions actually operate. In practice, the ABC often alleges violations of both the tied house and the free goods laws in a single case. However, the following cases turn primarily on judicial interpretation of the tied house laws. (For a discussion of the free goods law, see below.)

The leading tied house case is *California Beer Wholesalers Assn., Inc. v. Alcoholic Bev. etc. Appeals Bd.*,[100] in which the ABC denied a retailer's

---

88. *Id.* §25600.5.
89. *Id.* §25503.5.
90. *Id.* §25503.45. *See also infra* at 59 (text following note 119).
91. *Id.* §25503.4.
92. *Id.* §25503.24.
93. *Id.* §§25000.1, 25000.2.
94. *Id.*
95. *Id.* §§25503.6, 25503.8.
96. *Id.* §25503.85.
97. *Id.* §25503.26.
98. *Id.* §25503.23.
99. *Id.* §25503.61.
100. *Cal. Beer Wholesalers Ass'n*, 5 Cal. 3d 402.

application for a wholesale liquor license. The Court of Appeal stated what has become the controlling interpretation of the California tied house laws:

> Following repeal of the Eighteenth Amendment, the vast majority of states, including California, enacted alcoholic beverage control laws. These statutes sought to forestall the generation of such evils and excesses as intemperance and disorderly marketing conditions that had plagued the public and the alcoholic beverage industry prior to prohibition [citations]. By enacting prohibitions against "tied-house" arrangements, state legislatures aimed to prevent two particular dangers: the ability and potentiality of large firms to dominate local markets through vertical and horizontal integration [citation] and the excessive sales of alcoholic beverages produced by the overly aggressive marketing techniques of larger alcoholic beverage concerns [citations].
>
> The principal method utilized by state legislatures to avoid these antisocial developments was the establishment of a triple-tiered distribution and licensing scheme [citations]. Manufacturing interests were to be separated from wholesale interests; wholesale interests were to be segregated from retail interests. In short, business endeavors engaged in the production, handling, and final sale of alcoholic beverages were to be kept "distinct and apart."[101]

The ABC has been especially vigilant against *indirect* inducements, where suppliers try to do indirectly what they cannot do directly. In *Department of Alcoholic Beverage Control v. Alcoholic Beverage Control Appeals Board (Deleuze)*,[102] the Court of Appeal reinstated the ABC's decision (previously reversed by the ABC Appeals Board) that an indirect tied house violation existed where a winery purchased advertising space in a retailer's catalogue by paying the catalogue's printer, thereby reducing the cost of the catalogue to the retailer, who subsequently deposited the payment in the retailer's postal account. The court noted that Section 25502(a)(2) prohibits a winegrower from directly or indirectly giving money or other things of value to a retailer and deferred to the ABC's alcoholic beverage industry expertise.[103]

In *Department of Alcoholic Beverage Control v. Alcoholic Beverage Control Appeals Board (Schieffelin & Somerset Co.)*,[104] the court reinstated the ABC's decision (again, one the ABC Appeals Board had previously reversed) that payment by a distilled spirits supplier violated Sections 25502(a)(2) and 25503(h), which prohibit a wholesaler from directly or indirectly paying a retailer for placing advertising on or in a retailer's premises; the prohibited ads were logos on applications for the retailer's "fun run" event and on T-shirts distributed at the

---

101. *Id.* at 407 (citing 25 Ops. Cal. Atty. Gen. 288, 289 (1955)). Note that while courts frequently cite this language as controlling, it is not, strictly speaking, accurate that California law requires the separation of manufacturing from wholesale interests. While most retailers are prohibited from owning wholesale licenses, a California beer and wine importer can own a wholesale and Type 20 (limited) retail license; in fact, a few California breweries and wineries own their own wholesale operations.

102. 100 Cal. App. 4th 1066 (2002).

103. *Id.* at 1080.

104. 128 Cal. App. 4th 1195 (2005).

event. The court concluded that Schieffelin's payments to the event promoter (rather than the retailer) violated the indirect prohibitions of the tied house law and were not saved by Rule 106(i)(2), which permits sponsorship of races, contests, and similar activities by payments to "bona fide amateur or professional organizations established [to encourage and promote] the activities involved" because the promoter's principal focus was operating professional marketing promotions rather than promoting the sport of running.[105]

But the prohibition on indirect inducements has its limits. Anheuser-Busch was one of three alcoholic beverage suppliers that signed contracts with Shecky's, a New York–based event promoter, to sponsor a series of "Girls Night Out" shopping events throughout the United States. The brewery's contract left virtually all event details to Shecky's, which agreed to conduct each event in strict accord with local law. Shecky's was free to serve what beverages it wished and to hire a caterer of its choice, and it agreed to secure all necessary permits and licenses. Anheuser-Busch did give Shecky's logoed T-shirts to lend to caterers in those states (most states but not California) where this was legal. But, except for the payment of a sponsorship fee and the provision of point-of-sale material, the contract required Shecky's to handle all the details.

In 2007 Shecky's hired a retailer-concessionaire to obtain a license and serve alcohol beverages at an event in San Francisco. The concessionaire failed to get a license but did not tell Shecky's, which, in violation of its contract with Anheuser-Busch, lent the retailer a logoed T-shirt. The ABC filed an accusation against Anheuser-Busch for sales without a license, unlawful inducements (lending a T-shirt to a retailer), and several other related claims.

In 2009, an ABC administrative law judge (ALJ) found in the brewery's favor on all counts, and the ABC adopted the ALJ's decision.[106] The case stands for the proposition that mere sponsorship of an event by a supplier does not subject the sponsor to ABC sanctions on an indirect theory of liability for unlawful activities that may occur at the event, such as the unlicensed sale of alcohol and lending a T-shirt to a retailer, but, more broadly, a minor's consumption of alcohol at a ball game, concert, or even a county fair event sponsored by a supplier. Had ABC's accusation been proven and adopted by the Director, and sustained through appeals (a process with a standard of review according to the Director's great deference), it is possible that supplier sponsorships, including sponsorships of major league sports teams, would have disappeared from the California landscape. While Section 25505 of the ABC Act clearly prohibits commercial bribery, not every payment to a retailer or its employees is prohibited. For example, the ABC held that prizes awarded in a supplier-sponsored contest in which bartenders raced up California Street in San Francisco carrying trays of mixed drinks did not violate

---

105. *Id.* at 1209.

106. *In the Matter of Anheuser-Busch, Inc., California Department of Alcoholic Beverage Control*, Reg. No. 08069642 (Nov. 12, 2009). Because the ABC director "adopted" the ALJ's decision, it is technically a decision by the ABC. While this decision was not designated by the Department as precedential, the Department is unlikely to take a contrary position without issuing some type of prior guidance to the industry.

the tied house laws where the contest was not on a retailer's premises and there was no finding that the contest required the bartenders to promote or encourage the sale of the sponsor's products, and no such promotion or encouragement occurred.[107]

The Ninth Circuit more recently published a landmark decision in the *Retail Digital Network, LLC v. Prieto* (2017) ("*RDN*") case.[108] In this case, the Court upheld the statutory prohibition against a supplier paying for the privilege of advertising on a retail premises.[109] RDN installed and operated large digital screens displaying digital advertisements in California retail premises.[110] RDN solicited relationships with alcohol beverage suppliers, but the suppliers refused, relying on the statutory prohibition against paying for the privilege of advertising in a retail premises.[111] RDN brought a declaratory action challenging the constitutionality of the prohibition.[112]

Relying upon a 1986 Ninth Circuit decision, *Actmedia, Inc. v. Stroh*, the Court ultimately determined that the statute was constitutional.[113] The Court found that suppliers were prohibited from paying RDN, a third party, to have their advertising placed on the digital screens that were located within retail premises.[114]

The *Actmedia* case is also important here as it involved a third party that was leasing advertising space on shopping carts.[115] The Court in *Actmedia* determined that a supplier could not pay *Actmedia* to place its advertising on the shopping carts as the shopping carts were used within retail premises.[116]

In both cases, the Court noted that the prohibition in Section 25503(h) "addresses the California legislature's specific 'concern that advertising payments could be used to conceal illegal payoffs to alcoholic beverage retailers,' thereby undermining the triple-tiered distribution scheme."[117]

As such, the law in California is fairly established on this issue — a supplier may not pay anyone, including a third party, for advertising space in a retail establishment.

Although the ABC's rulemaking authority is broad, and courts usually defer to its expertise, the ABC cannot exceed statutory limits. Thus, tied house exceptions are the province of the legislature, not the regulatory agency.[118]

---

107. *In the Matter of Allied Domecq Spirits and Wine*, California Department of Alcoholic Beverage Control, Reg. No. 02052713 (Nov. 21, 2002).

108. *Retail Digital Network, LLC v. Prieto*, 861 F.3d 839 (9th Cir. 2017).

109. *Id.* at 851.

110. *Id.* at 842.

111. *Id.*

112. *Id.*

113. *Id.* at 851.

114. *Id.* at 851.

115. *Actmedia, Inc. v. Stroh*, 830 F.2d 957, 958 (9th Cir. 1986).

116. *Id.* at 968.

117. *Retail Digital Network, LLC v. Prieto*, 861 F.3d at 843.

118. *Cal. Beer & Wine Wholesalers Ass'n v. Dep't of Alcoholic Beverage Control*, 201 Cal. App. 3d 100 (1988) (provision of ABC Department Rule 106 permitting certain gifts of supplies by beer wholesalers to on-sale retailers, where such gifts are prohibited by ABC Act §25501(a), is

D. CALIFORNIA FREE GOODS LAW

1. STATUTE AND REGULATIONS

In addition to restrictions on tied houses and trade practices, California has a somewhat unique no-free-goods law. Set forth in Section 25600 [119] and substantially augmented by Rule 106,[120] California's no-free-goods law applies to all licensees (including retailers) and generally prohibits giving anything for free (including to consumers) in connection with the sale or distribution, which includes marketing, of alcohol beverages: "[n]o licensee shall, directly or indirectly, give any premium, gift, or free goods in connection with the sale or distribution of any alcoholic beverage except as provided by rules that shall be adopted by the [ABC] department to implement this section or as authorized by this division." Rule 106(e) distinguishes between retailer and consumer advertising specialties (the latter may be furnished by a supplier to a retailer or directly to consumers) and imposes a limit of $1 on the original cost of such specialties furnished by a wine supplier, of $5 by a distilled spirits supplier, and of $3 by a beer supplier. The statute requires that, with respect to *beer*, a "premium, gift or free goods," including advertising specialties, may not cost more than $0.25 per unit or, when given by a single supplier to a single retailer, be worth more than $15 per year;[121] however, as noted, a recent amendment permits breweries, but not wholesalers, to give consumer advertising specialties worth up to $3 directly to the consumer provided the brewer itself makes the gift.[122] Several exceptions to the general statutory prohibitions exist, and it is important to examine the rule and the cases whenever a trade practice issue arises. For the practitioner, the most important exceptions permit

- Retailers to accept returns and make refunds or exchanges;[123]
- Winegrowers to make refunds to consumers no matter where the wine was purchased;[124]
- Samples to be given to licensees;[125]
- Gifts to be given to non-licensees;[126]
- Certain inside signs to be given to retailers;[127]

---

invalid). *See also People ex. rel. Dep't of Alcoholic Beverage Control v. Miller Brewing Co.,* 104 Cal. App. 4th 1189 (2002). (ABC department rules cannot exceed statutory authority).

119. Cal. Bus. & Prof. Code §25600 (2022).

120. Cal. Code Regs., tit. 4, div. 1, §106 (2022).

121. Cal. Bus. & Prof. Code §25600(b)(1) (2022).

122. Cal. Bus. & Prof. Code §25600(b)(2)(A) (2022); Cal. Code Regs., tit. 4, §106(e) (2022).

123. Cal. Bus. & Prof. Code §25600(a)(2)(A) (2022).

124. *Id.* §25600(a)(2)(B).

125. Cal. Code Regs., tit. 4, div. 1, §52(a) (2022).

126. *Id.* §52(b).

127. *Id.* §106 (c)(1).

- Licensees to furnish certain services to specified communities and nonprofit organizations;[128] and
- Licensees to sponsor certain contests on or off their premises.[129]

Creative use of these provisions will often make possible a promotion that appears at first blush to be unlawful. But in order to fully utilize these exceptions, it is critical to do so in light of the case law they have generated.

2. FREE GOODS CASE LAW

The leading free goods case[130] *is Miller Brewing Co. v. Department of Alcoholic Beverage Control,*[131] in which the court addressed the definition of *distribution*, which the legislature added to the statutory prohibition against giving free goods in connection with the *sale* of alcohol beverages. In 1983 Miller sponsored a national tour featuring comedian Joe Piscopo. To promote the tour, Miller placed its logo on concert tickets and on jackets, both of which were to be given away by co-sponsoring radio stations. The department contended that the logoed tickets and jackets were illegal "premium[s], gift[s] or free goods," in violation of the statute. In sustaining the ABC's position, the court held that "distribution" included "marketing or merchandising … sales promotion as a comprehensive function including market research … and effective advertising and selling" of alcoholic beverages.[132] This expansive definition of "distribution" has significantly restricted the promotion of wine and other alcohol beverages in California.

There is interesting case law on the meaning of "premium, gift, or free goods," which Section 25600 now prohibits in connection with the sale or distribution of alcohol beverages. In a significant win for the industry, the court in *Gonzales & Co., Inc., v. Department of Alcoholic Beverage Control*[133] held that wine rebate coupons were not premiums, gifts, or free goods in violation of Section 25600. Subsequently, the ABC took the aggressive (some might say bizarre) position that although rebates were legal on beer and, of course, on non-alcoholic beverage items, a cash rebate on such items that was contingent on buying a licensed beverage (e.g., $1 off the purchase of a Miller beer product if the consumer also

---

128. *Id.* §106(h).

129. *Id.* §106(i).

130. California has very little precedential case law relating to tied houses and trade practices generally, and even less relating to free goods. It does, however, frequently go to hearing on such matters which has resulted in hundreds of written decisions issued by the Director. While such cases are instructive, they are not precedential unless designated as such by the Department. The Department exercised its statutory power to issue a precedential decision for the first time in 2019, in connection with a free goods case. California Department of Alcoholic Beverage Control Precedential Decision 19-04-E (Mundo Liquor & Market Inc. DBA Mundo Liquor & Market). Precedential decisions have the same force and effect of a regulation.

131. 204 Cal. App. 3d. 5 (1988).

132. *Id.* at 15.

133. 151 Cal. App. 3d. 172 (1984).

bought specified non-alcoholic products such as ground beef, pickles, soda, or buns) violated Section 25600 and Rule 106(j) because the rebate was more than the $0.25 then permitted for *premiums* given in connection with beer. In *People ex rel. Department of Alcoholic Beverage Control v. Miller Brewing Co.*,[134] the court continued the ongoing judicial exercise involving the definition of "premium, gift, or free goods" and determined that the contingent promotions at issue were none of the above and were therefore permissible.[135]

Despite the coupon victory, the industry has not fared as well in other challenges to Section 25600. For example, in *Department of Alcoholic Beverage Control v. Alcoholic Beverage Control Appeals Bd. (Anheuser-Busch, Inc.)*,[136] the court addressed the meaning of "gift" in an attempt to reconcile Rule 106 with Rule 52, which deals with both samples (Rule 52(a)) and gifts (Rule 52(b)) of alcohol beverages.[137] Although the court ultimately decided that the practice of trade sampling, whereby wholesaler employees offered bar patrons bottles or cans of the wholesaler's products, violated Rule 52(b)'s sampling requirements, it also urged "the Legislature, or the [ABC] Department, or both, to attempt a wholesale clarification of what items may be given away by licensees, to whom, and in what manner."[138] In 2010 the legislature partially addressed this issue by enacting Sections 25503.56 and 23396.6. These statutes permit retailers to obtain licenses that authorize suppliers to offer "instructional" tasting of beer, wine, and spirits to consumers at retail premises.[139]

E. WASHINGTON STATE TIED HOUSE AND TRADE PRACTICE LAW

In 1934, in response to the passage of the Twenty-first Amendment, the state of Washington passed the Steele Act, regulating the distribution and sale of alcohol beverages.[140] Through the Steele Act, Washington, unlike many other states, elected to implement a "mixed" form of regulation in which the state retained

---

134. 104 Cal. App. 4th 1189 (2002).

135. Rule 106(j) still prohibits most cross-merchandising promotions, at least presumably those that do not involve coupons.

136. 71 Cal. App. 4th 1518 (1999).

137. *See also* Rule 53.5, "Samples Used in Beer Tastings," adopted in 1994 after this case was decided.

138. *Anheuser-Busch*, 71 Cal. App. 4th at 1528-1529.

139. The court found no such ambiguity, however, in the case of sweepstakes where the prizes exceed the statutory minimums established in Business and Professions Code §25600 and Rule 106 ($0.25 (now $3) for beer, $1 for wine, and $5 for spirits) even when the ABC completely reversed a long-standing policy permitting sweepstakes. Although California subsequently legalized sweepstakes (Cal. Bus. & Prof. Code §25600.2), this part of the story is illustrative of the caution licensees must take regarding the ABC's apparent policies established by custom and practice. ABC policies, unless adopted under a formal rulemaking process as regulations, or as a precedential decision, are not precedent and are therefore subject to administrative amendment.

140. Codified as Title 66 of the Revised Code of Washington ("Wash. Rev. Code").

control over the sale of distilled spirits (through state and contract stores) but implemented a three-tier distribution system for the sale of beer and wine.[141] As such, Washington was known as a control state. The Steele Act also created the Washington State Liquor Control Board (WSLCB),[142] consisting of three members appointed by the governor and confirmed by the senate to oversee the licensed beverage industry.[143]

While multiple industry members voiced concern regarding the WSLCB's control, in 2004, Costco Wholesale Corporation initiated a push for comprehensive changes to the state's licensed beverage system. Costco filed an antitrust and Commerce Clause civil action against the WSLCB (and several other parties) in the Federal Court for the Western District of Washington alleging that Washington's laws and regulations, especially the trade practice laws, governing the sale of beer and wine restrict many of [Costco's] efficient and competitive practices as to wine and beer suppliers and create or facilitate agreement among distributors and among wineries and breweries ('manufactures') in restraint of competition....[Therefore] the challenged laws and regulations were restraints of trade preempted by Section 1 of the Sherman Act, 15 U.S.C. Section 1.[144]

Costco specifically challenged nine restraints including, among others, retailer-to-retailer sales.[145]The District Court upheld the retailer-to-retailer ban but found in Costco's favor with respect to all of the other statutes, holding that they irreconcilably conflicted with federal antitrust laws and, therefore, were invalid.[146] The state promptly appealed the decision to the Ninth Circuit Court of Appeals.

The Ninth Circuit Court of Appeals ultimately reversed in part and affirmed in part the district court's ruling. The court upheld the ruling that the retailer-to-retailer sales ban constituted a unilateral restraint of trade that is not subject to preemption by the Sherman Act, because "the potential anti-competitive effect is not the result of private pricing or marketing decisions, but the logical and intended result of the statute itself."[147] With respect to the other regulations, however, the Ninth Circuit found that they were all valid restraints except for the post-and-hold pricing system.[148] Costco subsequently announced that it would not appeal to the United States Supreme Court.

---

141. Wash. Rev. Code §66.16.010 (2009); Wash. Admin. Code §§314-01-005 to 314-76-035 (2010).

142. On July 24, 2015, SB 5052 (2015) took effect and changed the Board's name to Washington State Liquor and Cannabis Board.

143. Wash. Rev. Code §66.08.012 (2015).

144. *Costco Wholesale Corp. v. Maleng*, 522 F.3d 874, 882-883 (2008).

145. Wash. Rev. Code §§66.28.010(a) (2009); Wash. Admin. Code §§314-20-090, 314-13-015 (2010).

146. *Costco*, 522 F.3d at 884-885. The court found that the state did not properly supervise its regulatory scheme because "it neither reviewed resulting prices for reasonableness nor monitored market conditions." The state's lack of involvement prohibited it from seeking protection under antitrust immunity laws. Accordingly, the district court ruled that the regulatory scheme was subject to federal preemption.

147. *Costco*, 522 F.3d at 889-890.

148. *Id.* at 896-900.

Upon receiving the District Court's ruling, however, the Washington state legislature directed the WSLCB to establish a task force to conduct a comprehensive review of the state's regulatory system for the distribution and sale of beer and wine.[149] After years of debate, discussion, and previously failed ballot measures, in November 2011 voters approved Initiative 1183 (I-1183) ending the state's monopoly on distilled-liquor sales and allowing privatized retail sales as of July 2013.[150] Washington is the first control state to fully privatize both liquor distribution and retail sales.

1. RESTRICTED OWNERSHIP LAWS AND EXCEPTIONS

Following Washington's privatization, many of the state's tied house statutes and regulations were amended. Washington is arguably one of the more progressive states when it comes to permitting cross tier ownership interests. Washington generally permits cross tier ownership unless "such interest has resulted or is more likely than not to result in: (a) [u]ndue influence over the retailer or the industry member; or (b) [a]n adverse impact on public health and safety."[151] Washington defines "undue influence" as "one retailer or industry member[152] directly or indirectly influencing the purchasing, marketing, or sales decisions of another retailer or industry member by any agreement written or unwritten or any other business practices or arrangements..."[153] Examples of undue influence include the following:

- Coercion through acts or threat of physical or economic harm, including the threat of loss of supply or curtailment of purchase.
- A retailer involuntarily purchasing less of another industry member's product.
- Purchases made by a retailer or industry member as a prerequisite for the purchase of other items.
- A retailer purchasing a specific or minimum quantity or type of a product(s) from an industry member.
- An industry member requiring a retailer to take and dispose of a certain product type or quota of the industry member's products.
- A retailer having a continuing obligation to purchase or otherwise promote or display an industry member's product.
- An industry member having a continuing obligation to sell a product to a retailer.

---

149. 2SSB 6823.PL, 59th Leg. Reg. Sess. (Wash. 2006), §13.

150. Initiative Measure No. 1183 (2011).

151. RCW 66.28.290 and WAC 314-12-027.

152. Washington defines "industry member" as "a licensed manufacturer, producer, supplier, importer, wholesaler, distributor, authorized representative, certificate of approval holder, warehouse, and any affiliates, subsidiaries, officers, directors, partners, agents, employees, and representatives of any industry member." Wash. Rev. Code Ann §66.28.285(3).

153. Wash. Rev. Code Ann §66.28.285(6).

- A retailer having a commitment not to terminate its relationship with an industry member with respect to purchase of the industry member's products, and vice versa.
- An industry member being involved in the day-to-day operations of a retailer, and vice versa.
- Discriminatory pricing practices, or other practices that are discriminatory in that the product is not offered to all retailers in the local market on the same terms.[154]

"Adverse impact on public health and safety" means that "an existing or proposed practice or occurrence has resulted or is more likely than not to result in alcohol being made significantly more attractive or available to minors than would otherwise be the case or has resulted or is more likely than not to result in overconsumption, consumption by minors, or other harmful or abusive forms of consumption."[155]

2. RESTRICTED BENEFITS LAWS AND EXCEPTIONS

Washington does, however, take a more conservative approach when evaluating things of value. "No industry member shall advance and no retailer shall receive moneys or moneys' worth under an agreement written or unwritten or by means of any other business practice or arrangement."[156] Significantly, Washington's prohibition on proving any "moneys or money's worth" to a retailer applies even when exclusion and/or discrimination are not present.

Washington, like most other states, however, has established a number of exceptions to the "money's worth prohibition."[157] Industry members, for example, may provide services to special occasion licensee's including advertising and pouring wine.[158] Industry members may provide listings on their websites for retailers who sell or promote their products, and retailers may include listings on their websites to industry members whose products the retailers sell or promote.[159]A domestic winery or a certificate of approval holder may also, from time to time, provide personal services conducted at a licensed premises and intended to "inform, educate, or enhance customers' knowledge or experience of the manufacturer's products."[160] While not exhaustive, these exceptions identify the general type of permissible services or activities authorized between the tiers in Washington.

---

154. Wash. Rev. Code Ann §66.28.285(6).
155. Wash. Rev. Code Ann §66.28.285(1).
156. Wash. Rev. Code Ann. §66.28.305; see also W.A.C. 314-12-140.15.
157. Wash. Rev. Code Ann. §66.28.310; see also W.A.C. 314-12-140.
158. Id. §66.28.310(2).
159. Id. §§66.28.310(3) and (4).
160. Id. §66.28.310(5).

F. NEW YORK STATE TIED HOUSE AND TRADE PRACTICE LAW

New York's traditional trade practices statutory and regulatory scheme has been in place, in substantially the same form, since the Repeal of Prohibition. Following many other states, New York adopted a three-tier licensing system regulated by the State Liquor Authority (SLA).[161] The SLA is responsible for, among other things, regulating trade and credit practices related to the sale and distribution of alcohol beverages at the wholesale and retail levels, ensuring compliance with the ABC laws, and bringing disciplinary action where appropriate.[162] New York, like Washington and California, has many laws prohibiting close relationships between manufacturers and wholesalers, on the one hand, and retailers on the other. The general rule is clear and prohibits manufacturers and wholesalers from having an interest in a retailer:[163]

> It shall be unlawful for a manufacturer or wholesaler licensed under this chapter to:
>
> (a) Be interested directly or indirectly in any premises where any alcoholic beverage is sold at retail; or in any business devoted wholly or partially to the sale of any alcoholic beverage at retail by stock ownership, interlocking directors, mortgage or lien or any personal or real property, or by any other means.[164]

Similarly, manufactures and wholesalers are prohibited from making a loan or gift to a retailer. They may not:

> (b) Make, or cause to be made, any loan to any person engaged in the manufacture or sale of any alcoholic beverage at wholesale or retail.
>
> (c) Make any gift or render any service of any kind whatsoever, directly or indirectly, to any person licensed under this chapter which in the judgment of the liquor authority may tend to influence such licensee to purchase the product of such manufacturer or wholesaler. The provisions of this paragraph shall not be construed to prevent a manufacturer or wholesaler from entertaining a licensee at lunch or dinner, or to prevent a manufacturer or wholesaler from participating in or supporting bona fide retailer association activities such as, but not limited to, associate memberships, dinners, conventions, trade shows, product tastings and product education where such participation is in reasonable amounts and does not reach proportions that indicate attempts to influence the purchase of products of contributing manufacturers and wholesalers by the members of such retailer associations.[165]

---

161. Historical Overview, https://sla.ny.gov/historical-overview (accessed June 2022).

162. *Id.*

163. New York also has many exceptions to the general rule. *See, e.g.*, N.Y. Alcoholic Beverage Control Law §101 (2022). In fact, most manufacturers located in New York also hold a wholesaler's license. Thus, they may sell to traditional wholesalers (who then sell to retailers), but they may also sell directly to retailers.

164. N.Y. Alcoholic Beverage Control Law §101(1)(a) (2022).

165. *Id.* §101(1)(b), (c).

Although the laws were essentially the same as those of many other states, corruption was rampant and trade practice laws went largely unenforced.[166] A report by the New York State Law Revision Commission noted that "[s]ince its inception, the SLA has been plagued with problems of licensing delays, inadequate enforcement, inefficient and ineffective administration and, indeed, bribery and corruption."[167]

This alleged lack of enforcement provided ample opportunity for licensees to play fast and loose with the rules. Despite the enactment of price posting requirements and other trade practice laws, "[f]or decades, pay-to-play practices were rampant in the state's alcohol industry as retailers, wholesalers and suppliers used a variety of schemes to avoid the clear directive of the State's Alcohol Beverage Control Law.... The system benefitted a favored few, to the detriment of thousands of smaller stores, bars and restaurants."[168] Organized crime was prevalent and licensees commonly would operate a premises for six months to a year, "take whatever money they can out of it," and move the operation to another location once the license was revoked.[169]

Between 2005 and 2007 the Office of the Attorney General began an intense investigation into New York's licensed beverage industry and found many examples of violations against which the SLA was not taking action.[170] One example was the "game" licensees played in connection with price post-and-hold requirements.[171] The law is clear: manufacturers and wholesalers are prohibited from favoring select retailers with discounts, rebates, allowances, free goods, or other inducements.[172] The state's price posting system is designed to eliminate such favoritism.[173] The system requires wholesalers to send the SLA their current prices, which are then made available to retailers. Wholesalers are required to "hold" the published prices for a period of time, allowing all retailers to pay the same price, without any extra inducements, discounts, or rebates, for the same product.[174] Nevertheless, for many years, favored retailers were purchasing products at prices very different from those posted with the state.[175]

---

166. New York State Law Revision Commission, The New York State Law Revision Commission Report on the Alcoholic Beverage Control Law and its Administration 56-67 (Dec. 15, 2009), https://nyslawrevision.files.wordpress.com/2014/07/12-15-09-report-on-abc-law.pdf.

167. *Id.* at 5.

168. Agreement Is First in Ongoing Efforts to Remove Illegal Practices in State's Liquor Industry, Law Fuel (March 17, 2003), http://www.lawfuel.com/show-release.asp?ID=7601 (citing then attorney general Eliot Spitzer) (accessed December 13, 2010).

169. New York State Law Revision Commission, *supra* note 211 at 63.

170. *Id.* at 65-66.

171. Following the Repeal of Prohibition, price wars raged throughout New York. For example, before the price posting requirement was enacted, a four-day "price war" resulted in prices that were moving so quickly that stores posted hourly price changes on blackboards in the windows. *Id.* at 201-202. At the time, the State Liquor Authority claimed it had no jurisdiction over the price wars other than enforcing rules regarding signage. *Id.*

172. N.Y. Alcoholic Beverage Law §101(b) (2010).

173. *Id.*

174. *Id.*

175. New York State Law Revision Commission, *supra* note 171 at 201-221.

Wholesalers' ability to charge lower prices to favored retailers was a function of the SLA's unsophisticated price posting system. For many years, there was no easy way retailers could access the postings filed with the SLA. In fact, to view the postings, a retailer was required to physically go to SLA headquarters. Consequently, a publisher, working with wholesalers, published a book listing the prices at which retailers would purchase. Unfortunately, the prices listed in the book were not necessarily consistent with the postings filed with the state. Instead, the pricing book was based on verbal representations made by the wholesalers. This permitted wholesalers to provide favored retailers with illegal discounts without raising a red flag for the SLA.

In 2006, after more than a year of investigation, the state and several major manufacturers and wholesalers entered into a consent decree and judgment.[176] Among other things, the consent decree enjoined wholesalers and manufacturers from, directly or indirectly, providing retailers with things of value in connection with the sale of wine or distilled spirits and from discriminating between retailers. Specifically, the consent decree prohibited, subject to certain exceptions, payments or gifts to retailers, discrimination among retailers, discrimination in the distribution of limited items, tie-ins,[177] credits and rebates, payments to certain persons or entities that perform services for retailers,[178] payments for wine and drink menus, buy-back events, gifts of product, and payment for participation in retailer advertising. Although such practices were already prohibited by New York state law (again, subject to specified exceptions), the consent decree imposed substantial fines (ranging from $100,000 to $225,000) against several manufacturers and wholesalers for past practices and provided a vehicle for imposing similar fines upon a finding that the consent decree was violated.[179]

Most recently, New York's Law Revision Commission[180] conducted an examination of New York's licensed beverage control laws and the state's administration of such laws.[181] In connection with its study, the Commission, among other things, studied historical documents (such as statutes, judicial opinions, and journals) and conducted hundreds of interviews with stakeholders (producers, wholesalers, and retailers), attorneys, state and local law enforcement, community members, SLA staff, and legislative staff.[182] The Commission

---

176. *People (New York) v. Bacardi U.S.A., et al.*, I.2006-9782, Consent Decree and Judgment, State of New York, Supreme Court, County of Erie, October 31, 2006.

177. Requiring or compelling retailers to purchase a particular brand in order to purchase another brand.

178. Prohibited if payment constitutes an incentive, award, or rebate, if the entity is owned or controlled by retailer(s) or if the principal, officer, or employee of a retailer is an officer or employee of the entity.

179. Bacardi, Consent Decree and Judgment, *supra* note 181. The current consent decree technically applies only to those companies that signed it. In 2010, however, the SLA made clear to all industry members that they were expected to abide by the same rules.

180. About the Commission, New York State Law Revision Commission, http://www.lawrevision.state.ny.us/index.php (accessed December 7, 2010).

181. New York State Law Revision Commission, *supra* note 171 at 1.

182. *Id.* at 2-4.

essentially recommended a complete overhaul of the SLA — a process described by the Commission as "herculean."[183]

The Commission's recommendations were divided into two primary areas, the substantive law and the law's administration. As the Commission aptly noted, "statutory overhaul would be futile unless and until the dysfunctional and programmatically-challenged SLA is rehabilitated so that it can fulfill the mission for which it was designed."[184]

The Commission recommended changes to several different substantive laws, including the tied house laws. As noted above, manufacturers and wholesalers are prohibited from making any gift or rendering any service of any kind directly or indirectly to another licensee that "may tend to influence such licensee to purchase the product of such manufacturer or wholesaler." [185] Like California and Washington, New York law provides many exceptions to the general rule prohibiting tied house acts. For example, manufacturers are allowed to give retailers certain items, such as wine racks, bins, barrels, casks, and various advertising merchandise.[186]

The Commission recommended a two-pronged approach to controlling and preventing tied house abuse.[187] First, the state must "establish rules and regulations that clearly outline impermissible trade practices and permissible exceptions...." Second, the state must enforce the rules and regulations by responding to complaints and conducting routine and random compliance audits.[188] The SLA recommended incorporating the consent decree into the state's statutes and amending the tied house laws to apply uniformly to all licensed entities regardless of type of licensed beverage.[189]

Shortly before the Law Revision Commission published its findings, the governor appointed Dennis Rosen as the new SLA chairman. Notably, Mr. Rosen, a former assistant attorney general, had spearheaded the attorney general's 2005 investigation into the licensed beverage industry. Upon his appointment as chairman of the SLA, Mr. Rosen made many personnel changes throughout the agency.[190] The Commission commended this and other recent changes such as the reinstitution of basic administrative protocols and meetings with stakeholders and legal officials to discuss new policies and procedures. [191] The Law Revision Commission encouraged these efforts and expressed its hope that its report would help "facilitate [the SLA's] efforts and accelerate the much-needed reformation of the agency."[192]

---

183. *Id.* at 5.
184. *Id.*
185. N.Y. Alcoholic Beverage Control Law §101(1)(c) (2010).
186. N.Y. Alcoholic Beverage Control Law, Appendix §§86.1-86.17 (2010).
187. New York State Law Revision Commission, *supra* note 171 at 175.
188. *Id.* at 175-176.
189. *Id.* at 175-177.
190. *Id.* at 5-6.
191. *Id.*
192. *Id.* at 6.

In March 2010 SLA Chairman Rosen testified before the Senate Committee on Investigations and Government Operations.[193] He, too, recommended a complete overhaul of New York's licensed beverage law:

> One of the major hurdles facing the alcohol industry as well as the SLA is trying to do business in the 21st Century with a statute that was passed in 1934 coming out of Prohibition. Since its inception, there have been various amendments to the ABC Law. While many of these amendments have been well-intentioned and indeed necessary, what I believe is needed today is a total overhaul of the statute. I recently told a reporter that what we have with the ABC Law is not what one would typically call a statute. A statute is logically written. What we have with the ABC Law is a collage. This is because it has persistently been jerry-rigged to suit the perceived needs of the moment without much deference to its overall structure or logic. Thus, it is difficult for even attorneys to understand, and almost impossible for the average licensee to know exactly what their responsibilities are under the statute.[194]

Chairman Rosen identified additional steps the SLA had recently taken to address the problems identified in the Law Revision Commission's report. The agency hired many new professionals, including an internal auditor. Enforcement priorities were refocused: "[w]e are getting away from counting fruit flies in bottles to cracking down on underage drinking, sales to intoxicated patrons, and the bars and nightclubs that wreak havoc on their neighborhoods."[195]

One component of the SLA's refocused enforcement priorities relates to the consent decree's prohibition against wholesalers/suppliers providing a thing of value to retailers. In the summer of 2010, a wholesaler invited several retailers to attend a professional baseball game at its expense. The wholesaler rented a bus to transport the retailers to the event; the retailers sat in the wholesaler's luxury box, and after the game, the bus took them home. After learning of the incident, the SLA filed an accusation against the wholesaler on the grounds that such conduct violated the consent decree and N.Y. CLS Al. Bev. Section 101(c). Ultimately, the wholesaler agreed to pay a $50,000 fine.

News of the $50,000 fine spread quickly throughout New York, and many in the industry expressed concern over the SLA's position that such activities were unlawful and over the gravity of the fine. In August 2010 the SLA called an industry meeting to discuss regulatory reform in New York. Over 75 people, representing diverse industry interests, including representatives from the various trade associations, general counsel for several distilled spirits organizations, large wholesalers, private attorneys, and miscellaneous small beer wholesalers, attended the meeting.

---

193. New York State Liquor Authority, Division of Alcoholic Beverage Control, Media Advisory: Chairman Testifies Before Senate Committee on Investigations and Government Operations (March 24, 2010), http://www.abc.state.ny.us/newsletter/media-advisories/chairman-testifies-before-senate-committee-on-investigations-and-governm (accessed December 14, 2010).

194. *Id.* at 2.

195. *Id.* at 4.

The SLA continues to evaluate the permissible boundaries of "entertainment."

Cross tier ownership interests have also been strictly enforced in New York over the last several years. Licensed manufacturers and wholesalers are prohibited from having any interest, direct or indirect, in any premises where alcohol beverages are sold at retail unless expressly authorized.[196] Similarly, retail liquor and wine stores may not have an interest in a business that manufactures or wholesales alcoholic beverages.[197] The New York State Court of Appeals has held that even de minimis ownership is a disqualifying interest under the tied house laws.[198]

The tied house laws in New York, like many states, prohibit unlawful "interests," but are silent about "control." The SLA strictly construes its tied house laws as demonstrated in its 2014 enforcement action against Eataly, a well-known Italian marketplace located in New York. In that case, the SLA accepted a global settlement from licensee Eataly NY LLC principals, including Lidia Bastianich, Joe Bastianich, Mario Batali, Oscar Farinetti, and Luca Filangieri, who allegedly held winemaking interests. The penalty included a $500,000 fine, a six-month suspension of the Eataly Vini wine shop license, and removal of Lidia Bastianich from the Eataly Vini license. SLA officials alleged that the partners lied or "suppressed information" about their supplier interests.

G. TEXAS STATE TIED HOUSE AND TRADE PRACTICE LAW

1. RESTRICTED OWNERSHIP LAWS AND EXCEPTIONS

Texas has very strict tied house prohibitions, many of which were recently evaluated by the Courts. The statutory law provides that:

> [N]o person who owns or has an interest in the business of a distiller, brewer, rectifier, wholesaler, class B wholesaler, winery, or wine bottler, nor the agent, servant, or employee of such a person, may: (1) own or have a direct or indirect interest in the business, premises, equipment, or fixtures of a retailer.[199]

Texas' cross tier ownership prohibition is commonly referred to as the "one-share rule." This strict prohibition was unsuccessfully attacked in the legal system. *See Cadena Commercial USA Corp. v. Texas Alcoholic Beverage Comm'n*, 518 S.W.3d 318, 326 (Tex. 2017) (holding out-of-state brewer with Non-Residential Manufacturing Permit could not hold even "one share" of stock in Texas retailers).

---

196. ABCL §101(1)(a).
197. ABCL §105(16).
198. *Rihga International USA Inc. vs. State Liquor Authority*, 84 NY2d 876 (1993).
199. Tex. Alco. Bev. Code §102.07(a)(1).

In the *Cadena* case, the Texas Supreme Court considered whether Cadena Commercial USA Corp., a company formed to operate convenience stores throughout the United States, could hold a Texas retail license. *Cadena Commercial USA Corp. v. Texas Alcoholic Beverage Comm'n,* 518 S.W.3d 318, 326 (Tex. 2017). The issue presented was that Cadena's ultimate parent company, FEMSA (a foreign entity), also held interests in two Heineken companies, each of which operated breweries in other states; they also held non-resident manufacturer's permits in Texas.

The Texas Supreme Court ultimately upheld the TABC's decision to deny the retail license applications because, among other reasons, the term "interest" should broadly include both direct and indirect interests, including those based on "corporate stock, affiliate-subsidiary relationships, and a level of control" if the interests are "commercial or financial" in nature. Ultimately the Court determined that the phrase applies to both the entities and the stockholders themselves, and even parent company cross tier ownerships are prohibited.

2. RESTRICTED BENEFITS LAWS AND EXCEPTIONS

In addition to its very strict cross tier ownership position, Texas applies an equally strict prohibition on suppliers providing a thing of value to retailers.[200] Texas loosely characterizes any activity between industry members and retailers that influence business practices as "marketing practices" and has published a number of advisories outlining permitted and prohibited activities.[201]

Generally, unless an activity is expressly excepted, it is prohibited. Texas does, however, have a number of exceptions that, for example, authorize a supplier to provide limited merchandising and product displays,[202] provide advertising specialties to retailers subject to limitation,[203] and advertise where a supplier's product is available.[204] While not exhaustive, these exceptions identify the general type of permissible services or activities authorized between the tiers in Texas.

H. CONCLUSION

Since the repeal of Prohibition, tied house law has evolved from an apparently rational solution to a perceived social evil (the supplier-owned so-called open saloon) to something very different today. While in its pure form (prohibiting most suppliers from owning interests in most retailers) it restricts a supplier from forcing a retailer to buy the supplier's products, formulations like California's have given

---

200. See Tex. Alco. Bev. Code §102.07(a)(2).

201 . See Marketing Practices Advisories, https://www.tabc.texas.gov/texas-alcohol-laws-regulations/tabc-advisories-bulletins/.

202. Tex. Alco. Bev. Code §102.20.

203. Tex. Alco. Bev. Code §102.07.

204. Tex. Alco. Bev. Code §108.09.

wholesalers a potent weapon to maintain their monopoly status as members of the middle tier in the three-tier distribution system.

Wholesalers play a critical role in the licensed beverage industry; they are indispensable, especially to large suppliers who sell throughout the country and must deliver product to thousands of separate retailers (including restaurants) in vastly different markets. But the law in every open (as distinguished from monopoly) state requires licensed beverage suppliers outside the state to sell only to in-state wholesalers, who, in turn, are the only licensees permitted to sell and deliver to retailers.[205] Wholesalers cherish and generally do everything possible to protect and maintain this favored monopoly position.

And while there are many fewer wholesalers than in the past, those that have survived become increasingly powerful as they continue to grow through acquisition and consolidation. The chairman of one such wholesaler publicly favors a duopoly at the wholesale tier in every state. In practice, a duopoly already exists in California and several other states. In the 1960s, for example, nearly 35 full-service wholesalers sold wine and spirits in San Francisco; at the dawn of the twenty-first century that number had shrunk, effectively, to 2.[206]

Wholesalers often resist any regulatory or legislative initiative designed to promote programs to which they may be required to contribute money or effort, even when such programs are designed to increase their business. This attitude applies with special force to attempts to provide focused exemptions to the tied house laws, which most wholesalers view as a bulwark against the weakening of their monopoly status. They have acquired legislative influence through close and continual cultivation and support of their elected representatives; as a result, in many states, passage of even the least controversial supplier-sponsored tied house exceptions have become increasingly difficult to enact.

For example, in 2009 a large winery offered a generous gift of wine and cash to the San Francisco Symphony. But the Symphony held an on-sale general alcoholic beverage license for a small room in Davies Hall (its performance venue), in which it sold drinks and food to major contributors, and the winery conditioned the gift on the Symphony's finding its own solution to the resulting tied house problem.[207] California law permits wineries (but not other licensed beverage suppliers) to give wine to bona fide charities,[208] but no law permits similar gifts of cash or other alcohol beverages when the charity holds an on-sale license.

When the Symphony became aware that the tied house law blocked its receipt of a substantial portion of the proffered gift, it sought a surgically targeted tied

205. The most significant exception, of course, is the ability of out-of-state wineries to ship direct to consumers in other states whose laws permit such shipment by in-state wineries pursuant to the Supreme Court decision in *Granholm v. Heald*, 544 U.S. at 493 (2005).

206. These are Southern Wine and Spirits of California and Young's Market Company. Other wholesalers carry both wine and spirits, but none rank close to the aforementioned in size, economic power, reach, brand selection ("book"), and "feet on the street."

207. Sales of alcohol beverages to the general public before Symphony events and during intermission are handled by an outside caterer.

208. Cal. Bus. & Prof. Code §25503.9 (2009).

house exception. The only opposition to the bill came from the beer and wine wholesalers association, which demanded several changes — including a requirement that the Symphony pay an annual fee of $750 before it accepted any gift and that the ABC report all such gifts in its annual report to the legislature. The Symphony resisted the requirement and was forced, instead, to accept a five-year sunset clause as a compromise in order for the proposal to become law.[209]

The tied house and trade practice laws are difficult to amend. Amendments require substantial lawyer and registered lobbyist time and, as the preceding example illustrates, even the most benign proposals often face considerable political challenges.

Any lawyer who advises wineries must have at least a working knowledge of the trade practice laws. These laws are complex themselves and are also subject to changing regulatory interpretations. While the courts sometimes grant relief from overzealous enforcement, they are more inclined to defer to the administrative agency's regulatory expertise. Thus, open communication with state and federal licensed beverage regulators can greatly enhance a lawyer's understanding of the trade practice laws. But there are many gray areas in which the safest posture for a regulator is simply to deny permission to conduct the requested practice or promotion.[210] Lawyers must advise their clients when a given program falls into a gray area. If it does (and in trade practice and tied house law it often will), a counselor must analyze and explain the risks, and the client must make its own business decision, after considering the risks and rewards, about whether to test the agency's interpretation of the law.

In the meantime, an enlightened interpretation, which considers modern business realities, can help. The tied house laws, in particular, are vestigial remains of Repeal and now operate in and often control a commercial environment their drafters could never have imagined 75 years ago. They are mid-twentieth-century laws controlling an industry operating in a twenty-first-century environment.

Some have questioned the need for parallel state and federal regulation in the trade practices area. But neither the states nor Congress has shown interest in or appetite for relinquishing their power to control alcohol beverages. In 2010 the wholesalers, frustrated by frequent legislative and litigation losses in the states with regard to wine direct shipping under the *Granholm* doctrine, introduced H.R. 5034 (amended and reintroduced in 2011 as H.R. 1161, the "Community Alcohol Regulatory Effectiveness" Act of 2011, or, for short, the "CARE" Act), a bill that would permit states, under certain circumstances, to pass laws discriminating against alcohol beverages from out of state without regard to the Commerce Clause. At this writing the bill's fate is uncertain.

If tied house laws are designed to prohibit manufacturers from controlling the purchasing practices of retailers, it would not be unreasonable for the ABC to

---

209. *Id.* §25503.31. The section applies only to a charitable, nonprofit symphony association that has operated in San Francisco for at least 99 years and produces not less than 175 public musical events per season, among other restrictions, but it does permit gifts from brewers, spirits producers, and retailers (but not wholesalers) as well as winegrowers.

210. A sardonic adage holds that "No regulator ever got fired for saying 'No'!"

interpret them to reach that result. However, so far, licensed beverage regulators in California and some other states have often taken a safer and less controversial route by expressing sympathy for those who need a legitimate exception but doing nothing to grant it, referring the issue to the legislature, where, as we have seen, politics often has more to do with protecting vested interests than with facilitating the original and rational intent of those who wrote the laws.

CHAPTER 3

LABELING AND ADVERTISING

John Trinidad

A. INTRODUCTION

Members of the wine industry do not often garner sympathy from the public at large. People view wine as a luxury product and the "wine lifestyle" as aspirational, not something deserving of pity. But as you read this chapter, I ask you to put aside those preconceived notions and look at the wine industry with sympathetic eyes. Consider the wine label designer tasked with navigating a complex set of federal and state regulations that dictate what information must go on a wine label and how and where on the label it appears (even minute details regarding font size). And think of the winery trying to market a product in a regulatory environment that at its core is still aimed at limiting consumption of alcoholic beverages and requires bottles of wine to carry warnings of their potential ill effects. Finally, have sympathy for the attorneys who try to stay current on the ever-evolving laws and regulations that govern wine labeling and how wines can be marketed to consumers.

Wine labeling and advertising regulations are primarily aimed at protecting consumers from misleading labeling practices[1] and were not necessarily drafted with an eye towards making the lives of designers, wineries, or attorneys easier. Indeed, the Department of Treasury's Alcohol and Tobacco Tax and Trade Bureau (TTB), the agency charged with enforcing federal alcohol beverage labeling and advertising regulations, has conceded that these regulations should be modernized.[2] On top of that, the Treasury Department has identified labeling

1. Richard Mendelson, From Demon to Darling: A Legal History of Wine in America, 133 (2009).

2. Modernization of the Labeling and Advertising Regulations for Wine, Distilled Spirits, and Malt Beverages ("Notice 176"), 83 Fed. Reg. 60566 (Nov. 26, 2018) (to be codified at 27 C.F.R. pt. 4).

regulations as an area of potential regulatory reform as part of an overall effort to increase competition in the alcohol beverage industry.[3]

Adding to the complexity are several pending notices of proposed rulemaking aimed at, among other things, clarifying, updating, and consolidating wine labeling requirements.[4] Cross references to the proposed notices and amendments are contained in this article, but regardless of any final rulemaking, the principles that underpin alcohol beverage labeling and advertising regulations will remain intact.

B. FEDERAL WINE LABELING AND ADVERTISING REGULATONS — BACKGROUND ISSUES

1. JURISDICTION

The Federal Alcohol Administration Act (FAA Act)[5] provides the statutory standards for the regulations governing the labeling and advertising of wine over 7 percent alcohol by volume.[6] The labeling provisions of the FAA Act can be boiled down to two key principles: preventing consumer deception and providing consumers with sufficient and truthful information regarding the labeled product.[7] As noted during the hearings on the FAA Act:

> [Regulations to be adopted under the FAA Act are] intended to ensure that the purchaser should get what he thought he was getting, that representations both in labels and in advertising should be honest and straight-forward and truthful. They should not be confined, as the pure-food regulations have been confined, to prohibitions of falsity, but they should also provide for the information of the consumer that he should be told what was in the bottle, and all the important factors which were of interest to him about what was in the bottle.[8]

TTB administers the FAA Act labeling regulations. However, other federal agencies play a role in determining what appears on a wine label and in advertisements.

The Food and Drug Administration (FDA) maintains authority over wine under the Federal Food, Drug, and Cosmetic Act of 1938, and the agency has

---

3. Department of the Treasury, *Competition in the Markets for Beer, Wine, and Spirits* ("Competition Report") (February 2022) at 4, https://home.treasury.gov/system/files/136/Competition-Report.pdf (recommending that "TTB should reexamine its labeling and other practices to prioritize labeling rules that protect consumers and public health, while reducing or eliminating any regulatory requirements that create compliance costs and can be barriers to new entrants or burdens on small businesses.").

4. Notice 176, 83 Fed. Reg. 60566.

5. 27 U.S.C. §§201-219a.

6. 27 U.S.C. §205(e) – (f).

7. 27 U.S.C. §205(e); 6 U.S.C. §531.

8. Hearings on H.R. 8539 before the Committee on Ways and Means, House of Representatives, 74th Cong., 1st Sess. 10 (1935).

primary responsibility for labeling regulations that apply to wine with less than 7 percent alcohol by volume.[9] TTB's predecessor agency, the Bureau of Alcohol Tobacco and Firearms, and FDA entered into multiple different Memoranda of Understanding recognizing that TTB has primary responsibility over alcohol beverage labeling, without having FDA concede its jurisdiction.[10] The coordinated work of the FDA and TTB have come into play recently in connection with the use of health-related statements on labeling and advertising.

The Federal Trade Commission (FTC), whose primary mission is to protect consumers, also plays a role in wine labeling and advertising. In connection with alcohol advertising, the FTC is particularly concerned about advertising practices that may appeal to those below legal drinking.[11] However, due at least in part to First Amendment commercial speech concerns, the FTC has largely allowed the alcohol beverage industry to self-regulate.[12] For example, the Wine Institute's Code of Advertising Standards[13] sets forth responsible advertising guidelines, such as prohibiting the use of models or personalities who are or appear to be under age[14] and placing advertisements in "any media where more than 28.4% of the audience is underage."[15] Although these are voluntary guidelines for industry members, Wine Institute members are, as a condition of membership, required to comply.[16] The primary beer and spirits industry trade groups (the Beer Institute and the Distilled Spirits Council of the United States) have set out their own advertising standards. The FTC periodically audits the alcohol beverage industry's compliance with these guidelines; the agency's most recent report was issued in Mach 2014.[17]

With the rise of internet and social media advertising, TTB and industry groups have had to address how the regulations and industry codes apply to the online world. In 2013, TTB issued an Industry Circular making clear that the existing

---

9. TTB, Wine Labeling: Overview of Labeling Requirements for Domestic Wines Less than 7 Percent Alcohol by Volume (Jul. 19, 2021) https://www.ttb.gov/wine/7percentorless#:~:text=There%20are%20no%20Federal%20pre,approve%20labels%20for%20food%20products.

10. FDA & BATF,MOU 225-88-2000, *Memorandum of Understanding Between the Food and Drug Administration and the Bureau of Alcohol, Tobacco, and Firearms* (1987) https://www.ttb.gov/images/pdfs/atf-fda-1987.pdf (last visited Aug. 30, 2022).

11. Federal Trade Commission, *Alcohol Advertising* (Sep. 2013) https://consumer.ftc.gov/articles/0391-alcohol-advertising.

12. *Id.*

13. Wine Institute, *Wine Institute Code of Advertising Standards* (June 2011) https://wineinstitute.org/our-work/responsibility/social/ad-code/.

14. The Wine Institute's guidelines further recommend that all models should be at least 25 years old. *See id.*

15. *Id.*

16. Wendell Lee, in Wine in America Law and Policy, 139 (Richard Mendelson ed., 1st ed. 2011).

17. FTC, *Self-Regulation in the Alcohol Industry: Report of the Federal Trade Commission* (Mar. 2014) https://www.ftc.gov/reports/self-regulation-alcohol-industry-report-federal-trade-commission-0.

advertising regulations apply to websites and social media pages and posts.[18] A year later, Wine Institute issued its Digital Media Guidelines.[19] In addition to reinforcing that the advertisement placement provisions apply to online advertising, Wine Institute recommended that winery websites require age affirmation or verification in order to access the site.[20]

2. CERTIFICATE OF LABEL APPROVAL (AND EXEMPTION) PROCESS

The FAA Act requires that each wine sold in the United States go through a pre-approval process before entering the market.[21] Wineries wishing to sell their product in interstate commerce (and importers who wish to introduce foreign wine into the United States) must obtain a Certificate of Label Approval, commonly referred to as a "COLA," from TTB for each wine.[22] The COLA application and approval process provides two key benefits: (a) allowing TTB to undertake a review for compliance with federal regulations prior to the wine entering the market; and (b) providing a mechanism for the agency to keep illegal products from entering the market.[23] Domestic wineries wishing to sell a wine they bottle within the state of the bottling winery do not need to obtain a COLA but must apply for a COLA exemption and label the wine with the following statement: "For sale in [state name] only."[24] Currently, COLA-exempt wines fall outside the scope of the FAA Act and its wine labeling regulations.[25] However, as discussed in Section F.3 below, TTB has proposed some amendments to its regulations that would apply the FAA Act labeling regulations to both COLA and COLA-exempt wines.[26]

TTB is required to complete a review of each COLA or COLA-exemption application within 90 days.[27] In practice, however, the review time has recently

18. TTB Industry Circular 2013-01, *Use of Social Media in the Advertising of Alcohol Beverages* (May 13, 2013) https://www.ttb.gov/images/industry_circulars/archives/2013/13-01.html.

19. Wine Institute, *Wine Institute Digital Marketing Guidelines* (effective Jan. 2014) https://wineinstitute.org/our-work/responsibility/social/ad-code/.

20. Note that certain states may require age verification in connection with any online sale of wine.

21. 27 U.S.C. §205(e).

22. 27 C.F.R. §4.50(a); As noted by Wendell Lee in the prior edition of this textbook, TTB regulations require that a winery obtain a COLA prior to bottling. 27 C.F.R. §4.50. This may not necessarily line up with a winery's production timeline. One potential option that Mr. Lee highlighted was having a few generic red and/or white wine labels that could be approved and be sufficient to cover the winery's entire production portfolio. *See* W. Lee *supra* note 16 at 77.

23. Mendelson, *supra* note 1 at 133.

24. 27 C.F.R. §4.50(b).

25. COLA-exempt wines are, however, still subject to the labeling requirements found in the Internal Revenue Code.

26. Proposed Revisions to Wine Labeling and Recordkeeping Requirements, 81 Fed. Reg. 40584 (to be codified at 27 C.F.R. pt. 4); the current form of the COLA/COLA Exemption application is available at https://www.ttb.gov/images/pdfs/forms/f510031.pdf.

27. 27 C.F.R. §13.21(b).

been under one week, and in an effort to promote transparency, TTB lists the current COLA review timeframe on its website.[28]

Reviewers can deny an application but must provide the applicant with an explanation as to why they believe the proposed label does not comply with federal labeling regulations.[29] If an industry member believes that a reviewer has made a mistake in rejecting a label, it can appeal that decision.[30]

Once issued, COLAs can be revoked if TTB concludes that the label is not in compliance with either TTB-administered law or regulation or applicable law or regulation of other agencies.[31] As stated clearly on the application itself: "This certificate does not relieve you from liability for violations of the Federal Alcohol Administration Act, the Alcoholic Beverage Labeling Act of 1988, the Internal Revenue Code of 1986, or related regulations and rulings."[32]

Moreover, issuance of a COLA does not necessarily insulate a winery from third party claims that its labels are misleading or otherwise actionable.[33]

Over the years, TTB has been responsive to complaints that the COLA approval process is time consuming and creates a regulatory burden on wineries and importers and has taken active steps to streamline the process.[34] First, following complaints that the approval process took too long, Congress allocated funding to improve COLA application processing times, and that has borne significant results.[35] In fiscal year 2016, the average processing time for a COLA application was 27 days.[36] By fiscal year 2021, that number had been cut down to six days.[37] Also in 2014, 2018, and 2021, TTB announced expansions to its list of changes that can be made to a COLA-approved wine label without having to submit a whole new application.[38] For example, if a previously approved label is

---

28. TTB, Processing Times for Label Applications https://www.ttb.gov/labeling/processing-times (last visited Aug. 30, 2022).

29. 27 C.F.R. §13.23.

30. 27 C.F.R. §13.25.

31. 27 C.F.R. §§13.41, 13.51.

32. COLA/COLA Exemption application, *supra* note 26.

33. *Kay v. Copper Cane, LLC*, 549 F. Supp. 3d 1014, 1021-23 (N.D. Cal. 2021) (denying Copper Cane's motion for summary judgment and finding that COLA issued to Copper Cane did not trigger California safe harbor provisions based on the record before the court); *but see O'Hara v. Diageo-Guinness, USA, Inc.*, 306 F. Supp. 3d 441, 449 (D. Mass. 2018), *on reconsideration*, 370 F. Supp. 3d 204 (D. Mass. 2019) (dismissing certain claims to the extent they relied on COLA-approved alcohol beverage labels and holding that COLA approval for the labels in question were entitled to safe harbor protection under Massachusetts law).

34. U.S. Department of Treasury, Alcohol and Tobacco Tax and Trade Bureau, *TTB Announcement: Certificate of Label Approval (COLA) Streamlining Efforts* (Feb. 29, 2012), https://www.ttb.gov/images/pdfs/announcement-cola-streamlining-efforts.pdf. *See also* TTB, *Certificate of Label Approval (COLA) Streamlining Accomplishments and Long-term Initiatives* (Jun. 22, 2017) https://www.ttb.gov/labeling/streamlining-accomplishments.

35. Competition Report *supra* note 3 at 46.

36. *Id.*

37. *Id.*

38. TTB Industry Circular 2014-2, *Expansion of Allowable Revisions to Approved Alcohol Beverage Labels* (Sep. 29 2014) https://www.ttb.gov/images/industry_circulars/archives/2014/14-02.html; TTB Industry Circular 2018-2, *Expansion of Allowable Revisions to Approved Alcohol*

simply being updated to reflect a new vintage year for the wine, there is no need for the winery to submit a new COLA application.

Despite these efforts, the entirety of the COLA application process is being closely examined by the Department of Treasury as a result of President Biden's efforts to increase competition in the alcohol beverage industry.[39] While the Department noted that label preapproval may result in lower agency costs compared to launching enforcement actions for noncompliant products that already have entered the market, it noted that "the appropriate cost-benefit test is not cost to the government alone, but rather net national cost."[40]

C. MANDATORY AND OPTIONAL INFORMATION ALLOWED ON WINE LABELS

Federal wine labeling regulations require that all wines sold in the United States be labeled with certain mandatory information. In addition, federal regulations currently dictate whether such information must appear on a "brand label" (as defined below) or can appear anywhere on a wine bottle. To add a further level of specificity, there are also font size requirements for mandatory information, and certain mandatory information must appear in direct conjunction with certain other information.

Wine labels can contain certain optional information (such as a vineyard or "estate bottled" designations), but regulations also restrict when and how that information can be used.

Wineries are required to maintain "complete records" to substantiate and verify all information that appears on their label should TTB conduct an audit.[41] In addition, a "wine is not entitled" to have any information on its label unless there is a complete and accurate record trail from sourcing of fruit through removal of wine to verify that information.[42]

In the section below, we will discuss both the mandatory information (brand name, class/type designation, bottler's name and address, alcohol content, net contents, Health Warning Statement, and sulfite declaration) and the optional labeling information (appellation, fanciful name, vintage, estate bottled designation, and vineyard designation).

Beverage Labels (Mar. 26 2018) https://www.ttb.gov/industry-circulars/ttb-industry-circulars-18-2; TTB Industry Circular 2021-1, *Expansion of Allowable Revisions to Approved Alcohol Beverage Labels* (Oct. 15, 2021) https://www.ttb.gov/industry-circulars/ttb-industry-circular-2021-1.

39. Competition Report *supra* note 3 at 46.

40. *Id.*

41. 27 C.F.R. §24.314.

42. *Id.*

1. THE BRAND LABEL

If you were to ask the average wine consumer to identify a wine's "brand label," s/he will likely assume it is the consumer-facing label, i.e., the label you will likely see when you walk through the aisles of a retail store. In other words, most consumers think the "brand label" is the "front label." But in wine regulatory parlance, the "brand label" can be any label (whether it is a front, back, side, or strip label) so long as it is identified as such in the COLA and includes the following mandatory information: the wine's brand name and the class/type designation.[43] If the wine is labeled with an appellation, the appellation must appear in direct conjunction with the class/type designation and, as a result, must appear on the brand label.[44]

	Must appear on Brand Label	**Can Appear on Any Label**
Mandatory Information	Brand Name Class/Type Designation	Alcohol Content Bottler's Name & Address Health Warning Statement Net Content Sulfite Declaration
Optional Information	Appellation of Origin (while there is no requirement that a wine be labeled with an appellation name, an appellation is required if (a) class/type designation is a grape varietal name or (b) if a vintage date is utilized)	Estate Bottled Claim Fanciful Name Vineyard Designation Vintage Date Sustainability/Organic Claims

In November 2018, as part of Notice 176, TTB proposed eliminating the brand label distinction, thereby allowing mandatory information to appear anywhere on a wine container.[45] TTB believes this will provide producers with more "flexibility in the placement of the mandatory information"[46] and at the same time will not lead to consumer confusion because consumers are used to looking at the back and neck labels to find mandatory information on containers."[47]

43. 27 C.F.R. §4.32(a) (listing information required to appear on the brand label). *See* 27 C.F.R. §4.10 (defining the brand label as "The label carrying, in the usual distinctive design, the brand name of the wine.")

44. 27 C.F.R. §4.27(a).

45. Notice 176, 83 Fed. Reg. 60562 §§ 4.39(a), 5.42(a) (Nov. 26, 2018).

46. Notice 176, 83 Fed. Reg. 60575.

47. Notice 176, 83 Fed. Reg. 60582.

2. MANDATORY INFORMATION

a. Brand Name

Although federal regulations require that the brand label include the wine's "brand name," the federal regulations do not define that term. However, TTB typically refers to the brand name as "the name under which a wine or line of wines is marketed."[48]

There are some restrictions on the use of certain brand names under 27 C.F.R. Part 4.[49] First, a brand name cannot be found by TTB to be misleading as to the "age, origin, identity, or other characteristics" of the wine.[50] TTB can reject certificates of label applications for brand names it finds to be misleading or, in certain cases, it can conclude that the use of the word "brand" in conjunction with the selected brand name would negate the potential for consumer confusion.

Second, there are restrictions on the use of certain geographical brand names.[51] Specifically, federal regulations prohibit a wine from being labeled with a brand name "of viticultural significance" unless the wine meets the appellation of origin requirements for the named geographical area. Names of viticultural significance include state or county names (and foreign equivalents), names of approved American Viticultural Areas (AVAs), viticultural area names approved by a foreign government, and other names that TTB has determined to have viticultural significance.[52] For example, assume a new California-based winery wants to market its goods under a name that signals its primary location, such as "California & Sons." California, being the name of a state, is a name of viticultural significance under federal regulations. If that winery subsequently produces a wine primarily from Oregon's Willamette Valley AVA, it would be prohibited from selling that wine under the "California & Sons" brand name: The wine in that bottle does not meet the federal rules for a California appellation wine as the wine could not have been made from 75 percent fruit grown in California.

Of course, savvy consumers are likely aware of numerous examples of wine brand names that use a name of viticultural significance but produce wines from outside that geographic area. If the brand name was used in certificates of label approval issued before July 7, 1986, it can continue to be used on wine labels

48. Alcohol and Tobacco Tax and Trade Bureau, *Wine Labeling: Brand Name* (Sep. 23, 2019), https://www.ttb.gov/labeling-wine/wine-labeling-brand-name. NPRM 176 also proposes similar language as a regulatory definition for "brand name." Notice 176, 83 Fed. Reg. 7526 §5.1 (Mar. 11, 2022) ("The name under which a wine or line of wine is sold.") If in the rare case that a wine is not sold under a brand name, the name of the designated bottler or importer is treated as the "brand name" so long as it is shown on the brand label. 27 C.F.R. §4.33(a).

49. This chapter does not address trademark-related issues that may arise in the context of wine labeling. Please see Chapter 6 for more information on practical, intellectual property related concerns in choice of brand names.

50. 27 C.F.R. §4.33(b).

51. 27 C.F.R. §4.39(i).

52. 27 C.F.R. §4.39(i)(3).

provided that the wine complies with the requirements of 27 C.F.R. §4.39(i)(2).[53] Such wines can (a) meet the appellation of origin requirements for the named geographical area; (b) otherwise be labeled with its true appellation of origin; or (c) be labeled with some other statement that TTB has found sufficient to avoid a misleading impression as to the wine's true origin.

Finally, there are restrictions on wines labeled with brand names that use a vineyard, orchard, farm, or ranch name.[54] For such wines, 95 percent of the wine must be made from fruit grown on the named source. There is an exception, however, if the brand name is the same as the company or trade name utilized in the "bottled by" or "imported by" disclosure. Such wines do not need to meet the 95 percent sourcing requirement. In general, this exception allows for all sorts of wine brand names that incorporate a vineyard name but that are made primarily from grapes grown on other vineyards. Let's say, for example, the author owned Trinidad Vineyard in the Fort-Ross Seaview AVA in California and decided to produce wines under the TRINIDAD VINEYARDS brand name. The selected brand name does not prevent the winery from producing and selling wine sourced entirely from grapes from a Napa Valley AVA vineyard. The only requirement is that TRINIDAD VINEYARDS also appears as part of the required botting winery name/address disclosure (as discussed in the next section).

b. Bottler's Name/Address

All U.S. domestic wine must be labeled with the name and address (i.e., the city and state) of the bottling winery (for containers of 4 liters or less) or packing winery (for containers larger than 4 liters).[55] There are other optional terms that can accompany the name and address statement, but there are requirements for the use of such terms as outlined in the table below.[56] One of the most popular optional terms is the "Produced by" disclosure, which can only be used if the named winery fermented at least 75 percent of the wine; or conducted production activity that changed the class and type of the base wine by adding alcohol, flavors, or carbonation; or, for sparkling wine, had the wine undergo secondary fermentation at the identified location.

---

53. 27 C.F.R. §4.39(i)(2).
54. 27 C.F.R. §4.39(m).
55. 27 C.F.R. §4.35(a).
56. Alcohol and Tobacco Tax and Trade Bureau, *Wine Labeling: Name and Address* (Sep. 8, 2021) https://www.ttb.gov/labeling-wine/wine-labeling-name-and-address.

Use the Explanatory Phrase	If (at the Stated Address) the Named Proprietor...
Blended by	Mixed the wine with other wines of the same class and type
Cellared by	Subjected the wine to cellar treatment in accordance with 27 CFR 4.22(c)*
Made by	Fermented not less than 75%of the wine, OR Changed the class and type of the base wine by the addition of alcohol, brandy, flavors, colors, or carbonation, OR Produced sparkling wine by secondary fermentation
Prepared by	Subjected the wine to cellar treatment in accordance with 27 CFR 4.22(c)*
Produced by	Fermented not less than 75%of the wine, OR Changed the class and type of the base wine by the addition of alcohol, brandy, flavors, colors, or artificial carbonation, OR Produced sparkling wine by secondary fermentation.
Vinted by	Subjected the wine to cellar treatment in accordance with 27 CFR 4.22(c)

Imported wines must be labeled with a statement stating the name of the importer and address (city and state) of the importer's principal place of business.[57]

All name and address statements must be legible, on contrasting backgrounds, and appear separate and apart from, or be substantially more conspicuous than, other descriptive information on the wine label. In addition, there are specified type size requirements: 1mm for containers of 187 ml or less, and 2mm for containers larger than 187 ml.

c. Alcohol Content

All wines sold in the U.S. must be labeled with a statement of alcohol content.[58] Most wines are bottled with a quantitative statement that the wine has "Alcohol ___% by volume" or an approved abbreviation thereof.[59] TTB allows for some tolerance between the number stated on the label and the wine contained in the bottle. If the wine is 14 percent or less alcohol by volume, then a tolerance

57. 27 C.F.R. §§4.35(b)(1)(i), (b)(1)(iii).
58. 27 C.F.R. §4.36(a).
59. 27 C.F.R. §4.36(b)(1).

of 1.5 percent is permitted, but if the wine is over 14 percent alcohol by volume, then the tolerance is only 1 percent.[60]

Federal regulations also allow the alcohol content to be expressed as a range of 3 percent difference if the alcohol by volume is 14 percent or less (for example "9% to 12% Alc. by Vol."), or 2.0 percent if the wine is above 14 percent alcohol by volume, with certain qualifications as further discussed below.[61] However, there is no tolerance granted for such wines: The alcohol content must actually fall within the specified range.[62]

Wines that are between 7 percent and 14 percent alcohol by volume are not required to carry a quantitative statement about alcoholic content so long as the brand label includes the "Table Wine" or "Light Wine" class designation.[63] In essence, TTB deems "Table Wine" to be sufficient disclosure to consumers of the wine's alcohol content. Notably, "Dessert Wines," which are defined as wines between 14 percent and 24 percent alcoholic content,[64] are not granted the same exemption; they must still be labeled with one of the quantitative alcohol content statements referenced above.

Despite the tolerance provisions discussed above, the alcohol content statement cannot be contrary to the taxable grade of the wine or the class or type designation of the wine, if alcoholic content is part of the definition for that class or type (e.g., Table Wine or Dessert Wine).[65] Under current federal regulations, wines with ABV of 16 percent or less are taxed at one rate, and wines between 16.1 percent and 21 percent are taxed at a higher rate. Accordingly, a wine that is truly 16.3 percent cannot be labeled as 16 percent despite the 1 percent tolerance because the stated ABV is now contrary to the wine's true taxable grade.

d. Net Content

All wines sold in the U.S. must be in containers that hold specific and authorized "standards of fill."[66] In addition to the common 750 ml containers, there are eleven other approved standards of fill.[67]

---

60. *Id.*
61. 27 C.F.R. §4.36(b)(2).
62. *Id.*
63. 27 C.F.R. §4.36(a).
64. 27 C.F.R. §4.21(a)(6).
65. 27 C.F.R. §4.36(c).
66. 27 C.F.R. §4.71(a)(2).
67. 27 C.F.R. §4.72(a).

Approved Wine Standards of Fill

3 L	355 ml
1.5 L	250 ml
1 L	200 ml
750 ml	187 ml
500 ml	100 ml
375 ml	50 ml

TTB recently proposed the addition of six new standards of fill (180 ml, 300 ml, 360 ml, 550 ml, 720 ml, and 1.8 L) in response to a side letter signed in conjunction with the U.S.-Japan Trade Agreement as well as three additional standards of fill (620 ml, 700 ml, and 2.5 L) that TTB had previously proposed, but which did not garner much public comment.[68]

In addition to the limitation placed on container sizes through the standards of fill requirements, wine containers must be labeled with (or have embossed) a statement of its net contents.[69]

On multiple occasions, the federal government has considered eliminating the standards of fill requirement. In 2019, TTB published Notice of Proposed Rulemaking 182, requesting comments on the proposal to revise federal standards of fill regulations to only require that wine be bottled in a container size of at least 50 milliliters.[70] On December 29, 2020, TTB issued a final rule stating that it would not eliminate the standards of fill. Its decision to do so was influenced by public comments expressing concern that elimination of the standards of fill "would cause consumer confusion and potentially lead to a proliferation of differing State container size requirements that could cause further consumer confusion."[71]

But just two years later, TTB issued Notice of Proposed Rulemaking Number 210,[72] proposing yet again to eliminate the standards of fill requirement. The impetus for this reexamination was the February 2022 Competition report.[73] The Department concluded that "[c]ontainer size requirements can be a barrier to

68. Standards of Fill for Wine and Distilled Spirits ("Notice 210"), 87 Fed. Reg. 31787 (May 25, 2022) (to be codified at 27 C.F.R. pts. 4, 5, 19, 24, 26, 27); Robert E. Lighthizer, *Letter Exchange on Alcoholic Beverages* (Oct. 7, 2019) https://ustr.gov/sites/default/files/files/agreements/japan/Letter_Exchange_on_Alcoholic_Beverages.pdf.

69. 27. C.F.R. §4.37(a).

70. Elimination of Certain Standards of Fill for Wine (proposed Jun. 30, 2019) to be codified at 27 C.F.R. §4.

71. Addition of New Standards of Fill for Wine and Distilled Spirits; Amendment of Distilled Spirits and Malt Beverage Net Contents Labeling Regulations, 85 Fed. Reg. 85514 (Dec. 29, 2020).

72. Notice 210, 87 Fed. Reg. 31787 (May 25, 2022).

73. Treasury Report on Competition in the Markets for Beer, Wine, and Spirits (Feb. 9, 2022), available at https://home.treasury.gov/system/files/136/Competition-Report.pdf.

innovation and competition, insofar as producers must conform their packaging to the Treasury-mandated sizes" and recommended further proposed rulemaking to "examine whether their potential impact on competition outweighs potential consumer confusion."

In Notice 210, TTB makes clear that it believes standards of fill are no longer needed to assist in calculating excise tax due, and that the net content labeling requirement helps lower the risk of consumer confusion.[74] However, the agency did not address the biggest concern voiced by the industry in response to prior attempts to eliminate standards of fill: the likelihood that states would, in the absence of federal standards, create their own standards, creating a balkanized set of state rules for wine container sizes. As Wine Institute stated in its comment letter to Notice 182, federal standards of fill "create a uniform set of national standards for wine container sizes that the wine industry can rely on," and in their absence, "states would likely impose their own standards of fill, resulting in a patchwork of potentially 50 different sets of state standards."[75]

e. Class and Type Designations

Federal regulations, specifically 27 C.F.R. §4.21, categorize wine into nine distinct classes. Each class is further broken out into different "types" of wine. A wine's class, type, or other approved designation must appear on the brand label.[76] If a grape varietal name is used as the class/type designation, then the wine must also carry an appellation name, and the varietal name must appear in direct conjunction with, and in lettering substantially as conspicuous as, the wine's appellation.[77]

The most common class of still wine is Class 1 Grape Wine, and it can be further broken out into various types including: wines identified by their color (red wine, rose wine, white wine);[78] wines identified by one or more grape variety names;[79] and wines identified by certain specified semi-generic names or non-generic, such as Burgundy, Chablis, or Romanée-Conti.[80] In addition, grape wine (as well as certain other classes of wine) can be classified as Table Wine or Light Wine or Dessert Wine if the wine complies with certain alcohol content

---

74. Notice 210, 87 Fed. Reg. 31789 (May 25, 2022).

75 Robert Koch, Wine Institute Comment Letter on Notice 182, (Oct. 29, 2019) https://www.regulations.gov/comment/TTB-2019-0004-0164.

76. 27 C.F.R. §§4.32(a)(2), 4.34.

77. 27 C.F.R. §4.32(b)(1). There are certain other circumstances where the specified class / type designation must appear in direct conjunction with, and in lettering as conspicuous as, the named appellation including when the wine is labeled with a vintage year. 27 C.F.R. §4.32(b)(2)-(5).

78. 27 C.F.R. §4.21(a)(4).

79. 27 C.F.R. §4.23.

80. 27 C.F.R. §4.24.

restrictions.[81] The table below provides a summary of some of the more common types found within the Class 1 – Grape Wine category.[82]

Class: Class 1 Grape Wine 27 C.F.R. §4.21(a)	
Class Description: "Wine produced by the normal alcoholic fermentation of the juice of sound, ripe grapes (including restored or unrestored pure condensed grape must), with or without the addition, after fermentation, of pure condensed grape must, and with or without added grape brandy or alcohol, but without other addition or abstraction except as may occur in cellar treatment. The regulations at 27 C.F.R. §4.21(a)(1) also set forth the methods by which grape wine may be ameliorated before, during, or after fermentation."[83]	
Type	**Type Description**
Red Wine Rose Wine Pink Wine White Wine Amber Wine 27 C.F.R. §4.21(a)(4)	Wines identified by color
Single Grape Variety Name 27 C.F.R. §4.23(b)	Single grape variety name can be used as the type designation if wine is derived of 75% or more grapes of the named variety, the entire amount of which was grown in the labeled appellation of origin.
Two or more Grape Variety Name 27 C.F.R. §4.23(d)	All grapes used to make the wine must be of the named varieties and the percentage of the wine from each variety must be shown on the label (a tolerance of plus or minus 2% is permitted). Additional requirements apply if the wine is labeled with a multi-county or multi-state appellation of origin.
Certain Semi-Generic Grape Wines (examples: Burgundy, Chablis, Chianti,) 27 C.F.R. §4.24(b)	Grape wines produced in certain specified countries (unless grandfathered label under 27 C.F.R. §24.257(c))

81. 27 C.F.R. §4.21(a)(5)-(6).

82. Table information based on TTB, *The Beverage Alcohol Manual,* (May 12, 2022) https://www.ttb.gov/images/pdfs/wine_bam/c5-class-and-type-designation.pdf.

83. *Id.*

Foreign non-generic names (examples: Bordeaux, Mosel, Romanée-Conti) 27 C.F.R. §4.24(c)	Grape wine designations of certain foreign countries
Table Wine or Light Wine 27 C.F.R. §4.21(a)(5)	Wine containing at least 7% but not more than 14% alcohol by volume
Dessert Wine 27 C.F.R. §4.21(a)(6)	Wine containing over 14% but not more than 24% alcohol by volume

One of the common pitfalls for wineries is trying to use "Rosé" as a class/type designation. While "Rosé Wine" is an accepted class/type designation under 27 C.F.R. §4.21(a)(1)(4), "Rosé" on its own is not an approved class or type designation.

Other common labeling complications arise from the use of a name of a single grape varietal as the wine's class or type designation. Such wines have numerous additional requirements.

First, any such wine must also be labeled with an appellation of origin,[84] and the appellation of origin must appear in direct conjunction with, and in lettering as conspicuous as, the class/type designation.[85]

Second, at least 75 percent of the wine must be derived from grapes of the named varietal, the entire 75 percent of which must be grown in the named appellation.[86] So, for example, if you produced a wine that was made from 90 percent Cabernet Sauvignon and 10 percent Petit Verdot, and you wanted to label that wine as "Napa Valley Cabernet Sauvignon," then:

- At least 75 percent of the grapes in that wine must be Cabernet Sauvignon grown in Napa Valley;
- The remaining 15 percent of the Cabernet Sauvignon grapes used in that wine could be sourced from Napa Valley or some other region;[87] and
- Another 10 percent of grapes (whether Cabernet Sauvignon or Petit Verdot or a combination) must have been grown in Napa Valley in order to meet the AVA designation requirements described above.

84. 27 C.F.R. §4.23(a).

85. 27 C.F.R. §4.32(b)(1). In Notice 176, TTB proposed changes to the regulations which would eliminate this direct conjunction requirement. Notice 176, 83 Fed. Reg. 60586.

86. 27 C.F.R. §4.23(b).

87. As described below, state law would require that 100 percent of the grapes used in this wine be grown in California.

Finally, only approved grape varietal names can be used as a class or type designation.[88] The Code of Federal Regulations includes a list of approved names, including acceptable synonyms, in 27 C.F.R. §4.91. However, in addition to the approved names that are listed in the Code of Federal Regulations, other administratively approved grape variety names are listed on TTB's website.[89]

Wineries wishing to use names of grape varieties that have not been approved by TTB have found creative work-arounds. For example, Carol Meredith, a professor at University of California, Davis and a wine producer has conducted research confirming that California Zinfandel is genetically identical to a Croatian variety known as Tribidrag.[90] Wishing to draw attention to the historical roots of her wines while still complying with federal labeling regulations, Professor Meredith labeled her wine with the class designation "Red Wine" but then adopted "Tribidrag" as a fanciful name (similar to a sub-brand) on her wine labels.

88. 27 C.F.R. §4.23(d).

89. *See* TTB, *Grape Variety Designations on American Wine Labels* (May 10, 2022) https://www.ttb.gov/wine/grape-variety-designations-on-american-wine-labels.

90. Wine Business International, *I am Tribidrag* (Jun. 15, 2017) https://www.wine-business-international.com/wine/styles-regions/i-am-tribidrag.

f. Federal Government Warning Statement

As a result of a federal statute adopted in 1988,[91] all alcoholic beverages sold in the United States must be labeled with the following government warning statement:

> **GOVERNMENT WARNING:** (1) According to the Surgeon General, women should not drink alcoholic beverages during pregnancy because of the risk of birth defects. (2) Consumption of alcoholic beverages impairs your ability to drive a car or operate machinery, and may cause health problems.

The primary purpose of the law is to inform the public "about the health hazards that may result from the consumption or abuse of alcoholic beverages."

Codified in 27 C.F.R. Part 16, the regulation includes significant details regarding the appearance of the government warning. Specifically:

1. the information must appear separate and apart from all other information;[92]
2. the warning must be legible and appear on a contrasting background;
3. the words "government warning" must be in all capital letters and in bolded font;
4. there is a minimum font size requirement based on the size of the container;[93]
5. the statement has to appear in a maximum number of characters per inch, depending on the type size.[94]

Although the authorizing statute requires that the statement be "located in a conspicuous and prominent place,"[95] there is no requirement that the Government Warning appear on the brand label.

Despite the clarity provided by both the statute and regulation regarding how the government warning must appear on wine labels, improperly punctuated government warning or failure by the applicant to put the words "GOVERNMENT WARNING" in capital letters and in bold type are among the most frequent errors encountered by TTB label examiners.[96]

Of particular note, while the federal government and states have concurrent jurisdiction over most areas of wine labeling, in adopting the Alcoholic Beverage Labeling Act, Congress expressly preempted states from enacting laws requiring any other labeling statement "relating to alcoholic beverages and health."[97] Federal preemption has played a significant role for wines sold in California. In 1986, California voters approved Proposition 65, thus requiring products sold in

---

91. Alcoholic Beverage Labeling Act of 1988, 27 U.S.C. §§213-219a (2006).

92. 27 C.F.R. §16.21.

93. For containers of 237 ml or less, the typeface of the warning must be at least 1 millimeter; for containers over 237 ml and up to 3 L, the font size must be at least 2 millimeters; and for any larger containers, 3 millimeters. 27 C.F.R. §16.22(b).

94. 27 C.F.R. §16.22.

95. 27 U.S.C. §215(b).

96. Alex Jewell, TTB, *Wine Labeling Overview Presentation,* 20 https://www.ttb.gov/images/pdfs/presentations/2021-02-wine-labeling-overview.pdf (Feb. 2021).

97. 27 U.S.C. §216.

the state to disclose that certain products or ingredients contained therein may cause cancer, reproductive harm, or birth defects.[98] Because of federal preemption, these warnings cannot appear on wine labels, though may be required to appear at the point-of-sale or otherwise in connection with the sale of wine.[99]

g. Sulfite Declaration

Any wine with sulfur dioxide of 10 or more parts per million or greater must be labeled with a statement that the wine contains sulfites or contains sulfating agent(s).[100] If a wine does not carry a sulfite declaration, the bottling winery or importer (whoever applied for the certificate of label approval) must obtain a sulfite labeling waiver by submitting a laboratory report to support a finding that the wine has less than 10 parts per million (ppm) of total sulfites and submit that analysis in connection with its COLA application.[101]

This requirement was adopted in 1986 in connection with efforts by TTB's predecessor agency, the Bureau of Alcohol, Tobacco and Firearms, to address concerns that foods with "undeclared sulfites" posed a public health risk, specifically to individuals allergic to sulfites.[102] However, it should be noted that the 10 ppm figure represents an "analytical threshold" for the purpose of triggering disclosure and that the presence of such statements on wine does not "necessarily mean that adverse reactions will occur upon consumption."[103]

Although sulfur dioxide and similar agents have been used as an antioxidant in wine production for some time, of late, certain wineries espousing "minimal intervention" wine making have championed producing wine with limited use of (or outright exclusion of) sulfur dioxide (or other sulfur agents).[104] TTB has allowed certain additional sulfite-related disclosures, such as "no sulfites added" or "contains naturally occurring sulfites." However, TTB has stated that it will not permit wines to be labeled with a statement that it is "sulfite free."[105]

---

98. Cal. Health & Safety Code §25249.5 et seq.

99. Beer Institute, Proposition 65 https://www.beerinstitute.org/beer-policy/legislative-policy/proposition-65/#:~:text=Proposition%2065%20is%20a%20California,about%20exposure%20to%20such%20chemicals (last visited Aug. 21, 2022).

100. 27 C.F.R. §4.32(e).

101. TTB Beverage Alcohol Manual *supra* note 41 at 1-12 and 1-13.

102. 51 Fed. Reg. 34706 (September 30, 1986).

103. Wendell Lee, in Wine in America Law and Policy, 114-15 (Richard Mendelson ed., 1st ed. 2011).

104. Rupert Joy, *No sulphites added wine: the great debate*, Decanter (Jan. 11, 2021) https://www.decanter.com/learn/no-sulphites-added-wine-the-great-debate-451195/.

105. *See* Wine Labeling Overview Presentation *supra* note 55 at 17, TTB Beverage Alcohol manual *supra* note 41 at 1-12, 1-13.

3. OPTIONAL INFORMATION

a. Appellation of Origin[106]

"Wine is a product of place." Or so goes the common refrain for those that believe that one of the more interesting aspects of wine is that it reflects the "terroir" of where the grapes were grown and the wine produced.

Given all the discussion in the wine press and among wine connoisseurs about wine and terroir, you would think that place, above all other things, would be an essential and required element of any wine label. U.S. wine regulations, however, do not as a general rule require that wines be labeled with an appellation of origin or any "place" name other than the city and state of the bottling winery. Of course, as discussed above, if a grape variety is used as the type designation or (as discussed below) a vintage date is used, then an appellation designation must appear in direct conjunction with the class/type designation and appear on the brand label.

Current regulations require that if an appellation of origin is used on a wine, it appears in direct conjunction with, and in lettering substantially as conspicuous as, the class/type designation. In Notice 176, TTB has proposed eliminating this direct conjunction requirement, thereby allowing the appellation of origin to appear anywhere on a wine label.

Domestic wines can be labeled with either a political appellation (i.e., the name of the country, a state, or a county) or a petitioned appellation — i.e., an American Viticultural Area (AVA) approved by TTB following the submission of a petition and approval through the administrative notice of proposed rulemaking process.

Political Appellations

Wines labeled with a political appellation have both grape sourcing and place of production requirements. Such wines must be made up from at least 75 percent grapes grown in the indicated appellation.[107] If the wine is labeled with a state name, then under federal regulations, the wine must have been "fully finished"[108] within the named state or an adjacent state.[109] If a county name is used as the designated appellation, the wine must be fully finished in the state in which that

---

106. For the purposes of this chapter, we have limited the discussion of appellations of origin to focus on what is required in order to include an appellation on wine labels. For a more detailed discussion about the regulatory history of U.S. appellations, please see Chapter 6.

107. 27 C.F.R. §4.25(b)(1)(i). As discussed below, certain states have adopted laws that require a higher percentage of grapes from the named appellation, while others have required that any wine carrying a political appellation from within the state be made from fruit solely grown in that state.

108. Although the federal regulations do not include a definition of "fully finished," it has been interpreted to mean ready to be bottled except for blending and certain other cellar treatments, provided that the blending and cellar operations do not change the wine's class or type. 27 C.F.R. §4.22(c).

109. 27 C.F.R. §4.25(b)(1)(ii). As we discuss below, however, state laws may have stricter requirements.

county lies.[110] There is no requirement that such a wine be fully finished within the named county.[111]

In addition, any wine labeled with a political appellation must conform "to the laws and regulations of the named appellation area governing the composition, method of manufacture, and designation of wines made in such place."[112] This is one of the few instances in which federal wine labeling regulations recognize the concurrent regulatory powers of state and local laws.

Federal regulations also allow for wines to be labeled with up to three counties that are in the same state, but 100 percent of the grapes must come from those named counties and the percentage of wine derived from grapes grown in each county must be disclosed (with a tolerance of plus or minus 2 percent).[113] In addition, a wine can be labeled with an appellation comprised of two or three contiguous states, but 100 percent of grapes must come from the named states, the percentage of grapes grown in each identified state must be disclosed with a tolerance of plus or minus 2 percent, and the wine must be fully finished in one of the named states.[114] In Notice 176, TTB proposes loosening those requirements by (a) lowering the grape sourcing requirement so that only 85 percent of fruit need come from the identified counties or states and (b) eliminating the requirement that the percentage of grapes from each county or state be listed.[115] Under the proposed regulations, the only requirement is that the states or counties be listed in descending order of predominance and that the percentage of wine derived from each named county or state is greater than wine derived from grapes grown in any other county or state that is not named.[116]

Petitioned Appellations

AVA-labeled wines must meet slightly different grape sourcing and place-of-production requirements than those for political appellations. Under 27 C.F.R. §4.25(e)(3)(iv), an AVA name can be used on a wine label so long as not less than 85 percent of the wine is derived from grapes grown within the boundaries of the named AVA and the wine is fully finished within the state (or in the case of a multi-state AVA, in one of the states) in which the AVA is located. The producing winery must keep strict sourcing and production records to support its AVA labeling claim.[117]

Previously, the federal regulations expressly required that AVA-designated wines be made in compliance with "the laws and regulations of all the States

---

110. *Id.*

111. If a county name is used, the word "county" must also be used and appear in the same size of type and in letters as conspicuous as the name of the county. 27 C.F.R. §4.25(b)(1)(i).

112. 27 C.F.R. §4.25(b)(1)(iii).

113. 27 C.F.R. §4.25(c).

114. 27 C.F.R. §4.25(d).

115. Notice 176, 83 Fed. Reg. 60652.

116. *Id.*

117. *See* 27 C.F.R. §24.314.

contained in the viticultural area."[118] However, this language was removed as a result of the approval of the Columbia Valley AVA, a multi-state AVA that included portions of both Oregon and Washington.[119] TTB's predecessor was concerned that the regulations may unfairly require a winery to be subject to the laws of another state even though its grapes or wine may never have entered the other state.[120] As a result, the references to state laws in the regulations governing AVA-labeling were removed. However, the federal government made clear that this change was not meant to undermine concurrent state laws governing AVA labeling.

> Since §4.25a(e)(3)(iv) requires a wine claiming a viticultural area appellation to be fully finished within one of the states in which the viticultural area is located, State laws or regulations of that state would apply at the bonded winery where the wine is produced.[121]

As discussed in more detail below, a few of the major wine producing states, such as California and Oregon, have adopted laws to protect their well-recognized AVAs.

b. Vineyard Designation

In Section C.2.a above, we discussed 27 C.F.R. §4.39(m), which restricts brand names that use a vineyard, orchard, farm, or ranch name.[122] That same provision governs the use of a vineyard designation on a wine label. In short, any wine that is labeled with a vineyard designation must be able to show that 95 percent of the wine was made from fruit from that named vineyard.

Keep in mind, however, that unlike AVAs, there is no registry of vineyards or regulated boundaries of named vineyards: The names and boundaries are purely a construct of either the grape grower or the wine producer. There is no federal regulation that requires that a vineyard designation consistently refer to the same vineyard blocks or rows.

Assume that the Smith and Turner families own neighboring, eponymously named vineyard properties and that the Smith Family makes wine using "Smith Hillside Vineyard" as a vineyard designation for wines produced from their own vineyard. Despite their proximity, the Turner parcel is not particularly well suited to quality grape growing, and its grapes generally sell for less per ton than grapes grown on the Smith's property. If the Smiths were to purchase the Turner parcel, they could use those grapes in future vintages of "Smith Hillside Vineyard" designated wine so long as 95 percent of the grapes used in that wine are grown on whatever the Smiths have decided *post-acquisition* to identify as the Smith Hillside

---

118. 27 C.F.R. §4.25 (a),©(3) (1978).
119. 27 C.F.R. §4.25 (a)(vi).
120. ATF Notice No. 564, 50 Fed. Reg. 19384 (1985).
121. T.D. ATF-222, 51 Fed. Reg. 3773 (1986).
122. 27 C.F.R. §4.39(m).

Vineyard. Also, since the federal regulations do not define or require that a vineyard be comprised of contiguous vineyard blocks, this same example arguably would apply even if the Smith and Turner family parcels were not adjacent to each other.

c. Estate Bottled

Producers often try to find ways to distinguish their wines from their competitors and provide a rationale for charging a premium price. One way of doing so is signaling to the consumer that the producer has exerted significant control from grape growing through fermentation and bottling by use of the "Estate Bottled" designation. 27 C.F.R. §4.26 governs use of the term "Estate Bottled" on wines and requires that any wine labeled with that statement meet all of the following requirements:

1. The wine must be labeled with the name of a viticultural area appellation of origin (i.e., not a political appellation).
2. The bottling winery and the vineyard(s) in which all the grapes used in the wine were grown must be located in the named viticultural area.
3. The vineyard(s) from which all such grapes were sourced must be "owned or controlled" by the winery.
4. All production activity (crushing, fermenting, finishing, and aging) and bottling must be conducted "in a continuous process" whereby at no time the grapes, must, juice, or wine has left the bottling winery.

The regulation defines land "controlled by" the winery as "property on which the bottling winery has the legal right to perform, and does perform, all of the acts common to viticulture under the terms of a lease or similar agreement of at least 3 years duration."[123]

Wineries that purchase grapes under a grape purchase agreement that provides the winery with significant control over the farming practices often ask if such wines qualify for the "Estate Bottled" designation. A strict reading of 27 C.F.R. Section 4.26 provides no assurance that TTB would allow purchased grapes to be used in wines labeled as "Estate Bottled." Thus, in order to ensure compliance with federal regulations, it is advisable to limit the use of "Estate Bottled" for wines made from grapes grown on vineyards owned and farmed by the bottling winery or leased and farmed by the bottling winery where the lease is of at least three years duration.

Once a winery has adopted use of "Estate Bottled" on its wines, it generally wants to continue use of that designation as a quality endorsement to warrant any price premium for that wine and differentiate the wine from others in its portfolio as well as competitors' wines. There are some situations where that may not be possible. For example, nearby wildfires may cause a winery to move tanks or barrels of wine from its facility to another bonded facility for safe keeping.

123. 27 C.F.R. §4.26(c).

However, once the wine has been removed from the bottling winery, that wine has lost any ability to be labeled as "Estate Bottled." By way of example, assume that the owner of a vineyard located in the San Miguel District AVA (an AVA entirely within the Paso Robles AVA) produces wine solely from grapes grown on its vineyard in a facility also located in the San Miguel District AVA. The resulting wine may qualify as being designated as a San Miguel District AVA wine and estate bottled. But if the vineyard owner is forced to move his production premises to the neighboring Adelaida District AVA (also entirely within the Paso Robles AVA), even though the wine still qualifies as a San Miguel District AVA wine, it can no longer be labeled both as "Estate Bottled" and with the San Miguel District AVA name since the wine is now produced outside of the labeled AVA. If the winery wishes, however, it could use the Paso Robles AVA as the wine's designated appellation, in which case it may still qualify as "Estate Bottled" under §4.26.

Some wineries have expressed interest in using the term "Estate Grown" on their wine labels in an attempt to signal that the grapes used in the wine were grown on vineyards owned by the winery. Although current federal regulations do not directly address the use of the term "Estate Grown," TTB's policy has been that Estate Grown can only be used on a wine label if the wine meets the requirements for the use of the term "Estate Bottled."[124]

In Notice 176, TTB proposed allowing the term "Estate Grown" on wines that meet the following qualifications: (a) the wine is labeled with an appellation of origin; (b) the producing winery is located in that appellation; (c) the producing winery grew all the grapes on land owned or controlled by it within the named appellation and fermented 100 percent of the wine from those grapes; and (d) if the bottling winery is not the producing winery, the label must state that the wine was ''estate grown'' by the producing winery, and the name and address of both wineries must appear on the label.[125]

d. Vintage

Wine is an agricultural product subject to the unique growing conditions of each harvest year. For that reason, certain wine buyers rely heavily on vintage year labeling in forming their opinion about a wine's quality and making purchase decisions. Such buyers may be surprised to discover that U.S. laws do not require a vintage date to appear on wines, and they may be even more surprised to learn that the presence of a vintage year on a wine label does not necessarily mean that 100 percent of the wine was made from grapes harvested in that year.

If a wine is labeled with a vintage date (i.e., a "Vintage Wine"), it must also be labeled with appellation of origin, which must appear in direct conjunction with the class or type designation.[126] If the Vintage Wine is labeled with the name of an AVA or its foreign equivalent, 95 percent of grapes must have been harvested

---

124. 27 C.F.R. §4.26.
125. Notice 176, 83 Fed. Reg. 60562 §§ 4.92, 4.93.
126. 27 C.F.R. §4.27(a).

in the labeled year.[127] The standard is a bit lower for wines that carry non-AVA appellation names, such as the name of counties or states: Only 85 percent of the wine must have been made from grapes harvested in the stated vintage year.[128]

Federal regulations governing vintage date labeling have been adjusted over time to allow for more flexibility. Prior to 1972, Vintage Wines had to be made "wholly from grapes gathered in the same calendar year."[129] As a result of federal rulemaking, starting in 1972, Vintage Wines could include up to 5 percent of grapes from other vintage years.

Then, in 2006, as a result of a petition submitted by the California Wine Institute, the percentage for wines from non-AVA/AVA-equivalent appellations was further reduced. According to that petition, the vintage labeling standards for a number of other wine-producing countries (including Australia, New Zealand, the European Union, Chile, and South Africa) was 85 percent or less.[130] The Wine Institute argued that not only would the change help domestic wineries compete on a more even playing field with imported Vintage Wines, but also U.S. consumers would benefit from more regulatory flexibility regarding vintage date labeling. As stated in the final rule:

> The petitioner asserted that the proposed amendment would benefit both U.S. winemakers and American consumers because of the advantage derived from being able to use either a younger or older wine in a blend. The petition explained this advantage as follows: For instance, 15 percent of a wine from an older riper vintage will assist in achieving a style target when the current vintage has produced thinner, more acid wines. An 85 percent vintage date regulation, as proposed, would lead to improved taste appeal and quality perception of many wines. Young red wines would be smoother and less 'green' and would be more consistent across vintages. Older white wines would be fresher and fruitier and more consistent across vintages as well.[131]

e. Sustainability and Organic Claims

Federal alcohol beverage labeling regulations currently do not directly address claims regarding sustainability, environmental impact, social justice, and grape-growing and wine-making practices. Such information is considered additional information that must be truthful and non-misleading and cannot conflict with, or otherwise qualify, any of the mandatory information that appears on the wine label.[132]

---

127. 27 C.F.R. §4.27(a)(1).

128. 27 C.F.R. §4.27(a)(2).

129. 37 Fed. Reg. 7974 §4.10 (Apr. 22, 1972).

130. Letter from Robert Koch, President, Wine Institute, to John Manfreda, Administrator, TTB (Apr. 12, 2005), available at https://www.ttb.gov/images/pdfs/vintagedatereg042705.pdf.

131. Change to Vintage Date Requirements, 71 Fed. Reg. 25748-49.

132. 27 C.F.R. §4.38(f).

Wineries wishing to label their wines with the logos of certain certifying agencies such as Demeter Certified Biodynamic,[133] California Certified Sustainable,[134] or B Corp Certification[135] may do so as long as they are indeed certified and have complied with all obligations associated with the use of such certification marks.

In Notice 176, TTB proposed a new §4.85, which is meant to codify current TTB policy regarding sustainability and other similar statements.[136]

> **§4.85 Environmental, sustainability, and similar statements.** Statements related to environmental or sustainable agricultural practices, social justice principles, and other similar statements (such as, "Produced using 100% solar energy" or "Carbon Neutral") may appear as long as the statements are truthful, specific, and not misleading. Statements or logos indicating environmental, sustainable agricultural, or social justice certification (such as, "Biodyvin," "Salmon-Safe," or "Fair Trade Certified") may appear on wines that are actually certified by the appropriate organization.

Organic claims are treated differently than these other sustainability-related statements and information. Any wine labeled or advertised with the term "organic" must comply with the National Organic Program[137] (NOP) administered by the Agricultural Marketing Service division of the U.S. Department of Agriculture (USDA).[138] TTB and the USDA have worked in tandem to provide the industry with guidance regarding the use of organic claims on alcoholic beverages.[139]

The NOP sets forth standards on how agricultural products, such as grapes and wine, must be produced, handled, and processed in order to be labeled as "organic" as well as standards for facilities that process such crops. Third-party certifying agents authorized by the USDA conduct inspections and issue certifications to growers and processors (i.e., wineries).

In order for a wine to be labeled as "organic," 100 percent of the grapes used in the wine and the winery itself must be certified as organic.[140] Any additional agricultural ingredients that are used in the winemaking process, such as yeast, also

---

133. Demeter Association, Inc., *Biodynamic Certification Marks*, https://www.demeter-usa.org/about-demeter/biodynamic-certification-marks.asp (last visited Aug. 30, 2022).

134. California Sustainable Wine, *Certification Requirements*, https://californiasustainablewine.com/certification-requirements (last visited Aug. 30, 2022).

135. B Lab, *B Corp Certification*, https://www.bcorporation.net/en-us/certification (last visited Aug. 30, 2022).

136. Notice 176, 83 Fed. Reg. 60577, 60627.

137. 7 C.F.R. Part 205 (National Organic Program).

138. 27 C.F.R. §4.101.

139. TTB, *Memorandum of Understanding — Agreement on the Coordination of Organic Labeling and Advertising between the Alcohol and Tobacco Tax and Trade Bureau, United States Department of the Treasury and the Agricultural Marketing Service, United States Department of Agriculture* (Mar. 10, 2010), available at https://www.ttb.gov/images/pdfs/mou-ams.pdf.

140. U.S. Department of Agriculture, Agricultural Marketing Service National Organic Program, *Labeling Organic Wine*, 2 (Feb. 2014) https://www.ttb.gov/images/pdfs/wine-labeling-guide.pdf.

need to be certified as organic unless such strains are not available in organic form.[141] The wine can contain up to 5 percent of non-agricultural ingredients so long as those ingredients are allowed under the NOP's National List of Allowed and Prohibited Substances (7 C.F.R. §§205.600 - 205.607).[142] While wines can have naturally occurring sulfites, no added sulfites are permitted in organic wines. Wines that meet all these qualifications can be labeled as "organic wine" and can display the USDA Organic logo.

USDA ORGANIC

If a wine is labeled as "made with organic grapes," the standards are slightly different. All of the grapes used to make the wine must be certified organic, but the wine can (a) be made with other agricultural ingredients that are not organic (such as non-organic yeasts) and (b) contain up to 100 ppm total sulfites, including added sulfites.[143] Non-agricultural ingredients are permitted so long as they are allowed under the NOP's National List. These wines, however, cannot be labeled with the USDA organic logo nor can there be any claim that the wine itself is organic.

Wineries submitting a COLA application for a label that carries any organic claim must submit documentation to support their claim.[144] In addition, the label must include a certification statement (such as "Certified Organic by [insert name of certifying agent]") below the "bottled by" mandatory disclosure.[145]

4. PROHIBITED PRACTICES

Given TTB's mission to protect consumers, it should come as no surprise that federal wine labeling regulations expressly prohibit statements that are false or

---

141. *Id.* at 3.

142. *Id.*

143. Id. at 4.

144. TTB, *Alcohol FAQs, Organic Alcohol* at OA2 (Aug. 12, 2022), https://www.ttb.gov/faqs/alcohol.

145. *Id.* at OA10.

misleading.[146] A truthful statement may be considered to be misleading through ambiguity, omission, or inference.[147]

There are numerous specific categories of prohibited labeling practices found under 27 C.F.R. §4.39, including the following:

1. Disparaging statements of a competitor's products are expressly prohibited,[148] but TTB's policy has been to allow truthful and accurate comparisons with competitor products. As a result, in practice, this prohibition only applies to false or misleading claims about a competitor's products.[149]
2. Obscene or indecent statements, designs, devices, or representations are prohibited[150] although actual enforcement of this restriction would be ripe grounds for a First Amendment challenge.[151] TTB's enforcement of this provision seems lax given wine brands such as FAT BASTARD and the cheekily named IF YOU SEE KAY. As one alcohol beverage industry attorney has pointed out, TTB has become "more lenient in approving potentially immoral, scandalous or derogatory" brand names on wines.[152] Despite that, the proposed labeling regulations under Notice 176 still include a prohibition against "any statement or representation that is obscene or indecent."[153]
3. Utilizing the name or likeness of a living individual of public prominence or the name or logo of an existing private or public organization if such use may incorrectly lead a consumer to believe the product has been endorsed, produced, or used by that individual.[154]

---

146. 27 C.F.R. §4.39(a)(1).

147. *Id.*

148. 27 C.F.R. §4.39(a)(2).

149. *See* Notice 176, 83 Fed. Reg. 60577. In Notice 176, TTB proposed the following regulation to address the general prohibition against disparaging statements and noted in the comments that this is consistent with current TTB policy.

§ 4.124 Disparaging statements.

(a) General. Wine labels, containers, or packaging may not contain any false or misleading statement that explicitly or implicitly disparages a competitor's product.

(b) Examples.

(1) An example of an explicit statement that falsely disparages a competitor's product is, "Brand X is not aged in oak barrels," when such statement is not true.

(2) An example of an implicit statement that disparages competitors' products in a misleading fashion is, "We do not add arsenic to our wine," where such a claim is true but it may lead consumers to falsely believe that other winemakers do add arsenic to their wine.

(c) Truthful and accurate comparisons. This section does not prevent truthful and accurate comparisons between products (such as, "Our wine contains more grapes than Brand X") or statements of opinion (such as, "We think our wine tastes better than any other wine on the market").

150. 27 C.F.R. §4.39(a)(3).

151. *See Iancu v. Brunetti,* 139 S. Ct. 2294 (2019) (holding that Lanham Act prohibition on registration of immoral or scandalous marks violated the First Amendment).

152. Tracy Jong & Luis Ormaechea, *Trends to Note in Alcoholic Beverage Trademark Law That Can Impact the Decision Making Process for Businesses at Critical Points in the Alcoholic Beverage Product Life Cycle*, 12 Buff. Intell. Prop. L.J. 19, 68–69 (2018).

153. Notice 176, 83 Fed. Reg. 60631 §4.102 (2018).

154. 27 C.F.R. §4.39(a)(6).

In addition, federal regulations currently prohibit any statement or representation which "tends to create the impression" that the wine contains distilled spirits or has "intoxicating qualities."[155] This has been interpreted to prohibit wines from being labeled as "fortified" even though a number of dessert grape wines, commonly known as fortified wines, have been produced by adding brandy or other distilled spirits. TTB recently issued Notice of Proposed Rulemaking Number 211[156] to allow truthful and accurate statements that a wine contains added distilled spirits, including the use of the word "fortified" as part of a wine's statement of composition (for example, "Grape wine fortified with brandy").[157]

While health-related statements are not outright prohibited, they are highly restricted.[158] The term "health-related statements" covers a broad swath of content, including (a) statements of a curative or therapeutic nature that links wine (or alcohol or any substance found in the wine) and a health benefit or effect on health; (b) general references to alleged health benefits or effects on health; (c) claims implying physical or psychological sensation resulting from wine consumption; and (d) claims of nutritional value (other than those typically found in serving facts statement as discussed in Section F.1 below).[159] The federal regulations identify and define two types of health-related statements, listed below.

- SPECIFIC HEALTH CLAIMS:[160] Statements that, expressly or through implication, link wine (or alcohol or any substance found in the wine) to a "disease or health-related condition.
- HEALTH-RELATED DIRECTOINAL STATEMENTS:[161] Statements that direct a consumer to a third party for information regarding wine's effects on a person's health.

Wine labels cannot include any health-related statement that is "untrue in any particular or tends to create a misleading impression as to the effects on health of

---

155. 27 C.F.R. §4.39(a)(7).

156. Proposal Regarding Labeling Wines Containing Added Distilled Spirits (Notice 211), 87 Fed. Reg. 35693 (June 13, 2022).

157. Notice 211, 87 Fed. Reg. 35697. The new proposed language for §4.39(a)(7) would prohibit:

> (7) Any statement, design, device, or representation (other than a statement of alcohol content in conformity with §4.36), which tends to create a misleading or inaccurate impression that a wine:
>
> > (i) Contains distilled spirits. (A wine that contains added distilled spirits may be labeled with an accurate statement of composition which references the type of distilled spirits that have been added, for example, "grape wine fortified with apple brandy," or "apple wine with apple neutral spirits," and not be considered misleading.)

158. 27 C.F.R. §4.39(h)(1)(i). Similar restrictions apply to use of health-related statements on wine advertisements under 27 C.F.R. §4.64(i).

159. 27 C.F.R. §4.39(h)(1)(i).

160. 27 C.F.R. §4.39(h)(1)(ii).

161. 27 C.F.R. §4.39(h)(1)(iii).

alcohol consumption."[162] As part of the COLA review process, TTB evaluates such statements and assesses them on a case-by-case basis. During that process, TTB is free to reject the statement or require additional information, such as a disclaimer of qualifying language.

Additional rules apply to specific health claims and directional statements. Any specific health claim must be truthful and supported by "scientific or medical evidence."[163] The claim must disclose risks associated with both moderate and heavier levels of consumption and include qualifying language regarding the categories of individuals to whom the claim applies.[164] In assessing specific health claims, TTB consults with the Food and Drug Administration to ensure that such claims comply with the Federal Food, Drug, and Cosmetic Act.[165]

There is a regulatory presumption that health-related directional statements are misleading.[166] In order to overcome that presumption, the third party to whom consumers are directed must be a source of "balanced information regarding the effects on health of wine or alcohol consumption" and the statement must include qualifying language approved by TTB.[167] The following qualifying language has been approved by TTB: "This statement should not encourage you to drink or to increase your alcohol consumption for health reasons."[168]

The recent rise in wellness-focused marketing in the alcohol beverage industry,[169] including the rise of beverages touted as "clean," has led to controversies surrounding the regulatory restrictions governing the use of health statements.[170]

One such controversy arose from the launch by Bellion Spirits of a vodka product that was produced with a proprietary blend of ingredients known as "NTX."[171] In 2016, Bellion Spirits petitioned the TTB for approval to use certain health-related statements in connection with the NTX vodka product, including the following: (1) "NTX helps protect DNA from alcohol-induced damage," and (2)

---

162. 27 C.F.R. §4.39(h)(2)(i).

163. 27 C.F.R. §4.39(h)(2)(ii)(B).

164. *Id.*

165. 27 C.F.R. §4.39(h)(2)(ii)(A).

166. 27 C.F.R. §4.39(h)(2)(iii).

167. 27 C.F.R. §4.39(h)(2)(iii).

168. 27 C.F.R. §4.39(h)(2)(iii)(B)(1).

169. *See, e.g.,* Marissa Conrad, *Getting a Handle on the Wellness-Branded Beverage Trend,* SevenFiftyDaily (Jan. 20, 2020), https://daily.sevenfifty.com/getting-a-handle-on-the-wellness-branded-beverage-trend/.

170. For a historical perspective on of health-related statements and controversies that pre-date the 2003 amendments to those regulations, *see* Richard Mendelson, From Demon to Darling *supra* note 2 at168-72.

171. *Bellion Spirits, LLC v. U.S.*, 7 F.4th 1201, 1206–07 (D.C. Cir. 2021). According to the petition, NTX is a blend of glycyrrhizin (a licorice root extract); mannitol (a sugar alcohol), and potassium sorbate (a food preservative*). In re Bellion Spirits, LLC's Petition for Health Claims* under 27 C.F.R. §§70.701, 7.54(e), https://www.ttb.gov/images/pdfs/bellion-spirits-llc-petition-health-claims-under-27cfr-70-701-7-54e.pdf.

"NTX reduces alcohol-induced DNA damage."[172] Bellion also proposed including the following disclaimer on the product's label:

> NTX does not protect against all health risks associated with moderate and heavy levels of alcohol consumption, including, but not limited to, motor vehicle accidents, high blood pressure, stroke, cancer, birth defects, psychological problems, and alcohol dependency. Do not consume alcohol if: you are younger than the legal drinking age; you are pregnant or may become pregnant; you are taking medicine that can interact with alcohol; you have a medical condition for which alcohol is contraindicated; you plan to drive; or you cannot restrict your drinking to moderate levels. If you consume alcohol, only consume it in moderation. "Moderation" means up to one drink per day for women and up to two drinks per day for men.

TTB denied the petition finding that the proposed claims were "not truthful" and "not adequately substantiated by scientific or medical evidence."[173] TTB also noted that the proposed disclaimer did not alter its conclusion and, in any event, there is no requirement for TTB to consider a disclaimer in connection with specific health claims that have been found to be inadequately substantiated by scientific or medical evidence.[174]

Bellion filed suit in federal court, claiming, among other things, that TTB's denial of the petition violated First Amendment commercial free speech rights, that the health statement regulatory restrictions were an unconstitutional prior restraint on protected speech, and that the regulations were unconstitutionally vague in violation of Fifth Amendment due process rights.[175] The court granted defendant's motion for summary judgment, and the DC Circuit Court of Appeals upheld the lower court ruling on appeal.[176]

More recently, TTB has signaled increased concern related to the use of health-related statements on alcohol beverage labels and advertising. In March and April 2022, TTB issued five different public newsletters in light of "an increasing number of alcohol beverage advertisements that suggest a relationship between alcohol beverage consumption and purported health benefits or effects."[177] In those newsletters, TTB noted the following examples of statements that the agency considers to be health-related:

---

172. *Id.* at 1207.

173. Letter from Amy R. Greenberg, Director, Regulations and Rulings Division, to Jonathan W. Emord (May 3, 2017), https://www.ttb.gov/images/pdfs/2017-05-03-response-ntx-health-claim-petition.pdf.

174. *Id.* at 46.

175. *Bellion Spirits, LLC v. U.S.*, 393 F.Supp.3d 5, 11 (D.D.C. 2019).

176. *Bellion Spirits, LLC v. U.S.*, 7 F.4th 1201, 1206–07 (D.C. Cir. 2021).

177. TTB, TTB News (Mar. 25, 2022), https://content.govdelivery.com/accounts/USTTB/bulletins/3107f19; TTB, TTB News (Apr. 1, 2022), https://content.govdelivery.com/accounts/USTTB/bulletins/311798c; TTB, TTB News (Apr. 8, 2022), https://content.govdelivery.com/accounts/USTTB/bulletins/3128c9c; TTB, TTB News Apr. 15, 2022), https://content.govdelivery.com/accounts/USTTB/bulletins/3139893; TTB, TTB News (Apr. 22, 2022), https://content.govdelivery.com/accounts/USTTB/bulletins/3149be6.

- No headaches;
- Hangover free;
- Diabetic friendly;
- Recovery drink;
- Anti-inflammatory;
- Aphrodisiac; and
- Health benefits.

TTB also responded to inquiries regarding the use of the word "clean" on alcohol labels and advertising.[178] Noting that the term is not defined in the federal regulations, TTB concluded that in and of itself, the use of the term is not prohibited, and that there are instances when it is simply used as a taste descriptor or puffery ("a clean, crisp wine," for example). However, TTB warned that certain use of the term "clean" would be considered misleading health-related statements, such as any claim that "clean production methods" mean no hangover.[179]

The bottom line for anyone wishing to use any statement or representation that may link consumption of wine with any sort of health or therapeutic benefit: tread carefully.

D. STATE WINE LABELING LAWS AND REGULATIONS

Despite the breadth of federal wine labeling regulations, a number of states have adopted their own wine labeling laws. Many of those laws are aimed at protecting the state's key wine and grape producing regions by creating stricter regulations on how and when those appellations' names can appear on a wine label.

Producers who have run afoul of these stricter state wine labeling laws have been unsuccessful in claiming federal preemption. As the California Supreme Court concluded in 2004, "[T]he history of the 1935 FAA Act discloses no intent on the part of Congress to supplant or preempt state efforts to regulate wine labeling."[180] Indeed, as discussed above, federal labeling regulations have consistently made clear that state laws would also apply to the use of AVAs and political appellations.[181]

178. TTB, TTB News (Apr. 8, 2022), https://content.govdelivery.com/accounts/USTTB/bulletins/3128c9c.

179. *Id.*

180. *Bronco Wine Co. v. Jolly*, 33 Cal.4th 943, 975 (2004).

181. In Notice 176, TTB proposed adding in a new regulation that states: "Compliance with the requirements of this part relating to the labeling and bottling of wine does not relieve industry members from responsibility for complying with other applicable Federal and State requirements" 83 Fed. Reg. 60618.

In this section, we address four key state wine labeling regulations aimed at protecting appellations of origin: compositional and place of production requirements, conjunctive labeling laws, and statutory protections against misleading geographical brand names.

1. COMPOSITIONAL AND PLACE OF PRODUCTION REQUIREMENTS

Federal regulations allow for wines labeled with an appellation name to incorporate grapes from outside that appellation. For example, a wine labeled with the name of a county could, under federal law, include up to 25 percent of grapes grown anywhere outside of the county, in the same state or anywhere outside of the state.[182]

Certain states have adopted regulations that impose stricter compositional requirements for appellation-designated wines. For example, California regulations require that all grapes used to produce a wine labeled with (a) the California state appellation or (b) "geographical subdivision" of the state must be 100 percent composed of grapes grown in California.[183] Though the term "geographical subdivision" is not defined, the regulation arguably applies to counties and AVAs located entirely within the state.

Similarly, Oregon's laws impose a 100 percent state-grown grape requirement on wines carrying Oregon appellation names.[184] In addition, if the wine's "claimed or implied" appellation of origin is one or more Oregon counties or the name of an AVA entirely within the state of Oregon, 95 percent of the grapes used in that wine must have been grown within the named region.[185]

California regulations also have stricter place of production requirements. Federal regulations permit a wine labeled with a state name as its appellation of origin to be fully finished in that state or in any adjacent state.[186] California, however, requires that any wine labeled with the California state appellation be "fully produced and finished" within the state.[187]

---

182. 27 C.F.R. §4.25(b)(1).
183. Cal. Code Regs. tit. 17, §17015(a)(1).
184. Or. Admin. R. 845-010-0920 (2022).
185. *Id.*
186. 27 C.F.R. §4.25(b)(1).
187. Cal. Code Regs. tit. 17, §17015(a)(2).

2. CONJUNCTIVE LABELING

In the 1980s, Napa Valley Vintners (NVV), an organization whose mission is to protect and promote the Napa Valley AVA, grew increasingly concerned that the rise of new AVAs located entirely within Napa Valley "would divert trade focus and consumer focus from Napa Valley itself and dilute the reservoir of consumer goodwill about the valley."[188] In France, the growing prominence of Bordeaux's sub-appellations (such as Margaux, Paulliac, and St. Julien) served as a cautionary example. "[T]he name Bordeaux was nowhere to be found on many of those labels and had become known instead for regional and sometimes non-descript wines."[189]

Hoping to avoid the same fate, NVV proposed a "conjunctive labeling law," which would ensure "that Napa Valley remained on the label of every sub-AVA wine."[190] The proposed law complied with federal regulations which allow the use of more than one viticultural area name as an appellation of origin so long as at least 85 percent of the grapes come from the overlapping area of the identified AVAs.[191]

In 1989, the California legislature adopted California Business and Professions Code §25240 commonly referred to as the Napa conjunctive labeling law. Section 25240 requires any wine bottled after January 1, 1990 and labeled with an AVA located entirely within Napa County to also include Napa Valley on the label "in conjunction with the area designation of the wine." For example, an Oakville AVA wine must state on the label, Oakville — Napa Valley. Violators risk having their license suspended or revoked by the California Department of Alcoholic Beverage Control.[192]

Since the adoption of §25240, a number of other wine and grape regional associations have successfully lobbied for similar protections for their appellations. This includes AVAs such as Paso Robles (§25244) and Lodi (§25245) and counties such as Sonoma County (§25246), Monterey County (§25247), and Mendocino County (§24248). Not all of these regulations, however, require that the sub-AVA name appear in conjunction with the larger appellation. Under §25246, for example, a wine labeled with the name of an AVA located entirely within Sonoma County must have the sub-AVA appear on the brand label in order to comply with federal requirements, but the larger Sonoma County appellation can appear on the brand label or any other label, so long as it appears somewhere on the bottle.

---

188. Richard Mendelson, Appellation Napa Valley: Building and Protecting an American Treasure, 104-05 (2016).

189. *Id.* at 105.

190. *Id.*

191. 27 C.F.R. §4.25(e)(4).

192. Cal. Bus. & Prof. Code §25240(b).

Oregon also passed a conjunctive labeling law in 2020 which goes into effect on January 1, 2023.[193] The law applies to wine labeled with the name of an AVA that lies wholly or partially within the state's Willamette Valley AVA.

3. CALIFORNIA MISLEADING GEOGRAPHIC BRAND NAME STATUTE

In 2000, the California legislature adopted a new law to prohibit the deceptive use of the Napa Valley AVA names (as well as sub-AVAs of Napa) on wines not made from Napa County grapes. The law ensures that wine produced or sold in the state with brand names, packaging materials, or advertising referring to Napa appellations actually qualify for the Napa County appellation of origin (i.e., that the wine in question actually be made from at least 75 percent Napa County grapes and be fully finished within California). The background to this law and the lawsuit following its adoption are covered in detail in the chapter on Wine Brands and Appellations of Origin. California also has a misleading brand name law aimed at protecting Sonoma County wines.[194]

E. FEDERAL ADVERTISING REGULATIONS

Federal advertising rules adhere closely to the labeling regulations and can also be broken out into mandatory information, optional information, and prohibited practices.[195]

All wine advertisements must include a clear identification of the industry member responsible for the advertisement, the member's contact information (such as a website URL or phone number), and city and state as well as the class/type designation of the product.[196] There are general prohibitions against false and misleading statements appearing on advertising, and a specific set of prohibited statements that mirror the prohibited labeling statements discussed in Section C.1 above (no disparaging statements or obscene or indecent statements, for example).[197] And just as in labeling, any health related or therapeutic statement should be carefully reviewed to ensure compliance.

In addition to federal regulations under 27 C.F.R. Part 4, businesses engaged in wine advertising also need to be cognizant of FTC concerns and voluntary industry group advertising guidelines discussed in Section B.1. The FTC has been active in ensuring transparency in sponsored advertising and endorsements. Section 5 of the Federal Trade Commission Act prohibits misleading, deceptive, and unfair advertising.[198] The agency treats influencer sponsored posts as

193. Or. Admin. R. 845-010-0923 (2020).
194. Cal. Bus. & Prof. Code §25242.
195. 27 C.F.R. Part 4, Subpart G.
196. 27 C.F.R. §4.62(a)-(b).
197. 27 C.F.R. §4.64.
198. 15 U.S.C. §45.

endorsements which are defined as "any advertising message . . . that consumers are likely to believe reflects the opinions, beliefs, findings, or experiences of a party other than the sponsoring advertiser."[199] In order to prevent consumer deception, the FTC has made clear that influencer sponsored posts are endorsements and therefore must clearly disclose any sort of direct or indirect financial or compensatory relationship, including but not limited to the provision of samples.[200] Influencers must disclose such a relationship in any post that mentions or otherwise promotes the sponsor's product.[201] The disclosure must be clear and conspicuous and can include hashtags (such as #sponsored or #advertisement).[202]

F. CURRENT ISSUES IN WINE LABELING

1. SERVING FACTS

In 2007, TTB proposed requiring a serving facts statement on all alcohol beverage labels to disclose the number of calories, grams of carbohydrates, fat, and protein per serving as well as the number of servings per container and serving size.[203]

While Notice 73 was never finalized, in 2013, TTB issued a ruling on voluntary use of serving facts statements on wine and other alcohol beverages.[204] As a result, all serving facts statements must include the following information: serving size, number of servings per container, and the number of calories and the number of grams of carbohydrates, protein, and fat per serving size.[205] The serving facts statement can also include the alcohol content, and if it is shown as a percentage of alcohol by volume, the panel can also include a statement of fluid ounces of pure ethyl alcohol per serving.[206] Below is an example of an acceptable serving facts panel.[207]

---

199. FTC Guides Concerning use of Endorsements and Testimonials in Advertising, 16 C.F.R. Part 255.

200. FTC, *Disclosures 101 for Social Media Influencers* (Nov. 2019), available at https://www.ftc.gov/system/files/documents/plain-language/1001a-influencer-guide-508_1.pdf.

201. *Id.* at 2-3.

202. *Id.* at 4-5.

203. 72 Fed. Reg. 41860 (July 31, 2007).

204. TTB Ruling 2013-2, *Voluntary Nutrient Content Statements in the Labeling and Advertising of Wines, Distilled Spirits, and Malt Beverages* (May 28, 2013), available at https://www.ttb.gov/images /pdfs/rulings/2013-2.pdf.

205. *Id.* at 7.

206. *Id.* at 8.

207. *Id.* at 9 (image of serving facts panel).

Serving Facts	
Serving Size	5 fl oz (148 ml)
Servings Per Container	5
	Amount Per Serving
Alcohol by volume	14%
fl oz of alcohol	0.7
Calories	120
Carbohydrate	3g
Fat	0g
Protein	0g

TTB also permits serving facts to appear in a linear display.[208]

Serving Facts: Serving size: 5 fl oz (148 ml); Servings per container: 5; **Amount Per Serving:** Alcohol by volume: 14%; Calories: 120; Carbohydrates: 3g; Fat: 0g; Protein: 0g

Historically, industry groups have been wary about mandatory serving facts labeling requirements, noting the potential high cost of compliance for wineries if they were forced to conduct "expensive testing of multiple batches of wine close to the time of bottling."[209] In 2020, following input from industry members, TTB announced that the nutritional content information disclosed on statement facts can be based off of databases or typical value charts and need not rely solely on laboratory analysis.[210] Wine Institute celebrated this news, noting that it would reduce costs for wineries wishing to label their wines with serving facts statements.[211]

More recently, in its 2022 report on the status of competition in the beer, wine, and spirits markets,[212] the Department of Treasury appeared supportive of requiring serving facts statements on wines and other alcoholic beverages to ensure

---

208. *Id.* at 10 (image of linear form serving facts panel).

209. Wine Institute, *New TTB Ruling on Nutrition Labeling and Advertising* (Sep. 28, 2020), available at https://wineinstitute.org/press-releases/new-ttb-ruling-on-nutrition-labeling-and-advertising/; Wendell Lee *supra* note 9 at 131-34.

210. TTB Ruling No. 2020-1, *Expanded Tolerances for Voluntary Calorie Statements in the Labeling and Advertising of Wine, Distilled Spirits, and Malt Beverages* (Sep. 28, 2020), available at https://www.ttb.gov/rulings/r2020-1.

211. New TTB Ruling on Nutrition Labeling and Advertising *supra* note 24.

212. *See generally* Competition Report *supra* note 3.

that the FAA Act's labeling regulations address legitimate public health and competition concerns. "Serving facts labeling could be an effective means of conveying information relevant to health concerns (for example, calorie content and more detail about alcohol content) to consumers." The Department has recommended that TTB revive rulemaking on nutritional content, alcohol content, and serving sizes, and it would not be surprising if, as a result, TTB dusts off Notice 73.

2. INGREDIENT LABELING[213]

Over the past few years, ingredient labeling on wine labels has garnered significant attention from U.S. wine writers.[214]

> In the last few decades, Americans have become far more conscious of the ingredients in their meals. Categories like organic foods, once the province of eccentric health nuts, are now mainstream and big business. Shopping is no longer a clear-cut matter of driving the car to the supermarket and loading up; it carries a host of ethical, political and aesthetic considerations.[215]

With consumers asking for more information about how the food they consume is made, it seems to follow that they would be equally concerned about how the beverages they drink are produced.

Others believe that consumers may not necessarily be clamoring for this sort of information to inform their purchase decisions. One survey conducted by the Wine Market Council concluded, "Wine shoppers are looking for variety and flavor information when deciding on purchasing a bottle and most have little interest in learning more about how the wine was made, how the grapes were grown and ingredient labeling."[216] Other industry observers are unsure if disclosing certain wine making additions, such as "yeast" or "malolactic bacteria" may simply confuse consumers.

The Competition Report, however, made clear that the industry will see an increased regulatory focus on ingredient labeling in the near future. The Treasury Department identified ingredient labeling as another area where the FAA Act regulations could be amended to address public health and competition concerns and recommended that TTB "revive or initiate rulemaking" on that front.[217]

Some industry members are not waiting for additional action from TTB but have instead started including ingredient labeling as "additional information" on

---

213. In this section, we address the current regulatory focus on ingredient labeling. However, the debate over wine ingredient labeling has a long history. *See* Richard Mendelson, *From Demon to Darling: A Legal History of Wine in America* (Univ. of Cal. Press 2009) 167-68.

214. See, e.g., Eric Asimov, *Want to Pick Better Bottles? Repeat After Me: Wine is Food*, N.Y. Times (Mar. 6, 2017), available at https://www.nytimes.com/2017/03/06/dining/wine-is-food.html.

215. *Id.*

216. Andrew Adams, *Survey Finds Scant Interest in Wine Ingredients, Grape Growing* (Sep. 3, 2020) https://www.winebusiness.com/news/article/235923/.

217. Competition Report *supra* note 3 at 47, 61.

their wine labels. Such practices are permitted under existing regulations so long as the information is truthful and non-misleading. Below is an example of Ridge Vineyards wine labels which, since 2011, have included an ingredients statement.[218]

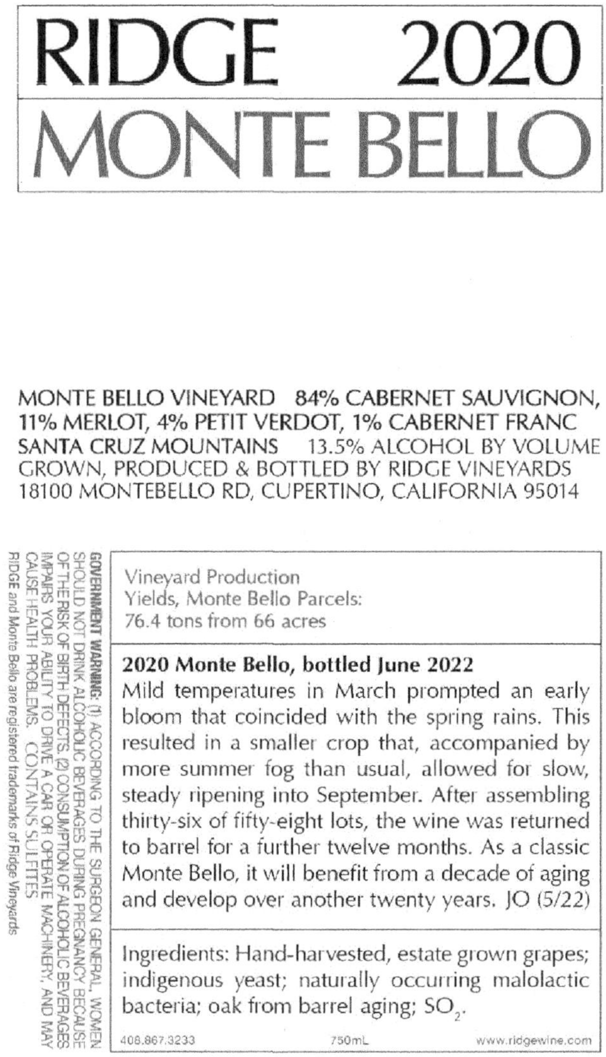

218. Paul Draper, *Ingredient Labeling: A Look Back* (Jun. 2021), available at https://www.ridgewine.com/about/news/ingredient-labeling-a-look-back-by-paul-draper/.

3. OPTIONAL GEOGRAPHICAL REFERENCES AND GRAPE SOURCE INFORMATION

One of the most hotly debated issues in wine labeling pits efforts to protect the U.S. wine appellation system against industry members who claim that transparency warrants a broader use of geographic references on wine labels specifically in connection with grape sourcing. Although this issue has been percolating for many years, it became a source of significant proposed regulatory activity over the past seven years.

The current iteration of this debate arose from what, on its face, appeared to be a simple goal: the creation of a single federal standard for wine origin labeling by applying the same standard to COLA and COLA-exempt wines.[219] As discussed above, wines sold solely within the home state of the bottling winery are not required to obtain a Certificate of Label Approval, but instead must apply for a COLA exemption. These COLA-exempt wines are not subject to federal wine labeling regulations found in 27 C.F.R. Part 4, including but not limited to 27 C.F.R. §4.25, which governs the use of appellation of origin. As a result, a New York winery could purchase grapes grown on a vineyard located in a California AVA; truck those grapes across the country; and then produce wine from it at their New York winery and label it with the AVA's name *even though the wine failed to meet the federal AVA labeling requirements* so long as the wine was solely sold in New York pursuant to a COLA-exemption. Some industry members believe that this loophole creates an opening for misleading labeling practices that ultimately undermined the integrity of the appellation labeling system.

> Currently, wineries operating under a COLA exemption are able to unfairly benefit from the goodwill and brand recognition of appellation names without having to comply with the appellation regulations that apply to all in-state wineries. This undermines decades-long efforts by federal and state governments to protect the integrity of wine appellations and by trade associations to educate consumers about, and to promote and protect, AVAs like Napa Valley. The COLA-exemption loophole creates an uneven playing field where in-state wineries must meet stringent requirements for using AVA names, while out-of-state wineries can use those place names without regard to those labeling laws.[220]

In 2016, TTB issued Notice of Proposed Rulemaking 160[221] to eliminate this COLA-exemption loophole. The proposed amendment would "require that a

---

219. For a more in-depth discussion of recent challenges to the U.S. appellation system, see Richard Mendelson & John Trinidad, *Recent Challenges to the U.S. Wine Appellation System*, in La vigne, le vin et le droit/Du local au global: Mélanges en l'honneur de Robert Tinlot, 459-73 (T. Georgopoulos, C. Leble, Y Juban, eds. 2021).

220. Napa Valley Vintners. Comment Letter on Proposed Revisions to Wine Labeling and Recordkeeping Requirements

(Aug. 22, 2016), https://www.regulations.gov/comment/TTB-2016-0005-0056.

221. Proposed Revisions to Wine Labeling and Recordkeeping Requirements, 81 Fed. Reg. 40584 (Jun. 22, 2016) (hereinafter, "Notice 160") (to be codified at 27 C.F.R. pt. 4, 24).

standard grape wine that contains 7 percent or more alcohol by volume and is covered by a certificate of exemption from label approval may not be labeled with a varietal (grape type) designation, a type designation of varietal significance, a vintage date, or an appellation of origin unless the wine complies with the relevant part 4 provisions for that label information."[222]

In light of the comments received in response to Notice 160, TTB reopened the comment period twice[223] and expanded its line of inquiry to ask more broadly whether geographical references could be used as optional information on wine labels. TTB specifically requested additional comments "regarding whether any geographic reference to the source of the grapes used in the wine could be included on a wine label in a way that would not be misleading with regard to the source of the wine."[224] In other words, could a wine that did not qualify as being from a particular AVA (such as the Russian River Valley AVA) under 27 C.F.R. §4.25 include a statement on its label that some of its grapes were sourced from that AVA? TTB also asked whether proposals submitted by commenters to achieve this goal should apply to all wines sold in the U.S., not just those subject to a COLA-exemption.[225]

This request hit on a broader tension in the industry: Are appellations of origin (including AVAs) simply an indication of where the wine's *grapes* were grown or are they indications of *wine* origin? Proponents of Notice 160 argued the latter,[226] noting that federal regulation imposes a place of production requirement for a wine to be labeled with an appellation name.[227] For example, as discussed above, an AVA located entirely within an individual state must be fully finished within that state's boundaries in order to be labeled with the AVA's name.[228] This is consistent with the idea that when an appellation name appears on a wine bottle, it is an indicator of where the wine (i.e., the finished product) is from, not just from where the raw materials were sourced. Opponents of Notice 160 argued that that consumers generally view appellations as just an indication of where the grapes were grown and at least one industry member argued for the elimination of the place of production requirement entirely.[229] Others avoided a direct challenge to the appellation labeling regulations but instead argued that truthful and accurate

---

222. Notice 160, 81 Fed. Reg. 40586.

223. Notice 160A, 81 Fed. Reg. 62046 (Sep. 8, 2016); TTB Notice 160B, Proposed Revisions to Wine Labeling and Recordkeeping Requirements – Comment Period Reopening, 82 Fed. Reg. 47165 (Oct. 11, 2017).

224. Notice 160B, 82 Fed. Reg. 47166.

225. Notice 160B, 82 Fed. Reg. 47167.

226. *See, e.g.,* Napa Valley Vintners and Wine Institute Comment Letter on Proposed Revisions to Wine Labeling and Recordkeeping Requirements (Dec. 8, 2016), https://www.regulations.gov/document?D=TTB-2016-0005-0111; Napa Valley Vintners and Wine Institute Comment Letter on Proposed Revisions to Wine Labeling and Recordkeeping Requirements (Jan. 10, 2018), https://www.regulations.gov/document?D=TTB-2016-0005-0122 .

227. 27 C.F.R. §4.25.

228. 27 C.F.R. §4.25(e)(3)(iv).

229. Brooklyn Winery Comment Letter on Proposed Revisions to Wine Labeling and Recordkeeping Requirements (Aug. 22, 2016), https://www.regulations.gov/document?D=TTB-2016-0005-0054.

geographical references to the source of grapes should be permitted, relying on First Amendment commercial free speech principles.[230]

Although to date TTB has not issued a final rule on Notice 160, in Notice 176, TTB included a proposed regulation that directly addresses the use of geographical references for grape source information.[231] The proposed rules for grape source information differ depending on whether or not the wine is labeled with an appellation of origin (political or petitioned) designation. If a wine is labeled with an appellation of origin, then it can include a statement regarding grape sourcing so long as that statement is "consistent with the appellation of origin that appears on the label."[232] If a wine is not labeled with an appellation of origin designation, it can be labeled with "truthful" information regarding grape sourcing so long as (a) the name of the place where grapes were sourced does not create a misleading impression regarding the wine's appellation of origin; and (b) any such information sets out the origin of 100 percent of the grapes used to make the wine in descending order of predominance along with the place where the wine was produced.[233]

This debate about use of geographical references highlights issues that impact numerous other wine labeling controversies: commercial free speech rights; fair use; and the need to protect consumers against misleading labeling practices. Add to that the concern of the potential erosion of goodwill associated with AVA names, and you have a tempest in a teapot.

G. CONCLUSION

Having now completed our journey through the regulatory labyrinth of wine labeling and advertising, I ask you again to consider whether wine industry professionals are deserving of your sympathy. Their task is seemingly simple: market and sell a product that has deep cultural and historic roots, is grounded in agriculture, and is widely associated with celebratory occasions. But faced with these numerous and detailed rules, pre-approval hurdles, and concurrent state and federal jurisdictions, the marketing of wine becomes hard work. As noted throughout this chapter, there is an effort underway to modernize the federal labeling and advertising regulations that may result in some more digestible and organized federal regulations, but would still leave in place the complexity of the current system as well as the guiding principles of providing consumers with truthful, non-misleading, and adequate information as they make their purchase decision.

---

230. Pacific Legal Foundation Comment Letter on Proposed Revisions to Wine Labeling and Recordkeeping Requirements (Aug. 22, 2016), https://www.regulations.gov/document?D=TTB-2016-0005-0038.

231. *See* Notice 176, 83 Fed. Reg. 60634 §4.135.

232. *See id.* at §4.135(b).

233. *See id.* at §4.135(c).

CHAPTER 4

BUSINESS MODELS FOR MAKING WINE AND GROWING GRAPES

James Terry and Erik Lawrence

The traditional view of the wine business is that wine is produced at a winery estate complete with on-site vineyards and winery facilities. While this romantic image is still common in the modern winemaking world, it is only one of several ways to make and market wine. A prospective winemaker has a myriad of options on how to enter the industry, including whether to grow or buy grapes and whether to produce the wine independently, to have it custom made by a third party, or to buy and blend bulk wine.

This chapter begins with an examination of the most popular business models for wine production, including the purchase of an existing winery, the development of a traditional bricks-and-mortar winery, operation as an alternating proprietor or as a négociant, and producing wine through the use of a custom crush wine company. Whatever choice is made, the winemaker must comply with a unique set of local, state, and federal regulations and must obtain all required licenses and permits to produce and sell the wine.

The discussion then turns to the vineyard side of the winery equation; without grapes, wine cannot be made. As in the case of wine production, there are many options for obtaining grapes, including owning a vineyard (farmed by the owner or by a vineyard management company), leasing a vineyard, and purchasing grapes. It is not unusual for a wine company to use all of these methods concurrently. We explore each of these options in turn, focusing on the specific laws that make the wine sector different from other industries that also must acquire raw materials.

Because 90 percent of domestic wine is made in California, this chapter focuses on California law and applicable federal law. Although state requirements for vintners and grape growers vary, many of the key concepts are similar throughout the wine-producing regions of the country.

A. THE TRADITIONAL MODEL: BRICKS-AND-MORTAR WINERIES

There are many reasons an aspiring vintner might want to own and operate its own production facility, including tradition, quality control, the opportunity to conduct on-site sales, and even ego gratification. A key threshold decision for a vintner is whether to purchase raw land and build a new winery, purchase an existing winery, or lease an existing winery. While the development of a new winery may seem appealing, the process is almost always complicated and expensive as a result of local and state land use and environmental laws and regulations. Although purchasing an existing winery is generally more costly, it provides more certainty to a prospective purchaser because most of the groundwork with respect to regulatory compliance and local permitting has been completed. No aspiring vintner, however, should acquire a property, even an agricultural property, without first assessing its general suitability for winery development and the likelihood of obtaining local, state, and federal approvals, licenses, and permits for the development of the property and the production of wine.

1. DEVELOPING A NEW WINERY FACILITY

Following is a brief summary of the process of acquiring land to be used for the construction of a new winery facility.

a. The Acquisition Process

The first phase of developing a traditional bricks-and-mortar winery is the purchase of unimproved land. After identifying a target property for development, the vintner will negotiate the key terms of the purchase transaction with the seller (ultimately captured in a definitive purchase and sale agreement) and investigate the property to ensure that it is both legally and practically suited for its intended purpose.

NEGOTIATING THE SALE

Term Sheet or Letter of Intent. Rather than immediately negotiating a definitive purchase and sale agreement, which can be a lengthy and costly process, many parties choose to first negotiate and come to agreement on the material terms of the transaction (including price, payment terms, and due diligence period) with the use of either a term sheet or letter of intent (LOI). A term sheet is merely a summary of key terms with no commitment by either party to take further action. By contrast, an LOI typically contains an agreement between the parties to prepare and enter into a final, binding purchase and sale agreement according to the terms outlined in the LOI.

Purchase and Sale Agreement. The purchase and sale agreement (PSA) is the definitive document binding the parties to their respective obligations to purchase and sell the specific real property. The PSA describes every facet of the transaction, including the parties involved (i.e., the buyer and seller), the property being acquired, the purchase price, and the payment terms. The PSA also includes representations and warranties by both parties, which are statements of fact that the parties explicitly rely upon in carrying out the various terms of the transaction. The buyer often will seek representations and warranties from the seller about the property's condition and suitability for the buyer's intended use, while the seller will typically seek to make as few representations as possible, preferring to sell the property "as is."[1] The PSA should contain provisions establishing pre-closing conditions that must be satisfied before the purchaser is obligated to buy the property, including satisfactory completion of the due diligence review by the buyer. Counsel for either party must be extremely careful in drafting the PSA because its provisions can be the focus of litigation resulting from a broken transaction.

INVESTIGATING THE PROPERTY: DUE DILIGENCE AND TITLE REVIEW

The PSA should provide a time frame and process for the buyer and the buyer's attorney and consultants to investigate the property being acquired (the "due diligence period"). The purpose of the due diligence period is to enable the buyer to determine whether the property is compatible with the buyer's intended uses, discover any problems that warrant a price reduction or rejection of the purchase, and identify any warranties with respect to the property or conditions to closing that should be included in the final transaction.

Due diligence can be divided into two categories, legal due diligence and non-legal due diligence. Legal due diligence requires a review of applicable land use laws and zoning ordinances, which may require, among other things, compliance with a county-supervised process for obtaining a use permit to develop and operate the property as a winery. The buyer will be able to assess the project's feasibility after a thorough review of all local restrictions affecting not only the development of the property, but also the operation of the business on the property. In Napa County, for example, the Winery Definition Ordinance[2] regulates many aspects of winery operations, including grape sourcing, tours,

---

1. Under California law, an "as is" provision puts the burden on the buyer to ascertain the condition of the property. Nevertheless, the seller must disclose all hidden material defects of which the seller has knowledge. Failure to do so constitutes fraud. *See, e.g. Lingsch v. Savage*, 213 Cal. App. 2d 729 (1963). Additionally, notwithstanding an "as is" provision, the seller must comply with other disclosure obligations imposed by statute. *See, e.g.*, Cal. Civ. Code §§1102-1102.17 (2021); Cal. Health & Safety Code §25359.7 (2021).

2. Napa County, Cal., Ordinance 947 (Jan. 23, 1990) (as amended by Napa County, Cal., Ordinance 1340 (May 11, 2010)) (codified at Napa County, Cal., Code §§12069-12072, 12418-12420, 12420.1, 12421-12422, 12602.3 (1993)).

tastings, special events, facilities size, facilities locations in relation to roads and streams, sales of non-wine items, and many other matters that are key to generating income. These types of land use restrictions vary widely from county to county in California, as discussed in Chapter 7.

Legal due diligence also includes a review of all matters affecting the title (i.e., legal right to possess the property) as revealed by all documents in the public record affecting the property. Recorded restrictions and encumbrances may affect the use of or access to the property to the same degree as local ordinances. For instance, title research will uncover all easements (i.e., rights concerning use of or access to the property by another) that benefit the property, including access and utility easements that are necessary to fully utilize the property. The scope of the access easements that benefit the subject real property over the lands of another must be sufficiently broad to include winery uses, and any described roadways that are part of an easement must be wide enough to meet local standards for roadways serving winery production facilities.[3]

The reviewing lawyer must ensure that the parcel or parcels constituting the targeted property have been legally created under state law. A legal parcel is one that has been created in compliance with the requirements of the California Subdivision Map Act or other county-level ordinances predating the Subdivision Map Act.[4] In many instances, a legal parcel is a requirement for obtaining development rights for the property. Proof that the parcel was legally created also is typically required by a lender, which may be relying on the property as collateral. Finally, proper title review will expose any burdens or encumbrances on the property, such as conservation easements, view easements held by others over the subject property, rights of first refusal, and, if the property is surveyed, encroachments of structures and fences on the property. Each of these burdens or encumbrances can threaten the intended use of the property or adversely affect the property's marketability.[5]

Non-legal due diligence similarly requires an assessment of the property's basic compatibility with its intended uses. In a land acquisition for purposes of winery development, this process includes, among other things, an evaluation of

---

3. For example, in Napa County, access driveways to off-site parking lots for wineries must be maintained at 18 feet for two-way traffic. *See* Napa County, Cal., Code §18.104.130(D)(12) (1993), available at http://library.municode.com.

4. *See generally*, Cal. Govt. Code §§66410-66499.37 (2021). In California, buyer's counsel should always ensure that the title policy includes a CLTA 116.7 endorsement, which establishes that the subject parcel was legally created under the Subdivision Map Act.

5. In California there are two basic types of title insurance: California Land Title Association (CLTA) basic coverage and American Land Title Association (ALTA) extended coverage. The primary distinction is that a CLTA policy is based only on a search of public records that affect the property. An ALTA policy is based on public records and a physical survey of the property, which will be used to evaluate the boundaries and any easements burdening or benefiting the property that only a physical inspection would reveal, and any interests in the property that may arise by adverse possession. For a more detailed discussion of title insurance policies, *see* CEB, California Title Insurance Practice (2d ed. 1999).

access to public roads, site suitability for the construction of a processing facility, and access to a suitable and sufficient water source.

b. The Development Process

After completing due diligence and acquiring the property pursuant to the terms of the PSA, the prospective vintner faces new challenges in developing and building a suitable winery facility. For example, a vintner seeking to construct a traditional stand-alone winery must do so in a manner that complies with local zoning and land use laws.

2. ACQUIRING AN EXISTING WINERY FACILITY

Many vintners choose to forgo the cost, uncertainty, and delays associated with building a new winery and instead purchase an existing winery facility. Frequently, the vintner who purchases a winery facility also purchases an established business with wine inventory, brands, other intellectual property, and ongoing liabilities, although this is not required. This section discusses some of the key business issues to be addressed in such acquisitions.

STRUCTURING THE ACQUISITION

There are several ways to acquire an existing winery business. The three most common methods are an asset purchase, an equity purchase, and a merger.

Asset Purchase. In an asset purchase, the buyer acquires some or all of the seller's assets, typically including real estate, and assumes none of the seller's liabilities (except those that the buyer chooses to accept). The aspiring vintner who wishes to acquire only a winery facility and not an ongoing business would purchase just the real estate assets, including the winery buildings and improvements. A buyer acquiring an entire bricks-and-mortar winery, including the business, typically would purchase the following assets: (1) real estate and improvements (i.e., the winery building); (2) equipment, including barrels and tanks, presses, crusher-destemmers, bottling equipment, pumps, hoses, and equipment and furniture in the tasting room and offices; (3) inventory, including bottled wine, bulk wine in tanks or barrels, bottles, corks, labels, and packaging materials; and (4) intellectual property, including trademarks, brands, and trade names used in the business and the associated goodwill of the enterprise.[6] The buyer also may choose to assume certain contracts, such as the winery's existing grape purchase agreements, distribution agreements, and winemaker consulting agreements.

6. Often a winery's intellectual property is its most valuable asset.

An asset purchase is the most common structure for acquisitions in the wine industry today because buyers prefer the ability to carefully select which assets and which liabilities they will acquire and assume. The seller will remain responsible for all non-assumed liabilities. In addition to the control afforded the buyer in an asset purchase, this structure provides the buyer with the opportunity for advantageous tax treatment: the buyer's tax basis in many assets will "step up" to the allocated purchase price,[7] leading to higher depreciation and lower income taxes and lower capital gains taxes in the future.[8] The disadvantages associated with an asset purchase include a complicated transaction structure requiring separate documentation for conveyance and assignment of various assets and obligations, the potential for application of the bulk sales law (which may be triggered by the sale of inventory),[9] and the seller's payment of sales tax.

Equity Purchase. In an equity purchase, the buyer purchases some or all of the current owner's interest in the winery, and the winery operations continue uninterrupted, with all existing assets and liabilities remaining in place. An equity purchase is the simplest acquisition structure because there is generally no separate documentation required to transfer assets and all contracts continue in effect (unless they contain a change-in-control provision, in which event the parties must obtain consent from the counterparty to the applicable contracts). The primary disadvantage of an equity purchase for the buyer is that all of the winery's liabilities continue in place, even those not disclosed to the buyer, which could result in some surprises for the new owners. In addition, if the buyer desires to acquire 100 percent of the winery's equity, a small minority shareholder could prevent the sale.[10] Finally, equity purchases, with limited exceptions, do not receive the same favorable tax treatment as asset purchases.

Merger. Mergers are extremely rare in the wine business. In a merger, one company, including all of its assets and liabilities, is merged into a surviving company, and the merged company ceases to exist. Depending on the facts and circumstances, mergers can be structured in many ways: a buyer may merge into the target company, the target company can be merged into the buyer, a buyer can form a subsidiary into which the target is merged ("forward triangular

---

7. In an asset sale, both the buyer and seller are required to file a Form 8594 with the IRS allocating the purchase price to seven separate asset classes. 26 U.S.C. §1060 (2020); 26 C.F.R. §1.1060-1(e)(1)(ii)(A) (2021). The allocation has real economic consequences to buyer and seller. For example, amounts allocated to a seller's covenant not to compete are taxed as ordinary income to the seller and are amortizable, intangible assets to the buyer.

8. Both buyer and seller should seek tax advice concerning the purchase price allocation. One common problem occurs when the amount allocated to accounts receivable and inventory (referred to as "hot" or "fast pay" assets) is less than those assets' fair market value. In such cases, the buyer may be forced to realize accelerated taxable income.

9. Cal. Comm. Code §§6101-6111 (2021).

10. Unless a shareholder is subject to a shareholders' agreement requiring him to sell under certain circumstances, he cannot be compelled to sell his shares. Therefore, a holdout shareholder can refuse to sell and prevent the buyer from acquiring 100 percent of the company's equity.

merger"), or the buyer can form a subsidiary that is merged into the target company ("reverse triangular merger"). The advantages of a merger are that it is simpler than an asset purchase, it is easier to structure as a "tax-free" transaction, and unanimous approval of the owners typically is not required (unless the owners of the target company are subject to an agreement that states otherwise, such as a shareholders' agreement, limited liability company operating agreement, or partnership agreement). As in the case of an equity purchase, the buyer will assume all unknown or undisclosed obligations of the merged company, and dissenting owners are afforded "dissenters' rights" by which they are permitted to protest the merger and demand payment in cash for their shares.[11]

THE ACQUISITION PROCESS

After the vintner has identified a target winery and determined the preferred acquisition structure, the acquisition process is quite similar to the raw land acquisition process described above. However, a vintner acquiring a stand-alone winery often is acquiring an ongoing business in addition to real estate. The additional due diligence required in investigating the ongoing winery business will make the process longer and more complicated compared to a land-only transaction. If structured as an asset purchase, the vintner should closely examine all assets, contracts (e.g., grape purchase agreements, equipment leases, and distributor agreements) and liabilities in order to determine which assets to purchase and which contracts and liabilities to assume, and what third-party consents, if any, must be obtained. In equity purchases and mergers, the vintner should use the due diligence period to fully evaluate the winery's business operations, which may lead to a renegotiation of the purchase price.

Regardless of the structure, the buyer must comply with local, state and federal regulations governing the production and sale of alcoholic beverages in order to operate the winery. This involves applications for state licenses and federal permits. The process can be lengthy, so it should be started as early as possible. However, there also are some important ways to close a purchase and sale transaction while the license and permit applications are pending.

For example, in California, if the acquisition is structured as an asset purchase, the existing winery may transfer its state alcohol beverage licenses via a "person-to-person" transfer to the new winery owner. When the buyer files the application for a person-to-person transfer of the existing winegrower's license at that location, the California Department of Alcoholic Beverage Control (ABC) will issue a temporary permit upon request, allowing the new vintner to operate the acquired winery on an interim basis until the ABC formally approves the license transfer to the new owner.[12] On the federal side, the new vintner in an asset purchase must apply for and obtain a new federal basic permit. However,

11. Cal. Corp. Code §§1300-13 (2021).
12. Cal. Bus. & Prof. Code §24045.5 (2021).

the new vintner will be permitted, following timely notice to the federal Alcohol and Tobacco Tax and Trade Bureau (TTB),[13] to operate under the prior owner's permit until the new permit issues, usually pursuant to the terms of a management agreement that will terminate when the TTB issues the new federal basic permit. If the acquisition is structured as an equity purchase, the licensed entity remains unchanged; only the underlying ownership changes. In such cases, the vintner must notify the state and federal agencies of the change in control, and the new control group must be qualified following the filing of appropriate applications.[14]

In addition to the notifications and applications that must be filed with the alcoholic beverage regulators in the state where the winery is located and at the federal level, wineries must notify state agencies in other states to which the existing winery ships its wines. Some states permit a simple name change on the license held by the existing winery in the case of an acquisition or change in control, but other states require a brand new application, complete with personal affidavits from the company owners and supporting entity documentation. A state-by-state analysis of the applicable rules and regulations, along with discussions with state agency personnel, typically are required to determine the appropriate steps to ensure the winery's continued operation.

3. LEASING AN EXISTING WINERY FACILITY

An excellent choice for a vintner seeking to operate a traditional winery without expending the capital necessary to build or acquire a winery facility is to lease an existing winery. Most provisions of a winery lease are identical to those in standard commercial leases and are not discussed here. However, one important consideration for a vintner relates to the winery's tasting room. A tenant winery that builds a strong tasting room presence becomes well known for that specific location and typically generates significant retail sales. If the tenant winery must relocate after lease maturity, consumers may be confused or have difficulty finding the new location, which could adversely affect retail sales and the winery's brand equity both in the short and long term. In order to ensure long-term occupancy of the winery facility, winery tenants often will negotiate for an option to purchase the property. Such options can be part of the lease (a "lease option"). Although leasing may be highly desirable to vintners because of the cost savings involved, there are, in fact, very few winery facilities available for lease, so these opportunities are few and far between.

A vintner leasing a winery will be required to obtain its own federal and state licenses to produce wine on the leased premises and will have to confirm that the landlord has a use permit authorizing the winery use.[15]

---

13. *See* 27 C.F.R. §1.44 (2021). New owners must file an application for a new basic permit with the TTB within 30 days after the transaction closes.

14. *Id.*

15. In California, use permits run with the land by operation of law. *See County of Imperial v. McDougal*, 19 Cal. 3d 505, 510 (1977); *Cohn v. County Bd. of Supervisors of L.A.*, 135 Cal. App.

4. LICENSES AND PERMITS FOR TRADITIONAL BRICKS-AND-MORTAR WINERIES

Regardless of whether a vintner develops a new winery or acquires or leases an existing winery, it will have to comply with the rules and regulations governing the production, sale, and distribution of alcoholic beverages imposed by state and federal agencies.

a. State Regulation

A vintner operating a traditional winery must comply with the home state's alcoholic beverage laws as well as rules and regulations imposed by other agencies within the state.

CALIFORNIA DEPARTMENT OF ALCOHOLIC BEVERAGE CONTROL

In California any person desiring to produce and sell wine must apply for a Type 02 winegrower's license from the ABC.[16] Under the California Constitution and California's Alcoholic Beverage Control Act (ABC Act), power is vested in the state, through the ABC, to license the manufacture, importation, distribution, and sale of alcoholic beverages.[17] The winery's operations and activities must be specifically permitted by the ABC Act or its implementing rules and must be conducted by a licensed individual or entity unless a specific exemption applies.[18] A license issued under the ABC Act is a permit to do that which would otherwise be unlawful. Such a license is not a right but a privilege that can be suspended or revoked by administrative action (e.g., because of a violation of the ABC Act).

To obtain a Type 02 winegrower's license, the vintner must submit an application to the ABC including information regarding, among other things, the type of business entity that owns the winery; the amount and source of funds invested in the business; the personal and financial qualifications, along with fingerprints, of the officers, directors, managers, and persons holding a 10 percent or greater interest in the business, including their spouses; the tied-house interests of the owners, directors, and managers, regardless of the amount of their

---

2d 180 (1955). Thus, the tenant will benefit from the landlord's use permit. Obtaining the use permit in the first place typically is the landlord's responsibility.

16. Cal. Bus. & Prof. Code §23356 (2021); see list of common licenses and associated privileges available at http://www.abc.ca.gov/forms/abc616.pdf (last visited Jan. 17, 2011).

17. Cal. Const. art. XX, §22.

18. Cal. Bus. & Prof. Code §23300 (2021).

ownership interest; and the location, layout, and proposed uses of the subject premises.[19]

The personal affidavits must include a statement that the affiant has not been convicted of a felony or, if such a statement cannot be made, an explanation of the facts and circumstances surrounding the felony conviction.[20] Before ABC will issue the Type 02 license, the applicant must show that it has complied with local permitting requirements and that the federal basic permit has been issued.

The privileges of a Type 02 winegrower license include the ability to (1) conduct wine tastings under certain specified conditions;[21] (2) sell wine to any person holding a license authorizing the sale of wine;[22] (3) sell wine to consumers for consumption off the premises, provided that at least 50 percent of the wine sold is produced on the winery's premises;[23](4) operate a public eating place on the licensed premises and sell beers, wines, and brandies, regardless of source, in that eating place for consumption on the premises;[24] (5) manufacture grape brandy for fortification purposes only;[25] (6) provide samples to retailers in certain circumstances;[26] and (7) sell wines for export.[27]

The ABC requires a license at each location where the winery accepts orders. Therefore, if the winery will use a separate or additional office location for accepting and processing orders, or if a winery has an off-site retail room, a separate application for a duplicate winegrower license is required for each of these locations. Although there is no limit to the number of duplicate winegrower licenses that a winery may obtain for additional office locations, wineries may only have one duplicate winegrower premise where wine tastings occur and/or where wine is sold to consumers for consumption off the premises.[28]

---

19. The ABC application package includes some or all of the following ABC forms, depending on the ownership structure: Form ABC-217, Application Questionnaire, disclosing, among other things, sources of funds and felony convictions; Forms ABC-208A and ABC-208B, Individual Personal Affidavit and Individual Financial Affidavit, respectively; Form ABC-253, Supplemental Diagram, with a drawing of the real property and an exterior view of the premises and surrounding area; Form ABC-257, Licensed Premises Diagram/Planned Operation, showing the floor plan, including overall dimensions of the licensed premises and description of proposed operations; Form ABC-069, Statement of Citizenship, Alienage, and Immigration Status for State Public Benefits and supporting documents; Form ABC-255, Zoning Affidavit, confirming compliance with local zoning; Form ABC-247, Statement Re: Residences, disclosing any residences within 100 feet of the proposed licensed premises; and Form ABC-251, Statement Re: Consideration Points, including nearby schools, hospital, churches, public playgrounds, parks, and youth facilities.

20. Cal. Bus. & Prof. Code §23952 (2021).

21. *Id.* §23356.1.

22. *Id.* §23356.

23. *Id.* §23358.

24. *Id.*

25. *Id.* §23359. Note that a winegrower licensee must obtain a separate license if manufacturing grape brandy for any purpose other than fortification.

26. *Id.* §23386.

27. *Id.* §23356.

28. *Id.* §23390.

Other wine-producing states, including Oregon[29] and Washington,[30] have laws and regulations covering the same subject matter that are similar to California's laws and regulations.

CALIFORNIA DEPARTMENT OF FOOD AND AGRICULTURE

In addition to the licensing requirements imposed by the ABC, a traditional bricks-and-mortar winery that purchases and crushes wine grapes, even if the grapes are from related entities,[31] for the purpose of making wine must register as a processor with the California Department of Food and Agriculture (CDFA) and annually renew the processor's license.[32] Because processor license fees are based on the volume of grapes purchased, a winery that crushes grapes must provide a report to the CDFA by January 10 of each year describing the total tons of grapes purchased during the preceding harvest, broken down by reporting district, tons harvested, variety, and price paid per ton.[33] Failure to comply with the reporting requirement could lead to investigation and audit by the CDFA and, potentially, fines, suspension, or revocation of the processor's license. This information is also used annually to produce the CDFA Final Grape Crush Report, discussed in more detail below.

---

29. In Oregon, the Oregon Liquor Control Commission (OLCC) regulates the production and sale of wine. The stated mission of the OLCC is to promote the public interest through the responsible sale and service of alcoholic beverages. The OLCC derives its authority from Oregon's Liquor Control Act. To operate a winery in Oregon, the vintner must apply for and obtain a Winery License. The application process is similar to that of California and can take two to four months to complete. The Winery License allows an Oregon vintner to import, bottle, produce, store, transport, and export wines. Additionally, the Winery License allows vintners to sell wine at wholesale to the OLCC, licensees of the OLCC, and consumers at retail. *See* About the OLCC, http://oregon.gov/OLCC/about_us.shtml (last visited Jan. 17, 2011); Or. Rev. Stat. §§471.223, 311, 313 (2021).

30. In Washington, the Washington State Liquor and Cannabis Board (WSLCB) regulates the production and sale of wine under Washington's Alcoholic Beverage Control Law. The stated role of the WSLCB is to contribute to the safety and financial stability of local communities by ensuring the responsible sale, and preventing the misuse, of alcohol and tobacco. To operate a winery in Washington, the vintner must apply for and obtain a Domestic Winery License. The application process is similar to that of California and can take up to 90 days to complete. The Domestic Winery License allows a Washington vintner to produce wine and sell it directly to consumers and to retail and wholesale licensees. Additionally, the Domestic Winery License allows a Washington vintner to operate up to two off-site tasting rooms. *See* Washington State Liquor Control Board, Board Information, http://liq.wa.gov/general.aspx (last visited Jan. 17, 2011); Wash. Rev. Code §66.24.170 (2021).

31. For example, sometimes a vintner owns a vineyard and sells those grapes to a separate winery entity that it also owns.

32. Cal. Food & Agric. Code §§55521, 55861-55862 (2021).

33. *Id.*§55601.5.

CALIFORNIA DEPARTMENT OF TAX AND FEE ADMINISTRATION

A winery, like any other California business that sells tangible personal property, must register for a seller's permit and pay sales tax to the California Department of Tax and Fee Administration (CDTFA) on a quarterly basis.[34] Wineries also must pay an excise tax on wine that varies depending on the wine's percentage of alcohol.[35] However, as a result of a surtax that was imposed in California, the state excise tax rate for all still wines is $0.20 per gallon.[36] CDTFA may require a winery to post some collateral, such as cash or a bond, to secure its excise tax payments, although this is not always required.[37]

b. Federal Regulation

A vintner operating a bricks-and-mortar winery must comply with federal laws governing the production, sale, and distribution of alcoholic beverages, including federal tied-house laws. The applicable federal permits must be issued by the TTB before winery operations can begin.

ALCOHOL AND TOBACCO TAX AND TRADE BUREAU

The TTB is charged with regulating the production and sale of alcoholic beverages under the Internal Revenue Code (IRC),[38] the Webb-Kenyon Act,[39] the Federal Alcohol Administration (FAA) Act,[40] and the Alcoholic Beverage Labeling Act.[41] The TTB's stated mission is to qualify and issue operating permits, known as basic permits, to wineries, importers, and wholesalers of wine; secure and collect revenue from winery operations; protect consumers by ensuring that alcohol products are labeled, advertised, and marketed in accordance with applicable laws; and ensure fair trade practices in the wine industry.

A bricks-and-mortar winery that will be producing or blending wine is required to apply for and hold a federal basic permit under the FAA Act to

---

34. Cal. Rev. & Tax. Code §§6051, 6066, 6452 (2021).

35. *See, e.g.*, Cal. Rev. & Tax. Code §32151 (2021). In other wine-producing states, the excise taxes are typically much higher. For example, in Oregon, for wines with less than 14 percent alcohol the tax rate is $0.67 per gallon, and for wines over 14 percent alcohol the tax rate is $0.77 per gallon. Or. Rev. Stat. §473.030 (2021). In Washington, for wines with less than 14 percent alcohol the tax rate is $0.87 per gallon, and for wines over 14 percent alcohol the tax rate is $1.72 per gallon. Wash. Rev. Stat. 66.24.210 (2009). *See also* State Taxes on Wine, available at http://www.taxadmin.org/fta/rate/wine.pdf (last visited Jan. 17, 2011).

36. *See* Cal. Rev. & Tax. Code §32220 (2021).

37. *Id.* §32102.

38. 26 U.S.C. §§5001-5008, 5010-5011, 5041-5045, 5051-5056, 5061-5062, 5064-5067 (2020).

39. 27 U.S.C. §122 (2020).

40. *Id.* §§201-208, 211 (2020).

41. *Id.* §§213-219(a) (2020).

produce and blend wine[42] and also to register as a Bonded Wine Cellar (BWC) under the IRC to operate the winery premises.[43] To obtain the BWC approval, a vintner must have a secure winery premise to protect the wine (and thereby preserve the government's revenue source) and obtain a wine bond from either an insurance company or some other surety, which acts as collateral to secure payment of the winery's estimated tax liability.[44] This is the derivation of the term "bonded wine premise." The applicant's excise tax liability is calculated based on the estimated number of gallons of wine produced and the particular types of wine produced.

As with the state licensing process, the vintner's applications to the TTB for a basic permit and a BWC registration must describe in detail the people who own, manage, and control the business, the premises, and the proposed operations. More specifically, the application provides the TTB with information regarding the personal and financial qualifications of the owners and various aspects of the operation such as the amount, source, and disposal of garbage and liquid waste; the source of power; operational noise sources; and discharges into navigable waters. Once the application is filed, the review and investigation process, which is run out of the TTB's National Revenue Center in Cincinnati, Ohio, can take two to four months. The TTB will conduct a telephone interview with the applicant and may conduct a field investigation to verify that (1) there is no hidden ownership of the applicant, a process that includes verification of the applicant's sources of funds; (2) the applicant is not prohibited from obtaining a permit;[45] (3) the applicant is likely to commence operations and comply with state and federal law;[46] (4) the government's source of revenue will be protected by adequately secured premises; and (5) the information contained in the application is accurate. When the TTB approves the applications, the vintner will receive a unique federal basic permit number and a unique IRC registry number.

After a winery begins operating, it must pay federal excise taxes on wine in accordance with, and at the times prescribed by, federal regulations.[47] A winery's federal excise tax is calculated based on wine type and alcohol content.[48] A domestic winery that produces fewer than 250,000 gallons of wine may qualify

42. *Id.* §§203, 204.

43. 26 U.S.C. §5351 (2020).

44. *Id.* §5551.

45. A person is prohibited from obtaining a permit if such person (or in case of a corporation, any of its officers, directors, or principal stockholders), within five years prior to the date of application, has been convicted of a felony under federal or state law or, within three years prior to date of application, has been convicted of a misdemeanor under any federal law relating to liquor, including the taxation thereof. 27 C.F.R. §1.24(a) (2021).

46. *Id.* §1.24(b).

47. 26 U.S.C. §§5041-5045 (2020).

48. *Id.* §5041. The tax rate is calculated as follows: from 0.5 percent but not more than 14 percent alcohol, $1.07 per gallon; from 14 percent but not more than 21 percent, $1.57 per gallon; from 21 percent but not more than 24 percent, $3.40 per gallon; artificially carbonated, $3.30 per gallon; and sparkling, $3.40 per gallon. *Id.*

for the Small Producer's Wine Tax Credit, which can reduce the excise taxes owed by as much as $0.90 per gallon.[49]

FOOD AND DRUG ADMINISTRATION

A new winery must register with the Food and Drug Administration (FDA) as a "food facility" pursuant to the Public Health Security and Bioterrorism Preparedness and Response Act of 2002 ("Bioterrorism Act")[50] before commencing wine production activities.[51] Congress passed the Bioterrorism Act following September 11, 2001, to enhance the security of the nation's food supply. The Bioterrorism Act imposes an ongoing recordkeeping obligation on food producers, including wineries. Wineries must establish and maintain, for two years, records that allow the FDA to identify the sources and recipients of their products to allow it to address credible threats to public health.[52]

B. "NON-TRADITIONAL" WINERIES

The acquisition and operation of a fully licensed and permitted bricks-and-mortar winery can be complicated, expensive, and time consuming. Two basic structures have evolved to allow new vintners to enter the wine industry without incurring these hefty acquisition and development expenses: the custom crush arrangement and the alternating proprietorship.

1. CUSTOM CRUSH

In a custom crush arrangement, an aspiring vintner (the client) hires a host winery to produce wine, from grapes provided by the client, to the client's specifications. The host winery, which holds a basic permit as a bonded winery, will handle all production, recordkeeping, and reporting to the TTB, with limited client oversight. In this arrangement, the client is not a bonded winery, does not own or lease a facility or equipment, and is not subject to any regulatory reporting requirements with respect to the winery premises. The client merely buys or grows grapes, delivers the crop to the host winery, and provides general instructions to the host winery for producing and bottling wine. In many cases, the client or a consulting winemaker hired by the client will closely supervise, and sometimes direct, production, but the client has no right to make its own wine at the host winery; that has to be done by the host winery itself.

No fermentation or production licenses are required of the client, and it has no bonded premises. The client relies upon the production permits and bond of

49. *Id.* §5041(c).
50. Pub. L. No. 107-188, 116 Stat. 594 (2002).
51. 21 U.S.C. §350d (2020).
52. 21 U.S.C. §350c (2020).

the host winery until the wine is bottled, labeled, and released by the host winery as "tax paid" (meaning that the federal excise tax on that wine has been paid, and the wine has been removed from the bonded premise) or the wine is transferred in bond to another bonded premise such as a warehouse.

A vintner may not bottle or sell wine until the TTB has approved the label for that wine by issuing a Certificate of Label Approval (COLA). Only the host winery as the bonded winery can apply for and obtain a COLA for the client's brands. Because the client is not a winery, the TTB will not allow the word "winery" as part of the client's brand or trade name (e.g., Client's Winery); this is considered misleading. The client can select some other brand or trade name, such as Client's Cellar.

In the custom crush model, before bottling and labeling the client's wine, the host winery will adopt the client's trade name by adding it to the host winery's federal basic permit.[53] The host winery first files and publishes a Fictitious Business Name Statement in the county in which it does business[54] and then files that statement with the TTB along with a written authorization from the client to the host winery to add the client's trade name as an "additional bottling trade name" on the host winery's basic permit. The label will reflect that the wine is "Produced and Bottled by [*Trade Name*]." For example, if the client intends to market wine under the brand Escalier Wines, the host winery will file and publish a Fictitious Business Name Statement indicating that the host winery is doing business as Escalier Wines. The host winery then will amend its federal basic permit to reflect Escalier Wines as one of its additional bottling trade names, specifying that it is for the account of the client. At that point, the wine label may report that the wine is "Produced and Bottled by Escalier Wines." Although the TTB could track the custom-produced wine back to the client, a consumer would find it difficult, if not impossible, to know that Escalier Wines is something other than a producing winery.

The custom crush arrangement allows aspiring vintners to enter the wine business and build a brand and distribution network with little capital investment and limited regulatory complications and responsibilities compared to brick-and-mortar wineries. The client has no need to purchase or lease property, facilities, and equipment. The client has no reporting responsibility to the TTB regarding the wine made for it and has no direct responsibility to pay wine excise taxes to the TTB upon release of the wine from the host winery's bonded premises. The client need not engage a winemaker, although many do so for purposes of quality control.

The custom crush model is commonly used in the industry. The Napa Valley Vintners Association reports that in 2010, 140 of its 400 vintner members practiced custom crush at a host winery.[55] While custom crush is often associated

---

53. Under 27 C.F.R. §4.35 (2021), the wine label must include the name of the entity bottling the wine, and that name must be identical to the name that appears on the producer's basic permit.

54. Cal. Bus. & Prof. Code §17915 (2020).

55. Author's conversation with Napa Valley Vintners, St. Helena, California (October 13, 2010).

with small companies and new entrants into the industry, there are numerous large and very profitable companies that operate under the custom crush model. Those companies are most likely perceived by consumers as being traditional bricks-and-mortar wineries.

a. Federal and State Regulation of Custom Crush Arrangements

The state licensing sought by a client will vary depending on the client's marketing plan as well as its state of domicile. In California a client typically will obtain both a Type 17 Beer and Wine Wholesaler's License, which allows sales of wine to other licensees in the state for the purpose of resale, and a Type 20 Off-Sale Beer & Wine License, which, when held in conjunction with a Type 17 license, allows the sale of wine directly to California consumers in a retail sales outlet and/or by telephone, Internet, and mail order.[56] A client also must obtain a wholesaler's basic permit from the TTB, which authorizes the client to sell wine that has been made for it to other wholesalers and retailers. Finally, clients must comply with state and federal tied-house regulations.

Although a custom crush arrangement provides an easy entry into the wine business, it has several limitations. The holder of a Type 17 wholesaler's license in California may not conduct wine tastings.[57] The client has limited rights to sell wines direct to consumers in other states compared to licensed producers.[58] Additionally, many state tied-house exceptions are available only to licensed winegrowers and not wholesalers or retailers.

b. Custom Crush Agreements

Although the ABC and TTB do not typically scrutinize custom crush arrangements, the custom crush contract should reflect the regulatory underpinnings of the relationship. Because the client has no licenses or permits for producing, fermenting, processing, storing, bottling, or packaging wine, those activities must be performed by the host winery. It is the obligation of the host winery to store the wine in bond, maintain all required licenses, comply with all reporting requirements, and comply with applicable labeling requirements. The

---

56. The licensing required in a custom crush arrangement differs based on the state in which the host winery is located. For example, in Washington clients can obtain a Wine Distributor/Importer License, which allows for the sale of wine to other licensees for resale but does not allow for sales directly to consumers. *See* Wash. Rev. Code. §66.24.170 (2009). In Oregon clients can obtain a Winery License, exactly as if they operated stand-alone wineries. *See* Or. Rev. Stat. §471.223 (2021).

57. This is one of the privileges conferred on the holder of a Type 02 winegrower's license but not on the holder of a Type 17 Beer and Wine Wholesaler's License or a Type 20 Off-Sale Beer & Wine License. Cal. Bus. & Prof. Code §23356.1. A wholesaler may pour wine in certain limited circumstances where the client donates wine to a qualified charitable organization. *Id.* §24045.18.

58. Many states only allow wineries, not custom crush clients who are licensed as wholesalers and/or as retailers, to ship their wines directly to in-state consumers. *See, e.g.*, Tex. Alco. Bev. Code Ann. §§54.01, 54.03 (2021).

contract should reflect that all of these responsibilities fall squarely on the host winery.

Custom crush contracts may allow a client to provide winemaking specifications to the host winery. Typically, title to the wine remains with the client at all times. The host winery then returns the finished wine to the client. The host winery is responsible for paying excise taxes upon release of the wine from the bonded premises, although contracts typically require the client to reimburse the host winery for the taxes paid. A host winery contracting with multiple custom crush clients must include all wine produced for all of its custom crush clients, as well as its own production, for purposes of calculating the federal excise tax and determining eligibility for the Small Producer's Wine Tax Credit.[59]

Because the winemaking responsibility necessarily falls on the host winery, which is required to produce wine according to the client's specifications, the custom crush contract tends to focus on risk allocation and liability protection for both parties. The host winery may seek broad indemnifications for its winemaking activities, coupled with releases of liability. Contracts generally recognize that a host winery may be liable for negligence, but the host winery often seeks to cap its liability in the amount of the bulk value of the wine, not its ultimate resale value. The host winery generally requests disclaimers of express and implied warranties of fitness, quality, and character of the wine; waivers of consequential damages; and disclaimers of responsibility for shrinkage and breakage, subject to negotiated limitations. Dispute resolution, arbitration, and mediation provisions are common.

Custom crush contracts generally provide that fees charged by the host winery are based on volume of production measured by tons, gallons, or cases. For example, a custom crush agreement might provide for specific services such as crushing, fermenting, and pressing at a fixed price per ton of fruit processed. Additional services typically are charged on a volume basis, such as barrel or cased goods storage for a monthly fee per barrel or case.

The host winery should obtain a security interest in the customer's wine under the California Commercial Code to secure the customer's payment obligations and should file a financing statement. The host winery also should conduct a UCC search and, at a minimum, obtain warranties and representations from the client with respect to competing liens such as grower's liens and liens of lenders, along with a representation by the client that its grapes and wine are free of encumbrances.

c. The Négociant Model

The term "négociant" generally refers to a producer who purchases bulk wine from different sources, blends that wine, and bottles the blend under its own

59. The host winery's total production also is relevant to compliance with any production (gallonage) limitations in the host winery's use permit.

label. The practice originated in the Burgundy region of France and now serves as the business model for many producers in the United States.[60]

Most négociants obtain licensing identical to that required for custom crush clients. Vintners are attracted to the négociant model for good reason. It requires little to no investment in facilities and equipment. Particularly in bad economic times, the négociant can obtain high-quality wine at low prices and react quickly to changing market conditions. On the other hand, the négociant may find it difficult to make (blend) a consistent product from vintage to vintage without a secure long-term grape source.

Wineries choose to sell bulk wine for many different reasons. In some cases, the winery holds more wine in inventory than it can sell at acceptable prices. In other cases, the bulk wine being sold does not meet the winery's quality standards. Therefore, wineries that sell bulk wine to négociants should ensure that the bulk wine sales agreement includes a confidentiality provision ensuring that the wine sold is never identified as that of the seller, as well as a liquidated damages provision quantifying the measure of damages in the event of breach by the buyer.[61]

2. ALTERNATING PROPRIETORSHIP

In an alternating proprietorship arrangement, an existing operating winery with excess production capacity (the "host winery") allows another wine producer (the "alternating proprietor"), and sometimes several other producers, to produce wine at the facility. This model is also commonly known as a "winery within a winery." The alternating proprietorship model is essentially a collaboration of independent bonded wineries, including the host winery, operating under one roof. The host winery and all alternating proprietors are separately bonded wineries, each responsible for its own production, recordkeeping, excise tax payments, and label approvals.

The alternating proprietorship model is conceptually similar to a residential condominium development consisting of commonly owned areas for the enjoyment of all condominium owners as well as separate, independently owned living spaces. In an alternating proprietorship, each bonded winery may have a designated area dedicated to the exclusive use of the winery for storage of its wine. The host winery and each alternating proprietor will also share the production facilities and winemaking equipment of the host winery. Since only one winery may use a particular tank or bottling line at any given time, the use of the facilities alternates between the host winery and the alternating proprietor. The shared production facilities and dedicated areas together comprise the bonded wine premises of the alternating proprietor, separate and distinct from the

---

60. Karen Macneil, The Wine Bible 196-197 (2001).

61. If a winery sells bulk wine without a written agreement, it is not without recourse if the buyer discloses the winery's identity. Common law and federal trademark rules prevent unlicensed use of the winery's trade name. In California and many other states, the right to publicity prevents the unauthorized commercial use of a winery's name. *See, e.g.*, Cal. Civ. Code §3344(a) (2021).

bonded wine premises of the host winery and those of other alternating proprietors.

a. Federal and State Regulation of Alternating Proprietorships

In states that allow alternating proprietorships, such as California, Oregon, Washington, and Colorado, the alternating proprietor is required to obtain its own state licenses for the production and sale of wine. For example, in California, an alternating proprietor is required to obtain a Type 02 winegrower license. An alternating proprietor also must obtain its own federal basic permit and is solely responsible for its own winemaking, recordkeeping, and reporting to the ABC, TTB, and other governmental agencies, including the payment of excise taxes.

New vintners are attracted to the alternating proprietorship for a variety of reasons. If the alternating proprietor's production is less than 250,000 gallons, it will qualify for the Small Producer's Wine Tax Credit.[62] Additionally, as the holder of a winegrower's license in California, the alternating proprietor enjoys the same rights and privileges as the bricks-and-mortar winery holding the same license, including the right to conduct wine tastings and operate an off-site tasting room. Consumers looking at an alternating proprietor's wine label typically would not know that the winery is anything other than a stand-alone, traditional winery. Finally, the alternating proprietor has no obligation to comply with burdensome and expensive local regulations and use permit processes, that being the responsibility of the host winery.

TTB SCRUTINY

Alternating proprietorship arrangements are specifically permitted by federal regulations.[63] However, because alternating proprietors as independent producers are eligible for the Small Producer's Wine Tax Credit, which has the potential of reducing revenue to the government, the TTB will carefully scrutinize an alternating proprietorship arrangement to verify that the alternating proprietor is truly acting as a separately bonded winery rather than as a client of the host winery under a custom crush arrangement.[64] In the custom crush situation, the excise tax is paid by the host winery, which, when it combines its own production with that of all its clients, might not qualify for the credit.

The TTB also wants to ensure that the alternating proprietor will itself engage in wine production. The TTB will consider the alternating proprietor's business history and development plans to demonstrate that commitment. If the alternating proprietor intends to rely on the host winery to make its wines and run

---

62. 27 C.F.R. §24.278 (2021).

63. *Id.*§§24.135, 24.136.

64. TTB, Alternating Proprietors at Bonded Wine Premises, TTB Industry Circular No. 2008-4 (Aug. 18, 2008), §6(a), available at http://www.ttb.gov/industry_circulars/archives/2008/08-04.html. TTB Industry Circular No. 2008-4 entirely supersedes TTB Industry Circular No. 2003-7.

its winery operations, the TTB will refuse to issue a bonded winery basic permit to that person or entity.

SCOPE OF THE BONDED PREMISES

Central to its function of securing and collecting revenue from winery operations, the TTB carefully regulates the definition and delineation of the bonded premises of each alternating proprietor. As noted above, an alternating proprietor's bonded premises must include the alternating production areas where the wine is produced by each proprietor and typically also a dedicated area where the alternating proprietor stores its wine in barrels, bottles, or finished cases. The shared and dedicated areas together constitute the bonded premises of each alternating proprietor.

The alternating proprietor must report the movement of the wine into and out of its bonded premises, even if the transfer is from one alternating proprietor to the host winery or between alternating proprietors. In order to facilitate such reporting and enable the TTB to locate and identify the wines of each alternating proprietor, the TTB may require visual or structural delineation of the dedicated premises of the alternating proprietor(s) and the host winery. This can involve signage or even lines on the ground or, depending on the design of the facility, fencing or other physical separation between the dedicated areas.

b. The Alternating Proprietorship Agreement

During its investigation and analysis of an alternating proprietor's application for a federal basic permit, the TTB will pay close attention to the written agreement between the alternating proprietor and the host winery. The alternating proprietorship agreement should expressly state that the alternating proprietor is responsible for its own production, recordkeeping, reporting, labeling, and payment of taxes, independent of the host winery.[65] The agreement should provide that the alternating proprietor will pay the host winery directly for its floor space, equipment use, and, where applicable, personnel time and material consumed if the host winery is to provide services or materials. Pricing should be structured around rental of space and rates for specific services rendered.[66] Payment to the host winery should not be based on volume rates (tons, gallons, or cases), a method of charging more appropriate for custom crush agreements.[67] The TTB reviews all of these factors to determine if the arrangement is a true alternating proprietorship and not a custom winemaking relationship in disguise.

Although it is acceptable for the alternating proprietorship agreement to provide for the use of the host winery's employees for certain services, it must be clear that such employees will be acting solely at the alternating proprietor's

---

65. *See* Industry Circular No. 2008-4, §6(a), *supra* note 64.
66. *Id.*
67. *Id.*

direction or be hired directly by the alternating proprietor.[68] The contract should clearly state that the alternating proprietor is in control of, and responsible for, bottling under its permit, storing of bulk wine in its premises, and removal of wine from the bonded premises.[69] The alternating proprietor must have absolute access to its bonded premises and its wine at all times.[70] The agreement also must allow the TTB unfettered right of access to the bonded premises.[71]

3. THE UNINTENTIONAL VINTNER: GROWER CUSTOM CRUSH

When grapes are in over-supply (or under-demand), many growers with unsold grapes choose to convert those grapes to wine to preserve their economic value. A grower without winery facilities must make arrangements with a winery to process its fruit. Commonly, the grower will deliver grapes to the winery, the winery will process and market the resulting bulk wine, and the grower and winery will split the profits, if any, when the wine sells. The legal issues arising out of this structure depend on whether the arrangement is characterized as a sale of wine or a sale of grapes.

a. Sale of Wine?

In some instances, the parties intend that the winery merely act as a processor and never take title to the grapes or bulk wine. Yet sharing profits implies that the winery and the grower share ownership of the wine, and growers that do not regularly produce and sell wine typically do not hold the requisite state licenses and federal permits to sell wine.

Recognizing how common this situation is, the California legislature in 1983 created the Type 29 Winegrower's Storage license specifically to address this circumstance.[72] The Type 29 license allows a grower to hire a winery to ferment its grapes and store the resulting bulk wine at the winery, and it also allows that grower to sell the bulk wine in California to wineries and blenders, but not to wholesalers or retailers. Under the Type 29 license, the grower may sell only wine produced from grapes that he has grown. With respect to federal permits, if the grower is engaged in the business of purchasing wine for resale at wholesale and if the grower has control over activities normally associated with wholesaling (price determination, buyer selection, and marketing), the grower may be required to obtain a wholesaler's basic permit.

---

68. *See* Industry Circular No. 2008-4, §6(c), *supra* note 64.
69. *Id.*
70. *See* Industry Circular No. 2008-4, §6(d), *supra* note 64.
71. *Id.*
72. Cal. Bus. & Prof. Code §23358.3 (2021).

b. Sale of Grapes?

If the transaction is not characterized as a sale of wine, it may constitute a sale of grapes by the grower to the winery. This poses a legal problem because the grape prices to be paid by the winery generally will not be determined until the wine is sold — many months, if not years, after the grape harvest. The Clare Berryhill Grape Crush Report Act of 1976 (the "Berryhill Act")[73] requires every processor who crushes grapes to deliver a report to the Secretary of Food and Agriculture by January 10 following harvest indicating the total number of tons of grapes purchased in California during the preceding harvest and the final prices of those grapes.[74] A violation of these provisions is a crime. Unless the grower and the winery can agree on the price of the grower's grapes before January 10 following harvest, the grower should obtain a Type 29 license.

C. GRAPE SOURCING

It is obvious that a winery must obtain grapes before it can produce wine.[75] What is not obvious are the many available choices. A winery may buy raw land and develop a vineyard, buy an existing vineyard, lease raw land and develop a vineyard, lease an existing vineyard, or buy grapes from a grower. Each of these options is discussed below.

1. PURCHASING RAW LAND OR AN EXISTING VINEYARD

a. Raw Land

Developing a vineyard from raw land allows the winery ultimate control over varietal selection and viticultural techniques. The winery will have a long-term stable source of fruit perfectly suited to its chosen wine style and marketing plan. There are many downsides to this approach, however. First, the winery must devote significant financial resources to acquiring, developing, and maintaining land and improvements. Second, it usually takes three to four years before a vineyard produces a commercially viable crop. Add this to the one to four years it takes to convert grapes into finished product, and the winery clearly may have to wait up to eight years before it realizes any cash return on its investment.

---

73. Codified at Cal. Food & Agric. Code §55601.5 (2021).

74. *Id.*§55601.5(g) provides that "all grape purchase contracts entered into on or after January 1, 1977, shall provide for a final price, including any bonuses or allowances, to be set on or before the January 10 following delivery of the grapes purchased. Any grape purchase contract entered into in violation of this subdivision is illegal and unenforceable." The Berryhill Act defines "purchase" as "the taking by sale, discount, negotiation, mortgage, pledge lien, issue or reissue, gift or any other voluntary transaction creating an interest in property." *Id.* §55601.5(i)(6). The Berryhill Act further defines "sale" as the passing of title from the seller to the buyer for a price. *Id.*

75. Alternatively, the winery can purchase bulk or bottled wine.

Finally, wine is a consumer product, and tastes change rapidly. The winery runs the risk that whatever variety it plants now will fall out of favor in the future. Nevertheless, many wineries choose this alternative.

b. Existing Vineyard

To save time and avoid the expense of developing a vineyard (development costs range from $30,000 to $250,000 per acre),[76] a winery may choose to purchase a mature vineyard. The winery will gain immediate possession of a crop that it can use to produce wine and will have control over farming practices. The downside is that a mature vineyard will cost more per acre than raw land and typically will have a shorter useful life than a newly developed vineyard. Additionally, the buyer is limited to the grape varietals and vineyard design (including, for instance, orientation of and spacing between the vines) that the seller selected.

c. Acquisition Process

The process of acquiring raw land or an existing vineyard is quite similar to acquiring land for winery development. The parties typically negotiate the key terms in a term sheet or LOI, which the parties will incorporate into a definitive purchase and sale agreement. The buyer, together with his advisors and counsel, will conduct a due diligence review of the property.

There are also several issues the buyer must focus on during due diligence that are unique to vineyard (or future vineyard) acquisitions.

d. Legal Due Diligence Concerns

ZONING

Counsel for the buyer should determine how the subject parcel is zoned. Zoning restricts the uses of a parcel and places other restrictions on the property, which may include minimum setbacks, water and septic requirements, and height restrictions for structures. In Napa County, California, for example, vineyard property is most frequently located in areas zoned as either Agricultural Preserve (AP)[77] or Agricultural Watershed (AW).[78] Each zoning district imposes unique restrictions on the uses to which a property may be put.

---

76. A number of variables affect the cost of development, including the location of the vineyard (flat valley floor vs. steep hillside), the availability of water (development of a reservoir may be required), and the desired viticultural practices.

77. Napa County, Cal., Code §§18.16.010-18.16.040 (1993).

78. *Id.*§§18.20.010-18.20.040.

MATERIAL CONTRACTS AND WATER RIGHTS

The buyer's attorney should review material contracts that affect the land, particularly if the buyer is acquiring an existing vineyard. Material contracts include, but are not limited to, loan documents, grape purchase agreements, farming agreements, and equipment leases. The buyer should determine whether it wants to assume any of the existing contracts. The buyer's attorney should review the desirable contracts to determine whether the seller can assign its rights and obligations under those contracts to the buyer and, if so, whether the seller must consent to the assignment. The buyer's attorney must provide in the PSA that the seller's written consent to assignment of all contracts to be assumed is a condition to closing the transaction. Buyer's counsel also should obtain documents related to water rights, which are particularly important to agricultural operations in California. These rights are reflected in state permits granting appropriative water rights,[79] reservoir permits, common law riparian rights,[80] and water pipeline and sharing agreements.[81]

NEIGHBORS

In agricultural areas, an experienced local land use attorney should know or ascertain the attitude and demeanor of the owners of neighboring parcels. This knowledge will be very useful if the buyer intends to seek approval to develop the property in the future and if the approval process will involve a public hearing and comment.

TITLE ISSUES

Buyer and buyer's counsel should examine whether the property is subject to any so-called Williamson Act contract or conservation easements during the title review process.

Williamson Act Contracts. It is very common for agricultural land in California to be subject to a Williamson Act contract.[82] In a Williamson Act

---

79. The California Water Resources Control Board was created in 1967 to oversee water allocation and water quality protection. Cal. Water Code §§13100-13197.5 (2021).

80. *See, e.g., In re Determination of Rights to Water of Hallett Creek Stream Sys.*, 44 Cal. 3d 448, 464 (1988) (citing *Lux v. Haggin*, 69 Cal. 255 (1886)).

81. These agreements generally are recorded and are discovered in connection with title review.

82. The California Land Conservation Act of 1965 (Cal. Gov't Code §§51200-51297.5 (2021)), commonly referred to as the Williamson Act, enables local governments to enter into contracts with private landowners for the purpose of restricting specific parcels of land to agricultural or related open-space use. In return, landowners receive property tax assessments that are much lower than normal because they are based upon farming and open-space values as opposed to full market value. Local governments receive an annual subvention of forgone property tax revenues from the state via the Open Space Subvention Act of 1971. As of 2005 more than half of California's 30 million acres of agricultural lands and open space was protected under the

contract between a property owner and the county, the property owner agrees to devote the property to agricultural use in exchange for lower property taxes. Typically, cancellation of such contracts requires 10 years' notice. Material breach of a Williamson Act contract could lead to stiff penalties, including a fine of up to 25 percent of the fair market value of the land and improvements.[83] Williamson Act contracts are recorded against the subject property and should therefore be discovered during title review.

Conservation Easements. The title review may reveal a conservation easement against the subject property. A conservation easement is created when a property owner donates or sells an easement, typically to a local nonprofit land trust, pursuant to which the landowner agrees to limit development on some or all of a particular parcel.[84] Limitations imposed by conservation easements bind the landowner and its successors in interest in perpetuity so long as the land is in private hands. Buyer's counsel should review conservation easements of record carefully to evaluate compatibility with the client's intended uses and development plans, including future land divisions or lot line adjustments. Buyer's counsel should pay special attention to the rights of any third-party land trusts to inspect, police, and enforce the terms of the easement.

e. Non-Legal Due Diligence Concerns

When evaluating an existing or potential vineyard property, the buyer should investigate, among other things, the site's soil quality, slope (particularly if excessive slope is a hindrance to development),[85] access roads, reservoirs and other water sources, and visible environmental hazards. The buyer should engage experts to evaluate the quality of the water source, the site's drainage, and the potential for discharge of waste and storm water.

The buyer who is acquiring an existing vineyard should obtain very detailed information about the property prior to closing the transaction. Specifically, the buyer should identify the vineyard developer, current farming company, and any

---

Williamson Act, including over 70 percent of the state's prime farmland. See California Dep't of Conservation, California Department of Conservation Celebrates 40 Years of the Williamson Act (2005), NR 2005-12, available at http://www.consrv.ca.gov/index/news/2005%20News%20Releases/NR2005-12_ Williamson_Act_at_40.htm.

83. Cal. Gov't Code §51250 (2021). Williamson Act amendments enacted in 2003 (A.B. 1492, Cal. Assemb. (Cal. 2003)) provide for enhanced penalties for material breach of a Williamson Act contract.

84. In addition to an altruistic desire to preserve agricultural and open space, a property owner may be motivated to grant a conservation easement by various tax benefits. For instance, the taxpayer may claim an immediate federal income tax deduction based on various factors, including a decrease in the property's value resulting from the imposition of restrictions (26 U.S.C. §170 (2020)), save substantially on federal estate taxes (*id.* §2031(c)), claim an immediate deduction against California income taxes (Cal. Rev. & Tax. Code §24357 (2021)), and receive California income tax credits (Cal. Pub. Res. Code §§37000-37042 (2021)).

85. *See* Napa County, Cal., Code §18.108.060 (1993).

viticultural consultants and, if possible, interview those people to learn about the vineyard. Additionally, the buyer should obtain an accurate count of producing and missing vines, vineyard maps, viticultural reports, and climate logs along with information such as the year the vineyard was planted or replanted, the varietal clone and rootstock, vine spacing, trellis system, irrigation system and schedule, soil preparation and amendments, ongoing soil or drainage issues, nutritional inputs, pest and disease issues, pesticide use reports, annual petiole analysis, harvest dates, yield history, and grape juice analysis. All of this information will provide the buyer with a realistic picture of the vineyard's health and performance and, depending on what is discovered, may result in a renegotiation of the purchase price.

2. LEASING RAW LAND OR AN EXISTING VINEYARD

Many vintners lease raw land for vineyard development or lease an existing vineyard rather than purchase vineyard property. Vintners and landowners have unique motivations for entering a lease, which become relevant when they negotiate the lease terms.

a. Vintner's Motivation to Lease

Purchasing raw land or an existing vineyard requires a large amount of capital. To obtain this capital, a buyer must either use its own cash, borrow, take on equity investors, or implement some combination of the above. Most vintners do not have enough cash to purchase land without outside financing, and may be adverse to the liability associated with borrowing money and the lack of control associated with additional equity investors. When capital limitations make acquiring a vineyard unattractive, a vintner who wants to control how his grapes are farmed should consider a vineyard lease. Importantly, a vintner who leases a vineyard is allowed to use the term "Estate Bottled" on his wine label, a benefit not allowed if the vintner were to purchase grapes under a typical grape purchase agreement.[86] Many vintners believe that the term "Estate Bottled" can increase the prestige and bottle price of wine.

b. Landowner's Motivation to Lease

An owner of raw land may lack the capital to develop the land into a vineyard. In a vineyard development lease, it is the vintner/tenant that pays the development costs and ongoing farming costs as well as other expenses typically

86. A winery may use the term "Estate Bottled" on its label if 100 percent of the wine came from grapes grown on land either owned or controlled by the winery, which must be located in a viticultural area that is identified on the label. 27 C.F.R. §4.26(a) (2021). "Controlled by" refers to property on which the winery has the legal right to perform, and does perform, all of the acts common to viticulture under the terms of a lease or similar agreement of at least three years duration. Id. §4.26(c).

associated with land ownership such as real property taxes, assessments, and insurance.

The landowner may be motivated by the opportunity to convert nonproductive raw land into income-producing property. During the lease term, the vintner/tenant will pay the landowner rent in the form of fixed annual payments or a certain percentage of the crop proceeds. At the end of the lease term, ownership of the developed vineyard and related improvements typically reverts to the landlord.

c. A Side Note on Sale-Leaseback Transactions

A common real estate transaction that is relatively new to the wine industry is the "sale-leaseback."[87] In these transactions, a real estate owner sells property to a buyer and immediately leases the property back for its own use. This option is attractive to vineyard and winery owners that need cash now, which they receive in the form of the purchase price, but who want to continue using the real estate for their vineyard and/or winery operations. While property owners can obtain bank loans for needed capital, banks will lend only up to a certain percentage of the property's value (60-65 percent is typical). A sale-leaseback is sometimes viewed as a method for obtaining 100 percent financing. In most sale-leaseback transactions, the seller/tenant will retain an option to purchase the property at the end of the lease term at a predetermined price or according to a pricing formula.

d. Process

Most vineyard leases are long-term commitments and are entered only after long periods of investigation and negotiation. Therefore, the process is very similar to a purchase. Often the parties will negotiate a term sheet or LOI to agree upon the material terms before negotiating all the details of the vineyard lease.

e. Unique Vineyard Development Lease Elements

Although a vineyard development lease and a lease of an existing vineyard are structured similarly, there are key distinctions between them. A development lease requires the tenant to spend significant sums early in the lease term to develop the vineyard. Additionally, the newly developed vineyard will not produce a commercially viable crop for several years. Accordingly, a development lease will generally have a longer term than an existing vineyard lease, allowing the tenant to recoup his investment over time. Often, in the first three to five years of a development lease, rent will be reduced or abated because

---

87. See, e.g., Lilly Vitorovich, Diageo Signs Sale, Leaseback Wine Deal in US, Dow Jones Newswire, June 24, 2010, available at http://www.advfn.com/news_Diageo-Signs-Sale-Leaseback-Wine-Deal-In-US_43355949.html.

of the development expenses and negative cash flow that the tenant experiences. Commonly, a development lease is contingent on the tenant's ability to obtain proper permits for the intended use. A development lease ordinarily will include additional provisions describing the construction plans and costs.

f. Subdivision Map Act Concerns (California Only)

In many cases, the landowner will continue living in a residence on the leased parcel while leasing the vineyard portion. In California, leasing a parcel of real property while retaining a portion of that parcel is considered a "subdivision" of the parcel, in violation of California's Subdivision Map Act.[88] If the lease is for "agricultural purposes," however, the Subdivision Map Act does not apply, and the landlord may retain an interest in a homesite on the leased premises.[89] Counsel for the landlord, therefore, should ensure that the tenant will use the leased premises only for agricultural purposes. If the landlord will retain a homesite, the lease should describe the method of allocating water between the residential and agricultural areas and provide for access to the home without interfering with farming activities.

g. Lease Term Issues

Vineyard leases, especially vineyard development leases, have lengthy terms. In California, the term of the lease can have adverse property tax consequences. If the lease term is 35 years or more, including options to extend the term, the lease transaction will constitute a "change in ownership," triggering a reassessment of the property by the county assessor and a resulting increase in real property taxes.[90] Leases often allocate property tax payment responsibilities between the vineyard and residential areas, or they may allocate any increase in property taxes to the tenant.

h. Rent Issues

Vineyard lease rates are often calculated as a fixed amount per acre, paid annually. Because the leases often are for long terms, the landowner typically will require adjustments to the rental amount over time to protect against inflation. Some vineyard leases include a standard adjustment based on changes in the consumer price index (CPI). More specific to vineyard leases are adjustments based on changes in average grape prices as published in the annual California Grape Crush Report.[91]

---

88. Cal. Gov't Code §66424 (2021).

89. *Id.* §66412(k).

90. Cal. Rev. & Tax Code §61(c) (2021).

91. The California Grape Crush Report is published annually by the USDA National Agricultural Statistical Service, California Field Office. The report publishes results from the prior

Vineyard leases also may involve the calculation of rental payments as a percentage of the proceeds of the crop plus a minimum fixed payment per acre. Such a lease, generally known as a "crop share," allows the landlord to enjoy a greater return in productive years while accepting reduced payments in years during which grape prices are down or yields are low. The sharing of the risk in the context of a material participation lease may enable the landlord to take advantage of special use valuations of the property, resulting in reduced estate taxes after death.[92]

i. Vineyard Improvements

Most often, vineyard improvements such as vines, stakes, trellising, and irrigation systems remain with the landlord at the end of the lease term. In vineyard development leases, the tenant may seek some compensation at the end of the lease term for the capital invested in these improvements, depending upon the length of the term and whether the tenant has the continuing obligation to maintain the vineyard in good condition, including vine replacement obligations through the end of the lease.

3. PURCHASING GRAPES

For some vintners, purchasing grapes is their only means of supply. Other vintners rely on purchased grapes to supplement the harvest from the vineyards that they own or lease. Grape purchase agreements vary from simple one-year agreements intended to fill a temporary need to multi-year contracts intended to create a lasting bond between grower and vintner.

As with many farmers, a culture exists among some grape growers, especially old-timers, to do business "on a handshake," dispensing with written agreements and avoiding the cost of engaging legal counsel. These trusting growers should be aware, however, that in most wine-producing states, a contract for the sale of goods, including grapes, for $500 or more is unenforceable unless it's in writing.[93] In bad economic times, wineries seeking to cut costs may seize the opportunity to terminate an oral agreement that is unenforceable. Although a grower with an oral grape contract is at risk, the parties may have exchanged sufficient writings such as e-mails and letters to establish a written contract,

---

harvest, including total tons harvested and price per ton, by district and grape varietal. The report is available at http://www.nass.usda.gov.

92. Under 26 U.S.C. §2032A (2020), taxpayers may lower the value of agricultural property by up to 75 percent for estate planning purposes. As one of several qualification tests, the taxpayer transfering the property at his or her death must have "materially" participated in operating the farm. The taxpayer can satisfy this test if he or she substantially participates in management decisions relating to production. A properly drafted material participation lease agreement should provide for the landlord's material participation in such decisions.

93. *See* Cal. Comm. Code §2201 (2020); N.Y. U.C.C. Law §2-201 (2021); Or. Rev. Stat. §72.2010 (2021); Va. Code Ann. §8.2-201 (2021); Wash. Rev. Code §62A.2-201 (2020).

leaving certain provisions unstated. In most states, the law will impose material provisions such as price and timing of payment even without a written contract.[94] If the parties desire certainty or wish to avoid litigation, they should enter into a formal written grape purchase agreement.

a. Grape Purchase Agreement

A written grape purchase agreement (GPA) is uniquely interconnected; almost every material provision affects other provisions. For example, the provision that states which party controls farming practices will affect the pricing mechanism, grape quantity, grape quality, term, and harvest provisions. Counsel for either party to a grape contract must be acutely aware of this interconnectedness and negotiate and draft the contract accordingly. The material provisions in a grape purchase agreement are described next.

PREAMBLE AND RECITALS

Like a PSA and a vineyard lease, the GPA generally begins with a preamble that describes the agreement and the parties, followed by recitals. It is critical to specify the source vineyard. Often a vintner will purchase only a portion of a vineyard's production. In such cases, the parties typically identify specific vineyard blocks or rows as the source of fruit; the rootstock and varietal clone also might be specified.

TERM AND TERMINATION

A GPA's term is determined primarily from the vintner's goals. In some cases, the vintner is seeking a short-term source of grapes to fill a temporary need. Here the GPA's term might be as short as one year or one harvest, with no automatic renewal provision. In other cases, the vintner might seek a long-term source of fruit for its most stable brands. The relationship between vintner and grower in a longer-term contract is closer to a partnership than an ordinary vendor relationship. A typical term for such a contract is five to seven years.

Longer-term contracts often contain a so-called evergreen provision where the final term is perpetually extended unless either party notifies the other of its intent to terminate the agreement. Usually after the notice of termination is given, the contract will continue for an additional one to five years, during which time the grower will seek a new buyer and the vintner will find replacement fruit.

Because long-term contracts create substantial financial obligations, vintners will not enter such contracts without ample due diligence. Often a vintner seeking a long-term source of grapes from a new grower will negotiate for an initial short-term "look-see" period. During this period, usually one to three years, the vintner has an opportunity to evaluate the quality of the grower's

94. *See, e.g.*, Cal. Food & Agric. Code §§55601.3(c) (2021).

vineyard, viticultural practices, and grapes. At the end of the look-see period, the vintner will have the option to extend the term of the GPA, in which case it will convert to a longer-term GPA with an evergreen provision. If the vintner elects to not continue, the GPA will terminate at the end of the look-see period.

QUANTITY

Historically, vintners typically purchased a fixed tonnage of grapes in each harvest year. Today, fixed-tonnage contracts are more common in short-term contracts in which the vintner has little input into farming practices. It is now common for vintners to purchase all the grapes produced from a specified vineyard or portion of a vineyard. Such "all-production" arrangements are often found in long-term contracts where the vintner has considerable, if not total, control over farming decisions. An all-production contract ensures that the grower will be adequately compensated if farming practices directed by the vintner lower the yield in the vineyard.

QUALITY

Almost all GPAs contain a provision describing the required quality of grapes that the grower will deliver. In addition to generally requiring the grapes to be sound, merchantable, and suitable for making a particular quality of wine, the GPA may include specific standards. For example, the GPA may set a cap on the amount of grape defects (for example, mold or rot) and material other than grapes (MOG) as a percentage of the grapes delivered. A typical cap is 1 percent. In most cases, if the defects or MOG exceed the cap, the vintner will be allowed to reject the load of grapes. Less frequently, if defects or MOG exceed a certain percentage of all grapes delivered, the vintner will have the ability to reject all the grapes. To resolve disputes over grape quality, including MOG, the parties may appoint a third party, such as an inspector from the Grape Inspection Service of the California Department of Food and Agriculture, to referee.[95]

PRICING AND PAYMENT

There are many different methods used to determine grape prices. Some GPAs use a fixed price per ton of grapes delivered; others use a fixed price per acre harvested; still others employ a pricing mechanism tying grape prices through a formula to the bottle price of the wine produced from the grapes purchased under the GPA. California, as previously noted, requires final grape prices to be determined on or before January 10 in the year following harvest.[96] If a vintner fails to comply with the Berryhill Act, the grower has the option of

---

95. *See* Cal. Code. Regs., tit. 3 §§1650.15, 1658.3, 1661, 1661.1, 1661.2, 1661.4 (1921). *See also* California Winegrape Inspection Advisory Board, Defect Inspection Information, available at http://www.cwiab.org/pdf/Defect-Inspection-Information.pdf.

96. Cal. Food & Agric. Code §55601.5(g) (2021).

terminating the GPA, and the vintner may be investigated by the California Department of Agriculture.[97]

Price per Ton. This is the most common pricing mechanism in GPAs. In most cases, the price per ton is a fixed dollar amount. If the contract is longer term, there typically is a pricing adjustment mechanism tied to an outside index. Although the CPI is used frequently, it is not directly tied to grape prices and thus can lead to odd results. In California, a common alternative to the CPI is the annual percentage change in the weighted average price per ton of grapes paid for the given varietal in the local reporting district, as published in the Grape Crush Report. A downside to relying on the Grape Crush Report for adjusting pricing is the lag effect: pricing adjustments in a given year are based on changes in the prior year's Grape Crush Report.

The price per ton itself may be calculated by reference to the Grape Crush Report — for example, by setting the price per ton at the price corresponding to a particular level of cumulative tonnage for a specific varietal in a certain district. As an illustration, the price for Cabernet Sauvignon grapes may be set at the per-ton price corresponding to the 95th percentile of the total tonnage of Cabernet Sauvignon grapes sold in Napa County.

Per-Acre Pricing. In situations where the vintner controls farming practices, the grower may be concerned that the vintner could manage the farming in a manner that will reduce the crop yields, thereby reducing the price the grower will receive in a price-per-ton contract. An alternative is a fixed price per acre; under this formulation, annual yield fluctuations will not affect the amount the grower receives. It is common for the parties to adjust the price per acre by reference to an outside index such as the CPI or Grape Crush Report. Additionally, the parties should consider price adjustments for replanted or diseased vines or other natural factors that could reduce the crop yield. If the vintner resists per-acre pricing, the grower might consider a price-per-ton formula with a per-acre floor; the floor (minimum price) should be set at a level sufficient to cover the grower's farming costs plus a reasonable return on the grower's investment.

Bottle Pricing. In premium wine production, a grower may seek to share in the profit that the vintner earns from wine produced from the grower's grapes. One method to achieve this goal is to include a bonus pricing mechanism that is based on the bottle price of wine produced from the grower's grapes. In California, a significant obstacle to bottle pricing is the Berryhill Act. Converting grapes to finished, saleable wine takes between one and four years following harvest, making it impossible to know the price of the bottle of wine made from the grower's grapes by January 10 following harvest. Some GPAs include a bottle pricing payment that ties the price of the current year's grapes to the most

97. *Id.*§55601.5(g), (h).

recent vintage of wine being sold by the winery that was made from the grower's grapes. This approach, however, does not work for new wine offerings.

Other Price Adjustments. Price adjustments can be used to protect both grower and vintner from various risks depending on the context. In some cases, a GPA will include pricing adjustments based on certain qualities of the grapes delivered. For example, many vintners prefer grapes to have a higher sugar content, measured in degrees Brix. However, to achieve higher sugar content, the grower must delay harvest until later in the season, known as a long "hang time," when the risk of crop loss or weight loss is greater. If price were calculated on a per-ton basis, the grower would realize less revenue absent a price adjustment. To compensate the grower for the higher risk of loss and lower yield, the grower may insist that the vintner make increasing bonus payments as the Brix level rises above a threshold stated in the contract. In a per-acre contract, the vintner may require a downward price adjustment in the event of low yields resulting from acts of God or blight. In other cases, the vintner might require a downward price adjustment if the percentage of grapes with defects or MOG is too high. There are many variations on this theme.

Timing of Payment. Although the Berryhill Act requires that the price paid for grapes be determined by January 10 following harvest, there is no requirement that payment be made by that date or any other specific date. If the GPA does not include a provision regarding the timing of payments, however, the vintner must pay the grower within 30 days after taking delivery or possession of the grapes.[98] Ordinarily the parties will include a provision regarding the timing of payment(s). For tax purposes, the grower may desire to defer some or all of the payment until after December 31 of the harvest year. A common payment schedule is for 50 percent of the price to be paid within 30 days after harvest, with the balance due by January 15 of the year following harvest.

VINEYARD DESIGNATION

Many vintners use a vineyard designation on the label to identify the vineyard from which the vintner's wine was produced.[99] Under TTB regulations, a vintner may not use a vineyard designation on its label unless 95 percent of the wine in the bottle was produced from fruit grown in the named vineyard.[100]

---

98. Cal. Food & Agric. Code §55601 (2021).

99. Two well-known examples of vineyard designation are Martha's Vineyard in Napa and the Sangiacamo Vineyard in Sonoma. See Heitz Cellar, Martha's Vineyard, http://www.heitzcellar.com/vineyards/marthas.cfm (last visited Jan. 7, 2011); Sangiacamo Family Vineyards, Our Clients, http://www.sangiacomo-vineyards.com/wines/clients (last visited Jan. 7, 2011).

100. 27 C.F.R. §4.39(m) (2021).

It is the grower, not the winery, that possesses rights in the vineyard name. However, according to the doctrine of "fair use," if a grower sells wine grapes under a vineyard name, the winery may fairly use that name, even without the grower's consent, on the wine produced from those grapes to designate origin so long as such use complies with TTB vineyard designation labeling requirements. A grower that wishes to control the winery's ability to use the vineyard name on wine should include language in the grape purchase agreement prohibiting the use of the vineyard name without the grower's prior consent.

If the parties envision the winery's use of a vineyard designation at the time of the contract negotiation, the contract should explicitly authorize that use and specify that, upon termination of the contract, the winery shall cease use of the vineyard name (except on wines already produced from the grower's grapes). A grower holding a trademark registration for a vineyard name might consider licensing the name to the winery for use as a vineyard designation on the winery's label.[101] Such an arrangement is more typical in a long-term relationship and provides the winery with clear rights to use the name and the grower with an additional economic return in the form of a royalty and additional goodwill value in the vineyard.[102]

FARMING PRACTICE AND VITICULTURAL CONTROL

The description of farming practices can be quite basic ("consistent with viticultural practices in Santa Barbara County") or quite detailed, with reference to a farming plan. Traditionally, the grower will control farming practices, but in some premium wine programs, the GPA gives that control to the vintner. Growers are understandably hesitant to cede control over farming, particularly when the grape price is set on a per-ton basis.[103] For that reason, if the GPA allows the vintner to control farming practices, the grower should negotiate for a per-acre price so that the grower will be unaffected by reduced yields. A compromise is to provide for cooperative control over farming, requiring consensus between grower and vintner for certain farming decisions. This approach may prove difficult in practice, however. Other provisions that should be negotiated in tandem with farming practices include risk-of-loss provisions

---

101. The owner of a new vineyard may file for an "intent to use" trademark application, which will reserve the grower's rights in the name pending maturation of the vineyard and sufficient use of the name in interstate commerce to qualify for trademark status. See 15 U.S.C. §1051(b)(1) (2020).

102. *See* J. Scott Gerien, The Vineyard Designation: Branding & Trademark Issues for Wineries & Vineyard Owners, Wine Business Monthly, Apr. 15, 2003, available at http://www.winebusiness.com/wbm/?go=getArticle&dataId=23622 (last visited Jan. 7, 2011). In some cases, the vintner and grower will jointly apply for and hold a trademark for a specific vineyard. This aligns the parties' interests and in some cases allows the vintner to continue using the mark after the GPA and license agreement have been canceled.

103. The concern is that a vintner might intentionally reduce crop yield to improve grape quality or for some nefarious purpose, thereby reducing the overall payment under the GPA.

and quality standards; greater vintner control makes it less fair for the grower to be forced to bear the risk of loss or meet rigid quality standards.

HARVEST, DELIVERY, AND RISK OF LOSS

Traditionally, the vintner instructs the grower when to harvest grapes. In most cases, the vintner will want the grapes to mature on the vine as long as possible to increase sugars and enhance flavor profiles. The grower, on the other hand, will be eager to harvest sooner rather than later because of the risk that late fall rains could cause mold or other damage. Additionally, the longer the grapes hang on the vine, the more water weight they lose, which affects price in a GPA with per-ton pricing. The grower should consider a "harvest notice" provision whereby the grower will notify the vintner that the grapes are ready for harvest as soon as they reach pre-determined Brix and pH levels. If the vintner elects to delay harvest beyond this point, the risk of loss passes to the vintner.

The harvest provision often describes the manner of harvest (e.g., manual or machine harvesting) and might even require a specific size of picking bin (e.g., a half-ton bin). The contract should address delivery scheduling. Harvest is a hectic time at a winery because grapes arrive throughout the day, often from multiple vineyard sources. The grower should provide a minimum notice time (24 or 48 hours, for example) before delivering grapes.

The parties should determine when the risk of loss passes. Typically, the risk of loss passes to the winery when the grapes are off-loaded at the crush pad, but the grower might request that risk of loss pass when the truck enters the winery's premises. The reason for such a provision is that the grower should not be held accountable if the grapes are damaged because of a delay at the winery's crush pad.

A BRIEF NOTE ON GROWER'S LIENS

In California, any farmer, including a grape grower, who delivers a crop to an agricultural processor,[104] including a winery, automatically obtains a lien on the crop and products made from the crop by operation of law until the grower is paid in full. Although the statute refers to this as the producer's lien, it is commonly known in industry vernacular as the "grower's lien."[105] This lien is superior to a secured lender's interest.

---

104. "Processor" means any person that is engaged in the business of processing or manufacturing any farm product, that solicits, buys, contracts to buy, or otherwise takes title to, or possession or control of, any farm product from the producer of the farm product for the purpose of processing or manufacturing it and selling, reselling, or redelivering it in any dried, canned, extracted, fermented, distilled, frozen, eviscerated, or other preserved or processed form. It does not, however, include any retail merchant that has a fixed or established place of business in this state and does not sell at wholesale any farm product which is processed or manufactured by him.

Cal. Food & Agric. Code §55407 (2021).

105. *Id.* §§55631-55653. In 2006 the grower's lien was greatly increased by California's Fifth District Court of Appeal in the case of *Frazier Nuts, Inc. v. American Ag Credit*, 141 Cal. App. 4th

While a powerful remedy for the grower, the grower's lien has limitations in practice. A grower may enforce a grower's lien only through judicial action, which can be very costly, especially if the GPA does not allow the prevailing party to recoup its attorney's fees. Additionally, many wine companies operate under a custom crush model and hold no processor's license.[106] If a grower sells grapes to such a buyer, the grower's lien will not apply by operation of law and, after delivering the grapes, the grower will simply be an unsecured creditor.

To enhance its position, particularly if it sells to a wine company that holds no processor's license, the grower should consider negotiating a provision allowing it to file a UCC-1 financing statement. By filing a UCC-1 financing statement, the grower could pursue non-judicial foreclosure or self-help repossession to enforce its security interest.[107] A vintner likely will resist granting the grower this right, particularly if doing so would violate the loan agreement between the vintner and its bank.

D. CONCLUSION

The American wine industry has evolved beyond a collection of traditional winery estates to a sophisticated modern industry with many options available for entering the industry. In view of the complicated and highly regulated nature of the wine business, the wine industry lawyer has an important role to play in advising vintners and growers about the various models for producing and selling wine and growing grapes.

1263 (2006). In this case, the court expanded the grower's lien to cover cash proceeds and accounts receivable arising from the sale of agricultural products, including wine.

106. Unless they also hold a CDFA processor's license, these companies are not considered "processors" under the California Food & Agriculture Code. *See* Cal. Food & Agric. Code §§55407, 55521 (2021).

107. *See* Cal. Comm. Code §§9601, 9609 (2021).

CHAPTER 5

THE COMMERCE CLAUSE AND THE TWENTY-FIRST AMENDMENT: AN EVOLVING CONSTITUTIONAL PUZZLE

Tracy Genesen and Justin McGuirk[1]

A. INTRODUCTION

The Commerce Clause provides that "Congress shall have the Power to regulate Commerce . . . among the several States."[2] Though phrased as a grant of interstate regulatory power to Congress, the Commerce Clause has long been understood to have a "negative" or dormant aspect that denies states the power to unjustifiably discriminate against or burden the interstate flow of commerce. This dormant Commerce Clause doctrine prohibits state economic protectionism—i.e., regulatory measures designed to benefit in-state economic interests by burdening out-of-state competitors.

The Supreme Court's understanding about whether and to what extent the dormant Commerce Clause limits a challenged state law has evolved over time. But when it comes to evaluating state alcohol regulations, the Court's decisions are more akin to a seesaw than an evolving continuum.

Prior to Prohibition, the Court struggled to draw the line between where the dormant Commerce Clause limitations began and state police powers and their legitimate interests ended. For the most part, the Court adopted a broad understanding of the dormant Commerce Clause which, in turn, limited the ability

1. Tracy Genesen and Justin McGuirk revised this section, which Margot Mendelson originally wrote. Margot is now the Litigation Director at the Prison Law Office, a non-profit organization headquartered in Berkeley, California, that protects the constitutional rights of people behind bars through advocacy, education, and litigation. Tracy and Justin extend their sincere gratitude to Margot and to Berkeley Law student Olga Baranoff, who assisted with research for this revised edition.

2. U.S. Const. art. I, §8, cl. 3.

of states to become fully "dry"—if they so desired—and frustrated advocates of the temperance movement. Indeed, the Court's decisions likely helped usher in Prohibition.

In the 1930s, after repeal of Prohibition, Supreme Court jurisprudence embraced "the dormant Commerce Clause" and readily struck down state laws that discriminated against out-of-state products: "states must sink or swim together . . . prosperity and salvation are in a union not division."[3] This was true for virtually all products sold in interstate commerce, except for alcoholic beverages.

The Court had a very different perspective when it came to state laws regulating alcohol in the years immediately after Prohibition ended. In a series of opinions that Justice Brandies wrote, the Court vigorously defended the absolute nature of states' authority to regulate alcohol under the Twenty-first Amendment.[4] In effect, the Amendment acted as a shield that could save even a discriminatory state law from any dormant Commerce Clause scrutiny. For almost 30 years, Justice Brandeis' broad interpretation of the Twenty-first Amendment was the law of the land, until the Court called that interpretation into question in *Hostetter v. Idlewild Bon Voyage Liquor Corp.*[5] Over the remainder of the Twentieth Century, the Court continued to broaden its view of the dormant Commerce Clause and narrow its understanding of whether and how the Twenty-first Amendment can "save" an otherwise discriminatory state law.

By 2005, in the landmark case *Granholm v. Heald*, the Court made clear that the non-discrimination principle of the dormant Commerce Clause applied to state regulation of alcohol.[6] There, the Court confronted the modern reality of e-commerce and struck down two state laws prohibiting out-of-state wine producers from shipping directly to in-state consumers. Then in 2019, the Court unequivocally reiterated its view and made clear its reasoning applied to state laws regulating any "tier"—i.e., alcohol producers, wholesalers, and retailers—of the three-tier distribution system.[7] In doing so, the Court struck down a state law requiring retailer licensee applicants to reside in the state for at least two years before applying for a retailer license. The Court's jurisprudence seemed in equipoise whereby the Twenty-first Amendment was not an absolute shield against the dormant Commerce Clause for otherwise discriminatory state laws.

Since the Supreme Court last addressed these issues, however, new theories appear to be taking hold in circuit and lower courts.[8] These theories and the

---

3. *Baldwin v. G. A. F. Seelig, Inc.*, 294 U.S. 511, 523 (1935).

4. The Amendment provides in part: "[t]he transportation or importation into any state … for delivery or use therein of intoxicating liquors, in violation of the laws thereof, is hereby prohibited." U.S. Const. amend. XXI, §2.

5. *See infra* at note 61 and related text.

6. 544 U.S. 460 (2005).

7. *Tenn. Wine & Spirits Retailers Ass'n v. Thomas*, 139 S. Ct. 2449 (2019).

8. *See, e.g., B-21 Wines, Inc. v. Bauer*, 36 F.4th 214, 229 (4th Cir. 2022) (holding that "although the [state law] discriminates against interstate commerce, it is nevertheless justified on the legitimate nonprotectionist ground of preserving North Carolina's three-tier system"); *Lebamoff Enters. v. Whitmer*, 956 F.3d 863, 867 (6th Cir. 2020) (holding that "the Twenty-first Amendment permits

resulting decisions posit that the three-tier distribution system is "unquestionably legitimate"—or, in essence, sacrosanct—under the Twenty-first Amendment. Thus, the Twenty-first Amendment "saves" state laws, including discriminatory laws, that regulate an "essential" feature of its three-tier system. The Supreme Court may soon need to decide whether it will get on the seesaw again.

B. AN OVERVIEW OF COMMERCE CLAUSE JURISPRUDENCE

The Supreme Court first interpreted the Commerce Clause in 1824—35 years after the Constitution's ratification. In the earliest cases, the Court navigated among broadly divergent interpretations of the Commerce Clause and its implications. By one account, the clause granted the federal government complete authority over interstate commerce to the exclusion of state legislative authority. By another account, the clause required deference to states in all matters about which Congress had not explicitly legislated. Although the Court wavered about the extent of permissible state authority over interstate commerce, the early cases paved a tentative middle path between extreme interpretations of the clause. Through these cases, the Court adopted a doctrine of partial federal exclusivity and recognized concurrent powers of state and federal legislation.

In its earliest interpretation of the Commerce Clause, the Supreme Court invalidated a New York state law that granted private individuals the exclusive right to operate in interstate waterways.[9] Although the case, *Gibbons v. Ogden,* turned on the Supremacy Clause, in which the Court construed a 1793 law as authorizing American vessels to engage in interstate trade,[10] it also raised critical questions about the relationship of state police power to federal commerce power. The opinion is considered an early articulation of the dormant Commerce Clause because it indicated that the constitutional grant of power to the federal government significantly limited state legislative authority over interstate commerce:

> Few things were better known, than the immediate causes which led to the adoption of the present constitution . . . that the prevailing motive was *to regulate commerce;* to rescue it from the embarrassing and destructive consequences, resulting from the legislation of so many different States, and to place it under the protection of a uniform law.[11]

Michigan to treat in-state retailers (who operate within the three-tier system) differently from out-of-state retailers (who do not)" and upholding state law); *Sarasota Wine Mkt., LLC v. Schmitt*, 987 F.3d 1171, 1184 (8th Cir. 2021) (finding "we should be no more invasive of the 'unquestionably legitimate' three-tiered system than the Supreme Court has mandated" and affirming dismissal for failing to state viable dormant Commerce Clause claims).

9. *Gibbons v. Ogden,* 22 U.S. 1 (1824).

10. Act of February 18, 1793, 1 Stat. 305 ("An Act for enrolling and licensing ships or vessels to be employed in the coasting trade and fisheries, and for regulating the same").

11. *Gibbons,* 22 U.S. at 11 (emphasis added).

Gibbons was a forceful assertion of exclusive federal power over interstate commerce. Indeed, *Gibbons* gave rise to the term "dormant Commerce Clause," in addition to articulating the logic of the concept. In dicta, Chief Justice John Marshall referred to a power to regulate interstate commerce which "can never be exercised by the people themselves, but must be placed in the hands of agents, or lie dormant."[12]

C. ALCOHOLIC BEVERAGES AND THE DORMANT COMMERCE CLAUSE BEFORE PROHIBITION

A constant march of liquor cases through the courts, as well as the interplay between Congress and the courts over liquor laws, left an indelible mark on Commerce Clause jurisprudence in years leading up to National Prohibition. Supreme Court decisions during that time left states with some—albeit limited—authority to legislate on matters that affect interstate commerce, but in general the Court's decisions provided increasingly robust understandings of the dormant Commerce Clause's limitations on states. As the political and jurisprudential winds shifted, the air of uncertainty pushed prohibitionists to seek what they hoped would be a more permanent solution in the form of a constitutional amendment.

1. THE ORIGINAL PACKAGES DOCTRINE

Three years after *Gibbons*, Chief Justice Marshall again considered the scope of the Commerce Clause in *Brown v. Maryland*, a case involving the states' power to regulate imported goods.[13] In this early liquor law case, the Court held that a state could not levy a license fee on foreign importers until the import had "become incorporated and mixed up with the mass of property in the country."[14] In reaching its decision, the Court had to define "commerce" and determine its scope. The Chief Justice built upon the expansive conception of "commerce . . . among the several States" that the Court had announced in *Gibbons,* defining commerce not just as traffic, but as "commercial intercourse" that necessarily extends beyond the external boundaries of each state and reaches from one state into another.[15] In the context of foreign trade, which Congress had explicitly authorized, the Court concluded that the state had no ability to impose a fee on an imported alcoholic beverage until the product "has become incorporated and mixed up with the mass of property in the country, . . . [and] lost its distinctive character as an import, and has become subject to the taxing power of the State; but while remaining the property of the importer, in his warehouse, in the original form or package in which it was imported, a tax upon

12. *Id.* at 189. The Chief Justice again referred to the federal "power to regulate commerce in its dormant State" in dicta in *Willson v. Black Bird Creek Marsh Co.,* 27 U.S. 245, 252 (1829).

13. 25 U.S. 419 (1827).

14. *Id.* at 441-42.

15. *Id.* at 451.

it is too plainly a duty on imports to escape the prohibition in the constitution."[16] This theory came to be known as the "original packages doctrine."

2. STATE AUTHORITY TO REGULATE ISSUES AFFECTING INTERSTATE COMMERCE

In *Willson v. Black Bird Creek Marsh Co.*, Chief Justice Marshall produced his third opinion involving the Commerce Clause, which departed somewhat from *Gibbons* in upholding a Delaware state law authorizing the construction of a dam that blocked passage through a navigable stream.[17] The Court found no conflict between the Delaware act and any federal law and concluded that the construction of the dam constituted a legitimate exercise of state police power, not "repugnant to the [federal] power to regulate commerce in its dormant state."[18] Thus, the Court afforded the states some measure of authority to legislate on matters that affect interstate commerce.

Eighteen years later, with Marshall no longer presiding, the Court returned to the subject of the states' ability to regulate trade in alcoholic beverages. In 1847 the Court considered three consolidated cases challenging the alcoholic beverage laws of Massachusetts, Rhode Island, and New Hampshire, known as *The License Cases*.[19] The Court issued a unanimous decision with six separate opinions that share little, if any, common ground. Nonetheless, the Court made two separate and important holdings. First, the Court upheld the Massachusetts and Rhode Island licensing requirements for alcoholic beverage retailers because, as applied to imported liquors, those licensing laws "act upon the article *after* it has passed the line of foreign commerce and become a part of the general mass of property in the state."[20] Second, with respect to interstate commerce, the Court upheld a New Hampshire licensing requirement for purveyors of distilled spirits and wines. The case involved an unlicensed importer of a barrel of gin from another state. The Court upheld the state's licensing law because Congress had not exercised its Commerce Clause authority by passing any law about interstate trade in liquor. The holding echoed the Marshall Court's approach in *Willson v. Black Bird Creek Marsh Co.* in its deference to the states' rights to regulate matters involving interstate commerce in the absence of federal action. As Chief Justice Taney wrote in the *License Cases*:

> [T]he mere grant of power to the general government cannot, upon any just principles of construction, be construed to be an absolute prohibition to the exercise of any power over the same subject by the states .... [T]he state may . . . for the safety or convenience of trade, or for the protection of the health of its citizens, make

---

16. *Id.* at 441-42.
17. 27 U.S. 245 (1829).
18. *Id.* at 252.
19. 46 U.S. 504 (1847).
20. *Id.* at 577 (emphasis added).

> regulations of commerce for its own ports and harbors, and for its own territory; and such regulations are valid unless they come in conflict with a law of Congress.[21]

It should be noted that this was only one approach that the Court would employ in deciding when the Commerce Clause deprives the states of their regulatory authority. In *Cooley v. Board of Wardens,* the Court upheld a state law that required ships entering and leaving the port of Philadelphia to hire local pilots.[22] In this ruling, the Court articulated a different test for the application of Commerce Clause principles. The Court reached its holding in *Cooley* based on the subject matter of the challenged law—i.e., states could appropriately legislate local subject matter, but national subject matter was reserved exclusively for uniform federal legislation. "[U]ntil Congress should find it necessary to exert its power, it should be left to the legislation of the states; that it is local and not national; that it is likely to be the best provided for, not by one system, or plan of regulations, but by as many as the legislative discretion of the several states should deem applicable to the local peculiarities of the ports within their limits."[23] The Court adopted yet another approach just over 10 years later, when it attempted to distinguish between *direct* and *indirect* burdens on interstate commerce in determining which laws to uphold. In *Smith v. Alabama,* the Court upheld state licensing of locomotive engineers on the grounds that it affected interstate commerce "only indirectly, incidentally, and remotely."[24]

3. INTERPLAY BETWEEN THE STATES, COURTS, AND CONGRESS LEADING UP TO PROHIBITION

Chief Justice Marshall's enunciation in 1827 of the "original packages doctrine" had a direct effect on the growing temperance movement in the United States. As the states began to adopt laws curtailing the sale of alcoholic beverages, the doctrine prevented them from banning the importation of wines, beers, and spirits from abroad that remained in their original packages. For that reason, the Maine Law of 1851, which spawned a wave of prohibitory laws across the U.S., expressly exempted alcoholic beverages "of foreign production . . . imported under the laws of the United States . . . contained in the original packages."[25]

During that time, the Court struck down restrictive state laws that discriminated against out-of-state or foreign interests. In *Walling v. Michigan,* the Court overturned a state tax imposed on persons residing outside the state who sold liquor to be shipped into the state; again, no such tax was imposed on in-state sellers of alcoholic beverages produced in the state.[26] In *Walling,* the Court specifically distinguished Michigan's tax from the occupational taxes on liquor purveyors that

21. *Id.* at 579.
22. 53 U.S. 299 (1851).
23. *Id.* at 319.
24. 124 U.S. 465, 482 (1888).
25. 1851 Me. Acts 211, §11.
26. 116 U.S. 446 (1886).

had been upheld in *The License Cases,* noting that unlike the tax at issue in *Walling,* those taxes did not "operate as a discriminative burden against the introduction and sale of the products of another State, or against the citizens of another state."[27]

In the last two decades of the nineteenth century, the Court broadened its understanding of the dormant Commerce Clause's limitations on states. The Court overturned prohibitory laws that, although not overtly discriminatory, restricted interstate and foreign commerce. In the eyes of temperance crusaders, the Court's opinions demonstrated its preference for interstate commerce over instate interests. With each decision, they became more incensed. The dry state of Iowa, surrounded by wet states like Illinois, provided the setting for several of the most significant cases in the period leading up to National Prohibition. In an 1888 case, *Bowman v. Chicago and Northwestern Railway Company*, the Court overturned Iowa's prohibitory law because it banned the importation of alcoholic beverages from other states.[28] The Bowman brothers sued the Chicago and Northwestern Railroad for refusing to ship 5,000 barrels of beer from a location in Chicago to a location in Iowa, where they intended to sell the beer. The railroad company sought to defend the law as a quarantine regulation or a sanitary measure. The Court acknowledged the defendant's argument that states possessed the power to prohibit the introduction of articles of trade that "would bring in and spread disease, pestilence and death, such as rags or other substances infected with the germs of yellow fever, or the virus of small-pox, or cattle or meat or other provisions that are diseased or decayed, or otherwise, from their condition and quality, unfit for human use or consumption."[29] Indeed, the Court declared that such articles "are not legitimate subjects of trade and commerce . . . . The self-protecting power of each state, therefore, may be rightfully exerted against their introduction, and such exercises of power cannot be considered regulations of commerce prohibited by the constitution."[30]

Nonetheless, in its *Bowman* decision, the Court rejected the argument that alcoholic beverages are inherently deleterious to human health and safety. The Court warned of the dangers of permitting states to prohibit the importation of *"any* . . . article, the use or abuse of which it may deem deleterious" and decried the confusion and protectionism that would result if each state could make its own determination about which commercial products could be outlawed.[31] Ultimately, the Court held that the states did not have the "right and power to prevent [the] introduction [of intoxicating liquors] by transportation from another State."[32] As the Court stated, "[t]he absence of any law of Congress on the subject is equivalent to its declaration

27. *Id.* at 461. The Court also overturned a state law imposing a "peddler's license tax" on persons selling various goods not manufactured in the state when there was no such tax on peddlers selling in-state goods. *Welton v. Missouri,* 91 U.S. 275 (1875). The goods in that case were sewing machines, not liquor.

28. 125 U.S. 465 (1888).

29. *Id.* at 489.

30. *Id.*

31. *Id.* at 494 (emphasis added).

32. *Id.* at 500.

that commerce in that matter shall be free."[33] The Court, however, did not decide at what point in the stream of commerce the state could permissibly regulate the liquor in question.

For the growing number of temperance activists, the Court's robust defense of open state borders meant that the "very existence of wet states" posed a "constant and insidious threat . . . to the order and security of dry states."[34] Not only could imported alcoholic beverages in their original packages enter a dry state (following *Brown v. Maryland*) but now also alcoholic beverages from other states. What began as judicial quibbling over a puzzling clause of the Constitution had arrived at the saloon, church, dinner table, and city hall.

The Court took another step toward dismantling state prohibition measures in the name of Commerce Clause principles two years later in *Leisy v. Hardin,* a decision that all but ushered in Congressional legislation to facilitate statewide prohibition.[35] Leisy Brewery, located in Illinois, shipped its packaged beer to an Iowa retailer who sold it in its original package, in violation of Iowa's prohibitory law.[36] Leisy challenged the law, and the Court struck it down as a violation of the Commerce Clause. In overturning the law, the Court for the first time established the point at which interstate commerce protection ended and the state's police power attached, holding that the plaintiffs "had the right to import this beer into [Iowa], and in the view which we have expressed they had the right to sell it, by which act alone it would become mingled in the common mass of property within the state. Up to that point of time, we hold that, in the absence of congressional permission to do so the state had no power to interfere by seizure, or any other action in prohibition of importation and sale."[37] Congressional silence no longer would be interpreted as an authorization of state action. After *Leisy,* which effectively overturned *The License Cases* of 1847, states could no longer bar out-of-state liquor from sale in its original package, notwithstanding congressional silence.

The Court's *Leisy* ruling confirmed temperance activists' worst fears. "The *Leisy* ruling," according to historian Richard Hamm, "flooded the dry states with liquor."[38] "Within a month of the ruling, 'original package houses'. . . had sprung up in every prohibition state."[39] Suddenly, dry states that had been waging war against the saloon for decades confronted a new and apparently lawful incarnation of their old foe.

The language of the *Bowman* and *Leisy* decisions suggests that the Court may have been pressing Congress to act. Both decisions are relatively deferential to the

---

33. *Id.* at 508.

34. Norman H. Clark, Deliver Us from Evil: An Interpretation of American Prohibition 118 (1976).

35. 135 U.S. 100 (1890).

36. After *Bowman* Iowa repealed its nuisance law and provided that no intoxicating liquor, domestic or foreign, could be sold in Iowa except for pharmaceutical and medical purposes or, in the case of wines, for sacramental use. 22d General Ass., Iowa Acts 91, ch. 71. It was this new law that *Leisy* challenged.

37. *Leisy,* 135 U.S. at 124.

38. Richard F. Hamm, Shaping the Eighteenth Amendment 70 (1995).

39. *Id.* at 69.

goals of temperance ideology, and they specifically point to the absence of congressional direction as the critical factor in their conclusions. In *Bowman,* the Court explained that it was legally bound to strike down the state's alcohol regulations "however desirable such [] regulation[s] might be," and that only the "consent of congress, express or implied" could enable such laws to advance.[40] The *Leisy* decision referred to "the absence of legislation on the part of congress" and pointed out that the outcome was unrelated to the Justices' "individual views" about "the deleterious or dangerous qualities" of the regulated items.[41]

Under pressure from temperance advocates, Congress passed the Original Packages Act, commonly known as the Wilson Act, in the summer of 1890. The Wilson Act provided that "all . . . intoxicating liquors . . . transported into any State . . . for use, consumption, sale or storage therein, shall upon arrival in such State . . . be subject to the operation and effect of the laws of such State . . . enacted in the exercise of its police powers, to the same extent and in the same manner as though such . . . liquors had been produced in such State . . . and shall not be exempt therefrom by reason of being introduced therein in original packages or otherwise."[42] The Act was intended not to implement prohibition at a national level but rather to overcome the constitutional barriers to state prohibitory laws. Simply stated, the law "empowered the States to regulate imported liquor on the same terms as domestic liquor."[43] If a state prohibited the sale of alcoholic beverages within its borders, it no longer would have to allow out-of-state and out-of-country imports of the prohibited goods. In this way, a dry state could seal its borders without running afoul of the law or exposing itself to costly constitutional litigation.

Although the Act survived an initial challenge in which the Court held that it did not constitute an impermissible delegation of Congress's commerce power to the states,[44] it soon fell to the same Commerce Clause challenges that had laid waste to so many of its state law antecedents. In *Rhodes v. Iowa,* a railway station agent in the state had been charged and convicted under an amended version of the state's prohibitory law for having received a wooden box containing liquor shipped from Illinois directly to an Iowa resident.[45] The railway company appealed the conviction, arguing that neither the Wilson Act nor Iowa's prohibitory law could lawfully apply to consumer-direct interstate liquor sales. The Court agreed, holding that the state law could not attach to imports before they reached their point of destination within the state. Acknowledging that the Wilson Act "[u]ndoubtedly" was

40. *Bowman,* 125 U.S. at 493.

41. *Leisy,* 135 U.S. at 110, 125.

42. Original Packages (Wilson) Act, ch. 728, 26 Stat. 313 (1890).

43. *Granholm v. Heald*, 544 U.S. 460, 461 (2005). In *Scott v. Donald*, 165 U.S. 58, 100 (1897), the Court held that under the Wilson Act, a "[s]tate cannot ... establish a system which, in effect, discriminates between interstate and domestic commerce in commodities to make and use which are admitted to be lawful."

44. *Wilkerson v. Rahrer*, 140 U.S. 545 (1891). The Court found that Congress had not "attempted to delegate the power to regulate commerce" but instead had "taken its own course, and made its own regulation, applying to these subjects of interstate commerce one common rule, whose uniformity is not affected by variations in state laws." *Id.* at 561.

45. 170 U.S. 412 (1898).

intended to enable states to control "intoxicating liquors" in original packages at an earlier date than would have been otherwise the case, the Court nonetheless interpreted the statutory language "upon arrival in such state" to mean following delivery to the consignee rather than upon crossing the state line.[46] Finding otherwise would have destroyed the right to contract for shipments beyond the state: "The right to contract for the transportation of merchandise from one state into or across another involved interstate commerce in its fundamental aspect."[47]

In so holding, the Court carved out yet another loophole for the entry of liquor into dry states. Although a drinker might be prohibited from purchasing liquor in a dry state, they could order it from out-of-state dealers without unreasonable state interference. Once again, Congress was called upon to fix an intolerable outcome. In 1913, it passed the Webb-Kenyon Act, which prohibits the interstate shipment of "spirituous, vinous, malted, fermented, or other intoxicating liquor [which] is intended, by any person interested therein, to be received, possessed, sold, or in any manner used, either in the original package or otherwise," in violation of any law of the state into which they are shipped.[48] In passing the Act, Congress expressed its unambiguous intent to allow dry states to stop direct-to-consumer interstate liquor shipments.[49]

The Webb-Kenyon Act, however, did not allay prohibitionists' fears that a future Congress or Supreme Court would reverse course. To protect their cause from wavering political and jurisprudential tides, they pressed for a constitutional amendment that, they hoped, would resolve the matter forever. Led by the politically powerful and astute Anti-Saloon League and bolstered by the Women's Christian Temperance Union, as well as church and business leaders, the prohibition movement propelled Congress to adopt the Eighteenth Amendment in December 1917. Thirty-six states ratified the amendment by 1919. The full Amendment provides:

> Section 1. After one year from the ratification of this article the manufacture, sale, or transportation of intoxicating liquors within, the importation thereof into, or the

---

46. *Id.* at 424.

47. *Id.* at 424.

48. Webb-Kenyon Act, ch. 90, 37 Stat. 699 (1913) (codified at 27 U.S.C. §122 (2006)). The Webb-Kenyon Act carried no specific provisions for federal enforcement and included no penalties; that was left to the states. Prosecutions for violation of the state prohibitory laws were to be in state courts. Interestingly, that issue was addressed 87 years after the enactment of the Webb-Kenyon Act, with the passage of the Twenty-first Amendment Enforcement Act, Pub. L. No. 106-386, 114 Stat. 1547 (2000) (codified at 27 U.S.C. §122a (2006)). That law for the first time granted state attorneys general federal court jurisdiction to pursue potential civil injunctive relief for alleged violations of state law regulating the importation or transportation of alcohol.

49. The Webb-Kenyon Act was challenged on constitutional grounds in *James Clark Distilling Co. v. Western Maryland Railway Co.*, 242 U.S. 311 (1917). There, a railway company that had transported liquor interstate for personal use argued that the Act was an impermissible delegation of Congress's Commerce Clause authority and was not uniform in its state-by-state application. The Supreme Court upheld the law, just as it had upheld the Wilson Act in *In re Rahrer*, 140 U.S. 545 (1891).

> exportation thereof from the United States and all territory subject to the jurisdiction thereof for beverage purposes is hereby prohibited.
>
> Section 2. The Congress and the several States shall have concurrent power to enforce this article by appropriate legislation.

The efforts of the federal and state governments to enforce National Prohibition are beyond the scope of this chapter. Suffice it to say that the liquor trade never really died; it simply went underground, with criminal syndicates, local gangsters, and even heretofore law-abiding citizens partaking in illegal liquor production and sale.[50]

Just as the onset of World War I prepared the nation for sacrifices that National Prohibition entailed, the Great Depression of 1929 advanced the cause of repeal of the Eighteenth Amendment. Among the groups advocating repeal were the Association Against the Prohibition Amendment, the Voluntary Committee of Lawyers, the Women's Organization for National Prohibition Reform, labor unions, medical societies, and business leaders. Ultimately, they succeeded, and Congress and the states for a second time enshrined "intoxicating liquors" in the U.S. Constitution.

D. PROHIBITION, REPEAL, AND THE JUDICIAL AFTERMATH: THE COMMERCE CLAUSE AND THE TWENTY-FIRST AMENDMENT

Repeal happened quickly. Congress passed the resolution proposing the Twenty-first Amendment on February 20, 1933. For the first time, Congress called for state conventions rather than state legislatures to ratify the Amendment under Article V of the Constitution.[51] Prohibition officially ended when Utah became the thirty-sixth state to ratify Repeal on December 5, 1933. With Repeal a new set of tensions arose surrounding the regulation of alcohol. The purposes of the Twenty-first Amendment were to repeal Prohibition (§1) and to restore to the states the ability to regulate their own liquor markets—even to the point of forbidding alcoholic beverage sales altogether (§2). Wisconsin Senator John Blaine, a member of the drafting committee, stated that the purpose of §2 was "to assure the so-called dry States against the importation of intoxicating liquor into those States."[52] Virginia Senator Carter Glass added, "Liquors may be shipped across a State in interstate commerce from one wet State to another wet State, but [§2] as I have drafted it prohibits the shipment of intoxicating liquors into a State whose laws prohibit the manufacture, sale, or

---

50. *See* Richard Mendelson, From Demon to Darling: A Legal History of Wine in America 78-85 (2009).

51. State conventions as a means of ratification were proposed largely "to circumvent the various state legislatures, where, it [was] feared, dry legislators from rural districts (because rural districts were represented with a strength so inconsistent with their actual population) might present a serious barrier to ratification." *Clark*, *supra* note 34, at 205.

52. 76 Cong. Rec. 4141 (1933).

transportation of liquors."[53] Thus §2 allowed states to remain dry after Prohibition ended, and many states did so:

> Section 2. The transportation or importation into any State, Territory, or possession of the United States for delivery or use therein of intoxicating liquors, in violation of the laws thereof, is hereby prohibited.

The challenge of interpreting this sentence and reconciling it with disparate sections of the Constitution has plagued courts since Repeal and continues to do so today.

Of course, the right of states to regulate the passage of alcohol into and through their borders was a subject of controversy well before Prohibition or Repeal, by virtue of the unique moral, religious, and social issues surrounding the consumption and distribution of alcohol. To suggest that the regulation of alcohol was ever a subject of scrutiny equivalent to the regulation of milk or other commonplace goods would vastly overlook the passions on all sides of the issue from the early days of the Union.[54] Nonetheless, the passage of Repeal set the stage for the battles waged in the courts today. These battles are not just philosophical and cannot be understood simply as functions of the evolution of Commerce Clause jurisprudence. Instead, they revolve around tensions between the language of the Twenty-first Amendment and the strictures of the dormant Commerce Clause.

1. EARLY AND EXPANSIVE VIEW OF THE TWENTY-FIRST AMENDMENT

By the 1930s, the Supreme Court well-understood the Commerce Clause's important role in preserving a national union and its force when applied to state laws that interfered with interstate commerce of products that were not alcohol. Justice Cardozo summarized that view well when he wrote that the Constitution "was framed upon the theory that the peoples of the several states must sink or swim together, and that in the long run prosperity and salvation are in union and not division."[55] In the immediate aftermath of Repeal, however, the Court also expressed the view that state action regarding alcohol, even if discriminatory, would be upheld on account of the Twenty-first Amendment's explicit grant of authority to the states. This position was set forth in a series of opinions that Justice Brandeis wrote, which vigorously defended the absolute nature of states' authority to

53. *Id.* at 4219.

54. As Justice Stevens stated in his dissent in *Brown-Forman Distillers Corp. v. New York State Liquor Auth.*, 476 U.S. 573, 590 (1986): "For some of us who were 'present at the creation' of the Twenty-first Amendment, there is an aura of unreality in [the] assumption that we must examine the validity of New York's Alcoholic Beverage Control Law (ABC Law) just as we would examine the constitutionality of a state statute governing the sale of gasoline'—or, I would add, of milk" (alterations in original). Justice Stevens quotes Judge Friendly in *Battigalia v. New York State Liquor Auth.*, 745 F.2d 166, 168 (2d Cir. 1984), but Judge Friendly refers only to gasoline; Justice Stevens added milk.

55. *Baldwin v. G. A. F. Seelig, Inc.*, 294 U.S. 511, 523 (1935).

regulate alcohol. Principal among those opinions was the 1936 case of *State Board of Equalization v. Young's Market Company,* in which the Court upheld a California law requiring a beer wholesaler there to obtain a $500 importer's license and a $50 wholesaler's license for the privilege of importing beer and then selling it in the state while wholesalers of beer produced in California needed only a wholesaler's license.[56] The Court held that §2 of the Twenty-first Amendment plainly "confer[s] upon the State the power to forbid all importations which do not comply with the conditions which it prescribes"—whether or not the regulations were reasonable.

Another Brandeis opinion three years later, *Indianapolis Brewing Company v. Liquor Control Commission,* went further.[57] There, the Court upheld a Michigan law that prohibited dealers in the state from purchasing, selling, receiving, or possessing beer manufactured in any state that discriminated against beer manufactured in Michigan—10 states at the time. The Court dismissed the plaintiff's challenges to the law despite claims that the law was retaliatory and patently violated the Commerce Clause, stating that "[f]or *whatever its character,* the law is valid. Since the Twenty-first Amendment, as held in the *Young* Case, the right of a state to prohibit or regulate the importation of intoxicating liquor *is not limited by the commerce clause. . . .*"[58]

The Brandeis opinions do not reveal the precise analysis that led the Court to its conclusion that the Twenty-first Amendment trumped the Commerce Clause. Perhaps the Court was following the logic that the more precise provision of the Constitution, namely the Twenty-first Amendment with respect to intoxicating liquor, prevailed over the more general provision—the Commerce Clause. The Court's decisions also could be rationalized based on plain meaning; certainly, the language of the Twenty-first Amendment includes no limitation on state regulatory authority over the transportation or importation of alcoholic beverages for delivery or use in the state. The legislative history offers some support for the Court's holdings.[59] Proponents of absolute state control over the delivery and use of alcoholic beverages within state borders pointed to the initial inclusion of §3 in the Twenty-first Amendment, which gave Congress and the states concurrent power over alcoholic beverage sales at on-site retail establishments like bars and restaurants. That section provided that "Congress shall have concurrent power to regulate or prohibit the sale of intoxicating liquors to be drunk on the premises where sold."[60] Congress later deleted the provision because of concerns about federal jurisdiction over purely intrastate businesses. Nonetheless, proponents of the Brandeis approach argue that the deletion of §3 and the absence of any discussion of concurrent powers in §2 suggest that the grant of state authority is exclusive and absolute.

---

56. 299 U.S. 59 (1936).

57. 305 U.S. 391 (1939).

58. *Id.* at 394 (citation omitted) (emphasis added).

59. *See generally* Todd Zywicki & Asheesh Agarwal, *Wine, Commerce, and the Constitution,* 1 N.Y.U. J. L. & Liberty 609, 625-39 (2005).

60. Boris I. Bittker, Bittker on the Regulation of Interstate and Foreign Commerce §13.02, at 13-15 (1999).

2. MODERN COMMERCE CLAUSE JURISPRUDENCE

Over time, however, the absolutist tone of the Brandeis opinions yielded to a more flexible interpretation of the competing concerns of the Twenty-first Amendment and the Commerce Clause. The Court's 1964 decision in *Hostetter v. Idlewild Bon Voyage Liquor Corporation* marked a significant retreat from its hardline approach following Repeal.[61] There, the Court examined the case of a company engaged in selling duty-free alcoholic beverages to departing international airline travelers at a New York airport, for delivery upon arrival at their foreign destinations. The New York State Liquor Authority sought to halt the business and to prohibit the passage of liquor through New York State territory to the airport liquor store. In examining the case, the Court considered "whether the Twenty-first Amendment so far obliterates the Commerce Clause as to empower New York to prohibit absolutely the passage of liquor through its territory, . . . acting under federal law, for delivery to consumers in foreign countries. For it is not disputed that, if the commodity involved here were not liquor, but grain or lumber, the Commerce Clause would clearly deprive New York of any such power."[62]

The *Hostetter* Court enjoined New York from interfering with Idlewild's business and, in so doing, rejected the complete subordination of the Commerce Clause to the Twenty-first Amendment in no uncertain terms: "To draw a conclusion from this line of decisions that the Twenty-first Amendment has somehow operated to 'repeal' the Commerce Clause wherever regulation of intoxicating liquors is concerned would, however, be an absurd oversimplification. If the Commerce Clause had been pro tanto 'repealed,' then Congress would be left with no regulatory power over interstate or foreign commerce in intoxicating liquor. Such a conclusion would be patently bizarre and is demonstrably incorrect."[63] Rather, the Court implemented a balancing test that, though vague, reflected the complexity of the question that confronted it: "Both the Twenty-first Amendment and the Commerce Clause are parts of the same Constitution. Like other provisions of the Constitution, each must be considered in the light of the other, and in the context of the issues and interests at stake in any concrete case."[64]

Hostetter can be understood in part as a reflection of the broader developments taking place in dormant Commerce Clause jurisprudence in the decades following Repeal. Many of the cases that define the modern approach to the dormant

61. 377 U.S. 324 (1964).

62. *Id.* at 329. Arguably, *Hostetter* did not actually invoke the Twenty-first Amendment because the liquor was not destined for "delivery or use" within the state. However, because the state had an interest in ensuring that alcoholic beverage imports destined for the retailer, Idlewild, were not diverted en route, the Twenty-first Amendment was implicated. Concerns about the diversion of alcohol constitute an important state interest that is directly related to the delivery and use of alcohol in the state. *See, e.g., North Dakota v. United States,* 495 U.S. 423 (1990) (alcoholic beverages destined for federal lands within the state fall under the Twenty-first Amendment because of the states' interest in prohibiting diversion of alcohol).

63. *Hostetter*, 377 U.S. at 331-32.

64. *Id.* at 332.

Commerce Clause arose during the 1960s and 1970s. Although the cases did not raise the unique concerns about alcohol that are at issue in the Brandeis cases and *Hostetter*—i.e., balancing the principles of the Commerce Clause and the scope of the Twenty-first Amendment's delegation of authority to states—they demonstrate the Court's changing perspectives on the power of states to regulate matters affecting interstate commerce in the absence of federal legislation.

Modern approaches to the dormant Commerce Clause have long discarded *Cooley's* subject matter-based inquiry and distinctions between direct and indirect burdens on interstate commerce, as did *Smith v. Alabama.*[65] Instead, the Court has adopted a two-step inquiry to determine whether laws that burden interstate commerce are nonetheless permissible. Courts first consider whether a challenged law or ordinance discriminates against interstate commerce. Then, if a court determines that the law regulates in a neutral manner (that is, it does not discriminate), the court assesses whether the law imposes a burden on interstate commerce that is clearly excessive in relation to the putative local benefits.

In 1970, the Court's decision in *Pike v. Bruce Church, Inc.*[66] crystallized this modern approach to Commerce Clause jurisprudence. There, the Court considered the Arizona Fruit and Vegetable Standardization Act, which required that all cantaloupes grown in Arizona and offered for sale be packed in closed standard containers that government officials approved. The state had issued an order under the Act prohibiting the plaintiff, a cantaloupe farming company, from transporting uncrated cantaloupes from its Arizona ranch to its California packing plant. Consequently, the plaintiff's only option was to build a packing plant within the Arizona state limits, at a high cost, to duplicate the function of its existing packing facility about 30 miles across the border. The Court determined that the "purpose and design" of the Act—namely, to "protect and enhance the reputation of growers within the State"—were "surely legitimate."[67] Nonetheless, the Court concluded that "the State's tenuous interest in having the company's cantaloupes identified as originating in Arizona [could not] constitutionally justify the requirement that the company build and operate an unneeded $200,000 packing plant in the State."[68] Because the state's interest was "minimal at best," it could not justify imposing "a straitjacket on the . . . company with respect to the allocation of its interstate resources."[69] Thus, the Court invalidated the law as an impermissible burden on interstate commerce, in violation of the dormant Commerce Clause.

In reaching its holding, the *Pike* Court enunciated a balancing approach that continues to govern in cases where laws affect interstate commerce but do so in a nondiscriminatory manner:

> Where the statute regulates evenhandedly to effectuate a legitimate local public interest, and its effects on interstate commerce are only incidental, it will be upheld

---

65. *Cooley,* 53 U.S. 299; *Smith v. Alabama,* 124 U.S. 465, 482 (1888).
66. 397 U.S. 137 (1970).
67. *Id.* at 143.
68. *Id.* at 145.
69. *Id.* at 146.

> unless the burden imposed on such commerce is clearly excessive in relation to the putative local benefits. If a legitimate local purpose is found, then the question becomes one of degree. And the extent of the burden that will be tolerated will, of course, depend on the nature of the local interest involved, and on whether it could be promoted as well with a lesser impact on interstate activities.[70]

Central to the modern approach to the Commerce Clause is the determination as to whether a law discriminates—that is, whether it is "basically a protectionist measure" or whether "it can fairly be viewed as a law directed to legitimate local concerns, with effects upon interstate commerce that are only incidental" (in which case the *Pike* test applies).[71] In a classic case, *City of Philadelphia v. New Jersey,* the Supreme Court determined that a law prohibiting importation of waste from out of state was discriminatory.[72] The Court found the law violated the principle of nondiscrimination "on its face," holding that "whatever New Jersey's ultimate purpose, it may not be accomplished by discriminating against articles of commerce coming from outside the State unless there is some reason, apart from their origin, to treat them differently."[73]

Decades later, the Court struck down another state statute as nakedly discriminatory, irrespective of the magnitude or impact of the discrimination. In *Wyoming v. Oklahoma,* the Court invalidated an Oklahoma law that required local coal-fired electric generating plants to burn a mixture containing at least 10 percent Oklahoma-mined coal.[74] In reaching its conclusion, the Court rejected the state's rationale for the law—that it "conserves Wyoming's cleaner coal for future use"—and found that the real reason "cannot be characterized as anything other than protectionist and discriminatory."[75] With that finding, the Court saw no need to analyze the scope of the interstate burden, which Oklahoma had argued was negligible.[76]

Even if a court determines that a state law does not discriminate on its face, it may nonetheless find that the law discriminates in effect or has a protectionist purpose. In 1977, for example, the Supreme Court struck down a North Carolina law requiring the use of U.S. Department of Agriculture grades and forbidding state grades on imported apples. The Court in *Hunt v. Washington State Apple* found that the law discriminated in impact because it raised the cost of doing business and stripped away the competitive advantage for certain out-of-state apple growers, particularly Washington growers, while leaving in-state growers unaffected.[77] As the Court explained, "[t]his discrimination resulted from the fact that North Carolina, unlike Washington, had never established a grading and inspection system. Hence, the statute had no effect on the existing practices of North Carolina producers . . .

---

70. *Id.* at 142 (citation omitted).
71. *City of Phila. v. New Jersey,* 437 U.S. 617, 624 (1978).
72. *Id.* at 626-27.
73. *Id.*
74. *Wyoming v. Oklahoma,* 502 U.S. 437 (1992).
75. *Id.* at 455, 457.
76. *Id.* at 456.
77. *Hunt v. Washington State Apple Advertising Comm'n,* 432 U.S. 333 (1977).

Washington growers and dealers, on the other hand, were forced to alter their long-established procedures, at substantial cost, or abandon the North Carolina market."[78] Finding that impact constituted discrimination against interstate commerce, the Court invalidated North Carolina's law.

If a law discriminates, facially or otherwise, it "invokes the strictest scrutiny of any purported legitimate local purpose and of the absence of nondiscriminatory alternatives."[79] As the Court set forth in *Maine v. Taylor,* "once a state law is shown to discriminate against interstate commerce . . . the burden falls on the State to demonstrate both that the statute 'serves a legitimate local purpose,' and that this purpose could not be served as well by available nondiscriminatory means."[80] As such, courts typically strike down discriminatory laws, as the Supreme Court has done in several cases involving local processing requirements.[81] *Maine v. Taylor* is a rare case in which the Court found a law to be facially discriminatory but upheld it nonetheless.[82] In that 1986 case, the Court decided that Maine's prohibition on the importation of baitfish discriminated against interstate commerce on its face, but upheld the law because Maine demonstrated both that the statute served a legitimate local purpose—namely, protecting its unique population of wild fish from nonnative species—and that available non-discriminatory means could not serve that purpose as well.[83] Given the rigor of the test to which discriminatory laws are held, cases like *Maine v. Taylor* are uncommon.

3. EVOLVING VIEW OF THE DORMANT COMMERCE CLAUSE AND THE TWENTY-FIRST AMENDMENT

Recent cases involving states' regulation of the liquor trade under the Twenty-first Amendment draw heavily on developments in dormant Commerce Clause analysis. As courts shifted away from the absolutist interpretations of the Twenty-first Amendment that were advanced shortly after its passage, they increasingly followed the analytical framework of *Pike* and its progeny. The evolving jurisprudence still takes the states' Twenty-first Amendment concerns into account, but the judicial inquiry tends to be limited to whether those interests can tip the balance or even "save" a law that could otherwise not withstand dormant Commerce Clause scrutiny.

---

78. *Id.* at 340.

79. *Hughes v. Oklahoma*, 441 U.S. 322, 337 (1979). State laws found to discriminate are held to "a virtually *per se* rule of invalidity." *City of Phila.*, 437 U.S. at 624.

80. 477 U.S. 131, 138 (1986) (citing *Hughes,* 441 U.S. at 336).

81. *See, e.g., Dean Milk Co. v. Madison, Wisconsin*, 340 U.S. 349 (1951) (invalidating municipal ordinance requiring all milk sold in Madison be pasteurized within five miles of the city on the grounds that "reasonable and adequate alternatives are available" to meet the city's professed concerns about ensuring that milk sold within its borders was properly pasteurized); *C & A Carbone, Inc. v. Clarkstown*, 511 U.S. 383 (1994) (overturning municipal ordinance that required all solid waste to be processed initially at a local site, after which it would be shipped to elsewhere for further processing).

82. *Taylor,* 477 U.S. 131.

83. *Id.* at 142, 151.

Bacchus Imports, Ltd. v. Dias is widely viewed as a decisive step in Twenty-first Amendment jurisprudence toward a more vigorous defense of the principles underlying the dormant Commerce Clause.[84] The case involved a 20 percent excise tax on alcoholic beverages that exempted certain locally produced products such as okolehao (a brandy distilled from the root of an indigenous plant) and pineapple wine. There, referencing classic dormant Commerce Clause cases such as *Hunt v. Washington State Apple* and *Philadelphia v. New Jersey*, the Court concluded that the liquor tax exemption "violated the Commerce Clause because it had both the purpose and effect of discriminating in favor of local products."[85]

The Court then embarked on a second analytical step that has come to characterize many cases that simultaneously consider dormant Commerce Clause principles and Twenty-first Amendment concerns. After determining that the challenged statute violates the dormant Commerce Clause, the Court inquired whether the Twenty-first Amendment "saves" the measure. With respect to the second inquiry, the Court in *Bacchus* developed a "core interests" analysis, holding that the law "is not saved by the Twenty-first Amendment" because it "violates a central tenet of the Commerce Clause but is not supported by any clear concern of the Amendment in combating the evils of an unrestricted traffic in liquor."[86] The Court explained:

> [O]ne thing is certain: The central purpose of [the Twenty-first Amendment] was not to empower States to favor local liquor industries by erecting barriers to competition. . . . State laws that constitute mere economic protectionism are therefore not entitled to the same deference as laws enacted to combat the perceived evils of an unrestricted traffic in liquor. Here, the State does not seek to justify its tax on the ground that it was designed to promote temperance or to carry out any other purpose of the Twenty-first Amendment, but instead acknowledges that the purpose was 'to promote a local industry.'[87]

In other words, the Court determined that the interests Hawaii's legislation advanced fell outside the "core interests" of the Twenty-first Amendment and therefore did not warrant protection from invalidation under the Commerce Clause.

In the years following *Bacchus*, the Court continued to affirm that the Twenty-first Amendment would not "save" measures that otherwise offended the dormant Commerce Clause. In *Brown-Forman Distillers Corporation v. New York State Liquor Authority*, the Court maintained the principle that states are prohibited from regulating interstate commerce by restricting commerce in other states.[88] The New York law in question stated that distillers could not sell liquor to New York distributors at a price higher than that charged anywhere else in the nation for that product for a prescribed period. Confusingly, several other states had similar "price affirmation" laws, so the practical result was that no distiller could sell its liquor

84. 468 U.S. 263 (1984).
85. *Id.* at 273.
86. *Id.* at 264.
87. *Id.* at 276.
88. *Brown-Forman*, 476 U.S. 573.

anywhere at a discount. The Court held that "[w]hen a state statute directly regulates . . . interstate commerce, or when its effect is to favor in-state economic interests over out-of-state interests, we have generally struck down the statute without further inquiry" on the grounds that it violates the Commerce Clause.[89] The Court did not stray from that approach, despite the argument that the Twenty-first Amendment should dictate a contrary outcome.

Similarly, in *Healy v. Beer Institute,* the Court struck down a Connecticut price affirmation law dealing with the prices of beer.[90] Unlike the prospective price affirmation law at issue in *Brown-Forman,* Connecticut's law was contemporaneous, meaning that the price affirmation only applied when the seller posted its prices. The Court analyzed the effects of the statute on interstate commerce and concluded that, like the price affirmation law at issue in *Brown-Forman,* Connecticut's contemporaneous price affirmation law had an impermissible extraterritorial effect. The Court also concluded that the law was discriminatory:

> Connecticut has claimed throughout this litigation that its price-affirmation laws are designed to ensure the lowest possible prices for Connecticut consumers. While this may be a legitimate justification for the statute, it is not advanced by, in effect, exempting brewers and shippers engaging in solely domestic sales from the price regulations imposed on brewers and shippers who engage in sales throughout the region.[91]

In contrast, in *North Dakota v. United States,* the Court upheld two North Dakota regulations requiring out-of-state shippers of alcoholic beverages to affix a label to each bottle sold to in-state military bases and to file monthly shipping reports identifying the products and quantities of alcoholic beverages shipped into the state.[92] The state's declared interest was to prevent liquor moving in transit through the state from being diverted for unauthorized uses within the state. The Court found that "[t]he risk of diversion into the retail market and disruption of the liquor distribution system is thus both substantial and real."[93] On that basis, the Court concluded that the North Dakota regulations were consistent with "the core of the State's power under the Twenty-first Amendment . . . In the interest of promoting temperance, ensuring orderly market conditions, and raising revenue, the State has established a comprehensive system for the distribution of liquor within its borders. That system is unquestionably legitimate."[94]

The Court emphasized in both the *Bacchus* and *North Dakota* cases that states can organize their alcoholic beverage markets as they wish to promote temperance.

---

89. *Id.* at 578-79.

90. 491 U.S. 324 (1989). Likewise, the Court in *324 LiquorCorp. v. Duffy*, 479 U.S. 335 (1987), decisively "rejected the view 'that the Twenty-first Amendment has somehow operated to 'repeal' the Commerce Clause wherever regulation of intoxicating liquors is concerned'" (quoting *Hostetter*, 377 U.S. at 331-32).

91. *Healy*, 491 U.S. at 339-41.

92. *North Dakota*, 495 U.S. 423.

93. *Id.* at 433.

94. *Id.* at 432.

The states also may take steps to prevent the diversion of alcoholic beverages to combat the "social evils" that occurred during Prohibition and to ensure an orderly market. Generally, when a state law is challenged, the state articulates the purpose of its alcoholic beverage regulations and the courts then endeavor to decide "whether the interests implicated by a state regulation are so closely related to the powers reserved by the Twenty-first Amendment that the regulation may prevail, notwithstanding that its requirements directly conflict with express federal policies."[95]

E. GRANHOLM v. HEALD AND BEYOND

That wine should be the subject of the next seminal Supreme Court case involving the dormant Commerce Clause and the Twenty-first Amendment was in many ways predictable. Beginning in the 1970s, the U.S. wine industry experienced a renaissance, with both wine production and consumption soaring.[96] For example, the number of wineries in California grew from 335 in 1976[97] to 2,275 in 2005, the year *Granholm* was decided, and there were more than 4,900 nationwide by that time.[98] Furthermore, wine purchasing patterns were shifting. The rise of the Internet beginning in the 1990s led to an explosion of online commerce and greater familiarity among consumers with direct shipment to buy and receive goods. Because consumers now expected to be able to access goods despite geographical barriers, they clamored for direct access to out-of-state wines.

Following Repeal, most states adopted rigid and carefully prescribed systems of distribution for wine and other alcoholic beverages to achieve an orderly market and to avoid the social evils that plagued the pre-Prohibition and Prohibition eras. Each state made its own decision in this regard, exercising its authority under the Twenty-first Amendment. However, broadly speaking, 18 states decided to become direct market participants, serving as wholesalers and/or retailers of alcoholic beverages in these so-called control states.[99] The remaining states relied on the licensure of private parties as producers, importers, wholesalers, and retailers of alcoholic beverages. Their distribution systems often took the form of a "three-tier system of distribution," under which wine and other alcoholic beverages pass from the producer or importer to a separately licensed wholesaler who, in turn, sells to retailers for resale to consumers. Not surprisingly, there are many variations on this theme, with strict regulations governing the marketing, sales, and distribution of alcoholic beverages

---

95. *Bacchus,* 468 U.S. at 275-76 (internal citation omitted).

96. *See supra* Chapter 1, Table 1.

97. *See* Wine History Project of San Luis Obispo County, Wine History by Decade: 1970s, available *at* https://winehistoryproject.org/wine-history-by-decade-1970s/ (last visited Aug. 22, 2022).

98. Alcohol and Tobacco Tax and Trade Bureau (TTB), List of Permittees, Bonded Wine Producers Count by State: January 1, 1999-June 30, 2022 *available at* https://www.ttb.gov/images/pdfs/bonded-wine-producers-by-state.xlsx (last visited Aug. 22, 2022).

99. *See* Chapter 1 for more information about control states and license states, which are the two main approaches the states used after Repeal to organize and regulate their alcoholic beverage markets.

between each tier. In a strict three-tier system, only in-state retailers are allowed to sell and ship wine directly to in-state consumers. Out-of-state wineries must sell and ship their wines to an in-state importer or wholesaler (depending on the laws of the state), which in turn sells them to a retailer for resale to in-state consumers.

Of course, this labyrinthine structure was of little concern to the growing numbers of Internet consumers in the burgeoning world of e-commerce. And, in fact, long before the Internet took hold, many states had authorized local wineries to sell their wines directly to consumers, typically when those consumers visited the winery, as legislative exceptions to the three-tier system. This concept of a "farm winery," first introduced in the 1970s, was intended to promote tourism and boost the local agricultural economy.[100]

As the Internet increased the demand from both consumers and wineries to allow interstate direct shipping, states expanded the wineries' direct-shipping privileges—often in ways that directly discriminated against other states. By 2003, 30 states permitted winery direct-to-consumer shipments within the state.[101] Of those, 24 states also allowed some form of direct interstate shipping.[102] Thirteen of these 24 passed "reciprocity" laws that granted out-of-state wineries the right to ship a certain amount of wine per month to an in-state consumer on the express condition that the winery's home state must afford wineries in the destination state a similar direct-to-consumer privilege.[103] Some of the remaining 11 states allowed direct shipping by out-of-state wineries but placed restrictions on interstate shipments that were not imposed on intrastate shipments.[104] Still, approximately half the states allowed no direct interstate shipments at all, and some of these states made it a felony for out-of-state wineries to ship wine to in-state consumers.[105] The states made these decisions under the authority of the Twenty-first Amendment, presumably without considering requirements of the dormant Commerce Clause.

Given the distance, both temporally and doctrinally, from the ratification of the Twenty-first Amendment and the absolutist interpretation that the Brandeis opinions advanced about the scope of the Amendment, the stage was set for a new round of

---

100. *See* Chapter 7 for a discussion of the history of "farm wineries" in the United States. These wineries were allowed to sell wines produced from local grapes directly to consumers inside the state.

101. Fed. Trade Comm'n, Possible Anticompetitive Barriers to E-Commerce: Wine 7 (July 2003), *available at* https://www.ftc.gov/sites/default/files/documents/reports/possible-anticompetitive-barriers-e-commerce-wine/winereport2_0.pdf (last visited Aug. 8, 2022).

102. *Id.*

103. *Id.* at 7-8; *see also* Iowa Code §123.187(2) (2003) (repealed 2010) ("A winery licensed or permitted pursuant to laws regulating alcoholic beverages in a state which affords this state an equal reciprocal shipping privilege may ship into this state by private common carrier, to a person twenty-one years of age or older, not more than eighteen liters of wine per month, for consumption or use by the person"). These laws were not unlike the law at issue in the famous case of *Indianapolis Brewing Co.*, 305 U.S. 391. *See supra* text surrounding note 58.

104. Fed. Trade Comm'n, *supra* note 101, at 8. In 2002, following a ban that the Transportation Security Administration imposed on passengers carrying liquids in containers larger than three ounces onto planes, Congress passed a federal direct shipment law, 27 U.S.C. §124, that allows a consumer who has purchased wine "while the purchaser was physically present at the winery" to ship it to their home in accordance with their state's rules on personal importation.

105. Fed. Trade Comm'n, *supra* note 101 at 8.

Commerce Clause litigation. Indeed, by the time *Granholm v. Heald* came before the Supreme Court, a circuit split had developed with respect to states' measures to foster their own wine industries through limitations on out-of-state direct shipping. In 2003, the Fourth Circuit invalidated a North Carolina law that required out-of-state manufacturers to use the three-tier system, while allowing in-state manufacturers to ship directly to consumers on grounds that it violated the Commerce Clause and the Twenty-first Amendment did not save it.[106] One year later, the Second Circuit upheld a New York law restricting direct shipment of out-of-state wine to New York consumers on the ground that the state's Twenty-first Amendment powers protected the law—recognizing the additional costs imposed on out-of-state manufacturers but finding that "New York's regulatory regime falls squarely within the ambit of section 2's grant of authority."[107] The Seventh Circuit, in reasoning that echoed that of the Second Circuit, held in *Bridenbaugh v. Freeman-Wilson* that the Twenty-first Amendment saved an Indiana statute prohibiting direct shipments from out-of-state producers to Indiana consumers.[108] The Fifth and Sixth Circuits, by contrast, adopted logic similar to the Fourth Circuit in finding that the direct shipping laws of Texas and Michigan violated Commerce Clause principles; accordingly, the courts invalidated these laws notwithstanding the Twenty-first Amendment.[109]

Broadly speaking, the Court took up the same issue in *Granholm,* considering the constitutionality of laws in Michigan and New York that allowed in-state wineries, but not out-of-state ones, to circumvent the three-tier system, thereby giving the in-state wineries a competitive advantage. Although Michigan's statute required out-of-state wineries to channel their sales through wholesalers and New York's statute permitted out-of-state wineries either to do likewise or to establish a physical presence as a so-called "branch winery" in the state, both states allowed in-state wineries to obtain licenses for direct sales to consumers without additional steps.[110] Considering whether "a State's regulatory scheme that permits in-state wineries directly to ship alcohol to consumers but restricts the ability of out-of-state wineries to do so violate[s] the dormant Commerce Clause in light of §2 of the Twenty-first Amendment," the Court invalidated both statutes on the grounds that they discriminated facially against interstate commerce.[111] In other words, the

106. *Beskind v. Easley,* 325 F.3d 506, 519-20 (4th Cir. 2003).

107. *Swedenburg v. Kelly,* 358 F.3d 223, 227 (2d Cir. 2004).

108. 227 F.3d 848, 854 (7th Cir. 2000).

109. *Dickerson v. Bailey,* 336 F.3d 388, 410 (5th Cir. 2003); *Heald v. Engler,* 342 F.3d 517, 527 (6th Cir. 2003). Interestingly, the Eleventh Circuit's decision on this issue relied on *Bacchus's* language with respect to the core concerns of the Twenty-first Amendment. In *Bainbridge v. Turner,* 311 F.3d 1104, 1106, 1114 (11th Cir. 2002), the court noted that Florida's prohibition against out-of-state wineries shipping directly to consumers could be upheld against a dormant Commerce Clause challenge if Florida could prove that the statute was closely related to a core concern of the Twenty-first Amendment and that the state's statutory scheme is "genuinely needed to effectuate the proffered core concern."

110. *Granholm,* 544 U.S. at 468-71.

111. *Id.* at 471. With respect to New York's in-state presence requirement, the Court found that it "runs contrary to our admonition that States cannot require an out-of-state firm 'to become a resident in order to compete on equal terms.'" *Id.* at 475 (quoting *Halliburton Oil Well Cementing Co. v. Reily*, 373 U.S. 64, 72 (1963)).

"object and design" of both statutes was "to grant in-state wineries a competitive advantage over wineries located beyond the states' borders."[112] The Court held, in a five-to-four decision, that such favoritism violates the Commerce Clause's implied restriction on state protectionism.

Granholm clarified that neither the Constitution nor Congress had authorized states to discriminate against interstate commerce. The Court rejected the argument that the Twenty-first Amendment permits states to legislate in ways that the dormant Commerce Clause doctrine would otherwise preclude, rejecting, as had *Bacchus,* the idea that the Twenty-first Amendment would "save" or "supersede" state laws that violate other provisions of the Constitution.[113] Instead, in *Granholm* the Court held that "state regulation of alcohol is limited by the nondiscrimination principle of the Commerce Clause."[114]

In reaching its holding, the Court rejected the argument that the Webb-Kenyon Act, still in effect today, had "removed any barrier to discriminatory state liquor regulations."[115] Instead, the Court interpreted the Webb-Kenyon Act as an extension of the Wilson Act, which also remains in effect and explicitly prohibits states from discriminating against interstate commerce.[116]

In keeping with the *Pike* test, the Court examined whether there was any reasonable, nondiscriminatory means to accomplish the states' legitimate objectives after it concluded that the New York and Michigan laws discriminated against interstate commerce on their faces. The states argued that their laws were necessary to prevent youth access to alcoholic beverages, to ensure the collection of the states' tax revenue, to hold out-of-state wineries accountable, and to maintain an orderly market. The Court rejected each claim, noting that either there was no evidence of a problem (for example, in the case of youth access to alcohol or failure to collect taxes) or there were nondiscriminatory means to address the problem (for example, licensing schemes and self-reporting requirements for all direct shipments).[117]

Importantly the Court fashioned no remedy in *Granholm.* The states were free to "level up" (allowing in-state and out-of-state wineries alike to ship directly to in-state consumers) or "level down" (allowing states to prohibit *all* wineries

---

112. *Id.* at 466.

113. *Granholm*, 544 U.S. at 486, 489.

114. *Id.* at 487.

115. *Id.* at 482.

116. Justice Kennedy authored the *Granholm* opinion and Justices Scalia, Souter, Ginsburg, and Breyer joined. Justices Stevens and Thomas both wrote dissenting opinions, in which Justice O'Connor and Chief Justice Rehnquist joined. Chief Justice Rehnquist and Justices Stevens and O'Connor were widely expected to vote to uphold the laws because they had dissented in *Bacchus*, in a clear case of a protective tariff—expressing their view that the liquor tax exemption for locally produced alcoholic beverages at issue in that case "plainly" constituted "an exercise of a power expressly conferred upon the States by the Constitution," *Bacchus Imports*, 468 U.S. at 287, and that the "wholesalers' Commerce Clause claim is squarely foreclosed by the Twenty-first Amendment," *Id.* at 279. Justice Stevens' dissent in *Granholm* was largely grounded in his historical experience—thus lending strength to the notion of Twenty-first Amendment and Commerce Clause jurisprudence as a product of time. *Granholm,* 544 U.S. at 494, 496.

117. *Granholm*, 544 U.S. at 490-92.

from shipping directly to consumers) to end discrimination. *Granholm* also left open a series of questions that would arise in its wake.

Granholm required all the state legislatures that discriminated in their direct shipping laws against out-of-state wineries to revisit and revise those laws. As they did, the rules of the game changed for interstate direct shipping. After *Granholm,* most states decided to level up. Today, 47 states allow both in-state and out-of-state wineries to ship to in-state consumers. All but one reciprocal shipment law has been repealed following the Court's pronouncement in dicta in *Granholm* that "the perceived necessity for reciprocal sale privileges risks generating the trade rivalries and animosities, the alliances and exclusivity, that the Constitution and, in particular, the Commerce Clause were designed to avoid."[118] No states "leveled down" by taking away an existing right to ship. Only three states currently prohibit direct shipping: Delaware, Mississippi, and Utah.[119] As this edition goes to press, wineries can ship their wines directly to 98 percent of adult Americans.[120]

The laws in the 50 states, however, are far from settled when it comes to direct shipping and regulation of the liquor trade. *Granholm* sent states scrambling to legislate around the dictates of the Court's holding. In the last several years, states have adopted new laws, tried new approaches, and then amended those laws and approaches. Among the more novel responses are the leveling up laws that seem to constitute discrimination in *effect.* Although their laws are not facially discriminatory like the laws the *Granholm* Court considered, they include criteria that burden out-of-state producers. The criteria fall into three general categories: volume caps, wholesaler exclusion, and face-to-face sales.

Volume or capacity caps eliminate the direct shipping privilege for wineries, in-state or out-of-state, that produce more than a stated number of gallons of wine per year. Although the laws are facially neutral as to the citizenship of the wineries they regulate, capacity cap laws draw suspicion when the effect of the gallonage cap set by the state is to allow all in-state wineries to engage in direct shipping but exclude a large percentage of out-of-state wineries. In such cases, there is a reasonable suspicion of a discriminatory purpose or effect. This was the finding of the First Circuit in the 2010 case, *Family Winemakers of California v. Jenkins*,[121] which overturned a Massachusetts law that made a "small winery shipment license" available to any winery that produces less than 30,000 gallons annually.[122] In 2006, when the law was enacted, "large" wineries produced 98 percent of domestic wine.[123] Thousands of "small" U.S. wineries—31 of which were in Massachusetts—produced the remaining two percent of domestic wine.[124] Importantly, all the

---

118. *Id.* at 472.

119. Free the Grapes! website, Issue Summary, *available at https://freethegrapes.org/issue-summary/* (last visited Aug. 21, 2022). The laws change sufficiently swiftly from state to state.

120. *Id.*

121. 592 F.3d 1, 9-10 (1st Cir. 2010).

122. Mass. Gen. Laws ch. 138, §19F(b) (2009).

123. *Family Winemakers,* 592 F.3d at 8, 11-12.

124. *Id.* at 8.

Massachusetts-based wineries fell within the "small" winery category, each producing between 200 and 24,000 gallons of wine per year.[125] Consequently, the impact of the law was to preserve the direct shipping privilege for in-state wineries but to eliminate it for wineries responsible for 98 percent of the nation's wine supply. The court found the Massachusetts law to be discriminatory in both purpose and effect, the latter as a result of "the statutory context, legislative history, and other factors."[126]

The second type of law, known as wholesaler exclusion, eliminates the direct shipping privilege for wineries that sell their wines to a wholesaler in the destination state. The logic underlying the exclusion is that only those wineries whose wines are not otherwise available in the state through the three-tier distribution system should be allowed to ship wines directly to in- state consumers. Because this criterion applies to both in-state and out-of-state wineries, it is facially neutral. Interestingly, Massachusetts combined the 30,000-gallon capacity cap with the wholesaler exclusion in the law at issue in *Family Winemakers.* Together, these two criteria, according to the First Circuit, forced large wineries to choose their distribution method:

> If ['large' wineries] choose direct shipping, . . . they are *forced* to terminate their existing wholesaler relationships, which also means that they lose all access to retailers in Massachusetts. Since this is a crucial way for a winery to build consumer awareness for the brand in Massachusetts, its unavailability means that these wineries are not able to compete on the same footing as §19F(b) 'small' wineries.[127]

Because the Massachusetts law "change[d] the competitive balance between in-state and out-of-state wineries in a way that benefits Massachusetts's wineries and significantly burdens out-of-state competitors," the First Circuit ruled it to be discriminatory in effect.[128] No balancing under *Pike* was required considering the statute's discriminatory purpose and effect.[129]

The court's concern about the forced termination of wholesaler relationships echoes *Pike* itself, which struck down the Arizona Fruit and Vegetable Standardization Act on the grounds that it imposed a "straight jacket on the. . . company with respect to the allocation of its interstate resources."[130] Courts have shown a consistent aversion to laws that so burden interstate commerce that businesses are forced to make specific choices about the allocation of their resources.

Courts, however, have not marched in lockstep with respect to their holdings on post-*Granholm* laws. Arizona, for example, imposed a 20,000-gallon capacity cap, maintaining direct shipment privileges for all but one Arizona winery. The state also restricted direct-to-consumer shipments to wineries, in-state or out-of-state, large or

---

125. *Id.* at 8-9.
126. *Id.* at 5.
127. *Id.* at 12 (emphasis added).
128. *Id.* at 5.
129. *Id.* at 10.
130. *Pike,* 397 U.S. at 146.

small, that sold their wines to consumers in a face-to-face transaction at the winery.[131] This is the third type of facially neutral direct shipping law that burdens out-of-state wineries. These laws, which allow direct shipment only after a mandatory trip to the winery, come in various forms. Some states require only an initial visit, after which consumers can make subsequent remote orders; others require that every shipment be the culmination of an on-premises purchase.

In contrast to the First Circuit's treatment of the Massachusetts law, the Ninth Circuit in *Black Star Farms v. Oliver* upheld the Arizona law—largely on the ground that the plaintiff offered inadequate evidence of the law's alleged discriminatory effect.[132] The plaintiff in the case argued that the face-to-face requirement, also known as the "in person" exception, favored in-state interests because most Arizona consumers were likely to buy wine directly from Arizona wineries that were closer than out-of-state wineries.[133] Hence, out-of-state wineries would be disadvantaged by the "in person" requirement.[134] The court rejected the argument because there was no differential treatment between in-state and out-of-state wineries, and the "geographical proximity" of in-state wineries to Arizona consumers is a "natural condition" not amounting to a discriminatory effect under the Commerce Clause.[135] The court held in no uncertain terms that "[a]n effect is not discriminatory . . . if it results from natural conditions."[136]

In reaching its conclusion, the court in *Black Star Farms* emphasized that Arizona's law, unlike the Massachusetts law at issue in the *Family Winemakers* case, did not force "large" wineries to choose between distribution methods. Arizona's law permitted all large wineries to distribute their wine through the three-tier system and through direct shipping.[137] To the contrary, Massachusetts required all large wineries to distribute their wine either through the three-tier system or through direct shipping.[138] The court concluded that "[the p]laintiffs proffer no evidence to suggest

---

131. Ariz. Rev. Stat. §4-203.040 (2010). The legislature created the gallonage cap and face-to-face sales regulations in direct response to *Granholm* as stated in the statement of purpose for the bill. *See* S.B. 1276, 47th Leg., 2d Reg. Sess. (Ariz. 2006).

132. *Black Star Farms LLC v. Oliver,* 600 F.3d 1225, 1231 (9th Cir. 2010). As an evidentiary matter, the court noted that merely demonstrating that a law grants a "de minimis benefit to instate wineries is ... insufficient" to warrant its invalidation.

133. *See id.* at 1234-1235 (discussing the plaintiff's challenge to Arizona's "in person" exception).

134. *Id.* at 1229 ("Black Star Farms filed an action under 42 U.S.C. [§] 1983 on the ground that the small winery and in-person exceptions to the three-tier distribution system violate the dormant [Commerce Clause] because, in practical effect, the two exceptions to the three-tier system discriminate against out-of-state wineries.").

135. *See id.* at 1234-1235. Both of these are relevant to the "in person" exception since Arizona's consumers are most likely to visit and make in-person purchases from in-state wineries, therefore allowing in-state wineries to take advantage of the benefits of shipping directly to consumers. *See id.*

136. *Id.* at 1234 (citing *Cherry Hill Vineyard, LLC v. Baldacci,* SOS F.3d 28, 38 n.7 (1st Cir. 2007)).

137. *See* Ariz. Rev. Stat. §§4-243.01, 4-244(6)-(7) (2010) (codifying the three-tier system); Ariz. R v. Stat. §4-203.040 (2010) (codifying the "in person" exception permitting all wineries to ship directly to consumers, with some conditions).

138. Mass. Gen. Laws ch. 138, §19F(a) (2010).

that such a limited [direct shipment] exception, applicable to both in-state and out-of-state wineries, erects a barrier to Arizona's wine market that in effect creates a burden that alters the proportional share of the wine market in favor of in-state wineries, such that out-of-state wineries are unable to effectively compete in the Arizona market.[139]

The post-*Granholm* litigation concerning these and other state liquor laws has produced divergent results. For example, a circuit split seemingly developed with respect to laws requiring in-person transactions as a precondition for direct shipment privileges. The Sixth Circuit invalidated a Kentucky law requiring in-person transactions because the evidence showed that the law was discriminatory in effect, favoring in-state wineries and wholesalers over out-of-state wineries.[140] However, the First and Seventh Circuits reached the contrary conclusion, sustaining state laws requiring in-person transactions because the evidence in those cases did not prove a discriminatory effect that altered the market share of in-state wineries.[141] Given the various combinations of provisions that can be included in these state laws and the complicated evidentiary issues related to market impact, such divergent results are likely to continue.

F. IS THE THREE-TIER SYSTEM SACROSANCT?

Although the facts in *Granholm* were limited to seeking a level playing field in winery direct-to-consumer sales, post-*Granholm* litigation also involved wine and beer producer "self-distribution" to retail, durational residency requirements for retailers, and interstate retail-to-consumer wine sales and shipping. In Washington state, Costco, the largest retailer of wine in the U.S., was authorized to purchase wine directly from in-state wineries but not from out-of-state wineries. Following the Supreme Court's nondiscrimination principle in *Granholm*, Costco sued the state to invalidate this facial discrimination.[142] In December 2005 the district court, in ruling on a motion for partial summary judgment, found that the Washington law discriminates against out-of-state producers and thus violates the dormant Commerce Clause because the law permits in-state wine and beer producers to distribute their products directly to retailers while withholding the same privileges from out-of-state wine and beer producers.

The court-ordered remedy was to eliminate the "self-distribution" privilege for in-state wineries and breweries; however, the court stayed the entry of judgment until April 2006 to provide sufficient time for the Washington legislature to determine

---

139. *Black Star Farms,* 600 F.3d at 1231 (alteration in original).

140. *Cherry Hill Vineyards, LLC v. Lilly*, 553 F.3d 423, 432-34 (6th Cir. 2008).

141. See *Baldacci*, 505 F.3d at 36-38; *Baude v. Heath*, 538 F.3d 608, 613-15 (7th Cir. 2008); *Black Star Farms*, 600 F.3d at 1231; *see also Kleinsmith v. Shurtleff*, 571 F.3d 1033, 1042 (10th Cir. 2009) (distinguishing *Lilly* on the ground that the plaintiffs in *Lilly* had presented sufficient evidence to establish a discriminatory effect).

142. *Costco Wholesale Corp. v. Hoen* (*Hoen I*), 407 F. Supp. 2d 1247 (W.D. Wash. 2005), *rev'd on other grounds*, *Costco Wholesale Corp. v. Maleng* (*Maleng I*), 514 F.3d 915 (9th Cir. 2008).

whether to extend the self-distribution privilege to out-of-state beer and wine producers. The legislature responded by passing a measure that extended the self-distribution privilege to out-of-state manufacturers, effectively "leveling up" so that producers in any state can distribute directly to Washington retailers.[143]

Retailers were the next tier of the three-tier system to join the post-*Granholm* litigation. They sought the right to ship their wines to consumers around the country, challenging state laws that prohibit out-of-state retailers, including auction houses, from shipping their wines directly to in-state consumers while authorizing such shipments by in-state retailers. Many of these retailers banded together to form the Specialty Wine Retailers Association (SWRA), whose mission was to strike down discriminatory interstate retailer-to-consumer laws.

Despite SWRA's efforts, the litigation results were not particularly encouraging. Because *Granholm* concerned only producers, courts did not feel compelled to follow the nondiscrimination principle when it comes to retailers' sales and shipments to consumers. Even when a state law facially discriminates against out-of-state retailers, the law was frequently upheld on the ground that such preferential treatment is within the state's prerogative of defining who is a retailer and what the retailer's privileges are within the three-tier system.[144] As the Fifth Circuit said in the 2010 case *Wine Country Gift Baskets.com v. Steen*, the in-state retailers' shipment right is inherent in the concept of retailing and does not constitute discrimination.[145] By 2011, only one district court had reached the opposite conclusion, and the appeal in that case was rendered moot when the legislature amended the statute.[146]

In 2019, however, the Supreme Court issued a decision in *Tenn. Wine & Spirits Retailers Ass'n v. Thomas* ("*Tennessee Wine*"), which proved instructive for the next wave of Commerce Clause challenges to discriminatory retailer-to-consumer cases. There, the Court reviewed a Tennessee law that imposed a durational residency requirement on retail license applicants that required all persons and companies applying for a liquor store retail license to demonstrate they were a "bona fide resident" of the state for the previous two years.[147] To renew the license, which the state required after one year of operation, the licensee had to show continuous in-state residency for 10 years.[148] Corporations could not get a retail license unless all its officers, directors, and owners of capital stock satisfied the durational residency requirements.[149]

---

143. 2006 Wash. Legis. Serv. 302, §4 (codified at Wash. Rev. Code §66.24.206 (2009)).

144. *Wine Country Gift Baskets.com v. Steen*, 612 F.3d 809, 815-821 (5th Cir. 2010); *Arnold's Wines, Inc. v. Boyle*, 571 F.3d 185, 188-191 (2d Cir. 2009); *Brooks*, 462 F.3d at 351-352.

145. *Wine Country Gift Baskets.com*, 612 F.3d at 819-20.

146. *Siesta Vill. Mkt., LLC v. Granholm*, 596 F. Supp. 2d 1035, 1039-1045 (E.D. Mich. 2008), *vacated as moot*, Order Dismissing Action, July 17, 2009; *see also Wine Country Gift Baskets.com*, 612 F.3d at 817 n.5 (noting that the *Siesta Village Market* appeal was rendered moot by a change in statute).

147. 139 S. Ct. 2449, 2457 (2019).

148. *Id.*

149. *Id.* (noting "[i]n practice, this meant that no corporation whose stock is publicly traded may operate a liquor store in the State").

The Tennessee Alcoholic Beverage Commission ("TABC") sought a declaratory judgment, and a federal district court, relying on *Granholm*, held that the durational residency requirements, including as they applied to corporations, were unconstitutional.[150] After the TABC declined to appeal, a trade association for retailers in the state did so and the Sixth Circuit affirmed.[151] The association petitioned the Court, challenging only the Sixth Circuit's decision on the two-year durational residency requirement as it applied to individuals and corporations.[152] The Supreme Court held that the two-year durational residency requirement violated the dormant Commerce Clause, and the Twenty-first Amendment did not shield it.[153] The Court found that §2 of the Twenty-first Amendment "gives each State leeway in choosing the alcohol-related public health and safety measures that its citizens find desirable. But §2 is not a license to impose all manner of protectionist restrictions on commerce in alcoholic beverages."[154] In other words, the Court's holding—which applied to laws in the retail tier—was consistent with *Granholm*.

The Court first reiterated that relevant history and case law established that "the Commerce Clause by its own force restricts state protectionism."[155] Under the dormant Commerce Clause, "if a state law discriminates against out-of-state goods or nonresident economic actors, the law can be sustained only on a showing that it is narrowly tailored to 'advanc[e] a legitimate local purpose.'"[156] The Court found that Tennessee's durational residency requirement "plainly favor[ed] Tennesseans over nonresidents" but the association argued that §2 of the Twenty-first Amendment shielded the law from the dormant Commerce Clause.[157] Accordingly, the Court undertook a comprehensive analysis §2 of the Twenty-first Amendment as it related to the dormant Commerce Clause.

The Court found that "[d]espite the ostensibly broad text of §2 . . . it must be viewed as one part of a unified constitutional scheme."[158] To understand how §2 and other provisions work together, the Court explained, "history has taught us that the thrust of §2 [wa]s to 'constitutionaliz[e]' the basic structure of federal-state alcohol regulatory authority that prevailed prior to the adoption of the Eighteenth Amendment."[159] The Court found, "as recognized during that period, the Commerce Clause did not permit the States to impose protectionist measures clothed as police-power regulations."[160] The Court concluded, "[a]s for the dormant Commerce Clause, the developments leading to the adoption of the Twenty-first Amendment

150. *Id.* at 2458.
151. *Id.*
152. *Id.* at 2459.
153. *Id.* at 2457.
154. *Id.*
155. *Id.* at 2461.
156. *Id.*
157. *Id.* at 2462.
158. *Id.* ("reading §2 to prohibit the transportation or importation of alcoholic beverages in violation of *any* state would lead to absurd results" whereby state alcohol laws would be immune from challenges under the Equal Protection Clause, First Amendment, Import-Export Clause, etc.).
159. *Id.* at 2463.
160. *Id.* at 2468.

have convinced us that the aim of §2 was not to give States a free hand to restrict the importation of alcohol for purely protectionist purposes."[161]

Citing cases like *State Board of Equalization v. Young's Market Company*, the Court acknowledged that its earliest opinions interpreting the Twenty-first Amendment "feint[ed]" in the direction that §2 overrides all previously adopted constitutional provisions.[162] The Court found, however, that its modern §2 precedents have "repeatedly rejected" the view "that §2 shields all state alcohol regulation—including discriminatory laws—from any application of dormant Commerce Clause doctrine."[163] Indeed, the association conceded that under *Granholm* the Twenty-first Amendment does not give states the power to discriminate against out-of-state alcohol "*products and producers*" but argued that "a different rule applies to state laws that regulate in-state alcohol *distribution*."[164] The Court found "no sound basis" for that assertion and made clear that *Granholm*'s holding was not limited to products or producers: "On the contrary, the Court stated that the [dormant Commerce] Clause prohibits state discrimination against all 'out-of-state economic *interests*,' and noted that the direct-shipment laws in question 'contradict[ed]' dormant Commerce Clause principles because they 'deprive[d] *citizens* of their right to have access to the markets of other States on equal terms.'"[165]

The Court then turned to whether the challenged requirement could be justified as a public health or safety measure or on some other legitimate non-protectionist ground—noting that "mere speculation" or "unsupported assertions" are insufficient to sustain a law that would otherwise violate the Commerce Clause.[166] The Court found that the law at issue "expressly discriminated against nonresidents and ha[d] at best a highly attenuated relationship to public health or safety."[167] Indeed, the record was "devoid of any 'concrete evidence' showing that the 2-year residency requirement actually promote[d] public health or safety" or "that nondiscriminatory alternatives would be insufficient to further those interests."[168] Nevertheless, the association asserted several health and safety concerns that the durational requirement purportedly addressed.[169] The Court found them all facially implausible or unpersuasive.

First, the association asserted that the requirement ensured retailers were subject to the state's jurisdiction but "did not explain why this objective could not easily be achieved by ready alternatives, such as requiring a nonresident to designate an agent

---

161. *Id.* at 2469 (internal citations omitted).

162. *Id.* at 2468.

163. *Id.* at 2469.

164. *Id.* at 2470-71 (emphasis added).

165. *Id.* at 2471.

166. *Id.* at 2474.

167. *Id.*

168. *Id.* According to the Court, there was no record-evidence because "[d]uring the course of this litigation, the Association relied almost entirely on the argument that Tennessee's residency requirements are simply 'not subject to Commerce Clause challenge,'... and the State itself mounted no independent defense." *Id.*

169. *Id.* at 2475.

to receive process or to consent to suit in the Tennessee courts."[170] Second, the association asserted that the requirement provided an opportunity to determine an applicant's fitness to sell alcohol, but the Court found that was possible without the burden of a durational requirement and state law already required criminal background checks for all applicants.[171] Besides, the Court noted, the TABC would have no reason to investigate a prospective applicant during the two years prior to their submission.[172] Third, the Court found that the requirement was not needed to enable oversight of retailers: if "improvements in technology" provided adequate means of monitoring out-of-state shipments in *Granholm,* then surely there were adequate means for monitoring in-state retailers such as on-site inspections and audits.[173] Finally, the Court rejected the argument that a durational residency requirement makes retailers more familiar with the communities they serve which, in turn, would lead to "responsible sales practices."[174] As the Court noted, licensees did not have to live in the communities where they owned stores and there was no durational requirement for the person making the actual sale or for licensees of on-premise establishments like bars.[175]

The Court ruled that the association fell "far short" of showing the durational requirement was valid under the dormant Commerce Clause and the Twenty-first Amendment did not save it.[176]

G. IS THE THREE-TIER SYSTEM "UNQUESTIONABLY LEGITIMATE"?

Granholm and *Tennessee Wine* did not end the debate. Courts continue to struggle with whether and to what extent the Twenty-first Amendment provides states with discriminatory "leeway" when it comes to alcohol laws, which are related to the three-tiered system. Seizing on the "unquestionably legitimate" reference to the three-tiered system in *Granholm* and *North Dakota,* recent lower court decisions suggest that any discriminatory law related to "essential features" of the three-tier system either avoids or overcomes Commerce Clause scrutiny. What is not yet clear is whether the Supreme Court shares that perspective. The Court's opinions in *Granholm* and *Tennessee Wine* suggest that it does not.

As mentioned, in *North Dakota v. United States,* the Court upheld North Dakota's labeling and reporting regulations that applied to out-of-state shippers of alcohol beverages.[177] In doing so, Justice Scalia referred to the three-tier system in

170. *Id.*
171. *Id.*
172. *Id.*
173. *Id.*
174. *Id.* 2475-76.
175. *Id.* at 2476.
176. *Id.*
177. 495 U.S. 423.

his concurrence as "unquestionably legitimate."[178] But considering the case resulted in a plurality opinion and did not implicate the Commerce Clause—rather, it involved the Supremacy Clause and federal preemption—some argue that Justice Scalia's comment was pure dicta.[179] Regardless, in *Granholm* the Court acknowledged in passing: "We have previously recognized that the three-tier system itself is 'unquestionably legitimate.'"[180] Lower courts have referenced the comment but come to different conclusions as to its significance and effect.

For instance, in *Arnold's Wines, Inc. v. Boyle*, the Second Circuit upheld a New York state law that prohibited out-of-state wine retailers from delivering directly to in-state consumers.[181] The court considered the challenge "a frontal attack on the constitutionality of the three-tier system itself," which was in its opinion "unquestionably legitimate" under *Granholm.*[182] Appellants argued that language was "merely dicta" but the court wrote "if dicta this be, it is of the most persuasive kind."[183] Notably, *Arnold's Wines* was before the Supreme Court's decision in *Tennessee Wine.*

Even after *Tennessee Wine*, however, courts continue to cling to the proposition that the three-tier system is sacrosanct such that the Twenty-first Amendment immunizes it from Commerce Clause scrutiny. In the wake of *Tennessee Wine,* the Fourth, Sixth, and Eighth Circuits have looked at retailer importation bars that prohibit out-of-state retailers from shipping wine directly to in-state consumers but permit in-state retailers to do so. Those courts found that retailer importation bars discriminate against interstate commerce, but the legitimate non-protectionist ground of preserving a state's three-tier system justified such discrimination.[184]

In *B-21 Wines, Inc. v. Bauer* ("*B-21 Wines*"), for example, the court conceded that a North Carolina statutory scheme by its nature discriminated "to some extent" against interstate commerce.[185] The court went on to frame what it considered to be the pivotal question: To what extent is such discrimination constitutionally permissible?[186] To answer that question, the court turned to *Tennessee Wine* and found it "did not suggest 'that §2 [of the Twenty-first Amendment] sanctions every

---

178. *Id.* at 432.

179. *See generally*, Amy Murphy, *Discarding the North Dakota Dictum: An Argument for Strict Scrutiny of the Three-Tier Distribution System*, 110 MICH. L. REV. 819 (2012); *see also Arnold's Wines, Inc.*, 571 F.3d at 191 ("Appellants reply that the language ... endorsing the three-tier system is merely dicta.").

180. *Granholm*, 544 U.S. at 489.

181. 571 F.3d at 187.

182. *Id.* at 190.

183. *Id.* at 191 (quoting *Arnold's Wines, Inc. v. Boyle*, 515 F. Supp. 2d 401,412 (S.D.N.Y. 2007)) (internal quotation marks omitted).

184. *Lebamoff Enters. v. Whitmer*, 956 F.3d 863 (6th Cir. 2020) (upholding Michigan's alcoholic beverage control regime that permitted in-state retailers to offer at-home deliveries while denying that option to out-of-state retailers); *Sarasota Wine Mkt., LLC v. Schmitt*, 987 F.3d 1171 (8th Cir. 2021) (upholding Missouri's alcohol beverage regime that barred out-of-state retailers, but not in-state retailers from shipping directly to Missouri consumers); *B-21 Wines, Inc. v. Bauer*, 36 F.4th 214 (4th Cir. 2022).

185. *B-21 Wines*, 36 F.4th at 227.

186. *Id.*

discriminatory feature that a State may incorporate into its three-tiered scheme.'"[187] Instead, according to the court's reading of *Tennessee Wine*, the Twenty-first Amendment authorized "essential features" of the three-tier system.[188]

Homing in on this "essential feature" concept, the court in *B-21 Wines* concluded that the discriminatory retailer importation bar was "an integral part of North Carolina's three-tier system" and should thus be upheld.[189] The court first found that the importation bar related to separation of the tiers as it required "nearly all" alcoholic beverages to pass through each of the three tiers before being sold to consumers.[190] Allowing interstate wine retail-to-consumer shipping would completely exempt those out-of-state retailers from the three-tiered requirement. That would open the North Carolina wine market to less regulated wine, as such wine would pass through an out-of-state wholesaler or possibly no wholesaler at all. In sum, citing the Sixth Circuit's decision in *Lebamoff Enters. v. Whitmer*, the court concluded that eliminating the role of North Carolina's wholesalers in this way would create "a sizable hole" in the three-tier system, such that "the least regulated (and thus the cheapest) alcohol will win."[191] Finally, the court dismissed the protectionist and competitive advantage that North Carolina retailers would enjoy via their ability to sell and ship wine to in-state consumers, a privilege not afforded to out-of-state retailers.[192] Interestingly, the court arrived at that conclusion by summarily determining that wine shipping, which is just another way for in-state retailers to sell wine, was an essential aspect of North Carolina's three-tier system.[193] And for those reasons, the *B-21 Wines* court ruled, as its colleagues in the Sixth and Eighth Circuits did when they faced similar situations, that although a retailer importation bar discriminates against interstate commerce, it was nevertheless justified on legitimate non-protectionist grounds of preserving North Carolina's three-tier system.

In a robust, often stinging, rebuke to the majority's cloaking a flatly discriminatory state alcohol law in Twenty-first Amendment immunity, Judge Wilkinson begins his dissent with the following: "By holding that North Carolina may flatly discriminate against out-of-state interests in its alcohol regulations, the majority has forsaken the commercial unity that makes this nation one."[194] The dissent carefully and thoughtfully outlined the majority's failure to subject North Carolina's law, which plainly discriminated on its face, to the necessary strictures of Commerce Clause scrutiny.

The dissent goes on to point out that North Carolina's statutory scheme grants in-state retailers access to the state's consumers on preferential terms.[195] Indeed, §2 of the Twenty-first Amendment authorized evenhanded, non-discriminatory laws for

187. *Id.* (quoting *Tennessee Wine*, 139 S. Ct. at 2471).
188. *Id.*
189. *Id.* at 228.
190. *Id.*
191. *Id.* (quoting *Lebamoff Enters.*, 956 F.3d at 872) (internal quotation marks omitted).
192. *Id.*
193. *Id.*
194. *Id.* at 230.
195. *Id.* at 232.

maintaining an effective and uniform system of controlling liquor—it did "not give states a free hand to restrict the importation of alcohol for purely preferential terms."[196] Judge Wilkinson observed that "[n]evertheless, the majority upholds the law as part of North Carolina's three-tiered scheme, which is itself 'unquestionably legitimate'" in the majority's view.[197] Judge Wilkinson offered the following rebuttal to the majority's insistence on a three-tier system Commerce Clause carve out: "[T]he majority commits the very same mistake identified in *Tennessee Wine* by 'read[ing] far too much into *Granholm*'s discussion of the three-tiered model' which exists to track and regulate the distribution of alcohol."[198] Judge Wilkinson found that "[a]lthough *Granholm* spoke approvingly of that basic model, it did not suggest that §2 sanctions every discriminatory feature that a state may incorporate into its scheme."[199] Besides, Judge Wilkinson continued, "at issue in the present case [wa]s not the basic three-tiered model of separating producers, wholesalers, and retailers" but rather North Carolina's choice to impose on the third tier what amounted to a physical presence requirement.[200] In the dissent's view, "that choice is not essential to maintaining a three-tiered scheme."

Prior to but consistent with the reasoning in Judge Wilkinson's dissent, a federal district court in Minnesota granted judgment on the pleadings to a wholesaler who brought a dormant Commerce Clause challenge to a state law that prohibited exclusive distribution agreements for alcohol produced out-of-state but not for alcohol produced (or "distilled, refined, rectified, or blended") in-state.[201] Citing *Granholm* and *Bacchus*, the court found:

> [A]lthough the three-tiered distribution system itself is unquestionably legitimate, previous cases establish that the ways in which a State implements a three-tiered system under the Twenty-first Amendment are not immune from dormant Commerce Clause scrutiny. Instead, the appropriate question is whether the principles underlying the Twenty-first Amendment are sufficiently implicated . . . to outweigh the Commerce Clause principles that would otherwise be offended.[202]

It is unclear whether the Eighth Circuit or the Supreme Court would agree with that district court. Perhaps the Supreme Court would view retailer "physical presence" requirements in the same light as the Fourth, Sixth, and Eighth Circuits—i.e., as "essential features" of the three-tier system that the Twenty-first Amendment saves from dormant Commerce Clause scrutiny. Or perhaps the Supreme Court would agree with Judge Wilkinson in his *B-21 Wines* dissent and require states to

---

196. *Id.* at 233 (quoting *Tennessee Wine*, 139 S. Ct. at 2469) (internal quotation marks omitted).

197. *Id.* at 234 (internal citations omitted).

198. *Id.* at 234 (quoting *Tennessee Wine*, 139 S. Ct. at 2471).

199. *Id.* (quoting *Tennessee Wine*, 139 S. Ct. at 2471) (internal quotation marks omitted).

200. *Id.*

201. *S. Glazer's Wine & Spirits, LLC v. Harrington*, No. 21-1254 JRT/ECW, 2022 U.S. Dist. LEXIS 57077, 2022 WL 912032 (D. Minn. Mar. 29, 2022).

202. *Id.*

meet the same dormant Commerce Clause standards applied in *Tennessee Wine* and with concrete evidence. Only time will tell.

H. WHAT WILL BE THE NEXT SUPREME COURT BATTLE?

The Supreme Court made clear in *Tennessee Wine* that durational residency requirements imposed upon retailers inherently discriminate against out-of-state individuals and entities and are thus subject to dormant Commence Clause scrutiny. As it stands, however, the Court has not had to decide whether imposing a "physical presence" requirement on a retailer is also inherently discriminatory and subject to dormant Commerce Clause scrutiny. At oral arguments in *Tennessee Wine*, the Court foresaw this issue of "physical presence" requirements in a telling exchange with counsel for the two retailers challenging the state's durational requirement:

> JUSTICE GORSUCH: . . . I would think that the next case would be . . . the requirement of physical presence in state, that . . . this three-tier system is, in fact, discriminatory by requiring some sort of physical presence in state. And under the dormant Commerce Clause jurisprudence, you have a point. You have a good point. So I — why isn't this just the camel's nose under the tent?
>
> MR. PHILLIPS: Well, if only because, under these circumstances, as the camel at least, or I guess I'm the nose of the camel, that's not what I'm looking for.
>
> JUSTICE GORSUCH: I think you may be, yes. (Laughter.)
>
> MR. PHILLIPS: I am not . . . you know, it is fundamentally at odds with my client's business model to be looking to undo the three-tier principle.[203]

In other words, the Court was already thinking about whether a "physical presence" requirement necessarily triggers dormant Commerce Clause scrutiny. Not surprisingly, counsel for the two in-state retailers—who benefitted from a physical presence requirement—reminded the Court that was not what his clients were asking for and it was an issue the Court could save for another day. At other times, the Court raised the issue of how states "can achieve all the regulatory interests it wants . . . dealing with virtual sellers from outside of the state, just as easily as it can with the physical presence sellers in state" but recognized, "that's tomorrow's argument, isn't it?"[204] Accordingly, the issue of whether a "physical presence" requirement for retailers would be subject to dormant Commerce Clause scrutiny remains, perhaps, unresolved.

To be sure, there is more to the issue. For instance, if the Twenty-first Amendment shields essential features of the three-tier system—which, as noted,

---

203. Transcript of Oral Argument at 49:19-50:17, *Tennessee Wine* (No. 18-96), *available at* https://www.supremecourt.gov/oral_arguments/argument_transcripts/2018/18-96_09m1.pdf (last visited Aug. 20, 2022).

204. *Id.* at 56:21-57:03.

some courts contend[205]—then one question would be whether a "physical presence" requirement for retailers constitutes an essential feature. Indeed, what remains unclear in the post-*Tennessee Wine* circuit court decisions is what, if any, criteria are used to determine whether a feature of the three-tier system is in fact "essential." In *Tennessee Wine*, the Court found that the state's durational residency requirement was *not* an essential feature of the three-tier system because "[m]any such schemes [in other states] do not impose durational-residency requirements—or indeed any residency requirements—on individual or corporate liquor store owners."[206] That suggests if "physical presence" is not required in some states, then it is not an essential feature of the three-tier system. In his dissent in *B-21 Wines*, Judge Wilkinson came to the same conclusion and cited examples of "many states with three-tiered systems [that] do allow out-of-state retailers to ship wine on the same terms as in-state retailers."[207] Moreover, *Granholm* made clear that "physical presence" requirements for producers to sell directly to consumers is inherently discriminatory and subject to dormant Commerce Clause scrutiny.

Another issue is whether or to what extent a state is relieved of all burdens once it asserts that an "essential feature" of the three-tier system is being challenged. Many of the post-*Tennessee Wine* circuit court decisions appear to accept unsupported assertions that a discriminatory aspect of the three-tier system is an "essential feature" and take to heart the *North Dakota* dicta that the three-tier system is "unquestionably legitimate." According to the court in *B-21 Wines*, "[w]hen . . . an essential feature of a state's three-tier system is challenged, a court's role is more limited and does not entail an examination of the effectiveness of the three-tier system."[208] That means a state need not provide concrete evidence that a challenged law—even if it discriminates against out-of-state commence—promotes public health or safety.[209] The court in *B-21 Wines* also did away with any burden on the state to explain why nondiscriminatory alternatives would not suffice: "Although consideration of nondiscriminatory alternatives could have some relevance to that inquiry, it does not transform the applicable framework into the test that ordinarily applies to a dormant Commerce Clause challenge when the Twenty-first Amendment is not implicated."[210]

At oral arguments in *Tennessee Wine*, Justice Gorsuch was almost certainly right that these issues will constitute "tomorrow's argument[s]." Given that nearly 15 years passed between *Granholm* and *Tennessee Wine*, what is less certain is when tomorrow will come. Until then, the debates will no doubt continue.

---

205. *See* note 184 *supra.*

206. *Tennessee Wine,* 139 S. Ct. at 2471-72.

207. *B-21 Wines*, 36 F.4th at 235 (citing Cal. Bus. & Prof. Code §23661.2; Conn. Gen. Stat. §30-18a; Idaho Code §23-1309A; La. Rev. Stat. §26:359; Neb. Rev. Stat. §53-123.15; N.H. Rev. Stat. §178:27; N.M. Stat. §60-7A-3; Or. Rev. Stat. §471.282; Va. Code §§4.1-206.3(F), - 209.1; W. Va. Code §60-8-6; Wyo. Stat. §12-2-204).

208. *B-21 Wines, 36 F.4th at 227 n.8.*

209. *Id.* at 228.

210. *Id.* at 225-26.

CHAPTER 6

WINE BRANDS AND APPELLATIONS OF ORIGIN

Richard Mendelson and Scott Gerien

The World Trade Organization (WTO) Agreement on Trade-Related Aspects of Intellectual Property Rights (TRIPS)[1] establishes the types of intellectual property rights that must be recognized by WTO members. The United States is a WTO member. Under TRIPS, intellectual property rights are generally divided into two areas: (1) industrial property, such as patents and distinctive signs and, in particular, trademarks and geographical indications;[2] and (2) copyright and related rights.

According to TRIPS, all intellectual property rights have equal stature. By and large, there is no conflict among the various types of intellectual property. The best-known and frequently used intellectual properties—copyright, trademark, and patent—rarely overlap. When multiple intellectual properties coincide, they usually coexist harmoniously because they serve distinct purposes.

Trademarks and geographical indications, however, are distinctive signs that serve different purposes and often do come into conflict. In the wine industry, the same term may be utilized as a trademark (a wine brand) to designate the producer of a product and as a geographical indication (an appellation of origin) to designate the geographical origin of the product. This dual usage can result in thorny questions about priority of rights, possible coexistence, and possible consumer confusion.

In the United States, the potential for conflict is exacerbated by the U.S. government, which acknowledges geographical indications as intellectual property

1. TRIPS: Agreement on Trade-Related Aspects of Intellectual Property Rights, Apr. 15, 1994, Marrakesh Agreement Establishing the World Trade Organization, Annex 1C, 1869 U.N.T.S. 299, 33 I.L.M. 1197 (1994) (hereinafter TRIPS Agreement).

2. TRIPS Article 22(i) defines geographical indications as "indications which identify a good as originating in the territory of a Member, or a region or locality in that territory, where a given quality, reputation or other characteristic of the good is essentially attributable to its geographical origin."

pursuant to TRIPS but has failed to fully define what constitutes a geographical indication under U.S. law. Neither statute nor case law clearly states whether geographical indications in the United States are geographical certification marks under the federal Lanham Act, appellations of origin for wine under the Federal Alcohol Administration (FAA) Act, or something else entirely.[3]

What is clear, however, is that in the United States one federal law protects trademarks as distinctive signs, and a separate body of federal law and a separate enforcement authority protect appellations of origins for wines as distinctive signs. The conflicts, inconsistencies, and commonalities between the rights offered under these laws, the procedures for obtaining these rights, and the forums for seeking redress for infringement of these rights make this area of law difficult to navigate. For that reason, a clear understanding of the laws governing brands and appellations of origin is of great value to members of the wine industry.

In Sections A and B, which follow, Scott Gerien addresses trademarks and copyrights, respectively. In Section C, Richard Mendelson discusses appellations of origin. The authors note at the outset that it is beyond the scope of this chapter to analyze TRIPS itself or the case law thereunder. We confine our discussion to U.S. law.

A. TRADEMARK LAW

The wine industry is one of the most fragmented industries for consumer goods in the United States. In 2021, the U.S. Patent and Trademark Office (USPTO) received 4,538 applications to register trademarks for wine and issued 2,295 trademark registrations for wine. The Alcohol and Tobacco Tax and Trade Bureau of the U.S. Treasury Department (TTB) approved 110,500 products relating to wine between July 2021 and July 2022.[4] In this market, crowded with wine brands, a foundational understanding of trademark law is critical.

In the United States, the Lanham Act defines trademark law at the federal level. Most states also have statutory provisions in addition to the common law that govern the protection of marks.[5] In terms of the scope of protection, federal trademark registration is more advantageous than state registration because federal trademark rights extend to the entire United States. Registration under state law only confers rights in the particular state in which the registration is obtained. In situations involving alleged trademark infringement or dilution, a party often seeks

3. The Lanham Act is at 15 U.S.C. §1051The FAA Act is at 28 U.S.C. §§201-212.

4. BW166, *TTB Approved 176K Products L12M through July 2022, A Decrease of -0.8K* (–0.4%), (Aug. 16, 2022) available at https://www.bw166.com/product/the-total-beverage-alcohol-overview/.

5. *See, e.g.*, Cal. Bus. & Prof. Code §§14200-14272, 17200-17210 (2021); N.Y. Gen. Bus. Law §§360-360-R (2010); Or. Rev. Statutes §§647.005-647.155 (2021); Wash. Rev. Code §§19.77.010-19.77.040 (2021).

protection under both federal and state law; the legal analysis in either jurisdiction is generally the same.[6]

As defined by the Lanham Act, a mark is a designation used to identify the goods and/or services of a party and to distinguish them from the goods and services of others.[7] A designation must be used in some prominent, distinctive manner in association with the particular product or service in order to communicate the mark's source-identifying purpose. The mark's use must communicate to the consumer that the designation is a brand identifying the particular producer of the product.[8] Using a designation in a manner that does not communicate its source-identifying function (e.g., as an aesthetic embellishment on packaging) will not establish the designation as a mark.

In the wine industry, the designation identifying the source of the goods is typically a word or group of words. Most commonly, the designation is the brand name of the wine, which is usually the most prominent term on the wine label. This designation is sometimes referred to as the "house mark." Brand names for wine include ROBERT MONDAVI, SUTTER HOME, and KENDALL-JACKSON, among many others with varying degrees of consumer recognition.

Other words on a label, which may serve as marks due to their source-designating symbolism, may be referred to as sub-brands. These label designations are usually subordinate in appearance or importance to the main brand, but they still assist the consumer in associating the particular wine with a particular producer. Sub-brands may be names of special proprietary wine blends or simply names used to differentiate various wines under the same house mark. For example, D'ARENBERG is a well-known Australian brand that features different wines under the D'ARENBERG house mark, all with unique names such as LAUGHING MAGPIE, THE FOOTBOLT, and THE DEAD ARM. All of these terms may be legally categorized as trademarks.

A "vineyard designation" also may appear on wine labels.[9] A vineyard designation functions like a sub-brand in that it usually appears on a wine label subordinate to the main brand; more specifically, it informs consumers about the source of the wine or, more particularly, the source of the wine grapes. A well-known vineyard designation is MARTHA'S VINEYARD, found on Heitz Cellars wine. This designation under TTB labeling regulations informs consumers that at least 95 percent of the wine is made from wine grapes grown on the vineyard property known as Martha's Vineyard. Section C below will cover this point in more depth.

---

6. *One Industries v. Jim O'Neal Distrib., Inc.*, 578 F.3d 1154, 1166 n.5 (9th Cir. 2009) (California trademark claims congruent to claims under Lanham Act) (citing *Acad. of Motion Picture Arts & Scis. v. Creative House Promotions, Inc.*, 944 F.2d 1446, 1457 (9th Cir. 1991).

7 .15 U.S.C. §1127 (2006).

8. Patent and Trademark Office, U.S. Dept. of Commerce, Trademark Manual of Examining Procedure (hereinafter TMEP) §1202 (July 2022).

9. *See* J. Scott Gerien, *The Vineyard Designation: Branding and Trademark Issues for Wineries and Vineyard Owners*, Wine Business Monthly, April 15, 2003.

Another example of a word mark is a tagline—a phrase used in the marketing and promotion of wine associated in the minds of consumers with a particular wine or producer. An early, classic example of a tagline in the wine industry was WE SHALL SELL NO WINE BEFORE ITS TIME, which consumers recognized as representing PAUL MASSON wine.

Logos, graphic presentations on a label, packaging elements, or even catalog covers, besides words, may also serve as symbols designating the source of particular own commercial impression; the logo may have independent significance as a mark. Figures 6-1 and 6-2 are two examples of wine logos with independent trademark significance.

Figure 6-1
Barefoot Logo (Registration No. 3,780,742)

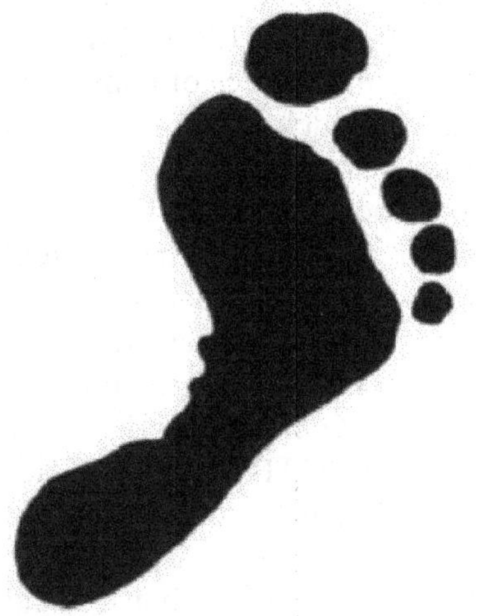

Figure 6-2
Ravenswood Logo (Registration No. 2,130,653)

The overall graphic representation of a label design also can have trademark significance. This is sometimes referred to as trade dress. Trade dress is the overall look and feel created by the packaging. Figures 6-3 and 6-4 are two examples of wine label designs protected as trademarks.

Figure 6-3
Vistamar Label (Registration No. 3,809,013)

Figure 6-4
Clancy's Label (Registration No. 3,712,315)

One of the most notable wine industry trademark cases involving trade dress is *Kendall-Jackson v. E. & J. Gallo.*[10] This case involved a dispute over the trade dress of two wine bottles, shown in Figure 6-5. Kendall-Jackson claimed that Gallo infringed its trade dress, consisting of a Bordeaux or Burgundy style wine bottle with a flanged lip, exposed cork, neck label, and a cream-colored rectangular main label with a multi-colored grape leaf bordered by gold bands.[11] Ultimately, the jury found that Gallo's trade dress for its TURNING LEAF product did not create a likelihood of consumer confusion, and on that basis no infringement was found.

Figure 6-5
KENDALL-JACKSON and TURNING LEAF Bottles

10. *Kendall-Jackson Winery, Ltd. v. E. & J. Gallo Winery,* 150 F.3d 1042 (9th Cir. 1998).

11. *Id.* The black-and-white bottle images reproduced here do not reveal the similar colors of the leaves on the two bottles.

As with logos, particular design elements of product packaging that create a distinctive commercial impression may be protected as marks. As shown in Figure 6-6, a unique presentation of alternating horizontal lines and rectangular boxes forming the background design for a label have been registered. Similarly, a unique presentation of swirls forming the background design for a label and the exterior and interior of a wine shipper have been registered (Figure 6-7).

Figure 6-6
Terra D'Oro Striped Capsule (Registration No. 3,122,409)

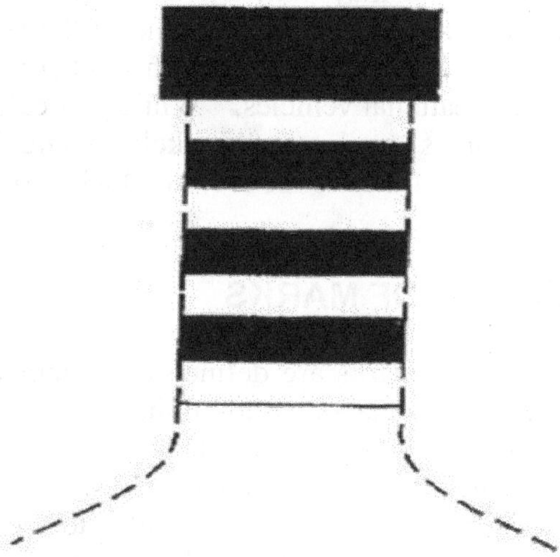

Figure 6-7
Clos Du Val Swirl Designs (Registration No. 3,066,515)

A single color may be protectable as a trademark although color alone is not inherently distinctive.[12] For a color to be protectable, it must acquire "secondary meaning" as a mark in the minds of consumers.[13] In the wine industry, producers have attempted to protect bottle color[14] and the color of labels[15] with mixed results. Even where color can be protected, the level of protection for such a mark may be diminished because, when evaluating the likelihood of confusion, the marks must be considered in the context of the entire packaging on which they appear. Often, the entire package has elements in addition to color that reduce any likelihood of confusion.

Although there do not appear to be any sound or smell marks in the wine industry, sound and smell also may function as symbols creating trademark significance. The distinctive sound of NBC's chime of the notes G, E, and C is protected,[16] as is the smell of cherry associated with synthetic lubricants for high-performance racing and recreational vehicles.[17] While particular wines are known for having distinctive aromas, such smells likely would be categorized as descriptive of the goods rather than distinctive, in which case they would not be protectable as marks.

1. CLASSIFICATION OF MARKS

This section explains how marks are defined as trademarks, service marks, certification marks, or collective marks based on their function. Any of the types of symbols identified in the previous section, including words, designs, and trade dress, can serve as any of the mark types discussed below.

The term "trademark" is commonly used to refer to the entire area of law dealing with marks as defined and protected under the Lanham Act. Technically, however, "trademark" only refers to marks used in association with goods as a means of designating the producer of the goods.

Service marks are marks used in association with services to designate the source of the services. Wine industry services include the retail sale of wine, wine club services, the production of wine for others, and vineyard management services.

Certification marks are terms or symbols that certify the quality and/or origin of a particular good or service. Some certification marks are intended solely to indicate that a product or service has met certain quality requirements. For instance, Underwriters Laboratories' "UL" certification mark indicates and

12. *See Qualitex Co. v. Jacobson Prods. Co.*, 514 U.S. 159 (1995).

13. *See Wal-Mart Stores v. Samara Bros.*, 529 U.S. 205 (2000).

14. *See Freixenet v. Admiral Wine,* 731 F.2d 148 (3d Cir. 1984) (black bottle protectable as part of overall trade dress, but no confusing similarity found due to label differences); *see also Sazerac Co. v. Skyy Spirits*, 95 F.3d 53 (5th Cir. 1996) (cobalt blue bottle used by Skyy Spirits not protectable due to numerous examples of third-party use of cobalt blue bottles for alcoholic beverages).

15. Veuve Clicquot Ponsardin Maison Fondee En 1772 is the owner of U.S. Trademark Registration No. 2,052,302 for the color "orangish-yellow" used on labels for wine.

16. Registration No. 916,522.

17. Registration No. 2,463,044.

certifies that products bearing that mark have met certain safety standards.[18] As another example, the Demeter Association certifies that certain goods produced from agricultural products, including wine, use agricultural ingredients that are grown with sustainable farming practices and produced with sustainable manufacturing processes. The certified goods are allowed to use the DEMETER certification mark.[19] Geographical certification marks certify the origin of goods. They also may, but do not necessarily, certify the quality of the goods.[20] Examples in the wine industry include ASTI,[21] NAPA VALLEY,[22] and LODI RULES.[23]

Unlike a trademark owner, the owner of a certification mark *cannot* use the certification mark; the mark may only be used to certify the goods of other parties who are entitled to use the mark.[24] This restriction is intended to maintain the integrity of the certification process. Additionally, any party whose products meet the certification standards may apply for certification and thereby be entitled to use the mark. The standards must be applied to all parties equally.[25] Finally, the certifier, not the government (unless the government is the owner of the certification mark), polices the users of the certification mark to ensure that the certification standards are being met.[26] However, an action to cancel a certification mark may be filed by any party with the USPTO.[27]

For geographical certification marks, the certifier must demonstrate that it has the authority to control the geographical term that is the subject of the certification mark. The certifier may be a government agency; if not, the certifier typically should be able to show that it is acting with the authority of a government agency.[28]

Geographical certification marks are an important way to protect the names of geographical regions known for the production of certain types of goods. In practice, however, the use of certification marks in the wine industry has been minimal. The main reason is that TTB's wine appellation program has made geographical certification marks for the wine industry superfluous. Nevertheless, geographical certification marks still may play an important role in protecting wine appellations at home and abroad.

Finally, collective marks are used on goods or services exclusively by members of an association or organization.[29] A certification process or standard is not required for a collective mark, although the organization may elect to set standards for its members. Compared to certification marks, the rules related to the

---

18. Registration No. 782,589.
19. Registration No. 2,097,887.
20. 15 U.S.C. §1127 (2006); TMEP §1306.02 (6th ed., May 2010).
21. Registration No. 3,369,276.
22. Registration No. 4,853,438.
23. Registration No. 3,736,972. *See* Section C for a discussion of the LODI RULES certification mark.
24. 15 U.S.C. §1127 (2022).
25. *Id.*
26. *Id.*
27. 15 U.S.C. §1064 (2022).
28. TMEP §1306.2(b) (July 2022).
29. 15 U.S.C. §1127 (2022).

use and availability of collective marks are less strict, making collective marks easier to maintain. In the wine industry, an example of a collective mark is WINE AND SPIRITS GUILD OF AMERICA.[30]

2. PROTECTABILITY AND THE SPECTRUM OF MARKS

All marks can be placed on a spectrum based on their degree of inherent distinctiveness and the protectability of the mark. Marks that are inherently distinctive and protectable upon their adoption are at one end of the spectrum. These marks are characterized as fanciful, arbitrary, or suggestive. At the other end of the spectrum are marks that are not inherently distinctive and either not protectable at the time of their adoption but capable of acquiring distinctiveness through use (i.e., descriptive marks) or not ever protectable, being non-exclusively used by all (i.e., generic marks).[31]

Fanciful marks consist of those terms or symbols that have no meaning and are completely original, the product of the imagination of their creators. An abstract design such as that found on the INTRINSIC label (Figure 6-8) or wine brands such as TRUVAY[32] and ZULAL,[33] which have no known meaning, are fanciful marks. Because the meaning of these marks is unknown, consumers will associate them exclusively with the producer owning the particular mark. For this reason, fanciful marks are inherently distinctive and are considered the most distinctive of all marks.[34]

Arbitrary marks are next on the spectrum of inherent distinctiveness. An arbitrary mark is a term or design that already exists in the consumer's consciousness but not in association with the product or service with which it is used. Arbitrary marks include a wine label featuring the image of a red truck and such wine brand names as APOTHIC,[35] MAYA,[36] and BANDIT.[37] Although these designations mean something to consumers, the meaning is not associated with wine. As a result, the apparently arbitrary use of the mark in association with an unexpected product may make a strong and distinctive impression on consumers.[38]

Situated near the dividing line between distinctive and non-distinctive marks are those that suggest, but do not describe, a quality or characteristic of the product. The consumer must go through a multi-step thought process to associate the suggestive mark with the quality or characteristic of the good or service on which it is used. For example, the process of "veraison" occurs when grapes mature and

30. Registration No. 2,277,008.
31. *See Kendall-Jackson*, 150 F.3d at 1047.
32. Registration No. 6,472,855.
33. Registration No. 6,530,928.
34. *Kendall-Jackson*, 150 F.3d at 1047 n. 8.
35. Registration No. 4,093,343.
36. Registration No. 2,508,401.
37. Registration No. 3,311,926.
38. *Kendall-Jackson*, 150 F.3d at 1047 n. 8

change color during the growing season.[39] Consumers seeing the brand VERAISON on a wine bottle will not immediately understand if the brand name relates to wine; they will follow a multi-part reasoning process: veraison is a stage of the grape growing process; grapes are used to make wine; therefore, VERAISON is suggestive of wine.[40] A suggestive mark such as VERAISON is distinctive upon adoption and immediately registerable.[41]

Figure 6-8
Intrinsic Label

39. According to Jancis Robinson, veraison is the "intermediate stage of grape berry development which marks the beginning of ripening, when the grapes change from the hard, green state to their softened and coloured form." The Oxford Companion to Wine 1017 (Jancis Robinson ed., 1st ed. 1994).

40. *See Kendall Jackson*, 150 F.3d at 1048-49 ("The use of a grape leaf as a mark for wine would normally be inherently distinctive because it suggests, rather than describes, the product. One has to go through two or three steps to associate the leaf with the product—i.e., a grape leaf comes from a grapevine, which has grapes from which wine is produced. Under the standard test, a grape leaf could be suggestive and thus inherently distinctive.")

41. Registration No. 2,753,822.

Certain suggestive marks are less distinctive than others. The less distinctive marks may be described as "highly suggestive." Such marks are protectable; however, they are harder to protect than marks that are arbitrary or fanciful.[42]

Descriptive marks describe a quality or characteristic of the product or services on which the marks are used. Descriptive marks are not protectable upon their adoption but may acquire distinctiveness through use as a brand in association with a product or service. Descriptive marks are said to acquire a secondary meaning in the minds of consumers over time.

Descriptive wine industry marks that have acquired the distinctiveness required for protection include DOUBLE BARREL AGED[43] and CUVEE ROUGE.[44] The USPTO often will find terms descriptive that are actually suggestive of wine, such as "barrel," "plump," and "oak." In these instances, practitioners in the wine industry may consider taking steps to challenge the USPTO's determination.

Another form of descriptive mark is the surname of the wine producer. More than in any other industry, surnames are commonly used as trademarks for wine. On adoption, surnames are not protectable because a person should not be able to claim exclusivity in a name shared by others absent a showing of acquired distinctiveness. Indeed, even some of the best-known surname brands coexist, such as ROBERT MONDAVI and CK MONDAVI, as a result of the strong judicial tendency in the common law to allow an individual to use their surname in association with the product they produce.[45] Therefore, while Georgina Gerien might be the first to use Gerien as a trademark for wine, her brother Cameron Gerien would not be precluded from using Cameron Gerien as his brand of wine absent some showing of strength and acquired distinctiveness of the Gerien mark. That being said, some of the best-known marks in the wine industry are surnames that have acquired distinctiveness as wine brands: WENTE,[46] ANTINORI,[47] and TAITTINGER,[48] for example.[49]

Because wine is a product of place, geographical terms are almost as commonly used as surnames in wine marks. Typically, geographical terms in trademarks are either "primarily geographically descriptive,"[50] in which case they

---

42. *See Minnesota Mining & Mfg. Co. v. Johnson & Johnson*, 454 F.2d 1179, 1180 (C.C.P.A. 1972) ("Often the best trademarks are highly suggestive, and it is well settled that a valid trademark may be highly suggestive.").

43. Registration No. 3,802,353.

44. Registration No. 3,374,998.

45. *See Friend v. H.A. Friend & Co.*, 416 F.2d 526, 531 (9th Cir. 1969), *cert. denied* 397 U.S. 914 (1970) ("the law is reluctant to preclude an individual's business use of his own name when no attempt to confuse the public has been made").

46. Registration No. 1,535,670.

47. Registration No. 1,155,028.

48. Registration No. 1,420,365.

49. *See, e.g., E. & J. Gallo Winery v. Gallo Cattle Co.*, 967 F.2d 1280 (9th Cir. 1992) (despite judicial reluctance to preclude one from using his own name, the court upheld injunction restricting brother of winery's principals from using GALLO as trademark on cheese due to strength of mark and consumer confusion).

50. A mark is primarily geographically descriptive if (1) the primary significance of the mark is geographic; (2) purchasers would likely think that the goods originate in the place identified in the

are not protectable, or they are misdescriptive of the wine's origin. But there are many exceptions. Some terms may have both geographical significance and non-geographical significance, but the overall significance is not primarily geographical. Even a term that is solely geographical may not be *primarily* geographically descriptive or misdescriptive if there is no goods-place association in the minds of consumers between the geographical term and the goods on which it is used.[51] For instance, San Lorenzo is the name of an Italian saint as well as a city in California that has no association with the cultivation or production of wine. Therefore, the mark SAN LORENZO is neither primarily geographically descriptive nor misdescriptive of wine and is protectable as a trademark for wine.[52] As another example, there is an area in California called Cuttings Wharf, where grapes are grown. Despite the descriptiveness of the name, CUTTINGS WHARF was found to be protectable as a trademark for wine because the area is not known to consumers and, therefore, is not primarily geographically descriptive.[53]

An important distinction between geographically descriptive and misdescriptive marks is that the former are not protectable absent acquired distinctiveness, but they still may be used on products so long as they are not misleading. Wine trademarks often include the name of the geographical area in which the grapes are grown in an effort to take advantage of the recognition of the particular region. Yet these brand owners know, or should know, that they cannot prevent others from using the same geographical term in their own marks.[54]

By contrast, trademarks that are primarily geographically misdescriptive and may deceptively influence consumer purchasing decisions violate the trademark laws and may not be used by anyone.[55]

Following the U.S. adoption of TRIPS, the use of a non-generic geographical indication on wine not from the place identified by the geographical indication is strictly prohibited for all wine brands adopted after 1996, regardless of whether the consumer is misled by the use of the geographical indication.[56] Thus, pursuant to Article 23 of TRIPS, the name of an obscure geographical area that produces a

---

mark (i.e., there is a place-goods association); and (3) the mark identifies the geographic origin of the goods. *See* 15 U.S.C. §1052(e)(2).

51. *See In re Brouwerij Nacional Balashi NV*, 80 USPQ 2d 1820 (TTAB 2006) (Balashi, Aruba is obscure to U.S. consumers and therefore registerable as a trademark for beer from that place).

52. Registration No. 3,003,575.

53. Registration No. 3,337,951.

54. Examples include the marks RUTHERFORD RIDGE, RUTHERFORD HILL, and RUTHERFORD RANCH, each of which refers to the Rutherford AVA situated inside the Napa Valley AVA. None of the owners of these marks has exclusive rights to the term "Rutherford," but each owner has exclusive rights in its own composite mark and benefits from the association of the brand with the AVA.

55. *See, e.g.*, *Bronco Wine Co. v. Jolly*, 33 Cal. 4th 943 (2004) (upholding state consumer protection law requiring wine labels using "Napa" to qualify for the Napa County or Napa Valley appellation because consumers otherwise would be deceived).

56. 15 U.S.C. §1052(a); *see* TRIPS, *supra* note 1, at art. 22 and 23; Uruguay Round Agreements Act (URAA), Pub. L. No. 103-465, 103 Stat. 4809. The 1996 grandfather date, set forth in TRIPS, is distinct from the TTB's grandfather date for geographical brands, 1986, which is discussed in detail below.

wine with particular characteristics may not be used or registered as part of a trademark for wine not from that area even if consumers in the United States have no familiarity with this geographical area. Presently, the USPTO appears to take a different approach to obscure geographical names. The use or registration of a geographical term on wine or spirits not from the identified area will only be prohibited if the name has developed a reputation among U.S. consumers. The USPTO's focus on whether the mark, in fact, misleads consumers is not required under Article 23 of TRIPS.[57]

Descriptive marks, including geographically descriptive marks and surnames, can cross the divide from non-distinctive to distinctive if they establish over time secondary meaning as brand names in the minds of consumers. Descriptive marks with secondary meaning are fully protectable in the same way as suggestive, arbitrary, or fanciful marks. The owner of the descriptive mark carries the burden of demonstrating acquired distinctiveness. In the context of trademark registration, this burden may be met by continuous exclusive use of the mark in U.S. commerce for a period of five years.[58] Secondary meaning also may be demonstrated by a significant sale of the product or significant advertising featuring the mark.[59] However, the best evidence of acquired distinctiveness, especially in an infringement action in federal court, is a consumer survey demonstrating consumer recognition of the mark as a brand.[60]

Different rules regarding the distinctiveness and exclusive use of geographical names apply to certification marks and collective marks. A geographical certification mark may be registered by the certifier under the name of the specific geographical area, and that name will receive instant protection and exclusivity without a showing that consumers have come to recognize the term as a distinctive geographical identifier. Thus, if the city of Chattanooga, Tennessee, wishes to obtain the certification mark CHATTANOOGA for wine made from grapes grown in Chattanooga, it would be able to claim exclusive rights in the trademark use of that term in association with wine even though the term is descriptive of a geographical place and has not acquired distinctiveness with consumers as a geographical indication. Once such a certification mark is registered, a winery in Chattanooga that makes wine from grapes grown there could not call itself Chattanooga Winery without the permission of the city of Chattanooga, the owner of the certification mark, to use the name Chattanooga.

On the other hand, the owner of a collective mark with geographical significance, for example, a regional trade association, may not claim exclusive use in the geographical term absent some evidence of fame or acquired distinctiveness. Thus, if a group of winegrowers from Lodi, California, wished to register LODI WINEGROWERS as a collective mark, it would have to disclaim

---

57. TMEP §1210.08(a) (July 2022).

58. 15 U.S.C. §1052(f).

59. *See In re Uncle Sam Chemical Co.*, 229 USPQ 233, 235 (TTAB 1986) ("over eighteen years of substantially exclusive and continuous use of the term together with evidence of considerable sales of products sold under the mark is sufficient to support a claim of acquired distinctiveness").

60. *See Yankee Candle Co. v. Bridgewater Candle Co.*, 259 F.3d 25, 43 (1st Cir. 2001).

exclusive rights to the term "LODI," and others would be allowed to use that name as part of competing collective marks (e.g., LODI WINERY ASSOCIATION) or as trademarks (e.g., LODI CELLARS). Put another way, the winegrowers' collective mark would not give them exclusivity in the use of the term "LODI."

Generic marks lie at the far end of non-distinctiveness. Under trademark law, a mark is generic if it functions to identify the product itself or has been used in such a way so as to become an identifier of the product type in the minds of consumers. "Wine" is and always has been the generic term for wine, as it identifies the product. The court in the *Kendall-Jackson v. Gallo* case found that grape leaves, although originally suggestive of wine, had become generic symbols due to their prevalent use on wine labels in the marketplace.[61] Similarly, the term "champagne" has come to be recognized as a generic term for sparkling wine in the United States despite the fact that it is also a winegrowing region in France and is recognized outside the United States as a geographical indication for sparkling wine from that region.[62]

Unlike descriptive marks, generic terms or symbols may not acquire distinctiveness through use. Therefore, to the extent that a mark encompasses a term that conceivably could be defined as generic or descriptive, a party hoping to claim exclusivity in that term through use must not allow it to be classified as generic by the USPTO or otherwise.

In conclusion, the most distinctive brands are the easiest to register as trademarks. They also receive the highest level of protection against any confusingly similar brands. The distinctiveness of a brand, however, does not imply the successful marketing of the brand. Brands resonate with consumers for different reasons; brands with strong impact are not always distinctive. If a brand resonates with consumers because it describes some characteristic of the wine, for example, its geographical origin or the family producing the wine, the brand owner may find it difficult to prevent others from capitalizing on that same point of appeal in their own brand names.

3. ADOPTION AND REGISTRATION OF MARKS

In the United States marks can only be protected if they are used in commerce. Under common law, once a mark is used in commerce, rights in the mark are established in association with the particular goods and services. However, common law rights are limited to the geographical area in which the mark is actually used.[63] For example, if a California wine brand is not federally registered as a trademark and is only sold in California, the California winery cannot stop a

61. *Kendall-Jackson*, 150 F.3d at 1048-49.

62. *See, e.g., Door Systems, Inc. v. Pro-Line Door Systems, Inc.*, 83 F.3d 169, 170-71 (7th Cir. 1996) (dictum that "champagne" is a generic term identifying the product). The TTB classifies "champagne" as semi-generic for reasons explained in Section C.

63. *See Hanover Star Milling Co. v. Metcalf*, 240 U.S. 403 (1916); *see also Grupo Gigane SA De CV v. Dallo & Co., Inc.*, 391 F.3d 1088 (9th Cir. 2004) (priority of use in one area of the United States does not necessarily suffice to establish priority in another area).

New York winery from subsequently using the same brand name for its wine sold only in New York. Furthermore, if the California brand wine were ever sold in New York, the California winery would be infringing on the New York winery's common law rights despite the California winery's earlier common law use of the brand name in California.

a. Use in Commerce Requirement for Federal Registration

Federal registration of trademarks avoids the confusion and conflicts caused by ambiguous or overlapping markets by granting rights throughout the United States and in all of its territories.[64] Like common law rights, federal trademark rights cannot be secured unless or until the mark is used in commerce.[65] The Lanham Act defines commerce as "all commerce which may be lawfully regulated by Congress."[66] According to the Commerce Clause of the U.S. Constitution, use in commerce means the sale or transport of marked goods across state lines or between the United States and a foreign nation.[67] However, because Congress regulates the production and sale of wine in the United States,[68] it can be argued that even the intrastate sale of wine is commerce regulated by Congress and, therefore, sufficient to meet the "use in commerce" requirement for federal registration of a mark.[69]

Use in commerce to support federal registration must be a "legal" use.[70] This means that the sale or shipment of any product that is the subject of an act of Congress, such as the Food, Drug and Cosmetic Act or the Meat Inspection Act, must comply with the applicable federal law to be considered a "legal" use for purposes of registration under the Lanham Act.[71] In the wine industry, the FAA Act requires all wineries to be qualified and permitted by the TTB; wineries also must obtain a COLA, or COLA exemption, for their wine labels before those wines are released from bond for sale.[72] The shipment or sale of wine that has not complied with these requirements arguably would not be a "legal" use sufficient to support a federal trademark registration. However, the USPTO is not inclined to make such determinations of "legality" under regulations established by other government agencies, including the TTB.[73]

---

64. *See Giant Foods, Inc. v. Nation's Foodservice, Inc.*, 710 F.2d 1565, 1568 (Fed. Cir. 1983).
65. 15 U.S.C. §1127 (2006).
66. *Id.*
67. U.S. Const., art. I, §8, cl. 3.
68. *See* Federal Alcohol Administration Act, 27 U.S.C. §202.
69. See *Christian Faith Fellowship Church v. Adidas AG*, 841 F.3d 986, 995 (Fed. Cir. 2016) (the reasoning in the Christian Faith holding of the Federal Circuit provides analogous support for this concept).
70. *See* C.F.R. §2.69 (2021).
71. *Id.*; *see also In re Stellar Int'l Inc.*, 159 USPQ 48 (TTAB 1968) (requiring compliance with Food, Drug and Cosmetic Act for registration); *In re Cook United, Inc.*, 188 USPQ 284 (TTAB 1975) (requiring compliance with Meat Inspection Act for registration).
72. 27 U.S.C. §204 (2021); 27 C.F.R. §13.21 (2021).
73. *See Churchill Cellars, Inc. v. Graham* (Opp. No. 77787019) 2012 WL 5493578, at *8 (TTAB Oct. 19, 2012).

A sale of goods to support federal registration is also inadequate if the goods themselves do not exist at the time of the sale.[74] Entering into a contract to buy goods that are not yet available does not constitute a use in commerce for purposes of federal registration.[75] Thus, where a winery has wine aging in barrel that has been advertised and sold on a "pre-release" basis, the sale of the pre-release wine is inadequate to demonstrate use of the mark in commerce.

Federal registration gives the registrant the right to stop any infringing activity by junior users anywhere in the United States. Because most wineries do not sell their wine in most, or even many, states when they commence operations, especially where distribution or direct sales may not be legally or economically feasible, federal trademark registration allows them to protect their rights to a brand before they expand into new markets. However, a mark holder's ability to enforce trademark rights against another winery located in a different market is contingent on the two products entering the same market.[76] Once there is such a product overlap, the federal registration allows the registrant to stop the junior user's use of the mark, regardless of how long the junior user has been using the mark prior to the registrant's entry into the market.

b. Trademark Screening

Prior to adopting a new brand, a party seeking to protect its brand and avoid trademark infringement liability should conduct a trademark clearance search. An experienced trademark attorney is the most qualified advisor to evaluate the nuances related to the risks of infringement and the availability of marks; however, parties can conduct their own searches to generally evaluate availability.

The Internet has increased access to information previously unavailable to those without specialized databases and other resources. Public information is readily available about products offered for sale in the marketplace. Any lawyer or non-lawyer evaluating the availability of a new name as a trademark for wine need only fire up her computer, select her favorite search engine, and input the proposed brand name in combination with generic terms such as "wine," "vineyard," and "cellars." Internet research is a good tool for making a preliminary evaluation of the marketplace; however, it is not determinative of the availability or protectability of a potential brand name.

---

74. *See Richardson-Vicks, Inc. v. Franklin Mint Corp.*, 216 USPQ 989 (TTAB 1982) (where the goods that are the subject of the trademark registration application have been sold but have not yet been created and marked, such sale is inadequate to prove the use of the mark on the goods in commerce).

75. *See Geovision, Inc. v. Geovision Corp.*, 928 F.2d 387 (11th Cir. 1991) (an as-yet unperformed contract of sale does not result in goods being "sold or transported" in interstate commerce; the term "sold" contemplates a product with the mark on it).

76. *See Dawn Donut Co. v. Hart's Food Stores, Inc.*, 267 F.2d 358 (2d Cir. 1959) (where the parties' goods or services are not yet offered to the same geographical markets, there can be no harm and no infringement).

The TTB's online COLA database is another excellent resource for evaluating the availability of a potential wine brand.[77] COLAs do not provide a brand owner with any statutory trademark rights, and the COLA database is sometimes incomplete or incorrect, but the existence of a COLA indicates that a brand name likely has been used in commerce. The COLA database is a valuable resource for discovering more obscure brands that may not be located easily through an Internet search. A discovery of a potentially conflicting brand on the COLA database should be followed up with research concerning the actual use of the brand to determine if a conflict does, in fact, exist. The COLA database is also a valuable resource for a brand owner policing infringing uses by others once trademark rights have been established.

The USPTO Trademark Electronic Search System is possibly the most important resource for locating potentially conflicting marks.[78] This resource is available to the public on the USPTO website; however, the database is not user friendly. Many trademark practitioners subscribe to proprietary search systems that simplify and improve searches of the USPTO Register database. A USPTO search can be simplified by restricting search results to international Class 33 for wine and alcoholic beverages other than beer. Although difficult to navigate, the USPTO Register must be searched to identify marks that are the subject of pending applications and not yet in use. If pending marks are eventually used and the applications mature to registration, these marks could preempt the intervening use of a similar mark initiated after the trademark application date. Given the investment required to establish a new wine brand and the potential liability for infringing on the trademark rights of another brand owner, the cost of hiring experienced trademark counsel to perform a USPTO search and analyze potential likelihood of confusion with the proposed brand name may be money well spent.

Wine marks with geographical significance require particular attention. A trademark for wine should not include a geographical term associated with a particular wine region unless the wine is from that region. Use of a geographical reference on wine not from the identified region violates TRIPS Article 23, as recognized by the United States in the Lanham Act, even if the region is not well known in the United States so long as it is a region in which wine with a given quality, reputation, or other characteristic is produced.[79] In addition to violating TRIPS Article 23, labeling wine with the name of a winemaking region in which

---

77. *See* Alcohol and Tobacco Tax and Trade Bureau, U.S. Department of the Treasury, COLA Registry, https://www.ttb.gov/labeling/colas.

78. *See* USPTO, Department of Commerce, Trademark Electronic Search System, https://tmsearch.uspto.gov/bin/gate.exe?f=login&p_lang=english&p_d=trmk.

79. While the United States indicated that it did not need to amend the Lanham Act to enact TRIPS Article 23 with respect to the improper *use* of geographical indications on wine because the TRIPS Article 23 protections already are encompassed within the Lanham Act, this interpretation of U.S. law is questionable. Because no case has been brought in a U.S. court attempting to enforce an Article 23 violation through a Lanham Act claim, one cannot say for certain whether such a claim would be recognized by a U.S. court.

the subject wine was not produced would give rise to claims of consumer deception and false designation of origin under the Lanham Act.[80]

The use of wine brands that include geographical names is also regulated by TTB, as discussed in more detail in Section C. A brand name featuring a recognized American viticultural area (AVA) or any other "name of viticultural significance"[81] can only be used on wines that meet the AVA requirements, namely, that at least 85 percent of the wine be made from grapes grown in that AVA.[82] Although not all geographical names used or locally recognized in winemaking areas are, or will become, names of viticultural significance, a brand owner runs the risk that a brand name that includes a known, or even a relatively obscure, geographical name could become the subject of a future AVA petition. If that AVA were established, the brand could only be used on wines that comply with the 85 percent grape source requirement for that AVA.

At times, the USPTO is overly aggressive in rejecting trademarks for wine on the basis of geographical descriptiveness or deceptiveness when, in fact, the primary significance of the marks is not geographical. For example, marks that reference the name of a road located in a wine region are not necessarily geographically descriptive or deceptive because most consumers would not recognize the road name or know that it is located in that wine region. Nevertheless, the USPTO routinely refuses applications to register marks on the basis of geographical distinctiveness or deceptiveness. Applicants should be prepared to challenge the USPTO on such refusals.

c. The Application Process for a Federal Trademark Registration

Once a party has determined that a mark is available for use, the brand owner must consider whether the mark should be protected, and if so, to what degree. A brand owner is not obligated to protect its mark through registration of the trademark.[83] A party develops common law rights in a mark just by using it. However, as we have seen, a registered mark carries more benefits than a mark protected by common law principles. Contrary to some popular misconceptions,

---

80. If a mark encompasses the name of a wine region and the wine is from that region, the use of the mark is permissible unless the region also owns a certification mark that controls the use of the regional name on wine and that requires compliance with certain production guidelines. Nevertheless, the rights in a descriptive mark are fairly limited, and the use of the regional name by others in marks for wine from the region usually is allowed.

81. 27 C.F.R. §4.39(i)(3) (2021) provides that "a name has viticultural significance when it is the name of a state or county (or the foreign equivalents), when approved as a viticultural area in Part 9 of this chapter, or by a foreign government, or when found to have viticultural significance by the appropriate TTB officer."

82. *Id.* §4.25. There is a grandfather exception to this rule, at 27 C.F.R. §4.39(i) (2021), which is discussed in Section C below.

83. While certain states require that a winery "register" its brand with the state's alcoholic beverage regulatory agency, this does not constitute registration of the trademark for protection purposes; that information is provided to the state for the state's own regulatory purposes, similar to the application for a COLA from the TTB.

trademark registration is the only way to obtain statutory protection for a mark. This section discusses the application process for a federal trademark registration.

A federal trademark registration will only issue after a mark has been used in commerce in association with the goods or services identified in the application. However, a mark need not be used in commerce before the mark holder initiates the trademark application process. A U.S. trademark application may be filed on three bases: (1) use of the mark in commerce;[84] (2) intended use of the mark in commerce;[85] and (3) ownership of a foreign application or registration by a foreign applicant intended for use in commerce.[86]

When a mark is already in legal use in commerce on wine, a trademark application may be filed based on such use. A "use-based" application may proceed immediately to registration after it has been examined and published for opposition.

Use-based applications often present practical problems for winery owners. The one-to-three-year production process for wine means that a wine brand may be developed many years before the wine is slated for release. Fortunately, the Lanham Act allows a trademark registration application to be filed where there is intent to use the mark on the particular goods or services. An "intent-to-use" (ITU) application need only include a verified statement that the applicant has a bona fide intent to use the mark on wine in the future,[87] as opposed to a verified statement and evidence that the mark is in use in commerce as required for a use-based application.[88]

An ITU application is examined and published for opposition in the same manner as a use-based application. However, once the application has successfully proceeded through the opposition period, a "notice of allowance" is issued against the ITU application.[89] To obtain registration, the applicant then must use the mark in commerce and submit an allegation of use within six months of issuance of the notice of allowance.[90] An ITU applicant may obtain one six-month extension to allege use and, upon a simple showing of good cause, an additional four six-month extensions to allege use before an application will be abandoned.[91] An ITU applicant may take up to three years in total after the issuance of a notice of allowance to use the mark in commerce and file a statement of use to perfect the registration.

Once an allegation of use is submitted and the registration issues, the registrant's rights in the mark are effective as of the original filing date of the application. The registrant may rely on registration to stop any party who adopted a confusingly similar mark after the registrant's trademark application filing date.[92]

---

84. 15 U.S.C. §1051(a) (2021).
85. *Id.* §1051(b).
86. *Id.* §1051(d)-(e).
87. *Id.* §1051(b).
88. *Id.* §1051(a).
89. *Id.* §1063(b)(2).
90. *Id.* §1051(d)(1).
91. *Id.* §1051(d)(2).
92. *Id.* §1057(c).

An ITU application can give a wine brand owner peace of mind that, once his wine is ready for release, he can use the brand name selected years earlier and stop any winery that adopted a similar mark in the intervening years.

Pursuant to the U.S. accession to the Paris Convention, which is an international treaty, a person whose country of origin is a Paris Convention signatory[93] may seek registration of her mark in the United States based upon her trademark registration in her country of origin.[94] Under the Paris Convention, that party also may file a "priority application" in the United States based upon the first trademark application she filed for the mark in another Paris Convention country, provided the U.S. application is filed within six months after the filing date of the foreign application.[95] Upon filing, the U.S. application will be given the same effective date as the previously filed foreign application.[96]

A Paris Convention application requires a statement of intended use of the mark in the United States, but the foreign applicant need not actually use the mark in U.S. or foreign commerce or submit any statement for the registration to issue once examination and publication for opposition have been completed.[97] This relief from the use-in-commerce requirement allows foreign wineries to gain a foothold for their brands in the United States before they export any goods here. However, registrations without proof of use in commerce are susceptible to attack on the basis of abandonment after three years of non-use following registration or upon a showing of registrant's intent not to use the mark in the United States.[98] To maintain the validity of the registration, the foreign registrant must use the mark in U.S. commerce and submit a statement of such use between the fifth and sixth anniversaries of the registration.[99] Use in commerce is also a prerequisite to proving likelihood of confusion under the Lanham Act; a registrant cannot rely on a Paris Convention—based U.S. registration to bring an infringement action absent proof of use of its mark in U.S. commerce.[100]

A person who is not a citizen of the United States and whose domicile or residence is in a country that is a signatory to the Madrid Protocol, another international treaty, may obtain a U.S. registration based on a foreign registration by filing an International Registration application through its home country with a request for extension of protection to the United States. As with a Paris Convention application, the foreign applicant need only submit a declaration of a bona fide

93. *See* WIPO, Contracting Parties: Paris Convention, https://wipolex.wipo.int/en/treaties/textdetails/12633 (last visited Aug. 15, 2022).

94. 15 U.S.C. §1126(c), (e) (2006).

95. *See id.* §1126(c)-(d); *In re Fisons, Ltd.*, 197 USPQ 888 (TTAB 1978) (a claim of priority must be based on the first application filed in a Paris Convention country, not on any application filed in any Paris Convention country).

96. 15 U.S.C. §1126(d) (2006).

97. *Id.* §1126(e).

98. *See Oromeccanica, Inc. v. Ottmar Botzenhardt GmbH & Co. KG*, 223 USPQ 59 (TTAB 1983).

99. 15 U.S.C. §1058 (2021).

100. *See* 3 J. Thomas McCarthy, McCarthy on Trademarks and Unfair Competition §19:27 (4th ed. 2010).

intent to use the mark in the United States; no actual use of the mark in U.S. or foreign commerce is required prior to obtaining registration.[101] Madrid Protocol registrations also are susceptible to cancellation and abandonment based on non-use; they cannot be invoked in infringement proceedings absent actual use of the mark in commerce.

Procedurally, a U.S. trademark or service mark application may be filed with the USPTO at the USPTO website through the Trademark Electronic Application System. Within seven to nine months after the filing, a USPTO trademark examining attorney will review the application for registrability. If the application is deemed not registerable, the USPTO issues an "office action" outlining the problems with the application. The applicant has six months to respond to the office action by either correcting the problems or contesting the examining attorney's assessment. The examining attorney may either accept the corrections and contentions or issue a final office action. An applicant has a right to respond to the final office action or to appeal the decision to the Trademark Trial and Appeal Board (TTAB) of the USPTO. If an applicant fails to timely respond to an office action, the application is deemed abandoned. If the applicant inadvertently fails to respond, the applicant may revive the application within two months after the issuance of the notice of abandonment by paying an additional fee.

Within three to four months after the examining attorney's approval of an application, the application is published for a 30-day period in the USPTO *Official Gazette* to allow possible third-party opposition. A third party may file a request with TTAB for a 30-day extension to oppose the application without cause and an additional 60-day extension upon a showing of cause, such as the need to investigate the applicant and its mark. An interested third party may oppose registration on any grounds on which the application could have been refused initially. Most often, applications are opposed on alleged likelihood of confusion with the opposer's mark. A claim of likelihood of confusion may be based on registered or common law trademark, or service mark rights or trade name rights.

If no opposition is filed and the application was based on use of the mark in commerce or on a foreign registration under the Paris Convention or Madrid Protocol, the USPTO normally will issue a registration certificate within three to four months following the end of the opposition period. If the application was based on intended use of the mark, a registrant must file a statement of use within six months following the issuance of the notice of allowance or during an extension period in order to perfect the registration. The USPTO will issue a registration certificate upon receipt of an acceptable statement of use. If the USPTO deems the statement of use insufficient, it will issue an office action, similar to the procedure used during the examination period.

During the first five years after registration, a third party may seek cancellation of a trademark registration based on likelihood of confusion with another's mark. After the fifth anniversary of the registration, the registration may only be canceled under limited circumstances, including deceptive use or genericness; the

---

101. 15 U.S.C. §1141(f) (2021).

registration cannot be canceled based on likelihood of confusion with another's mark even if the other mark was used in commerce before the registrant's mark. The five-year period thus serves as a type of statute of limitations that gives registrants security in their registrations.

To maintain the registration, a registrant must file a declaration of current use of the mark between the fifth and sixth anniversaries of the registration.[102] The declaration must include a specimen of current use of the mark in commerce and be accompanied by a filing fee.[103] There is also a six-month "grace period" following the sixth anniversary; unless a declaration of current use is filed in that "grace period" with the payment of an additional surcharge, USPTO will abandon the registration.[104]

Together with the registrant's filing of a declaration of current use or at any time after the fifth anniversary of the registration, a registrant may file a declaration of *continuous* use of the mark in commerce for the preceding five years.[105] After the USPTO accepts the registrant's declaration of continuous use and the accompanying filing fee, the registration becomes incontestable, and the registrant may claim an exclusive right to use the registered mark for the registered goods or services and assert exclusivity without challenge, except on limited statutory bases.[106]

The USPTO also requires that trademark registrants file a declaration of current use and a declaration of renewal in the year preceding the ten-year anniversary of the registration.[107] The declaration of use must include a specimen of current use of the mark in commerce, and both the use and renewal declarations must be accompanied by a filing fee.[108] A registrant's failure to file the current use declaration in the year preceding the tenth anniversary of the registration will result in abandonment of the registration. A registrant can cure the abandonment in the six-month period after the tenth anniversary for an additional charge.[109]

d. State Trademark Registration

All U.S. states and Puerto Rico have trademark registration systems independent of the federal system. State trademark registration only applies within the boundaries of the state in which registration is obtained. State trademark registration is superfluous if the registrant has obtained a federal registration because federal registration rights apply in all U.S. states and territories. However, a small winery or other wine business that conducts business exclusively in one state may prefer state registration as a less expensive alternative to federal registration. State registration also may be an alternative means of protection if

102. 15 U.S.C. §1058 (2021).
103. *Id.*
104. 37 C.F.R. §2.182 (2021).
105. 15 U.S.C. §1065 (2021).
106. *Id.* §1065; *see also Park N' Fly, Inc. v. Dollar Park and Fly, Inc.*, 469 U.S. 189 (1985).
107. 15 U.S.C. §§1058-1059 (2021).
108. *Id.*
109. 37 C.F.R. §2.182 (2021).

prior use or registration of the mark by someone else is blocking a federal registration but does not conflict with the winery's intended use of the mark.[110]

e. Legal Systems That Provide No Statutory Trademark Protection

Not all registration systems for wine brands provide statutory protection against trademark infringement. In the wine industry, many brand owners mistakenly believe that obtaining a COLA for their wine label guarantees their right to use the brand name or a fanciful name identified on the COLA. In fact, the COLA application form expressly states: "This certificate does not constitute trademark protection."[111]

Registering a company name with the state in which a winery conducts business, receiving a certificate of incorporation from a state, or filing a fictitious business name statement with a state or county does not provide any statutory protection for a brand name. These types of filings are not intended to create rights in names, but rather to identify the business entity to the government and third parties for purposes of taxation, accountability for legal actions, and the like.

As a final example, the registration of an Internet domain name does not create any legal name rights. While the registration of an Internet domain name may create value in a marketing sense by securing a party's address in cyberspace, registration does not give the owner standing to take legal action against those who use terms similar to the domain name as a trademark.

4. ENFORCEMENT OF MARKS

Although some brand owners obtain trademark registration solely for the defensive purpose of preempting an infringement action against them, the business value of a mark is its exclusivity and its role in directing consumers to the owner of the mark or the goods or services on which the mark is used in the marketplace. To retain the trademark's value, the trademark owner must enforce his trademark rights against infringement by others. If a trademark owner does not stop others from using similar marks, the owner must live with the confusing or infringing uses.

In the case of *Russell v. Caesar*, the owner of the mark RABBIT RIDGE for wine obtained an injunction against the owner of the mark RABBIT HILL for wine. In that case, the judge noted,

---

110. For instance, the USPTO may refuse a registration for wine based on the use of the same mark for restaurant services. If the owner of the registration for restaurant services does business only in a state in which the winery does not intend to sell its wines, the winery might decide to register its mark in those other states.

111. Alcohol and Tobacco Tax and Trade Bureau, Department of the Treasury, Application for and Certification/Exemption of Label/Bottle Approval Form 5100.31 (2009).

> Because "Rabbit" is the single dominant or substantive term used by Rabbit Ridge on all of its products—including the 14.4 million bottles of wine already sold—Rabbit Hill's use of the term "Rabbit" even on a facially distinctive label or in conjunction with other terms cannot dissuade this Court from concluding that the marks are significantly similar for purposes of a finding of a likelihood of confusion.[112]

The court essentially acknowledged that the owner of RABBIT RIDGE had a monopoly in the term "RABBIT" in association with wine.

Interestingly, after the RABBIT HILL litigation, the RABBIT RIDGE owner ceased enforcing its judicially decreed right to the term "RABBIT." There are now several subsequent trademark registrations for wine encompassing the term "RABBIT."[113] The continuous enforcement of exclusive trademarks rights is difficult and costly, but the consequences of failing to enforce those rights can be the weakening of a mark's exclusivity.

Once a party has demonstrated a senior right in a trademark, the test for infringement is whether there is a likelihood of consumer confusion between the marks at issue. In determining likelihood of confusion, each federal circuit uses a different list of foundational factors.[114] As noted by Professor Thomas McCarthy, the eight basic factors are: (1) similarity between the marks at issue; (2) similarity of marketing methods and channels of distribution; (3) characteristics of prospective purchasers and degree of care; (4) degree of distinctiveness in the senior user's mark; (5) whether the goods or services at issue are competitive; (6) where the goods are sold in different territories and, if so, whether the senior user's mark is known in the junior user's territory; (7) the intent of the junior user; and (8) evidence of actual confusion.[115]

While these factors apply regardless of the nature of the goods or services at issue, many courts have applied these factors specifically to cases involving the alleged infringement of wine brands, sometimes with inconsistent results. These courts have found the following:

---

112. *Russell v. Caesar*, 62 U.S.P.Q. 2d 1125, 1129 (N.D. Cal. 2001).

113. See, e.g., FRENCH RABBIT, Registration No. 3,298,908; RABBIT RANCH, Registration No. 3,350,161; and RABBIT ISLAND, Registration No. 3,798,617.

114. *See Pignons S.A. de Mecanique de Precision v. Polaroid Corp.*, 657 F.2d 482 (1st Cir. 1981); *Polaroid Corp. v. Polaroid Electronics Corp.*, 287 F.2d 492 (2d Cir. 1961), *cert. denied*, 368 U.S. 820 (1961); *Interpace Corp. v. Lapp, Inc.*, 721 F.2d 460 (3d Cir. 1983); *Pizzeria Uno Corp. v. Temple*, 747 F.2d 1522 (4th Cir. 1984); *Roto-Rooter Corp. v. O'Neal*, 513 F.2d 44 (5th Cir. 1975); *Frisch's Rests v. Elby's Big Boy*, 670 F.2d 642 (6th Cir. 1982); *Helene Curtis Indus., Inc. v. Church & Dwight Co.*, 560 F.2d 1325 (7th Cir. 1977), *cert. denied*, 434 U.S. 1070 (1978); *SquirtCo v. Seven-Up Co.*, 628 F.2d 1086 (9th Cir. 1980); *AMF, Inc. v. Sleekcraft Boats*, 599 F.2d 341 (9th Cir. 1979); *Team Tires Plus, Ltd. v. Tires Plus, Inc.*, 394 F.3d 831 (10th Cir. 2005); *Frehling Enterprises, Inc. v. Int'l Select Group, Inc.*, 192 F.3d 1330 (11th Cir. 1999); *Am. Ass'n for Advancement of Sci. v. Hearts Corp.*, 498 F. Supp. 244 (D.D.C. 1980); *In re E.I. Du Pont Nemours & Co.*, 476 F.2d 1357 (C.C.P.A. 1973).

115. *See* 4 J. Thomas McCarthy, McCarthy on Trademarks and Unfair Competition §24:29 (4th ed. 2010).

1. Generally, wine consumers tend to exercise less care when purchasing wine because of the lower cost of the goods.[116]
2. Champagne and sparkling wines are not necessarily expensive goods that are always purchased by sophisticated purchasers, and even sophisticated purchasers might be aware that Champagne houses offer both expensive and less expensive sparkling wine products under similar marks[117]
3. It is difficult to generalize about the degree of care that consumers of wine are likely to exercise in making their wine selections because the standard for the reasonable consumer includes the ignorant and credulous and must include as well the portion of wine consumers who are not especially savvy.[118]
4. Even at $30 a bottle, a wine could be an impulse purchase made by an ordinary consumer without a great deal of care.[119]
5. The wine-buying public, insofar as their selection and purchase of wine is concerned, is a highly discriminating group[120]
6. The fact that the TTB requires source-identifying information on a wine label does not diminish the likelihood of confusion because consumers are more interested in the distinctive label design than in textual information regarding geographical origin, the dangers of alcohol to pregnant women, the presence of sulfites, or any other legally required verbiage that appears on the less interesting side of the bottle.[121]
7. If both parties laying claim to a trademark market their products through retail establishments such as wine shops and liquor stores and utilize magazines for advertising purposes, they use similar marketing channels for their wine as a matter of law.[122]

---

116. *E. & J. Gallo Winery v. Gallo Cattle Co.*, 967 F.2d at 1293; *see also Taylor Wine Co. v. Bully Hill Vineyards, Inc.*, 569 F.2d 731, 734 (2d Cir. 1978) (the average American who drinks wine on occasion can hardly pass for a connoisseur of wines and remains an easy mark for an infringer); *E. & J. Gallo Winery v. Consorzio del Gallo Nero*, 782 F. Supp. 457, 465 (N.D. Cal. 1991) (there is little doubt that wine purchasers typically fall into the category of unsophisticated impulse buyers where confusion is more likely); *Nova Wines, Inc. v. Adler Fels Winery LLC*, 467 F. Supp. 2d 965, 981 (N.D. Cal. 2006) (same); *In re Vina Lo Miranda Limitada*, 2002 WL 732146 at *3 (TTAB 2002) (many purchasers of wine are members of the general public who would not necessarily exercise the high degree of care necessary to prevent confusion).

117. *Palm Bay Imps., Inc. v. Veuve Clicquot Ponsardin Maison Fondee en 1772*, 396 F.3d 1369, 1376 (Fed. Cir. 2005).

118. *Vigneron Partners, LLC v. Woop Woop Wines Pty. Ltd.*, 2006 WL 1214859 at *8 (N.D. Cal. 2006)

119. *In re Saviah Rose Winery, LLC*, 2006 WL 2414518 *4 (TTAB 2006).

120. *E. & J. Gallo Winery v. Ben R. Goltsman & Co.*, 172 F. Supp. 826, 830 (M.D. Ala. 1959), criticized by *Gallo Nero*, 782 F. Supp. at 465; *see also Banfi Products Corp. v. Kendall-Jackson Winery, Ltd.*, 74 F. Supp. 2d 188, 199 (E.D.N.Y. 1999).

121. *Nova Wines*, 467 F. Supp. 2d at 981-982.

122. *Gallo Nero*, 782 F. Supp. at 464.

8. The fact that one wine is sold through mass market channels and the other is sold only through the defendant winery's tasting room weighs against a finding of likelihood of confusion.[123]
9. If the wines at issue are different in price, varietal, and origin, they still can be found to be similar due to the common practice in the wine industry of using the same brand for different wine varieties sold at different price points.[124]
10. Differences in varietal, price, and origin of wines diminish the likelihood of confusion.[125]
11. Differences in trade dress and differences in brand cannot be relied upon to distinguish the parties' products in an "on-premise" setting in which consumers may order a glass of wine at a bar or make their purchasing decisions based on a restaurant wine list, although it is worth noting that wine lists usually include the source of the wine.[126]
12. Although different products, wine and spirits are related such that consumers seeing the same or similar marks on both products would likely believe the products emanate from the same source.[127]

As these cases demonstrate, there are no hard-and-fast rules concerning the foundational factors for trademark infringement claims related to the sale of wine. Therefore, a claim of infringement should be based, to the extent possible, on all of Professor McCarthy's eight factors.

Another means of protecting a select subset of trademarks is an action for trademark dilution. Trademark dilution is distinct from trademark infringement and is reserved for marks that can be shown to be famous among the general consuming public of the United States.[128] In a claim of dilution, the goods or services on which the parties' marks appear need not be competitive, nor do consumers need to be confused by the similarity of the marks.[129] A claim of trademark dilution alleges that a junior mark somehow dilutes a famous senior mark by blurring or tarnishing it.[130] Dilution can make a mark less distinctive or bring the mark into disrepute.[131]

---

123. *Sutter Home Winery, Inc. v. Madrona Vineyards, L.P.*, 2005 WL 701599 at *7 (N.D. Cal. 2005); *see also Banfi Products*, 74 F. Supp. 2d. at 197 (where one wine is sold in discount drugstores, supermarkets, and mid-range Italian restaurants, and another is sold exclusively in fine restaurants and retail wine stores, there is a lower likelihood of confusion).

124. *Vigneron Partners*, 2006 WL 1214859 at *5; *see also Gallo Nero*, 782 F. Supp. at 464 (wines of all types constitute a single class of goods).

125. *Banfi Products*, 74 F. Supp. 2d at 197.

126. *Sutter Home*, 2005 WL 701599 at *11.

127. *White Oak Vineyards & Winery LLC v. White Oak Spirits, LLC*, 2015 WL 12731903, at *6 (C.D. Cal. Mar. 9, 2015); *Fleischmann Distilling Corp. v. Maier Brewing Co.*, 314 F.2d 149, 152–55 (9th Cir. 1963).

128. 15 U.S.C. §1125(c) (2021).

129. 15 U.S.C. §1127 (2021).

130. *Id.* §1125(c).

131. *See Nike, Inc. v. Nikepal Int'l, Inc.*, 85 USPQ 2d 1820 (E.D. Cal. 2007) (distinctiveness of NIKE mark for apparel and footwear diluted by NIKEPAL for medical laboratory syringes); *Pepsico,*

To prevail in a dilution action, the diluted trademark owner must prove that the mark is famous. Proving fame within a particular market segment is not sufficient to invoke the protection of the federal dilution laws.[132] Nationwide fame is the required showing. In the wine sector, because a large percentage of the American public does not drink wine and the wine market is highly fragmented, fame and dilution of a wine trademark are difficult to prove.[133] Wineries, however, are susceptible to claims of trademark dilution from non-wine producers if their wine brand is too similar to a famous mark outside of the wine sector.[134]

5. LICENSING OF MARKS

While the uncontrolled use of an identical or similar mark on wine by a third party will jeopardize a winery's legal exclusivity in its mark, use of an identical or similar mark on wine by a third party subject to the control of the senior trademark owner will preserve the senior trademark owner's exclusivity. This arrangement is referred to as a trademark license.

A license agreement need not be in writing to be legally effective, but preparing a written license agreement is good business practice. Specific monetary consideration for the grant of a trademark license, known as a royalty, also is not a legal requirement of a license agreement. The licensor receives consideration when the licensee uses the licensed mark, which use inures to the benefit of the licensor and strengthens the protection of the licensed mark. The single critical element to make any license arrangement enforceable is the licensor's control over the quality of the licensed goods being sold under the licensed mark. A licensor's failure to exert or impose quality control on the licensee's use of a mark is a "naked license," which puts the licensor's trademark rights at risk.[135] Examples of licensed

---

Inc. v. #1 Wholesale, LLC, 84 USPQ 2d 1040 (N.D. Ga. 2007) (using PEPSI cans to manufacture "stash can" storage containers for concealing illegal drugs tarnishes the PEPSI mark).

132. *See Bd. of Regents, Univ. of Texas Sys. ex rel. Univ. of Texas at Austin v. KST Elec., Ltd.*, 550 F. Supp. 2d 657, 675 (W.D. Tex. 2008) (fame of longhorn design among college football fans is insufficient to establish fame under federal dilution statute).

133. *See Maker's Mark Distillery, Inc. v. Diageo N. Am., Inc.*, 2010 WL 1407325 at *16 (W.D. Ky. 2010) (Maker's Mark dripping red wax top not famous: "While annual sales of 800,000 cases is somewhat significant, Maker's Mark is not the nation's largest whisky producer and its sales do not make it a behemoth in the distilled spirits world.").

134. *See Chanel Inc. v. Savannah-Chanel*, C-99-1790 (N.D. Cal. 1999) (dilution claim based on use of SAVANNAH-CHANEL as a mark for wine; case settled with change of brand to SAVANNAH-CHANELLE).

135. *See Barcamerica Int'l USA Trust v. Tyfield Imps., Inc.*, 289 F.3d 589 (9th Cir. 2002). In *Barcamerica*, plaintiff accused defendant of infringement of its LEONARDO DA VINCI mark on wine and alleged rights in the LEONARDO DA VINCI mark based on licensed use by a third party. Defendant attacked such rights on the grounds that the license agreement failed to include a quality control provision and plaintiff failed to produce any evidence that it actually exerted any control over the quality of the licensed wine on which the mark was used. Plaintiff was found to have abandoned its rights in the mark based on the naked license and the failure to exert control over the use of the mark.

marks are NEWMAN'S OWN[136] and ARNOLD PALMER[137] for wines sold under these brand names.

A licensor can exert control over the quality of the licensed goods simply by asserting that the licensor is relying on the reputation of the licensee as a producer of high-quality wine.[138] However, to ensure that there is no challenge to the quality control mechanism, a written license should include a more specific provision for quality standards and control, for example, requiring the licensee to provide the licensed product to the licensor before the product is released. If the license agreement requires the licensee to provide product samples, the licensor should test the product and keep internal records concerning the inspection. The licensed goods do not need to be of superior quality, but rather have consistent quality. To further define consistency, license agreements often specify a standard such as a quality similar to that of licensee's other wine products or similar to that of other wine on the market at a similar price point.

In the fractured and highly competitive wine market, license arrangements allow a trademark owner to legally control its mark by licensing a use that may not present any true threat of diluting the licensor's brand in the market. For instance, if a large winery finds a small winery using its mark on a limited production run of wine sold only in a tasting room, the large winery may elect to license its name to the small winery rather than initiate federal infringement proceedings, which can be costly and generate negative publicity.

In the wine industry, license arrangements are frequently a part of grower and producer relationships. Wineries often purchase grapes from vineyards with particular vineyard names and use the vineyard name on the wine as a vineyard designation.[139] Does the producer need a license from the grower to use his vineyard name as a vineyard designation? The legal concept of "fair use"[140] suggests not; the producer is merely identifying the place from which the grapes originated. However, the "fairness" of the use also depends on the way in which the vineyard name actually appears on the label. If the winery uses the vineyard name prominently on the label, so that it looks like an independent brand, the use may not be deemed fair.

A grower should establish limits on the use of his vineyard name at the outset of a grape purchasing relationship, preferably in a written grape purchase agreement. By taking the position that the producer may *not* use the vineyard name on the wine absent permission from the grower, the grower can ensure that the vineyard name is not used on wine that the grower finds to be of substandard quality.

---

136. Registration No. 3,679,763.

137. Registration No. 3,113,028.

138. Reliance on the reputation of the licensee was rejected as sufficient exercise of quality control in the *Barcamerica* case but was accepted in other cases. *See, e.g., Embedded Moments, Inc. v. Int'l Silver Co.*, 648 F. Supp. 187 (E.D.N.Y. 1986) (quality control satisfied where there is evidence that the licensor relied on the integrity of the licensee based on their prior relationship).

139. *See* 27 C.F.R. §4.39(m) (2021).

140. Fair use occurs when a term is used in a non-trademark manner to provide descriptive information about the product.

The use and establishment of vineyard designations can impact the bargaining power of grower and winery. A grower may be desperate for a winery to use his vineyard name so that he can establish a reputation for his vineyard. Alternatively, a new winery anxious to establish the quality of its brands may seek out vineyards with established reputations for growing quality grapes. In terms of compensation, the license royalty payment can serve as a pricing variable apart from the commodity value of the grapes. A well-drafted license agreement can address all these issues and assist the grower and the winery in establishing their respective rights relative to the use of the vineyard name.

B. COPYRIGHT

A trademark is a business symbol with an attached legal right that promotes the trademark owner's business and that protects consumers. By contrast, copyright is a distinct intellectual property that protects creative works and promotes and encourages the authorship of creative works. Copyright protects literary works; pictorial, graphic, and sculptural works; musical works and dramatic works; and others. Titles, names, short phrases, and taglines are not protectable by copyright, nor are ingredient lists and recipe instructions. Generally, trademarks offer more protections to wine brand owners and wine industry participants than copyright. However, copyright is an important overlay to trademark as well as an independent right that can benefit wineries, particularly in the context of retail sales. For example, logos and label designs are often pictorial and graphic works protected by copyright as well as trademark law. Similarly, advertising and promotional materials, including websites, can be protected by copyright as pictorial, graphic, and literary works.

A copyright attaches upon the creation of the work, when pen is put to paper.[141] Registration is not required.[142] The author or creator of the work owns the copyright. A work created by a salaried employee of a winery in the context of the employee's job responsibilities, for example, the text for a tasting sheet created by the winemaker or the director of marketing, is a "work for hire," and the copyright in the work is owned by the winery.[143] However, an independent contractor or outside design company owns the copyright in a work created at the instruction of a winery (for example, a label design).[144]

Absent a work-for-hire arrangement or assignment of the copyright, the author of the work retains all copyright in it even if the work was created at the direction of, or commissioned by, a winery. However, a winery has the right to use the commissioned work. The winery paid for the work, and the work was created at

141. This is true of works created after January 1, 1978. Prior to 1978, works were not protected by copyright unless copyright registration was obtained.

142. While copyright registration is not required for protection, it is available, provides certain benefits such as statutory damages, and is a prerequisite to filing a copyright infringement lawsuit.

143. *See Cmty. for Creative Non-Violence v. Reid,* 490 U.S. 730 (1989).

144. *See id.*

the direction of the winery with the understanding that it would be used for a specific purpose—for example, a label design for bottles of wine. There is an implied license to use commissioned work based on the specific facts of the relationship.[145]

The implied license, however, only extends to the use of the work as the parties clearly understood in their contractual relationship. If the agreement between the winery and the label designer is unclear (for example, whether the label design can be used on promotional items such as posters, postcards, or coasters), the winery could find itself defending a copyright infringement claim. The author is aware of an incident in which a producer retained a famous label designer to design its label; when the producer used the label design on promotional items beyond the product itself, the label designer did not hesitate and, in fact, felt an obligation to assert his copyright in the design to extract further payment from the producer for the use of the design on promotional goods.

Wineries must take great care in using art on labels when the art was not directly commissioned for that use. If a winery owner purchases a piece of fine art for his art collection, he merely takes title to the physical piece of art. Absent an express written assignment from the artist, the artist retains all copyright in the art. The winery owner has no right to use an image of the artwork he purchased on his wine label simply because he bought the work of art. While the winery can request that the artist permit the use of that artwork on wine labels, permission should be expressly obtained in writing from the artist to avoid ambiguity. Copyright law presumes that the copyright belongs to the artist.

Finally, an image or text that appears on the Internet is not free for third-party use.[146] The author of the image or text, or some other party, likely owns a copyright in that image or text, and use of the copyrighted material without the permission of the copyright owner may constitute blatant copyright infringement. Stock image companies allow use of images for a set fee. Wineries are advised to pay for photographs from stock image companies rather than copy them from the Internet.

C. APPELLATIONS OF ORIGIN

We now turn from trademarks and copyrights and the federal and state laws governing them to wine appellations and the separate and distinct laws concerning their establishment and use. Appellations of origin are not a new concept,[147] nor

---

145. *See Effects Assocs., Inc. v. Cohen*, 908 F.2d 555 (9th Cir. 1990).

146. Older works for which there is no copyright or for which the copyright has expired are free for use as they are considered to be in the public domain. However, works that are not at least a few hundred years old may be subject to a variety of copyright laws, depending upon the creation of the work and the term of protection, which could be from 28 years, the life of the author plus 70 years, or 120 years from the date of creation. It is also very difficult to research the existence of copyright registrations.

147. The Paris Convention for the Protection of Industrial Property, adopted in 1883, applies to industrial property in the widest sense, indications of source and appellations of origin. Last amended

are they restricted to wines. But wine labels in the United States for well over a century have routinely referred to the wine's appellation of origin, just as they have included wine brand names.[148]

After Repeal, American wine producers once again were allowed to state the geographical origin of the wine's grapes on their labels.[149] However, many of these place names were undefined in terms of their precise location. In 1978 TTB's predecessor agency, the Bureau of Alcohol, Tobacco and Firearms (ATF),[150] adopted a formal wine appellation system in the United States. The structure of this appellation system, the various appellations established to date, the use of other geographical terms on wine labels and in wine advertising, and the future of American appellations are the subjects of this section.

1. DEFINING WINE APPELLATIONS

One of the fundamental tenets of the FAA Act, which was adopted by the U.S. Congress in 1935, is to protect consumers and ensure that they get accurate and meaningful information to guide their purchase decisions. From the 1930s to the 1960s, as the U.S. wine industry gradually reestablished itself after Prohibition, vintners did not make widespread use of wine appellations on their labels. The references that they did use typically were states and counties that had pre-established boundaries.

During the Wine Renaissance of the 1970s, this practice changed, and wineries increasingly referred to places and regions that had no clear boundaries. Examples include Northern California (Figure 6-9), California Mountain (Figure 6-10), Napa Valley, Howell Mountain, and North Coast.[151]

To prevent consumers from being misled by these references and to prevent unfair competition among wine producers, in 1978 TTB adopted a formal framework for wine appellations in the United States. That multi-tiered framework consists of various types of appellations, each of which can be used on a wine label if the prescribed percentage of grapes from that area is used to make the particular wine.

September 28, 1979, 21 U.S.T. 1583, 828 U.N.T.S. 305; https://wipolex.wipo.int/en/text/287556 (accessed July 23, 2022).

148. According to 27 C.F.R. §4.32 (2010), "[t]he [wine] product shall bear a brand name, except that if not sold under a brand name, then the name of the person required to appear on the brand label shall be deemed a brand name for the purpose of this part." The person referenced above is the bottler, who perhaps also is the producer of the wine. *Id.* §4.35. Appellations of origin, unlike brand names, are not mandatory information on wine labels.

149. Amending Certain Provisions of the Wine Labeling and Advertising Regulation Relative to Standards of Identity and Other Matters, 3 Fed. Reg. 2093 (Aug. 26, 1938) (defining an "appellation of origin" for the first time as a "place or region of origin").

150. The Homeland Security Act of 2002 transferred responsibility from the ATF to TTB. *See* Reorganization of Title 27, Code of Federal Regulations, 68 Fed. Reg. 3744 (Jan. 24, 2003) (to be codified at C.F.R. pts. 447, 448, 479, 555, and 646). The ATF was, and TTB now is, part of the U.S. Treasury Department. For consistency, we use the term "TTB" to refer to both ATF and TTB.

151. The Lohr's Northern California non-vintage wine had a handwritten back label describing the counties in which the grapes were grown.

Figure 6-9
J. Lohr Label

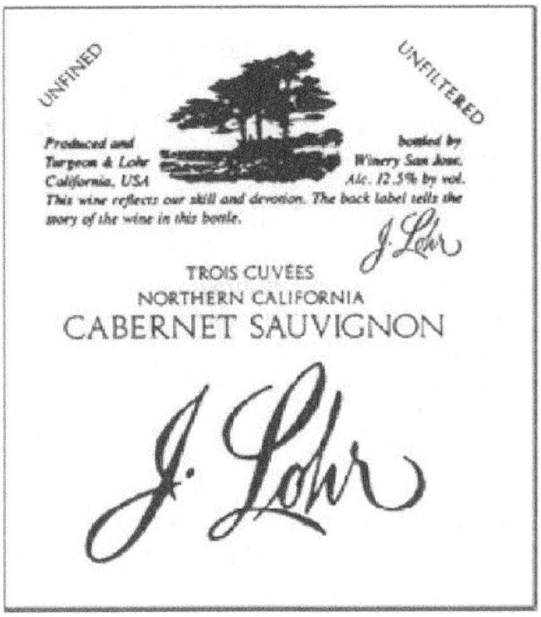

Figure 6-10
Louis M. Martini Label

TTB's practice of allowing the use of state and county names as appellations continued. As before, 75 percent of the wine bearing such an appellation has to be derived from grapes grown in the named state or county, and the wine has to be fully finished within the named state or an adjacent state in the case of a state appellation or within the state in which the named county is located.[152] Multi-county and multi-state appellations are authorized as long as no more than three counties in a state or three contiguous states are listed on the label and the percentage of grapes from each county or state is shown, adding up to 100 percent (with a tolerance of 2 percent).[153]

For previously undefined places, TTB established a new type of appellation known as the "American viticultural area," or AVA. AVAs are defined as "delimited grape growing regions distinguished by geographical features, the boundaries of which have been recognized and defined" by TTB.[154] An AVA can be used on a wine label if at least 85 percent of the wine is made from grapes grown inside that AVA and the wine is fully finished in the state, or one of the states, in which the AVA is located.

If a winery also includes a vineyard designation on its label, TTB requires that 95 percent of the grapes used to make that wine be grown in the named vineyard. However, TTB did not establish formal vineyard appellations in the same way it did for AVAs. The location of the vineyard is left to the discretion of the vineyard owner.[155]

Foreign wine appellations can be used on labels of wine imported into the United States. They consist of two types. First, foreign political appellations include a country, state, province, territory, or other political subdivision of a country equivalent to a state or county. A foreign political appellation can be used on labels of wine sold in the United States if at least 75 percent of the wine is derived from grapes grown in the named appellation, and the wine conforms to the requirements for the use of that appellation in the country of origin. The second type of foreign appellation is a viticultural area, defined as a "delimited place or region, the boundaries of which have been recognized and defined by the country of origin for use on labels of wine available for consumption within the country of origin."[156] Like a domestic AVA, a foreign viticultural area can be used if at least

---

152. 27 C.F.R. §4.25(b)(1)(i) (2021).

153. *Id.* §4.25(c), (d).

154. 27 C.F.R. §4.25(a)(1)(vi), (e) (2021).

155. The dispute between Robert Mondavi Winery and grapegrower Andy Beckstoffer over the To-Kalon Vineyard designation is one of the consequences of the TTB's decision not to establish formal vineyard designations. H. W. Crabb had established the 359-acre To-Kalon vineyard in 1868. Around a century later, Mondavi acquired 250 of those acres and registered To-Kalon Vineyard as a federal trademark for wine. Mondavi later acquired some adjoining vineyards and called its entire 550-acre vineyard holding To-Kalon Vineyard. In 2000 Beckstoffer, who had previously purchased 89 acres of Crabb's original vineyard not owned by Mondavi, sold those grapes to Schrader Winery, which used the vineyard designation, Original Tokalon Vineyard. Mondavi sent Schrader a cease and desist letter for infringing its mark, after which the litigation commenced. Beckstoffer and Schrader argued that Mondavi's mark was deceptive and should be canceled. The case ultimately settled, and both parties now use the Tokalon name.

156. 27 C.F.R. §4.25a(e)(1)(ii) (2021).

85 percent of the wine is made from grapes grown in that area and the wine conforms to the production, composition, and designation requirements of the country of origin.

a. American Viticultural Areas

As a part of TTB's 1978 rulemaking process, the agency set up a procedure to establish AVAs. Any interested party may petition TTB to establish an AVA, and a petition must contain the following information:

1. Evidence that the name of the viticultural area is locally and/or nationally known as referring to the proposed area;
2. Historical or current evidence in support of the boundaries of the viticultural area;
3. Evidence relating to the geographical features, such as climate, soil, and topography, which distinguish the viticultural area from surrounding areas; and
4. The specific boundaries of the area based on features found on the topographic maps of the U.S. Geological Survey.[157]

Upon receipt of a complete petition from any person—grower, vintner, or other—TTB commences a public rulemaking process under the Federal Administrative Procedure Act.[158] Typically, the process includes at least one Notice of Proposed Rulemaking (NPRM), a public comment period of between 30 and 90 days, and a Final Rule, each of which is announced in the Federal Register. In controversial cases, TTB may hold a public hearing, generally at the site of the proposed AVA.

As of July 2022, 266 viticultural areas had been established in 34 states.[159] There is no prescribed size of a viticultural area. Consequently, they range from the very large (e.g., the over 16-million-acre (6.7 million hectare) Ohio River Valley, spanning parts of four states) to the very small (e.g., the 160-acre (64.7 hectare) Cole Ranch viticultural area in California).

There also is no prescribed order for the creation of AVAs. Some larger viticultural areas have been carved into smaller, "nested" AVAs, often referred to by the trade and consumers as sub-appellations or sub-AVAs. Examples include

---

157. *Id.* §9.3(b).

158. 5 U.S.C. §§551-559 (2018).

159. 27 CFR §§9.22 et seq. TTB has on its website an AVA Map Explorer showing the locations of all approved AVAs, at ttb.gov/wine/ava-map-explorer (last visited August 17, 2022.

Napa Valley (Figure 6-11), which now consists of 16 nested appellations;[160] Lodi (Figure 6-12), consisting of seven sub-appellations; Willamette Valley (six sub-appellations); and Paso Robles (Figure 6-13), with its 11 sub-appellations.

Figure 6-11[161]

160. The "nested" AVAs of Napa Valley, sometimes referred to as sub-appellations, are, in order of their establishment, Carneros (1983), Howell Mountain (1984), Wild Horse Valley (1988), Stags Leap District (1989), Mt. Veeder (1990), Atlas Peak (1992), Spring Mountain District (1993), Rutherford (1993), Oakville (1993), St. Helena (1995), Chiles Valley (1999), Yountville (1999), Diamond Mountain District (2001), Oak Knoll District of Napa Valley (2004), Calistoga (2010), and Coombsville (2011). Carneros and Wild Horse Valley AVAs lie partially inside and partially outside of the Napa Valley AVA.

161. Napa Valley Appellation Map, Napa Valley Vintners, http://www.napavintners.com/downloads/Napa_Valley_Appellation_map.pdf (last visited Aug. 15, 2022).

Figure 6-12
Lodi and Its Sub-AVAs[162]

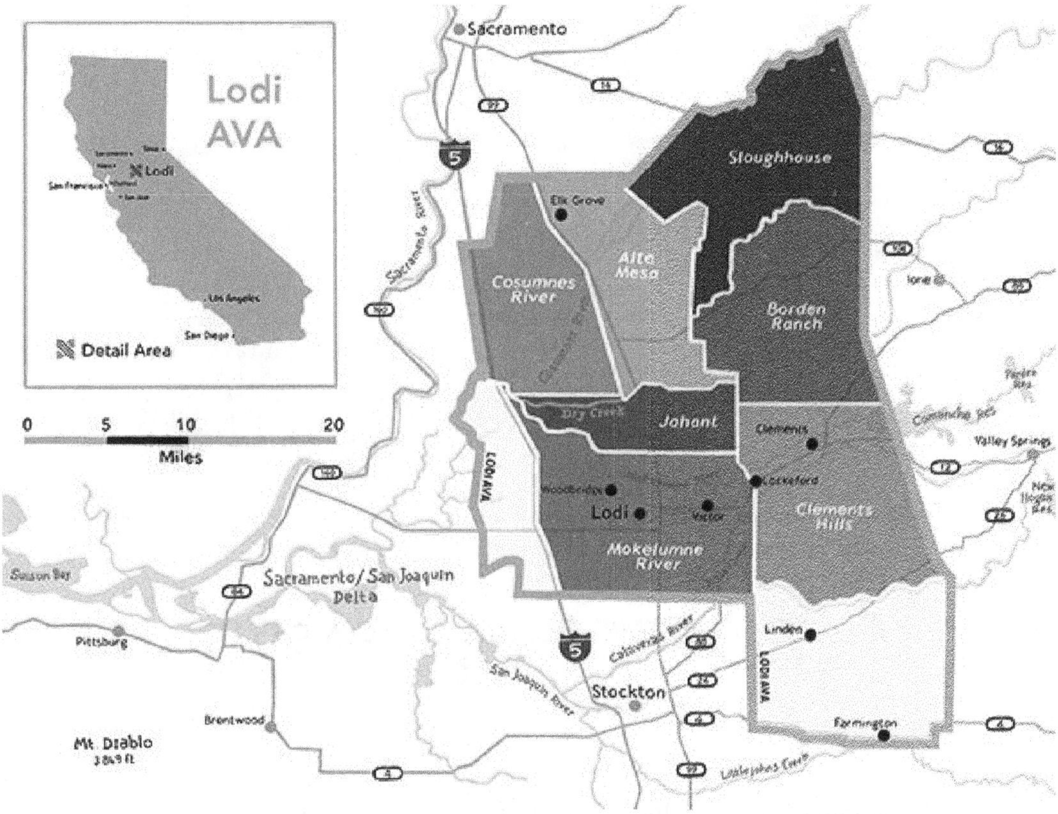

This process of subdividing AVAs is partially the result of the early tendency to create very large AVAs that included any outlying property with roughly similar viticultural characteristics; it also is a natural evolution as vintners and growers come to better understand their terroir and desire to express the differences in growing conditions and wine characteristics within those larger AVAs. Less frequently, large viticultural areas have been formed around preexisting smaller AVAs, as with the San Benito viticultural area in California.

162. Viticultural Areas, Lodi Winegrape Commission, https://www.lodiwine.com/About/Place/Viticultural-Area (last visited Aug. 15, 2022).

Figure 6-13
Paso Robles and Its Sub-AVAs[163]

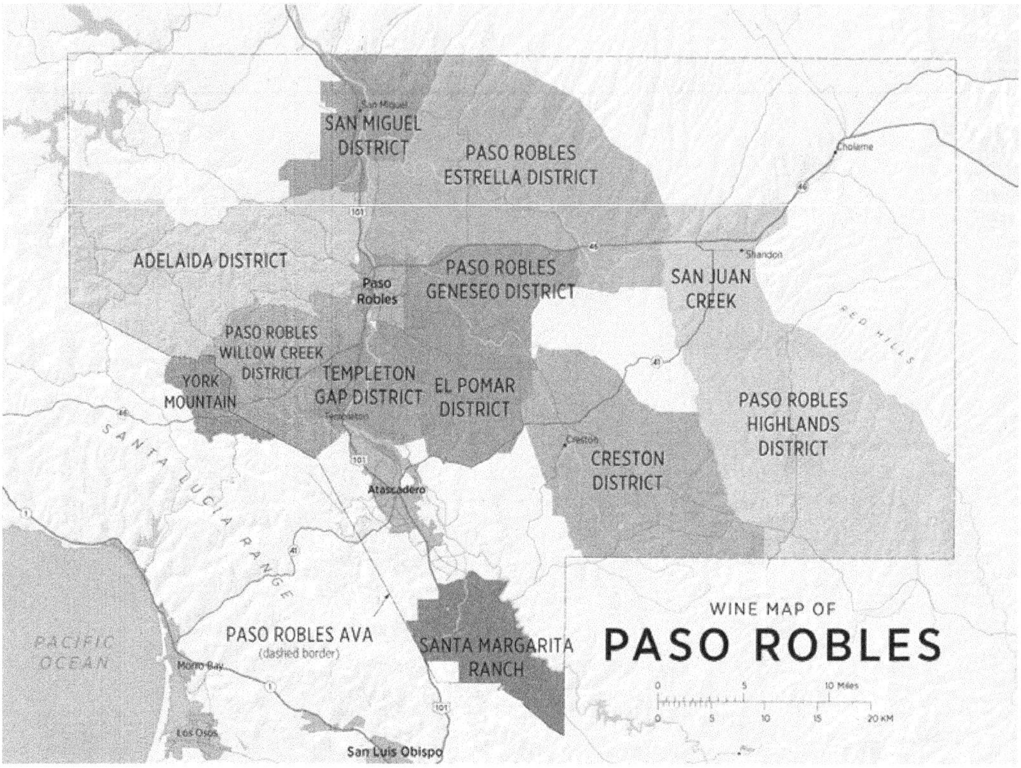

In Sonoma County, which is home to 16 AVAs, there are several wholly and partially nested AVAs, which can be confusing. For example, the 15,400-acre Rock Pile AVA in northern Sonoma County is partly in the Dry Creek Valley AVA. Dry Creek Valley is inside the larger Northern Sonoma AVA, but the portion of Rock Pile that is outside of Dry Creek Valley is also outside of the Northern Sonoma AVA. Russian River Valley, consisting of 154,984 acres, entirely encompasses two smaller AVAs—the Chalk Hill AVA, in the northeastern corner, and the Green Valley of Russian River Valley AVA (formerly known as Sonoma County Green Valley), in the southwest. The Russian River Valley lies within the Northern Sonoma AVA, but the Russian River Valley also is largely but not entirely within the Sonoma Coast AVA. The Northern Sonoma and Sonoma Coast AVAs partially overlap.[164] The order of establishment of these AVAs followed no particular rhyme or reason.

163. Get to Know the Paso Robles AVA Through Its Diversity, Paso Robles Wine Country Alliance, https://pasowine.com/get-to-know-the-paso-robles-ava (last visited Aug. 15, 2022).

164. TTB has an AVA Map Explorer at https://www.ttb.govwine/ava-map-explorer that shows the boundaries of each AVA.

Early on, TTB determined that one AVA can partially overlap another. The Carneros AVA is situated in part in the Sonoma Valley AVA and in part in the Napa Valley AVA. Initially, Carneros was envisioned as a sub-AVA of the Napa Valley, but after the petition was filed, neighboring owners in Sonoma Valley west of the proposed AVA petitioned for inclusion. TTB stated in the Final Rule establishing the Carneros AVA: "Based on written comments submitted and oral testimony from the hearing, ATF determined that the boundaries of Los Carneros should extend into Sonoma County."[165] The agency pointed to climate and soils as the key physical features distinguishing the Carneros AVA.

Unlike the traditional European appellation systems, U.S. wine appellations indicate grape origin only and do not involve or imply any quality controls. None of the criteria for establishing an AVA refers to the taste, character, or quality of the wine, and there is no organoleptic aspect to the U.S. appellation system.[166] TTB makes no endorsement of the wine made from an AVA. TTB's standard approval language follows:

> The establishment of viticultural areas allows vintners to describe more specifically the origin of their wines to consumers and allows consumers to attribute a given quality, reputation, or other characteristic of a wine made from grapes grown in an area to its geographical origin. Establishment of a viticultural area is neither an approval nor an endorsement by TTB of the wine produced in that area.[167]

Although TTB requires evidence of viticultural distinctiveness, it makes no attempt to control grape varieties or viticultural practices through the appellation system.[168] AVAs, in this sense, are analogous to the original French *appellations simples* established in 1919, prior to adoption of the *appellations d'origine contrôlées* in 1935. They are provenances of origin, without associated, appellation-specific viticultural or enological controls.

i. AVA NAMING

The proposed AVA name need not have any specific wine meaning or following in the wine industry or among wine consumers. Any name that has local or national recognition will suffice, including Native American names (Napa was named by the Onasatis-Wappo indigenous people), Mexican land grants (Carneros derives its name from Rancho El Rincón de los Carneros), and surnames of

165. 48 Fed. Reg. 37366 (Aug. 18, 1983).

166. Under the FAA Act, 27 USC §205(e), (f) (2018), and its implementing regulations, 27 C.F.R. §§4.39, 4.64 (2010), government endorsement of wine, organoleptic or otherwise, in labeling or in any other manner is specifically prohibited.

167. 74 Fed. Reg. 64602 (Dec. 8, 2009) (establishing the Calistoga AVA).

168. It is not clear that the FAA Act confers sufficient authority for TTB to dictate which grape varieties may be grown in which locations. In all likelihood, it would take an Act of Congress to implement such a program, and Congress is not likely to require a farmer to replant a vineyard in view of the expenses involved.

individuals that are now attached to particular places (the town and AVA of Rutherford were named after Thomas Rutherford). TTB, in its 2011 revisions to the AVA regulations, discussed in detail below, states:

> The name and the evidence in support of [an AVA] must come from sources independent of the petitioner. Appropriate name evidence sources include, but are not limited to, historical and modern government or commercial maps, books, newspapers, magazines, tourist and other promotional materials, local business or school names, and road names. Whenever practicable, the petitioner must include with the petition copies of the name evidence materials, appropriately cross-referenced in the petition narrative. Although anecdotal information by itself is not sufficient, statements taken from local residents with knowledge of the name and its use may also be included to support other name evidence.[169]

TTB expresses concern over any name that is misdescriptive and confusing to consumers. In 1981, Paul Masson Vineyards, Inc., objected to a TTB proposal to establish an AVA named The Pinnacles, which had been proposed by vintner Chalone Vineyard.[170] Paul Masson Vineyards objected on the basis that it had acquired trademark protection for the terms "Pinnacle" and "Pinnacles" and for the phrase "A Pinnacles Selection." Paul Masson Vineyards argued that consumers who recognized those terms in connection with Paul Masson wines would be confused and misled because Paul Masson's Pinnacles brand wine was not made from grapes grown in the proposed AVA; in fact, its vineyard sources were located nearby and had been excluded from the AVA. TTB agreed with Paul Masson Vineyards and asked Chalone if it would accept a different name for the AVA. Chalone agreed to use its own Native American name, and TTB established the Chalone AVA.[171]

In the petition for the Temecula AVA, TTB refused to include vineyards within the neighboring city of Murrieta because of possible consumer confusion.[172] TTB reasoned that grapes grown in the city of Murrieta were never known by the name of Temecula, which is a separate city. Although the Temecula AVA is not confined to the city of Temecula, TTB modified the proposed boundary to exclude the neighboring town. Otherwise, TTB reasoned, consumers might be misled as to the origin of the grapes.

One of the more novel efforts to create name evidence was the proposed "Alexander Mountain" AVA. After TTB rejected a petition to establish "Alexander Mountain" as an AVA for lack of name evidence, a winery petitioned the U.S.G.S. to change the name of the land that it owns, which is identified as

---

169. 76 Fed. Reg. 3489, 3501 (Jan. 20, 2011).

170. ATF Notice of proposed rulemaking (Notice No. 386), 46 Fed. Reg. 49600 (Oct. 7, 1981).

171. ATF Final Rule (T.D. ATF-107), 47 Fed. Reg. 25517 (June 14, 1982) (to be codified at 27 C.F.R. pt. 9). It is somewhat surprising that Chalone agreed to call the AVA by its own brand name, which is also a registered trademark. This solution worked only because Chalone owned or controlled, and intended to use, all the grapes in the Chalone AVA. In this sense, the Chalone AVA is a monopoly like the Condrieu appellation in France, with all the grapes in that appellation owned by a single winery, Château-Grillet.

172. ATF Final Rule (T.D. ATF-188), 49 Fed. Reg. 42563 (Oct. 23, 1984).

"Black Mountain" on current U.S.G.S. maps, to "Alexander Mountain," some say to take advantage of the reputation of the nearby Alexander Valley viticultural area. That petition made it to the quarterly Review List of the U.S. Board on Geographic Names' Domestic Names Committee.[173] In 2011, the Committee voted not to approve the change, citing the negative recommendation of the State Names Authority, as well as widespread local opposition and a reluctance to change a longstanding name.[174]

ii. AVA BOUNDARIES

TTB requires historical or current evidence that the boundaries of the proposed AVA match the name. This requirement is deceptively complicated. Petitioners have pointed to a variety of types of evidence to make their case, from phone directories (in the case of the Napa Valley AVA) to school districts (e.g., the Yamhill-Carlton Union High School and the Yamhill-Carlton School District in support of the Yamhill-Carlton AVA) to historical maps (Stags Leap, for example, is printed on the same U.S.G.S. topographical map on which TTB requires AVA boundaries to be plotted).

Rarely do the boundaries of an AVA match exactly those of the cited examples. From TTB's perspective, the problem is greater when a portion of the proposed AVA has never been known by the proposed name than when the name has applied historically to an area larger than that of the proposed AVA. In other words, from an evidentiary perspective, over-inclusiveness is more acceptable than under-inclusiveness.

Unlike in France and other countries of the Old World, the boundaries of AVAs are mostly geographical features (roads, rivers, elevation contours, mountain peaks), not property lines. It is not uncommon for an AVA boundary to divide a property, in which case the grower must separate the grapes from different parts of the vineyard and indicate the correct AVA on each load of grapes. This is especially important if the AVA wine made from those grapes is blended very close to the 85 percent grape source standard. As noted below, the burden of proof is on the bottling winery, which obtained the COLA but may not have grown the grapes, to justify any and all label claims.

iii. VITICULTURAL DISTINCTIVENESS

Although the regulatory definition of an AVA as a geographically distinctive grape-growing region would suggest that viticultural distinctiveness is the most important AVA criterion, TTB has not accepted that argument. All of the regulatory criteria for AVA establishment are weighted equally. The failure to prove any one criterion will prove fatal to an AVA petition. More importantly,

173. U.S. Board on Geographic Names, Quarterly Review List 401 (Jun. 17, 2009), https://geonames.usgs.gov/docs/pubs/DNCReviewLists/ReviewList401_Jun17_2009.pdf.

174. U.S. Board on Geographic Names, Seven Hundred and Thirty-fourth Meeting, Council of Geographic Names Authority Annual Conference, §4.2 (Oct. 27, 2011).

when the evidence in support of a particular AVA criterion (e.g., name or boundary) fails to coincide on the ground with evidence of viticultural distinctiveness (e.g., distinguishing geography, geology, or soils), TTB has to exercise its discretion in establishing, modifying, or rejecting the particular proposal.

Over time, AVA petitioners have become increasingly sophisticated in their assertions and preparation of supporting data concerning viticultural distinctiveness, as seen quite clearly in the field of climate and its effects on the grapes grown inside and outside of a proposed AVA. In the first decade of the AVA program, most climate discussions focused on degree days, which is a measurement of the heat available for vine development during the growing season.[175] Although the degree day classification scheme proposed by Professor Albert Winkler of the University of California—Davis was widely accepted, data often were sparse, making it difficult to compare areas inside and outside of a proposed AVA boundary.

Today, climate data are more readily available, with many growers owning their own weather-monitoring stations that collect measures of temperature, humidity, precipitation, wind direction, and speed every 15 minutes. This abundance of data allows for more detailed analysis of microclimates within a proposed AVA. In 2009, these data were used to help defeat the proposed Paso Robles Westside AVA.[176] The opponents hired a meteorologist to analyze the long-term data from a multitude of monitored stations inside and outside of the proposed AVA. TTB summarized these data as follows:

> Mr. Donald Schucraft, a certified consulting meteorologist with the Western Weather Group, explains in his opposing comment (comment 122) that in the mid-1990's he led a team of meteorologists and physical scientists that established a network of automated weather stations in the Paso Robles region, and that these stations continue to provide key information for localized Paso Robles weather forecasts. Based on the data from these stations, Mr. Schucraft states that the Salinas River does not provide a suitable boundary line for the many different microclimates found in the Paso Robles viticultural area. He notes that there are distinct microclimates to the west of the Salinas River within the proposed Paso

---

175. Professor Winkler first advanced the concept of growing degree days (GDD) in his seminal book, A. J. Winkler et al., General Viticulture 61 (2d ed. 1975). By convention, grape degree days are tallied between April 1 and October 31, and a base temperature of 50° Fahrenheit is used. *Id.* Winkler's formula for calculating degree days follows: GDD = Sum of ([(Daily Maximum Temperature—Minimum Temperature) ÷ 2]—50) for all days from April 1 to October 31. Winkler established five grape-growing regions based on seasonal degree day accumulations: Region I, less than 2,500 degree days; Region II, 2,501-3,000 degree days; Region III, 3,001-3,500 degree days; Region IV, 3,501-4,000 degree days; and Region V, above 4,000 degree days. *Id.* at 61-64.

176. TTB Withdrawal of Notice of Proposed Rulemaking (Notice No. 94), 74 Fed. Reg. 19917 (April 30, 2009). TTB withdrew the Paso Robles Westside AVA petition because it could "not conclude that a delimited grape-growing region exists that is recognized by the name Paso Robles Westside." *Id.* at 19917.

Robles Westside viticultural area, and that these microclimates change from north to south as well as east to west.[177]

iv. AMENDING AVA NAMES OR BOUNDARIES

TTB will consider petitions to amend the name or boundaries of existing AVAs. In the first two decades after the AVA system took effect, such petitions were routinely granted. For a boundary expansion, the petitioner had to present evidence showing that the added acreage shares the same viticultural characteristics as the rest of the AVA.[178] Generally, the enlargement area was not planted to vines or not considered plantable at the time of the AVA establishment, and the Final Rule did not specifically address that area. This gave the TTB some leeway in altering the boundaries.

TTB, however, was and still is reluctant to expand an AVA that was controversial at the time of its original establishment. For example, the bureau carefully scrutinized and rejected the petition of Sonoma-Cutrer Winery to expand the Carneros AVA. The TTB generally contacts the petitioners for the existing AVA to ensure that they have an opportunity to comment on the proposed expansion.

Today, TTB, since the 2011 revisions to its AVA regulations, scrutinizes AVA expansion petitions more carefully. The agency requires, among other things, detailed evidence of the distinguishing features of the expansion area that justify its inclusion in the existing AVA. The petitioner must show that these same features are not found in the surrounding, excluded areas.

TTB also will amend an AVA name so long as there is national or local recognition of that name in relation to the proposed area. Temecula was later renamed Temecula Valley,[179] and Yamhill-Carlton District became Yamhill-Carlton.[180] TTB also will modify AVA names to avoid a fight between brand owners and AVA proponents over a particular geographical name so long as the modified name meets the AVA regulatory criteria. An example is the name change from Santa Rita Hills to Sta Rita Hills, which is discussed more fully below.

---

177. *Id.* at 19920.

178. Almost all amendments have sought to enlarge, not contract, AVAs. The exception is when boundaries of adjacent AVAs are being realigned; an example is Santa Lucia Highlands and Arroyo Seco AVAs (moving approximately 200 acres from Arroyo Seco to Santa Lucia Highlands). TTB Final Rule (T.D. TTB-49), 71 Fed. Reg. 34525 (June 15, 2006).

179. The Temecula Valley Winegrowers Association, which petitioned for the change, argued that the new name would provide a more accurate description of the region's geography and "provide greater clarity as to the area's location for wine consumers and the public." The new name also distinguished the winegrowing area from the City of Temecula. TTB Final Rule (T.D. TTB-10), 67 Fed. Reg. 64573 (Oct. 21, 2002).

180. TTB Final Rule (T.D. TTB-87), 75 Fed. Reg. 67616-67618 (Nov. 3, 2010). The petitioners for the name change said that the AVA name was too long to use on wine labels. They argued that Yamhill-Carlton was locally recognized as referring to the AVA, and the TTB agreed.

2. PROTECTING WINE APPELLATIONS

TTB enforces its appellation requirements through the federal label review process and audits of winery production records. No wine, domestic or foreign, can be sold in the United States without a COLA.[181] TTB issues a COLA following a review of the proposed label to ensure compliance with federal law. TTB also has a list of prohibited labeling practices. Any label information that is false or misleading or tends to create a misleading impression, including as to origin, is prohibited.[182] TTB has the right to conduct an inspection of the bonded winery and its required recordkeeping to verify any winery's labeling claims.

If a label claim cannot be justified, the COLA will be rejected or revoked, the wine may be seized, and/or the winery's or importer's federal operating permit can be suspended or revoked.

3. OTHER GEOGRAPHICAL DESIGNATIONS ON WINE LABELS

Appellations are not the only geographical references that are authorized on wine labels in the United States. Other approved uses include brand names of geographical significance; generic, semi-generic, or non-generic classes or types of wine with geographical significance; and varietal names with geographical significance. Each of these uses is discussed below.

a. Brand Names of Geographical Significance

Just as Chateau Margaux in France incorporates the name of the appellation in which it is located, there are numerous U.S. wineries whose brand names have viticultural significance. Examples include Napa Wine Company in the Napa Valley viticultural area, Carneros Creek Winery in the Carneros viticultural area, and Santa Cruz Mountain Vineyard in the Santa Cruz Mountain viticultural area.

In many of these cases, the wineries have selected these brand names because of their geographical significance. At the same time, as noted in Section B, wineries typically wish to protect these brand names as trademarks to prevent others from adopting and using similar brand names to identify their wines. Under U.S. trademark law, there is no inherent inconsistency in claiming trademark rights in a term that has geographical significance. However, to the extent that a geographical term describes the location from which a product originates, it cannot function as a trademark because it does not operate to distinguish products of multiple manufacturers located in the region to which the term applies.[183]

As previously noted, the Lanham Act provides that a geographically descriptive trademark may not be registered as an inherently distinctive

---

181. 27 C.F.R. §4.50 (2021).

182. *Id.* §4.39(a)(1).

183. *See* 1 J. Thomas McCarthy, McCarthy on Trademarks and Unfair Competition, §14.1 (4th ed. 2010).

trademark.[184] However, such a mark may be entitled to registration and the associated protections if it can be shown that the mark "has become distinctive of the applicant's goods in commerce."[185] Thus, for example, "Chalone Vineyard" is registered as a trademark with the U.S. Patent and Trademark Office despite TTB's designation of "Chalone" as a viticultural area. Misdescriptive geographical trademarks, however, cannot be registered if they were first used after January 1, 1996.[186]

Geographical terms, we know, also can function as certification marks. TTB, however, does not defer to certification marks in defining wine appellations. TTB stated its position on this subject very clearly in the case of the North Coast AVA in California. The California North Coast Grape Growers Association (CNCGGA) relied on its existing North Coast certification mark for grapes to justify its position on the proposed boundaries of the North Coast AVA. TTB was not persuaded:

> CNCGGA claims that use of the "North Coast" appellation by wineries using grapes from outside of Napa, Sonoma, and Mendocino Counties constitute infringement of the mark under the Lanham Act, 15 USC Chapter 22. In the event a direct conflict arises between some or all of the rights granted by a registered certification mark under the Lanham Act and the right to use the name of a viticultural area established under the FAA Act, it is the position of [TTB] that the rights applicable to the viticultural area should control. Since the evidence shows that portions of Napa, Sonoma, Mendocino, Solano, Lake, and Marin Counties meet the requirements for a viticultural area as set forth in 27 CFR 4.25a(e), the North Coast viticultural area includes portions of all six counties.[187]

Even if a winery were to acquire trademark rights in a geographical term, it could not prevent certain uses of the term by others. In particular, the owner of rights in a geographically descriptive term cannot prevent others from making non-trademark uses of that term to describe the geographical origin of their products.[188] Such use of a term, referred to as a "fair use," provides an outer limit on the trademark monopoly that one may acquire in a geographical term.

In its early AVA rulings, TTB often ignored claims by the owners of registered trademarks that their names were being infringed and diluted by the government's establishment of AVAs by the same or similar names. In 1985, TTB approved the petition of Chicama Vineyards of West Tisbury, Massachusetts, for an AVA known as Martha's Vineyard.[189] TTB established the AVA over objections of the much better-known Heitz Wine Cellars of Napa Valley, which claimed that approval of the AVA would undermine its common law trademark rights in the

---

184. 15 USC §1052(e) (2021).

185. *Id.* §1052(f).

186. *Id.* §1052(a).

187. ATF Final Rule (T.D. ATF-145), 48 Fed. Reg. 42973, 42976 (Sept. 21, 1983).

188. 15 U.S.C. §1115(b)(4) (2006); *see also In Re Nantucket*, 677 F.2d 95, 102-03 (C.C.P.A. 1982) (Nies, J.,concurring).

189. ATF Final Rule (T.D. ATF-193), 50 Fed. Reg. 255 (Jan. 3, 1985).

name of its most famous wine, Martha's Vineyard Cabernet Sauvignon, named after the grower's wife, Martha May.

In 1988, TTB issued a very clearly worded position statement on the issue of conflicts between geographical brands (in TTB parlance, "brand names of viticultural significance") and AVAs. The statement is included in the Final Rule establishing the Wild Horse Valley viticultural area over the objection of the owner of the Wild Horse brand, whose wine was not made from grapes grown in the proposed AVA:

> It is not the policy of ATF to become involved in purely private disputes involving proprietary rights, such as trademark infringement suits. However, in the event a direct conflict arises between some or all of the rights granted by a registered trademark under the Lanham Act and the right to use the name of a viticultural area established under the FAA Act, it is the position of ATF that the rights applicable to the viticultural area should control.[190]

TTB followed the same logic in the battle involving the Santa Rita Hills AVA and the Santa Rita trademark held by Santa Rita Winery in Chile. TTB established the Santa Rita Hills AVA in 2001 over the objection of the Chilean winery, which feared infringement, tarnishment, and dilution if the Santa Rita name were used by other wineries.[191] The Chilean winery responded by commencing a legal action against TTB in federal district court. TTB prevailed, largely because the court determined that legal redress could not be sought from TTB, which established the AVA, but from users of the AVA in commerce.[192] The outcome of such an action no doubt would depend on the way in which the AVA name appeared on the subject label. For example, if the AVA name were prominently displayed and led consumers to believe that the wine was the product of the Santa Rita Winery, a trademark infringement action might be appropriate.

Santa Rita Winery has never filed such an action. Instead, the Chilean winery and other wineries in the Santa Rita Hills AVA agreed to change the name of the AVA to "Sta Rita Hills" to avoid consumer confusion between the brand and the appellation. TTB consented, and the name change was approved in 2005.[193]

TTB has wrestled with conflicts between brand names and AVA names since the passage of the FAA Act. It has adopted and then abandoned a series of solutions. For example, TTB once required wineries to modify their geographic brand names with the word "brand," or with ™ or ®, to indicate to consumers that this is only a brand name and does not imply the geographical origin of the fruit. In 1986, after a lengthy rulemaking, TTB adopted what appeared to be its final regulatory solution. In that rulemaking, TTB concluded that brand names of viticultural significance, which typically are the most prominent feature on a wine

---

190. ATF Final Rule (T.D. ATF-278), 53 Fed. Reg. 48244 at 48246 (Nov. 30, 1988).

191. ATF Final Rule (T.D. ATF-454), 66 Fed. Reg. 29476-29480 (May 31, 2001).

192. *Sociedad Anomina Vina Santa Rita v. U.S. Treasury Dep't,* 193 F. Supp. 2d 6 (D.D.C. 2001).

193. TTB Final Rule (T.D. TTB-37), 70 Fed. Reg. 72710-72713 (Dec. 7, 2005).

label, can mislead consumers about the origin of the grapes used to make the wine.[194] For that reason, the bureau decided that if a brand name incorporates the name of a state, county, or viticultural area or is otherwise found to have viticultural significance by TTB, the wine must comply with the appellation requirements for the named area.

The discretion afforded TTB allows the agency to determine whether the full AVA name or any part thereof has viticultural significance (known as a "term of viticultural significance"). For example, TTB has stated that "Napa" alone, instead of the full AVA name Napa Valley, has viticultural significance. Because "Napa" is so distinctive, unlike "Green" in the AVA Green Valley of Solano County, "Napa" alone cannot be used in a brand unless the wine qualifies for the Napa Valley AVA or Napa County appellation, or is otherwise grandfathered, as explained below.

In its 1986 ruling, TTB also established an exception for preexisting brand names of viticultural significance. Under this grandfather provision, wineries that obtained label approval from TTB for a brand name of viticultural significance prior to July 7, 1986, are allowed to continue to use that brand name, and even to sell it to other proprietors who could use it, so long as the label includes an appropriate appellation of origin for the wine or a label disclaimer.[195] An appropriate appellation or disclaimer is defined as follows:

> A county or a viticultural area, if the brand name bears the name of a geographical area smaller than a state, or . . . [a] state, county or a viticultural area, if the brand name bears a state name; or . . . [t]he wine shall be labeled with some other statement which the appropriate TTB officer finds to be sufficient to dispel the impression that the geographical area suggested by the brand name is indicative of the origin of the wine.[196]

As an example, the brand Napa Ridge was first used in a COLA approved by TTB before 1986, so the winery can continue to use that name, including for wines that are not made from Napa Valley grapes, so long as the label includes an appropriate appellation of origin. An example of such a grandfathered label would be Napa Ridge Central Coast Cabernet Sauvignon. (Napa Valley is not a part of the Central Coast AVA.) By contrast, a hypothetical new wine sold under the brand Napa Valley Oaks would have to include at least 85 percent Napa Valley grapes, or that brand name could not be used.

The TTB's grandfather exception provided an opportunity for the owners of pre-1986 brands to profit by sourcing lower-cost grapes for wines labeled with a well-known geographical brand name that would fetch a higher price. Bronco Wine Company (Bronco) purchased three such brands: Napa Ridge, Rutherford

---

194. 27 C.F.R. §4.39(i) (2021), which is set forth in full in Chapter 3; *see also* Wine Labeling and Advertising; Use of Geographic Brand Names, T.D. ATF-229 (May 16, 1986).

195. 27 C.F.R. §4.39(i) (2021).

196. *Id.*

Vintners, and Napa Creek Winery, sample labels of which are shown in Figure 6-14.

Figure 6-14
"Napa" Labels

Because these brands were grandfathered, Bronco could use the names and source grapes from any AVA as long as an appropriate appellation was identified on the label. Recognizing the potential for confusion and damage to the reputation and economy of Napa Valley, the California legislature passed Business and Professions Code §25241, which prohibits the use of a brand name with the word Napa, or any federally recognized viticultural area wholly within Napa County, or any confusingly similar name on the label, packaging material, or advertising of wine produced, bottled, labeled, offered for sale, or sold in California, unless at least 75 percent of the grapes used to make the wine are from Napa County. The legislature adopted the following findings in support of the bill:

> (1) The Legislature finds and declares that for more than a century, Napa Valley and Napa County have been widely recognized for producing grapes and wine of the highest quality. Both consumers and the wine industry understand the name Napa County and the viticultural area appellations of origin contained within Napa County (collectively "Napa appellations") as denoting that the wine was created with the distinctive grapes grown in Napa County.
>
> (2) The Legislature finds, however, that certain producers are using Napa appellations on labels, on packaging materials, and in advertising for wines that are not made from grapes grown in Napa County, and that consumers are confused and deceived by these practices.
>
> (3) The Legislature further finds that legislation is necessary to eliminate these misleading practices. It is the intent of the Legislature to assure consumers that the wines produced or sold in the state with brand names, packaging materials, or advertising referring to Napa appellations in fact qualify for the Napa County appellation of origin.[197]

Bronco challenged the state law, claiming, among other things, that federal law preempted the more restrictive California legislation and that the court "should

197. Cal. Bus. & Prof. Code §25241(a) (2009).

find implied preemption . . . because Section 25241 stands as an obstacle to the accomplishment and execution of the full purposes and objectives of Congress."[198]

The court found that:

> nothing in the history of the underlying federal statute or the federal regulations suggest[s] that, although the [ATF] may have determined that as a *general matter* its grandfather clause was appropriate so as to avoid destroying an "entire class" of brand-name labels, states would or should be precluded from adopting more stringent brand-name labeling requirements as necessary to address local concerns.[199] [Emphasis in original.]

California's labeling rule therefore was not preempted by federal law and did not "frustrate Congress's intent or stand as an obstacle to the accomplishment and execution of the full purposes and objectives of Congress." In conclusion, the court ruled without dissent as follows:

> Bronco has failed to carry its burden of demonstrating federal preemption of a long-established and legitimate exercise of state police power with respect to the subject regulated by section 25241. As we have seen, there is no express preemption in the present context, and Bronco's assertions of implied preemption are contradicted by the long history we have described of concurrent state and federal regulation of wine labels including, historically, the representations appearing on labels suggesting the place of origin of the grapes used to make wine. Nor has Bronco succeeded in providing any persuasive indication that this long-standing concurrent regulatory scheme no longer is compatible with Congress's overall purposes which have been to support the states' efforts to protect consumers from misleading labeling, not to permit the type of labeling at issue here. Finally, Bronco has not established that, by purchasing a brand name that had been used prior to 1986, it acquired a federally recognized right or license exempting it from stricter state regulation.
>
> California is recognized as a preeminent producer of wine, and the geographical source of its wines—reflecting the attributes of distinctive locales, particularly the Napa Valley—forms a very significant basis upon which consumers worldwide evaluate expected quality when making a purchase. We do not find it surprising that Congress, in its effort to provide minimum standards for wine labels, would not foreclose a state with particular expertise and interest from providing stricter protection for consumers in order to ensure the integrity of its wine industry.[200]

---

198. *Bronco Wine Co. v. Jolly*, 33 Cal. 4th 943, 956 (2004). In addition to its preemption cause of action, Bronco claimed that the California law violated the First Amendment, the Commerce Clause, and the Takings Clause of the U.S. Constitution. *Id.* at 955.

199. *Id.* at 994.

200. *Id.* at 997. California's action to codify Business & Professions Code §25241 was not the first time that the Napa Valley wine industry had turned to the state to protect the Napa Valley brand. In 1989 California adopted a law requiring "conjunctive labeling" for Napa Valley wines. Cal. Bus. & Prof. Code §25240 provides that any wine labeled with a Napa Valley sub-AVA must also say "Napa Valley" on the label. Oregon also has adopted wine labeling standards that are stricter than the federal labeling regulations—for example, for varietal wines (Oregon Administrative Rules

Both before and after the *Bronco* case, TTB has tried to avoid conflicts between brand names and AVA names in a number of ways. Perhaps the most common solution mentioned above is to modify the name of the AVA, such as Diamond Mountain District or Eola-Amity Hills, to differentiate those AVAs from the brands Diamond Mountain and Eola Hills. The full name of the AVA is then established by TTB as the name of viticultural significance so that the brand names are unaffected by the provisions of 27 C.F.R. 4.39(i). But sometimes this solution has not worked.

The most recent contentious battle, described briefly in Section B, was fought over the name Calistoga.[201] Although TTB found a "substantial basis for the establishment of the viticultural area"[202] under the Calistoga name in the northern part of the Napa Valley AVA and no evidence was presented to contradict the petitioners' evidence of viticultural distinctiveness, TTB was troubled by the claims of Calistoga Partners, L.P., doing business as Calistoga Cellars (its brand name), and Chateau Calistoga (Calistoga Estates brand name) that their brands would be adversely impacted or eliminated altogether by the TTB's action. Calistoga Cellars and Calistoga Estate did not source enough grapes from the proposed Calistoga AVA to meet the 85 percent grape sourcing requirement. In its rulemaking notice, TTB made it clear that it "do[es] not believe that, in the context of the labeling provisions of the FAA Act, it is an appropriate government role to make choices between competing commercial interests, if such choices can be avoided."[203] That is, the TTB would be hard-pressed to establish an AVA that would cause an existing winery to "forfeit" its trademark rights and invested capital in its brand name.

The preferred resolution of revising the AVA name was unavailable; petitioner Chateau Montelena would not accept Calistoga District as the AVA name and as the name of viticultural significance. After the Bronco saga, Chateau Montelena feared that there would be a variety of brands with Calistoga name variations (Calistoga Caves, Calistoga Hills, Calistoga Wine Cellars), none of which would have to use Calistoga AVA grapes because the brands did not include the precise words "Calistoga District."

Although the TTB might have solved the problem by denying the petition altogether, the agency proposed a new compromise and, in doing so, sparked a hotly contested and heavily politicized AVA rulemaking proceeding. The agency's proposal, in the form of Notice of Proposed Rulemaking No. 77, published in the

---

(OAR) 845-010-0915 requires 90 percent varietal content for some varietals and 75 percent for others compared to the federal requirement of 75 percent) and appellations of origin (OAR 845-010-0920 requires 95 percent grape sourcing from Oregon appellations, including Oregon AVAs, counties, and the state, compared to the federal requirement of 85 percent).

201. Given the role that Calistoga played in Napa Valley's rise to prominence in the wine world, it is surprising that it was not a recognized AVA sooner. Chateau Montelena's 1973 Chardonnay, produced in Calistoga, took first prize for white wine in the Paris Tasting of 1976. George M. Taber, Judgment of Paris: California vs. France and the Historic 1976 Paris Tasting 201-02 (New York: Simon & Schuster 2005).

202. TTB Final Rule (T.D. TTB-83) at 64605.

203. *Id.*

Federal Register on November 20, 2007, was to expand grandfather protection beyond the pre-1986 limit to include brands that had been in actual commercial use for a "significant period" prior to the filing of the AVA petition and to require additional information on the allowed labels sufficient to dispel the impression that the wines qualified as Calistoga AVA wines.[204] The solution was essentially a one-brand fix for Calistoga Cellars. Calistoga Estates would be left out because its first COLA was approved after TTB issued the first Notice of Proposed Rulemaking for the Calistoga AVA in March 2005.

TTB received over 1,350 comments in response to Notice No. 77. Of the comments received, over 1,160 were in the form of letters and postcards championing "the little guy" brand owners being denied their "due process right."[205] Most of these comments were form letters submitted by "Stand Up for the Little Guy," a group supporting Calistoga Cellars.[206]

In forming its response to the debate, TTB stated that many commentators got it wrong. The issue was not about large versus small wineries:

> The present rulemaking raised the question of what to do about viticultural area petitions that are received long after the issuance in 1986 of §4.39(i) on the use of geographical brand names of viticultural significance where the petition proposes a name that results in a conflict with a brand name first used on an approved COLA not covered by the grandfather provision in §4.39(i). Such a circumstance may occur for legitimate reasons because exact terms of viticultural significance are not always universally agreed upon, and relevant facts and issues regarding terms and areas of viticultural significance are not always brought forward until a petition is published for rulemaking.[207]

TTB concluded in December 2009 that the "adoption of a specific, limited grandfather provision would not be appropriate in this case."[208] TTB also abandoned the notion that a back label disclaimer could adequately dispel consumer confusion. The TTB's ultimate compromise was to create a three-year "use up period," during which the Calistoga-named brands could be transitioned to new names or brought into compliance with the AVA grape-sourcing requirements.[209]

204. TTB Notice of Proposed Rulemaking (Notice No. 77), 72 Fed. Reg. 65257-65261 (Nov. 20, 2007).

205. TTB Final Rule (T.D. TTB-83) at 64606.

206. *Id.*

207. *Id.* at 64610.

208. *Id.* at 64611.

209. *Id.*

b. Generic, Semi-generic and Non-generic Names of Geographical Significance

The same distinction between generic and geographically descriptive designations under the Lanham Act discussed in Section A is recognized by TTB. Under the FAA Act, TTB has the authority to establish "Standards of Identity for Wine," which include various classes of wine (e.g., grape wine, sparkling grape wine, fruit wine) and types of wine within each class (e.g., table or dessert wine, champagne, berry wine as well as varietal types).[210] A generic wine name is a designation for a particular class or type of wine. Generic names also can have geographical significance. In the United States, vermouth and sake now are considered to be generic names that have lost their original geographical significance. These terms may be used on wine labels without any indication of origin.

Other names retain their original geographical reference but also indicate a type of wine under U.S. law.[211] There are 16 authorized semi-generic names—generic as to product characteristics but not as to origin—that may be used to designate wines from the original source or, when modified by an appropriate appellation of origin displayed in direct conjunction with the name, from some other source (e.g., California Sherry).[212] The 16 semi-generics are Angelica, Burgundy, Claret, Chablis, Champagne, Chianti, Malaga, Marsala, Madeira, Moselle, Port, Rhine Wine, Sauterne, Haut Sauterne, Sherry, and Tokay.

Finally, names deemed non-generic may be used only to designate wines of the origin indicated by such names.[213] Non-generic status under TTB regulations is of two sorts. First, certain non-generic designations are deemed to be "distinctive designations" of particular wine types and suffice as class and type designations in their own right. These designations include Chateau Margaux, Graves, Medoc, Rhone, and over 100 other names listed in 27 C.F.R. Part 12, Subpart D. To be so classified, the names must be found by the director of TTB to be known to the U.S. consumer and trade as designating a specific wine from a particular place and distinguishable from all other wines.[214]

The second type of non-generic name can be used only to designate wine of the origin indicated by such name but is not sufficiently well recognized to serve as a class and type designation under U.S. law. Such wine names, including Bandol, Piemonte, Rheinfalz, and others listed in Part 12, Subpart C, still must be accompanied by an acceptable class or type designation on the label.

The difference between these categories of non-generic names is not well understood. Although both are non-generic, the second category seems to imply a lesser degree of protection. Additionally, those foreign wine names not entered on either list appear to be unprotected. In fact, Subpart C of Part 12 lists only

---

210. 27 U.S.C. §205(e); 27 C.F.R. §§4.20-4.23 (2021).
211. 27 C.F.R. §4.21 (2021).
212. 26 U.S.C. §5388(c) (2021); 27 C.F.R. §4.24(b) (2021).
213. 27 C.F.R. §4.24(c) (2021).
214. *Id.* §4.24(c).

"examples" of foreign non-generic names rather than a comprehensive list (as is the case for Subpart D, concerning foreign distinctive designations), further confusing the status, use, and protection afforded non-generic names.

c. Varietal Names with Geographical Significance

Another possible geographical reference on a U.S. wine label is as part of a varietal name. TTB initiated rulemaking in 1986, and completed it in 1995, establishing an approved list of wine grape varietal names.[215] Certain contentious varietal names such as Johannisberg Riesling and Gamay Beaujolais were phased out.

4. THE FUTURE OF WINE APPELLATIONS IN THE UNITED STATES

The wine appellation system in the United States is now over 30 years old. Its future will be shaped by two separate and independent processes. The first is governmental; the TTB has recently completed a comprehensive review of the appellation rules and regulations and amended certain of the AVA regulations. The second is private; various vintner-grower groups are taking steps on their own to give their appellation wines added meaning and value.

a. Revisiting the Regulations

In 2007 TTB decided that it was time for a comprehensive review of the appellation system. On its own initiative, the bureau issued Notice of Proposed Rulemaking No. 78, with a series of questions and reform proposals.[216] Not surprisingly, disputes between brand names and AVAs were first on the list. TTB described the problem as follows:

> Since July 1986, more than 100 AVAs have been established in response to petitions from industry members and grape growers, reflecting the increased interest in, and spread of, viticulture throughout the United States. In addition, in recent years an increasing number of petitions have been submitted that, if the AVA were to be established with the petitioned-for name, would affect established brand names. As noted above, our intent in administering the AVA program, consistent with the intent behind the original grandfather approach, is to recognize established grape-growing regions while avoiding interference with established brand names.
>
> While TTB will continue to work with future AVA petitioners to limit the adverse impact on established brand names, we recognize that sometimes it will not be possible to amend a petition to achieve this result. In such cases, we believe that application of a new prospective grandfather approach would achieve the

215. Grape Variety Names for American Wines, 61 Fed. Reg. 522 (Feb. 13, 1996).

216. TTB Notice of proposed rulemaking (Notice No. 78), 72 Fed. Reg. 65261-65275 (Nov. 20, 2007).

> most balanced result. Accordingly, we are proposing to amend §4.39(i) by adding a new grandfathering standard that would apply in the case of AVAs established after adoption of the final rule in this matter and that would be based on a specified number of years that a COLA was issued, and whether the brand label was in actual commercial use, before receipt by TTB of a perfected AVA petition. This approach would permit the establishment of the AVA and at the same time afford appropriate protection of existing labels.[217]

TTB's specific proposal provided that, for a post-1986 geographical brand to be grandfathered, it must be used in a COLA issued at least five years before the establishment of an AVA bearing that geographical name and that wine brand must have been commercially sold for at least three of those five years. Further, a geographical brand, if used on a wine that does not qualify for the named AVA, must include a label disclaimer.[218] Although no particular disclaimer language was proposed, presumably it would be something like "This ABC brand wine is not from the ABC appellation." This is commonly referred to as a rolling grandfather rule because the precise grandfathering date would be decided on a case-by-case basis, depending on the date of "perfection" of the AVA petition.

In Notice 78 the TTB also addressed the issue of AVAs that are nested inside of other AVAs and AVA expansions. Regarding the former, the bureau described its concerns as follows:

> TTB has come to recognize that [petitions for AVAs that would be entirely or partially within the boundaries of existing AVAs] can create the appearance of a conflict or inconsistency because, with reference to the criteria set forth in §9.3(b), the new petition might draw into question the accuracy and validity of the evidence presented in support of the establishment of the existing AVA or the legitimacy of the justification for establishing the AVA.[219]

For that reason, TTB proposed to reserve the right, when establishing an AVA within an AVA, to carve it out of the larger area of which it is part.[220] For example, a future "Coombsville" AVA in the southeastern portion of Napa Valley might be considered so distinct that it would no longer be considered part of the Napa Valley AVA. If that were to happen, grapes grown there would not count toward the 85 percent grape source requirement for Napa Valley wines.

TTB also proposed to clarify in Notice 78 that amendments to existing AVAs will only be approved if the expansion area shares "essentially the same" distinguishing viticultural features as the rest of the AVA and the petitioner can show that the area outside the expanded AVA has different features.[221] Additionally, "[t]he petition must explain how the boundary of the existing AVA was incorrectly or incompletely drafted or is no longer accurate due to new

---

217. *Id.* at 65263.
218. *Id.* at 65267.
219. *Id.* at 65262.
220. *Id.* at 65268.
221. *Id.*

evidence or changed circumstances with reference to the name evidence and distinguishing features" of the AVA.[222]

Finally, TTB sought to clarify the grounds upon which an AVA petition can be rejected and to more completely describe the submission and review processes, including the actions that the TTB is empowered to take at each stage of the process.[223]

TTB's Final Rule on Notice 78 was published on January 20, 2011.[224] TTB carefully analyzed the 191 comments that it received from U.S. senators and representatives, state government representatives, local government officials, wine industry members, trade associations, interest groups, and others. The large majority of the comments opposed part or all of TTB's proposed changes; some commenters recommended their own changes to the AVA regulations.[225]

In the Final Rule, TTB amended Part 9 of 27 C.F.R. in the following areas: the submission of AVA petitions (§9.11), AVA petition requirements (§9.12), initial processing of AVA petitions (§9.13), and the AVA rulemaking process (§9.14). The new regulations take effect on February 22, 2011. Petitions received prior to that date are processed under the pre-existing rules.

TTB decided to abandon its proposal for a rolling grandfather rule to resolve conflicts between brand names and appellations. This was not surprising in light of TTB's earlier decision on the Calistoga AVA brand name conflict and the fact that 105 of 107 comments that the bureau received on this issue opposed TTB's proposal. TTB noted in the Final Rule that in almost all instances of name conflicts, the parties have been able to reach a satisfactory compromise. It cited specific examples involving AVA name modifiers like "District" (e.g., Diamond Mountain District AVA), the consent of the affected brand owners to comply with the AVA's grape sourcing requirement (e.g., Lake Chelan), the change of an AVA's name (e.g., Chalone AVA), and the rejection of an AVA petition (e.g., the Tulocay AVA in Napa Valley). TTB then referred to the transitional three-year period that it adopted in the Calistoga situation, which gave the affected brand owners time to modify their grape sourcing or adopt a new brand name. And the bureau added that "we continue to believe that dispelling information [a disclaimer] is appropriate in certain situations."[226] With all these tools at its disposal, TTB decided that future brand name—appellation conflicts can be resolved on a case-by-case basis without

---

222. *Id.*

223. *Id.* at 65269.

224. TTB Final Rule (T.D. TTB-90), 76 Fed. Reg. 3489 (Jan. 20, 2011).

225. Jess Jackson, owner of Kendall-Jackson and many other wine brands, recommended that TTB classify appellations based on their size, viticultural distinctiveness, and homogeneity in grape growing attributes; specifically, he recommended the establishment of AVA zones, regions and districts. Proposed Revision of American Viticultural Area Regulations, 76 Fed. Reg. 13 (Jan. 20, 2011) (comment of Jess J. Jackson on Mar. 19, 2008), accessible as Docket no. TTB-2007-0068-0106. This scheme harkens back to a proposal made earlier by geographer Harm Jan de Blij who recommended the establishment in the U.S. of regional appellations (e.g., Ohio River Valley, Pacific Northwest), state and county appellations, and smaller AVAs. Harm Jan De Blij, *Viticultural Areas and Mental Maps,* 21 East Lake Geographer, Sept. 1, 1986.

226. *Id.* at 3499.

a "new grandfather provision as a default resolution."[227] The bureau reserved the right to revisit the issue in the future should circumstances warrant and, in the meantime, encouraged all concerned parties, including consumers, to resolve any name conflicts on their own rather than rely on rulemaking.

On a related issue, TTB chose not to adopt any new regulation about "terms of viticultural significance" but instead will continue to rely on 27 C.F.R. §4.39(i)(3) to make those determinations. That subsection reads: "A name has viticultural significance when it is the name of a state or county (or the foreign equivalents), when approved as a viticultural area in part 9 of this chapter, or by a foreign government, or when found to have viticultural significance by the appropriate TTB officer." The bureau cited a comment that it received on this subject stating that no rule on "terms of viticultural significance" should be promulgated by TTB "without explaining the criteria for the selection so that the industry can provide meaningful comments."[228] Since December 2005 TTB has stated the "terms of viticultural significance" in each of its Final Rules establishing AVAs.[229]

With respect to nested AVAs, TTB received strong opposition to its stated concerns and proposal. TTB agree with the commenters that "consumer interests are served by greater specificity within a hierarchy, where a true hierarchy exists."[230] But TTB restated its belief that some AVAs formed within larger, existing AVAs might be so distinct as to confuse consumers if both AVA names could be used on wine labels. TTB gave the following example:

> [I]f an existing AVA is defined as being a large valley and its distinguishing geographical features are those that are found on the valley floor, it may be appropriate to approve a proposed AVA described as being situated in whole or in part on the same valley floor within the existing AVA if the proposed AVA shares some of the geographical features with the existing AVA but at the same time has other geographical features that are sufficiently distinctive as to warrant its own AVA designation. On the other hand, if within that large valley AVA there is a mountain on which a petitioner proposes to establish a new AVA above the 500-foot elevation line, the evidence provided in the petition might demonstrate that the distinguishing features of the proposed AVA bear no relationship to those of the valley floor. In the latter case, the new petition has demonstrated that this is not a hierarchical situation involving some sharing of common features but rather is a proposal to establish an entirely distinctive AVA. In such a case, TTB believes it may be inappropriate to take a regulatory action that could cause consumers mistakenly to conclude that wine produced from grapes grown within the petitioned-for AVA has the same characteristics as wine produced from grapes grown in the existing AVA.[231]

227. *Id.* at 3498.

228. *Id.* at 3499.

229. *See, e.g.*, 27 C.F.R. §9.185 (Texoma AVA), established by T.D. TTB-38, 70 Fed. Reg. 72716 (Dec. 7, 2005).

230. TTB Final Rule (T.D. TTB-90) at 3499.

231. *Id.* at 3496.

This prompts the question of how TTB might react to a future petition for a high-elevation, mountain-named AVA that is entirely within a low-lying, valley-named AVA. Many such AVAs already exist, such as Sonoma Mountain in Sonoma Valley and Diamond Mountain District or Howell Mountain in Napa Valley. Fortunately, TTB stated in the Final Rule that carving out a nested AVA from the larger AVA of which it is part is likely to occur only in "very rare instances in which no notable common geographical features between the two AVAs can be found."[232]

In the Final Rule, TTB modified the evidentiary requirements for an AVA petition, although in practice these requirements have been in effect for several years.[233] The requirements vary with the three different types of AVA petitions: those seeking to establish new AVAs that do not overlap or lie wholly within an existing AVA, those seeking to establish AVAs that are partially or wholly within another AVA, and those that modify the boundaries or name of existing AVAs. For a new, free-standing AVA, the petition must still provide evidence of the name, boundary, and viticultural distinctiveness of the area, but the regulations now provide more detail on the types of information that are required or disallowed. The petition must contain sufficient information, data, and evidence so that TTB does not need to conduct any independent verification or research. With respect to the proposed AVA name, "[t]he name … must be currently and directly associated with an area in which viticulture exists. All of the area within the proposed AVA boundary must be nationally or locally known by the name specified in the petition, although the use of that name may extend beyond the proposed AVA boundary."[234] The petition must completely explain the manner in which the name is used for the proposed area. That evidence must come from sources independent of the petitioner. Statements from local residents may be included, although they are not sufficient in and of themselves.

With respect to the proposed boundary, the new regulation, 27 C.F.R. §9.12. states, "The petition must explain in detail the basis for defining the boundary.… In support of the proposed boundary, the petition must outline the commonalities or similarities within that boundary and must explain with specificity how those elements are different in the adjacent areas outside that boundary."[235]

Finally, the petition for a new AVA must explain the viticultural distinctiveness of the area compared to the adjacent areas. Distinguishing features affecting viticulture are defined to include (1) climate, including temperature, precipitation, wind, fog, solar orientation and radiation, and other information; (2) geology, including the underlying geologic formations, landforms, and geophysical events such as earthquakes, eruptions, and major floods; (3) soils, including the soils series denoting parent material, texture, slope, permeability, soil

---

232. *Id.*

233. The TTB itself stated that the new requirements do not impose new standards but "represent a codification of longstanding administrative authority and practice and address a need for greater transparency." TTB Final Rule (T.D.-90) at 3499.

234. *Id.* at 3500-01.

235. *Id.* at 3501.

reaction, drainage, and fertility; (4) physical features such as flat, hilly, or mountainous topography, geographical formations, bodies of water, watersheds, irrigations resources, and other features; and (5) elevation. As always, the petition must include the boundaries on U.S.G.S. maps; the boundaries also must be described in narrative.

For petitions proposing to establish an AVA entirely within or partially overlapping an existing AVA, the same evidence is required as for a new AVA, as described above, but it must be supplemented by evidence identifying the attributes of the proposed AVA that are "consistent with" and "sufficiently distinct from" the existing AVA so as to justify separate recognition of the proposed AVA.[236] As noted previously, when a smaller AVA has name recognition and features that clearly distinguish it from a larger AVA of which it is part, TTB may determine in the course of the rulemaking that the new AVA is not a part of the larger AVA.

The third type of AVA petition seeks to modify an existing AVA boundary or name. With respect to the former, the petitioner must include all of the evidence required for a new AVA along with the following additional information: (1) name evidence showing that the name applies to the new area, whether expanded or reduced in size; (2) distinguishing features affecting viticulture that are essentially the same as those of the existing AVA and different from those outside the proposed boundary; and (3) boundary evidence and description, including an explanation of how the boundary of the existing AVA was incorrectly or incompletely defined or is no longer accurate due to new evidence or changed circumstances. For petitions that seek to change the name of an existing AVA, the petition must establish the suitability of the new name by providing the name evidence required for a new AVA petition.

Finally, TTB has spelled out in more detail its AVA procedures. After a petition is filed, TTB will notify the petitioner of receipt within 30 days. TTB then will review the petition to determine whether or not it is a "perfected petition," defined as "a petition containing all of the evidence meeting the requirements of §9.12 and containing sufficient supporting information for TTB to decide whether or not to proceed with rulemaking to establish a new AVA or to change an existing AVA."[237] TTB will return petitions that are not perfected without prejudice to the later filing of a revised petition. If a petition is perfected, TTB will decide whether to proceed with rulemaking and advise the petitioner of its decision in writing. TTB will place a notice on its website when a perfected petition has been accepted for rulemaking.

If TTB determines that rulemaking is appropriate, it will prepare and publish a NPRM to solicit public comment. After receiving comments, TTB can prepare a Final Rule, adopting the proposed AVA with or without changes, withdraw the proposal, prepare a new Notice of Proposed Rulemaking, or take any other action it deems appropriate as authorized by law. TTB must cite the reasons for withdrawing an AVA petition, which must include at least one of the following:

236. *Id.*
237. *Id.* at 3500.

(1) insufficient viticulture within the proposed AVA, with no objective standard to determine that in terms of the number of planted vineyard acres or the percentage of the AVA land mass planted to vines (TTB, however, did provide one example in the Final Rule: five acres of grapes in a 10,000-square-mile AVA will not suffice to designate a new AVA[238]); (2) insufficient evidence of name, boundary, or distinguishing features; or (3) inconsistency with one of the purposes of the Federal Alcohol Administration Act or other federal statute, or a decision that the proposal is contrary to the public interest, which is a nebulous grab bag of potential grounds for withdrawal.

Although it is impossible to know how these changes will affect future AVA petitions, three things seem fairly certain. First, petitions for nested or overlapping AVAs will be scrutinized more closely and will have to meet a higher burden of proof than in the past. That being said, the movement to establish nested AVAs will not be stymied by the increased governmental scrutiny. Second, TTB will look to the concerned parties in most instances to resolve disputes between brands and appellation names. Clearly, the bureau does not want to become embroiled in another multi-year Calistoga-style dispute. Third, AVA petitions will become increasingly detailed and sophisticated. This is a welcome development.

b. Privatization

Separate and apart from these regulatory reforms, grower-vintner groups in numerous appellations are taking private steps to promote the particular characteristics and qualities of their wines to the wine trade and consumers. Several examples follow.

In the viticultural area of Augusta in the state of Missouri, the local town council has awarded a special town seal, the Owl Seal, for those wines that abide by the city's viticultural and enological controls and have passed the required organoleptic evaluation. The Montelle label shown in Figure 6-15 includes the Owl Seal. The required taste test was largely designed to weed out defective wines. The program is now defunct.

For many years in the viticultural area of Carneros in southern Napa and Sonoma counties, the local vintners produced a cooperative, master blend of Pinot Noir and Chardonnay, marketed by the local trade association previously known as Carneros Quality Alliance (CQA), and today as Carneros Wine Alliance, under the association's label (Figure 6-16). The purpose of the joint undertaking was to showcase the unique characteristics and quality of the appellation's two most distinctive varietals.

The Napa Valley Vintners (NVV), a trade association with over 400 vintner members located in that appellation, registered a certification mark in the form of a logo that can be used only on wines that are entirely produced and bottled in the Napa Valley AVA and made from 100 percent Napa Valley grapes, not 85 percent

238. *Id.* at 3494.

as federal law requires.[239] The mark is shown in Figure 6-17. The use of the certification mark is voluntary. Any winery whose wines meet the certification criteria can use the mark on those wines, whether or not that person or entity is a member of NVV.

Figure 6-15
Montelle Label

Figure 6-16
Carneros Label

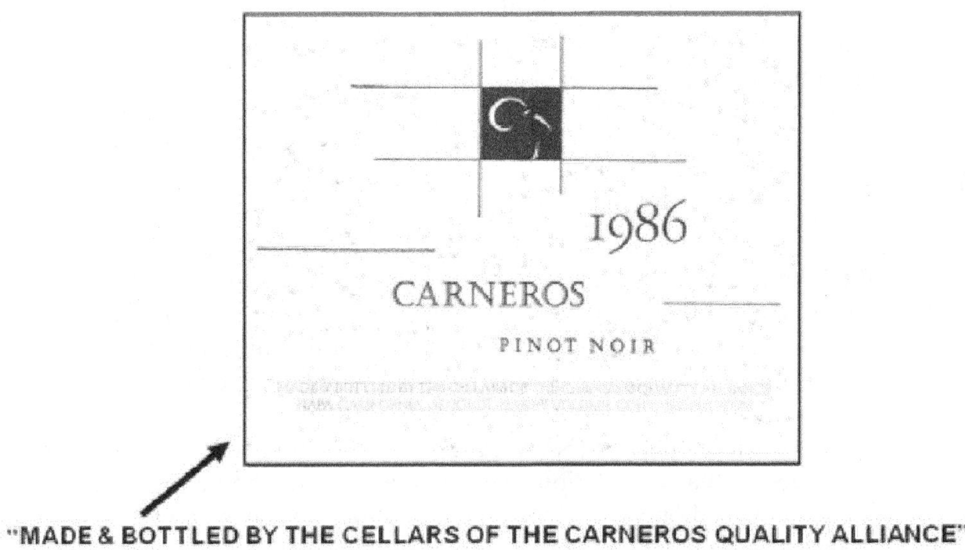

239. Registration No. 3232326.

Figure 6-17
100% Napa Valley Mark

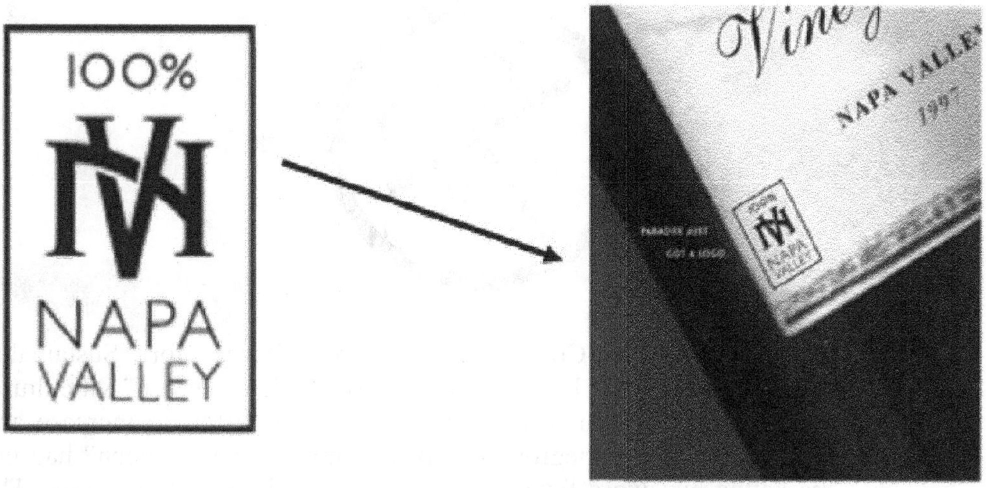

In Mendocino County, the group Coro Mendocino created a protocol for the production of wine distinctive to that appellation. Coro Mendocino's mission is to "increase the awareness and value of Mendocino wine and winegrape products through the production of Coro Mendocino, a controlled, ultra premium blended wine that reflects the quality and commitment of the Mendocino County wine industry."[240] Coro Mendocino requires wine to be produced according to specific winemaking parameters and to be submitted to a blind tasting panel.[241] If the wine passes, it is then packaged in uniform bottles with labels bearing the individual brand in conjunction with the Coro Mendocino trademark and trade dress. The Coro Mendocino protocol requires Zinfandel to be the dominant varietal in the wine, comprising a minimum percentage of 40 percent and a maximum of 70 percent. There are nine allowed second-tier varietals, but any one of the second-tier varietals cannot exceed the quantity of Zinfandel. An additional 10 percent of the wine can be made from any varietal. Coro Mendocino also designates basic chemistry and sensory limits and prescribes the details of both cooperage and aging. The group does not place any restrictions on viticultural practices. The Coro Mendocino mark is shown in Figures 6-18.

---

240. Consortium Mendocino By-Laws as amended August 2005, http://www.coromendocino.com/img/CoroBylaws.pdf.

241. *See* http://www.coromendocino.com/ProductionProtocol.htm (accessed December 8, 2010).

Figure 6-18
Coro "Mark"

The Lodi Winegrape Commission's "Lodi Rules for Sustainable Winegrowing" have become a benchmark for sustainable or "green" viticultural practices.[242] The project began in the early 1990s in an effort to increase and encourage sustainability in winegrowing. At the time, the term "green" had not become a marketing buzzword for pro-environment products and processes. The program, which was developed with extensive input from growers, vintners, scientists, academics, and environmentalists, has culminated in the publication of the nearly 300-page *Lodi Winegrower's Workbook.*[243] The *Workbook* serves as a guide for vintners and growers to make measurable improvements in the health of their property's ecosystem and society at large and to improve wine quality and purity.

The Lodi Rules program has two components: sustainable winegrowing standards and pesticide assessment that measures the impact of all pesticides, both organic and synthetic, used in a vineyard. In order to qualify for certification and earn the right to place the "Lodi Rules" certification mark on wine labels, the winery or vineyard must achieve a minimum number of sustainable farming points, as defined in the *Workbook*, and must not exceed a maximum number of pesticide impact points. The Lodi Rules mark and sample labels are shown in Figures 6-19, 6-20, and 6-21.

---

242. *See* Lodi Winegrape Commission, *Lodi Rules for Sustainable Winegrowing*, https://www.lodigrowers.com/wp-content/uploads/2013/04/Lodi-Rules-Binder-intro-and-standards-3rd-Ed.-2017-website.pdf (2017).

243. Chris Storm, Clifford Ohmart & Steve Matthiasson, Lodi Winegrowers' Workbook, 2d ed. (San Francisco: Wine Appreciation Guild 2010).

Figure 6-19
Lodi Rules Mark

Figure 6-20
Lobo Loco Label

Figure 6-21
Mohr-Fry Ranches Back Label

Lodi Rules has led numerous growers to adopt more sustainable and eco-friendly farming practices, but the Lodi Rules program is also a marketing effort to re-brand the Lodi AVA as a winegrowing region that values sustainable farming. The Lodi Rules program is not touted as creating qualitative sensory differences in wine produced under the standards. The Lodi Rules also do not define the characteristics of wine produced from Lodi grapes. Instead, the Lodi Rules promote Lodi as a region distinctive for its farming and values.

D. CONCLUSION

The United States is a brand-driven market economy that does not have the same tradition as, say, Europe with respect to products of place. Wine is the exception, but even then wine appellations are less important to most consumers than wine brands. The United States embarked more than 30 years ago on the path of defining its wine appellations. That evolution has had noticeable successes and failures.

Interestingly, some of the most prestigious wine appellations, such as Napa Valley, today have to protect their good names from impostors at home and abroad who seek to profit from consumer confusion.[244] For example, the NVV has fought against the following Napa-named brands around the world: Ca' de Napa (Italy), Varon de Napa (Spain), Napa Crest (United Kingdom), Napatina (Argentina), Napa (Taiwan and Vietnam), and Valley Napa (China). None of the wines sold under these brand names is made from Napa Valley grapes.

In its present form, TRIPS does not provide any form of automatic international protection for geographical indications. The holder of these intellectual property rights must establish the existence of, and protect, the geographical indication in each country based on the particular uses of that name there (as a brand, generic name, wine appellation, or otherwise), all in keeping with the laws of that particular country, in accordance with the principle of territoriality. This rule respects all intellectual property rights, including brands (trademarks) and appellations (geographical indications). But it also means that the tensions between brands and appellations are not likely to be resolved in the near term. Each name and each situation will present unique facts, and each country will have its own legal regime to resolve conflicts. As domestic wine production and wine exports continue to expand in the United States, the role of intellectual property lawyers is secure.

244. Author Richard Mendelson should and could have predicted this evolution based on the following personal observation: "When I first worked in the wine industry in Burgundy, France, in the late 1970s, before Napa Valley began its meteoric rise, I visited the Comité Interprofessionel du Vin de Champagne and met with the chief counsel of that organization. As I walked into his office, I saw a slew of Champagne-designated non-Champagne products, including Spanish Champagne, Champagne toothpaste, Champagne cigars, and Champagne cookies. When I asked the chief counsel to explain what he did, those imposter Champagne-named products figured prominently in his response."

CHAPTER 7

LAND USE: RURAL WINERIES AND URBAN BARS

Richard Mendelson[1] and Erin Kelleher[2]

Wine is directly tied to the soil and grape growing, so it should come as little surprise that land use law is important to the wine industry. However, the myriad ways in which land use controls affect the wine industry may not be obvious to even an industry veteran. Let us recite some simple examples. Wine appellations would not mean much if the zoning of an area prohibited agricultural uses, namely the growing of grapes. If wineries could be located only in industrial zones or if winery tasting rooms could be established only in commercial areas, much of the mystique of wine country would be lost.

Land uses are regulated by states and their political subdivisions—cities, counties, wards, parishes, and the like—in the exercise of their police powers. This

1. Richard Mendelson authored the section on rural wineries, with contributions from Terri Cofer Beirne (Virginia) and Elaine Albrich (Oregon). Ms. Beirne is Eastern Counsel of San Francisco-based Wine Institute, representing the California wineries on various legal and policy issues. Before that, she practiced administrative law in Virginia, representing wineries, among other clients. Ms. Albrich is a partner in the law firm of Davis Wright Tremaine in Portland. She is a land use lawyer whose alcohol beverage practice focuses on manufacturers, retailers, and event venues.

2. Erin Kelleher revised the section on urban retailers that was originally written by Lynne Carmichael, a name partner, now retired, in Ms. Kelleher's law firm, Hinman & Carmichael. Contributing to the chapter are Susan Johnson and Claire Mitchell (Washington), Kimberly Frost (Texas), and Leonard Fogelman (New York). Ms. Johnson is a partner at the law firm of Stoel Rives LLP in Seattle. She practices solely in the area of alcoholic beverage law. Ms. Mitchell is also an attorney at the law firm of Stoel Rives LLP in Seattle where her practice focuses on regulatory compliance and licensing for the alcoholic beverage industry. She leads her firm's Beverage Subgroup, a subsection of Stoel Rives' broader Agribusiness, Food, Beverage, and Timber Industry Group. Ms. Frost is a shareholder at the law firm of Martin Frost & Hill, where she practices administrative law, specializing in the representation of members of the alcoholic beverage industry, with a particular expertise in Texas Alcoholic Beverage Commission and TTB matters and transactions. Mr. Fogelman, of Fogelman & Fogelman, LLC, practices alcoholic beverage law in New York and Massachusetts.

typically takes the form of specific land use laws. But land use controls also may be embodied in other laws, including specific alcoholic beverage control laws. This assortment of laws and regulations determines where bars and liquor stores are located, their hours of opening and other aspects of their operations, and what constitutes a "disorderly house" and what can be done about it.

This chapter focuses on the particular land use issues involved with wineries situated in agricultural settings, and bars and bottle shops located in urban areas. Although rural wineries and urban liquor retailers are commonplace, the ways in which states and cities control their establishment and operations vary considerably.

A. RURAL WINERIES

The quintessential image of a winery is an agricultural estate in the middle of farm country, with a vineyard, winery, and estate home. Although there are numerous exceptions to this rule in the form of urban and suburban wineries, the tie to the land remains a distinguishing feature of wine and the wine industry, setting it apart from beer and spirits. This special place-goods association is captured in the concepts of *terroir*, defined as the natural features of the vineyard, and *goût de terroir*, the effects of *terroir* on the characteristics of the grapes and the resulting wine. These concepts underscore the fact that grape growing is an agricultural use.[3] To survive and prosper in a rural setting, wineries typically do more than grow grapes.[4] They also make wine (an industrial operation) and engage in a variety of marketing and sales activities (commercial operations), all of which are critical to their success.

After Repeal, the wine industry had to completely retool, in the vineyards as well as the wineries, in terms of both physical and human capital. State and local governments in the wine-producing regions of the United States were hopeful that wine would become an engine of economic development, leading to higher land values, spurring agri-tourism, and generally helping states to revive their lagging post-Depression economies. It was not until the 1960s that this dream began to be realized.

By the 1970s, as the Wine Revolution took hold across the United States, many states established "farm wineries," emphasizing the local agricultural roots of grape growers and wine producers. Farm wineries were allowed to sell to consumers at the winery premises wines made from local grapes, however "local" might be defined under the applicable local or state law. For example, New York's 1976 Farm Winery Law authorized farmers to make wine from the grapes grown on their own properties and to sell those wines directly to the public from tasting

---

3. *See, e.g.*, Sarah Bradshaw, Winery, Town Battle over Meaning of "Agricultural," Poughkeepsie J., Feb. 27, 2010, at BPJ.1.

4. As noted in Chapter 4, some wineries do not grow their own grapes but purchase grapes or bulk wine from independent grape growers or wineries, respectively, as the raw material for their own branded wines.

rooms at the winery. As Jim Trezise, president of the New York Wine and Grape Foundation, explains: "The concept [of a farm winery] was derived from the commonly understood view that winemaking was a natural extension of the grape growing process, and that the production of grapes into wine was a value-added process that a grower could utilize for his crop."[5] In 1978, the New York law was amended to allow farm wineries to sell at their premises wines made from grapes grown anywhere in New York State.

While this rooting in agriculture is a distinguishing feature of wineries, rural wineries present complicated land use issues because they are mixed uses, often combining farming, winemaking, marketing, and retail sales at a single location on agricultural land. The following sections review the basic precepts of land use law and address the various approaches adopted by several states and localities to regulate rural wineries.

1. LAND USE BASICS

The Tenth Amendment to the U.S. Constitution reserves to the states all powers not delegated to the federal government.[6] This "police power" affords states the authority to regulate land uses within their jurisdictions to promote the health, safety, and welfare of their residents.[7]

Many states delegate the police power to local governments by state constitution, state law, or charter.[8] Early jurisprudence in the United States held that, absent an express or implied delegation, the states alone retain the police power. This is known as Dillon's rule, after the judge who formulated the doctrine in 1865.[9]

---

5. Letter from Jim Trezise, president, New York Wine and Grape Foundation,, to Town of New Paltz Zoning Board of Appeals (Oct. 15, 2007), available at http://www.rivendellwine.com/Lawsuit%20Files/Support%20Letters/nywgf10.15.07.pdf.

6. The Tenth Amendment reads, "The powers not delegated to the United States by the Constitution, nor prohibited by it to the States, are reserved to the States respectively, or to the people." U.S. Const. amend. X.

7. A land use regulation lies within the police power if it is reasonably related to the public welfare. *Associated Home Builders Inc. v. City of Livermore*, 557 P.2d 473, 485 (Cal. 1976) (quoting *Miller v. Bd. of Pub. Works*, 234 P. 381, 385 (Cal. 1925)). Justice Douglas in *Berman v. Parker*, 348 U.S. 26, 33 (1954), elaborated on the concept of public welfare, stating that it "is broad and inclusive. The values it represents are spiritual as well as physical, aesthetic as well as monetary" (citation omitted). In a later case, *Village of Belle Terre v. Boraas*, 416 U.S. 1, 9, (1974), Justice Douglas added: "The police power is not confined to elimination of filth, stench, and unhealthy places. It is ample to lay out zones where family values, youth values, and the blessings of quiet seclusion and clean air make the area a sanctuary for people."

8. Municipalities are creatures of the state, and the states grant them their legal existence, typically in the form of a charter. The charter grants certain powers to the municipality, places limits on its powers, and sets forth its boundaries.

9. "It is a familiar and elementary principle that municipal corporations have and can exercise such powers, and *such* only, as are expressly granted, and such incidental ones as are necessary to make those powers available and essential to effectuate the purposes of the corporation; and these powers are strictly construed." *Clark v. City of Des Moines*, 19 Iowa 199, *7 (1865) (opinion by J. John Dillon).

Subsequently, many states established what is known as "home rule" whereby a city or county government is allowed to exercise any function reserved to the state, including land use planning, so long as it is not prohibited under the state constitution or by state statute. Home rule may be established legislatively or constitutionally.

By far the majority of states today adhere to home rule. One wine-producing state, Virginia, strictly follows Dillon's rule. California, by contrast, expressly allows its cities to regulate land uses to benefit the public health and welfare. The California constitution specifically provides, "A county or city may make and enforce within its limits all local, police, sanitary, and other ordinances and regulations not in conflict with general laws."[10]

Zoning is the primary, though not the only, means by which governments control land uses. Most jurisdictions establish zoning districts to regulate the location, type and intensity of land use and land development.[11] In any given county, one may find residential (single-family or multi-family), commercial, industrial, and agricultural zoning districts. Zoning ordinances allow some uses in each district and prohibit others; the regulations often vary significantly from one district to the next. For example, bars serving alcohol may be excluded from certain zoning districts inside a city. Or a county might establish an agricultural zoning district to preserve and protect valuable farmland, prohibiting non-agricultural uses there. Mixed-use zones allow a variety of activities to occur in the same zoning district.

Most jurisdictions also allow certain uses by conditional use permit or by special exception. The conditional use permit (CUP) allows a local government to make an individualized determination about the suitability of a proposed use in a particular location. The local government, generally in the form of an appointed planning commission or elected council or board of supervisors, decides on a case-by-case basis whether a particular use is detrimental to the public health, safety, or general welfare and whether it is compatible with existing, neighboring uses. The government can impose particular conditions to mitigate any potential adverse impacts. With respect to grape growing and winemaking, agricultural zones typically allow vineyards as a matter of right, and wineries often require a CUP, perhaps because they themselves are mixed uses.

---

10. Cal. Const. art. XI, §7. The court in *Candid Enterprises, Inc. v. Grossmont Union High School District*, 39 Cal. 3d 878, 885 (1985), elaborated on just how broad this delegated authority is.

> Under the police power granted by the Constitution, counties and cities have plenary authority to govern, subject only to the limitation that they exercise this power within their territorial limits and subordinate to state law. Apart from this limitation, the "police power [of a county or a city] under this provision ... is as broad as the police power exercisable by the Legislature itself" (alterations in original) (citations omitted).

11. The U.S. Supreme Court validated zoning in *Village of Euclid v. Amber Realty Co.*, 272 U.S. 365 (1926). Amber Realty claimed that the restricted uses under the zoning ordinance of Euclid, Ohio, substantially reduced the value of its property. Its suit was denied and the zoning ordinance was upheld based on the court's finding of a valid governmental interest in maintaining the community's character in the face of burgeoning industrial growth in Cleveland, which threatened to subsume Euclid.

Another form of special exception to zoning regulations is a variance.[12] By granting a variance, the decision maker(s) can waive or modify quantitative standards such as setbacks to avoid hardships.

There are constitutional limits to a state's or municipality's land use authority. These include the takings provision of the Fifth Amendment to the U.S. Constitution, the Due Process and Equal Protection Clauses of the Fourteenth Amendment, and the First Amendment guarantee of free speech and freedom of religion. Each area has spawned significant jurisprudence seeking to balance private property rights and other basic rights of individual landowners against the public good as expressed by the state or local government.

2. CALIFORNIA

California, as a home rule state, delegates a large portion, but not all, of its police powers to local agencies to protect the public health, safety, and welfare. Municipalities oversee the uses of land within their boundaries—the cities within city limits and the counties in the remaining, "unincorporated" lands.

Local government avails itself of a wide variety of land use planning and development controls. For example, elected municipal council members and elected members of county boards of supervisors adopt a general plan (the equivalent of a local constitution), pass zoning ordinances, issue CUPs, and create parcels (legal lots of record), typically by subdividing existing parcels. As we shall see, each locality can chart its own course in this regard; some might decide to facilitate growth, whereas others might stifle it.

In California, voters wield power in the land use arena in several ways. First, they elect government officials who, in turn, vote to approve or reject particular development projects, public infrastructure projects, and land use ordinances. Second, they can comment directly on particular development proposals. Finally, they can submit initiatives or referenda affecting particular development projects or policies in the form of a petition signed by a required number of voters.[13] If passed in a local election, these initiatives and referenda bind local elected bodies.

Normally, changes to land use regulations and specific development projects are proposed by the local agency (often, the local planning department) and/or by private parties. These changes and proposals are reviewed by the professional staffs of the various local agencies. The planners, engineers, and environmental experts ensure that the proposal meets the jurisdiction's general plan and zoning requirements as well as applicable state laws and local ordinances. If public notice and a public hearing are required, the planning department staff prepare and

12. A variance is a permit issued to a landowner to build a structure or engage in a use not otherwise permitted under the current zoning regulations. Typically, the landowner must prove that he or she would suffer unique hardship under the zoning regulations because the parcel in question is different from others to which the regulations apply because of its size, shape, topography, location, or other special circumstances. *See, e.g.*, Cal. Gov't Code §65906 (2021).

13. Cal. Const. art. II, §§8-9.

present a report on the proposed project to the elected officials and the public prior to holding the hearing on the project.

In the case of an initiative or referendum that qualifies for the ballot, staff review is limited to the potential consequences of the ballot measure, if passed.[14] This report, prepared at the discretion of the local board of supervisors, is presented to the elected body and to the public to help voters understand the issue at election time.

California law mandates that any governmental action that is discretionary be taken in full public view. Thus, general plan adoption and amendment, zoning ordinance changes, use permit issuance, and parcel creation, among other actions, can occur only after public notice through a published agenda, a public hearing, and deliberation by the elected officials in open session. The issuance of a building permit, by contrast, is generally a ministerial action rather than a discretionary one. If the jurisdiction's building code requirements are met, the building permit will issue without need of a public hearing.

The distinction between ministerial and discretionary actions also is important in determining the extent of environmental review appropriate for any proposed project. The California Environmental Quality Act (CEQA)[15] requires that every discretionary project be analyzed in terms of its direct, indirect, and cumulative environmental effects. The project cannot be approved until all significant adverse effects that are likely to result from the project are reduced to less than significant levels. The mitigation measures that serve to eliminate or reduce the project's significant adverse impacts are included as conditions for the project's approval. Alternatively, the governing body may lawfully approve the project notwithstanding the identification of unmitigatable impacts by adopting "findings of overriding consideration"; through such findings, the agency determines that the economic, legal, social, technological, or other benefits outweigh the significant environmental impacts.

a. Napa County, California

Napa County, one of California's original counties (established in 1850), has a land area of 754 square miles (1,953 square kilometers) and a population of approximately 140,000. Within the county are five municipalities: Napa, Yountville, St. Helena, Calistoga, and American Canyon. The county is governed by a five-member board of supervisors and the municipalities by their respective city or town councils. Land use planning and development controls were not established in the county until the mid-1900s. The first building permits were issued by the county in 1955, and the first general plan was adopted in 1969. That first general plan, and every general plan since then, has recognized agriculture as the highest and best use of land in Napa County.

---

14. Cal. Elec. Code §9111 (2021).
15. Cal. Pub. Res. Code §§21000-21177 (2021).

As the San Francisco Bay Area expanded in the latter half of the twentieth century, the recognition of Napa's unique value as a grape-growing and wine-producing area took on added importance. Other parts of the region, such as Santa Clara County, long known as a fertile agricultural area, were gradually overtaken by urban sprawl. As former Santa Clara County planner Karl Belser said of the decade of the 1960s, "Wild urban growth attacked the [Santa Clara] valley.... What so recently had been a beautiful, productive garden was suddenly transformed into an urban anthill."[16] Napans had the foresight and courage to take bold steps to avoid the same fate.

In 1968, after heated debate among vineyard and winery owners, the Napa County Board of Supervisors by unanimous vote approved an Agricultural Preserve (AP) zoning district[17] covering 25,950 acres (10,768 hectares) on the floor of the Napa Valley. The new zoning district established a minimum parcel size for a legal lot of 20 acres (8.3 hectares), which was a substantial increase over the 1 acre (0.4 hectare) minimum that applied before AP zoning was established. This "large-lot" zoning was the first in the United States. designed to protect a specific agricultural resource.[18]

AP zoning was highly controversial. Many property owners believed their property rights and their economic value were being taken by the government without compensation. Proponents, by contrast, argued that large-lot zoning was the only way to prevent Napa County from being overtaken by urban sprawl, as had occurred in Santa Clara Valley. Joseph Peatman, who served as Napa County Supervisor from 1969 to 1973 and supported the Agricultural Preserve, recalls: "The opponents didn't want anyone telling them what they could or couldn't do with their land. They wanted to be able to subdivide their land into several one acre parcels, each with the right to have a single family home. The proponents were not flaming liberals, but they didn't want to repeat the Santa Clara Valley story. They argued that development should occur in the cities and in the hills, not on the valley floor."[19]

---

16. Leonard Downie Jr., The Santa Clara Valley's "Appointment with Destiny," APF Newsletter (Alicia Patterson Foundation) (October 1971), available at https://aliciapatterson.org/stories/santa-clara-valley%E2%80%99s-%E2%80%9Cappointment-destiny%E2%80%9D. .

17. Napa County, Cal., Ordinance 274 §1 (Apr. 9, 1968) (amending Ordinance 186 of Jan. 25, 1955) (codified as amended at Napa County, Cal., Code §§18.16.010-.040"' (1993), available at http://library.municode.com/HTML/16513/book.html.

18. Tax incentives offered by the state of California through the California Land Conservation (Williamson) Act, 1965 Cal. Stat. 3377 (codified as amended at Cal. Gov't Code §§51200-51297.4 (2021)), also helped to keep land in agriculture. Under its provisions, counties may enter into 10-year continuously renewable contracts with landowners under which the landowners agree to retain their land in agricultural and compatible uses for 10 years and in return pay property taxes based on the value of the land as farmland rather than as land available for subdivision and urban development.

19. Telephone interview with Joseph Peatman, former supervisor, Napa County, Cal. (July 29, 2010).

Not surprisingly, AP zoning was challenged in court, but it was upheld.[20] In the 42 years since the Agricultural Preserve was established, the only changes have been to add vineyard land to the AP zone; in 1979, to raise the minimum parcel size within the zone to 40 acres (16.6 hectares); and more recently to permit new uses in the AP zone, including farm management and farmworker housing.

Since 1968 the county has adopted other important land use regulations designed to preserve Napa Valley's agricultural heritage and to avoid urban sprawl. The county subjected wineries to using permit control beginning in 1974, following a controversy over the construction of a modern barrel storage building that blocked the view of the historic 1879 Inglenook Winery. The requirement for a CUP allows the county to deny any given project if required findings cannot be made or to impose conditions of approval and mitigation measures.

To ensure that farming would continue unabated, the county adopted the Right to Farm Act in 1990 whereby each person buying property or building in or near an agricultural zone would receive a notice about the possible negative impacts of agricultural activities (spraying, noise, odors, etc.). The Act prohibits a nuisance finding as long as the agricultural operation is conducted according to "proper and accepted customs and standards" and has existed at the same location for more than three years.[21]

In 1973 the minimum parcel size in the remaining unincorporated area outside of the Agricultural Preserve, largely in the hills and mountains surrounding the valley floor (known as the Agricultural Watershed (AW) zoning district), was raised from 1 acre (0.4 hectare) to 40 acres (16.6 hectares) in order to protect the county's watersheds. Over two decades later, in 1994, the minimum parcel size of the then 450,000 acres (186,722 hectares) of Agricultural Watershed zoned lands was raised from 40 acres to 160 acres (66.4 hectares).[22]

In 1983 Napa County adopted urban growth boundaries for the City of Napa, which limit the development of urban infrastructure outside established municipal boundaries.[23] This serves to limit the development potential in those areas. In a related move in 1990, the voters of the county adopted, by initiative, restrictions on the conversion of agricultural land for urban uses, requiring until the year 2020 a county-wide vote on any proposal to redesignate agricultural lands to non-agricultural purposes or to change the building intensity of such lands.[24] That deadline has since been extended to 2058, at which time the original Agricultural Preserve zoning will have had a 90-year history.[25]

---

20. *Napa Valley United Farmers v. County Bd. of Supervisors* (Napa County Super. Ct. 1971); *see* judgment at Official Records of Napa County, Book 15, p. 574 (1971).

21. Napa County, Cal., Code §2.94.020 (1993).

22. Napa County, Cal., Ordinance 1058 §2 (Jan. 11, 1994) (increased minimum parcel size from 40 to 160 acres) (codified at Napa County, Cal., Code §18.104.010 (1993).

23. Napa County Dep't. Conservation, Dev. & Planning, Napa County General Plan 243-44 (Conservation and Open Space Element) (1983).

24. Agricultural Lands Preservation Initiative ("Measure J") (1990) (amending Napa County General Plan Land Use Element).

25. Agricultural Lands Preservation Initiative ("Measure P") (1990), Napa County, Cal., Ordinance 08-03 (Nov. 4, 2008).

Also in 1990 county government began to regulate more closely the establishment of new wineries and the expansion of existing wineries, restricting their commercial and industrial operations on agriculturally zoned lands and further protecting the valley from encroaching urbanization and the pressures of tourism.[26] The impetus for the restrictions was the existence of several wineries in Napa County that made wine from grapes grown outside the county and engaged in extensive marketing and sales activities with only limited winemaking facilities (essentially, a few outdoor tanks). In the county zoning ordinance, these kinds of winery activities were unregulated. Grapes could be sourced from anywhere, and the winery's accessory uses such as marketing, wine tastings, and sales were largely unregulated.

The county decided to impose new, more restrictive rules in the newly enacted Winery Definition Ordinance (WDO).[27] The WDO, which applies in the county's AP and AW zoning districts but not in the cities or in the other zoning districts of the county, first defines what a winery is and does as its primary activity, namely, fermenting grapes into wine.[28] But no longer would it be just any grapes; 75 percent of the wine produced at a new winery located in the county's agricultural zoning districts would now have to be derived from Napa County grapes.[29] Existing wineries were exempted from this grape source rule for the production levels authorized in their pre-WDO use permits.[30] However, for those wineries that later expand their footprint (known as the "winery development area") in order to

---

26. Winery Definition Ordinance, Napa County, Cal., Ordinance 947 (1990) (codified as amended in scattered sections of Napa County, Cal., Code tit. 18 (1993).

27. *Id.*

28. Napa County, Cal., Code §18.08.640 (1993).

29. *Id.* at §18.104.250(B).

30. Other California counties have adopted similar grape sourcing rules to tie the industrial operation (winemaking) to the local land (grapes). Santa Barbara County has a 50 percent local grape sourcing requirement for its wineries but defines local to include both Santa Barbara County and San Luis Obispo County. *See* Santa Barbara County, Cal., Code §35-42.280(D) (1985), available at http://search.municode.com/html/16322/book.html. Santa Barbara County is presently considering new Agricultural Preserve rules, including a new grape sourcing requirement that 51 percent of the winery's case production derive from grapes grown on the premises and/or from other contracted land *under the same ownership* in Santa Barbara County, provided that at least 20 percent of the case production comes from grapes grown on the parcel where the winery is situated. In Sonoma County certain land use categories refer to agricultural processing facilities as those facilities used for the processing of agricultural products "of a type grown or produced primarily on site or in the local area." *See, e.g.*, Sonoma County, Cal., Code §26-04-020(g) (1996), available at https://library.municode.com/ca/sonoma_county/codes/code_of_ordinances?nodeId=CH26SOCOZORE (permitted uses in Land Intensive Agriculture zoning district). Typically, this would mean that a winery must source grapes primarily from Sonoma County, although this is subject to interpretation on any given project. Finally, Riverside County followed Napa County's lead in adopting a 75 percent local grape source rule with certain exceptions. Riverside County, Cal., Code §17.136.040(D)(3)(a) (2000) (effective Jan. 24, 2011), available at https://library.municode.com/ca/riverside_county/codes/code_of_ordinances?nodeId=TIT17ZO_CH17.136CVCIVIZO.

increase production capacity beyond the originally approved annual gallonage, the increased production is subject to the 75 percent grape source rule.[31]

The WDO also spells out the specific "accessory uses" that are allowed at wineries; all other accessory uses are prohibited.[32] This supplanted the pre-existing rule, which allowed any accessory use, whether or not enumerated in the county code, that was "incidental or subordinate to the principal use."[33] The accessory uses allowed in the WDO include tours, wine tastings, the display but not the sale of art and items of ecological or viticultural significance, and child care centers to care for the children of winery employees.[34] Within each category of approved use, there may be additional restrictions. For example, the WDO for the first time prohibited drop-in public tours and tastings at any newly approved winery. Pre-existing wineries with approved public tasting privileges are unaffected, but they cannot increase the size of their pre-WDO tasting room. New wineries have to engage in by-appointment-only, private tours and tastings.[35] This visitation restriction is designed to control traffic congestion on local roads.[36] New wineries also have to be located on parcels of at least 10 acres,[37] must observe expanded setbacks from public roads and private roads used by the public,[38] and must meet strict accessory-to-production square footage ratios.[39]

As another example of Napa County's strict controls over winery operations, retail sales are now limited to wine fermented and bottled at the winery, wine produced by or for the winery from grapes grown in Napa County, and wine-related items.[40] Authorized marketing activities specifically exclude commercial food service (restaurants) and social events that are not directly related to consumer education and development.[41] Weddings, for example, are not allowed to be conducted at rural Napa Valley wineries; the only exceptions involve non-commercial weddings of the winery owners' immediate families. Even when winery marketing rights under the WDO were slightly expanded in 2010 as part of an economic stimulus package, these marketing restrictions remained, as did the 75 percent grape source rule.

---

31. Napa County, Cal., Code §18.104.250(C) (1993); *see also id.*§18.104.210. Although never challenged in court, the local grape source requirement might violate the dormant Commerce Clause, just as the local milk bottling requirement did in *Dean Milk Co. v. City of Madison, Wis.*, 340 U.S. 349 (1951).

32. Napa County, Cal., Code §§18.16.030(H) (AP zone), 18.20.030(J) (AW zone) (1993); *see also id.*§18.08.020 (defining "accessory use").

33. Napa County, Cal., Code §4.03 (1963).

34. Napa County, Cal., Code §§18.16.030(H) (AP zone), 18.20.030(J) (AW zone) (1993).

35. *Id.*§18.08.620 (defining "tours and tastings").

36 Use permit conditions typically limit the hours and visitor numbers for private tours and tastings. The hours are set so as to avoid the peak travel time on the nearby roadways.

37. Napa County, Cal., Code §18.104.240(B) (1993). Prior to this change, the minimum parcel size for a winery was 1 acre. *Id.* §18.104.240(A).

38. *Id.* §18.104.230; *but see* exceptions at *id.* §§18.104.235, 18.104.245.

39. *Id.* §18.104.200.

40. *Id.* §§18.16.030(G)(5)(c), (H)(4) (AP zone), 18.20.030(I)(5)(c), (J)(4) (AW zone).

41. *Id.* at §18.08.370 (defining "marketing of wine").

Wine tastings, wine sales, and even food service at wineries are also regulated by the California Alcoholic Beverage Control Act. Wineries are allowed under state law to conduct tastings of wine produced or bottled by, or produced and packaged for, the licensee.[42] They can sell wine and brandy to customers to be consumed off-site, and they also can sell beers, wines, and brandies, regardless of source, for consumption at a restaurant on the winery premises.[43]

Do these more liberal provisions of state law trump the restrictive, locally adopted WDO? While a preemption argument might be asserted, it would not prevail in California because of Business and Professions Code §23790, under which the state defers to a valid zoning ordinance of a county or city.[44]

In 1991 agriculturalists and environmentalists worked together to put in place regulations designed to minimize the environmental impacts of vineyard development. Concerned about the continuing development of hillside vineyards, these local regulations, known as the Conservation Regulations, supplement state and federal environmental laws and mandate the inclusion of erosion control measures, riparian and wildlife corridors, protections for streams and wetlands, and other environmental controls in vineyard development and farming operations.[45] The regulations apply to any new or redeveloped site with a slope of more than 5 percent. Because the regulations make the planting of a vineyard on other than flat land a discretionary action, CEQA also applies.

It is worth noting that not all California counties share Napa's concerns about protecting agricultural lands from urban sprawl. In some cases, the counties simply do not have the same development pressures caused by proximity to a large metropolitan area. For example, Mendocino County, located northwest of Napa County on the California coast, has an active wine production industry but does not impose the same level of restrictions on wineries or their operations. Wineries are classified as "packing and processing facilities" and are a permitted use in most of the county's agricultural and rural areas, without the requirement that a CUP be obtained.[46] As such, there is no public hearing or CEQA environmental review; all that is needed is a building permit for the winery structure. The only limitation on accessory uses is that the tasting room cannot exceed 25 percent of the total floor area of the production building. There is no requirement that the grapes be grown in Mendocino County, no restrictions on the type or number of wine tastings and marketing events, and no visitor limitations. This tendency to welcome and stimulate winery development with attendant commercial uses is a rural economic development strategy that is prevalent in many newer "wine countries" across the United States.

---

42. Cal. Bus. & Prof. Code §23356.1(a) (2021).

43. *Id.* §23358(a)(2), (4).

44. The deference to local law is explicit with respect to retail licenses but is also applied in practice by the California Department of Alcoholic Beverage Control to manufacturer licenses.

45. Napa County, Cal., Ordinance 991 (1991) (codified at Napa County, Cal., Code §§18.108.010-18.108.140 (1993)).

46. All development proposals in coastal areas require special review for compliance with the California Coastal Act of 1976, Cal. Pub. Res. Code §§30000-30900 (2021).

In southern California, where viticultural areas such as Temecula Valley are situated in close proximity to urban areas, counties have attempted to protect the wine industry from incompatible development. For example, in Riverside County, where Temecula is situated, regulations similar to those of Napa County establish minimum parcel sizes for wineries and require that 75 percent of the local winery's grapes be sourced from the winery property or elsewhere in the county. Unlike Napa County, however, Riverside County allows a winery to incorporate non-agricultural commercial facilities such as a delicatessen, restaurant, bed and breakfast inn, special-occasion facility for weddings and similar social events, and even a hotel. This allows Temecula Valley wineries to sell most of their wines directly to visitors from the large, surrounding metropolitan area.

A study commissioned in 2007 by the Temecula Valley Convention and Visitors Bureau concluded that the Temecula wine country can achieve its tourism potential only if it can master the tricky combination of supporting wine-related growth that maintains the rural character of the area and resisting residential and strip mall development.

3. VIRGINIA

Agriculture has been the backbone of Virginia's rural economy for four centuries, generating $70 billion in output and providing at least 334,300 jobs in 2015, the latest year for which data is available.[47] However, the total number of farms and acres under cultivation in the commonwealth has decreased from more than 47,000 farms covering 8.1 million acres in 2005 to 43,225 farms covering 7.8 million acres in 2015.[48] Despite shrinking acreage, the Virginia General Assembly continues to promote agricultural investment with numerous laws and policies that encourage the use of land for production of food, craft beverages, and other agricultural products.

Contrary to trends in agriculture elsewhere, the popularity of grape-growing and winemaking continues to expand with Virginia wineries growing in number, size, and reputation during the first two decades of this century. The number of employees at Virginia wineries has risen to more than 10,000 workers in 2019 earning nearly $400 million in wages.[49] When the General Assembly initially defined a farm winery in 1980, there were six wineries and merely 286 acres of vineyards in Virginia. In 2005 the Virginia Wine Board estimated there were 120 farm wineries and 2,000 acres of vineyards in Virginia. In 2019 there were 357 bonded wineries making wine from 3,809 acres of vineyards sprinkled across the

---

47. The Economic Impact of Virginia's Agriculture and Forest Industries, Terance J. Rephann, Ph.D., Weldon Cooper Center for Public Service, University of Virginia, May 2017.

48. USDA Economic Research Service, *2017 USDA Census of Agriculture* (Apr. 11, 2017), available at https://www.nass.usda.gov/Publications/AgCensus/2017/index.php.

49. Economic Forensics and Analytics, Inc., *The Economic Impact of the Wine and Wine Grape Industries on the Virginia Economic 2019 Summary Report* (Apr. 2022), available at https://vaw-public-prod.s3.amazonaws.com/1d80df21e685a927e1647af1583c76a5.pdf.

95 Virginia counties, with concentrations in Albemarle, Loudoun, Fauquier, Orange, and Nelson counties.[50]

Total economic activity surrounding grape growing, wine production, and consumer sales in Virginia totaled $1.73 billion in 2019, an increase of 26.5 percent over 2015. In 2009 Virginia wineries sold 399,745 cases of wine; a decade later, wineries sold 604,000 cases. New data demonstrates that 65 percent of those sales were direct to consumer, either via common carrier shipments or visits to a tasting room.[51] Of greatest impact on rural counties that are home to most of these wineries were the 2.6 million tourists driving rural routes to visit Virginia wineries in 2019. Those visitors made weekend trips to tasting rooms and also attended weddings and other private events that generated additional revenue, estimated at more than $37 million in 2019. It is these many visitors that often spark conflict between farm wineries, unhappy neighbors, and local officials.

Blurry lines between where state regulation of a Virginia winery stops and local regulation starts is at the core of many disputes between wineries and localities. There are few lawsuits memorializing these conflicts, but the Legislature has passed an abundance of laws supported by the wine industry to draw clearer lines. In the early 2000s, the General Assembly enacted statutory protections that enabled trail-blazing wineries to fend off complaints that winery tourism had grown too quickly to manage. Then, capitalizing on that success, in the decade between 2010 and 2020 wineries encouraged two policy changes that contributed to the dramatic increase in the production capacity and number of wineries. The first allowed farm wineries to become and utilize contract winemaking facilities; the second eliminated long-standing distinctions between farm and "commercial" wineries by allowing winery licensees on-site tasting privileges reserved for farm wineries with producing vineyards. These policy changes are highlighted in this article.

a. Source of Land Use Authority for Virginia Localities

While production of alcohol has always been strictly controlled by the Virginia Department of Alcoholic Beverage Control (ABC), localities have attempted to regulate public safety under land use authority to firm up the edges of local control over wineries. Local ordinances have been crafted by each county after the first winery locating there necessarily educated the board of supervisors, county attorney, and zoning officials on how wineries operate. And, to the frustration of local officials, wineries have also reminded localities how statewide ABC law can limit local land use authority. This complex blend of agricultural activity at a state-licensed production facility making direct-to-consumer sales in rural localities has made wineries a unique challenge for Virginia localities to govern.

---

50. *Id.*
51. *Id.*

Virginia localities are expressly granted power by the General Assembly to regulate territorial land use, with the option and right to divide jurisdictions into zoning districts with differing uses, including agriculture. Farming and agriculture are permitted by right in agricultural districts and occasionally within more intense land use categories, depending on the county. Counties may create, name, and classify zoning districts in unique ways. Within each district, a locality may regulate the use of land as well as the size, height, location, removal, and maintenance of structures; the area and dimensions of land, water, and air space occupied by various structures and uses; open space; and the size of lots based upon the availability of public utilities.[52] Farm wineries benefit immensely from zoning restrictions on agricultural lands that encourage grape growing as an agricultural enterprise, while protecting the rural character and scenic views that draw visitors. At the same time, wineries and local officials disagree over local attempts to regulate public safety by restricting the number of visitors, limiting tasting room hours, and otherwise controlling on-site sales and marketing activities.

Dillon's rule of construction, discussed previously, is rigorously applied in evaluating the effect of Virginia local governmental action upon farm wineries. Under that rule in Virginia, a locality may exercise those powers expressly granted to it by statute or charter, but no other powers unless necessarily implied in or incident to the powers expressly granted or essential to the declared purposes. Once the grant of authority is affirmed in statute, the question becomes whether a local ordinance is consistent with it. An ordinance is deemed to be inconsistent with state law when state law preempts it, either expressly by prohibiting local regulation or by enacting state regulations so comprehensive that the state may be considered to occupy the entire field.[53] The domain of state alcoholic beverage control law has repeatedly been found to preempt local ordinance. In *Board of Supervisors v. Pumphrey*,[54] a county ordinance dealing with beer container returns was held to be invalid because state statutes regulating alcoholic beverages preempt the field. Narrowing that opinion regarding preemption of local decisions by the ABC Board, the Virginia Supreme Court in *City of Norfolk v. Tiny House, Inc.*,[55] and later in County of *Chesterfield v. Windy Hill, Ltd.*,[56] opined that local zoning ordinances may regulate the location of businesses selling alcoholic beverages, but the legislature did not intend for localities to be able to preempt other aspects of ABC licensing.

Beyond case law, over the last 40 years the Virginia General Assembly has passed several statutes that increasingly limit local control over the agricultural exercise of grape growing and over wine making conducted under a state-issued ABC license. While these statewide laws are recognized by local governments during the zoning approval and building permit processes, they often preclude

---

52. Va. Code §3.2-6400 (2022).

53. King v. County of Arlington, 81 S.E.2d 587, 590 (Va. 1954).

54. 269 S.E.2d 361 (Va. 1980).

55. 281 S.E.2d 836 (Va. 1981).

56. 559 S.E.2d 627 (Va. 2002).

local involvement in most aspects of a winery's operation. Other statutes discussed within highlight buffers against local regulation of wineries and include the Virginia Right to Farm Law, exemptions from Uniform Statewide Building Code requirements, and limits on liability under the Virginia Agritourism Liability Act. Sprinkled throughout the Code of Virginia, these laws guide most interactions between Virginia farm wineries and their rural homes.

b. Growing and Harvesting Under the Right to Farm Statute

Virginia wineries benefit from a long history of protections granted to traditional commodity agriculture that were in place well before grape growing became a popular use of rural land. One law in particular has tamped down claims that agricultural uses create a public or private nuisance. Growing pressure from conflicting rural land uses prompted the General Assembly to protect agricultural operations from lawsuits by adjacent residential and commercial development through passage of the Virginia Right to Farm Act.[57] Effective in 1995, Virginia expressly recognized that potentially conflicting land uses, such as housing, were bleeding into areas with existing agricultural operations, often triggering lawsuits by those arriving later in time. Three short and direct Virginia Code sections form a backstop against nuisance claims and prohibit localities from adopting ordinances requiring a special exception or special use permit for agriculture activity in a district zoned as agricultural. Under the Act, localities shall not enact zoning ordinances that "unreasonably restrict or regulate farm structures or farming" in an agricultural district unless such restrictions bear a relationship to the health, safety, and general welfare of its citizenry. Va. Code section 3.2-302 states that "no agricultural operation or any of its appurtenances shall be or become a nuisance, private or public, if such operations are conducted in substantial compliance with any applicable best management practices . . ..." What constitutes best management practices in grape growing and harvesting is untested under this law to date. Further, the Right to Farm Act limits private nuisance claims to only those persons with an ownership interest in property affected by the alleged nuisance. It also permits localities to adopt setback, minimum area, and similar requirements for farmland in agricultural districts. The Right to Farm Act maintains a protective barrier around bona fide agricultural production against those moving into rural landscapes.

Notably, the Act only protects farmers engaged in actual production or harvesting of agricultural or silvicultural products, not the processing of those products. As applied to Virginia wineries, for example, the Right to Farm Act would protect against nuisance claims based on planting, spraying, tending, and harvesting of grapes. It would also spare a winery from ordinances placing unreasonable limits on noise or lighting from harvesting, temporary labor activity, or farm vehicle traffic, among other things. However, the Act stops short of

---

57. Virginia Right to Farm Act, 1994 Va. Acts 779 (codified as amended at Va. Code §§3.2-300 to -3.2-303 (2022)).

defending farm wineries against nuisance claims based on important tasks of making, bottling, and selling wine. To find the boundaries of the Right to Farm Act, ask a winery proprietor with unhappy neighbors how much energy she has spent defending allegations of trespass from dust kicked up from a gravel road to a tasting room, from a noise ordinance violation for a summer evening concert, or from allegations of an unsafe turning lane off a rural highway. While the Virginia Right to Farm Act provides invaluable protection from complaints against grape growing and harvesting activity, it has left many wineries far short of protections needed to do these things to sell value-added wine. As described below, Virginia wineries have had hard-fought but generally successful battles in the Legislature to shore up protections for those other essential activities.

c. Statutory Protection for On-Site Wine Production and Sales

Like wineries nationwide, those in Virginia generate tasting room wine sales by publicizing unique events or leasing space on their premises for weddings or community meetings. In the early 2000s, counties resisting growth in the wine industry characterized advertised activities as "special events" that required advance notice to the locality and/or special use permits. They also began crafting ordinances to limit the production capacity of wineries, the size of tasting rooms, hours of operation, the number of people that could visit wineries, and vehicle access to wineries, among other things. This tension between growing wineries and counties prompted the wine industry to appeal to the General Assembly for statutory relief from local management of their affairs.

In 2006, one winery holding large-scale, on-site marketing events in a county resistant to growth supported an aggressive bill before the General Assembly to exempt wineries from any local control. The Virginia Wineries Association (VWA) and Virginia Association of Counties (VACO) quickly jumped into the debate and nominal legislative progress was made. Most importantly, the legislation required the Virginia Secretary of Agriculture and Forestry to convene a study group to develop recommendations on how to address the ongoing relationship between farm wineries and their communities.[58] The goal was a more efficient and streamlined process for permitting wine tastings, special events such as wine festivals, and other promotional activities.[59] VWA, VACO, and numerous other stakeholders spent much of 2006 renegotiating language that ultimately passed the 2007 General Assembly.

Codified at Va. Code §15.2-2288.3, that law lists farm winery activities that a locality may not regulate under any circumstances, including the production and harvesting of fruit; on- premises sale, tasting, or consumption of wine during regular business hours; direct-to-consumer sales and shipment of wine; sale and shipment of wine to the ABC, wholesalers, and out-of-state purchasers; storage,

58. A Report on the Relationship Between Counties and Farm Wineries (Part I) by Robert S. Bloxom, Secretary of Agriculture and Forestry, 2006.

59. 2006 Va. Acts 794 (codified as amended at Va. Code Ann. §15.2-2288.3 (2022)).

warehousing, and wholesaling of wine; and sale of wine-related items incidental to the sale of wine. Finally, the new law exempted from regulation personal gatherings at the winery and permitted local regulation of outdoor amplified music equal to that in the jurisdiction's general noise ordinance.[60]

However, despite months spent searching for a solution, stakeholders could still not agree on how to address local regulation of winery special events outside regular business hours. A policy statement in the law posits that local restriction of events "shall be reasonable and shall take into account the economic impact on the farm winery of such restriction, the agricultural nature of such activities and events, and whether such activities and events are usual and customary for farm wineries. Usual and customary activities and events at farm wineries shall be permitted without local regulation unless there is a substantial impact on the health, safety, or welfare of the public."[61] There is no interpretation of what constitutes "reasonable" local restrictions or "usual and customary" events and activities, but this law has encouraged localities to review and coordinate with other local governments when drafting ordinances to ensure any restrictions are reasonable and commonly used. Note that this statute has not precluded local regulation of special events entirely. Albemarle County, with its many wineries, established 200 attendees as the threshold above which a winery must obtain a special use permit for a gathering, for example.

In 2017, the General Assembly was again asked to mediate simmering disputes between wineries and local governments. Based on a directive in the budget bill, the Virginia Secretary of Agriculture and Forestry convened another panel of representatives from 19 stakeholder organizations. Facilitated by the University of Virginia Institute for Environmental Negotiation, the panel surveyed constituencies, reviewed six previous studies, and compiled information on local ordinances and other approaches. Key issues relating to special events, noise, and traffic were identified, and the panel agreed by consensus on six recommendations. The panel recommended no new statewide legislation but encouraged the sharing among localities of best practices and protocols across all three topics. Specifically, the stakeholder panel encouraged farm wineries, in conjunction with localities, to evaluate and expand existing guidance on events, noise, and traffic for winery startup and expansion.[62]

d. Industry Growth from Contract Winemaking

As more tourists and brides wanted to visit and host events at Virginia wineries, new players saw the demand and opportunity to enter the beverage alcohol marketplace. Unfortunately, the business of growing grapes was slower than the market's desire for more wine. And since Virginia does not permit

60. 2007 Va. Acts 657 (codified as amended at Va. Code §15.2-2288.3 (2022)).

61. Va. Code §15.2-2288.3(A) (2022).

62. House Document No. 16 — A Study of Virginia Farm Wineries — 2017 Appropriation Act, Chapter 836, Item 88. Report to the Governor and the General Assembly of Virginia, November 1, 2017.

alternating proprietorships or other structures under federal law that increase production at wineries, there was growing pressure to produce more wine than new vineyards would permit. Wineries were selling all they could make out of their tasting rooms and pulling product back from the wholesale distribution system. Therefore, the 2013 General Assembly was convinced by industry to amend the definition of farm winery in Va. Code §4.1-100. That section initially defined a farm winery as one "located on a farm in the Commonwealth on land zoned agricultural with a producing vineyard, orchard, or similar growing area and with facilities for fermenting and bottling wine on the premises." It also granted the important privileges of tastings in on-site tasting rooms and the sale of wine for on and off premises consumption, as well as five additional "remote" outlets to participate in weekend wine festivals statewide. Meeting these definitional requirements enabled an applicant to obtain a farm winery license pursuant to Va. Code §4.1-207(5). This definition was the last vestige of traditional public policy that only allowed alcohol production and sale in rural areas if it supported local farmers.

The 2013 law change prompting the most dramatic increase in the number of wineries in Virginia allowed farm wineries to utilize "agreements for purchasing grapes or other fruits from agricultural growers within the Commonwealth" instead of being required to harvest their own grapes from a producing vineyard they owned or leased. No longer must a farm winery invest in land and labor to grow enough grapes to meet its market demand. It can have a token producing vineyard, acquire basic equipment for fermenting and bottling, meet other minimal requirements, and contract with another winery to produce wines under its own label. Pursuant to Va. Code §4.1-100, contract winemaking facilities are licensed farm wineries that obtain agricultural products from other licensees and are paid to "manufacture" such products into wine for the contracting winery. "Manufacturing" constitutes numerous services, including crushing, processing, fermenting, bottling, and any combination thereof. Critics have argued that this provision takes the "farm" requirement away from a farm winery and gives rural "party barns" all the privileges of a farm winery without investing time and resources in growing grapes. Alternatively, wineries are grateful for the ability to contract out winemaking so they can increase the pace of growth by focusing on marketing facilities and building the reputation of brands.

e. Objections to Initial Winery Licensure

Many new wineries faced neighbor or community objections to initial licensure by Virginia ABC. To the frustration of those that object to sharing rural space with commercial enterprises, the statutory process for granting a winery license in Virginia greatly favors the applicant. Procedurally, when a winery license application is filed, Virginia ABC provides notice to the relevant locality of such filing and offers that locality 30 days to submit objections.[63] In addition,

---

63. Va. Code §4.1-230(B) (2022).

the applicant must post a notice of the application filing in a newspaper of general circulation in the jurisdiction. If there are founded citizen objections, ABC may hold a public hearing on issuance of the license. Additional guidance in Va. Code §4.1-222(2) outlines specific conditions under which the ABC Board may refuse to grant a license, namely that the intended location will interfere with the normal conduct of affairs at public facilities such as churches or schools, or is so located with respect to a residential area that it will "adversely affect real property values or substantially interfere with the usual quietude and tranquility of such . . . residential area." In practice, proving one of these conditions is difficult, so while ABC takes note of local objections, it commonly issues the license without conditions.

Because of this presumption, the General Assembly was again pulled into a dispute between a winery and the community following lingering animosity over ABC issuance of a farm winery license in 2009 to Paradise Springs Winery in Fairfax County. Fairfax is a highly developed suburb of Washington, D.C. with a wealthy southern corner filled with small residential farms on narrow country roads. Well-heeled and determined activists and Washington Post reporters fanned the flames of this high-profile dispute, to the pleasure of local readers. After a fruitless lawsuit by neighbors and several years of failed attempts by a local Senator to change winery laws statewide, the 2016 General Assembly acted. It amended the siting requirements for a farm winery in Va. Code §4.1-100 to specify that a farm winery must be on agricultural land, which is "(1) land zoned as an agricultural district or classification or (2) land otherwise permitted by a locality for farm winery use." To appease Fairfax residents, the following language was added: "[F]or purposes of this definition, 'land zoned agricultural' does not include land zoned 'residential conservation.' Except for the limitation on land zoned 'residential conservation,' nothing in the definition of 'land zoned agricultural' shall otherwise limit or affect local zoning authority."

This 2016 law change was a paper victory, as Paradise Springs had been licensed since 2010, and the new law could not retroactively revoke its farm winery license. Further, classification of local zoning districts in Virginia is unique to each county and "residential conservation" exists in Fairfax; it is unknown how many other counties use that term to classify land. While triggered by community opposition, the amendment was a victory for the wine industry in affirming that a farm winery must locate in "land zoned agricultural" without granting localities any additional authority to limit farm winery siting. Fairfax County may have more control over future farm wineries, but counties elsewhere in Virginia likely gained no benefit from this law.

f. Uniform Statewide Building Code Exemption

Another objection to issuance of a new farm winery license centers on the safety of the winery structure itself. Whether the winery intends to use an existing structure or build something new, another important statutory protection for wineries always shocks the building inspector charged with approving the renovation or construction of the first winery in that county. Pursuant to Va. Code §36-99, "farm buildings and structures" are exempt from the provisions of the Uniform Statewide Building Code ("Building Code"), except for a building or a portion of a building located on a farm that is operated as a restaurant. Va. Code §36-97 defines "farm building or structure" as one "not used for residential purposes, located on property where farming operations take place, and used primarily for any of the following uses or combination thereof: 1. Storage, handling, production, display, sampling or sale of agricultural, horticultural, floricultural or silvicultural products produced in the farm . . . ."

Without question, a licensed farm winery satisfies the definition of a farm building or structure and is, therefore, exempt from Building Code requirements. It is easy to envision the legislature's intent in adopting this exemption when imagining existing farm buildings being refurbished or expanded into a quaint tasting room, for example. However, farm wineries also construct massive and elaborate structures housing production facilities and tasting rooms that can accommodate thousands of visitors a year. These are difficult projects for a county building inspector to ignore. Rather than litigating the matter or being accused of compromising visitor safety, many winery proprietors have voluntarily complied with the Building Code in building new facilities.

The General Assembly was prompted to revisit this issue in 2018, triggered by legislation challenging this exemption for all agritourism facilities. This resulted in a legislative study presented to relevant Committee leadership in November of 2018. The report examined "public safety and welfare and the impact of building codes applied to agritourism facilities, discussed possible definitions for farm structures used for gathering people, explored potential building attributes for agritourism facilities, and considered a process for revisions to the Virginia Uniform Statewide Building Code that would require agritourism facilities to incorporate specific building features."[64] One conclusion of this report was that Virginia's agritourism activities are complex and diverse, and that legislative changes to the existing Building Code or creation of a specialized Building Code for farm structures was premature. Another was that such changes would be cost prohibitive for small farmers who rely on agritourism to generate revenue that compliments other sales channels. And finally, the report noted that continuing dialogue between stakeholders about this topic is needed. While this exemption is yet another protection that Virginia's wineries enjoy that causes local officials some angst, its recent revisiting has likely deflected more legislative scrutiny of it for years to come.

64. 2018 Virginia Agritourism and Building Codes Review, Prepared at the Request of the Virginia House and Senate General Laws Committees by Martha A. Walker, Ph.D. Virginia Tech/Virginia Cooperative Extension, November 2018.

g. Virginia Agritourism Liability Act

Finally, back in 2006 the General Assembly passed another law to benefit all businesses engaged in agricultural activity, expressly including wineries and vineyards. It was the first time Virginia defined the term "agritourism" in statute and represented a significant development in encouraging tourism on Virginia farms. Under the Virginia Agritourism Liability Act, the law limits the liability of proprietors for death or injury to anyone engaged in agritourism, defined as "any activity carried out on a farm or ranch that allows members of the general public, for recreational, entertainment, or educational purposes, to view or enjoy rural activities, including farming, wineries, ranching, historical, cultural, harvest-your-own activities. . . ."[65] By posting the statutorily prescribed warning, proprietors may assert an affirmative defense of assumption of the risk. They are not liable for injury or death of a participant resulting from the inherent risks of these agritourism activities unless there is negligence or willful or wanton disregard for safety, actual or reasonable knowledge of a dangerous condition, or intentional injury to the participant. No lawsuit has been brought against a winery under this Act to date.

This sampling of hard-fought protections contained in the Code of Virginia have greatly benefitted the wine industry, which wrapped their operations under the cloak of agriculture to secure them. Wineries have provided economic growth for rural Virginia and opportunity for new generations of farming families to preserve traditional rural lifestyles. The model has been so successful that producers of beer, distilled spirits, mead, and cider have stepped up behind wineries asking the Legislature for the same exemptions and protections from local control over their operations. Public policies that took the wineries decades to procure have taken only a short time for other craft beverages to expand for their benefit as craft alcohol beverages producers have become combined in the minds of legislators. Consequently, if one type of producer asks for a new privilege, the others will expect to be covered as well. This expansion may lead to challenges in the future as wineries may not be as successful as they have been to date at convincing the General Assembly of the need for new protections from local government oversight.

4. OREGON

In 1972 Oregon passed Senate Bill 100 mandating visionary statewide land use planning.[66] The foundation of the state's land use program is a set of 19 statewide planning goals. The goals express the state's policies on land use and related topics, including housing, natural resources, recreation, and transportation. The goals are accompanied by guidelines, which are suggestions, not mandates, on how each goal should be applied.

65. Va. Code §3.2-6400 (2022).
66. 1973 Or. Laws ch. 80.

The state goals are implemented and achieved through local comprehensive planning. Oregon law requires each city and county to adopt a comprehensive plan, similar to California's General Plans.[67] The local comprehensive plans must be consistent with the statewide planning goals. They are reviewed for consistency by the Oregon Land Conservation and Development Commission (OLCDC). After OLCDC approval, the plan is said to be *acknowledged* and becomes the controlling document for land uses in the area covered by the plan. The local jurisdiction then adopts various land use ordinances to put the plan into effect.

Oregon land use laws designate lands into categories, generally described as agricultural, forest, residential, commercial, industrial, institutional, and recreational zones. Agricultural zoning is most commonly implemented through the Exclusive Farm Use (EFU) zone. Wineries located on rural land typically are located in EFU and other agricultural zones. However, wineries (not vineyards) also may be located in both rural and urban commercial or industrial zones, often without any land use approvals other than an approved site plan and various ministerial permits such as building and septic permits.

In an EFU zone, a winery is regarded as a permitted use if certain statutory requirements are met.[68] If the winery's maximum annual production is less than 50,000 gallons, the winery must have an on-site or contiguous vineyard of at least 15 acres, a long-term contract to purchase grapes from at least 15 acres of vineyards contiguous to the winery, or some combination of these sources totaling at least 15 acres. If the winery's maximum annual production is between 50,000 and 100,000 gallons, the minimum vineyard size is increased from 15 to 40 acres. If the winery can meet these criteria, the development can proceed, subject only to site plan review and the issuance of any required ministerial permits. A permitted use winery must still meet certain development standards for parking, access, circulation, and setbacks from neighboring properties.

If a proposed winery cannot qualify as a permitted use winery, it still may be allowed as a "commercial activity in conjunction with farm use," subject to review by the local government as a conditional use.[69] This applies to wineries in EFU and other agricultural zones such as the farm-forest or agriculture-forest zones. This process involves an application to the local planning department, public notice of the proposed development, and, in some cases, a public hearing. The project proponents must demonstrate that the development meets specific approval criteria such as consistency with the jurisdiction's comprehensive plan, enhancement of farming enterprises in the local agricultural community, and lack of adverse impact on farming and other approved uses on adjacent lands.[70]

A less common but viable way to establish a winery on agricultural land is as a "farm processing facility." This use is permitted subject to site plan review if the farm provides at least 25 percent of the crops (grapes) processed and if less than

---

67. Or. Rev. Stat. §197.175 (2022).

68. Or. Rev. Stat. §215.452(1) (2022).

69. *Id.* §§215.213(2), 215.283(2).

70. Or. Rev. Stat. §215.296(1) (2022); see, e.g., Marion County, Or., Zoning Code §§17.136.050(D)(2), 17.136.060(A), (D) (2022).

10,000 square feet of buildings space is used for processing.[71] There is no proscribed production limit for farm processing facilities. These are permitted uses subject to standards, not conditional uses.

The subject of accessory activities allowed at the various categories of wineries is as complicated as in California and Virginia. Wineries in an EFU zone are closely regulated in terms of their on-site marketing and sales activities. In addition to marketing and selling wine "produced in conjunction with the winery," a permitted use winery may engage in a variety of wine-related activities as long as the activities are "directly related to the sale or marketing of wine produced at the winery."[72] These activities include wine tastings in the tasting room or elsewhere on the premises, wine club activities and events, winemaker luncheons and dinners, vineyard tours, meetings or business activities with wine-industry members, open house promotions of wine, and as a final catch-all, "similar activities conducted for the primary purpose of promoting wine produced in conjunction with the winery."[73] The catch-all of "similar activities" is a generous statutory allowance that allows permitted use wineries to creatively market and sell wine with music, art, and other promotional events to bring people to the winery to taste and buy wine. There is no limit on these types of activities as long as the winery can demonstrate that such activities are "directly related" to the marketing and sale of the winery's wine.

Permitted use wineries may also sell non-wine items as long as such sales are directly related to wine and *incidental* to the on-site retail sale of wine.[74] Such items include food and beverages, as long as the service is part of a wine-related activity and does not "utilize menu options or meal services that cause the kitchen facilities to function as a café or other dining establishment."[75] Unlike wine-related activities and sales that have no limit, sales of incidental items and services must not exceed 25 percent of the income from the retail sale of wine on site.[76] This threshold is a mechanism established by the Oregon legislature to ensure that wine-related marketing and sales remain the predominant activity at a permitted use winery.

A permitted use winery may also hold up to 18 agritourism or other "commercial events."[77] These are events such as outdoor concerts, celebratory gatherings (e.g., weddings), facility rentals, lifestyle events, and other events where admission is charged where the "promotion of wine produced in conjunction

---

71. Or. Rev. Stat. §215.283(1)(r) (2022); Or. Admin. R. 660-033-0130(28) (2022).

72. Or. Rev. Stat. 215.452(2)(b) (2022).

73. Or. Rev. Stat. 215.452(2)(b)(a)-(g) (2022).

74. Or. Rev. Stat. 215.452(2)(c) (2022).

75. Or. Rev. Stat. 215.452(3) (2022). In 2013, the Oregon legislature adopted Senate Bill 841 that gave wineries greater flexibility when it comes to wine-related marketing activities and food service. See also *Guidance for Food Service at Wineries on Farmland under Oregon Senate Bill 841* (January 2017), published by the Oregon Liquor Control Commission, Oregon Department of Land Conservation and Development, Oregon Winegrowers Association.

76. Or. Rev. Stat. 215.452(4) (2022).

77. Or. Rev. Stat. 214.452(5) (2022).

with the winery is the secondary purpose of the event."[78] While permitted by state law, counties may adopt conditions of approval related to the number of attendees, hours of operation, traffic management, noise, and sanitation.[79] Consequently, it is not uncommon to find that some counties are more stringent when regulating the intensity of agritourism or other commercial events at wineries. With the adoption of Senate Bill 841 in 2013, however, regulation of permitted use wineries has become more uniform across the state. Senate Bill 841 (2013) provided clarity on permissible wine-related activities and established standards to better regulate commercial events on agricultural land

For conditional use wineries operating as a "commercial activity in conjunction with farm use," counties often look to the permitted use winery statute (ORS 215.452) for what wine-related and non-wine-related activities may take place. But because there is no overarching state law regulating this type of winery, counties have discretion to impose a range of conditions of approval and, consequently, one county may be more lenient than another when approving the intensity and scale of a conditional use winery.

A winery, regardless of whether it a permitted or conditional use, may look to "layer" approvals to have greater flexibility for the types or size of events. For example, a winery may seek an "outdoor mass gathering" permit that allows the winery to hold an outside event of 3,000 or more people for at least 24 hours as long as certain health and safety standards are met.[80] A common use of an outdoor mass gathering permit is to host music festivals with overnight camping. Regardless of the zone, the county can issue a permit for such events only if the applicant demonstrates that there will be adequate water supply, drainage and sewage facilities, toilet facilities, refuse storage and disposal facilities, emergency medical facilities, communication systems, fire protection, security personnel, traffic control, and sanitary food service (if food is offered). The applicant also must have casualty insurance, and the county may require whatever plans, specifications, or reports are necessary to properly review the event and facilities.[81]

Farm processing facilities cannot conduct any accessory activities, but state law does recognize "farm stands" as a permitted use in all agricultural zones.[82] Although farm stands cannot engage in winemaking, they can and do conduct many of the same accessory activities as wineries in the same zones. Specifically, the farm stand structure must be designed and used for the sale of crops grown on the farm and other farms in the local agricultural area. "Farm crops" include the processed form of the crops (e.g., wine from grapes) but not prepared food items.

---

78. Or. Rev. Stat. 215.452(14) (2022).

79. Or. Rev. Stat. 215.452(7) (2022).

80. *Id.*§§433.735-433.770.

81. Note that a mass gathering permit for an activity lasting less than 120 hours in any three-month period is not a land use decision. Local governments may not regulate these gatherings except to ensure adequate health and safety precautions. *See* Landsem Farms, LP, 44 Or. Land Use Bd. App. 611, 617 (2003). Napa County has a similar approval process for so-called temporary events that involve the exercise of First Amendment rights (singing, music, etc.) to the public.

82. Or. Admin. R. 660-033-0120, tbl.1 (2022).

"Local agricultural area" is defined to include the entire state."[83] Farm stands can sell incidental retail items; they also can collect a fee for activities to promote their products, although they cannot include structures intended for banquets, public gatherings, or public entertainment. As with wineries in EFU zones, farm stands' annual sales of incidental items plus their fees from promotional activities cannot exceed 25 percent of their total annual sales.

In addition to controls on land uses, including accessory uses, Oregon regulates land divisions in an effort to control urban and suburban sprawl. In 1993 the state legislature restricted the ability of landowners to subdivide lands in the EFU zones by requiring that newly created parcels be at least 80 acres in size.[84] The law included important grandfather exceptions, including the ability to sell any EFU-zoned land that existed as a legal "lot of record" before 1993 for winery or vineyard use, no matter the size of the lot.

Even with these exceptions, the restrictions were regarded by many as too stringent and resulted in a ballot initiative in 2004 known as Measure 37. This measure, which the voters passed, allowed landowners to seek compensation from the state or local government or, if the government is unwilling to pay such compensation, to obtain a waiver of land use restrictions that had been imposed since the time the land was acquired and that resulted in a diminution of the value of the land. Many voters thought Measure 37 went too far to weaken Oregon's land use laws, and in 2007, Ballot Measure 49 was passed to limit the relief available under Measure 37.[85]

Measure 49 "modif[ies] Ballot Measure 37 (2004) to ensure that Oregon law provides just compensation for unfair burdens while retaining Oregon's protections for farm and forest uses and the state's water resources." More specifically with respect to farmland, Measure 49 modified Measure 37 by providing for relief in two ways: a so-called express option that may allow up to three home sites on a given parcel,[86] and a "conditional option" that may allow up to 10 home sites. The conditional option requires proof that the value of the

---

83. Or. Rev. Stat. §215.283(1)(o) (2022); Or. Admin. R. 660-033-0130(23) (2022).

84. 1983 Or. Laws ch. 792 (codified as amended at Or. Rev. Stat. §215.780 (2022)).

85. Ballot Measure 49 (Or. 2007) (codified as amended at Or. Rev. Stat. §§195.300-195.336 (2022)). Ballot Measure 49 modified Ballot Measure 37, adopted by voters in 2004, to roll back Ballot Measure 37 to limit only certain types of compensation, land divisions, and development.

86. The details of the express option are extremely complicated. Consider this explanation in the Oregon Department of Land Conservation and Development's Measure 49 Guide, at 4 (Mar. 7, 2008), available at http://www.oregon.gov/LCD/MEASURE49/docs/general/m49_guide.pdf:

> The number of lots, parcels or dwellings that may be approved under the Express option is limited to three. In addition, the number cannot exceed the number in the claimant's Measure 37 claim or waiver, if one was issued. If the property already contains one or more dwellings or more than one parcel, then neither the total number of dwellings nor parcels can exceed three. However, if a claimant's property already contains three or more parcels and three or more dwellings, the claimant may receive one more parcel and one more dwelling if the claimant otherwise qualifies under Measure 49. If a claimant's property already contains three parcels and has two or fewer dwellings, the claimant can receive only additional dwellings.

claimant's property was reduced by the government's land use restrictions. To qualify for either option, the claimant must have had the right to develop the additional home sites when the property was acquired.

Many wine industry veterans supported efforts to unwind the measure. David Adelsheim, of Adelsheim Winery and former president of the Oregon Winegrowers Association, supported Measure 49, stating,

> Oregon winegrowers know the importance of preserving prime agricultural land. Oregon's land use laws are the reason our industry exists today. Without the establishment of Exclusive Farm Use zoning and Oregon's comprehensive land use system, the hillsides our industry needs to produce the best grapes would have been dotted with housing developments instead of rows of Pinot Noir vines. No visitor would want to come to a wine country filled with rural subdivisions. We need to be able to count on the same protections going forward, to ensure that Oregon's wines will continue to flourish.[87]

Wineries in Oregon are not only regulated by land use laws but are also subject to public health and safety regulations including but not limited to food, drinking water, and worker safety. In addition, there are environmental regulations like stormwater and wastewater disposal that apply to winery operations. When seeking permit approvals to operate a winery, these non-land use regulations are considered in the project's design and future operation.

B. URBAN RETAILERS

Retail licensees, or the third tier of the three-tier system, sell beer, wine, and spirits to consumers for drinking on or off the licensed premises. Most states have different classifications of alcoholic beverage licenses for on-sale consumption (restaurants, bars, clubs, and hotels) and off-sale consumption (wine shops, liquor stores, package stores, and, in some states, grocery stores and state liquor stores). Most states also distinguish between on-sale premises where minors are allowed because meals are served (restaurants, cafes, hotels), and bars and nightclubs where no or only minimal food is served and no one under 21 may be present. In this section, unless otherwise specified, "bars" refers to on-sale premises, including both bars and restaurants, and "liquor stores" refers to all off-sale premises selling alcoholic beverages in closed containers for consumption off the licensed premises. These may be liquor stores, wine shops, grocery stores, or even department stores. Of course, retailers, like wine producers, can be found in both urban and rural settings, but urban bars and bottle shops pose particular land use problems that are the topic of this part of the chapter.

Some states allow wineries to exercise retail privileges from locations away from the winery premises, either through operations of a "duplicate" tasting room

---

87. Jane Firstenfeld, Oregon Vineyards Protected From Developers, Wines & Vines, Sept. 2, 2010, http://www.winesandvines.com/template.cfm?section=news&content=78177.

which is a supplier-tier privilege, or through exceptions to state tied-house laws which allow the winery to own and/or operate a retail license. New Jersey's wineries, for example, may have up to six retail outlets, apart from winery premises, from which to sell closed bottles to consumers.[88] California allows two duplicate tasting rooms,[89] and there are numerous tied-house exceptions, which allow a winery to own an ownership interest in a retail license.[90] Washington allows four additional locations away from the winery premises,[91] from which the winery can exercise off-sale, closed bottle privileges and on-sale tasting room privileges, excluding restaurants.

Importantly, whether they are exercising retail privileges as a winery or operating as a retail licensee, wineries may be subject to the same limitations faced by bars and liquor stores for operations in urban areas. The discussion below is divided into two main parts: the controls and requirements for establishing a business in a new location, with separate sections on the laws of Washington State, Texas, New York, and California; and the increased restrictions on and changes to operating conditions that can be imposed on existing businesses in certain situations, using California as the example.

1. NEW LOCATIONS

The steps required for alcoholic beverage licensing vary depending on the locality. As noted above, some states, such as California, primarily vest alcohol licensing authority across all tiers with a dedicated state agency. Some states, such as Nevada and Illinois, delegate retail licensing approvals to county and city governments. The federal Alcohol and Tobacco Tax and Trade Bureau (TTB) licenses manufacturers of alcohol, including wineries, as well as importers and wholesalers, but it does not license retail establishments.[92]

While the principal focus of the following discussion of controls on the issuance of retail alcoholic beverage licenses in new locations is California, the first part includes descriptions of the licensing process applicable to retailers in Washington, Texas, and New York. Washington is a state that entirely controls the sale of spirits; Texas has wet and dry areas through the exercise of local control over sales of alcoholic beverages; and New York restricts the off-sale of wine to package liquor stores only, not convenience stores or grocery stores. The urban retail licensing requirements in these states are generally similar, but they differ with respect to local controls and ease of issuance.

---

88. New Jersey wineries may not ship wine ordered by phone, mail, or Internet. All winery retail transactions in New Jersey must be in person.

89. Cal. Bus. & Prof. Code §23390.5 (2021).

90. *See, e.g.,* Cal. Bus. & Prof. Code §§25503.15 and 25503.30 (2021).

91. Wash. Rev. Code §66.24.170(a)(ii) (2009).

92. TTB does require special occupational tax registration, without payment of tax, upon start-up of a retail alcoholic beverage business. 26 U.S.C. §§5122, 5124 (2006).

a. Washington

In Washington State, the Liquor and Cannabis Board (WSLCB), formerly the Liquor Control Board, is charged with protecting the "welfare, health, peace, morals, and safety" of the public and is the sole governmental body that holds the power to license and tax the sale and distribution of alcohol.[93] Until 2011, Washington was a control state, which meant that the WSLCB was the only authorized wholesaler and operator of liquor stores for the sale of distilled spirits. Washington Initiative 1183 (I-1183) appeared on the November 2011 ballot and was approved by approximately 59 percent of voters. The initiative directed the WSLCB to close its state-run retail liquor stores and the distribution center, liquidate the assets, and allow privately owned retail stores and distributors to begin selling and distributing spirits in 2021.[94] Today, the WSLCB issues retail licenses to on- and off-sale retailers for the sale of beer, wine, and spirits. By and large, the licensing process as it relates to zoning and land use issues is fairly straightforward. As in all states, the local zoning ordinances govern the use of the premises; in Washington there are generally no complex roadblocks to operating an on- or off-sale retail business. That said, since the passage of I-1183, the WSLCB has imposed certain requirements on applicants seeking an off-premises retail license allowing the sale of packaged spirits. In particular, applicants for this license type are required to demonstrate that the premises to be licensed consists of "at least ten thousand square feet of fully enclosed retail space within a single structure, including store rooms and other interior areas."[95] Washington law grants a limited exception to the ten-thousand-square-foot requirement for former state contractor run liquor stores and for premises located in a trade area with no other off-premises spirits retailers.[96] In addition to the aforementioned spatial requirements, off-sale spirits retail license applicants must provide a written security plan at the time of licensure addressing inventory management, employee training and supervision, and how the physical security of spirits products will be maintained.[97]

Washington differs from California and the handful of other states that treat certain on-sale licenses as personal property that can be bought and sold. In addition, there is a statutory cap on the combined number of two types of on-sale liquor licenses that may be issued by the WSLCB: (i) the spirits, beer, and wine nightclub licenses and (ii) the spirits, beer, and wine restaurant. At the time of writing, the aggregate number of spirits, beer, and wine nightclub and restaurant licenses cannot exceed "one license for each one thousand two hundred of population in the state."[98] Historically, however, each time the existing statutory limit has been approached, the legislature has amended the statute to make more

93. Wash. Rev. Code §66.08.010, 66.08.120 (2009).
94. Washington State Initiative 1183 (2011), i1183.pdf (wa.gov).
95. WAC 314-02-107(1)(a).
96. WAC 314-02-107(3).
97. WAC 314-02-107(b).
98. *Id.*§66.24.420(4).

licenses available. There is no statutorily imposed limit on the number of certain other on-sale retail liquor licenses that may be issued by the WSLCB, such as beer and wine only restaurant licenses or tavern licenses.

Even though an applicant for a spirits, beer, and wine restaurant or a spirits, beer, and wine nightclub license will likely not face an obstacle due to the statutory cap, other potential hurdles could arise. The WSLCB is directed to refuse to issue a spirits, beer, and wine restaurant license to an applicant "if in the opinion of the board the spirits, beer, and wine restaurant licenses already granted for the particular locality are adequate for the reasonable needs of the community."[99] The WSLCB is also directed to, "so far as in its judgment is reasonably possible," confine spirits, beer, and wine restaurant licenses to business districts and not approve such licenses in residential districts.[100]

During the licensing process, retail applicants submit a license application packet, after which the WSLCB will direct the applicant to post a public notice at the premises naming the interested parties and the license type and will send notice of the application to the local authority, be it a city or county.[101] The WSLCB also will notify public institutions, churches, and schools that are within 500 feet of the proposed premises.[102] The local authority has 20 days to object to, or request additional time to evaluate, the application. At this stage, the local authority generally circulates the application to various departments, including the law enforcement and zoning departments. Typical land use issues that may arise include building occupancy and zoning issues, which can cause a delay in the application process.

Along with the public notice posted at the premises, the process allows interested parties to comment on and object to the application. Objections usually are based on land use issues or public safety concerns.[103] Based on the response to the notices, a physical inspection of the premises, and investigation of the applicant, the WSLCB will grant or deny the application. Either an objecting party or the applicant can request a hearing to appeal the decision. In general, licenses are not subject to special conditions or restrictions, but there are two interesting exceptions.

The first exception applies to those off-sale retail premises and on-sale retail premises with off-sale privileges that are located within an alcohol impact area (AIA). There are currently mandatory AIAs located in Seattle, Tacoma, Spokane, Olympia, and Everett and a voluntary AIA located within the city of Vancouver. An AIA is an area within a municipality or county where chronic inebriation or illegal activity connected with alcohol consumption has been determined by the locality to require special treatment. The WSLCB's purpose in adopting AIA rules was to "establish a framework under which the board, in partnership with local

---

99. *Id.* §66.24.420(5).

100. *Id.* §66.24.420(2).

101. Apply for a Liquor License, available at https://lcb.wa.gov/licensing/apply-liquor-license; *see also id.* §66.24.010(8)(a).

102. Wash. Rev. Code §66.24.010(9)(a) (2009).

103. *Id.* §66.24.010(8)(c), (9)(a), (c), (12).

government and community organizations, may act to mitigate negative impacts on a community's welfare, health, peace, or safety that result from the presence of chronic public inebriation."[104] After the local government has created the AIA and the WSLCB has recognized it, an "enhanced" licensing procedure goes into effect for all new and renewal applications. The local authority notice period is extended from 20 days to 60 days, and the WSLCB is permitted to place restrictions on the license, such as limiting hours of operations and banning the sale of certain products.[105] For example, the most recent AIA—approved on September 7, 2016, for Everett—included a list of 32 banned malt beverage products, such as Keystone Ice, Olde English 800, and Four Loko.[106] The WSLCB notifies licensed distributors of the banned products and actively enforces the AIA restrictions.

The second exception relates to the spirits, beer, and wine nightclub license established by the legislature in 2009, which is intended specifically for businesses that will primarily be open to the public between 9 p.m. and 2 a.m. and has food sales and service that are merely incidental to the sale and service of alcohol.[107] Previously, these businesses typically held a spirits, beer, and wine restaurant license, which had more stringent food service and operational requirements. In creating this license type, the legislature built in a mechanism for the local authority to request that the WSLCB impose additional restrictions on the license.[108] Seattle, for example, requires nightclub applicants to submit safety plans and employ security personnel;[109] they must also participate in police training. The city will request these restrictions in response to the notice of a nightclub application; if the WSLCB approves them, the applicant is required to comply. Any restrictions imposed by the city of Seattle are considered conditions that must be satisfied before the WSLCB will issue the permanent license.

b. Texas

Following the repeal of Prohibition, the Texas Constitution was amended to allow the residents of each city, justice precinct, and county to determine whether and to what extent alcoholic beverages should be made available for sale within its jurisdiction. The range of possible local options includes 10 categories, primarily determined by the range of beverages to be made available (i.e., beer, wine, and/or distilled spirits) and whether on-premises consumption will be allowed.[110] In fact, while much of Texas remains largely dry in aerial extent, all of the major population areas are "damp" to some degree. In any case, the possession of

---

104. Wash. Admin. Code §314-12-210(1)(c) (2010).

105. *Id.*§314-12-215(3), (6)(a).

106. Recognizing the City of Everett's Core Commercial Area Alcohol Impact Area, available at https://lcb.wa.gov/publications/AlcImpactAreas/Everett/Everett-Resolution.pdf.

107. Wash. Rev. Code §66.24.600 (2009).

108. *Id.* §66.24.600(5).

109. Seattle, Wash., Mun. Code §§10.11.010(E), 10.11.015 (2010).

110. *See* Tex. Elec. Code §501.035. The right to manufacture or distribute alcoholic beverages is determined by whether the class of beverages can be sold at retail there. Tex. Alco. Bev. Code §§11.01, 251.71(a).

alcoholic beverages for personal consumption in the home is legal everywhere, as are private clubs that make alcoholic beverages available to their members for consumption on the club's licensed premises.

The manufacture, importation, distribution, marketing, and sale of alcoholic beverages are governed by the Texas Alcoholic Beverage Code (TAB Code), which is administered by the Texas Alcoholic Beverage Commission (TABC). Under the TAB Code, local control is limited to determination of local option, whether late-hours sales for on-premises consumption will be allowed (i.e., past midnight Sunday through Friday and past 1 a.m. on Sunday mornings),[111] and the adoption of prohibitions on (i) the issuance of permits in residential areas or to locations within prescribed distances from schools, child care facilities, churches, and hospitals; or (ii) the possession of open containers of alcohol within a "central business district"[112] or within 1,000 feet of homeless shelters or substance abuse treatment centers located outside of a central business district. Cities and counties are expressly prohibited from imposing stricter regulatory standards upon the holders of alcoholic beverage permits than other businesses unless the permit holder derives in excess of 75 percent of its gross revenues from the sale of alcoholic beverages for on-premises consumption or is operating a sexually oriented business.[113] Nonetheless, cities and counties occasionally adopt ordinances or require specific use permits that impose restrictions in excess of those seemingly allowed by the TAB Code. This can be quite problematic for the applicants because the TABC will not second-guess a city or county. If a city or county refuses to certify an application, the applicant's only recourse is a hearing before the county judge to contest the refusal to certify.[114]

The TAB Code does not restrict the number of permits that TABC may issue to an individual person or company, except with respect to package store permits.[115] The initial step of the application process is to obtain certification by the local city and county that operations of the type applied for are authorized at that location by the local option, that the issuance of the permit is not prohibited by the jurisdiction's charter or ordinance (to the extent such charter or ordinance is authorized by the TAB Code), and that late hours are authorized if a late hours permit is being sought. While this certification should be a straightforward determination based upon the location of the proposed business, cities and counties often use this process as leverage to ensure that the applicant has obtained any

111. Late hours are specifically authorized in cities or counties that had populations in excess of 500,000 at the time of the 2021 federal census or 800,000 or more at the time of the last preceding federal census (i.e., this will be a moving target in the future). Tex. Alco. Bev. Code §§105.03(c), 105.04, 105.05(c).

112. A "central business district" is defined as "a compact and contiguous geographical area of a municipality in which at least 90 percent of the land is used or zoned for commercial purposes and that is the area that has historically been the primary location in the municipality where business has been transacted." *Id.* §109.35(d).

113. *Id.* §109.57(a)-(b), (d).

114. *Id.* §§11.37(d), 61.37(d).

115. "A person may not hold or have an interest, directly or indirectly, in more than 250 package stores or in their business or permit." *Id.* §22.04(a).

other licenses and certifications that may be required in its business, including its certificate of occupancy. This can create unwarranted delay in the licensing process.

An applicant must also obtain a sales and use tax permit from the Texas comptroller and certification from the comptroller that the applicant satisfies all legal requirements for the issuance of a sales tax permit.[116]

Notice of the filing of an application must be published in two consecutive issues of a newspaper of general circulation published in the city where the proposed site is located or, if it is not located in a city, a newspaper published in the county.[117] A sign must be posted at all locations where a permit authorizing the sale of alcoholic beverages for on-premises consumption is being sought, giving notice of the application to the public, unless a permit authorizing the on-premises consumption of alcohol had been active at that location in the last 24 months or the applicant is applying for a winery permit.[118]

Finally, if a permit authorizing the on-premises consumption of alcoholic beverages is being sought, notice of the application must be mailed to every resident and neighborhood association located within 300 feet of the proposed location unless the applicant is also seeking a food and beverage certificate.[119]

A food and beverage certificate may be issued to a restaurant or to a business whose receipts from the sale of alcoholic beverages are 60 percent or less of the total receipts from the location.[120] To be eligible for a food and beverage certificate, the business must have permanent food service facilities for the preparation and service of multiple entrees for consumption at the location.[121]

The issuance of permits authorizing the manufacture, distribution, or sale of alcoholic beverages does not require a public hearing. If TABC recommends denial of an application on one or more grounds set forth in TAB Code §11.46, the applicant may request a hearing.[122]

c. New York

In New York State, there are several types of on-premises liquor licenses, including On-Premises Liquor (for the sale of liquor, wine, and beer), Restaurant Wine (for the sale of wine and beer), and Eating Place Beer (for the sale of beer). Prior to filing an application with the New York State Liquor Authority ("Liquor Authority"), the Original Notice Application Form must be mailed to the Town Clerk of the municipality of the proposed premises or, in New York City, to the appropriate community board. There generally is no response from the local authorities, except in certain parts of New York City, where a community board

116. *Id.* §11.46(b).
117. *Id.* §§11.39, 61.38.
118. *Id.* §§11.391, 61.381.
119. *Id.* §§11.393, 61.382.
120. *Id.* §§25.13(a), 28.18(a), 69.16(a).
121. *Id.* §§25.13(b), 28.18(b), 69.16(b).
122. *Id.* §11.43(d).

may require the applicant to fill out a questionnaire and perhaps attend a community board meeting to describe the type of premises and the proposed method of operation.

Thirty days after the mailing of the Original Notice form, the license application can be filed with the Liquor Authority. The multi-page application describes in great detail all aspects of the proposed licensed premises and includes personal questionnaires for the principals of the applicant. An applicant also must provide adequate "source-of-funds" documentation. If the principals have borrowed money, loan agreements, personal questionnaires, and source-of-funds declarations from the lenders must be submitted to the Liquor Authority.

For On-Premises Liquor license applicants, if there are three or more similarly licensed premises within 500 feet of the proposed premises, the applicant must attend a "500 Foot Hearing" at the Liquor Authority. At such hearing, testimony is presented advising the Authority of the names and addresses of any other licensed premises within 500 feet. The applicant must convince the Liquor Authority that the "public convenience and advantage" will be served by the granting of a license for the location. Although there are no restrictions on the number of on-premises licenses the Authority can issue, if the applicant cannot make this showing, the Liquor Authority has the discretion to reject the application.

In New York State, unlike the practice in about 35 other states, liquor and wine for off-premises consumption are sold in "package-stores," and beer is sold in grocery stores, drug stores, and convenience stores. In nearly every annual legislative session, attempts are made to allow grocery stores with an off-premises license to sell wine, but, year after year, these attempts have failed. Beer also can be sold in a "beer & soda" store that has a Wholesale "C" license (a wholesale license with a retail privilege). By statute, the Liquor Authority cannot issue any new "C" licenses; if one wants a "C" license, it must be purchased from an existing licensee, and the license then can be transferred to a new buyer and/or a new location.

Although there are no restrictions on the number of off-premises liquor or wine stores, the Liquor Authority considers applications on a case-by-case basis. The applicant, who cannot have any interest in any other liquor or wine store and cannot have any interest in a wholesale or production license, must provide the Liquor Authority with the names, addresses, and distances of the four "closest" liquor stores. The Liquor Authority then writes to the four stores and asks them to provide their gross sales for the previous three years. If, in the opinion of the Liquor Authority, the proposed store is too close (not defined) to the other stores and/or if the other stores' gross sales are too low (not defined), or perchance are diminishing over those three years, the members will reject the application. The applicant generally attempts—by submitting as part of the application demographic material, including photos of new construction, census data, and supporting petitions—to convince the members that the "public convenience and advantage" would be served by the addition of a new liquor or wine store in the neighborhood. Commonly, at a meeting of the Liquor Authority, the nearby liquor store owners appear and present their case to try to convince the Liquor Authority that the neighborhood is currently well served by the existing stores and that the public convenience and advantage will not be served by the issuance of a new liquor/wine store license to a prospective competitor.

d. California

The California Department of Alcoholic Beverage Control (ABC) issues all alcoholic beverage licenses in the state. An amendment to the California Constitution, effective 1955, created the ABC as the state's sole license-issuing entity, replacing the Board of Equalization, the state agency that collects excise and sales taxes.[123] The ABC's mission is to ensure "strict, honest, impartial, and uniform administration and enforcement of the liquor laws throughout the State."[124] Applications for all new liquor licenses, and transfers of existing licenses, in the state are submitted to the ABC. Applications for retail licenses are processed by local ABC District Offices.

NEW ESTABLISHMENTS

To examine the controls on the establishment of new bar and liquor store businesses in California, this discussion focuses on San Francisco. There are many hurdles for a new business to surmount and, depending on the type of business proposed, many opportunities for neighbors to protest and delays to ensue.

Limits on the Number of Licenses Issued. Licenses allowing the sale of beer, wine, and spirits ("general" licenses), for both bars and liquor stores, are limited in number based on county population.[125] In San Francisco and certain other counties, because the limitation on the number of licenses is severe (e.g., because of a small population relative to the demand for licensed premises or resorts), the legislature has authorized new restaurant licenses, which are made available through a lottery process,[126] to encourage economic development.[127] In counties where licenses are not available for original issuance, in order to start a new business with a general alcoholic beverage license, the business owner must purchase an existing license from a closed (or about to be closed) business and transfer the license to the new owner at the premises or at a new premises through a statutory escrow process.[128]

---

123. Cal. Const. art. XX, §22 note (1954 amendment).
124. Cal. Bus. & Prof. Code §23049 (2021).
125. Cal. Bus. & Prof. Code §§23816, 23817 (2021).
126. *Id.* §§23691, 23692; Cal. Code Regs. tit. 4, §69 - §69.4 (2022).
127. *Id.* §23862.5 - §23862.7 and §23862.9 - §23862.15.
128. *Id.* §24073 - §24075.

Until 1994, original beer and wine off-sale licenses were freely issued by the ABC in most counties without regard to the population of the county,[129] but this was curtailed in 1994, when the state legislature imposed a moratorium on any new beer and wine off-sale licenses in any city or county where the number of off-sale beer and wine licenses exceeds one for each 2,500 residents.[130] In San Francisco, however, the computation combines off-sale beer and wine licenses with off-sale general licenses and imposes a moratorium on the issuance of new off-sale beer and wine licenses if the combined total exceeds one off-sale license for every 1,250 inhabitants.[131] The proponents of the moratorium believed that it would reduce community problems associated with the sale of alcoholic beverages. The same law that restricted the issuance of licenses also increased police and ABC powers to deal with outlets that caused or supported "public nuisance activities" as discussed in more detail below. Thus, similar to general licenses discussed above, in many instances business owners must purchase existing off-sale beer and wine licenses as well and transfer the license to the new owner at a new premises through an escrow.

In contrast to the restrictions on the issuance of general licenses and beer and wine off-sale licenses, the issuance of new beer and wine on-sale licenses, whether for bars or restaurants, is not restricted by population, a reflection of reduced public health, safety, and welfare concerns at establishments where spirits are neither sold nor served.

Even if the ABC can issue a license or the applicant can find a license to purchase and move to its new business location, there are many other opportunities for the application to be denied or for the operations of the business to be restricted, as described in subsequent sections.

Zoning. All new retail license applications must confirm as part of the application to ABC that zoning permits the use and whether a CUP is needed, which is typically accomplished by discussions with local planning offices. As a practical matter, local zoning and other ordinances negate the uniformity in licensing that was one of the reasons for establishing the California ABC as the statewide agency for alcoholic beverage licensing. As noted above, the ABC Act itself restricts the ABC's ability to issue new licenses in contravention of a valid zoning ordinance of the city or county where the premises are to be located.[132]

As with many cities in California, San Francisco's Planning Code divides the city into more than 20 classes of use districts, which are further divided by

129. One exception to this was Los Angeles County, which had restricted the issuance of new beer and wine off-sale licenses beginning in 1985, except for operations in which the annual sale of products other than beer and wine would exceed the annual sales of beer and wine. Cal. Bus. & Prof. Code §23826.2 (2021).

130. *Id.* §§23817.5(a)(1).

131. *Id.* §23817.5(a)(2).

132. "No retail license shall be issued for any premises which are located in any territory where the exercise of the rights and privileges conferred by the license is contrary to a valid zoning ordinance of any county or city." *Id.* §23790.

additional categories such as residential, commercial, and industrial uses, with many variations based on neighborhood characteristics and mixed-use districts.[133] In most commercial districts, bars and liquor stores are permitted uses "as of right," without need of a CUP. In other mixed residential-commercial districts, a CUP is required for liquor stores or bars. In some districts, particularly districts zoned for predominantly residential uses, new bars and liquor stores are not permitted at all.

In addition to the zoning controls, some San Francisco areas have designated special overlay districts that conform to the neighborhood's official or unofficial boundaries in order to limit the number of bars or liquor stores, even in commercial districts. Some neighborhoods prohibit additional eating and drinking establishments in order to maintain convenient access to other types of neighborhood-serving businesses such as gyms, dry cleaning establishments, small markets, and other retail shops.[134] Other neighborhoods prohibit or limit the establishment of any new liquor stores because of the perceived problems they cause, such as "loitering, littering, public drunkenness, defacement and damaging of structures," which "leads to serious impacts on the health, safety, and welfare of residents of nearby single- and multiple-family areas, including fear for the safety of children, elderly residents and visitors to the area" and "the deterioration of the neighborhood and concomitant devaluation of property and destruction of community values and quality of life."[135]

Zoning limitations can often create significant or insurmountable obstacles to new businesses and fail to accommodate new business models. For example, COVID-19 accelerated a trend towards grocery and alcohol delivery, which was gaining in popularity even before the pandemic. Many new grocery businesses desire to operate delivery-only models from warehouse locations that are not intended to be open to the public. Often, zoning limitations in industrial areas (where warehouses may be located) prohibit retail operations or off-premises alcohol sales. While sometimes local municipalities will work within their existing framework to permit a use (for example, through special permissions or as "accessory uses" with a CUP), this is not always possible, and highlights the importance of ascertaining land use possibilities and limitations before signing leases.

Use Permits and Conditions. While zoning or designation as an overlay district may prevent the establishment of any new liquor stores or bars in some areas, zoning in other areas may permit the use but require that a new business apply for a CUP. CUPs for urban bars and liquor stores in San Francisco (and many other localities) typically involve the same steps as a rural winery: (1) submission of an application to the Planning Commission describing the proposed use, (2) a staff investigation and report recommending denial or issuance with conditions,

---

133. City and County of S.F., Cal., Mun. Code, Planning Code §201 (2022) available at https://codelibrary.amlegal.com/codes/san_francisco/latest/sf_planning/0-0-0-19790 (last accessed August 28, 2022).

134. *See, e.g., id.* §718 (Upper Fillmore Street Neighborhood Commercial District).

135. *Id.* §784 (Lower Haight Street Alcohol Restricted Use District).

based on an assessment of the requirements of the general plan, the planning ordinance, and the potential for negative impacts on the surrounding neighborhood,[136] (3) a public hearing, with notice mailed to certain property owners and interested parties as well as a notice posted on the property (informing interested persons of the time and place of the hearing and inviting them to appear),[137] and (4) a determination made by the Planning Commission based on the recommendations of the staff report and on testimony from the applicant and the public at the public hearing which may "condition" the use by imposing operational conditions aimed at mitigating neighborhood concerns (hours of operation, security, noise controls) as well as other conditions that may be required by the planning ordinance or building code, such as sufficient parking or landscaping and sign controls.[138] As with rural winery use permits, either the applicant or members of the public may appeal the Planning Commission's determination to the elected governing body, which is the Board of Supervisors in San Francisco.[139]

In 2020, voters in San Francisco approved Proposition H, the "Save Our Small Business Initiative," which ostensibly shifts approvals for many small business uses from a CUP authorization to an over-the-counter administrative approval and reduces other hurdles faced by small businesses operating in San Francisco both during and after the pandemic. The information and Legislative Text are available at https://sfplanning.org/save-our-small-businesses-initiative#permit-anchor-0 (last accessed October 25, 2022). Proposition H does not obviate the need for CUPs for all alcohol businesses; however, it could provide relief to new businesses depending on the exact location of the premises in the City.

In some jurisdictions, the CUP process, even for an application that is not protested, can take up to a year, although there may be provisions for shortening the process by payment of an expediting fee.[140] Persons wishing to establish a new business may apply for a liquor license before any necessary CUP is obtained, but the license cannot issue until the use permit is approved.

Public Convenience or Necessity. Additionally, the ABC Act itself restricts the ABC's ability to approve a new retail alcoholic beverage business in a particular area. The ABC is required to deny a license application if issuance "would tend to create a law enforcement problem" or "result in or add to an undue concentration of licenses."[141] An area of undue concentration is defined as (1) a crime-reporting district where the number of reported crimes is 20 percent greater than the average of all crime-reporting districts of the local law enforcement

---

136. *Id.* §303.

137. *Id.* §333.

138. S.F. Planning Dep't, Application Packet for Conditional Use Authorization (May 20, 2021), *available at* https://sfplanning.org/sites/default/files/forms/CUA_SupplementalApplication.pdf (last accessed August 19, 2022).

139. City and County of S.F., Cal., Mun. Code, Planning Code §308.1 (2022).

140. *See, e.g.*, City of L.A., Cal., Mun. Code §19.01(R) (2022).

141. Cal. Bus. & Prof. Code §23958 (2021).

agency, or (2) a census tract with a ratio of off-sale or on-sale retail licenses to the population in that census tract that exceeds the ratio of off-sale or on-sale retail licenses to the population in the county as a whole.[142]

Census tracts are small, relatively permanent statistical subdivisions of a county or statistically equivalent entities that can be updated by local participants prior to each census. The primary purpose of census tracts is to provide a stable set of geographic units for the presentation of statistical data.[143] The boundaries normally are based on visible features but may follow the government's jurisdictional boundaries or other non-physical features. They never cross county lines. Designed to be relatively homogeneous units with respect to population characteristics, economic status, and living conditions, census tracts average about 4,000 inhabitants but may have as few as 1,200 or as many as 8,000 inhabitants.[144] Census tracts with predominantly commercial zoning and fewer residents tend to be "over-concentrated" because of zoning policies that encourage business development outside residential areas.

If an undue concentration exists and the application is for a restaurant or a hotel, the ABC can issue the license if the applicant presents a simple letter describing its planned operations, including the type of food it intends to serve and the clientele it hopes to reach, and showing how the public convenience or necessity (PCN) would be served by the issuance of the liquor license. The burden is on the applicant to make a showing of PCN, but typically for new restaurants and hotels, if the police and the neighbors do not object, the ABC will act positively on the applicant's letter describing the proposed operations, the number of jobs created, perhaps the particular food philosophy or specific food that will be served, and the sales tax revenues to be generated for the local jurisdiction.

For bars (without meal service) and liquor stores, the governing body or its designee must make a determination within 90 days of notification of a completed application that PCN would be served by the license issuance.[145] There are no specific statutory standards to guide the governing body in this determination. Again, the applicant has the burden of establishing PCN.

In some jurisdictions, the governing body has designated the planning commission or the police department to make the PCN finding. In some jurisdictions, notice and a public hearing are not required, and the determination is made by a zoning administrator or a police representative. When the planning commission has been designated, if a CUP is required, findings from the conditional use hearing can include a determination that PCN would be served by the issuance of the ABC license. In San Francisco, the board of supervisors has not delegated such responsibility. The board asks the Police Department (Alcohol

---

142. *Id.* §23958.4(a).

143. U.S. Census Bureau, Census Tracts , *available at* https://www.census.gov/programs-surveys/geography/about/glossary.html#par_textimage_13 (last accessed August 19, 2022).

144. *Id.*

145. If the governing body does not make the determination within 90 days, the ABC may still issue the license if the applicant shows that the public convenience or necessity would be served. Cal. Bus. & Prof. Code §23958.4(b) (2021).

Liaison Unit) and the Planning Department to make findings of PCN, but all such requests are first heard in committee (City Operations and Neighborhood Services) and then by the full board. Applicants and those opposed to the issuance of the license may appear at the committee hearing and at the full board hearing. In San Francisco, determinations of PCN may be issued with conditions on operations if so requested by the Planning Department or the Police Department.[146]

In other local jurisdictions, different public bodies are involved in issuing the use permit and making the public convenience or necessity finding, so it is not possible to combine the two functions or even obtain them at the same time.

ABC Notifications: Mailing, Posting, and Publication. Anyone planning to open a new ABC-licensed business, change the ownership, or move an existing business to a new location must give notice to the public and to local officials in certain ways. For example, when an application is filed with the ABC for a retail license at a location that is not currently licensed or is not currently licensed with the same type of license, the applicant must mail a Notice of Intention to Sell Alcoholic Beverages to all residential addresses within 500 feet of the new premises.[147] If the city or county provides free lists of names and addresses, the applicant also must mail the notice to all owners of property within 500 feet, whether or not they reside on the premises.[148] A large poster announcing the applicant's intention to engage in the sale of alcoholic beverages is posted near the entrance to the premises for 30 days,[149] and a notice is published in a local newspaper of general circulation.[150] In addition, upon receipt of the application, the ABC mails a notice of the application to the sheriff, chief of police, and district attorney of the locality in which the premises are situated; to the city or county planning director, as appropriate; to the county board of supervisors if the premises are in an unincorporated area; and to the city council or other governing body if the premises are in an incorporated area. The public officials have up to 30 days to respond and can request an additional 20 days if they are preparing a protest or proposing conditions to be placed on the license.[151]

Neighborhood Groups. In some local jurisdictions, both the licensing and conditional use approval processes include a requirement that the applicant meet with neighborhood groups and obtain their approval of the proposed operations. Even if there is no formal process for involving them, neighborhood groups, if they exist, can be a powerful force for organizing the neighborhood to support or protest

---

146. *See* Public Convenience and Necessity Determinations, City and County of San Francisco, *available at* https://sfbos.org/sites/default/files/PC_or_N_Request_Fact_Sheet.pdf (last accessed August 28, 2022).

147. Cal. Bus. & Prof. Code §23985.5(a) (2021).

148. *Id.* §23985.5(b).

149. *Id.* §23985; Cal. Code Regs. tit. 4, §109 (2022).

150. Cal. Bus. & Prof. Code §23986(a) (2021).

151. *Id.* §23987.

a liquor license application. Engaging with these groups early is recommended to help ensure the success of a project.

Protests and Protest Hearings. Any person—not just public officials, residential neighbors, and property owners who receive the public notices—can protest the issuance of a license to the new business by lodging a written protest with the ABC within 30 days of the license posting or mailing, whichever is later.[152] While the ABC can reject a protest as "false, vexatious, frivolous, or invalid or unreasonable, or without reasonable or probable cause,"[153] in practice it rarely does. Once any protests are accepted, the ABC investigator responsible for the application conducts an investigation, interviews the protestors, proposes possible measures to mitigate the objections, and recommends either denial or issuance, typically with conditions aimed at addressing the protestors' concerns.[154]

After the investigation is complete, if the ABC is recommending license issuance, with or without conditions, it mails a notice to every protestor with information about the conditions and its recommendation.[155] If it is recommending issuance in spite of a protest by a public agency that received notice by post of the application, the ABC also must provide that agency with a written notice of its determination, including the reasons for the recommendation to issue the license.[156] Persons who have protested the issuance of the license, including any public agency protestors, may withdraw their protests if they are satisfied that the conditions imposed address their concerns. Again, in practice, the ABC rarely if ever issues a recommendation for issuance when a public agency, particularly the police department or sheriff, has objected to the issuance. More commonly, if the decision is to recommend issuance, the ABC and the police will have agreed upon conditions in advance, and the public agency will have withdrawn its protest.

Hearings in front of an administrative law judge may be held on valid protests, and the protestor must attend. The judge will issue a proposed decision (which is a ruling) for review by the ABC Director, and ABC may adopt or reject the proposed decision. After a decision, either party may appeal the decision to the ABC Appeals Board. The ABC Appeals Board decision can then be appealed to the State Courts of Appeal and to the State Supreme Court.[157]

At the time of this writing, ABC is considering updated guidelines or regulations for protest procedures, but they have not yet been proposed. The delays involved with protests, including scheduling a hearing, plus the additional time required for any appeals from the administrative law judge's ruling, can add

152. *Id.* §24013(a).

153. *Id.* §24013(b).

154. *Id.* §23800. *See also* information available on ABC's website regarding the protest process, *available at* https://www.abc.ca.gov/information-regarding-alcoholic-beverage-license-applications-and-protests/ (last accessed August 19, 2022).

155. Cal. Bus. & Prof. Code §§24015(a) (2021).

156. *Id.* §24013(b)(1).

157. *See* information available on ABC's website regarding the protest process, *available at* https://www.abc.ca.gov/information-regarding-alcoholic-beverage-license-applications-and-protests/ (last accessed August 19, 2022).

significantly to the time it takes for ABC to process an application. It may be possible for the applicant to obtain an interim permit while waiting for the hearing,[158] but some applicants will not want to expend the money to start the business or make tenant improvements if there is a chance that the protest hearing will result in denial of the license or will impose conditions that would make the operations uneconomical.

ABC- and Police-Imposed Conditions. Even if no protests are filed against the issuance of a license by the neighbors or other interested citizens, the ABC and the police department are allowed separate and independent grounds for imposing "reasonable" conditions by the ABC Act in certain situations.[159] Significantly, applying for a license for an operation that will be located within 100 feet of a residence is grounds for denial.[160] In an urban setting, many if not most commercial properties are within 100 feet of residential properties. Further, the ABC can deny a license if issuance would tend to create a law enforcement problem.[161] Conditions may cover any matter relating to privileges to be exercised under the license, the personal qualifications of the licensee, the conduct of the business or the condition of the premises which will protect public welfare and morals.[162] The ABC and the local police often work together to impose "standard" conditions for a city in an effort to mitigate such law enforcement problems. These conditions can include restrictions on hours of operations, on sales of single bottles, and on noise, signs, and lighting. Because the language is "standard," ABC does not typically engage in negotiations regarding language for conditions, despite the fact that the conditions may be vague, thus making them difficult to enforce. Examples of standard conditions imposed on liquor stores in urban areas include the following:

(1) Sales of alcoholic beverages shall be permitted only between the hours of 7:00 a.m. and 12:00 a.m. (midnight) each day of the week.
(2) Petitioner(s) shall actively monitor the area under their control in an effort to prevent loitering of persons on any property adjacent to the licensed premises as depicted on the most recently certified ABC-253.
(3) Wine shall not be sold in bottles or containers smaller than 350 milliliters.

For bars and restaurants, examples of typical conditions include:

(1) No noise shall be audible beyond the area under the control of the licensee as depicted on the most recently certified ABC-257.
(2) The licensee shall not permit its patrons or the general public to loiter or congregate on the sidewalks adjacent to the licensed premises.

---

158. Cal. Bus. & Prof. Code §24044.5 (2021).
159. *Id.* §23800(a).
160. Cal. Code Regs. tit. 4, §61.4(a) (2021).
161. Cal. Bus. & Prof. Code §23958 (2021).
162. *Id.* §23801.

(3) Petitioner shall provide sufficient security personnel who shall be readily identifiable as premises' security personnel to facilitate the orderly conduct of patrons whenever premises is providing entertainment.

These conditions track very closely restrictions proposed in a publication titled "How to Use Local Regulatory and Land Use Powers to Prevent Underage Drinking."[163] This publication proposes restricting the number and location of commercial alcohol outlets, keeping them away from schools and other youth facilities, and restricting the hours of operation, container sizes, and types of products available. Query whether the imposition of these conditions actually results in a decrease in underage drinking or drinking in general, or an increase in overall public safety. As discussed more fully in Chapter 9, jurisdictions throughout California and elsewhere in the country impose virtually identical conditions on liquor outlets in the belief that they are effective.

Once imposed, it can be difficult to change conditions. Similar to CUPs, ABC conditions are imposed on successor operators at the same premises and can only be removed upon petition to ABC (for a fee) showing that the grounds for the conditions no longer exist. ABC must also consult with the local governing body regarding the removal or modification of conditions.[164]

Entertainment Commission. In addition to CUPs, other local operational restrictions or requirements may apply. For example, the San Francisco Entertainment Commission was established to regulate, promote, and enhance the field of entertainment in San Francisco and issues permits for events and brick and mortar businesses. The seven-member commission has the power to gather, accept, and review information and to conduct hearings for entertainment-related permit applications, including live performances and extended hours operations.[165] The applications are considered in a hearing at which members of the public may voice their support or opposition. The Commission may issue one or both permits with Commission-drafted conditions on operations, including conditions for noise control, patron supervision, and security. The police may also contribute conditions, and if the business requires a CUP, those conditions will be imposed as well. There is no requirement that only one set of conditions be imposed by only one agency. Typically, the police, ABC, and Entertainment Commission will attempt to avoid imposing conflicting conditions on a business. More stringent requirements are usually the result of escalating protests, particularly involving clubs and other entertainment venues, as the applications move through the

---

163. James F. Mosher & Bob Reynolds, How to Use Local Regulatory and Land Use Powers to Prevent Underage Drinking, Pacific Institute for Research and Evaluation (January 2000, revised August 2013), *available at* https://web.archive.org/web/20150919212207/http://www.udetc.org/documents/LocalRegulLandUse.pdf (last accessed August 28, 2022). *See also* Chapter 9, *infra.*

164. Cal. Bus. & Prof. Code §23803 (2021).

165. City and County of S.F., Cal., Mun. Code, Admin. Code §§90.3(a), 90.4(a) (2021). *See also* https://sf.gov/departments/city-administrator/entertainment-commission (last accessed August 19, 2022).

Planning Commission to the ABC protest procedures to the Entertainment Commission hearing.

Entertainment Zones. Not all land use controls focus on prohibiting or regulating urban bars and liquor stores. Some jurisdictions have established particular areas of a city that are dedicated to restaurants, music clubs, bars, sports arenas, and other entertainment venues. Entertainment zones include organized redevelopment projects such as LA Live, San Diego's Gaslamp District, and other urban areas "occupying the margins of downtowns in former commercial and industrial areas, underutilized retail corridors or underdeveloped waterfronts."[166] The French Quarter in New Orleans is one of the oldest entertainment zones. For older, more established entertainment zones such as the French Quarter, the interface (and interference) with residential neighbors may be less contentious, but in areas where the proliferation of clubs and bars is relatively new and the established residents must adapt to late-night hours, crowds, and noise in previously quiet areas, community opposition can be substantial.

Summary: California's Controls on New Establishments. Although a new business rarely requires a conditional use permit, public convenience or necessity finding, *and* an entertainment permit, a bar or club without food and with entertainment will require the latter two and may also face neighbor protests to the issuance of the liquor license and entertainment permit. If persons or groups are determined to prevent or restrict the operation of a new urban bar or liquor store, they have many formal opportunities to object and appeal. In addition to the formal opportunities to protest, neighborhood groups opposing a particular licensed business can apply pressure on the individual members of the board of supervisors and the police personnel responsible for the neighborhood. This array of opportunities can result in substantial delays for the developer of a new bar or restaurant, particularly one that does not want to incur costs until it becomes clear that the license will be issued. Balancing the competing interests of nightlife businesses and city dwellers is often a complex dance.

2. CONTROLS ON EXISTING BUSINESSES IN CALIFORNIA

Although the applicant proprietor of a bar or liquor store may have satisfied all the requirements for beginning a licensed business and dealt with any protests, resulting in the issuance of all licenses and permits necessary to commence operations, the applicant may still face land use restrictions on the business during its ongoing operations. In addition to an ABC action to close a disorderly house or impose conditions on a business that has violated the ABC Act, several jurisdictions have enacted alcohol-specific ordinances that examine the operations

---

166. Daniel Campo & Brent D. Ryan, The Entertainment Zone: Unplanned Nightlife and the Revitalization of the American Downtown, 13 J. Urb. Design, 291, 292 (October 2008).

of existing businesses and provide the community with options to close or restrict those operations to mitigate any disturbances they may cause.

a. Non-Conforming Uses

Depending on their age and when their zoning ordinances were adopted, many liquor stores and bars will not conform to the current requirements of a zoning ordinance, either because the use is not permitted under the new ordinance or because a CUP is now required. These are "grandfathered" or "non-conforming" uses. Generally, as long as the use continues without change or interruption, it will be allowed to continue in spite of its non-compliance with current ordinances. However, if there is a change of ownership, a transfer of the license for any reason, an interruption in the operation of the business, or a material change in operations (for example, from a restaurant to a bar, from a bar to a club with entertainment, or from a beer and wine liquor store to a beer, wine, and spirits store), the requirement for a use permit modification may be triggered.

In addition, the ABC Act allows the ABC to impose "reasonable" conditions on an existing business, whether it is a non-conforming use or not, upon a transfer of 50 percent or more of the ownership of a licensed entity[167] or where any physical changes or alterations are made to the premises that materially or substantially alter the premises of the usage.[168] The conditions may be based on the ABC's own investigation, or they may be requested by the local governing body or its designated officer or agency, such as the police department, within 40 days of the filing of an application to transfer the license. The conditions imposed could substantially reduce the value of the business being transferred because, as noted above, they can significantly impact the operating permissions of the premises.[169]

b. Disorderly House Action

The ABC Act provides that keeping a disorderly house or allowing a disorderly house to exist is a misdemeanor and can subject the liquor license to revocation. A disorderly house is defined as a "place in which people abide or to which people resort, to the disturbance of the neighborhood, or … for purposes which are injurious to the public morals, health, convenience, or safety."[170] Any liquor store or bar that is characterized by loitering, noise, or petty crimes, or that exists in a neighborhood in which such behaviors cause more police action than other parts of the city, is at risk for a revocation action against its license. A substantial number of police calls to the vicinity, even if not pertaining to the liquor store or bar itself, can be grounds for a revocation action against the license on the grounds that the business is creating a police problem, even if the problem is with the neighborhood generally. Historical perceptions of neighborhoods experiencing persistent poverty

167. Cal. Bus. & Prof. Code §23800(e)(1) (2021).
168. *Id.* §23800(g).
169. *Id.* §23801.
170. *Id.* §25601.

suggested that if the liquor outlets were closed or reduced in number, issues of crime, drunkenness, loitering, noise, and perhaps even poverty would be eliminated. As a result, licensees in these neighborhoods have experienced increased enforcement activity and conditions placed on licenses. Typical conditions on convenience store operations in such neighborhoods require the proprietor to prevent loitering and noise, remove graffiti and trash, and not be a magnet for criminal activity. The responsibility for solving problems caused by systemic racism, such as unemployment, alcohol abuse, crime, violence—even graffiti, loitering, and litter—may impose an impossible burden on a neighborhood grocery and liquor store and raise important questions about social equity, policing, and fairness.

c. Deemed Approved Ordinances

Several cities in California, including San Francisco, have adopted "deemed approved ordinances" (DAOs) to regulate alcohol sales by imposing a uniform set of conditions on premises that were permitted, conditionally permitted, or nonconforming before the adoption of the DAO, or that are permitted or conditionally permitted after adoption. In San Francisco, a DAO was adopted in 2006[171] and is aimed at ensuring that liquor store sales occur in a manner that protects the health, safety, and welfare of San Francisco residents. The San Francisco Department of Public Health, the San Francisco Police Department, City Attorneys Office, and the San Francisco Tax Collector's Office work together to implement the DAO.[172]

Under San Francisco's DAO, a use is "Deemed Approved" if it conforms to all of the "Deemed Approved Performance Standards," which include: (1) not participating in illegal activities, (2) not causing repeated nuisance activities, (3) keeping advertising or signs at not more than 33 percent of the total square footage of window and door space and allowing clear sight lines from the exterior to the interior for law enforcement personnel (unless physical limitations prevent this), and (4) not resulting in violations to any local, state, or federal regulation, ordinance, or statute. A copy of these "Performance Standards" must be posted at the entrance of the premises.[173]

The "repeated nuisance activities" described in the San Francisco ordinance also can be evidence of, and grounds for, eliminating a disorderly house. But one of the reasons San Francisco and other cities have adopted DAOs is that an alleged violation of the DAO can be prosecuted at the city level under the local land use laws, without having to rely on the ABC to take action against the license or a criminal court to find the business owner guilty of a disorderly house

---

171. City and County of S.F., Cal., Mun. Code, Admin. Code Chapter 26 (2022).

172. *See* San Francisco Department of Public Health Deemed Approved Uses Ordinance Overview available at https://www.sfdph.org/dph/comupg/oprograms/CHEP/alcoholOrdInfo/DAO.asp (last accessed August 19, 2022).

173. City and County of S.F., Cal., Mun. Code, Admin. Code §26.12 (2022).

misdemeanor.[174] As with conditions on licensee operations imposed by ABC or local law enforcement, whether DAOs achieve their intended goals is subject to debate.

C. CONCLUSION

Land use clearly affects the wine business in more ways than even an industry veteran might imagine. From the establishment and operations of a rural winery to the location and activities of an urban retailer, land use laws delve into the nuts and bolts of these businesses. The adoption and implementation of land use laws involve many groups and many interests. Complying with the laws is both time-consuming and complicated, but often land use policy will determine whether a rural winery or an urban bar can be started and can succeed.

---

174. *Id.* §26.13.

CHAPTER 8

THE IMPACT OF CLIMATE CHANGE ON WINERIES AND VINEYARDS: MITIGATION, ADAPTATION, AND PREVENTION

Katie Jackson, Carol Kingery Ritter, and Viviann Stapp

Of the centuries of recorded wine production, the wine grape farmer's calendar has always been unpredictable: drought, pests, hail, heavy rain, frost, and fire are among the constant variables that threaten a farmer's invested time and finances each harvest. In recent years, however, the risks and uncertainty have become greater, with fires burning bigger, hotter, and more frequently. Although winegrowers have learned in recent years that vineyards can be good firebreaks, they have also learned that a fire hundreds of miles away can have a devastating impact on a harvest. Smoke from fires can drift, resulting in a near or total loss of an impacted region's particular vintage. The frequency and intensity of these fires, along with historic drought, have been attributed to climate change, a long-term shift in temperature and weather patterns that can be naturally occurring, but are now accelerated due to human activities from the past two centuries from the burning and release of hydrocarbons.[1]

With detailed records stretching back for some regions over 900 years, winegrowers have been at the forefront of noticing the effects of climate change in their vineyards. On the West Coast, for example, harvest picks are getting called

1. United Nations, What Is Climate Change, https://www.un.org/en/climatechange/what-is-climate-change (accessed July 2, 2022).

earlier, in part due to warming weather and earlier ripening,[2] but also to beat the fires that are typically seen during the Northern hemisphere's harvest months of September and October. Meanwhile, winegrowers are exploring new areas typically considered inhospitable or too cold for grape growing.

This chapter captures a moment in time as to what winegrowers and wineries are currently seeing and what they are doing to address the short-, medium-, and long-term impacts of climate change. It is by no means exhaustive of all the problems experienced or the potential solutions being explored. This chapter is in some respects limited to the experiences of wineries in Napa and Sonoma Counties, where the authors reside, but also because many of the fire and smoke impacts have hit this region more dramatically and frequently than others in the United States. We are hopeful that the wine industry's creativity, resilience, and cooperation will lead to better adaptations to climate change and result in long-term solutions for a better planet.

A. MITIGATION

Many wineries have taken steps to reduce the severity of predicted climate change impacts and, in some cases, accommodate them. As an immediate issue, most winegrowers are confronted with potential smoke taint issues, fire preparedness, and reduced water resources from drier conditions in the Western United States.

1. SMOKE TAINT AND GRAPES

The success of the wine industry rests on the quality of an annual wine grape crop. Growers invest and toil for a year to produce one crop that will become a vintage. Because of the relative humidity of vineyards and limited amount of dry fuel for fires, vineyards are not often devastated by fire. Direct fire impacts, when they occur, are usually minimal—end posts burn and drip irrigation melts. But wildfire smoke originating from fires even hundreds of miles away can threaten a vintage. As of the writing of this chapter, growers and vintners have few effective tools to mitigate the adverse impacts of smoke exposure on grapes and are still learning how to predict the degree to which smoke exposure will impact wine quality.

Grape purchase agreements (GPAs), like all commercial contracts, balance risk between contracting parties. Prior to the explosion of wildfire in wine country,

2. Scientists in Europe studied historical harvest dates using data from Beaune in the Burgundy region of France. From the dataset compiled between 1354-2018, scientists noted that the harvest date traditionally fell after September 28 from 1354 to 1987, and that harvests between 1988 through 2018 began 13 days earlier. Moreover, hot and dry years were typically outliers in the years 1354 to 1987 but have become the norm since 1988. T. Labbé, C. Pfister, S. Brönnimann, D. Rousseau, J. Franke, and B. Bois, The longest homogeneous series of grape harvest dates, Beaune 1354–2018, and its significance for the understanding of past and present climate, Clim. Past, 15, 1485–1501, 2019, https://doi.org/10.5194/cp-15-1485-2019 (accessed August 7, 2022).

crop quality risks were largely limited to grape defects that could be clearly identified in the vineyard or sorted on the crush pad. Most GPAs provide tolerances for grape defects and remedies for addressing defects in excess of tolerance. Absent a negotiated provision in the GPA or an implied provision such as the parties' past practices or generally accepted norms in the industry, the grower would hold the risk of crop damage or loss and is the only party with the ability to insure a crop against catastrophic loss through the federal crop insurance program managed by the USDA Risk Management Agency (RMA). The pressing climate change challenge of wildfires is that smoke exposure risks and defects cannot be managed, measured, and allocated like other crop risks and can be catastrophic, putting entire crops and vintages at risk. As a result, growers and vintners have found themselves at odds over a risk negotiation that is both extreme in scope and evolving.

Although wildfire had impacted California wine grape crops prior to and during the early 2000s, the 2017 wildfires in Napa and Sonoma Counties were the first to bring natural disaster-level wildfire impacts to the industry.[3] On the afternoon of Sunday, October 8, 2017, warm winds picked up north of the San Francisco Bay. Harvest was well underway, and many wineries had scheduled their final red grapes picks for the upcoming weeks. But by 10:30 PM that evening, fire was racing down the slopes of Atlas Peak. Within a few hours, the Tubbs Fire and the Partrick Fire had erupted, and Napa Valley was nearly surrounded by fire. Thousands were evacuating the Napa Valley while the greatest life and safety threat was barreling in on the population in and around Santa Rosa.

The 2017 wildfires caught the region by surprise, and given the date late into the harvest season, wineries and growers were under intense time pressure to manage harvest activities and grape inspection, all while keeping employees safe from fire and smoke risks and navigating access to vineyards and wineries located in evacuation zones.[4] Some lucky wineries in the hillsides had generators; others were scrambling to manage fermentations without power or in between outages. Under these trying circumstances, many wineries accepted and paid for smoke-exposed fruit and found that the fruit quality was not suitable for making wine consistent with the quality of prior vintages. Over the following months, and without public comment, many wineries destroyed their 2017 red wines.

From the 2017 learnings, many wineries reconsidered their GPAs and contractual guidance on smoke exposure and the testing processes and protocols that should be deployed as tools to analyze impact. Smoke testing is conducted in two primary forms: (a) whole cluster testing where clusters of grapes are analyzed for "free" guaiacol and 4-methylguaiacol (two of the primary indicators of smoke taint) that has not bound to grape sugars; and (b) wine testing where guaiacol and 4-methylguaiacol are measured in wine that has been fermented or micro-

---

3. The authors note that the Australian wine industry has been impacted by wildfires well before the issue arrived on our doorsteps in California, and that our industry's response has been aided by the research and learnings of our Australian counterparts.

4. Although not addressed in this chapter, legal issues concerning worker health and safety are another impact of wildfires that require industry consideration and adaptation.

fermented to capture "free" compounds and those broken away from sugars during primary fermentation.

Whole cluster testing was the methodology used by most wineries and growers during the 2017 fires, given the pressure to harvest an already mature crop as soon as possible. For most wineries, there was no time to micro-ferment grapes and test the resulting wine even though it was known that smoke taint characteristics would increase after sugar bonds broke during fermentation and would be exacerbated by barrel and bottle aging. After the 2017 harvest, many wineries modified their GPAs to include pre-harvest testing covenants specifically providing for whole cluster testing if grapes were exposed to wildfire smoke in the growing season. The negotiation of these GPA provisions required winery and grower to agree upon a level of "free" guaiacol in the grapes at which the winery would have the right to reject fruit as having reached unacceptable levels of smoke taint characteristics. Without any accepted industry standards for guaiacol levels in specific varietals,[5] and depending on the timing of smoke exposure in grape sugar development and the type of smoke in the vineyard, these negotiations strained grower and vintner relationships at a time when both were experiencing acute impacts on their businesses.

In 2018, while the industry was still regrouping after the 2017 wildfires, large early harvest season fires originating in Mendocino County brought smoke to Napa and Sonoma Counties. With more time before harvest, many wineries micro-fermented small batches of grape clusters and tested the resulting juice to better evaluate the actual impact of smoke exposure on the grapes. Some growers objected to this testing process because they lacked transparency into the micro-fermentation methodology and because the California grape grower and winemaking industry groups had not developed a uniformly recognized industry standard for micro-fermentation testing. As a result, growers claimed that smoke-related grape rejections were actually a red herring for wineries correcting supply in a supply glut.[6]

After a brief respite in 2019, the industry was tested by both early and late season smoke events in 2020. Three massive fires, and a fourth smaller but also devastating fire, raged in Northern California as a result of lightning storms in mid-August 2020. The fires covered almost 3,000 square miles—an area larger than Delaware. The breadth of these fires created an enormous demand for smoke testing. Even with technicians working around the clock, laboratories could not keep up with the demand. On September 10, Napa Valley's go-to laboratory was estimating that testing results for samples delivered that day would be ready on October 20.

---

5. Certain grape varietals have naturally high levels of guaiacol, e.g., Petit Verdot.

6. In fact, many wineries followed the small-lot fermentation method advocated by the Australian Wine Research Institute, but in-house fermentations and, in some cases, the use of in-house testing equipment increased grower mistrust. The Australian Wine Research Institute, Fact Sheet Winemaking, January 2021, https://www.awri.com.au/wp-content/uploads /small_lot_ fermentation_method.pdf (accessed August 28, 2022).

Testing delays, which were about to get worse, caused significant problems for wineries and growers. Wineries could not evaluate smoke impacts in real time to make informed grape harvest and acceptance decisions. And, further, even if a winery received test results prior to harvest, smoke exposure was ongoing in certain vineyards past the date that original grape samples were picked. For growers, the problem was more severe and immediate. Growers across the state watched their entire grape crop mature on the vine without definitive answers from wineries regarding a pick and delivery date or rejection of the grapes.

The situation got worse when the Glass Fire started burning on September 26. The Glass Fire originated in the northeast of the Napa Valley AVA, but after creating its own weather, fire winds picked up burning embers and blew them across the Napa Valley to the west and into Sonoma County. At this point in the 2020 growing season, lacking qualitative data concerning grape quality, and faced with tons of wine grapes that were maturing or past maturity, growers and wineries had few good choices. Wineries did not want to unnecessarily give up on the 2020 vintage, but if growers harvested their crop without knowing whether the fruit would ultimately be accepted, they risked voiding crop insurance coverage or simply incurring additional farming costs without any guarantee of revenue to cover the expense.

At this time, a viable crop insurance claim required rejection of the crop by the grape purchaser, laboratory analysis of the crop showing smoke taint, and a crop insurance adjuster's evaluation of the size of the rejected crop in the vineyard. The longer winery and grower were delayed in determining whether smoke taint was present, the lighter the tonnage as a result of desiccation, which further reduced the crop insurance claim. Under the best circumstances, a crop insurance claim will not provide growers the revenue they would receive if the GPAs were performed and fruit accepted. After a year of investment and work, growers were watching their revenue shrink with each day of delay.

In 2020, the RMA responded to the struggling wine industry and modified their claim guidance to allow growers to preserve their crop insurance claims after harvest if grape samples were taken for testing on the day of harvest and third-party weigh tags provided the grape tonnage to be covered by the claim. This modification allowed wineries that wanted to evaluate the fruit after fermentation, and growers who wanted to take a chance on their GPAs, to bring fruit into the winery for evaluation before a rejection or acceptance determination was made.

The strain of the 2020 harvest gave the industry an in-winery option for evaluating smoke impacts while preserving grape grower insurance claims, but wildfire challenges are far from resolved. Grower and vintner industry groups have not agreed on phenol levels in grapes or micro-fermented wine that indicate the presence of smoke taint characteristics; such an agreement may never be reached given the variability in wine grape varietals, wine quality requirements, and winemaking styles, among other complications. As technology advances, the industry will be able to more accurately and readily test important smoke-related phenols other than guaiacol and 4-methylguaiacol, such as cresols and syringol. As the industry has learned from each wildfire event in the vintages discussed here, technology may outpace the industry stakeholders' ability to agree on what the advances mean as far as allocating the risks of wildfire smoke.

The evolution of testing and diagnosis has been central to the wildfire and wine discussion as smoke impacts are complex and hidden from view, but the industry is working to manage the wildfire threat in other ways. Industry-leading institutions such as the University of California-Davis, Washington State University, and the University of Oregon are involved in the innovation and testing of barrier products to safely protect grapes from absorbing smoke phenols while not impacting fruit quality and allowing the uptake of good phenols that result in the diversity of the beautiful wines we love to drink. California counties are investing deeply in early detection technology to identify wildfires in remote areas, growing and mobilizing air support to create firebreaks that cannot be established with ground resources and reducing wildfire fuels but, for the wine industry, the life and safety concern of wildfire is not the only threat. To prevail against wildfire impacts, the wine industry must be able to consistently deliver a quality product to consumers. Quality depends on accurately evaluating smoke exposure impacts and, ultimately, on protecting grapes from the smoke that will surround them.

2. WILDFIRE PREPARATION

Although vineyards make good firebreaks, the toll of fire on wineries and vineyards in recent years has been tremendous. In the 2020 fires alone, the California wine industry is expected to lose $3.7 billion in total revenue through 2023 due to destroyed property, lost vintages, and sales from closed tasting rooms.[7]

Many vintners and winegrowers have joined efforts to fight fire directly. It is no longer uncommon to see wine industry owners and employees volunteering as firefighters, training for fire defense and landscape hardening with private contractors, or learning to cut firebreaks and extinguish spot fires. Wineries are investing in fire protection equipment, fire trucks, water storage tanks, and bulldozers. These actions are being undertaken to protect properties from reigniting after a fire has swept through an area and the firefighters have left.[8]

Despite the California Department of Forestry and Fire Protection (CAL FIRE)'s concern about these private firefighting efforts, many insurance companies now expect this type of preparation in extending fire insurance policies,

---

7. Calculated by industry analyst Jon Moramarco of the consulting firm bw166 llc, and editor of Gomberg, Fredrikson & Associates. For example, based on the USDA Grape Crush Reports, the fires in 2020 resulted in a nearly 50% reduction in the wine grape crop value in Napa County (from $906.1 million in 2019 versus $440.3 million in 2020) and Sonoma County (from $645.4 million in 2019 down to $347.7 million in 2020). Eric Schwartzman, Wine Country Fires Vindicate Climate Fears, Wine-Searcher.com, June 3, 2022.

8. Esther Mobley, $2 million helicopters and vintage fire trucks: How frustrated Napa residents are taking wildfire protection into their own hands, S.F. Chronicle, August 4, 2021, https://www.sfchronicle.com/food/wine/article/2-million-helicopters-and-vintage-fire-trucks-16365020.php (accessed July 4, 2022) (recounting efforts by wineries like Silver Oak and Castello di Amorosa to train staffers to put out spot fires and use equipment and fire engines in the event of a fire).

many of which still leave property owners underinsured relative to the cost of rebuilding. Napa Valley, which includes the most expensive vineyard land per acre in the U.S., has taken it upon itself to raise funds and develop a comprehensive action plan to reduce fire risk. To assist the wine industry with its firefighting and insurance concerns, Napa County launched in 2021 a multi-year Community Wildfire Protection Plan (CWPP) spearheaded by Napa Communities Firewise Foundation. Funded in large part by a CAL FIRE Climate Change Investment Fund Fire Prevention Grant, the CWPP was recently awarded $6.4 million in funding to be allocated over five years and potentially another $35 million to address fuels reduction, creation of 115 new fuel breaks, maintenance of existing fuel breaks, education, wildfire response support, and critical infrastructure protection.[9] This kind of public-private partnership seems likely to become more common for the wine industry in other fire-prone regions.

Another area of public-private cooperation that is growing in prominence is controlled burning. Controlled burns were legally authorized in California more than 40 years ago when they were signed into law by Governor Brown on July 16, 1980.[10] The California Legislature authorized CAL FIRE to partner with private landowners to use controlled burns through the Vegetation Management Program, which allows cost-sharing and the use of prescribed fire and mechanical methods to reduce fuels on non-federal lands. However, controlled burns were adopted sparingly by landowners and the public. Controlled burns are complicated to schedule and perform, and neighbors often complain about smoke, a blackened landscape, and fire risk. However, after catastrophic fires across California in 2017-2021, landowners and the public have quickly become much more accepting of controlled burns to reduce fuels and restore wildlands to native vegetation.

In 2021, the California Legislature further encouraged prescribed burns through passage of SB 332 (Dodd), to provide immunity from civil liability to burn bosses who are otherwise following an approved burn plan and meet specified conditions. The bill retains civil liability for burn bosses who are grossly negligent during a prescribed burn but reflects the popular sentiment of most Californians today after witnessing consecutive historic fires, noting in its preamble California's inability to meet fuel management goals without the aid of private entities for prescribed burning.[11]

3. WATER SCARCITY AND DROUGHT MANAGEMENT

As of the time of this writing, California has been in its third year of drought and one of its worst since the 1970s. The January, February, and March period in

9. Napa County Community Wildfire Protection Plan, Prepared for Napa Communities Firewise Foundation, March 15, 2021, https://ncff-cwpp-dms-usa.hub.arcgis.com/documents/177b4d28ea304594b4120edcb60d2e2f/explore (accessed July 4, 2022).

10. Cal. Code Regs. Tit. 14 §1560 et seq.

11. Cal. Civil Code §3333.8(a):

> The Legislature finds and declares that in order to meet fuel management goals, the state must rely on private entities to engage in prescribed burning for public benefit.

2022 was the driest in over 100 years.[12] According to the State of California's Drought Action website, weather extremes brought on by climate change have reduced the California water supply.[13] In the Russian River watershed, which includes numerous vineyards in Mendocino and Sonoma counties, state regulators are in their second year of curtailing the riparian rights of ranchers, winegrowers, and other users to draw water from the Russian River and its tributaries.[14] Although some water users may have other sources of water in the form of reservoirs, springs, and wells that were built prior to the drought, winegrowers without such sources will confront a summer of dry farming, delivered water, aggressive fruit drop, or an abandoned crop when the other solutions are not technically or economically viable. The number of curtailed users could increase through the summer based on water usage and weather conditions as California subordinates junior water rights holders to those with more senior rights through California's longtime "first in time, first in right" system.

However, for the first time in California, and in a remarkable example of collective action to address climate change, this year riparian rights holders in one watershed agreed to a voluntary water sharing agreement approved by the California State Water Resources Control Board. This allows senior water rights holders in the Russian River watershed to share their supply with junior rights holders who might otherwise be subject to the state's curtailment orders.[15] The State Water Board approved the water sharing agreement after determining that it would not adversely impact water availability for non-signatories or result in an unreasonable impact on fish and wildlife.[16]

Farmers and city officials are also working together to transfer treated wastewater from municipalities to agricultural lands to irrigate crops for a negotiated fee. For example, in the Petaluma Gap and Carneros AVAs, farmers and cities constructed purple pipelines (purple lines) to convey water from municipal treatment systems to vineyards. This also helps cities, which frequently have an excess of treated wastewater and an inability to discharge the wastewater into rivers and other waterways in the summer months, when treated wastewater cannot be diluted easily.[17] Although the purple lines may seem like a win-win solution for vineyards and cities, especially in times of drought, farmers will need to develop creative ways to work around the potentially higher salt, potassium, and

---

12. State of California, California Drought Action, https://drought.ca.gov/ (accessed July 2, 2022).

13. *Ibid.*

14. Cal. Code Regs tit. 23 §877.2, 877.3.

15. Mary Callahan, State Water Board approves historic Russian River water sharing agreement, The Press Democrat, June 7, 2022, https://www.pressdemocrat.com/article/news/state-water-board-approves-historic-russian-river-water-sharing-agreement/?artslide=0 (accessed August 7, 2022).

16. Cal. Code Regs. Tit. 23 §878.2

17. Esther Mobley, Desperate for water, Wine Country grape growers build expensive pipelines to cities' recycled sewage, San Francisco Chronicle, April 27, 2022, https://www.sfchronicle.com/food/wine/article/Desperate-for-water-Sonoma-grape-farmers-build-17130682.php (accessed July 23, 2022).

heavy metal content of treated wastewater through soil amendments or more advanced filtration techniques to protect soil and vineyard health.

In addition to sharing water with one other, winegrowers are experimenting with ways to reduce water needs. Winegrowers are testing smart sensors and weather stations on or near the vines to decide when to irrigate. Winegrowers are also conducting trials on the duration and amount of water needed to yield best results, including whether a sustained but less frequent watering of vines is preferred over more frequent, shorter bursts of irrigation activity. These answers differ by vineyard and topography, suggesting that a heavy-handed regulatory approach that dictates time and frequency is counter-productive. Similarly, winegrowers have been debating the merits of till vs. no-till farming, deficit irrigation to stress vines so that water in the root zone available for uptake is less than the rate of plant transpiration,[18] the utility of maintaining a cover crop (which can compete for water resources but also maintains soil moisture for the benefit of grape vines), and the use of herbicides. The industry does not have conclusive results in hand for these farming methods, but the existence of these tests indicates that winegrowers are questioning traditional practices with an eye toward farming in ways that are more productive, drought-resistant, and climate-friendly.

Finally, winegrowers have been working with local authorities to regulate and recharge groundwater basins to avoid over-depletion of groundwater sources and impacts on surface streams. In 2014, the State of California passed the Sustainable Groundwater Management Act (SGMA), which established a framework by which local groundwater sustainability agencies (GSAs) would be responsible for developing and implementing groundwater sustainability plans (GSPs) to mitigate overdraft of groundwater basins within the next 20 years. In coordination with regional GSAs, Jackson Family Wines[19] is identifying opportunities to recharge groundwater through a voluntary resource management strategy called Flood-

18. Terry Prichard, Mark Battany, Rhonda Smith, Larry Schwankl, Irrigation Management of Winegrapes with a Limited Water Supply, UC Drought Management, University of California at Davis, https://ucmanagedrought.ucdavis.edu/PDF/WINEGRAPE%20DROUGHT%20LONG-1.pdf (accessed August 22, 2022).

19. Jackson Family Wines is a family-owned and operated wine company with headquarters in Sonoma County, California. Founded by Jess Jackson and Barbara Banke in 1982, Jackson Family Wines owns 40 wineries and vineyard properties across the winemaking regions of California, Oregon, Washington, France, Italy, Australia, Chile, and South Africa. In August 2021, Jackson Family Wines launched its Rooted for Good: Roadmap to 2030 climate action and corporate social responsibility initiative. This 10-year plan outlines the company's long-term goals to become climate positive by 2050, implement smart water management, adopt regenerative farming practices across 100 percent of its estate vineyards, and champion social responsibility and Diversity, Equity, and Inclusion (DE&I). These and previous sustainability efforts have been recognized by the wine industry. Jackson Family Wines received the 2022 Green Medal for Business Leadership, 2022 Business Intelligence Sustainability Leadership Award, 2020 Green Company of the Year Award by Drinks Business, Climate Leadership Award in 2020, and the EPA Green Power Leadership Awards in 2018, 2016, and 2011.

Managed Aquifer Recharge (Flood-MAR).[20] This strategy entails applying flood water from rainfall and using it for flood irrigation in vineyards in the winter months, when the vines are dormant, to replenish the groundwater basin without comprising vine health. Initial study results at a Jackson Family Wines pilot site indicate that the water table can be recharged by up to six inches per acre, which exceeds or is net of the pilot vineyard's typical three to six acre-inches of water per acre per year use.[21] The project's findings thus far are promising and may allow vineyards to help recharge aquifers in the wet years between drought years, or what climate scientists have been calling a "climate whiplash" from an increasingly intense drought-flood cycle. Groundwater recharge opportunities will be site-dependent, as some sites may be prone to saltwater intrusion.

B. ADAPTATION

Given that grape vines stay in place for 30 to 40 years, most wineries are committed to mitigation efforts to reduce the impacts of climate change, knowing that it is unrealistic, logistically and financially, to pick up stakes and grow elsewhere. However, wineries and regulators are being creative in adapting to climate change through trials and experimentation. We expect that some of these efforts will force regulations, wine labels, and marketing to adjust to these climate change adaptation efforts.

For instance, England, which was historically seen as too cold and inhospitable for growing wine grapes, has become a popular site for sparkling wine. Champagne houses have expanded their holdings into English vineyards.[22] Producers are also growing grapes further north and south than in the past, from Scandinavia to Patagonia.[23] Some winegrowers are even curious enough to experiment with growing vines in space.[24] Back on earth, growers are reorienting

---

20. California Department of Water Resources, Flood-Managed Aquifer Recharge (Flood-MAR), https://water.ca.gov/programs/all-programs/flood-mar#:~:text=%E2%80%9CFlood%2DMAR%E2%80%9D%20is%20an,%2C%20floodplains%2C%20and%20flood%20bypasses (accessed August 29, 2022).

21. Will Carruthers, (Re)Charging into the Future, Made Local Magazine, May/June 2019, https://madelocalmagazine.com/2019/05/recharging-into-the-future/ (accessed August 11, 2022).

22. Eric Asimov, How Climate Change Impacts Wine, The New York Times, October 14, 2019, https://www.nytimes.com/interactive/2019/10/14/dining/drinks/climate-change-wine.html (accessed July 4, 2022).

23. *Ibid.*

24. There was a recent study to grow 320 vines in zero gravity conditions on the International Space Station after 10-14 months and compare them to vines on Earth to determine how grape vines deal with stress and can adapt to changes brought on by climate change. Scientists noted increased resistance to mildew and phylloxera, and changes to growth rates, polyphenol content, and bacterial and fungi composition associated with the plants grown in space. The vines will be further studied by Space Cargo Unlimited, the private European group funding the research, to better understand the impact of zero gravity conditions on the vines and attendant wines produced from the grapes of the space vines. Eloise Feilden, Vines grown in space show greater resistance to climate change, The

the direction of their vines from orientations that maximize afternoon sun exposures (traditionally south-facing vineyards in the Northern Hemisphere, and north-facing vineyards in the Southern Hemisphere) to orientations that reduce sun exposure, in addition to planting higher-elevation vineyard sites.[25] Meanwhile, some winegrowers are looking at ways to reduce sun exposure through shade solutions in the vineyard, with some experimenting with clay "sunblock" for grapes and shade cloth.[26]

Vintners are also experimenting with different varietals in their wine regions. For instance, researchers see potential in late-ripening varieties like Syrah, Grenache, and Mourvèdre if winegrowing regions rise by two degrees. The noble, early-ripening varietals of Pinot Noir and Chardonnay will spread further north and south as climate warms.[27]

The Bordeaux and Bordeaux Supérieur AOC winemakers, who in the past have restricted Bordeaux wine grapes to the same six red grape varieties[28] and seven white varieties,[29] approved the addition of seven new grape varieties in 2019[30] to combat the effects of climate change. Although subject to the approval of France's national appellation authority, the Institut National des Appellations d'Origine (INAO), Bordeaux winemakers may potentially add up to 10 percent of a final blend or 5 percent of a producer's vineyard area except in St. Julien or Margaux.[31] For watchers of Bordeaux, this move was made uncharacteristically fast, especially for a wine region that has prided itself on closely hewing to tradition.

Similarly, climate change concerns have spurred another French wine region, Châteauneuf-du-Pape, to avail itself of a 1930s appellation rule to include more white varieties in red blends to reduce the amount of alcohol and increase acidity in its wines.[32] Winemakers in the United States will likely continue to experiment with more climate resistant grape varieties. However, unlike the French, who

---

Drinks Business, June 16, 2022, https://www.thedrinksbusiness.com/2022/06/vines-grown-in-space-show-greater-resistance-to-climate-change/ (accessed July 4, 2022).

25. *Ibid.*

26. Christopher Flavelle, Scorched, Parched and Now Uninsurable: Climate Change Hits Wine Country, The New York Times, July 18, 2021, https://www.nytimes.com/2021/07/18/climate/napa-wine-heat-hot-weather.html (accessed August 7, 2022).

27. University of British Columbia. Switching grape varieties can help save world's wine-growing regions, ScienceDaily, www.sciencedaily.com/releases/2020/01/200127164337.htm (accessed July 4, 2022).

28. Merlot, Cabernet Sauvignon, Cabernet France, Petit Verdot, Malbec, Carménère, and Petit Verdot.

29. Semillon, Sauvignon Blanc, Muscadelle, Colombard, Merlot Blanc, Sauvignon Gris, and Ugni Blanc.

30. The approved red wine varieties are Marselan, Touriga Nacional, and Arinarnoa, and the approved white varieties are Alvarinho, Petit Manseng, and Liliorila.

31. Chris Mercer, Bordeaux winemakers allow new grapes to fight climate change," Decanter, July 19, 2019, https://www.decanter.com/wine-news/bordeaux-new-wine-grapes-419730/ (accessed July 4, 2022).

32. Panos Kakviatos, Châteauneuf-du-Pape red wines to contain more white grapes, Decanter, July 1, 2019, https://www.decanter.com/wine-news/chateauneuf-du-pape-white-grapes-blend-419213/ (accessed July 10, 2022).

prescribe certain varietals for certain winegrowing regions, the United States allows for more flexibility and allows a single varietal to be listed on a wine label as long as 75 percent of the volume of the wine is made from that varietal.[33]

C. PREVENTION

Adaptation strategies will only go so far: To ensure its future, the wine industry will also need to decarbonize and curb climate change.[34] This belief has led to winery commitments to meet the goals of the Intergovernmental Panel on Climate Change (IPCC) to bring emissions to net zero by 2050. This will allow global temperature to stabilize and limit warming to 1.5°C (2.7°F).[35] This section details some of the collective efforts of wineries, trade associations, and wine regions to raise collective environmental consciousness to grow wines in a more environmentally friendly manner and become solutions to the climate crisis.

1. THE REGULATORY REGIME

As of the date of this writing, the United States has not legislated comprehensive carbon emissions reductions, ratified the Kyoto Protocol,[36] or developed a cap-and-trade system for carbon emissions.[37] However, through the Inflation Reduction Act of 2022, the United States recently passed legislation that will inject $370 billion into climate and energy programs to extend electrical vehicle tax credits, provide rebates for energy-efficient appliances, tax credits for

---

33. 27 C.F.R. 4.23(b).

34. Amanda Little, Your Glass of Wine May Depend on This California Winery, Bloomberg, August 26, 2022, https://www.bloomberg.com/opinion/articles/2022-08-26/french-vineyards-can-take-hope-from-california-s-jackson-family-winery?srnd=opinion (accessed August 28, 2022).

35. Intergovernmental Panel on Climate Change, The evidence is clear: the time for action is now. We can halve emissions by 2030, April 4, 2022, ipcc.ch/2022/04/04/ipcc-ar6-wgiii-pressrelease/#:~:text=The%20global%20temperature%20will%20stabilise,is%20in%20the%20early%202070s (accessed August 8, 2022). *See also*, Paul Hawken, Regeneration: ending the climate crisis in one generation, at 9 (New York: Penguin Books 2021) (noting the change in scientific consensus from the previous assumption that warming would continue for centuries to the now-held belief that global warming can recede upon achievement of zero carbon emissions, quoting Dr. Joeri Rogelj, lead author of the Sixth Assessment of the IPCC: "It is our best understanding that, if we bring carbon dioxide [emissions] down to net zero, the warming will level off. The climate will stabilize within a decade or two. There will be very little to no additional warming. Our best estimate is zero.").

36. The United States signed the Kyoto Protocol, an international treaty intended to commit countries to a reduction of greenhouse gases, on November 12, 1998. The treaty has never been ratified by the U.S. Senate, which is required to become binding on the United States. The United States refused to ratify the treaty on the basis that the Kyoto Protocol did not require developing nations like China and India to commit to similar reductions targets as developed Annex I countries and would cause considerable harm to the U.S. economy.

37. Title IV of the Clean Air Act Amendments of 1990 established the world's first large-scale cap-and-trade or allowance trading system for pollutants by regulating sulfur dioxide and nitrous oxide emissions to curb acid rain.

companies to invest in clean energy, create a financial penalty for metric tons of methane emissions that exceed federal limits starting in 2024, and provide incentives for the fossil fuels industry to expand and modernize.[38] Billed as the United States' largest climate change investment to date, the legislation is projected to allow the United States to cut greenhouse gas emissions (GHGs) by 40 percent below 2005 levels by 2030. The bill also defines carbon dioxide produced from the burning of fossil fuels as an "air pollutant," potentially paving the way for the U.S. Environmental Protection Agency (EPA) to further regulate GHG emissions.[39]

U.S. federal regulation prior to the Inflation Reduction Act of 2022 in the climate arena has been limited to administrative rulemaking through the EPA to reduce emissions from certain sectors. For example, the American Innovation and Manufacturing (AIM) Act of 2020 directs the EPA to phase down the production and consumption of certain hydrofluorocarbons (HFCs), which are potent greenhouse gases and ozone-depleting substances commonly found in air conditioning, refrigeration, fire suppression, and foam blowing agents. A global phasedown of HFCs could theoretically avoid up to 0.5°C of global warming by 2100. The EPA has also finalized rulemaking with respect to greenhouse gas emissions standards for light-duty and heavy-duty motor vehicles for vehicles in model years 2023-2026 and has plans to initiate separate rulemaking for model years 2027 and beyond.[40]

The U.S. has periodically evaluated regulating carbon emissions on a national level, possibly as part of the Clean Air Act, but has taken no definitive action. Currently there is a regional cap-and-trade system among Northeastern and Mid-Atlantic states to reduce carbon dioxide emissions from large power plants. Under this Regional Greenhouse Gas Initiative, the country's first cap-and-trade system for carbon emissions, power plants in participating states began purchasing allowances in 2008 during quarterly auctions for each ton of carbon emitted. The number of allowances available for purchase in each auction will decline over time, ultimately resulting in a 50 percent reduction of carbon emissions.[41]

Most wineries and vineyards have yet to be impacted by greenhouse gas regulations on the federal or state levels, but this seems likely to change, at least on regional and state levels. In California, which produces approximately 81

---

38. Inflation Reduction Act of 2022, H.R. 5376. The Act also makes changes to health care policy through drug pricing reform and a 3-year extension to the Affordable Care Act.

39. Lisa Friedman, Democrats Designed the Climate Law to Be a Game Changers. Here's How. The New York Times, August 22, 2022, https://www.nytimes.com/2022/08/22/climate/epa-supreme-court-pollution.html (accessed August 23, 2022).

40. United States Environmental Protection Agency, Climate Change Regulatory Actions and Initiatives, https://www.epa.gov/climate-change/climate-change-regulatory-actions-and-initiatives (accessed July 30, 2022).

41. Wilson, Miranda, Does the nation's first CO2 cap and trade system work?, E&E News, April 6, 2022 (https://www.eenews.net/articles/does-the-nations-first-co2-cap-and-trade-system-work/#:~:text=There%20is%20no%20benefit%20to,28%20hearing%20on%20the%20initiative, accessed July 30, 2022).

percent of total U.S. wine produced,[42] wineries are slowly coming under the umbrella goals of the California Global Warming Solutions Act of 2006 (AB 32) and the 2016 extension bill (SB 32), which seek to limit GHGs to 1990 levels by 2020 and reduce GHGs to 40 percent below 1990 levels by 2030. While wineries are not specifically regulated under these bills, the bills' directives towards municipalities and planning departments have a direct impact on winery development and expansion projects. Through executive order, California has sought to further reduce emissions reduction targets by 80 percent of 1990 levels by 2050 and achieve carbon neutrality by 2045.[43] The California Air Resources Control Board (CARB), which is responsible for achieving the goals of this legislation, has had a cap-and-trade system to achieve emissions reductions since 2013. Thus far, the program covers electricity generators, large industrial facilities, and distributors of transportation, natural gas, and other fuels.

AB 32 required CARB to develop a Scoping Plan to reduce GHGs to achieve the emissions targets of the Act. Since 2008, CARB has updated its Scoping Plan twice and is on target to implement a revised Scoping Plan in 2022. The 2017 Scoping Plan attempts to merge the goals of AB 32 and the Sustainable Communities and Climate Protection Act of 2008 (SB 375), which is the first law in the United States to consider reductions in GHG emissions through land use and transportation planning considerations. SB 375 establishes incentives and exceptions within the California Environmental Quality Act (CEQA) that allow state and local agencies to approve development projects in line with the climate goals of SB 375.[44]

For instance, winery development projects in the Bay Area Air Quality Management District (BAAQMD), which includes Sonoma and Napa counties, may, depending on what is ultimately adopted by local agencies, need to show that

42. California Wine Institute, California & US Wine Production, https://wineinstitute.org/our-industry/statistics/california-us-wine-production/#:~:text=California%20produces%20an%20average%20of%2081%20percent%20of%20total%20U.S.%20wine%20production. (accessed July 30, 2022).

43. Executive Orders S-3-05, B-30-15, and B-55-18.

44. CEQA requires governments to consider the environmental consequences of a project prior to approval and may require an agency to prepare an Environmental Impact Report (EIR) when the project will have a significant impact on the environment. California Environmental Quality Act (Pub. Resources Code, §21000 et seq.) SB 97, which was passed by the California Legislature in 2007, requires CEQA to analyze and mitigate greenhouse gas emissions. For instance, under the CEQA Guidelines, which were amended and became effective on March 18, 2010, lead agencies must analyze GHGs of proposed projects and consider a range of potential mitigation measures to reduce emissions. CEQA Guidelines, Section 15064.4, Section 15126.4(c). This requirement has played out dramatically for over a decade with the Walt Ranch development project in the Napa Valley. The most recent EIR requires the owners to permanently protect 267.7 acres of woodland habitat to offset the GHGs from the development of 209 acres of vineyard and loss of 14,000 trees. Barry Eberling, Napa County endorses Walt Ranch greenhouse gas plan, Napa Valley Register, June 22, 2022, https://napavalleyregister.com/news/local/napa-county-endorses-walt-ranch-greenhouse-gas-plan/article_caffdbe8-d624-11ec-8bdd-1b8a140792c9.html (accessed August 11, 2022); Kerana Todorov, Napa County STILL Needs Time to Evaluate Walt Ranch Vineyard Project, Wine Business, April 20, 2022, https://www.winebusiness.com/news/article/257991 (accessed August 11, 2022).

a project is either (a) consistent with the local GHG reduction strategy of CEQA Section 15183.5(b), or (b) meets certain minimum design elements in the future. Examples of these design elements are (i) exclusion of natural gas appliances or natural gas plumbing inside a building; (ii) limiting wasteful, inefficient, or unnecessary energy usage as determined by the analysis required under CEQA Section 21100(b)(3) and Section 15126.2(b) of the State CEQA Guidelines; and (iii) reducing project-generated vehicle miles traveled (VMT).[45]

Although there are no specific mandates to do so yet, some wineries are starting to catalog greenhouse gas emissions in the event of future cap-and-trade regulation, or to show regulators and county officials that a project has done its "fair share" of what is required to meet California's long-term climate goals as part of future development approvals.

2. INTERNATIONAL WINERIES FOR CLIMATE ACTION

Regardless of any regulation on the horizon, many wineries and enterprises have taken it upon themselves to be part of climate solutions. For example, Jackson Family Wines is currently on track to cut carbon emissions in half by 2030 and become carbon positive by 2050 without reliance on carbon offsets. To do this, the company has measured its carbon footprint and that of its suppliers and partners since at least 2015, a baseline from which it has been able to reduce its carbon footprint by 17.8 percent.

In 2019, Jackson Family Wines co-founded International Wineries for Climate Action (IWCA) with Spain's Familia Torres, a five-generation wine company founded in 1870. IWCA provides a forum for like-minded, environmentally committed wineries to reduce carbon emissions in the wine industry by sharing best practices in vineyard management and winery operations and to reduce carbon output without reliance on carbon offset credits.

IWCA membership is tiered in three stages based on the scoping progress established for carbon emissions monitoring.[46] Applicant Members are those who

45. Arthur F. Coon, BAAQMD Adopts 'Fair Share' Based CEQA Thresholds of Significance For Evaluating Climate Change Impacts of Land Use Projects And Plans," Miller Starr Regalia, May 2, 2022, https://www.ceqadevelopments.com/2022/05/02/baaqmd-adopts-fair-share-based-ceqa-thresholds-of-significance-for-evaluating-climate-change-impacts-of-land-use-projects-and-plans/.

46. The GHG Protocol, in partnership with World Resources Institute and the World Business Council for Sustainable Development, has developed a scoping protocol and accounting standard for greenhouse gases upon which most corporate reporting programs rely. The GHG Protocol classifies emissions into Scopes 1-3: Scope 1 emissions are direct emissions from a company's owned or controlled sources; Scope 2 emissions are indirect emissions from purchased energy used by the company; and Scope 3 emissions are indirect upstream and downstream emissions from the value chain of the reporting company. GHG Protocol FAQ (https://ghgprotocol.org/sites/default/files/standards_supporting/FAQ.pdf, accessed July 31, 2022). The U.S. EPA follows the same definitions for Scopes 1-3 emissions. United States Environmental Protection Agency, EPA Center for Corporate Climate Leadership, Scope 1 and Scope 2 Inventory Guidance, https://www.epa.gov/climateleadership/scope-1-and-scope-2-inventory-guidance (accessed July 31, 2022); Scope 3 Inventory Guidance, https://www.epa.gov/climateleadership/scope-3-inventory-guidance (accessed July 31, 2022).

are interested in becoming members but have yet to complete a GHG inventory requirement for Scopes 1-2; Silver Members have completed the baseline third-party-verified GHG inventory across Scopes 1-3 and have committed to becoming net zero by 2050; and Gold Members, in addition to achieving the Silver Member requirements, must have at least 20 percent onsite renewable energy generation and demonstrate a consistent reduction in emissions from a baseline emissions inventory year. Wineries are required to show tangible progress towards climate neutrality by 2050 to retain membership in IWCA and the United Nation's Race to Zero campaign to achieve net zero emissions by 2050.[47]

INTERNATIONAL
WINERIES FOR
CLIMATE ACTION

One of IWCA's founding goals is to create a standardized accounting methodology for wineries and vineyards across Scopes 1-3 that allows wineries to identify emissions hotspots and mitigation options. IWCA has developed the U.S., Australia, and New Zealand versions of the emissions calculator and is in the process of developing additional calculators for other regions. Based on averages calculated from IWCA members' 2018 GHG emissions data, the hotspots from Scopes 1-2 take up less than a quarter of all emissions. However, Scope 3 emissions comprise a significant source of emissions, mostly from bulk purchases of grapes and wine (20 percent); wine packaging in the form of bottles, labels, and closures (19 percent); and case goods transport (16 percent). This inventory illuminates participant members' existing efforts in reducing carbon emissions from light-weighting glass, since the wine bottle typically comprises one of the largest source of emissions for wineries.

---

47. International Wineries for Climate Action, 2021 Annual Report, October 2021, at 1, 3, https://www.iwcawine.org/_files/ugd/dffd34_3f14bfc5c26f43c8b2293dbbbaeb04d5.pdf (accessed August 28, 2022).

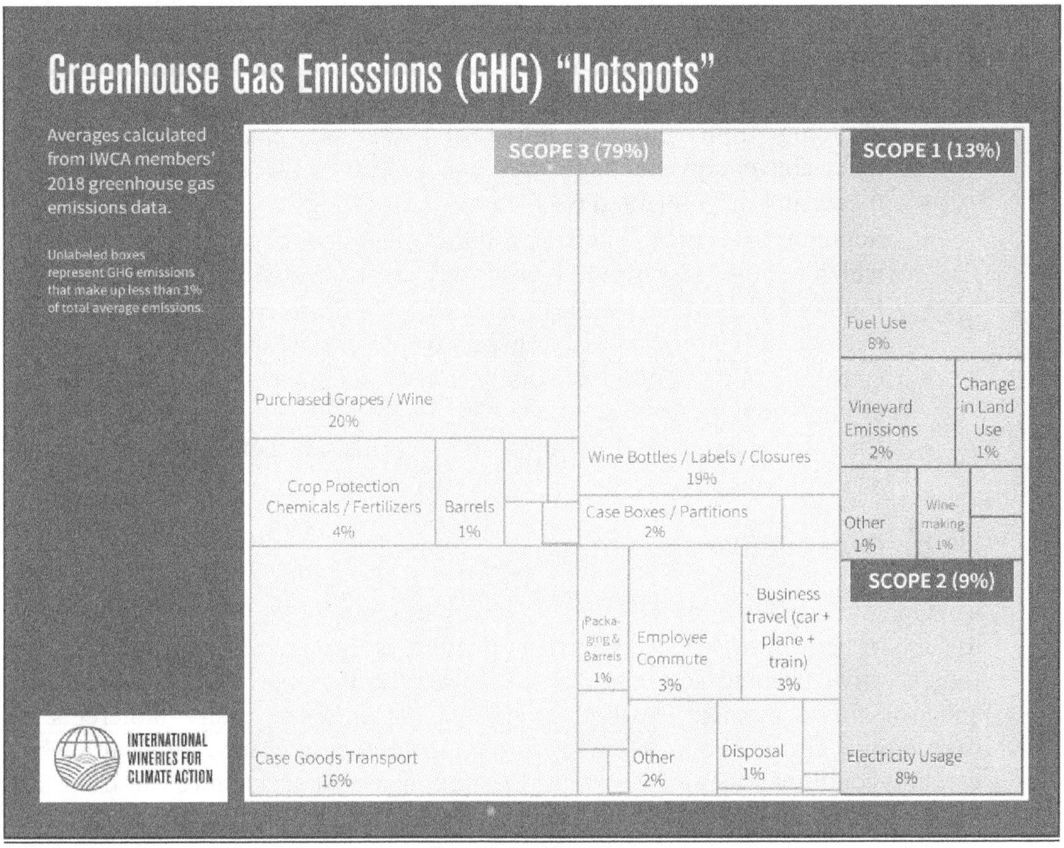

Reprinted with permission from International Wineries for Climate Action, www.iwcawine.org.

a. Glass Bottles

Packaging, and glass bottles in particular, are a significant source of emissions in the wine life cycle. Glass manufacturing worldwide (for all uses) produces at least 86 million tons of carbon dioxide annually.[48] While some wineries are pursuing aluminum cans and boxed wine options, these solutions are unlikely to become the only solution due to concerns about taste, environmental impacts from plastic liners, and ageability. Although glass wine bottles are recyclable and can be one of the most sustainable vessels for beverages, wineries seeking to reduce

48. Glass is the hidden gem in a carbon-neutral future, Nature, November 3, 2021, https://www.nature.com/articles/d41586-021-02992-8#:~:text=Worldwide%2C%20glass%20manufacturing%20produces%20at,of%20carbon%20dioxide%20every%20year (accessed July 31, 2022).

their carbon impact from glass packaging will have to adopt the following practices to reduce the impact of their carbon emissions[49]:

- Sourcing from glass manufacturing facilities that are powered by renewable energy sources rather than traditional fuel sources.
- Increasing recycling and reuse rates of glass bottles.
- Sourcing from manufacturing facilities that use recycled glass, or cullet, which requires less heat and has lower carbon emissions than raw glass.
- Light-weight glass bottles to reduce carbon emissions from the manufacturing process and transport of finished goods.
- Changing bottle molds, especially to reduce the indentation of the bottle, or punt, on wine bottles.
- Changing consumer perceptions of a correlation between bottle weight and wine quality.[50]

b. Regenerative Farming

One of the avenues by which IWCA sees an opportunity for member wineries to support their efforts in becoming net positive is through regenerative farming. Regenerative farming seeks to increase biodiversity, improve soil health, and enhance the ecosystem. Although still in its infancy, many adherents of regenerative farming believe that the following practices enhance soil health while creating conditions for soil carbon sequestration so that agriculture can transition from a net emitter to a source of carbon capture.[51] Thus far, member wineries have noticed some positive sequestration impacts from the following regenerative farming practices:[52]

- No tilling or minimally tilling between vine rows.
- Planting cover crops, especially grass-based instead of legume-only cover crops.
- Planting perennial rather than annual cover crops.

---

49. Betsy Andrews, The Shrinking Footprint of Glass Wine Bottles, SevenFiftyDaily, July 18, 2022, https://daily.sevenfifty.com/the-shrinking-carbon-footprint-of-glass-wine-bottles/ (accessed July 31, 2022).

50. Rupert Joy, Wine bottles: A heavy price, Decanter, March 15, 2022, https://www.decanter.com/learn/wine-bottles-a-heavy-price-475453/ (accessed July 31, 2022).

51. Although this view is shared by some regenerative farming proponents, the World Resources Institute is skeptical of the claim, noting that any carbon sequestering effects at a particular farm or vineyard cannot be translated when one farm's activities are moved to another area and/or potentially decrease or offset food production. International Wineries for Climate Change, Regenerative Farming & Carbon Sequestration, February 16, 2021, at 6, https://www.iwcawine.org/_files/ugd/dffd34_896e057865a14fd5ab68abd30c16a192.pdf (accessed July 31, 2022).

52. *Ibid.* at 11.

- Integration of beneficial insects and animals to enhance soil health, including for grazing.
- Spreading nutrient, carbon rich compost to build microbes and soil health.

3. PORTO PROTOCOL

Another winery association that is focused on climate change is the Porto Protocol. Currently comprised of over 220 members, including wineries and many non-wineries such as retailers, packaging companies, accounting firms, colleges, and car manufacturers, the Porto Protocol seeks to encourage thought leadership and engagement among members to adopt and promote climate solutions. Membership is free, and there are no minimum criteria for participation, regardless of actual practices or commitments. Members can progress along the stages of participation from Signatory to Mentor, with the latter being required to commit to recruiting new companies as members, being a face for the Porto Protocol, and active coaching and engagement of fellow members.

the PORTO PROTOCOL

4. GREEN CERTIFICATIONS

Although not specific to climate change, there are many wine-based sustainability certifications, often specific to a region or a governing trade association. The list below is by no means comprehensive, but it provides an overview of common certifications in the American wine industry. Most of these certifications were developed in the last two decades, and some of these certifications are evolving to directly address the impact of climate change.

Organic Certification. The rules governing organic claims in the United States are governed by the United States Department of Agriculture (USDA) as part of its National Organic Program (NOP) at 7 CFR Part 205. These rules apply to alcoholic beverages, and TTB takes an active role in reviewing label applications that include organic claims as part of its COLA review process. TTB will not approve proposed alcohol beverage labels that are inconsistent with the NOP.[53] Any wines labeled as Organic must be overseen and certified by a USDA third-

53. Memorandum of Understanding, Agreement on the Coordination of Organic Labeling and Advertising Between the Alcohol and Tobacco Tax and Trade Bureau, United States Department of the Treasury and the Agricultural Marketing Service, United States Department of Agriculture, signed March 10, 2010, by John Manfreda, Administrator, TTB, and June 3, 2010 by Rayne Pegg, Administrator, AMS, https://www.ttb.gov/images/pdfs/mou-ams.pdf (accessed June 10, 2022).

party accredited certifying agency (ACA) certifier.[54] The USDA allows three designations for organic claims:

a. "100% Organic"—this claim allows use of the USDA Organic seal. It means that 100 percent of the grapes are organic, with no added sulfites, and no ingredients using prohibited methods like genetic engineering. Both the growing and processing must be ACA-certified.

b. "Made with Organic Grapes"—100 percent of the grapes must be certified organic and no more than 100ppm of sulfites can be added. The USDA Organic seal may not be used.

c. Other Designations—The USDA and TTB allow "organic" to be placed in the ingredients statement on a label (nowhere else) if certain ingredients are organic and accompanied by an organic crop certificate/crop report for each claimed ingredient. This category is most often used when:

- Less than 100 percent of the grapes are certified organic.
- Sulfites exceed 100 ppm.
- An ingredient was produced through genetic engineering or other prohibited methods.

Although the USDA organic seal is seen on many food products in the United States, it is not widely seen on wine products, since the vast majority of winemakers rely on the use of sulfites, a natural preservative, to ensure shelf stability and prevent oxidation. In fact, one wine writer advises consumers to store USDA organic wines in their refrigerators and chillers and not to be surprised if the wines do not cellar well.[55]

The USDA has trade partnerships with multiple countries that allow the organic products certified in one country to be recognized in the destination country. The U.S. and the European Union signed an equivalency agreement on February 15, 2012, that covered an array of agricultural products, including wine,

---

54. In California, the ACA most frequently used is CCOF, which provides certification to growers for grape growing and processors for winemaking. California also has its own registration requirements requiring compliance with the federal NOP. The California Department of Food and Agriculture (CDFA) has jurisdiction over grape growers; the California Department of Public Health (CDPH) has jurisdiction over processors like wineries.

55. M. Puckette, Better Than Organic: Sustainability and Wine, Wine Folly, https://winefolly.com/tips/beyond-organic-certified-sustainable-wine/ (accessed July 17, 2022).

but which does not specifically create an equivalency for the use of sulfites in organic wine.[56] The organic standards in the European Union are different in that they allow winemakers to add sulfites to wine labeled as "organic wine" and include a corresponding EU organic seal.[57] Since the U.S. does not allow wines to be designated as "organic" or include the USDA organic seal when sulfites are added, European organic wines must be labeled as "made with organic grapes" or "made with organically grown grapes" once they are in the United States.[58]

Biodynamic: Based on a 1924 agricultural course given by Rudolf Steiner, a scientist and philosopher, biodynamics is a form of certification that combines regenerative, sustainable, and organic agricultural practices certified and enforced by two organizations: The Biodynamic Federation Demeter International ("Demeter"), a non-profit umbrella organization with authorized biodynamic organizations and certification bodies in 36 countries; and Biodyvin, which certifies wines from France, Belgium, Germany, Italy, Portugal, Switzerland, and Spain. Biodynamics are based on seven principles: soil fertility, GMO-free agriculture, animal welfare, biodiversity, organic certification, recognition of ecological interdependencies, and social responsibility.[59]

One of the notable features of biodynamic viticulture is its dependence on rhythm in determining when to prune, apply preparations, or harvest. Moreover, soil preparations can include self-described homeopathic remedies for the soil including horn silica for grape formation, horn manure for soil health, oak bark for insecticidal properties, and yarrow, chamomile, nettles, dandelion, and valerian to stimulate compost maturation.[60] Demeter USA has trademarked the term "biodynamic," such that only Demeter-certified wineries and vineyards are licensed to use the term subject to a trademark contract with the organization.

---

56. Philip L. Hinerman, Fox Rothschild LLP, "Organic" wines—it depends on where you drink it, Lexology.com, August 9, 2012, https://www.lexology.com/library/detail.aspx?g=a59f6d1d-e452-4849-8db2-0a7cf8ad86fa (accessed August 15, 2022); National Organic Program, U.S.-European Union Organic Equivalency Arrangement, Questions and Answers 1 and 13, July 2015, https://www.ams.usda.gov/sites/default/files/media/US_EUQAs.pdf (accessed July 10, 2022).

57. In the European Union, red wines may include up to 100mg/liter sulfite and white wines may include up to 150 mg/liter.

58. D. Nigro, U.S. and Europe Have Different Definitions of Organic Wine, Wine Spectator, February 24, 2012, https://www.winespectator.com/articles/us-and-europe-have-different-definitions-of-organic-wine-46432 (accessed July 10, 2022); Ryan Puszka, Reds, Whites, and Sulfites: Examining Different Organic Wine Regulation Practices in the United States and the European Union, 40 NW. J. INT'L L. & BUS. 251 (2020), at 265. https://scholarlycommons.law.northwestern.edu/njilb/vol40/iss2/4.

59. https://demeter.net/biodynamics/ (accessed July 17, 2022).

60. Demeter Biodynamic Winegrowers International at 5, https://demeter.net/wp-content/uploads/2021/05/200228_dem_winzerliste2020_int.pdf (accessed July 17, 2022).

Certified California Sustainable Winegrowing (CCSW): Established in 2003 by the California Wine Institute and the California Association of Winegrape Growers (CAWG), the California Sustainable Winegrowing Alliance (CSWA) administers the CCSW certification for wineries and vineyards in California. CCSW certification considers the “three Es” of sustainability: environmental soundness, economic feasibility, and social equity. The CCSW certification requires wineries and vineyards to self-score on more than one hundred criteria ranked on a 1-4 scale in the areas of water and energy efficiency, pest management, soil health, waste management, wildlife habitat, neighbors and community, employees, and supply chain. Wineries and vineyards must have an overall score of 85 percent with scores in Category 2 or higher by Year 2 of certification. The certifications must be audited by a third party annually, and wineries and vineyards are expected to improve each year with more stringent baselines for crop protection materials, and the measurement and recording of water use, nitrogen use, energy use, and GHGs annually by Year 2.[61] Recently, the CCSW logo was authorized for use on wine labels provided the winery is certified and 85 percent or more of the grapes are from CCSW, SIP-Certified, or LODI RULES vineyards.

61. California Sustainable Winegrowing Alliance, https://www.sustainablewinegrowing.org/sustainable_winegrowing_program.php (accessed July 17, 2022).

SIP Certified (Sustainability in Practice): Established in 2008 in California, SIP Certification is also based on the "three Es" of sustainability. Similar to CCSW in terms of requirements, SIP Certified allowed use of its logos on wines before CCSW. SIP prohibits the use of specific pesticides and requires wineries and vineyards to achieve a minimum score of 75 percent of total available points on nearly 200 practices and 50 requirements. The certification is also verified by a third party.

LODI RULES Certified Green Sustainable Winegrowing: Originally from Lodi, California, the LODI RULES were established in 2005 to encompass the six factors of ecosystem management, water management, soil management, pest management, business management, and human resources. The LODI RULES program is regional but has expanded to encompass wineries and vineyards in other parts of California, Washington, and Israel through the adoption of the seals, LODI RULES, CALIFORNIA RULES, and the CERTIFIED GREEN seal.

Napa Green: The Napa Green Land program was launched in 2004 to ensure the health of the Napa River and watershed. It then developed its own narrowly focused sustainability certification program for vineyards. In 2022, however, the Napa Green program will transition to a new, broader sustainability certification program that will focus on climate action, regenerative farming, and social equity. The new Napa Green Vineyard certification will require growers to become carbon neutral to negative within six to nine years; incorporate social equity, justice, and inclusion standards; increase water efficiency; practice tree and forest protection and enhancement; adhere to a prohibited and restricted pesticide list; and commit to conservation burning or burning alternatives.

Napa Green Wineries are required to implement standards to save energy and water; prevent waste through recycling, composting, and environmentally preferable purchasing; reduce GHG emissions; commit to social equity; and certify via a third party.

LIVE Certified (Low Input Viticulture and Enology): Based in the Pacific Northwest, LIVE certification is an annual process that is also third-party accredited. LIVE began certifying vineyards in Oregon in 1999, in Washington in 2006, and in Idaho since 2012. LIVE certification considers the entire chain of wine production, and members are audited by a third-party inspector in the first two years of membership and every third year afterward. Wines carrying the LIVE Certified Sustainable Gapes must be at least 97 percent certified, and wines carrying the LIVE Certified Sustainable Wine Logo must contain 97 percent certified grapes and be processed in a certified winery.

Salmon Safe: Also based in the Pacific Northwest, Salmon-Safe farm certification is included with LIVE's certification at no additional cost to the grower. Salmon-Safe is an organization focused on multiple food products and aiming to ensure that farming practices and land development projects protect water quality, maintain watershed health, and restore salmon habitat in key agricultural and urban watersheds. Salmon-Safe partners with certification organizations like Oregon Tilth, LIVE Certified, and Demeter to encourage landowners to plant trees on streams for shade, control runoff with beneficial cover crops and adopt natural methods for weed and pest control.

5. GREEN WASHING CONCERNS AND REGULATORY RESPONSES

As illustrated above, the number of certifications for a winery to pursue or a consumer to research is dizzying. Most of the certification groups require a third-party audit to ensure integrity with the certification processes, prevent dilution, and avoid consumer confusion. The U.S. Federal Trade Commission ("FTC") has also developed a set of "Green Guides" to help marketers make environmental claims without misleading consumers. The Green Guides are not regulations; they describe the types of claims from which the FTC can make a finding of deceptiveness and take enforcement action under Section 5 of the FTC Act. The last set of Green Guides was updated in 2012 to include new sections on the use of carbon offsets, green certifications and seals, and renewable energy and materials claims. The Guides themselves do not address the terms "sustainable," "natural," or "organic" (especially because the latter is covered by the USDA's NOP Program). However, misuse of these terms could still be subject to scrutiny by consumer protection plaintiffs' firms, the FTC, or the TTB, to the extent these claims could be deemed false or misleading.

D. CONCLUSION

Wine grapes, like people, thrive in regions that are not too hot, not too cold, and ideally have a bit of maritime influence. The wine grapes' sweet spot of the Mediterranean clime will be challenged in the next few years as temperatures rise and climate impacts become more variable. However, the wine grape—like its human minders—tends to be adaptable. The wine industry has shown this already, and we can expect more innovation and solutions in response to a changing climate and regulatory regime. Consumer preferences and moral imperative will prompt these changes: Wine producers know that they must adapt to survive. Flexibility and creativity will be the keys for wine in the years to come, ensuring that "wine country" and *la dolce vita* will continue to inspire future generations.

CHAPTER 9

PUBLIC HEALTH AND SOCIAL RESPONSIBILITY

Richard Mendelson, with Allyson Malecha[1]

> Wine [provides] cheerfulness, strength and nourishment, when taken only at meals, and in moderate quantities.
>
> Dr. Benjamin Rush, 1790[2]

> What do we know today about the risks and benefits of moderate alcohol consumption? While all may not agree, I believe that, for most people for whom alcohol is not contra-indicated by health, ethical, or religious reasons, there are "intelligent" ways of consuming alcohol that minimize the risks while providing health benefits. If consumed in "moderation" (when that term is defined to exclude binge or irresponsible drinking), alcohol can be considered as a component of a healthy lifestyle (along with not smoking, avoiding obesity, eating a healthy diet, and getting regular exercise).
>
> R. Curtis Ellison, M.D., May 2007[3]

The World Health Organization (WHO) has identified the harmful use of alcohol as "one of the main risk factors for poor health globally."[4] Alcohol in any

---

1. Allyson Malecha, a member of the Class of 2024 at the University of California, Berkeley, Law School, was integrally involved in researching and writing an updated version of this chapter. She has a background in life sciences and public health and is primarily interested in intellectual property and regulatory law. Mr. Mendelson and Ms. Malecha thank Charles Jefferson, Wine Institute's Vice President of Federal and International Public Policy, for his helpful comments and suggestions.

2. Benjamin Rush, An Inquiry into the Effects of Spirituous Liquors 12 (Boston, Thomas & Andrews, 1790).

3. R. Curtis Ellison, Closing Remarks, *in* Health Risks and Benefits of Moderate Alcohol Consumption: Proceedings of an International Symposium, published in 17 Supplement to Annals of Epidemiology S1, S114 (2007).

4. World Health Organization, Strategies to Reduce the Harmful Use of Alcohol, Report of the Secretariat A61/13, 1 (March 20, 2008).

form—cider, wine, beer, or spirits—can damage one's health and jeopardize public safety if used irresponsibly or excessively. Alcohol-related harm can include, but is not limited to, adverse health effects, intentional and unintentional injuries, crime and public disorder, other anti-social behavior and lost workplace productivity. The specific harm depends on the beverage, its alcoholic strength, the manner of consumption, and the personal attributes of the drinker.

In order to prevent the harmful use of alcohol and control its adverse effects on drinkers and society at large, almost every country, including the United States, regulates the production, sale, and consumption of alcoholic beverages in some manner. The particular approach to alcohol control depends on the country's religious and sociocultural context and on how it balances competing ideological, social, health, and commercial agendas.

In this chapter, we focus first on the public health and safety issues surrounding the sale and consumption of alcoholic beverages generally and wine specifically. We then examine the various legal approaches to reduce the harmful effects of alcoholic beverage consumption and assess their effectiveness. Finally, we propose a model of social responsibility for wine producers to ensure that the product is properly produced and moderately consumed.

A. HEALTH EFFECTS

Excessive alcohol use is the third leading preventable cause of death in the United States, following tobacco and poor diet/lack of exercise.[5] Approximately 95,000 deaths in the United States are attributable to excessive consumption of alcoholic beverages each year.[6] What is excessive consumption? Generally, it is defined as the opposite of moderate consumption, much like temperance is defined as the opposite of intemperance. There is no universal standard for moderate drinking; the standard varies from country to country.[7] In the United States, the 2020 edition of the *Dietary Guidelines* defines moderate drinking as no more than one standard drink per day for women and no more than two standard drinks per day for men.[8]

---

5. A. H. Mokdad et al., *Actual Causes of Death in the United States*, 2000, 291(10) JAMA 1238 (2004), available at http://jama.ama-assn.org/content/291/10/1238.full.pdf.

6. National Institute on Alcohol Abuse and Alcoholism, *Alcohol Facts and Statistics – Alcohol Use in the United States*, (Mar. 2022) https://www.niaaa.nih.gov/publications/brochures-and-fact-sheets/alcohol-facts-and-statistics#:~:text=Alcohol%2DRelated%20Emergencies%20and%20 Deaths%20in%20the%20United%20States&text=An%20estimated%2095%2C000%20people%20(approximately,death%20in%20the%20United%20States.

7. Some countries recommend no more than three drinks per day for men, including France, Greece, Hungary, Italy, and Switzerland. Countries with a recommended limit of three or more drinks per day for men and two for women include New Zealand, Chile, Belgium, and Spain. International Organization of Vine and Wine, *Comparison of International Alcohol Drinking Guidelines*, 25-54 (2019) https://www.oiv.int/public/medias/7169/oiv-report-alcohol-drinking-guidelines-collective-expertise.pdf.

8. USDA and U.S. Department of Health and Human Services, *Dietary Guidelines for Americans, 2020-2025*, 49 (9th ed. 2020), https://www.dietaryguidelines.gov/sites/default /files/2020-12/Dietary_Guidelines_for_Americans_2020-2025.pdfThere was a major effort on the

A "standard drink" contains 14 grams or 0.6 fluid ounces of pure alcohol, which can be found in 12 fluid ounces of beer (fcei percent alcohol by volume), five fluid ounces of wine (12 percent alcohol by volume), or 1.5 ounces of 80-proof distilled spirits (40 percent alcohol by volume).[9]

FIGURE 9-1[10]

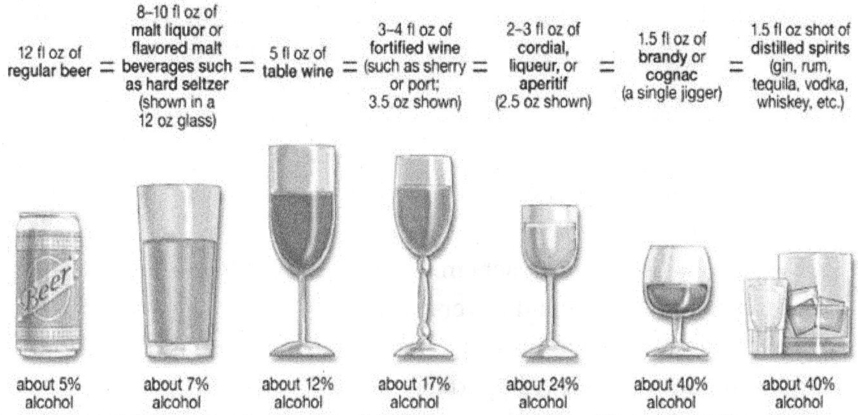

Notwithstanding the standard for moderate drinking, the *Dietary Guidelines* caution that "if adults age 21 years and older choose to drink alcoholic beverages, drinking less is better for health than drinking more." The Guidelines also warn that there are some groups of people who should not consume any alcohol. At-risk groups include children and adolescents, those who are pregnant or are trying to become pregnant, those who are breastfeeding, those who cannot restrict their alcohol intake, those who plan to drive or engage in other activities that require attention or skill, and those taking certain medications or who have certain medical conditions.[11]

---

part of health activists during development of the 2020 Dietary Guidelines to change the definition of moderate consumption for men from no more than two drinks per day to one drink per day. This was a recommendation of the Scientific Advisory Committee which was ultimately overruled by USDA and HHS. It is expected that similar efforts will be launched during development of the 2025 Dietary Guidelines.

9. *Id.*

10. Illustration of Standard Drink Sizes available at National Institute on Alcohol Abuse and Alcoholism, *What is A Standard Drink?* https://www.niaaa.nih.gov/alcohols-effects-health/overview-alcohol-consumption/what-standard-drink#:~:text=In%20the%20United%20States%2C%20 one,which%20is%20about%2040%25%20alcohol (2022).

11. *Id.* at 31-32, 131. While the Dietary Guidelines state that not drinking alcohol is the safest option during lactation, "moderate consumption of alcoholic beverages by a woman who is lactating (up to 1 standard drink in a day) is not known to be harmful to the infant, especially if the woman waits at least 2 hours after a single drink before nursing or expressing breast milk."

1. ALCOHOL'S EFFECT ON THE BODY

Although this section is not an exhaustive discussion of the effects of alcohol on the body, it must be acknowledged that alcohol directly causes or is associated with a variety of health conditions. The World Health Organization recognizes ethanol (the type of alcohol consumed by humans) as a toxin, psychoactive substance, and carcinogenic agent. Worldwide, alcohol contributes to three million deaths a year and is responsible for 5.1 percent of the global burden of disease.[12]

The following is a brief summary of alcohol's health effects:[13]

1. Cancers: head and neck cancers, liver cancer, colorectal cancers, breast cancer;
2. Neuropsychiatric conditions: alcohol dependence syndrome, alcohol abuse, depression;
3. Neurologic conditions: ischemic stroke, hemorrhagic stroke;
4. Diabetes (protective and adverse effects);[14]
5. Cardiovascular conditions: cardiac arrhythmias, cardiomyopathy, ischemic heart disease, hypertension;
6. Lung conditions: acute respiratory distress syndrome, pneumonia;
7. Gastrointestinal conditions: liver cirrhosis, steatosis (fatty liver), fibrosis, alcohol-associated hepatitis, pancreatitis;
8. Infectious diseases: tuberculosis, pneumonia, respiratory syncytial virus, increased susceptibility to other respiratory viruses;[15]
9. Maternal and perinatal conditions: low birth weight, fetal alcohol syndrome;[16]
10. Acute toxic effects: alcohol poisoning;

---

12. World Health Organization, *Alcohol*, WHO Health Topics (2022), https://www.who.int/health-topics/alcohol#tab=tab_1.

13. National Institute on Alcohol Abuse and Alcoholism, *Alcohol's Effects on the Body*, National Institutes of Health (2021), https://www.niaaa.nih.gov/alcohols-effects-health/alcohols-effects-body. The footnotes in the table are not in the original; they present additional information and explanations.

14. The impact of alcohol on Type 2 diabetes is challenging to assess and understand. There is high-quality evidence to suggest that moderate intake of alcohol (between 12-24 g/day) is associated with a lower incidence of diabetes. However, alcohol may worsen complications of diabetes and can cause blood sugar levels to rise (in addition to the fact that alcoholic drinks often contain sugar). Furthermore, studies with moderate-quality evidence show an association of light intake of alcohol or moderate intake of beer specifically with higher incidence of diabetes. Manuela Neuenschwander et al., *Role of diet in type 2 diabetes incidence: umbrella review of meta-analyses of prospective observational studies*, 8206 BMJ, 366-368 (Jul. 2019).

15. Samantha M. Simet et al., *Alcohol's Effects on Lung Health and Immunity*, 37(2)Alcohol Research 199-208 (2015).

16. Katherine DeJong et al., Alcohol Use in Pregnancy, 62(1) Clinical Obstetrics and Gynecology, 142-155 (Mar. 2019).

11. Accidents: road and other transport injuries, falls, drowning and burning injuries, occupational and machine injuries;
12. Self-inflicted injuries: suicide;
13. Violent deaths: assault injuries.[17]

There are other deleterious health conditions not listed above for which alcohol is the cause or a contributor. For example, heavy consumption of alcoholic beverages can interfere with the way the body digests and absorbs nutrients from food. Alcohol also can influence the effectiveness of various medications. Alcohol may either compete with a drug for a set of metabolizing enzymes, causing the drug to remain in the body for longer before it is broken down, or it may enhance the metabolism of a drug, causing it to be eliminated before it is fully absorbed by the body.

2. FACTORS IMPACTING HEALTH EFFECTS

Certain individuals are at a higher risk of developing health conditions as a result of alcohol consumption. Biological, behavioral, and social factors all contribute to an individual's risk of adverse health impacts from alcohol.[18] This is by no means an exhaustive discussion of these factors, but should serve as a brief overview of some of the most salient factors impacting health.

a. Amount of Alcohol Consumed

It is difficult to establish the level at which alcohol consumption becomes "harmful." This is referred to as the "risk threshold," and is defined differently by different health authorities across the world, as evidenced by the recommended amount of alcohol set forth in dietary guidelines from different countries. While some studies show that no level of alcohol consumption improves health, others show that the relationship between alcohol and all-cause mortality (death from any cause) is a "J-shaped" curve such that moderate drinkers appear to live longer than both those who drink in excess and those who do not drink. In a 2018 study of nearly 600,000 drinkers in high-income countries, those who had the lowest risk of all-cause mortality were those who drank about 100g of alcohol per week.[19]

17. Tanya Chikritzhs and Michael Livingston, *Alcohol and the Risk of Injury*, 13(8) Nutrients (Aug. 13, 2021), available at https://www.ncbi.nlm.nih.gov/pmc/articles/PMC8401155/.

18. Biological factors include age, sex, and health conditions. Behavioral and social factors include socioeconomic status, religious association, community association, social norms, and availability of alcohol. Race, ethnicity, and sexual orientation can fall into both of these categories. For the purposes of this chapter, we recognize that some ethnic communities disproportionately carry genetic markers that render them more susceptible to disease but acknowledge that the majority of negative health effects seen in marginalized communities are the result of social factors such as racism and discrimination.

19. Angela M. Wood et al., *Risk thresholds for alcohol consumption: combined analysis of individual-participant data for 599 912 current drinkers in 83 prospective studie*s, 391 The Lancet 1513-23 (Apr. 14, 2018).

However, when broken down by disease type, the reduced risk of death was only seen in ischaemic diseases (coronary heart disease, coronary artery disease) and diabetes. For other diseases, such as most cancers, neuropsychiatric disorders, gastrointestinal diseases, and even infectious diseases, the relationship between alcohol and disease is linear, where increased alcohol consumption is associated with increased risk of disease.[20]

Binge drinking is of particular concern for the development of adverse health outcomes. Binge drinking is defined as consuming five or more drinks in one occasion (for men) or four or more drinks in one occasion for women. Nearly 25 percent of American adults binge drink, and among them, a quarter of them report binge drinking five or more days a week.[21] In a study that compared moderate drinkers who never binge with those who binge drink, binge drinkers had three times as many problems related to alcohol (including emotional and psychological problems). In a follow-up that took place nine years after the initial data was collected, those who binged had a 40 percent increase in these problems over those who did not, demonstrating that it is not only the amount of alcohol, but also the pattern of drinking that is of concern.[22] Binge drinking is also associated with higher rates of other drug use, unintentional injury, and violence.

b. Gender and Sex

In general, men drink more than women and are more likely to abuse alcohol. A landmark Global Burden of Disease study of 204 countries published in 2022 in the Lancet found that, in 2020, 1.34 billion people drank alcohol in an unsafe amount. While 35.1 percent of the male population consumed alcohol in an unsafe amount, only 10.5 percent of the female population did the same.[23] Although seemingly drastic, the data for the United States is similar. In the U.S., men are twice as likely to binge drink, and seven percent of men have an alcohol use disorder (compared to four percent of women).

Nevertheless, drinking can be riskier for females than for males.[24] Estrogen regulates both body fat and the distribution of fat throughout the body. As a result, more estrogen leads to a higher percentage of body fat, and consequently, a lower

---

20. Jürgen Rehm et al., *The relationship between different dimensions of alcohol use and the burden of disease—an update*, 112(6) Addiction 968-1001 (Feb. 20, 2017).

21. U.S. Dept. of Agric. and U.S. Dept. of Health and Hum. Serv., *Scientific Report of the 2020 Dietary Guidelines Advisory Committee,* .https://www.dietaryguidelines.gov/sites/default /files/2020-07/PartD_Ch11_AlcoholicBev_first-print.pdf (July 2020).

22. Charles J. Holahan et al., *Binge Drinking and Alcohol Problems Among Moderate Average-Level Drinkers*, Am. J. of Preventive Medicine, 1-7 (2022) *available at* https://www.sciencedirect.com/science/article/pii/S0749379722001787.

23. GBD 2020 Alcohol Collaborators, *Population-level risks of alcohol consumption by amount, geography, age, sex, and year: a systematic analysis for the Global Burden of Disease Study 2020*, 400 Lancet 185-235 (2022).

24. U.S. Dept. of Health and Hum. Serv., NIAAA, Alcohol: A Women's Health Issue 6 (2008), available at http://pubs.niaaa.nih.gov/publications/brochurewomen/women.htm (last visited October 30, 2010).

percentage of water in the body. Even if a female and a male weigh the same amount and drink the same amount of alcohol, the blood alcohol content of the female will likely be higher due to the lower percentage of body weight attributable to water weight.[25] This is often cited as the justification for reducing alcohol consumption in women. However, other biological differences related to hormones as well as socio-cultural factors contribute to the differences between men and women and their respective alcohol risk.[26] Guidelines often fail to acknowledge whether the "one drink a day" limit for women is based on physiological sex characteristics (such as hormones) or gender identity. This is particularly important as it relates to the transgender community, who drink more than their cisgender[27] counterparts, often as a coping mechanism for stress related to discrimination and internalized negative attitudes. Further research is needed in this field to better understand the relationship between sex hormones, gender identity, and safe alcohol use.[28]

c. Race and Ethnicity

Studying the impact of alcohol on the health of different racial and ethnic groups is often challenging, as research is limited by complex factors such as national origin, birthplace, ancestry, and the existence of significant differences between subgroups of an ethnic group.

The prevalence of alcohol use disorders (consisting of both alcohol abuse and alcohol dependence) varies by ethnicity. The National Epidemiological Survey on Alcohol and Related Conditions found that the prevalence of alcohol use disorder at any point in one's lifetime is 32.6 percent for White Americans, 22.0 percent for Black Americans, 22.9 percent for Hispanic Americans, 43.4 percent for Native Americans, and 15.0 percent for Asian Americans/Pacific Islanders.[29] These national surveys often fail to account for differences in ethnic groups—for example, a 2016 study found that within the past 12 months, Mexican Americans had a seven percent rate of alcohol dependence, compared to six percent in Central/South Americans, four percent in Puerto Ricans, and three percent in

---

25. National Institute on Alcohol Abuse and Alcoholism, *Women and Alcohol*, https://www.niaaa.nih.gov/publications/brochures-and-fact-sheets/women-and-alcohol (Apr. 2021).

26. A full discussion on the variety of gender- and sex-related factors has been omitted in the interest of brevity. For a review that discusses many of these factors, refer to: Almila Erol and Victor M Karpyak, *Sex and gender-related differences in alcohol use and its consequences: Contemporary knowledge and future research considerations*, 156 Drug and Alcohol Dependence 1-13 (2015).

27. A person whose gender identity aligns with their physiological sex at birth.

28. Paul A. Gilbert et al., *Alcohol research with transgender populations: A systematic review and recommendations to strengthen future studies*, 186 Drug and Alcohol Dependence 138-146 (Mar. 10, 2018).

29. Patrice A.C. Vaeth et al., *Drinking, Alcohol Use Disorder, and Treatment Access and Utilization among U.S. Racial/Ethnic Groups*, 41(1) Alcoholism 6-19 (Dec. 16, 2016).

Cuban Americans.[30] Similar differences exist between Asian American national groups and American Indian/Alaska Natives both across regions and tribes.

Even after accounting for the differences in alcohol use and dependency between groups, certain ethnic groups are more likely to be injured or harmed in a situation where alcohol is involved. A 2011 review of studies of injuries where alcohol was involved showed that Native Americans have higher rates of fatal motor vehicle crashes, suicide, and falls. Asian Americans have the lowest rate of alcohol-attributable injury compared to other ethnic groups.[31] There are also differences between genders among races; when compared to other groups, both men and women, Black and Hispanic men had the highest rates of injuries, accidents, and health consequences. This is in line with many of the other alcohol-related health outcomes in the United States, where Black and Hispanic men are more likely than other groups to develop alcohol-related cancers and cirrhosis.[32]

Despite a common perception in the United States that certain groups, particularly Native Americans, have higher rates of alcohol abuse due to genetic factors, current evidence does not support this belief. In a 2013 study, researchers analyzed a variety of genetic markers involved in alcohol metabolism and drug-reward pathways, and ultimately determined "that the genetic influences contributing to substance use, abuse, and dependence in Native American populations are likely similar in kind and magnitude to the genetic influences contributing to the liability for these phenotypes in other ethnic groups."[33] Like other marginalized groups, increased levels of alcohol dependence in Native Americans are likely the result of personal and historical trauma, as well as lack of access to basic resources that would aid in sobriety.

d. Age

According to the 2020 Global Burden of Disease study published in the Lancet, harmful use of alcohol is concentrated in males between the ages of 15 and 39 and was the leading risk factor for mortality in males between 15 and 49. This study is of particular interest to those who study the impact of alcohol on health; per the study methods, the theoretical amount of alcohol per day that would allow for no health losses to those who drink in the 15-39 age group (versus non-drinkers) was calculated to be zero grams. Although the study methods are decidedly too complex to fully explain here, the authors' intended takeaway was clear: There are no "benefits" to any alcohol consumption among 15 to 39-year-olds, and for those over 40, drinking more than a small amount increases health risks.

---

30. Katelyn Jetelina et al., *An Investigation of the Relationship Between Alcohol Use and Major Depressive Disorder Across Hispanic National Groups*, 40(3) Alcoholism 541 (Mar. 2016).

31. Katherine M. Keyes et al., *The Role of Race/Ethnicity in Alcohol-attributable Injury in the United States*, 34(1) Epidemiologic Reviews 89-102 (Sep. 2011).

32. Jane Witbrodt et al., *Racial/Ethnic Disparities in Alcohol-related Problems: Differences by Gender and Level of Heavy Drinking*, 38(6) Alcohol Clinical and Experimental Research 1662-1670.

33. Cindy L. Ehlers and Ian R. Gizer, *Evidence for a Genetic Component for Substance Dependence in Native Americans*, 170(2) American Journal of Psychiatry 154-164 (Feb. 1, 2014).

FIGURE 9-2[34]

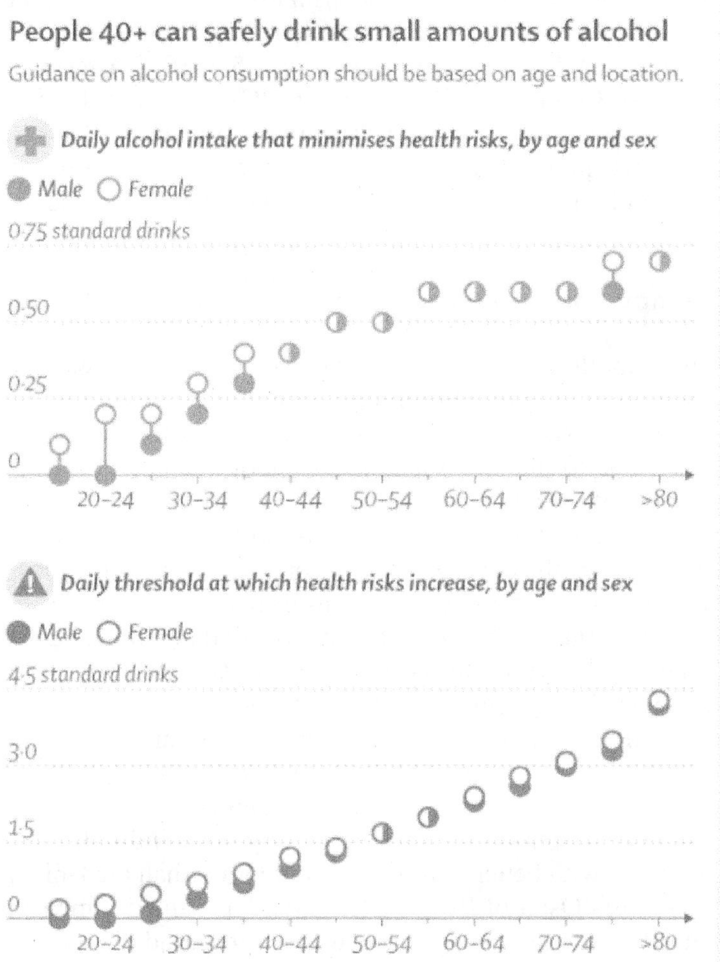

According to the 2020 The National Survey on Drug Use and Health (NSDUH) report, about 6.03 million Americans between the ages of 12 and 20 report current alcohol consumption; this represents 16 percent of this age group for whom alcohol consumption is illegal. Fortunately, among 12 to 20-year-olds, reported rates of past month consumption, binge drinking, and heavy alcohol

34. Image of alcohol intake to minimize health risks and daily threshold of alcoholic drinks at which health risks increase from GBD Alcohol Collaborators *supra* note 23, available at https://www.thelancet.com/pb-assets/Lancet/infographics/health-risks-alcohol/health-risks-of-alcohol.png.

consumption have declined steadily from 2011 to 2020, reaching historical low levels in 2020.[35]

Compared to abstainers and moderate drinkers, youth who drink heavily are at greater risk of death by unintentional injury, homicide, and suicide, which are the three leading causes of death among persons age 15 to 19.[36] A recent study by the Centers for Disease Control and Prevention (CDC) spells out the particular risks in more detail: driving after drinking; riding with a driver who has been drinking; sexual activity and pregnancy of self or partner; tobacco use; interpersonal violence; consideration of or attempt at suicide; and use of marijuana, cocaine, or inhalants.[37]

e. Pregnancy and Fetal Development

Pregnancy is another area in which alcohol poses risks to health. While many people are aware that they should not drink while pregnant for the health of the fetus, there is an increased risk of adverse health effects for both the fetus and the pregnant person, due to the direct health effects of alcohol as well as secondary factors associated with alcohol use.

Alcohol during pregnancy can cause miscarriages, still births, fetal alcohol syndrome, pre-term birth, and low birth weight.[38] The belief that one should abstain from alcohol while pregnant is enshrined as the first sentence of the government warning that is carried on the labels of all alcoholic beverages sold in the United States: "According to the Surgeon General, women should not drink alcoholic beverages during pregnancy because of the risk of birth defects."[39] Yet, despite the risks, the idea that one can consume a small amount of alcohol during pregnancy is contested. While the CDC and the American Academy of Pediatrics state unequivocally that there is "no safe amount of alcohol use during pregnancy,"[40] this has been called into question by some individuals citing studies from other countries with better infant health outcomes than the United States. Dr. (of economics) Emily Oster of Brown University has gained some traction for her assessment of 200+ studies on the topic, where she found "no credible evidence

---

35. "*The Fight Against Underage Drinking | Stats on Teen Alcohol Use* responsibility.org, https://www.responsibility.org/alcohol-statistics/underage-drinking-statistics (last visited June 13, 2022). National Survey on Drug Use and Health data reveal a decline in underage drinking. From 2002 to 2019, the prevalence of past-30-day alcohol use decreased 41.1 percent for 16- to 17-year-olds, 54.7 percent for 14- to 15-year-olds, and 61.9 percent for 12- to 13-year-olds. National Institute on Alcohol Abuse and Alcoholism, *Alcohol Facts and Statistics – Alcohol Use in the United States*, supra n. 5.

36. CDC: Wonder, *About Underlying Cause of Death*, https://wonder.cdc.gov/controller/saved/D76/D266F033 (last visited Aug. 11, 2022).

37. Tammy Chung et al., *Adolescent Binge Drinking* 39(1) Alcohol Rsch. 5-15 (2018).

38. DeJong, *supra* note 14.

39. *See* 27 U.S.C. § 215(a)(1) (2020).

40. Centers for Disease Control and Prevention, *Alcohol Use During Pregnancy* (2022), https://www.cdc.gov/ncbddd/fasd/alcohol-use.html.

that an occasional alcoholic beverage has any consequences."[41] While it is accurate that the risk of fetal alcohol syndrome increases with increasing amounts of alcohol, and that therefore, a low level alcohol might not result in fetal anomalies, Dr. (of medicine) Ruta Nonacs, MD, PhD of Harvard says the following:

> Some doctors may say that it's OK to have a drink of wine with dinner, but at this point we don't have enough data to support that recommendation. Because we don't have enough information to indicate the safety of "light" alcohol use and because alcohol is not medically necessary or beneficial during pregnancy, we recommend that women refrain from drinking alcohol during pregnancy.

In a California study, maternal death in those who used alcohol or drugs while pregnant was 2.7 times higher than in the general pregnant population.[42] In a study of females across the U.S. from 2015-2019, pregnant or recently pregnant females (within the last year) were 2.8 times more likely to die of alcohol or drug poisoning than the total female population. Deaths due to motor vehicle collisions and homicide were also higher in pregnant or recently pregnant females.[43] Given that alcohol is involved in about 30 percent of fatal crashes and in 48 percent of homicides,[44] the risk of alcohol to pregnant people includes not only their own consumption of alcohol, but also the consumption of those around them.

Although there is a great interest in reducing alcohol use during pregnancy due to these risks, research does not suggest that current policies regarding alcohol use during pregnancy actually reduces the risk of harm. Such policies include mandatory warning signs, limits on criminal prosecution, giving priority to pregnant women seeking substance abuse treatment, creating reporting requirements for Child Protective Services, and defining alcohol use during pregnancy as child abuse/neglect. Studies from Advancing New Standards in Reproductive Health (ANSIRH) at the University of California, San Francisco and the Alcohol Research Group show that these policies do not seem to be associated with lower alcohol consumption, nor better health outcomes.[45] A study of data spanning 1972-2015 found that these policies were associated with an increase in the number of low birthweight and preterm births. Furthermore, policies that place limits on criminal prosecution generally prevent the use of medical tests as

---

41. Leslie Goldman, *Parenting Rules You Can Break*, Brown Alumni Magazine (Apr.-May 2020), *available at* https://www.brownalumnimagazine.com/articles/2020-04-12/parenting-rules-you-can-break.

42. Wolfe et al., *Mortality Risk Associated with Perinatal Drug and Alcohol Use in California*, 25(2) Journal of Perinatology 93-100 (2005).

43. Howard et al., *Trends in Mortality Among Pregnant and Recently Pregnant Women in the US, 2015-2019*, 326(16) JAMA 1631-33 (Oct. 26, 2021).

44. National Highway Traffic Safety Administration, *Traffic Safety Facts: Alcohol Impaired Driving 2019 Data*, U.S. Dept. of Transp. (2019), https://crashstats.nhtsa.dot.gov/Api/Public/Publication/813120; Kuhns et al., *The Prevalence of Alcohol-Involved Homicide Offending: A Meta-Analytic Review*, 18(3) Homicide Studies, 251-270 (Aug. 1, 2014).

45. Roberts et al., *State Policies Targeting Alcohol Use during Pregnancy and Alcohol Use among Pregnant Women 1985–2016: Evidence from the Behavioral Risk Factor Surveillance System*, 29(3) Women's Health Issues 213-221 (May 1, 2019).

evidence against women who may have caused harm to a fetus or infant, and as a result often end in more pregnant people being prosecuted. However, they do not seem to decrease the likelihood of alcohol consumption during pregnancy, nor are they associated with improved infant health outcomes.[46]

3. WINE, AN EXCEPTION?

Although alcoholic beverage consumption over time can lead to the development of a variety of health problems, it has been thought that moderate alcohol consumption may have protective effects for certain health conditions. Perhaps the most notable beneficial health effect of alcohol is the correlation between moderate alcohol consumption and lower risk of coronary heart disease (CHD), which accounts for one in five deaths in the United States.[47] The association between reduced CHD risk and moderate alcohol consumption was popularized in 1991, when CBS aired its 60 Minutes segment on the "French Paradox." The program revealed that the French have a lower rate of heart disease than Americans, even when controlling for factors such as diet, exercise, and lifestyle choices, and suggested that this is the result of moderate consumption of alcohol, particularly red wine.[48]

French epidemiologist and nutritionist Serge Renaud, who first espoused the French Paradox, suggests that the health benefits derived from moderate alcohol consumption vary with the type of alcoholic beverage consumed. Most alcohol researchers generally do not address the differences among wine, beer, and spirits; they only measure absolute alcohol (ethanol).[49] It was thought that the French Paradox could therefore be explained by the fact that wine differs from other alcohol due to the presence of polyphenols, micronutrients that act as antioxidants. Antioxidants protect against aging and disease by neutralizing free radicals, which are unstable atoms that can cause damage to cells.

However, decades of research fail to support this hypothesis resolving the French Paradox for two reasons: (1) polyphenols are weak antioxidants with low bioavailability (meaning that they don't significantly impact the cell's pre-existing ability to target free radicals), and (2) the majority of studies on wine polyphenols in animals use such large quantities of polyphenols that it could not be replicated in humans drinking a "moderate" amount of wine.[50]

Unfortunately, more recent evidence does not conclusively show that moderate alcohol consumption reduces CHD risk. While a number of studies demonstrate a reduction in CHD risk among moderate drinkers, primarily in those over the age

---

46. Subbaraman et al., *Costs associated with policies regarding alcohol use during pregnancy: Results from 1972-2015 Vital Statistics*, 14(5) PLoS One (May 8, 2019).

47. Centers for Disease Control and Prevention, National Center for Health Statistics. *About Multiple Causes of Death, 1999–2020*, Centers for Disease Control and Prevention, 2022.

48. Richard Mendelson, From Demon to Darling: A Legal History of Wine in America 169 (2009).

49. *Id.*

50. Betul Catalgol et al., *Resveratrol: French Paradox Revisited,* 3 Frontiers in Pharmacology 141 (Jul. 17, 2012).

of 55,[51] others have found that the cardiovascular benefits of light to moderate drinking are instead the result of confounding lifestyle factors.[52] Moderate drinkers of wine may appear healthier, not because of any substance found in wine, but because wine drinkers in general tend to live healthier lifestyles than beer or spirits drinkers.[53] Furthermore, the alcohol itself may not matter; it is the fact that those who drink a light to moderate amount of alcohol live healthier lives that accounts for lower rates of CHD.[54] This might be the underlying reason for the French Paradox: differences in the French diet and lifestyle. Possibly drinking wine with meals, eating smaller portion sizes, and consuming more fruits and vegetables explains the paradox. These lifestyle differences might even account for the differences in CHD rates between different French regions.[55] Creina Stockley, a clinical pharmacologist in Australia, says the following about wine consumed with food:

> This pattern of wine consumption attenuates the blood alcohol concentration achieved, prolongs any short-term plasma anti-oxidative and anti-thrombotic effects, promotes any long-term effects, and prevents any rebound effects of the ethanol and phenolic components of the beverage. Populations that regularly consume a moderate amount of alcohol with a meal, such as those of the Mediterranean countries, and of central and southern France, have a significantly lower risk of cardiovascular disease.[56] [Citations omitted.]

These possible benefits might seem counter to the previously mentioned Lancet study on the Global Burden of Disease and Alcohol. In particular, the Lancet study questions cardiovascular health benefits, leading some health activists to claim that there is "no safe level" of alcohol consumption for those under age 40.[57] However, critiques of the Lancet study demonstrate the major problems with large-scale studies aimed at understanding lifestyle factors: It is difficult to combine data from countries with different base levels of disease, different social and cultural norms on drinking (and reporting drinking), and different socioeconomic statuses.[58] In countries like the US, where ischemic

---

51. Jinhui Zhao et al., *Alcohol Consumption and Mortality From Coronary Heart Disease: An Updated Meta-Analysis of Cohort Studies*, J Stud Alcohol Drugs, 78(3) 375-386 (May 2017).

52. Kiran J. Biddinger et al., *Association of Habitual Alcohol Intake With Risk of Cardiovascular Disease,* 5(3) JAMA Network Open (Mar. 25, 2022).

53. Wine: A Scientific Explanation, 103 (Merton Sandler & Roger Pinder eds., 2003) at 103; Philip Cook, Paying the Tab: The Costs and Benefits of Alcohol Control 114 (2007).

54. *See* Biddinger, supra note 52.

55. ASN Staff, *The French Paradox: Was it Really the Wine?, American Society for Nutrition*, https://nutrition.org/french-paradox-really-wine/ (Jan. 18, 2013).

56. Creina Stockley, *Evidence of the Specific Benefits of Wine Consumption on Human Health—An Update on the Cardiovascular and Other Physiological Mechanisms*, 446 The Australian and New Zealand Grapegrower and Winemaker 72, 77 (2001), available at www.aim-digest.com/gateway/pages/moderate/articles/evidence.htm (last visited Aug. 14, 2022).

57. GBD Alcohol Collaborators, *supra* note 23.

58. International Scientific Forum on Alcohol Research, *Critique 219: A global overview of alcohol consumption and health* (Sep. 3, 2018) https://www.alcoholresearchforum.org/critique-219/.

diseases and diabetes are among the leading causes of death, the protective effects of moderate alcohol consumption could be significant in reducing total mortality. In countries where ischemic diseases are less common, moderate alcohol consumption may only have a minor effect on total mortality (and may instead be associated with increases in other types of disease). In combining results from multiple countries, this nuance is lost, making it more difficult for policy makers to create appropriate guidance for the health of their constituents. As discussed elsewhere in this chapter, an approach that pushes abstention in all individuals is often ineffective and fails to reflect that moderate alcohol consumption can indeed be part of a healthy lifestyle.[59]

B. PUBLIC SAFETY

While moderate use of alcoholic beverages can have social benefits such as increased support systems and feelings of trust and happiness,[60] harmful use has adverse social consequences, including disorderly conduct, threats to public safety through crime, workplace problems, accidental injuries, drinking and driving, and intentional self-harm. With respect to these adverse consequences, heavy drinkers and chronic alcohol abusers are at a significantly higher risk than moderate drinkers.[61] Yet, epidemiological evidence reveals that acute intoxication among all drinkers, both moderate and heavy, is the main cause of alcohol-related injury. That is, the number of heavy-drinking occasions is a stronger predictor of injury than the average level of consumption.[62] As Ingeborg Rossow, et al., write in *Mapping the Social Consequences of Alcohol Consumption*,

> [M]ost of the accidents and injuries in established market economies are caused by unusually light to moderate drinkers who were exposed to heavy drinking occasions. Thus, it has been argued that the prevention paradox applies here, namely that preventive measures to reduce the occurrence of accidents and suicidal behavior due to alcohol should take the form of population-based strategies aimed at more moderate drinkers, who contribute the most to alcohol-related accidents and intentional injury.[63]

The fact that alcohol-related harm is "distributed on a continuum throughout the drinking population and is certainly not limited to the small number of consistently

---

59. *See* Yanping Li et al., Healthy lifestyle and life expectancy free of cancer, cardiovascular disease, and type 2 diabetes: prospective cohort study, BMJ 368, I6669 (Jan. 8, 2020).

60. R.I.M. Dunbar et al., *Functional Benefits of (Modest) Alcohol Consumption,* Adaptive Human Behavior and Physiology, 3, 118–133 (2017).

61. Ingeborg Rossow et al.,Accidents, Suicide and Violence, in Mapping the Social Consequences of Alcohol Consumption 105 (Harald Klingermann & Gerhard Gmel eds., 2001).

62. Jürgen Rehm, et al., *On the Emerging Paradigm of Drinking Patterns and Their Social and Health Consequences*, 91 Addiction 1615, 1619 (1996).

63. Rossow et al., *supra* note 62.

heavy drinkers,"[64] however, does not necessitate eliminating drinking among all individuals to reduce harm. As discussed in more detail in the following section, reducing the frequency of heavy drinking rather than reducing overall alcohol consumption may be more prudent and more acceptable to the general public.

C. REGULATIONS AND INTERVENTIONS

Given the array of problems associated with drinking, various policies have been adopted over time to keep health hazards and social harms to a minimum. This is generally known as "harm reduction," "harm minimization," or the "public health perspective." These alcohol policy measures generally fall into the following 6 categories: access and availability; taxation and pricing; altering the drinking context; drinking and driving; advertising and marketing; and prevention, specifically including education and treatment. Each of these approaches is discussed in turn below.

1. ACCESS AND AVAILABILITY

Perhaps the most heavily relied-upon alcohol control policy is to limit the availability of and access to alcoholic beverages. Supply-side controls can take many forms, from outright prohibition, as occurred (with certain exceptions) during National Prohibition, to government alcohol monopolies such as those that exist today in the 18 control states. As we learned during National Prohibition, a total ban may not be sustainable because of its numerous adverse side effects, including illegal production (moonshining), illegal trade (bootlegging), and a widespread disrespect for the law. By the end of that 13-year period, even John D. Rockefeller, oil magnate, philanthropist, and ardent prohibitionist, had become disillusioned with the "noble experiment."

After studying all the alcohol control systems around the world, Rockefeller proposed that the states establish alcohol monopolies after Repeal. He wrote, "[O]nly as the profit motive is eliminated is there any hope of controlling the liquor traffic in the interest of a decent society. To approach the problem from any other angle is only to tinker with it and to insure failure."[65] Rockefeller believed, as did his researchers Raymond Fosdick and Albert Scott, that the profit motive makes inevitable the stimulation of sales and over-consumption. The "authority plan," which they recommended and which Rockefeller endorsed, would establish a public monopoly in each state over the wholesale and/or retail sale of alcoholic beverages, particularly those with higher alcoholic strength sold for off-premise

---

64. Tim Stockwell, Eric Single, David Hawks & Jürgen Rehm, *Sharpening the Focus of Alcohol Policy from Aggregate Consumption to Harm and Risk Reduction*, 5 Addiction Rsch. 1, 4 (1997).

65. Raymond Fosdick & Albert Scott, Toward Liquor Control, x (Center for Alcohol Policy ed. 2011) (1933).

consumption.[66] The state authority plan, they said, would achieve a social, rather than a profit, objective by curtailing the consumption of alcoholic beverages through price controls, advertising restrictions, educational campaigns, elimination of the saloon, and establishment of carefully located and designed package stores, known today as state stores, run by salaried government employees.

Whether the individual states after Repeal adopted a government monopoly or a licensing system for the private sector, they were able to, and did, restrict the supply of alcoholic beverages through controls on the location and density of on-sale and off-sale premises, the days and hours of sale, and the minimum legal drinking age. Typically, states limit the density of retail outlets by population or geographic area. Certain locations may be prohibited—for example, if they are too close to churches or schools. In the college setting, for example, the numbers of package stores and other sales outlets may be restricted directly by placing a limit on their density within a certain radius of campus.[67] Sometimes these controls are part of the state's alcoholic beverage control laws, or they may be included in state or local land use laws.

All states limit the days and hours during which alcoholic beverages may be sold. The so-called blue laws,[68] originally designed to enforce religious standards, generally prohibit the off-premise sale of alcohol on Sundays. Many states have repealed or amended their blue laws to permit alcohol sales on Sundays, such that only seven states currently prohibit the sale of spirits on Sundays.[69] Similarly, states, in the exercise of their Twenty-first Amendment rights, decide which types of retail outlets can sell alcoholic beverages. Some states allow alcoholic beverage sales at drugstores, convenience stores, gas stations, grocery stores, fast food and other restaurants, and sports stadiums. Other states prohibit alcoholic beverage sales at one or more of these locations, or they may specify other products such as food or non-alcoholic beverages that may, may not, or must be sold there.

States may decide to apply specific control measures to specific alcoholic beverages, depending on their alcoholic strength and susceptibility to abuse. For example, state stores in some control states sell only distilled spirits, leaving lower-strength wines and beers to be sold at licensed establishments, including convenience stores and grocery stores. Many state and local jurisdictions through land use laws restrict, in some or all areas, the sale of single bottles of beer, spirits

---

66. *Id.* at 64. Off-premise consumption refers to alcoholic beverages that are sold in closed containers at a package store (also known as an off-sale premise) and are consumed away from the licensed premise. On-premise or on-sale establishments such as restaurants and bars sell and serve alcoholic beverages for consumption at the licensed premise.

67. Task Force of the NIAAA, A Call to Action Changing the Culture of Drinking at U.S. Colleges 19 (2002) https://www.collegedrinkingprevention.gov/media/taskforcereport.pdf (last visited Aug. 14, 2022).

68. "Blue laws" are those laws "forbidding certain secular activities on Sunday." Britannica, Editors of Encyclopaedia, "blue law." Encyclopedia Britannica (Feb. 13, 2020), available at https://www.britannica.com/topic/blue-law.

69. Patrick Gleason, *States Continue To Ease Restrictions On Alcohol Sales,* Forbes (Apr. 18, 2022), https://www.forbes.com/sites/patrickgleason/2022/04/18/states-continue-to-ease-restrictions-on-alcohol-sales/?sh=3eb69f923e86.

in bottles of one-half pint or less, and more recently, caffeinated alcoholic beverages (alcohol energy drinks).[70] That said, during the COVID pandemic, some jurisdictions liberalized the sale and delivery of alcoholic beverages. For example, California, as of January 1, 2022, allows the sale of cocktails to go, and in 2023, as many as eighteen states will have passed similar legislation.[71]

Another means of restricting access to alcoholic beverages is through the minimum legal drinking age. Today, all 50 states have established 21 as the minimum drinking age, although they vary in terms of the exceptions granted for home consumption or for religious, medical, or educational purposes. In the 1970s and early 1980s, following the adoption of the Twenty-sixth Amendment to the U.S. Constitution,[72] most states adopted 18 or 19 as the minimum drinking age. They accepted the logic that if 18-year-olds can vote and serve in the military, they are old enough to drink alcoholic beverages. In 1982, President Ronald Reagan appointed the Commission on Drunk Driving that recommended, among other things, the establishment of 21 as the national minimum drinking age.[73] This was achieved by withholding federal highway funds from any state that failed to adopt the recommended minimum drinking age. By 1988, all states had done so.

According to Thomas Babor and his co-authors, "[a] comprehensive review [citation omitted] based on all published studies on legal drinking published between 1960 and 2000 (a total of 135 documents) concluded that increasing the legal age for purchase and consumption of alcohol to 21 years is the most effective strategy for reducing drinking and drinking problems among high-school students, college students, and other youth, compared to a wide range of other programmes and efforts."[74] The argument in favor of a minimum drinking age is especially compelling when viewed in tandem with research that suggests that other interventions to reduce underage drinking, such as school-based interventions, are ineffective.[75]

Regardless, there are those who advocate for lowering the drinking age outright, and others who propose different strategies that lower the drinking age and combat irresponsible underage drinking. A statutory initiative to lower the drinking age to 18 was proposed in 2015 in California,[76] and South Carolina State Representative Todd Rutherford introduced a bill in 2021 that would reduce the

---

70. For a review of land use laws related to alcoholic beverages, *see* Chapter 7.

71. Cal. Bus. & Prof. Code Sec. 23401.5 (2020). The cocktail must be packaged in a container with a secure lid or cap, sealed in a manner designed to prevent consumption without removal of the lid or cap; the drink cannot contain more than 4 ½ ounces of distilled spirits; and the container must be clearly and conspicuously labeled or otherwise identified as containing an alcoholic beverage; Gleason *supra* note 68.

72. Section 1 of the Twenty-sixth Amendment, adopted in 1971, reads, "The right of citizens of the United States, who are eighteen years of age or older, to vote shall not be denied or abridged by the United States or by any State on account of age."

73. Presidential Commission on Drunk Driving: Final Report 10 (1983).

74. Thomas Babor et al., Alcohol: No Ordinary Commodity 140 (2d ed. 2010).

75. Martineau et al., *Population-level interventions to reduce alcohol-related harm: An overview of systematic reviews*, 57-4 Preventive Medicine 278-296 (2013).

76. A.G. File No. 2015-054, California Legislative Analyst's Office (2015).

state's drinking age to 18.[77] Neither was successful. Currently, 31 states allow underage drinking on private property with a parent's consent, and six states allow underage drinking on private property without a parent's consent.[78]

Other proposals to lower the minimum drinking age include: allowing those over 18 to drink in a bar or restaurant with a parent's consent or with someone over 21, a "learner's permit" and licensing structure for new drinkers that operates similarly to a driver's license and includes comprehensive education, a reduced drinking age for wine and beer only, and allowing 18-year-olds to purchase alcohol only in bars and restaurants, where their drinking can be monitored by knowledgeable staff.[79]

The other supply-side measures discussed in this section have not been as effective as the minimum drinking age in preventing harm, nor are they as widely supported. Certainly, these laws reduce total alcohol consumption. For example, there is strong evidence that state retail monopolies decrease alcohol consumption levels.[80] Between 1997 and 2007, the average annual alcohol consumption in the 18 control states was around 0.65 gallons per capita for people over the age of 14.[81] License states had a higher consumption rate of 0.76 gallons during the same period.[82] However, the decrease in alcohol consumption levels in control states is not distributed evenly across the population. A study from the Alcohol Research Group found that while white men living in a control state were 17 percent less likely to drink than those in license states and drank 0.14 percent less than their counterparts, living in a control state did not decrease the likelihood of drinking nor the amount consumed by African-American men and Hispanic women.[83] While total alcohol consumption may be reduced by state retail monopolies, differences among groups based on race, ethnicity, and other sociocultural factors suggests the importance of understanding demographic differences in creating policy to reduce harms from alcohol.

---

77. *State representative pre-files bill to lower S.C. drinking age to 18*, WYFF4 (Nov. 10, 2021 11:24 PM), https://www.wyff4.com/article/bill-to-lower-sc-drinking-age/38215016.

78. ProCon.org, *States That Allow Underage (under 21) Alcohol Consumption*, Britannica (Mar. 10, 2016), https://drinkingage.procon.org/states-that-allow-underage-under-21-alcohol-consumption/#A.; NYRA, *Solutions and Alternatives to the Drinking Age,* National Youth Rights Organization, (2020), https://www.youthrights.org/issues/drinking-age/solutions/.

79. *See* NYRA *supra* note 79.

80. Thomas Babor, Alcohol Policy and the Public Good: As Simple as One, Two, Three?, in From Science to Action? 100 Years Later—Alcohol Policies Revisited 36 (Richard Miller & Harald Klingermann eds., 2004), citing Alexander Wagenaar, & Harold Holder, Changes in Alcohol Consumption Resulting from the Elimination of Retail Wine Monopolies: Results from Five US states, 56 Journal of Studies on Alcohol 566 (1995).

81. Brian Sonntag, Washington State Auditor, Report No. 1002726, State Government Performance Review: Opportunities for Washington 32 (2010), available at https://portal.sao.wa.gov/ReportSearch/Home/ViewReportFile?isFinding=false&arn=1002726 (last visited Aug. 6, 2022).

82. *Id.*

83. Subbaraman et al., *Relationships between US state alcohol policies and alcohol outcomes: Differences by gender and race/ethnicity,* 115(7) Addiction 1285-1294 (Jul. 2020).

There also is evidence that the replacement of state monopolies with privatization leads to increased total annual alcohol consumption.[84] The Alcohol Research Group, in a publication prepared for the National Association of Beverage Control Authorities (NABCA) entitled *Alcohol Control Systems and the Potential Effects of Privatization*, concludes that "privatization results in higher outlet density, greater physical availability, longer and later hours of sale and new elements in the marketing and sales process, such as a greater commercial orientation towards alcohol sales and additional economic vested interests."[85]

This, in tandem with data confirming that total alcohol consumption is directly related to adverse health and social consequences, bolsters calls to reduce the access to and the availability of alcohol. However, a population-based strategy designed to reduce total alcohol consumption may be ill advised if it unnecessarily and unfairly burdens moderate drinkers, who far outnumber heavy drinkers. One commentator refers to this approach as "draining the ocean to prevent shark attacks."[86] Instead, harm reduction might focus on modifying heavy-drinking patterns (chronic or episodic),[87] altering the environments that promote heavy drinking,[88] and promoting beneficial drinking patterns in society. This may be more effective and more politically feasible than the across-the-board alcohol reduction approach.

2. TAXATION AND PRICING

The WHO has asserted that "[p]rice is an important determinant of alcohol consumption and, in many contexts, of the extent of alcohol-related problems."[89]

---

84. *See* Hahn et al., *Effects of alcohol retail privatization on excessive alcohol consumption and related harms: a community guide systematic review*, Am J Prev Med 42(4):418-27, (Apr. 2012).

85. Alcohol Research Group, *Alcohol Control Systems and the Potential Effects of Privatization* 7 (2009).

86. Martin Plant, Harm Minimization, in Harald Klingermann & Gerhard Gmel, Mapping Social Consequences of Alcohol Consumption 146 (2001).

87. On the Emerging Paradigm of Drinking Patterns and Their Social and Health Consequences, *supra* note 63 at 1619.

88. The Alcohol Research Group's analyses of the NIAAA's National Epidemiologic Survey on Alcohol and Related Conditions indicate that while drinking in bars, taverns, and cocktail lounges accounted for 24 percent of the overall volume reported in 6 drinking contexts, these "on premise" bar settings accounted for 37 percent of the hazardous drinking (5 or more drinks per day). Conversely, restaurants accounted for 14 percent of the total volume but only 3 percent of the volume attributable to hazardous amounts. Thomas Greenfield, Alcohol Policy, presented at the Alcohol and Alcohol Actions (Psychosocial) Lecture Series, Annual Meeting of the Research Society on Alcoholism (June 23-24, 2006), available at http://www.rsalectures.com/pdf/greenfield.doc. Excessive drinking also tends to occur at private parties and in public places such as parking lots and street corners. Patricia McDaniel & Thomas Greenfield, Somewhere between the Bars and Home: Drinking Locations and Drinking Norms among Women and Men in the United States, presented at the 129th Annual Meeting of the American Public Health Association (Oct. 21-25, 2001), abstract available at http://apha.confex.com/apha/129am/techprogram/paper_24218.htm.

89. World Health Organization, Strategies to Reduce the Harmful Use of Alcohol, Document A61/13 4 (March 2008).

Professor Philip Cook, in *Paying the Tab: The Costs and Benefits of Alcohol Control*, is more direct.

> Quite simply, alcohol taxation and other measures that increase the price of ethanol are effective in promoting public health and safety. Higher prices are conducive to lower rates of underage drinking, traffic fatalities, and sexually transmitted disease. There is less direct evidence on the effects of higher prices on the prevalence of chronic excess drinking and related medical conditions, but the indirect evidence is compelling on that score as well.[90]

Whether price intervention is good public policy depends on how sensitive consumers are to price changes and whether the reduced consumption has a corresponding effect on adverse health and social consequences. Price sensitivity is known as the price elasticity of demand. It is measured as the percentage change in consumption resulting from a 1 percent change in price. For example, a price elasticity of –0.49 for wine, which is a reasonable estimate, means that a 10 percent price increase will cause just under a five percent decline in the volume consumed.[91] Wine demand, we would say, is relatively inelastic. This makes intuitive sense because of the number of ways, other than buying less, in which consumers can compensate for price increases such as drinking more at home, drinking cheaper brands, or substituting other alcoholic beverages. If the price rise is too steep, consumers may turn to illegal alcoholic beverages (adulterated, counterfeit, etc.), as they did during Prohibition.

There has not been adequate study of price elasticities for particular groups of drinkers, but it is important in adopting alcohol policies to know which drinkers are affected by a price increase and by how much. On the whole, increased taxes decrease heavy episodic drinking and discourage excess drinkers, with a 2022 global umbrella review finding that a one percent increase in price resulted in a 0.28 percent decrease in demand for alcohol among heavy drinkers.[92] A 2016 U.S. study found that "excess drinkers" (defined as two or more drinks a day for men and one or more drinks a day for women) would feel the greatest burden associated with a state-specific tax increase of about $0.25 a drink, and would account for 72 percent of the total tax burden.[93]

In the case of youth, the evidence is more conflicting: Some studies find that they are more sensitive to pricing than adults, yet other studies find the opposite.[94] In the instance of youth binge drinking, a study found that as price increases, the tendency for binge drinking tends to decrease, but the relationship between the two

---

90. Paying the Tab, *supra* note 53 at 167.

91. *See* Table 5.2 in Paying the Tab, *supra* note 53.

at 72; cf. Table 8.1 in Alcohol: No Ordinary Commodity, *supra* note 73 at 113 (wine elasticities calculated by 3 separate researchers at -0.77, -0.70 and -0.69).

92. Guindon et. al., *Prices, taxes and alcohol use: a systematic umbrella review,* Addiction (Jun. 6, 2022), https://onlinelibrary.wiley.com/doi/10.1111/add.15966?af=R

93. Naimi et al., *Who Would Pay for State Alcohol Tax Increases in the United States?* 13 Preventing Chronic Disease, 5 (May 19, 2016).

94. Guindon, *supra* note 91.

varied greatly depending on age, sex, and ethnicity.[95] Furthermore, in response to price increases, youth are more likely to engage in substitute behavior such as drinking at home and buying less expensive alcoholic beverages.[96] The Committee on Developing a Strategy to Reduce and Prevent Underage Drinking, created by the National Research Council and the Institute of Medicine (NRC/IOM), concluded in 2004 that higher alcoholic beverage prices achieved by higher excise taxes "are potentially important instruments for preventing underage drinking and its harmful consequences and for generating revenue to fund a broad prevention strategy."[97]

Because of the diversity of research results, the policy prescriptions about alcohol taxation and pricing vary. For example, Godfrey Robson, senior consultant at the International Center for Alcohol Policies, argues that "taxes and price controls are regressive upon responsible consumers while failing to achieve their goal of reducing harm."[98] That is, these measures only distinguish between consumers and abstainers, not between moderate and heavy drinkers. There are other possible disadvantages of taxes as an alcohol control measure. Typically, taxes are imposed for revenue generation, not for prevention. Taxes also may not translate directly into higher prices because of the intervening complex market decisions of producers, wholesalers, and retailers. Finally, high taxes can have unintended negative consequences such as illicit production, adulteration, counterfeiting, and smuggling.

By contrast, Dr. Babor and his co-authors in *Alcohol: No Ordinary Commodity* conclude that "[a]lcohol taxes are thus an attractive instrument of alcohol policy, as they can be used both to generate direct revenue for the state and to reduce alcohol-related harms. Even setting aside their contribution to government revenue, they are among the most cost-effective ways for a government to reduce alcohol-related harm."[99] A report from the CDC Task Force on Community Preventive Services agrees, finding "strong evidence that raising alcohol taxes is an effective strategy for reducing excessive alcohol consumption and related harms."[100]

In terms of the specific measures used to raise prices, the most common is the state, federal, or local excise tax on alcoholic beverages.[101] Because the tax is applied to products that some consider as vices, such as tobacco and gambling, it often is referred to as a "sin tax." Excise taxes are paid by the manufacturer or

---

95. *Id.*

96. Godfrey Robinson, Pricing Beverage Alcohol, in Working Together to Reduce Harmful Drinking 100-101 (Marcus Grant & Mark Leverton eds., 2010).

97. Reducing Underage Drinking: A Collective Responsibility 244 (Richard J. Bonnie & Mary Ellen O'Connell eds., 2004)

98. *Id.*

99. Alcohol: No Ordinary Commodity, *supra* note 75 at 125.

100. Randy Elder et al., *The Effectiveness of Tax Policy Interventions for Reducing Excessive Alcohol Consumption and Related Harms*, 38 American Journal of Preventative Medicine 217, 226 (2010).

101. Environmental Influences on Young Adult Drinking, NIAAA, http://pubs.niaaa.nih.gov /publications/arh284/230-235.htm (last visited Aug. 14, 2022).

wholesaler rather than the retailer and are based on the volume of the product, not its value. The amount of excise tax varies depending on the type of alcoholic beverage, with the highest rates imposed on the highest-strength beverages—distilled spirits.[102]

Many policy analysts note that the United States has failed to increase alcoholic beverage excise tax levels to keep pace with inflation. Indeed, the last federal excise tax increase on beer, wine, or spirits was in 1991. This has led to many proposals to index the federal alcoholic beverage excise taxes to inflation, but no such proposal has been adopted.

The excise tax rates on beer, wine, and spirits also are not proportional to their respective levels of absolute alcohol. Specifically, the tax on spirits is far higher than on other alcoholic beverages. This was done purposefully after Repeal to dissuade the consumption of "ardent spirits" in favor of lower-alcohol fermented beverages. In fact, there was a recommended ratio: the excise tax on table wines was one-twentieth of the spirits tax, and the tax on fortified wines was one-tenth of the spirits rate.[103] Not surprisingly, distillers, in particular, want to eliminate this tax discrimination against spirits, but that proposal has had no traction in Congress.

In addition to imposing excise taxes, many states directly or indirectly regulate wine prices. State monopolies can set prices by administrative fiat. License states influence alcoholic beverage prices through a variety of mechanisms, including mandatory markups, impact fees to pay for alcohol-related externalities (health and social services, criminal justice, etc.), minimum prices, resale price maintenance, and price postings.[104] From a policy perspective, not all of these measures have similar effects. Minimum prices, for example, are thought to dampen heavy drinking, while imposing only minimally on moderate wine drinkers. Dr. Chris Record and Professor Chris Day describe the advantages of minimum alcohol pricing in the United Kingdom as follows:

> The current policy of low alcohol prices means that responsible drinkers are subsidi[z]ing the behavior of the 25% of the population who are drinking at hazardous or harmful levels. The introduction of a 50p/unit minimum price would mean that this sector would be selectively targeted and would pay more for the alcohol they consume thus removing the subsidy they are currently enjoying. Alcohol consumption in this group is therefore likely to fall with substantial advantages to public health, law and order.[105]

---

102. The excise tax on distilled spirits is disproportionally high compared to beer and wine in relation to their respective alcoholic strength. Also, Champagne, as a luxury product, is subject to a disproportionately high excise tax.

103. From Demon to Darling, *supra* note 48 at 229 n.10.

104. Price postings on retail prices are equivalent to resale price maintenance because they prevent retailers from lowering their prices below posted levels, although the prices typically can be changed monthly or quarterly.

105. Chris Record & Chris Day, *Britain's Alcohol Market: How Minimum Alcohol Prices Could Stop Moderate Drinkers Subsidizing Those Drinking at Hazardous and Harmful Levels*, 9 Clinical Medicine 421, 425 (2009).

The states do not have free reign in selecting alcoholic beverage price controls because some of the measures are unlawful. Generally speaking, states increase alcoholic beverage prices in order to decrease demand and promote temperance. Although these are valid goals under the Twenty-first Amendment, state laws may violate federal or state antitrust laws. For example, state fair-trade laws require manufacturers to file fair-trade contracts with the state, including the prices of all their brands; no wholesaler can sell these products to a retailer at prices other than those stated in the contracts. In the 1980 case of *California Retail Liquor Dealers Ass'n v. Midcal Aluminum*, the U.S. Supreme Court invalidated this form of resale price maintenance as a per se violation of the federal Sherman Antitrust Act (Sherman Act).[106] The Supreme Court specifically rejected California's argument that its price-setting program was saved by the Twenty-first Amendment. "The national policy in favor of competition," Justice Lewis Powell wrote, "cannot be thwarted by casting such a gauzy cloak of state involvement over what is essentially a private price-fixing arrangement.[107] *Midcal Aluminum* stood as the law of the land until 2007, when the court, in the case of *Leegin Creative Leather Products v. PSKS, Inc.*, reversed course, holding that resale price maintenance is no longer per se illegal and is to be judged under the so-called rule of reason.[108]

Similarly, "post and hold" pricing provisions have been invalidated by the courts, most recently in the state of Washington. In *Costco Wholesale Corp. v. Maleng*, the Ninth Circuit Court of Appeals invalidated the requirement that wholesalers in that state file with the Washington State Liquor Control Board a listing of all their wholesale prices.[109] Once the prices are posted, they are made public, and the posted prices must be held constant for at least 30 days. The court found the post and hold scheme to be a per se violation of the Sherman Act. While "each wholesaler is only required to adhere to its own posted price and is not compelled to follow others' pricing decisions, the logical result of the restraints is a less uncertain market, a market more conducive to collusive and stabilized pricing, and hence a less competitive market."[110] The restraint, the court concluded, is "highly likely to facilitate horizontal collusion among market participants."[111]

The court examined whether the Twenty-first Amendment would bar the application of the Sherman Antitrust Act in that case. While acknowledging that the Twenty-first Amendment confers wide latitude upon the states to regulate the intrastate distribution of alcoholic beverages, especially when the goal is to promote temperance, the court found that there was "little empirical evidence" that post and hold had any effect on the rate of alcohol consumption and therefore the

---

106. 445 U.S. 97 (1980); Sherman Antitrust Act, 15 U.S.C. §§ 1-7 (2006) (original version at ch. 647, 26 Stat. 209 (1890)).

107. *Cal. Retail Liquor Dealers Ass'n.*, 445 U.S. at 106.

108. 551 U.S. 877 (2007).

109. *Costco Wholesale Corp. v. Maleng*, 522 F.3d 874 (9th Cir. 2008).

110. *Id.* at 894.

111. *Id.* at 896.

state's interest was entitled to less deference than the federal interest in promoting competition.[112]

Price controls are used by some states for purposes other than the promotion of temperance. For example, some state "price affirmation" laws require manufacturers to affirm that they will sell their products to wholesalers at prices that are no higher than the lowest prices that they charge to wholesalers anywhere else in the United States during a prescribed future period, typically one month. These so-called prospective price affirmation laws ensure that consumers in the state will receive the lowest available alcoholic beverage prices, but these laws also interfere with the manufacturers' ability to change their prices in other states during the time that the price affirmation is in effect. The U.S. Supreme Court in 1986 invalidated New York's prospective price affirmation law in *Brown-Forman Distillers v. N.Y. Liquor Authority*, stating: "While New York may regulate the sale of liquor within its borders, and may seek low prices for its residents, it may not 'project its legislation into [other States] by regulating the price to be paid' for liquor in those States."[113] Because of this extra-territorial effect, the Supreme Court found New York's price affirmation law to be unconstitutional under the Commerce Clause.[114]

3. THE DRINKING CONTEXT

Controlling the context in which drinking occurs is an important way to reduce the negative consequences of intoxication. Responsible beverage service (RBS) is a common approach.[115] RBS requires that servers check the identification of anyone appearing to be under the age of 30. Servers learn how to recognize fake identification cards and driver's licenses. They themselves must be over 21. They also learn how to recognize intoxication, to refuse sales to obviously intoxicated patrons, and to deal with problem patrons to prevent violence.[116]

Although RBS programs are important, their effectiveness is modest. As reported in *Alcohol: No Ordinary Commodity*, "[o]verall, the findings suggest that RBS training and house policies [for staff and customers] are likely to have at best a modest effect on alcohol consumption, and this effect will depend on the nature of the programme and the consistency of its implementation."[117] RBS is greatly enhanced by the active enforcement of alcoholic beverage control laws by alcoholic beverage regulatory authorities and local law enforcement officials.[118]

---

112. *Id.* at 903.

113. *Brown-Forman Distillers Corp. v. N.Y. Liquor Auth.*, 476 U.S. 573, 582-83 (1986) (citing *Baldwin v. G.A.F. Seelig, Inc.*, 294 U.S. 511, 521 (1935)).

114. *See, e.g., Brown-Forman Distillers v. N.Y. Liquor Auth.*, 476 U.S. 573 (1986); *Healy v. U.S. Brewers Assn*, 464 U.S. 909 (1983).

115. *See, e.g.*, Reducing Underage Drinking *supra* note 98.

116. *Id.*; Environmental Influences on Young Adult Drinking, *supra* note 102.

117. Alcohol: No Ordinary Commodity, *supra* note 75 at 152.

118. Murray Sim, Elizabeth Morgan & Julie Batchelor, *The Impact of Enforcement on Intoxication and Alcohol Related Harm* 16 (2005), https://www.police.govt.nz/about-us/publication/impact-enforcement-intoxication-and-alcohol-related-harm.

Community groups also play an important role in controlling the drinking context and enhancing public safety. Community approaches include advocacy, outreach, alternative events, and education. While there is not much evidence to suggest that they reduce overall alcohol consumption, community programs are successful in reducing hazardous alcohol use and alcohol-related harms.[119] Some communities also have lobbied to change the legal environment, for example, by proposing local ordinances that mandate RBS training for all alcoholic beverage licensees, including their managers, servers, and security staff.[120]

Another way in which states can alter the drinking context is to adopt a dram shop law. Dram shop laws authorize legal actions to be brought against establishments that serve alcohol in a willful, wanton, or reckless manner (e.g., to a minor, an obviously intoxicated person, or after hours) if the intoxicated customer inflicts injury or causes property damage to himself or others. More than 40 states have adopted such laws. The laws vary widely. Some states have imposed damage caps, and others allow a "responsible business practices" or contributory negligence defense. Other states only hold establishments liable if they serve liquor without a license or serve liquor to a minor. The purpose of these laws is twofold: to compensate persons who suffer harm due to the intoxication of another and to incentivize licensed establishments to be responsible when serving alcoholic beverages to patrons.[121]

Some states also recognize dram shop liability as a common law cause of action for negligence.[122] Early common law principles precluded the imposition of liability on liquor servers because of the requirement of proximate cause. Specifically, the owner of the alcoholic beverage premise was not held liable for damages inflicted by the drinker on himself or a third party because the intoxicated person, not the owner or the server, was the proximate cause of the damage. While this remains the rule in several states, most states now impose liability under a dram shop statute or by following more recent judicial precedent that establishes proximate cause on the basis of public policy rather than foreseeability. As one judge noted, "[t]he law endures no injury, from which damage has ensued, without some remedy."[123] Dram shop laws are further justified by the fact that they have proven to be effective in reducing harmful drinking-related behaviors, including a

119. Stockings et al., *Community Approaches for Reducing Alcohol-Related Harms: an Overview of Intervention Strategies, Efficacy, and Considerations for Future Research,* Current Addiction Reports 5, 274-86 (2018).

120. *See, e.g.*, Ventura County Behavioral Health Department, Best Practices in Responsible Alcoholic Beverage Sales and Service Training with Model Ordinance, Commentary and Resources (Apr. 2008).

121. Heather Morton, *Dram Shop Liability State Statutes, National Conference of State Legislatures,* https://www.ncsl.org/research/financial-services-and-commerce/dram-shop-liability-state-statutes.aspx (Jun. 14, 2013).

122. Ronald Beitman, Practitioner's Guide to Liquor Liability Litigation 2-3 (1987).

123. *Id.* at 5 (citing *Harrison v. Berkley*, 32 S.C.L. (1 Strob.) 525, 47 Am. Dec. 578 (1847)).

6.4 percent reduction in alcohol-related motor vehicle fatalities in jurisdictions where dram shop liability applies.[124]

In some states, dram shop liability principles have been expanded to apply to non-commercial servers of alcohol such as social hosts, employers, fraternities, and other non-licensed entities.[125]

Social-host liability is important because, in the post-Repeal era, much drinking has moved from the saloon into the home. Today, for example, underage drinking at a home, hotel, or outdoor area is commonplace. For this reason alone, the social availability of alcoholic beverages needs to be addressed along with commercial availability.[126]

Social-host liability laws typically impose liability on non-commercial individuals who serve alcoholic beverages on property they own, lease, or otherwise control, or who provide the location at which alcohol is served to minors or intoxicated adults who, in turn, inflict some harm to person or property.[127] Generally, social-host liability is of two types: criminal, which may include fines or imprisonment, and civil, which may include reimbursement to local government for the cost of law enforcement and emergency services. Social-host laws vary significantly from state to state and locality to locality.[128]

There are other important laws that affect the drinking environment, particularly for youth drinking. Examples include the following: keg registration laws that require the purchaser of a specific numbered keg to be identified at the point of purchase; "shoulder tap"[129] and similar prevention programs that target adults who buy alcoholic beverages for minors; restrictions on drinking in public places such as parks, beaches, parking lots, and sports arenas; and laws that criminalize public drunkenness.[130] Additionally, some states control the activities that can accompany drinking in licensed establishments, such as gambling and nude dancing.[131]

The drinking context also includes the social and physical environment of drinking establishments. The environment includes the physical layout of the premises and the availability of various types of entertainment (gambling, topless

---

124. Rammohan et al., *Effects of dram shop liability and enhanced overservice law enforcement initiatives on excessive alcohol consumption and related harms: Two community guide systematic reviews,* 41, 3 Am J Prev Med (Sep. 2011).

125. Alcohol: No Ordinary Commodity, *supra* note 75 at 177.

126. *Id.* at 143.

127. *Id.*

128. Underage Drinking: Prohibitions against Hosting Underage Drinking Parties, Alcohol Policy Information System, https://alcoholpolicy.niaaa.nih.gov/apis-policy-topics/prohibitions-against-hosting-underage-drinking-parties/41/variables (last visited Aug. 6, 2022).

129. Shoulder tap programs involve a minor decoy who solicits adults outside a liquor store to buy alcoholic beverages for the minor decoy. Any person who furnishes alcohol to the minor decoy is arrested. *See, e.g.,* Cal. Bus. & Prof. Code § 25658(a) (2021).

130. For a discussion on the laws against public drunkenness, *see* Alcohol and Public Policy: Beyond the Shadow of Prohibition 87-89 (Mark Moore & Dean Gerstein eds., 1981).

131. Challenges to the nude dancing laws at licensed alcoholic beverage establishments have been brought under the First Amendment but generally have failed. *See, e.g., California v. LaRue,* 409 U.S. 109 (1972); *N.Y. State Liquor Auth. v. Bellanca,* 452 U.S. 714 (1981).

or nude dancing, recreational activities such as billiards or darts, etc.), security, transportation options, and food and non-alcoholic beverages. Interestingly, the drinking environment may play a greater role in encouraging aggression and violence than either the pharmacological effects of alcohol or the personality traits of the patrons.[132] Murray Sin, Elizabeth Morgan, and Julie Batchelor, authors of *The Impact of Enforcement on Intoxication and Alcohol Related Harm*, write:

> Aspects of the physical environment that are associated with increased aggression within the licensed premises environment include unclean or poorly maintained venues, poor ventilation, inconvenient access to the bar, inadequate seating, high noise level, crowding, dancing, and pool playing. The availability of food has been associated with reduced risk of aggression.[133]

History provides some excellent examples of how the drinking environment sets the tenor for the activities that occur there. Norman Clark vividly describes a pre-Prohibition saloon in *Deliver Us from Evil: An Interpretation of American Prohibition:*

> What is difficult ... to remember is that the saloon was more than an altar of fellowship. It was also a place where dirty old men spat on the floor and conspired toward the subversion of public and private moralities, where the fathers of young children floated away a week's wages that could have gone to food, clothing and education. It was a place where addiction enslaved many a man, insulating him from the lifestyle of decency and responsibility by sinking him into a blurred phantasmagoria of whores, drug fiends, pimps, thieves, and gamblers. Such phrases are in part an exercise in literary license, but they evoke images essential to understanding a reality as it was understood by Prohibitionists. To approach that reality is to fix the mind's eye ... upon a sort of metaphorical slave ship in middle passage, upon the images of sodden drunks, of hideously fat men sucking stale cigars, of toilets fouled with vomit and urine in the haze of alcoholic narcosis, of the blind idiocy of drunken violence. But the license is not mere local color. To dismiss these images as high camp would be to dismiss the absolute seriousness of millions of men ... and it would be to ignore a crucial issue in two hundred years of American life.[134]

After Repeal, the universal goal was to prevent the return of the saloon. Some states prohibited saloons outright and only allowed restaurants, hotels, and private clubs.[135] Other states required all on-sale establishments to serve food. Still other states did not allow women to be served at a bar or excluded them altogether from the licensed establishment.[136] States also strictly controlled the activities that could accompany drinking.

---

132. The Impact of Enforcement on Intoxication and Alcohol Related Harm, *supra* note 119 at 11.

133. *Id.*

134. Norman Clark, Deliver Us from Evil: An Interpretation of American Prohibition 2 (1976).

135. Randolph Childs, Making Repeal Work 146 (1947).

136. *Id.* at 157.

For several decades after Repeal, the state stores in the monopoly jurisdictions looked more like pharmacies than modern-day liquor stores. The consumer could not even view the bottles to be purchased, having rather to submit an order form for products that would be taken out of the storage room. There were no floor displays, no point-of-sale materials, and no advertising. All of this affected buying and drinking patterns.

Today, many, if not most, of these post-Repeal restrictions have been relaxed. Yet there still are particular settings that pose a high risk for harmful drinking. In *Alcohol: No Ordinary Commodity*, Dr. Babor and his co-authors suggest that by focusing on particular places such as problem bars, problem drinking can be limited without targeting the drinkers themselves.

[T]he focus on high-risk environments such as commercial drinking establishments has several advantages. First, it can have a broader impact than individual approaches would have on persons who are at high risk, especially young people and subcultures with risky drinking practices. Second, a variety of approaches can be applied at one time (e.g., training, enforcement, reduction of environmental risk factors). Finally, most approaches targeting high-risk environments are generally perceived as acceptable in most cultures and may be easier to implement than less-accepted prevention strategies such as general alcohol control and tax measures.[137]

4. DRUNK DRIVING

Considerable attention in the United States has been devoted to reducing the occurrence of drinking and driving. These laws are perhaps the most visible and widely discussed of the various alcohol control policies because of the sobering facts about drinking and driving. In a 2012-2013 survey on alcohol use, 3.9 percent of Americans reported driving after they had drunk too much, and 5.9 percent of Americans reported driving while drinking. Men were more than twice as likely as women to drive drunk or drink while driving.[138] In 2019, there were 10,142 motor vehicle fatalities involving an alcohol-impaired driver, totaling 28 percent of all traffic-related deaths in the year. 84 percent of fatal crashes involving alcohol occurred when drivers had a blood alcohol content (BAC) over the legal limit of 0.08 percent, and in 56 percent of these fatal crashes, drivers also had BAC levels above 0.15 percent. As with those who reported driving drunk, men were more likely than women to be involved in a fatal crash: There were four male alcohol-impaired drivers for every female alcohol-impaired driver.[139]

---

137. Alcohol: No Ordinary Commodity, *supra* note 75 at 162-63.

138. Amy Z. Fan et al., *Drinking and driving among adults in the United States: Results from the 2012–2013 national epidemiologic survey on alcohol and related conditions-III*, 125 Accident Analysis Prevention. 49-55 (Apr. 2019).

139. National Highway Traffic Safety Administration, *Traffic Safety Facts: Alcohol Impaired Driving 2019 Data*, U.S. Dept. of Transp. (2019), https://crashstats.nhtsa.dot.gov/Api/Public/Publication/813120.

The facts are clear and uncontroverted: Drunk drivers are more likely to get into serious crashes than sober drivers, and the relative risk increases with the driver's BAC.[140]

Over the past 30 years, state governments, under strong pressure from Mothers Against Drunk Driving and Congress, have made considerable strides in reducing the level of drinking and driving. Many of these state laws revolve around BAC standards. In 1968, many states allowed BAC limits of 0.15 percent. In 1983, President Reagan's Commission on Drunk Driving recommended, among other things, lowering the so-called legal limit for drivers to 0.10 percent BAC, establishing 21 as the minimum legal drinking age, and imposing tough sanctions for all drinking and driving violations. Since that time, there has been a deluge of anti-drunk driving laws.

Achieving a national standard on the minimum drinking age and BAC limits is no simple feat. Congress succeeded in establishing 21 as the minimum legal drinking age by offering monetary incentives to the states,[141] a practice that was upheld by the U.S. Supreme Court in 1987.[142] Congress subsequently promised supplemental highway grants to those states that lowered the BAC limit to 0.02 percent for persons under the age of 21.[143] By 1998, all the states had adopted that standard. These so-called zero tolerance laws, according to Dr. Christopher Carpenter, resulted in a 13 to 20 percent decrease in heavy drinking (defined as five drinks or more at one sitting) and in the overall number of drinks consumed in the previous month by males under the age of 21.[144]

In 2000 Congress imposed reductions in highway funding as a penalty on those states that failed to adopt 0.08 percent as the legal limit for adults by 2004.[145] All the states have now adopted that standard. However, some states seek to go further. In 2013, the National Transportation Safety Board issued a report recommending lowering the legal limit to 0.05 percent. Public health researchers agreed with this recommendation, citing studies from Europe and Australia that demonstrated a five to 18 percent reduction in fatal crashes after the legal limit was lowered from 0.08

---

140. Paying the Tab, *supra* note 53 at 89.

141. The National Minimum Drinking Age Act of 1984, 23 U.S.C. §158, also called the Federal Uniform Drinking Age Act, required all states to establish 21 as the minimum age for the purchase and public possession of alcoholic beverages. States that did not comply faced a reduction in highway funds under the Federal Highway Aid Act. Pursuant to the provisions of the Drinking Age Act, many states have adopted specific exceptions for underage consumption when a family member consents or is present and for educational, religious, and medical purposes.

142. *South Dakota v. Dole*, 483 U.S. 203 (1987).

143. 23 U.S.C.A. § 410 (1991); 23 U.S.C.A. § 161 (1994).

144. Christopher Carpenter, *How Do Zero Tolerance Drunk Driving Laws Work?*, 23 Journal of Health Economics 61, 81 (2004).

145. 23 U.S.C. § 163. The law allows the federal government to withhold 2 percent from federal highway funds, starting in 2004, if the state did not comply with the federal mandate. Each subsequent year, until 2007, an additional 2 percent would be withheld from states that had not complied. Therefore, any state that did not adopt legislation to lower the BAC to 0.08 would have 8 percent of the state's federal funding withheld in 2007. *See* Christopher O'Neill, *Legislating under the Influence: Are Federal Highway Incentives Enough to Induce State Legislatures to Pass a 0.08 Blood Alcohol Concentration Standard?*, 28 Seton Hall Legislative Journal 415, 416 (2004).

to 0.05 percent. They estimated that such a measure would result in at least 500 lives being saved a year across the United States.[146] In 2019, Utah became the first state to implement a 0.05 percent legal limit. In the first year under the new law, Utah's fatal crash rate dropped by 19.8 percent. Despite concerns from the beverage industry that the law would stifle economic growth, alcohol sales increased at a steady pace akin to that of similar industries.[147]

According to long-time alcohol policy advocate and attorney Jim Mosher, the deterrent effect on drinking and driving requires three components: certainty, swiftness, and severity. More specifically, effective deterrence depends on the drunk driver's *perception* that he or she will be caught and then promptly and harshly punished. For this reason, most state laws focus on open and active enforcement, which has made drunk driving one of the most commonly prosecuted offenses in the lower criminal courts.[148]

There is a wide range of drinking and driving laws and policies in the 50 states. The primary legal interventions include (1) administrative per se laws that authorize the state licensing agency to suspend a driver's license administratively if the driver's BAC exceeds a certain level, separate and apart from a court action for "driving under the influence" (DUI); (2) criminal per se laws that make it a crime to operate a motor vehicle at or above a specified BAC; (3) laws prohibiting plea bargaining between a prosecutor and defense counsel that might otherwise reduce a DUI charge to a lesser offense; (4) laws establishing a mandatory sentence of imprisonment or community service for a first or second DUI conviction; (5) open container laws that prohibit open containers of alcohol inside the passenger portion of a motor vehicle; (6) sobriety checkpoints at which drivers are stopped at random and checked for signs of driving under the influence, which may involve breathalyzer tests to measure the driver's BAC; (7) vehicle impoundment laws that authorize seizure and holding of the driver's vehicle; and (8) zero tolerance laws that impose 0.02 percent BAC on drivers under the age of 21.[149] Beyond legal interventions, education, treatment, and prevention measures also serve to enhance enforcement with the ultimate goal of reducing drunk driving.

Educational measures vary between states, with some states requiring coursework only after the second offense, while others such as California require a 30-hour, three month drug education and counseling program after the first offense and a 60-hour, nine month drug education for those with a BAC of 0.20 or higher.[150] However, education alone has been shown to be ineffective, and the lack of high-quality studies on the preventative effect of combined programs leaves

---

146. James Fell et al., *The effectiveness of a 0.05 blood alcohol concentration (BAC) limit for driving in the United States*, 109(6) Addiction, 869-74 (2014).

147. Thomas et al., *Evaluation of Utah's .05 BAC Per Se Law, U.S. Dept. of Trans. Natl. Highway Traffic Safety Admin.*, (2022), https://rosap.ntl.bts.gov/view/dot/60428.

148. James B. Jacobs, Drunk Driving: An American Dilemma, at xviii (1989).

149. William Evans, Doreen Neville & John Graham, General Deterrence of Drunk Driving: Evaluation of Recent American Policies, 11 Risk Analysis 279, 281 (1991).

150. California Department of Healthcare Services, *Driving-Under-The-Influence Programs* (May 5, 2021 10:15 AM), https://www.dhcs.ca.gov/individuals/Pages/DUI_Programs .aspx#:~:text =First%20Offender%20Programs,drug%20education%20and%20counseling%20program.

little evidence demonstrating their overall effectiveness. Furthermore, even for those programs that have been shown to be effective, the results do not last long-term, with both a control group and a group having completed an educational program showing the same recidivism rates after 12 months. Programs that utilize treatment such as cognitive behavioral therapy or motivational interviewing appear to be more effective, but future research is required to determine whether these interventions' ability to reduce drunk driving is evidence-based.[151]

Two preventative measures for repeat offenders have been shown to be effective: ignition interlock devices (IID) and transdermal alcohol monitoring. Ignition interlock devices are essentially breathalyzers installed on the dashboard of the vehicle, sometimes following a DUI conviction. Thirty states and the District of Columbia have laws that require all persons convicted of a DUI to install an IID, and 13 other states require an IID to be installed for repeat offenders or those who were convicted with a high (over 0.1) BAC.[152] Plans to make IIDs a permanent vehicle feature have gained traction, with the Reduce Impaired Driving for Everyone Act (RIDE Act) introduced in the Senate in 2021 and the Honoring Abbas Family Legacy to Terminate Drunk Driving Act (HALT Act) in the House in 2019. The acts proposed that motor vehicles be equipped with an IID or similar device that determines the BAC of the operator and prevents operation if the driver is intoxicated. The bill in the Senate would direct the National Highway Traffic Safety Administration (NHTSA) to create a rule implementing these devices as safety standards to be included in all new vehicles within three to five years of the bill's enactment.[153]

Another tool to prevent drunk driving, called transdermal alcohol monitoring, works by measuring alcohol expiration through the skin through a continuously worn anklet or bracelet. When used for a period of 90 days, recidivism rates have been reduced by up to 113 percent, with only two percent of individuals re-offending.[154]

While these programs do not treat alcoholism or other related disorders, they have proven to be effective in reducing repeat arrests, which is often accompanied by abstinence from drinking.[155]

All of these interventions, along with the national minimum drinking age of 21, have significantly reduced alcohol-related motor vehicle accidents in the United States and changed the social norms surrounding drinking and driving.

---

151. Peter G. Miller et al., *Effectiveness of interventions for convicted DUI offenders in reducing recidivism: a systematic review of the peer-reviewed scientific literature*, 41 Am. J. of Drug and Alcohol Abuse 1 (2015).

152. National Conference of State Legislatures, *State Ignition Interlock Laws* (2021) https://www.ncsl.org/research/transportation/state-ignition-interlock-laws.aspx.

153. H.R. 4354, 116th Cong. (2019); S.1331, 117th Cong. (2021).

154. A.S. McKnight et al., *Transdermal alcohol monitoring: Case studies. Report No. DOT HS 811 603,* National Highway Traffic Safety Administration, (Aug. 2012).

155. *See* James Fell et al., *The effectiveness of alcohol monitoring as a treatment for driving-while-intoxicated (DWI) offenders: A literature review and synthesis*, 22 Traffic Injury Prevention, S1-S7 (Oct. 2021).

Since 1982, drunk driving fatalities in the U.S. have decreased 45 percent (compared to a 12 percent reduction in total traffic fatalities). In the last decade, the rate of under 21 fatalities from drunk driving has declined 14 percent.[156] The reduction has been so dramatic that currently, according to Professor Cook, "the bulk of the damage to public safety from underage drinking is the result of violent crime rather than impaired driving."[157] Any further reductions in drunk driving, according to Jim Mosher, are likely to come from controls on access to alcoholic beverages through increased taxes and a focus on problem bars.

The attitudes surrounding drinking and driving, especially among young adults, are dramatically different than they were 30 years ago. My children in their 30s and their friends will not drive after drinking and always appoint a designated driver or take public or private transportation when they plan to drink.

5. ADVERTISING AND MARKETING

Advertising and marketing of alcoholic beverages occur in both traditional (also known as measured) media—radio, television, magazines, newspapers, outdoor billboards, and signs—and non-traditional (or unmeasured) venues such as the Internet, sponsorship of music concerts and sporting events, consumer contests and giveaways, product placement in movies and television programs, and in-store point-of-sale material and promotional items. Since Repeal, the propriety of alcoholic beverage advertising has been debated in Congress and state legislatures on numerous occasions. In the 1940s and 1950s, there were serious efforts, all unsuccessful, to ban all alcoholic beverage advertising in interstate commerce. Robert Laforge, in his dissertation, *Misplaced Priorities: A History of Federal Alcohol Regulation and Public Health Policy*, writes that

> the proponents of an alcohol ad ban were opposed to the increased volume of alcoholic beverage advertising, to its irrelevant appeals and to the use of puffery and "glamorous" or lifestyle advertising. [They] repeatedly contrasted this type of alcohol promotion with the social damage caused by alcohol, including alcoholism, driving deaths, accidents and family problems.[158]

The same concerns resurfaced in the 1970s and 1980s. Led by the Center for Science in the Public Interest (CSPI),[159] critics claimed that the beer and spirits industries, in particular, engaged in unfair and deceptive advertising and marketing practices that had significant adverse health and social consequences, especially among underage and heavy drinkers. These lifestyle advertisements, they said, portray alcoholic beverages in conjunction with appealing images of social

---

156. Responsibility.org, *Drunk Driving Fatality Statistics*, https://www.responsibility.org/alcohol-statistics/drunk-driving-statistics/drunk-driving-fatality-statistics/ (2021).

157. Paying the Tab, *supra* note 53 at 188.

158. Robert G. Laforge, Misplaced Priorities: A History of Federal Alcohol Regulation and Public Health Policy 292-293 (1987) (unpublished Ph.D. dissertation, Johns Hopkins University).

159. *See, e.g.*, Michael Jacobson, Robert Atkins & George Hacker, The Booze Merchants: The Inebriating of America (1983).

camaraderie, social success, wealth, elegance, sex, sports, and various risk-taking activities.[160] Regulation was "necessary to protect consumers from the presumed negative effects of advertising of alcoholic beverages—especially those consumers thought to be particularly vulnerable to such effects, such as children and adolescents."[161]

The Treasury Department's alcoholic beverage advertising regulations, which have changed little since 1940, are reviewed in Chapter 3. As a reminder, the TTB does not pre-approve alcoholic beverage advertisements as it does with alcoholic beverage labels. The Bureau prohibits false or misleading statements, statements that are disparaging of a competitor's products, obscene or indecent statements, therapeutic claims, health statements, and statements or designs that create the impression that a wine has intoxicating qualities.[162] But the TTB does not address what are socially acceptable or unacceptable standards for alcoholic beverage advertisements.

In 1983, the CSPI proposed that the federal government expand its regulations of alcoholic beverage advertising. Specifically, the CSPI proposed that (1) the Federal Trade Commission (FTC) or Bureau of Alcohol, Tobacco and Firearms (the TTB's predecessor) should ban all advertising and marketing efforts aimed at heavy drinkers and young people, including activities on college campuses, advertisements on rock music stations and in youth magazines, and commercials on sports broadcasts; (2) advertisements in print or on radio or television should contain, or be balanced by, equally well-disseminated public health information; (3) the Federal Communications Commission should encourage all broadcasters to run health-oriented and other alcohol-related public service announcements in prime-time, sports, and family-viewing time slots; and (4) the content of alcoholic beverage advertisements should be limited to consumer information about the taste, price, and composition of products (known as "tombstone advertising"), with no puffery and no association with social, sexual, or financial success.[163] None of the CSPI's suggestions have ever been adopted.

Nevertheless, the concerns expressed by the CSPI, the Center for Alcohol Marketing and Youth, and other advocacy groups prompted Congress to investigate the impact of alcoholic beverage advertising on underage drinking. In 1998, 2003, 2008, and 2014, at Congress' request, the FTC conducted these

---

160. Misplaced Priorities: A History of Federal Alcohol Regulation and Public Health Policy, *supra* note 138 at 415.

161. Sober Reflections: Commerce, Public Health and the Evolution of Alcohol Policy in Canada, 1980-2000, 209 (Norman Giesbrecht et al. eds., 2006).

162. 27 C.F.R. § 4.64. Unlike in the case of wine labels, the TTB does not pre-approve wine industry advertisements.

163. *Id.*

investigations.[164] Additionally, in 2002 Congress requested the NRC/IOM to develop a national strategy for reducing and preventing youth alcohol problems.[165]

All these reports recommended voluntary self-regulation as the primary strategy for protecting young people from the adverse effects of alcoholic beverage advertising.[166] As the FTC wrote in 1999,

> [s]elf-regulation often can be more prompt, flexible, and effective than government regulation. It can permit application of the accumulated judgment and experience of an industry to issues that are sometimes difficult for the government to define with bright line rules. With respect to advertising practices, self-regulation is an appropriate mechanism because many forms of government intervention raise First Amendment concerns.[167]

In the same report, the FTC pointed out certain weaknesses of industry self-regulation and recommended that industry implement best practices to reduce alcohol advertisements directed towards youth such that only 30 percent of the expected audience would be underage.[168] These suggestions included banning alcoholic beverage advertisements on media with large underage audiences, prohibiting advertisements with substantial underage appeal, and restricting promotional placement of alcoholic beverages in movies to films rated R and NC-17.[169] The recommendation also included prohibiting marketing activities on college campuses (except at licensed establishments) and industry sponsorship of

---

164. FTC, *Self-Regulation in the Alcohol Industry: A Review of Industry Efforts to Avoid Promoting Alcohol to Underage Consumers* (1999), available at http://www.ftc.gov/reports/alcohol/alcoholreport.shtm (last visited Aug. 8, 2022); FTC, *Alcohol Marketing and Advertising: A Report to Congress* (2003), available at http://www.ftc.gov/os/2003/09/alcohol08report.pdf (last visited Aug. 8, 2022); FTC, *Self-Regulation in the Alcohol Industry: Report of the Federal Trade Commission* (2008), available at http://www.ftc.gov/os/2008/06/080626alcoholreport.pdf (last visited Aug. 8, 2022); FTC *Self-Regulation in the Alcohol Industry Report of the Federal Trade Commission* (2014), available at https://www.ftc.gov/system/files/documents/reports/self-regulation-alcohol-industry-report-federal-trade-commission/140320alcoholreport.pdf (last visited Aug. 8, 2022).

165. Reducing Underage Drinking: A Collective Responsibility, *supra* note 98 at 2.

166. Self-regulation takes the form of industry advertising codes. Separate codes have been adopted by the Beer Institute (Brewing Industry Advertising Guidelines), Wine Institute (Code of Advertising Standards), and the Distilled Spirits Council of the United States (Code of Good Practice).

167. Self-Regulation in the Alcohol Industry: A Review of Industry Efforts to Avoid Promoting Alcohol to Underage Consumers, *supra* note 165 at 3.

168. The wine industry was the first to embrace a 30 percent threshold, that is, not more than 30 percent of the expected viewers shall be under the age of 21. This standard is consistent with the 2000 census data showing that 30 percent of the American public is under the age of 21.

169. Placement restrictions include bans on outdoor alcoholic beverage advertising in locations where children are present such as schools and playgrounds, near colleges and churches, and inside the retail store where point-of-sale advertising and other promotions might stimulate sales, particularly among at-risk groups such as young adults and problem drinkers. Center for Alcohol Marketing and Youth (CAMY), *State Alcohol Advertising Laws: Current Status and Model Policies* (2003). For a discussion of point-of-sale advertising, *see* Graeme Willersdorf, Selling and Serving Beverage Alcohol, in Working Together to Reduce Harmful Drinking, *supra* note 84 at 123-125.

spring break activities such as beach promotions and outdoor concerts. With respect to the youth audience standard, the NRC/IOM recommended that the industry immediately decrease the youth composition in traditional media to 25 percent (cited as a "best practice" in the 1999 FTC report), phasing in a 15 percent standard over time.[170]

In its subsequent reexaminations of alcoholic beverage advertising practices, the FTC again endorsed voluntary advertising codes. But the FTC required industry members to "check reliable audience composition data before placing an ad and . . . make a placement only if that data showed that, historically, at least 70 percent of the audience consisted of adults 21 and older."[171] The 2014 recommendations from the FTC included detailed guidelines for online and digital media advertising. These included (1) "age gates" on websites requiring that consumers enter their date of birth rather than asking them to simply verify that they are of legal age; (2) utilizing age-gating technologies on social media platforms to limit advertisements to their intended audience; and (3) utilizing blocking technologies and frequent monitoring to reduce the likelihood of code violations resulting from user-generated content.[172]

In addition to the federal government, state governments regulate advertising content and placement, typically with the stated goal of achieving temperance. Several of these laws have been carefully scrutinized under the First Amendment to the U.S. Constitution.[173] Generally speaking, restrictions on the "time, place, and manner" of alcoholic beverage advertising are more permissible than restrictions on content.[174]

In the seminal 1996 case of *44 Liquormart, Inc. v. Rhode Island*,[175] the Supreme Court invalidated Rhode Island's ban on price advertising of alcoholic beverages. Rhode Island had enacted a law that prohibited licensed vendors inside or outside of the state from advertising the price of any alcoholic beverage offered for sale in the state. The law also prohibited Rhode Island media from publishing

---

170. Reducing Underage Drinking: A Collective Responsibility, *supra* note 98 at 138.

171. Self-Regulation in the Alcohol Industry: A Review of Industry Efforts to Avoid Promoting Alcohol to Underage Consumers, (1999), *supra* note 165 at i.

172. Self-Regulation in the Alcohol Industry: Report of the General Trade Commission, (2014), supra note 165 at 33.

173. The First Amendment reads in pertinent part: "Congress shall make no law . . .abridging the freedom of speech, or of the press" The states also must consider federal preemption under Article VI, Section 1, Clause 2 of the U.S. Constitution, also known as the Supremacy Clause ("This Constitution, and the Laws of the United States which shall be made in Pursuance thereof ... shall be the supreme Law of the Land; and the Judges in every State shall be bound thereby, any Thing in the Constitution or Laws of any State to the Contrary notwithstanding.") *See, e.g., Capital Cities Cable, Inc. v. Crisp*, 467 U.S. 691 (1984) (state cannot interfere with the transmission of electronic media signals from outside the state because of the authority granted to the Federal Communications Commission to regulate cable television systems in the United States).

174. "Time, place, and manner" regulations are more acceptable to courts so long as they target a legitimate state interest (e.g., reducing youth exposure) and permit the advertising in at least some venues for the intended (adult) audience. *See, e.g., Metromedia, Inc. v. City of San Diego*, 453 U.S. 490 (1981).

175. 517 U.S. 484 (1996).

or broadcasting any advertisements making reference to alcoholic beverage prices. Not even a placard or sign visible from the exterior of a package store could make reference to alcoholic beverage prices. In fact, Liquormart did not advertise any alcoholic beverage prices; instead, its advertisement included low prices for non-alcoholic items and the word "WOW" in large letters next to pictures of vodka and rum bottles. When the State Liquor Administration imposed a fine, litigation commenced.

To judge the constitutionality of Rhode Island's advertising ban, the Supreme Court applied the 4-part commercial free speech test that it had enunciated in *Central Hudson Gas & Electric Corp v. Public Service Commission of New York*:

1. The speech must concern lawful activity and not be misleading;
2. The government's interest asserted to justify the regulation must be substantial;
3. The regulation must directly advance the government interest asserted; and
4. The regulation must not be more extensive than necessary to serve that interest.[176]

The justices unanimously found that the Rhode Island law did not directly advance the state's substantial interest in promoting temperance and that the ban was more extensive than necessary to serve that interest. Regarding the third prong of the *Central Hudson* test, Justice John Paul Stevens, who authored the unanimous decision, found that "the State has presented no evidence to suggest that its speech prohibition will *significantly* reduce marketwide consumption."[177] With respect to the fourth prong of the test, Justice Stevens added that "it is perfectly obvious that alternative forms of regulation that would not involve any restriction on speech would be likely to achieve the State's goal of promoting temperance. As the State's own expert conceded, higher prices can be maintained by direct regulation or by increased taxation."[178]

Under *Central Hudson*, a state must have an evidentiary basis for any content-based advertising ban. Where only "anecdotal evidence and educated guesses" support a ban, the Supreme Court will invalidate the law. That occurred in the case of *Rubin v. Coors Brewing Co.*[179] Coors challenged a federal law that prohibited beer labels from displaying alcohol content in order to prevent "strength wars" (battles over whose beer is stronger in alcoholic content).[180] Justice Clarence Thomas, who wrote the unanimous decision, found that the government's interest could be advanced in a less intrusive manner, for example, by directly limiting the alcoholic content of beers, prohibiting marketing that emphasizes high alcoholic

---

176. *Central Hudson Gas & Electric Corp. v. Public Service Comm'n of N.Y.*, 447 U.S. 557, 566 (1980).

177. *Liquormart*, 517 U.S. at 506 (emphasis in the original).

178. *Id.* at 507.

179. 514 U.S. 476 (1995).

180. *Id.* at 484.

strength, and limiting the ban to malt liquors, the segment of the beer market that allegedly is threatened with a "strength war."[181]

Does alcoholic beverage advertising encourage excess consumption, create an environment in which alcoholic beverage consumption is normalized, or simply capture market share?[182] Terrel L. Rhodes, in *Social and Economic Control of Alcohol: The 21st Amendment in the 21st Century*, argues: "There is little concrete evidence of a positive effect of controls on the advertising or presentation of alcoholic beverages . . . on levels of consumption."[183] Indeed, a four-decade long study from researchers at the University of Texas at Austin reaches a similar conclusion. Despite alcohol advertising expenditures in the United States increasing nearly 400 percent between 1971 and 2012, per capita alcohol consumption has remained largely the same. The small increase in per capita alcohol consumption of wine, beer, and spirits seen over this period was rather associated with an increase in per capita disposable income, with increased wine consumption having a significant relationship with increased per capita income.[184]

While it cannot be said based on the evidence that alcoholic beverage advertising necessarily *causes* youth alcohol consumption, a review of studies from 2008 to 2016 demonstrated positive associations between young people's exposure to alcohol marketing and alcohol consumption. Those with more exposure to alcohol marketing were more likely to start drinking, continue drinking, and engage in binge drinking or other problem drinking behaviors.[185]

Clearly, more research and monitoring need to be done on overall youth exposure to alcoholic beverage advertising, particularly including unmeasured media such as sponsorships, Internet promotions, and viral marketing. Even in the absence of a causal link between advertising and young persons' beliefs and behavior, it might be advisable to further limit youth exposure to alcoholic beverage advertising on the basis of the "precautionary principle." Knowing the potential for harm, the principle prescribes preventive action in the face of uncertainty. How the Supreme Court would react to this policy prescription is another matter altogether.

It is not only advertisements that may lead youth to drink, but products as well. There is no better example than energy drinks that combine beer or spirits with caffeine, inducing what one FDA Commissioner called a state of "wide awake

---

181. *Id.* at 490-91.

182. Mike MacAvoy & Meg Mackenzie, Government Regulation, Corporate Responsibility, and Personal Pleasure: A Public Health Perspective from New Zealand, in Corporate Social Responsibility and Alcohol: The Need and Potential for Partnership 88 (Marcus Grant & Joyce O'Connor eds., 2005).

183. Terrel L. Rhodes, Policy, Regulation and Legislation, in Social and Economic Control of Alcohol: The 21st Amendment in the 21st Century 87 (Carole Jurkiewicz & Murphy Painter eds., 2008).

184. Wilcox et al., *Beer, wine, or spirits? Advertising's impact on four decades of category sales*. Intl. J. of Advertising, 34(4), 641–57 (2015).

185. David Jernigan et al., *Alcohol marketing and youth alcohol consumption: a systematic review of longitudinal studies published since 2008*, 112 Addiction 7-20 (Aug. 26, 2016).

drunk."[186] Products such as Four Loko were widely criticized because of their appeal to youth drinkers. As David Jernigan and James O'Hara write in "Alcoholic Beverage Advertising and Promotion,"

> [s]uccessful youth brands not only attach themselves to the subculture, but . . . position themselves to be among its defining features. Some of the newest alcohol products attach themselves to the all-night clubbing scene. Energy drinks, loaded with caffeine, help young people to stay awake through all-night activities like clubbing. Premixed energy drinks were a natural successor to the common practice of mixing nonalcoholic energy drinks such as Red Bull with vodka or other distilled spirits.[187]

In November 2010, following hospitalizations and even deaths of young drinkers, the FDA issued warning letters to four manufacturers in which it stated that caffeinated energy drinks are not "Generally Recognized as Safe" (GRAS)[188] and are adulterated under the Federal Food, Drug, and Cosmetic Act.[189] Following pressure from the FDA and state governments, in December 2010, Four Loko removed the caffeine and guarana from their product and reintroduced a caffeine-free version that was not marketed as an energy drink. The product's "irresponsible marketing to young people" ultimately resulted in a 2014 settlement agreement with 20 attorneys general that included specific bans on advertising to those under 25 and a $400,000 payment to each state.[190]

---

186. Abby Goodnaugh, *F.D.A. Issues Warning Over Alcoholic Energy Drinks*, N.Y. Times (Nov. 17, 2020),
https://www.nytimes.com/2010/11/18/us/18drinks.html.

187. Reducing Underage Drinking: A Collective Responsibility, *supra* note 98at 632.

188. The FDA sent warning letters on November 17, 2010, to Phusion Projects, LLC (Four Loko), Charge Beverages Corp. (Core High Gravity HG Green, HG Orange, and Lemon Lime Core Spiked), New Century Brewing Co. (Moonshot), and United Brands Company Inc. (Joose and Max). Each letter states:

> To establish that the use of a substance in food is GRAS under its specific conditions of use (for example, the GRAS status of caffeine when directly added to an alcoholic beverage), there must be consensus among qualified experts that the substance is safe under its conditions of use, based on publicly available data and information. FDA is aware that, based on the publicly available literature, a number of qualified experts have concerns about the safety of caffeinated alcoholic beverages. Moreover, the agency is not aware of data or other information to establish the safety of the relevant conditions of use for your product. Therefore, the criteria for GRAS status have not been met for the caffeine in your beverages.

See, e.g., Letter from Joann M. Given, Acting Director, Office of Compliance, Center for Food Safety and Applied Nutrition, to Jaisen Freeman, Chris Hunter, and Jeff Wright, of Phusion Projects, LLC (Nov. 17, 2010), https://www.azag.gov/sites/default/files/2018-10/PhusionProjectsInc.pdf.

189. 21 U.S.C. §342(a)(2)(C). The FDA's regulations on food additives are located at 21 C.F.R. §170.

190. Ricardo Lopez, *Legal settlement restricts marketing of Four Loko alcoholic drinks*, L.A. Times (Mar. 24, 2014, 12:00 AM), https://www.latimes.com/business/la-xpm-2014-mar-25-la-fi-mo-four-loko-settlement-20140325-story.htm.

6. PREVENTION

Prevention includes both treatment and education. The former involves individualized services and programs for problem drinkers (heavy drinkers, binge drinkers, and alcoholics) as well as screenings for early detection and intervention. Therapeutic interventions include inpatient and outpatient treatment, medications,[191] behavioral counseling, and mutual help groups. In terms of their effectiveness, Dr. Babor writes, "In general, when patients enter treatment, exposure to any treatment is associated with significant reductions in alcohol use and related problems, regardless of the type of intervention used."[192]

Education also can directly influence drinking patterns, although it is generally less effective than treatment. Education may occur in schools, universities, and the home, as well as through mass media campaigns and community-based health programs. From a policy perspective, the educational approach is attractive because it does not infringe on consumer sovereignty. Indeed, this was the policy preferred by Ernest Cherrington of the Anti-Saloon League (ASL) before and during Prohibition. But Cherrington was overruled by ASL boss Wayne Wheeler, who believed that Prohibition could not succeed without tough laws and severe sanctions. Although this approach seems severe, Wheeler was, in part, correct because there is little direct evidence that education succeeds in any appreciable way.[193] In a 2016 review of 40 different alcohol education programs in schools, only three showed strong evidence of a positive effect. These programs used different methods to educate students. While these programs were different in approach, they used some of the same techniques, such as:

- Being based on accurate information and supported by empirical research;
- Using up-to-date materials, skills, knowledge, and cultural norms for the target group;
- Using an approach that promotes student resilience, social connectedness, and communication;
- Providing feedback on social acceptance and normative expectations that highlights that drug and alcohol use is less widespread than students might think; and
- Focusing on harm minimization and reducing risky behavior.[194]

Health warnings on alcoholic beverage labels are another form of consumer education that supplement public service announcements (PSAs) and counter-advertising. The Government Warning, adopted in 1988, refers to the following alcohol-related risks: birth defects caused by drinking when pregnant, impairment

---

191. Medications for alcohol dependence include benzodiazepines, glutamate inhibitors, and opiate antagonists.

192. Alcohol Policy and the Public Good, in From Science to Action?, *supra* note 85 at 40.

193. Alcohol and Public Policy: Beyond the Shadow of Prohibition, *supra* note 114 at 98.

194. Nicole K. Lee et al., *What works in school-based alcohol education: A systematic review,* 75(7), 780-96 Health Education Journal (Jan. 28, 2016).

when driving or operating machinery, and health problems.[195] The evidence, however, suggests that even this explicit warning is generally ineffective in changing drinking behavior,[196] despite the fact that consumer awareness of the warning, in the sense of recalling the wording, is significant and the law is widely accepted.[197] In 2021, the Consumer Federation of America, joined by organizations like the American Institute for Cancer Research and the American Public Health Association, petitioned the TTB to update warning labels with information about alcohol's potential to cause cancer.[198] The TTB has not responded to this petition, despite a clear gap in knowledge about the "health problems" alcohol can cause: Only 33 percent of American adults identify alcohol as a cancer risk factor, with 27 percent of American adults reporting that alcohol is *not* a cancer risk factor.[199]

The message is clear: Any single strategy is likely inadequate to address drinking problems and change consumer behavior. But synergies can be achieved in prevention by implementing multi-faceted strategies. The TTB has adopted this approach in the area of wine labeling and advertising. In addition to the health warning on labels, the federal government prohibits any health or therapeutic claim about wine or other alcoholic beverages on labels or in advertising. Even if the claim can be proven, such as "moderate wine consumption is associated with a reduced risk of coronary heart disease in persons age 55 or older," the TTB will

---

195. 27 U.S.C. §§ 213 et seq. The government warning is not required in alcoholic beverage advertising.

196. *Id.*

197. Harm Minimization, in Harald Klingermann & Gerhard Gmel, Mapping Social Consequences of Alcohol Consumption *supra* note 87 at 152. The health warning serves purposes other than consumer education. It also has legal consequences. Wine Institute chairman John DeLuca recalls the form of the warning label legislation when it was first introduced by Senator Strom Thurmond:

> The Thurmond bill would *not* preempt the other states. In other words, even though the federal government was asking for a warning label, it wasn't going to be preemptive legislation . . . [Y]ou could have a tank trap system of fifty different states, all desirous of putting on their own warning. We already had experience with Prop 65 that California was in the forefront of the states that wanted to put on warnings.
>
> The most critical aspect of the provisions was a section in the Thurmond bill that indicated that the warning label, if passed, could not be used by any of the companies as a defense in product liability lawsuits. [Emphasis in original.]

Each of these provisions was stricken in the final legislation. John DeLuca, Ph.D., President and CEO of the Wine Institute, 1975-2003, an Oral History Conducted in 1986-2007, by Victor Geraci, Ruth Teiser & Carole Hicke, 90, Regional History Office, The Bancroft Library, University of California, Berkeley, 2007.

198. Alcohol Justice, American Institute for Cancer Research, American Society of Clinical Oncology, American Public Health Association, Breast Cancer Prevention Partners, Consumer Federation of America, Center for Science in the Public Interest, and U.S. Alcohol Policy Alliance. *Petition for a Report to Congress Supporting a Label on Alcoholic Beverages Warning the Public that Consumption Can Cause Cancer, Including Breast and Colon.* (Oct. 21, 2020), https://consumerfed.org/wp-content/uploads/2020/10/Citizen-petition-re-alcohol-cancerwarning.pdf.

199. Marc T. Kiviniemi et al., *Limitations in American adults' awareness of and beliefs about alcohol as a risk factor for cancer*, 23 Preventative Medicine Reports, 101433 (Sep. 23, 2021).

not allow such a statement because it might mislead particular persons older than 55 for whom *any* alcohol consumption may be ill advised because of their particular health conditions or genetic propensities. Because we are a polymorphic species, it is inconceivable that information on a wine label could spell out all the possible risks of wine consumption for each and every consumer. For this reason, the only health claims that the TTB has approved in the last decade are so-called health-related directional statements, and even those must be qualified. The pertinent TTB regulations, 27 CFR §§ 4.39(h) for labels and 4.64(i) for advertising, are identical, and they state:

> A statement that directs consumers to a third party or other source for information regarding the effects on health of wine or alcohol consumption is presumed misleading unless it—
>
> (A) Directs consumers in a neutral or other non-misleading manner to a third party or other source for balanced information regarding the effects on health of wine or alcohol consumption; and
>
> (B) (1) Includes as part of the health-related directional statement the following disclaimer: "This statement should not encourage you to drink or to increase your alcohol consumption for health reasons"; or
>
> Includes as part of the health-related directional statement some other qualifying statement that the appropriate TTB officer finds is sufficient to dispel any misleading impression conveyed by the health-related directional statement.[200]

In conclusion, policymakers have used many measures to combat the harmful effects of alcoholic beverage consumption. In the 1970s, Selden Bacon, former director of the Center of Alcohol Studies at Rutgers University, summarized the various approaches used in the United States.

> This complex set of problems over the past 150 years has been defined as a moral weakness problem and turned over to the churches, defined as an economic problem and turned over to market and price control authorities, defined as a youth learning problem and turned over to educators, defined as a crime problem and turned over to law enforcement and correction agencies.[201]

The policy debate is ongoing, as is the research. Not surprisingly, on certain subjects there are wide disagreements. To illustrate the range of viewpoints and advance the public discussion of the available policy options, Appendix 9-1 presents a table derived from "Population-level interventions to reduce alcohol-related harm: An overview of systematic reviews," by Fred Martineau, Elizabeth Tyner, Theo Lorenc, Mark Petticrew, and Karen Lock. They provide an overview of 52 systematic reviews on the evidence supporting population-level interventions in ten distinct policy areas.

---

200. 27 C.F.R. §§ 4.39, 4.64 (prohibited labeling and advertising practices, respectively).

201. *Hearings Before the Special Subcommittee on Alcoholism and Narcotics of the Committee on Labor and Public Welfare*, 91st Cong. 115 (1970) (statement of Seldon Baken).

D. A MODEL OF SOCIAL RESPONSIBILITY

Even a cursory review of the positive and negative effects of alcohol consumption and of the effectiveness of the various regulations and interventions discussed in this chapter reveals that there still is considerable debate about the proper selection and mix of policy approaches to prevent and manage alcohol-related problems. No specific course of action is recommended in this section. Rather, a series of principles are presented, which the wine industry might consider as it charts its own course on issues of public health and as it interacts with public health advocates and local, state, national, and international government officials in setting the policy agenda.

The 2020-2025 Dietary Guidelines for Americans acknowledges that 60 percent of American adults report drinking alcohol in the past month, but simply states: "[d]rinking less is better for health than drinking more."[202] This statement acknowledges that alcohol is associated with harms to health, but recognizes that those who choose to drink can minimize the potential for harm by choosing to drink less and doing so more responsibly.

The wine industry cannot hide from the problems of alcoholism, binge drinking, and chronic drinking in an effort to ward off concerns about alcohol consumption in the broader population. But this does not mean that alcohol control policies should address only—or even primarily—the population at large. Where appropriate, policies should be designed to focus on specific at-risk drinkers, including those who consume alcoholic beverages to excess, those who engage in risky drinking patterns such as binge drinking, and those who drink when they should not, including drunk drivers and underage drinkers.

The question of how to affect drinking patterns so that they do not lead to harmful results is complicated because of the numerous factors that are involved, including individual predispositions, social pressures, cultural factors, commercial practices, and government intervention. Not surprisingly, no single policy is effective in all circumstances. Various measures need to be considered and carefully assessed in terms of their risks and benefits in reducing the harmful effects of alcohol consumption. The wine industry should insist and rely on empirical evidence of policy effectiveness and promote policies that balance the benefits and risks while still allowing for moderate and responsible drinking.

The wine industry should promote continued research by independent experts on the harms *and benefits* of moderate wine consumption. The funding sources should be acknowledged by the researchers to ensure transparency and full disclosure of potential conflicts of interest. Additionally, the results should be widely disseminated, and the full effects of drinking wine and the variables that determine those effects should be presented in a clear, accurate, and balanced way, including the amount of alcohol consumed, the pattern of drinking, the characteristics of the consumer, and the circumstances in which the drinking occurs. Because wineries are not allowed to make health claims, the dissemination

---

202. Dietary Guidelines 2020-2025, *supra* note 8 at 49.

of research results will need to be done by third parties who are not industry members. Education may not change people's drinking habits overnight, but informed decision making is critical to fostering responsible drinking and empowering responsible choices.

How, when, and what should young people learn about alcohol? They should know sooner rather than later that wine can be consumed sensibly, provide pleasure, and be part of a healthy diet; but, if consumed in excess, it can cause harm to the drinker and others. Although this may not alter their risk-taking activities, which often are part of youthful development, adolescents must be made aware of the difference between responsible and irresponsible drinking, the importance of moderation, and the dangers of binge drinking. The "Monitoring the Future" survey conducted by the National Institute on Drug Abuse measures drug and alcohol use in 8th, 10th, and 12th graders. The percentage of youth who drink has declined over the last decade; for example, 12th graders who report having drank alcohol in the past year decreased from 65.2 percent in 2010 to 55.3 percent in 2020.[203] Although this overall decline is perhaps positive, the way in which young people consume alcohol is still concerning. More than 90 percent of the drinks consumed by those age 12 to 20 are consumed in an episode of binge drinking.[204]

Advertising that associates alcohol with risk-taking activities, sex, and power does not encourage responsible drinking. Self-regulation through an industry advertising code has been an important means to ensure responsible marketing and promotion. The Wine Institute's Code of Advertising Standards aims to promote responsible consumption and prohibits advertising that implies wine is essential to success, social acceptability, sex appeal, or achievement. In 2014, the Wine Institute added Digital Marketing Guidelines to ensure that these standards keep pace with social media and digital communications.[205]

The wine industry must understand that, if its voluntary advertising code is shown to be ineffective, governments can and will intervene with laws on advertising content and placement. Any such laws should include effective administrative and deterrence systems for infringements. The laws, however, must not prohibit truthful communication about wine. The First Amendment protects commercial speech, and the wine industry must rely on that protection to invalidate misguided and overreaching advertising restrictions.

---

203. National Institute on Drug Abuse, *Monitoring the Future 2020 Results,* National Institutes of Health (Dec. 15, 2020), https://nida.nih.gov/research-topics/related-topics/trends-statistics/infographics/monitoring-future-2020-survey-results. Data in 2020 was collected before the COVID-19 pandemic and thus does not reflect the impact of the pandemic on teen drinking.

204. Calculated using past 30-day quantity and frequency of alcohol use and past 30-day frequency of binge drinking (4+ drinks for females and 5+ drinks for males on the same occasion) from the 2019 NSDUH public-use data file. SAMHSA, Center for Behavioral Health Statistics and Quality, *National Survey on Drug Use and Health* (2019), https://www.datafiles.samhsa.gov/study-dataset/national-survey-drug-use-and-health-2019-nsduh-2019-ds0001-nid19016.

205. Wine Institute, *Wine Institute's Code of Advertising Standards* (2014), https://wineinstitute.org/our-work/responsibility/social/ad-code/.

Consumers should have access to full and accurate information about the characteristics of the wines offered for sale. Tombstone advertising that would restrict wine labeling and advertising to the product name and type, its price, and where it is available is unnecessary and should be resisted on the grounds of free speech.

The wine industry should include in its advertising proactive communications about responsible alcohol consumption and the risks associated with misuse. And the industry should be careful not to use marketing and advertising to recruit underage drinkers, lest wine consumption be perceived, as it already is by some, to be part of a wider alcohol or even drug problem. The fact that there are no wine-based energy drinks is a good sign. The industry should remain on this high ground.

To address the drinking environment, the wine industry should work with retailers and community groups to ensure the responsible service of all alcoholic beverages. This includes not serving alcoholic beverages to intoxicated or underage persons and training servers about how to identify and deal with those situations. The consumer should be offered choice and value in the selection of wines but should not be induced in any way to drink to excess. Wherever alcoholic beverages are served, non-alcoholic beverages should be made available as an alternative. In addition to providing options to those who choose to abstain, the wine industry would benefit from the business opportunity presented by the growing demand for non-alcoholic alternatives.[206]

The wine industry also should support reasonable licensing restrictions to limit the availability of and access to alcohol. Restrictions on what, when, where, and how alcohol can be sold are an important way to deter inappropriate drinking (e.g., drinking and driving and sales to minors or those who are intoxicated). But these laws and regulations should not interfere with the right of consumers to buy wine at reasonable prices and drink responsibly. In this respect, governmental tax and pricing policies should take into account the consumers' demand for reasonably priced wines, the government's need for tax revenue, and the demonstrated effects of any particular measure on discouraging inappropriate drinking patterns. Of course, the devil is in the details of any particular licensing, pricing, or taxation scheme, but the guiding principle should be to assess the full set of effects before adopting the measure, lest it have unintended consequences such as substitution or displacement.[207]

On the subject of commerce and trade, the wine industry must support steadfastly the principle, enshrined in the Commerce Clause, that the states cannot discriminate against producers or products from another state unless there is no

---

206. *See* BevAlc Insights, *Category on the Rise: Non-Alcoholic Wine, Beer, and Spirits* (2022), https://bevalcinsights.com/category-on-the-rise-non-alcoholic-wine-beer-and-spirits/. Non-alcoholic wine sales are up 300 percent year over year from 2020.

207. For example, as Graeme Willersdorf, long-time consultant to the International Center for Alcohol Policies, writes, "where a neighboring jurisdiction has cheaper or more widely available alcohol, a state-owned monopoly that restricts availability may shift demand across the border." Graeme Willersdorf, Selling and Serving Beverage Alcohol, in Working Together to Reduce Harmful Drinking, *supra* note 84 at 126.

reasonable, non-discriminatory means to accomplish the state's legitimate objectives. Denying out-of-state wineries the right to ship their wines directly to in-state consumers while granting that same privilege to in-state wineries cannot be condoned, as the Supreme Court held in *Granholm v. Heald.* This is true whether the discrimination is obvious on its face, as was the case in *Granholm*, or in its effects. The states should not be allowed to stand behind platitudes such as "the three-tier system of wine distribution is inviolable," "direct shipping from out of state must be banned to protect youth," and "state tax revenue will be jeopardized if wine is shipped from out of state directly to in-state consumers." Justice Stephen Breyer was brilliant in his questioning of the attorneys general of New York and Michigan at oral argument in *Granholm.* Each time the state tried to rationalize discrimination against out-of-state wineries, whether it was on the basis of preventing underage purchases, collecting taxes, or ensuring an orderly market, Justice Breyer pointed out that the states could adopt reasonable, non-discriminatory measure to achieve their legitimate objectives without discriminating against interstate commerce. Justice Breyer suggested that the states require the shipper to obtain the signature of the adult purchaser at the time the wines are delivered and require the out-of-state producer to obtain a license in the destination state that can be suspended or revoked in the event of a violation; as part of that licensing process, the state could require the producers, in state and out of state, to post a surety bond to ensure excise tax payments to the destination state.

The wine industry must not forget wine's agricultural roots. This tie to the land distinguishes wine from beer and spirits. After Repeal, many states issued licenses to so-called farm wineries (there are no such things as "farm breweries" or "farm distilleries") and afforded them the privilege of direct sales to consumers. The states hoped that wineries would stimulate the local economy and promote agritourism, which they, in fact, did. This agricultural heritage explains in large measure why the direct sales litigation (*Granholm* and its progeny) is about wine, not beer or spirits.

Given wine's special role as an agricultural commodity and a significant one at that (wine is the number one finished agricultural product in California), the wine industry must embrace grape growing and winemaking practices that are environmentally, socially, and economically sustainable. This is an essential ingredient of the industry's social responsibility. The California Sustainable Winegrowing Alliance, established by the Wine Institute and the California Association of Winegrape Growers, is taking important steps in that direction. For example, in the field of viticulture, the Alliance addresses such diverse issues as climate change, carbon footprint, pesticide use, and farmworker housing.[208] There are also a variety of certification programs, such as Fish Friendly Farming, that promote environmentally beneficial management practices and carry out important ecological restoration projects.

---

208. California Sustainable Winegrowing Alliance (2022), https://www.sustainablewinegrowing.org/.

The enological side of the business is just as important. The wine industry must ensure product quality and integrity and protect consumers from adulterated and contaminated wines. Climate health is inextricably linked with human health, and wineries should be at the forefront of efforts to conserve water and energy, prevent pollution, and reduce solid waste. Programs such as Napa Green certify both vineyards and wineries that embrace practices advancing the environmental, economic, and social equity goals of sustainability.[209]

In conclusion, wine is now an integral part of American culture. The wine industry must accept its responsibility to address the harms associated with excessive drinking and find ways to promote a responsible role for wine in our society. Of course, there is no single prescription that can be offered. But as a core principle, wineries must accept their role as stewards of responsible corporate behavior and continue to monitor the activities of those in their world, such as tasting room and hospitality staff, brokers, distributors, advertisers, and the like. Of course, the wine industry cannot act alone. It must partner with governments, health care providers, educators, special interest groups, and community groups to achieve and maintain the rightful place of wine in American society as "the temperate, civilized, sacred, romantic mealtime beverage."[210]

---

209. Napa Green (2022), https://napagreen.org/.

210. Larry Walker, The Back Page, Wines & Vines 30 (Jan. 1991). The quote is from the Mondavi Mission Statement that is quoted in Walker's article.

APPENDIX 9-1

SUMMARY OF EFFECT OF POPULATION LEVEL INTERVENTIONS WITH LEVEL OF EVIDENCE RANKED ACCORDING TO AVAILABILITY OF EVIDENCE[211]

Policy Area	Description	Number of reviews (H=high quality, M=medium quality, L=low quality)	Outcome indicators used in category	Types of intervention	Main findings
Alcohol server setting	Interventions and policies targeting on- and off-premises server behavior, physical environment, or other night-time environment interventions	5 (H:1, M:3, L:1)	Sales, total consumption, consumption pattern, alcohol-related crashes and driving under the influence, violence, intoxication, disorder, server behavior, alcohol-related medical conditions	Server training, responsible beverage service, community nightlife interventions, dram shop liability/overservice law, on-site health promotion, stronger drink glasses, driving-home service	Mixed results. Dram shop liability reduces vehicle related deaths. Some studies demonstrated significantly beneficial effects on alcohol consumption, vehicle crashes, and on-premises violence, others showed no effect. Free driving-home service reduced injury crashes.

211. Martineau et al., *supra* note 76.

Policy Area	Description	Number of reviews (H=high quality, M=medium quality, L=low quality)	Outcome indicators used in category	Types of intervention	Main findings
Availability	Interventions and policies that reduce the physical availability of alcohol vendors, opening times, or types of saleable alcohol	8 (H:1, M:5, L:2)	Alcohol sales or consumption, violence, alcohol-related crashes/driving/ medical conditions, crime	Restricting opening days/hours, reducing alcohol outlet density, increasing minimum legal drinking age, government sales monopolization	Reduced availability in certain communities reduces consumption but is more effective when surrounding areas have similar policies. Privatization of government monopolies leads to increased consumption and related harm. Minimum legal drinking age policies create significantly beneficial effects on both consumption and drunk driving.
Illicit alcohol	Targeting unrecorded production, illegal importing or surrogate alcohol products	1 (L:1)	Reduced purchase of illicit alcohol	Educational campaign	Study demonstrated that education reduced illegal spirit purchase but the decrease coincided with increase in legal sales, suggesting a substitution effect rather than a reduction.
Taxation	Interventions to increase the tax and/or price of alcohol	3 (M:3)	Consumption, violence, crime, traffic outcomes, STDs/risky sexual behaviors	Increasing tax on some or all alcoholic products	Clear and consistent evidence that increased price or taxation reduces overall consumption and related harms, including morbidity, mortality, traffic crashes, crime, violence, and sexually-transmitted disease rates.
Mass media	Interventions using or restricting mass media to change consumption or behavior	3 (M:2, L:1)	Alcohol use, consumption behaviors	Health promotion campaigns, social marketing, advertising bans/ restrictions, counter-advertising	Beneficial effect of mass media campaigns, which are associated with better behavior outcomes than controls. Effects are strongest in the short-term. No substantive evidence supports the effectiveness of counter-advertising, but the body of evidence for its effectiveness is small.

Policy Area	Description	Number of reviews (H=high quality, M=medium quality, L=low quality)	Outcome indicators used in category	Types of intervention	Main findings
Drunk driving	Interventions and policies specifically aimed at reducing driving under the influence of alcohol or alcohol-related crashes	11 (H:3, M:7, L:1)	Alcohol-related/total/fatal/injury/single night-time crashes, traffic violations, hospitalizations, blood-alcohol concentration, self-reported drunk-driving or riding with a drunk-driver	Increased police patrols, sobriety checkpoints, graduated driving licenses, awareness campaigns, school-based interventions, on-premises incentives, multi-component programs	Random drunk driving checkpoints reduce vehicle crashes, with the most significant impact seen in the short-term after checkpoints are introduced. Graduated licensing programs reduces teen crashes. Significant beneficial effects seen with a variety of road safety campaigns and educational programs. Multi-component community programs that involve education, checkpoints, media advocacy, etc. are more effective than single component programs.
School	Interventions targeting general alcohol consumption and related harm in pre-school, primary and secondary school settings	11 (H:3, M:7, L:1)	Alcohol consumption or initiation, alcohol consumption without permission, problem drinking, risky sexual behavior	Classroom or extra-curricular programs, life skills or behavioral programs, whole school programs, peer support, general health education programs	Inconclusive evidence of effectiveness in school programs, with no clear pattern that distinguishes effective programs from ineffective programs. Interventions targeting early secondary-school (middle school) populations are more effective than those aimed at older pupils.

Policy Area	Description	Number of reviews (H=high quality, M=medium quality, L=low quality)	Outcome indicators used in category	Types of intervention	Main findings
Higher education	Interventions delivered in tertiary educational institutions	4 (H:1, L:3)	Alcohol consumption, alcohol misuse, anxiety or depression	Alcohol-free housing, fear appeal, social norm mass media campaign, multi-component	Only one study, utilizing social norm interventions, demonstrated a significant beneficial effect, but this was not replicated in studies of the same intervention. Alcohol-free housing had no effect on drinking. Prevention programs targeted at athletes was not effective. Increased enforcement and decreased access had no effect on self-reported alcohol use or alcohol-impaired driving.
Family and community	Interventions targeting a child or young person by influencing their family; community interventions delivered outside of educational institutions directly to young people	3 (H:2, M:1)	Alcohol consumption, problem drinking, health and social outcomes relating to alcohol use, personal and social skills	Mailed postcards, computer-mediated interventions, parental interventions in schools, youth agency and after school club interventions, community-wide campaigns targeting adolescents	Parenting interventions that are most effective actively involve parents and emphasize social skills or personal responsibility among young people. Interventions have a more significant effect on daughters than sons, No significant effect seen in interventions delivered in social or community settings.
Workplace	Interventions in workplace settings, both general and in occupations at risk of alcohol-related harm	3 (H:1, M:1, L:1)	Alcohol consumption, workplace injuries and fatalities, alcohol-related morbidity and mortality, problem consumption	Mandatory testing policy, health promotion mail-out, staff training sessions, peer-referral program	Mandatory random and for-cause alcohol testing associated with an initial decrease in injuries for occupational drivers. All studies demonstrated some beneficial effects on alcohol consumption or harm, but due to heterogeneity of studies, is difficult to generalize to overall effectiveness.

CHAPTER 10

INTERNATIONAL TRADE: U.S. RULES IN LAW, POLICY, AND PRACTICE FROM TRADE DISPUTES TO TRADE AGREEMENTS AND ACCORDS TO INTERNATIONAL ORGANIZATIONS

Robert M. Tobiassen

A. INTRODUCTION

The United States of America is a major wine-producing country, a major wine-consuming country, a major exporter of wine, and a major importer of wine. From colonial times until the turn of the twentieth century, imported wines were the ones most available to consumers, whereas beer and distilled spirits of domestic production were available widely.

From George Washington's love of Madeira[1] to Thomas Jefferson's affection for the wines from France following his ambassadorship, wines from other countries were a central part of the daily lives of many founders of the new republic. Even First Lady "Lemonade Lucy" Webb Hayes, 1877 to 1881, who banned alcohol beverages from the White House events, made some rare exceptions for wines, which most likely were imported.[2]

---

1. Joshua Malin, *George Washington: A Profile in Wine, Beer, and Whiskey*, Vine Pair (Feb. 16, 2015), https://vinepair.com/wine-blog/george-washington-whiskey-history/.

2. Callie Hopkins, *Lucy Hayes, Temperance, and the Politics of the White House Dinner Table*, The White House Historical Association (Oct. 25, 2018), https://www.whitehousehistory.org/lucy-hayes-temperance-and-the-politics-of-the-white-house-dinner-table.

As domestic wine production grew after the Repeal of Prohibition in December 1933, and the superpower role of the U.S. in the international community emerged from the winning side in World War II, the role of the U.S. increased both in its regulation of the domestic wine industry and in the development of many international trade and financial organizations with broad mandates that at times impact the global wine market.

From a U.S. legal and policy perspective, this chapter principally examines the post-1933 legal and regulatory regimes developed for domestic and imported wines and the role that the U.S. envisioned and advocated in several international organizations to carry forward on the global stage.[3]

Let me be clear: Nothing in this chapter diminishes the important culture, history, and tradition of wine production in Europe, South America, Central America, Oceania, Africa, and Asia. Rather and simply put, this chapter is focused on wine law, politics, and policy in the U.S. Policy is rarely pure, and politics is an influence here.

B. BASIC FRAMEWORK

We have to start with a basic framework in the U.S. legal and political regimes in order to lay the foundation for understanding how the U.S. manages its role in international trade today and its evolution in wine or any other agricultural commodity.[4] First, there are two legal systems that interact: domestic trade laws and international obligations arising from treaties, free trade agreements, and executive agreements, among others. Second, there are both trade policy and trade politics. As noted, policy is not pure, and political balancing considerations are always present. There is "free trade" policy, "fair trade" policy, and "freedom trade" politics.[5] "Fair trade" has two meanings. Commonly, it involves ensuring

---

3. "Sanctions" imposed by the United States directly impact trade though they are not part of a general trade policy. Sanctions are imposed on countries, companies, and individuals and cover goods that originate in those countries even if exported to the U.S. through a third country. In the United States, the Office of Foreign Asset Control (OFAC), Department of the Treasury, administers these sanctions. This chapter does not examine sanctions other than to note that there is a very detailed legal and regulatory framework governing sanctions, as explained on the OFAC website. U.S. Dep't of Treasury, Office of Foreign Assets Control—Sanctions Programs and Information, https://home.treasury.gov/policy-issues/office-of-foreign-assets-control-sanctions-programs-and-information (last visited Sep. 6, 2022).

4. Economies generally are within one of three categories: agricultural, industrial, and services. Wine, beer, distilled spirits, ciders, and meads are products representing an agricultural economy. The processing of raw materials through fermentation and, in some cases distillation, along with barrel aging does not convert these beverage alcohol products into "industrial products."

Obviously, some economies fall within all three categories in some respects, but it is still important to look at what is the real driver of a country's economy. For example, we are a consumer-driven economy, the People's Republic of China (PRC) is an export-driven economy, and the Russian Federation and the Kingdom of Saudi Arabia are energy-driven economies.

5. Craig Fuller, *Free trade is dead, welcome to 'Freedom Trade'*, Freight Waves (May 16, 2022), https://www.freightwaves.com/news/free-trade-is-dead-welcome-to-freedom-trade.

that the workers behind these goods and services are treated fairly and that human rights and environmental protections are maintained throughout the supply chain.[6] Recently, in political terminology,[7] it means there are no unreasonable barriers to trade in place, or a country is not using artificial measures, such as subsidies, to make its goods less expensive for the importing country.[8]

1. TWO SYSTEMS, ONE TRADE FRONT FOR THE UNITED STATES

Essentially, the U.S. has two separate legal regimes constituting the international trade policy system: domestic law and the international obligations arising from numerous international trade agreements, the prime one being the Uruguay Round Agreements under the auspices of the World Trade Organization (WTO) in Geneva, Switzerland.

"All politics are local" means that a country like the U.S. has a complex set of federal trade laws that were enacted over a 60-year period based on the two-fold goals of a fair-trade rules policy for U.S. commerce and a trade policy that protects the economy and security interests of the U.S. These laws are discussed in detail in later sections, but for illustration purposes, the Trade Act of 1974 is the prime example of such domestic laws.

There also are legal obligations imposed by multilateral and bilateral trade agreements. These instruments may be treaties, free trade agreements,[9] and other Executive Branch agreements between the U.S. and another country or a regional entity like the European Union through the European Commission. The Wine Accord Agreement reached in 2006, with the European Commission as discussed in detail below, is one example.[10] Another example is the Mutual Acceptance Agreement on Oenological Practices[11] (MAA), negotiated in 2001 and signed by the U.S. and other New World wine countries including Argentina, Australia,

---

6. Fair-trade, Merriam-Webster.com Dictionary, https://www.merriam-webster.com/dictionary/fair-trade (last visited Aug. 31, 2022).

7. Trump White House Archives, *President Donald J. Trump's Policy Agenda and Annual Report for Free, Fair, and Reciprocal Trade* (Feb. 28, 2018), https://trumpwhitehouse.archives.gov/briefings-statements/president-donald-j-trumps-policy-agenda-annual-report-free-fair-reciprocal-trade/.

8. The People's Republic of China is cited as a country that does not engage in "fair trade" with other countries. Buy American Campaign, *Fair Trade with China* (Aug. 22, 2018), https://buyamericancampaign.org/fair-trade-with-china/.

9. For a complete list and texts of all of the Free Trade Agreements (FTA) signed by the U.S., *see* Office of the United States Trade Representative, *Free Trade Agreements*, https://ustr.gov/trade-agreements/free-trade-agreements (last visited Aug. 31, 2022).

10. TTB, Agreement between the United States and the European Community on Trade in Wine (Sep. 4, 2012), https://www.ttb.gov/agreements/us-ec-wine-trade-agreement.

11. This Agreement was negotiated by the World Wine Trade Group (WWTG), formerly known as the New World Wine Trade Group. World Wine Trade Group, *Agreement on Mutual Acceptance of Oenological Practices*, https://legacy.trade.gov/td/ocg/wwtg.htm (last visited Aug. 31, 2022); World Wine Trade Group, *About*, https://www.wwtg-gmcv.org/ (last visited Aug. 31, 2022). In the Wine Accords of 2006, the U.S. and the European Commission agreed on a mutual recognition framework.

Canada, Chile, New Zealand, Republic of Georgia, South Africa, and Uruguay as members of the World Wine Trade Group.

The General Agreement on Tariffs and Trade (GATT), signed in 1947, is a multilateral agreement at regulating trade.[12] It continues today under the multiple disciplines covered by agreements that are all under the umbrella of the World Trade Organization (WTO), which came into existence on January 1, 1995. They are known either as the "Uruguay Round Agreements" (in recognition of the opening rounds in Punta del Este) or the "Marrakesh Agreements" (in recognition of their adoption at the Marrakesh Ministerial Meeting).

But overlaying this rules-based international framework of obligations is a second structure that is domestic in nature but international in impact. This dichotomy is found in the laws of many countries but varies in degree between nations depending on their economic power (and prior to World War II, their military power). The U.S. has numerous trade laws that were enacted to protect U.S. businesses and U.S. consumers against unfair trading practices by other countries.

While this dichotomy is examined in greater detail below, let us look at one example for illustration: the steel and aluminum dispute.[13] Currently, the U.S. has concluded that the global steel market has a large overcapacity in production that, in turn, reduces the economic incentives or even economic viability of the domestic steel industry. Recall that steel is an essential material in the time of war for the U.S. government, so the Executive Branch needs to ensure that U.S. capacity remains high enough to meet any supply needs for a potential upcoming war or for providing military hardware assistance to other countries. Globally, the overcapacity in steel production results from state-government subsidies in other countries to their local steel producers. The U.S. has two enforcement tools available: one is the "trade dispute settlement procedure" (DSP) under the WTO Agreement, which is initialed by consultations, and the other is the national security trade law. The U.S. could initiate a WTO proceeding against the country responsible for the over-capacity through state subsidies. However, a timelier and speedier result is necessary for national security protection. DSP is a very lengthy process and takes years if not a decade to complete.[14] Moreover, the enforcement

---

12. The GATT was one of several institutions set up after World War II to foster economic development around the world. The viewpoint in the late 1940s was that economic insecurity was the cause of wars. If people were economically secure so they could feed their families, have homes to live in, education for their children, and an adequate public health system, among other things, then the incentives for war would decrease, if not be extinguished. *See* John H. Jackson, The Word Trade Organization, Constitution and Jurisprudence, ch. 2 (Routledge, 1st ed., 1998).

13. This dispute indirectly impacts wine because the UK threatened to add U.S. wine to its retaliatory tariffs against the U.S. in response to the U.S.'s May 31, 2022 amendment of section 232 of the Trade Expansion Act of 1962, which created additional duties of 25 percent ad valorem on steel from the UK. As examined later, there are political reasons for the goods or services on a retaliation list.

14. The Airbus and Boeing trade disputes were both handled through the DSP and took over 14 years before the final decision and dollar amount of harm could be imposed through "retaliatory tariffs" (technically "additional duties") by the U.S. on EU goods until the EU came into compliance on the Airbus subsidies.

mechanism of a favorable WTO decision is the removal of trade concessions, usually in the form of retaliatory tariffs (or "additional duties"). This result would not address the national security concern arising from the insufficient steel production capacity in the U.S.

U.S trade law offers USTR an alternative enforcement tool. Section 232 of the Trade Expansion Act of 1962[15] authorizes the President to impose sanctions unilaterally against countries harming the U.S. through harmful trading practices, such as very widespread excessive industry subsidies that distort trade with other counties. Section 232 is generally called the national security exception and authorizes the U.S. to breach any international trade obligation where the President determines that national security is at risk or undermined by the allegedly harmful practice of the country of origin of the goods. Section 232 authorizes the President through tariffs or other means to adjust the imports of goods or materials from another country (even if that country is not the direct cause of the underlying national security threat) if the President deems the quantity or circumstances surrounding those imports to threaten national security. For example, the state subsidies in the Peoples Republic of China (PRC) is the cause of the overcapacity in steel production, but steel imports from other countries such as Canada, European Union nations, Japan, and the United Kingdom were subject to these section 232 tariffs.[16] In the steel (and aluminum) dispute, the President decided to use the Section 232 authority rather than avail the U.S. of the lengthy dispute settlement procedure at the WTO.

In response to the section 232 tariffs, the EU and UK imposed retaliatory tariffs on whiskey from the United States and threatened to extend these tariffs to wine from the United States. However, the resolution of this dispute with the EU and UK through the tariff rate quota (TRQ) ended these tariffs and the threats of tariffs on additional products.[17]

The Uruguay Round Agreements recognize a national security exemption from compliance with the country's trade obligations under the WTO agreements,[18] so the concept is recognized by the 164 member countries of the WTO, as of 2022.

---

15. 19 U.S.C. §1862. The Secretary of Commerce, in coordination with the Secretary of Defense, conducts an investigation and makes a recommendation to the President.

16. At present, the U.S. has agreements with Canada, the European Union, and Japan establishing a tariff rate quota (TRQ) that applies the section 232 tariffs only to quantities of steel that reflect the historic volume of steel exported to the U.S. by each of those countries. Section 232 National Security Investigation of Steel Imports (May 31, 2022), https://www.bis.doc.gov/index.php/232-steel.

17. Distilled Spirits Council of the United States, Statement by the Toasts Not Tariffs Coalition on the agreement between the U.S. and EU to End the Retaliatory Tariffs on American Whiskeys as part of the Steel and Aluminum Dispute Settlement (Oct. 30, 2021),

https://www.distilledspirits.org/news/statement-by-the-toasts-not-tariffs-coalition-on-the-agreement-between-the-u-s-and-eu-to-end-the-retaliatory-tariffs-on-american-whiskeys-as-part-of-the-steel-and-aluminum-dispute-settlemen/.

18. One point of current debate is whether the WTO agreements allowing unilateral measures that are inconsistent with the country's trade obligations under the WTO agreements to be imposed for purposes of national security are reviewable by the WTO through the Dispute Settlement

2. TRADE WARS MATTER TO YOUR PRACTICE OF THE LAW

Trade wars have all of markings of a military war. There are winners and losers, collateral damage to civilians, strikes strategically designed to inflict maximum damage, and a trade war is far easier to start then it is to end. There are spies and saboteurs. Peace agreements are rarely clearcut and may have ambiguities when the end of the war is a stalemate (which is frequently the case).

As a legal practitioner representing wine industry clients who are producers, distributors, importers, exporters, brokers, and retailers, among others, your clients frequently are collateral damage in a trade war. As in the steel and aluminum trade war grounded on national security, you wonder what does that have to do with wine trade? Retaliation lists of goods and services are strategic strikes to apply maximum pressure on the other side to settle. They appear asymmetrical when comparing the goods or services that are targeted to the core goods or services sparking the trade dispute.

Wine and distilled spirits are frequent commodities on these retaliation lists; they are the civilian collateral damage of the trade war. For the U.S., wine is frequently on the retaliation list because of the influence of domestic agriculture in France and Italy, for example, and distilled spirits are on these retaliation lists because Scotch whisky, cognac, and cream liqueurs are key industries in a number of EU Member States and the UK. For the EU and UK, wine is frequently on the retaliation list because California has the largest delegation in the House of Representatives and key leaders in the House, at present, are from California. Bourbon whiskey is on the retaliation because for many years the Majority or Minority Leader in the Senate has been from Kentucky, the home of bourbon.

The finalizing of the retaliation lists has its own intrigue. Before imposing a retaliatory tariff, USTR publishes a proposed list of goods and/or services in the Federal Register for public comment. Usually, a public hearing is scheduled in Washington, DC, as well. The hearing panel is chaired by an official from USTR, and each Executive Branch department may have a panel member. The Departments of Agriculture, Commerce, Labor, State, and Treasury will have a panel representative at a minimum. The written public comments and hearing statements from industry representatives (not under oath) form the basis for compiling the final list of goods and/or services that will be tariffed.

Trade associations group together to submit coalition comments opposing the inclusion of their products. For example, beer, wine, and spirits associations join as a coalition to oppose the inclusion of any beverage alcohol products on the final retaliation list. Individually, however, they may be advocating or lobbying privately for keeping their product category off the final list while including the other product categories on the list if the United States Trade Representative (USTR) decides some beverage alcohol must be on the final retaliation list. This

---

Proceedings (DSP). The U.S. position is "no." *See* GATT, Article XXI, Security Exceptions, https://www.wto.org/english/res_e/booksp_e/gatt_ai_e/art21_e.pdf (last visited Sep. 4, 2022).

is a continuing process because USTR may revise the final list later by removing one good and replacing it with another good, provided the latter good was subject to notice and comment on the original proposed list. This is called "carouselling."[19] Under U.S. trade law, USTR is required to review the list after the first 120 days and then regularly every 180 days thereafter.[20]

Wine law practitioners may have clients wishing to participate in these public comment and public hearing opportunities, including having their attorney prepare a comment letter or prepare and/or present oral remarks at the public hearing. In doing so, there is a straightforward formula. USTR does not want to place goods or services on the final retaliation list that are essential for the U.S. Government, businesses, and consumers. Computer chips, for example, will never be on a retaliation list and frequently certain medical equipment and public health goods are not on the retaliation list. The panel members are looking for public comments and remarks that focus on and establish why a specific good or service should not be on the retaliation list. French wines are an example from the Airbus retaliatory tariff public hearings. Burgundy is produced from pinot noir grapes in France. Pinot noir wine is widely (and well) produced in Oregon and other States as well as in South America, among other continents. At the hearings on the Airbus retaliatory tariffs, the speakers were trying to justify the unique character of Burgundy from France, and the panel members were asserting that many good pinot noirs are available, so placing Burgundy on the retaliation list would not harm U.S. consumers.[21]

Even if your client's wine is not targeted on a retaliation list, your client may suffer indirectly as components like imported glass bottles or wooden pallets are on the retaliation list and either become more expensive or less available, or both.[22]

And peace agreements are hard to come by. The five-year resolution period of the Airbus and Boeing retaliatory tariffs is just that, a temporary "suspension" based on an agreed set of State subsidy principles.[23] Another example is the

---

19. In the Airbus case, USTR "determined to alter the composition of the list of non-aircraft products subject to additional duties." The revision was minor in the commodities it removed and added. Importantly, however, this is the first instance where the U.S., in fact, put into effect the "carouselling" approach. Likely, USTR did this to establish a precedent for its use in future trade wars. *See* Notice of Modification of Section 301 Action: Enforcement of U.S. World Trade Organization (WTO) Rights in Large Civil Aircraft Dispute, 85 Federal Register 50866, 50867 (August 18, 2020).

20. 19 §U.S.C. 2416(c).

21. Office of the United States Trade Representative, *Section 301- Large Civil Aircraft,* https://ustr.gov/issue-areas/enforcement/section-301-investigations/section-301-large-civil-aircraft (last visited Aug. 31, 2022).

22. The domestic beer industry is suffering from the lack of aluminum cans and steel kegs. Beer Institute, *Beer Industry CEOs Send Section 232 Letter to President Biden* (Jul. 1, 2022), https://www.beerinstitute.org/press-releases/beer-industry-ceos-send-section-232-letter-to-president-biden/; Beer Institute, *Beer Institute Urges Immediate Removal of Section 232 Tariffs on Aluminum* (Jun. 6, 2022), https://www.beerinstitute.org/press-releases/beer-institute-urges-immediate-removal-of-section-232-tariffs-on-aluminum/ .

23. Office of the United States Trade Representative, *Section 301 Large Civil Aircraft supra* note 22.

terminations of the numerous Digital Services Taxes[24] investigations that are contingent on a sufficient number of countries enacting the two-pillar international tax framework[25] agreed upon by the Member States of the Organization for Economic Cooperation and Development (OECD). The original Section 301 DST investigation of France included "sparkling wine, made from grapes" on the proposed retaliation list[26] which could resurface if the OECD framework does not eventually enter into force.

For all of these reasons, knowing the provisions of trade law in the United States, be they derived from domestic law or compliance with the international trade obligations under treaties, free trade agreements, or Executive Agreements, is essential if your legal practice includes advisory work. Mitigation measures to protect your client, or at least minimize the impact of being collateral damage in a trade war or a lesser trade dispute require that you understand the frameworks and guardrails.

Even so, expect the unexpected that will disrupt smooth trade, such as President Trump's trade wars, sanctions, etc. One morning at a multi-country meeting hosted by the Embassy of Italy in Washington, DC, the agenda was immediately upended when President Trump tweeted that Champagne should be added to the active retaliation list in force at the moment.

3. TRADE POLICY VS. TRADE POLITICS

"Free trade," "fair trade," and "freedom trade" are trade policy descriptors that conveniently describe fundamentally different outlooks on the goal of trade. "Free trade" is described, in part, by David Ricardo's law of comparative advantage[27] positing that, if each country manufactures or produces the goods or services that it can do best, then the total supply of goods and services are optimal and maximized and, therefore, the world's population benefits. Jobs are optimal in the producing or manufacturing country, and the quantity of goods and services are maximized in quantity and quality. "Free trade" means that there are no artificial barriers preventing the free flow of goods across the borders. Tariffs, quotas, pre-import laboratory tests, sanitary and phyto-sanitary standards, and lengthy border inspections delaying imported goods in ports of entry are all trade barriers that may be reasonable but can be used unreasonably to disrupt or increase the costs of

---

24. Office of the United States Trade Representative, *USTR Welcomes Agreement with Austria, France, Italy, Spain, and the United Kingdom on Digital Services Taxes* (Oct. 21, 2021), https://ustr.gov/about-us/policy-offices/press-office/press-releases/2021/october/ustr-welcomes-agreement-austria-france-italy-spain-and-united-kingdom-digital-services-taxes.

25. OECD, *130 countries and jurisdictions join bold new framework for international tax reform* (Jul. 1, 2021), https://www.oecd.org/newsroom/130-countries-and-jurisdictions-join-bold-new-framework-for-international-tax-reform.htm.

26. *See* Notice of Determination and Request for Comments Concerning Action Pursuant to Section 301: France's Digital Services Tax 84 Fed. Reg. 66959 (Dec. 6, 2019) Harmonized Tariff Schedule of the United States (HTSUS), Chapter 22, subheading 2204.10.00, Sparkling wine, made from grapes.

27. https://www.britannica.com/topic/comparative-advantage.

imported goods compared to domestically manufactured or produced goods that are similar or equivalent.

"Freedom trade" is a "fair trade plus" concept. It incorporates social values in deciding which countries the U.S. wants to have free or fair trade with and which economies it wants to support and which ones it wants to deal with solely on a need-only basis. We only want to build or support economies that share our values. These social values include human rights, worker rights and protections, and combatting climate change. The Biden-Harris Administration has a two-pillar approach to commercial trade arrangements that the U.S. joins into with other countries; they must be worker-centric and focus on climate change mitigation.[28] For example, under the United States – Mexico – Canada Agreement (USMCA), USTR is aggressively pushing the Government of Mexico to protect worker rights in Mexico for free and fair elections on whether to unionize.[29]

Another example is the Forced Labor Initiative by Customs and Border Protection (CBP), Department of Homeland Security[30] and, more recently, The Uyghur Forced Labor Prevention Act (UFLPA).[31] CBP has a broad definition of "forced labor," and it applies to every stage of manufacture or production including the vineyard workers who harvest the grapes in the country of origin of the wine you import from to the factory in another country manufacturing the new empty wine bottles you use.[32]

Social values are starting to overlay on trade relations between the U.S. and the UK. Following Brexit, the UK has pursued trade agreements with countries around the world, including the U.S. While negotiations for a free trade agreement with the UK were on a fast track under the Trump Administration, the movement forward has slowed under the Biden-Harris Administration.[33] More recently, it is

---

28. Office of the United States Trade Representative, *Fact Sheet: USTR Releases 2022 Trade Policy Agenda and 2021 Annual Report* (Mar. 2022), https://ustr.gov/about-us/policy-offices/press-office/fact-sheets/2022/march/fact-sheet-ustr-releases-2022-trade-policy-agenda-and-2021-annual-report (last visited Aug. 31, 2022).

29. Office of the United States Trade Representative, *United States Announces Successful Resolution of Rapid Response Labor Mechanism Matter at Panasonic Auto Parts Facility in Mexico* (Jul. 14, 2022), https://ustr.gov/about-us/policy-offices/press-office/press-releases/2022/july/united-states-announces-successful-resolution-rapid-response-labor-mechanism-matter-panasonic-auto; Office of the United States Trade Representative, *United States Seeks Mexico's Review of Labor Rights Issues at Teksid Hierro Facility* (Jun. 6, 2022), https://ustr.gov/about-us/policy-offices/press-office/press-releases/2022/june/united-states-seeks-mexicos-review-labor-rights-issues-teksid-hierro-facility.

30. U.S. Customs and Border Protection, *Forced Labor* (Aug. 3, 2022), https://www.cbp.gov/trade/forced-labor.

31. U.S. Customs and Border Protection, *Uyghur Forced Labor Prevention Act* (Jun. 28, 2022), https://www.cbp.gov/trade/forced-labor/UFLPA.

32. "CBP defines forced labor as all work or service which is exacted from any person under the menace of any penalty for its nonperformance and for which the worker does not offer work or service voluntarily. Indentured labor is defined as work or service performed pursuant to a contract, the enforcement of which can be accomplished by process or penalties. This includes forced or indentured child labor." U.S. Customs and Border Protection, *Forced Labor supra* note 31.

33. Office of the United States Trade Representative, Joint Statement on the U.S./UK Dialogues on the Future of Atlantic Trade (Mar. 22, 2022),

thought that a political policy concern was in play about the border between Northern Ireland and the Republic of Ireland. When the UK was a Member State of the EU, as is the Republic of Ireland, the Irish border was uncontrolled and unimpeded. This open border is a key element of the Good Friday Peace Agreement,[34] of which President William Clinton was an essential proponent. The "divorce papers"[35] between the UK and EU under Brexit called for a continuation of this open border. Former Prime Minister Boris Johnson lately revealed he is reconsidering that portion of the UK-EU Withdrawal Agreement and decided to establish a controlled border.[36] Former Foreign Secretary Liz Truss, the new prime minister, supports "tearing up" parts of the Northern Ireland Protocol that would impact the border question.[37] President Biden made it clear that this would be unacceptable to the U.S., and the implications are now that the negotiations on the U.S.-UK free trade agreement are on hold for this reason.[38]

Disruptions to trade may arise in unexpected arenas. In the event the UK decides to reintroduce a controlled border between Northern Ireland and the Republic of Ireland, the European Commission would have to respond and could respond with a trade war and trade sanctions. The U.S., in turn, may feel compelled to support the European Commission and the Republic of Ireland (the latter wants an open border). Trade sanctions in retaliation by the UK could well target U.S. wines and whiskies. Again, this is the asymmetrical character of international disputes that spill over from politics into trade policies and practices.

Accordingly, U.S trade law and policy is embedded in many domestic laws and international agreements that are multilateral, plurilateral, and bilateral. However, the political dynamics surrounding many trade policy decisions must take into account these dynamics.

---

https://ustr.gov/about-us/policy-offices/press-office/press-releases/2022/march/joint-statement-usuk-dialogues-future-atlantic-trade.

34. Good Friday Agreement, Encyc. Britannica Online, https://www.britannica.com/topic/Good-Friday-Agreement (last visited Aug. 31, 2022).

35. European Commission, *The EU-UK Withdrawal Agreement* (Feb. 1, 2020), https://ec.europa.eu/info/strategy/relations-non-eu-countries/relations-united-kingdom/eu-uk-withdrawal-agreement_en.

36. The European Commission in Brussels strongly opposes any changes to the Northern Ireland Protocol. *See* Catherine Barnard, *A Northern Irish compromise is a balancing act of conflicts*, City A.M. (Aug. 17, 2022 6:00 AM), https://www.cityam.com/a-northern-irish-compromise-is-balancing-act-of-conflicts/.

37. David Young, *Key questions on the latest twist to the Irish Sea Border Saga*, Independent (May 17, 2022 07:09 PM), https://www.independent.co.uk/news/uk/northern-ireland-liz-truss-irish-sea-dup-uk-government-b2081111.html.

38. Brian O'Donovan, *Biden: No change to 'Irish accords' that results in 'closed border'*, RTE (Sep. 22, 2021 1:59 PM), https://www.rte.ie/news/world/2021/0921/1248226-biden-irish-accords-border/; George Parker & Katrina Manson, *Joe Biden warns Boris Johnson not to let Brexit upend Northern Ireland peace process*, Financial Times (Nov. 10, 2020), https://www.ft.com/content/57c02222-1634-4b88-9b46-0ebd89e89832.

C. U.S. TRADE LAWS AS UNILATERAL LEGAL AUTHORITIES

The United States has enacted trade laws that apply when determining whether specific foreign trade situations are harmful to the U.S. economy, discriminate against U.S. businesses and commercial entities, or when foreign trade must be limited or restricted in order to allow U.S. businesses to develop to a degree that they are equipped to face competition in global trade. USTR is the principal Executive Branch entity to administer these laws though the Secretaries of Commerce, Treasury, and Labor; the International Trade Commission also has a vital role here. As one might expect, the evolution of U.S. trade laws and the principal trade official role today in USTR corresponds to the expansion of global trade.

1. ROLE OF USTR AND ITS IMPACT ON WINE TRADE

Prior to 1962, the U.S. Department of State held principal authority over trade agreements. In that year, the White House, under President Kennedy, established the Special Trade Representative that in 1980 was redesigned and expanded as the USTR.[39] While the State Department remains an important player in the trade agreements sphere, it is now more of a partner with USTR than the leader.

The creation of USTR ultimately has worked to the benefit of the domestic wine industry especially, as well as generally, to the distilled spirits industry. Its core focus is protecting the trade interests of the U.S. including both the U.S. consumer and U.S. exporters, such as wineries. The wine industry has been very successful in getting attention from USTR officials involved in agricultural negotiations with the EU and the USTR officials heading U.S. delegations to the WTO in Geneva. These are long-term commitments by USTR of its resources because negotiations between governments and trading blocks move at a snail's pace. For example, the Wine Accord (2006) with the European Commission resulted from talks or consultations and then negotiations dating back to 1983, when TTB's predecessor agency, Bureau of Alcohol, Tobacco and Firearms (ATF), published a notice in the Federal Register asking for comments on Foreign Nongeneric Names of Geographic Significance Used in the Designation of Wines.[40] The Wine Accord (2006) is discussed below.[41]

---

39. Office of the United States Trade Representative, History of the United States Trade Representative, https://ustr.gov/about-us/history (last visited Aug. 31, 2022).

40. Foreign Nongeneric Names of Geographic Significance Used in the Designation of Wines, T.D. ATF-296, 55 Fed. Reg. 17960 (April 30, 1990) (codified at 27 C.F.R. §12) listing these foreign non-generic names. The Treasury Decision-Final Rule published in the Federal Register lays out the administrative history that started in 1983. The dissatisfaction of the European Commission and the EU wine industry with the outcome of this rulemaking created the impetus for more formal negotiations leading to the Wine Accord (2006).

41. The 1980s were truly a time of transition and change by ATF to respond the global trade in wine. In one sense, it was the period of "wake up calls" on the importance of (and the inability to

2. LEGAL PRACTICAL REASONS FOR LAWYERS TO KNOW—UNIQUE FEATURES

Unique to the practice of trade law in the U.S. is the inability to go to court to enforce your client's rights under a trade agreement. No private rights of action exist. Unless specified in a trade agreement, private parties do not have the right to seek judicial enforcement of a trade benefit in a trade agreement; rather the international obligations in the trade agreements are government-to-government arrangements. Only the government has the right of enforcement through either a mechanism in the agreement, such as the Dispute Settlement Procedure at the WHO or unilaterally under U.S. trade laws.

Private parties may have litigation rights against the United States (but not another country alleged to be in violation of its international obligations) depending on the precise terms of the laws enacted and/or regulations promulgated to implement the obligations under the trade agreement. For example, your client may have a route to judicial review under the Administrative Procedure Act of the agency regulations implementing a provision in the trade agreement.

So, how do you represent your client's interests here? Knowing the many tools under U.S. laws that are used to develop and finalize U.S. trade policy as it impacts wine and how to influence the decision makers behind those tools is a start. The following sections discuss a few of these tools.

a. Federal Advisory Committees for USTR

USTR has eight formal advisory committees (with subcommittees),[42] including ones on Agriculture Trade Policy, Agriculture Technical Policies, and Trade Policy and Negotiations. Representatives from industries and trade associations, among others, serve on these advisory committees. Members are required to sign nondisclosure agreements in order for them to provide candid advice to USTR officials and receive details from internal meetings within USTR.[43] Individuals may apply to be selected to serve on an advisory committee.

---

avoid) global trade in wine and the clashes arising from cultural, traditional, economic, and commercial stakeholders in the traded wines. The United States joined the International Office of Wine and Vine (OIV), as it was known then. The reality that trade resulted in clashes in importing markets was driven home to ATF in the 1980 Administrative Decision in Kaiser-Stuhl Brand wine from Australia and the label objection filed by the German Stabilization Fund to protect the German wine commune by that name. ATF held an administrative hearing that was reviewed by the ATF Deputy Director that concluded a reasonable intelligent wine consumer would not be misled and, therefore, both wines could co-exist in the U.S. domestic market. *See* In the Matter of Certificates of Wine Label Approval Issued to: Victoire Imports Company, San Francisco, California and Peartree Imports Company, Inc, New York, New York, Docket No. LA 1, Administrative Law Judge Recommended Decision, dated February 11, 1980, and Decision of the Deputy Director, dated May 15, 1980.

42. Office of the United States Trade Representative, Advisory Committees, https://ustr.gov/about-us/advisory-committees (last visited Aug. 31, 2022).

43. The advisory committee system, established by the U.S. Congress in 1974 in the Federal Advisory Committee Act, was created to ensure that U.S. trade policy and trade negotiating

b. Trade Act of 1974

The Trade Act of 1974, as amended, enacted very comprehensive unilateral and multilateral enforcement tools. These enforcement tools are used to respond to commercial threats by other countries, such as the Digital Services Tax imposed by France[44] and other countries,[45] and to implement favorable dispute settlement decisions from the World Trade Organization dispute settlement procedure, such as the Airbus decision rendered by the WTO.[46]

c. Trade Expansion Act of 1962—19 USC 1862

Section 232 provides a national security ground for the U.S. to abrogate one of its international obligations under trade agreements.[47] This section was discussed earlier with the steel and aluminum tariffs, and the material here only briefly expands on the section.

Any "interested person" or an Executive Branch department may raise a potential Section 232 case with the Department of Commerce. The Secretary of Commerce is the key decisionmaker on a recommendation to the President, and the Secretary relies on the investigative work of the Bureau of Industry and Security (BIS).[48] The very detailed process in determining whether to impose

---

objectives adequately reflect U.S. public and private sector interests. The advisory committee system consists of 26 advisory committees, with a total membership of approximately 700 citizen advisors. USTR's Office of Intergovernmental Affairs & Engagement (IAPE) manages the advisory committee, in cooperation with other agencies, including the Departments of Agriculture, Commerce, and Labor. IAPE is also designated as the state coordinator for the World Trade Organization and the North American Free Trade Agreement, and provides outreach to official state points of contact, governors, legislatures, and associations on all trade issues of interest to states.

44. Notice of Action in the Section 301 Investigation of France's Digital Services Tax, 85 Fed. Reg. 43292 (Jul. 16, 2020), https://ustr.gov/sites/default/files/enforcement/301Investigations/France_Digital_Services_Tax_Notice_July_2020.pdf (last visited Aug. 31, 2022).

45. *Id.*

46. Notice of Modification of Section 301 Action: Enforcement of U.S. WTO Rights in Large Civil Aircraft Dispute, 86 Fed. Reg. 13961 (Mar. 11, 2021), https://ustr.gov/issue-areas/enforcement/section-301-investigations/section-301-large-civil-aircraft.

47. For a list of the Section 232 reports prepared over the last 40 years, *see* Bureau of Industry and Security, U.S. Department of Commerce (2020), https://www.bis.doc.gov/index.php/other-areas/office-of-technology-evaluation-ote/section-232-investigations (last visited Aug. 31, 2022).

48. The Bureau of Industry and Security (BIS) at Commerce conducts the investigation (15 C.F.R. §705). In terms of national security, Commerce considers (1) existing domestic production of the product; (2) future capacity needs; (3) manpower, raw materials, production equipment, facilities, and other supplies needed to meet projected national defense requirements; (4) growth requirements, including the investment, exploration, and development to meet them; and (5) any other relevant factors. On imports, Commerce must consider (1) the impact of foreign competition on the domestic industry deemed essential for national security; (2) the effects that the "displacement of domestic products" cause, including substantial unemployment, decreases in public revenue, loss of investment, special skills, or production capacity; and (3) any other relevant factors that are causing, or will cause, a weakening in the national economy. Commerce may request public comments or hold hearings, if appropriate. An Executive Summary of the final report (excluding any confidential or classified material) must be published in the Federal Register.

Section 232 tariffs on steel and aluminum is transparent, and the steps can be followed on the Department of Commerce website.[49]

d. International Economic Emergency Powers Act (1967) —50 USC 1701-07

The International Economic Emergency Powers Act (IEEPA)[50] authorizes the President to regulate international commerce after declaring a national emergency in response to any unusual and extraordinary threat to the U.S that has its source in whole or substantial part outside the U.S. It has been used to impose sanctions on countries like Iran and Sudan.

IEEPA was not generally viewed as a trade enforcement tool, but the Trump Administration used it to threaten tariffs against Mexico for not doing more to control illegal immigration on the Southern border. The sanctions that would have been imposed were never made clear by the Administration. Perhaps a tariff on tequila? This is a reminder, however, of the breadth and unexpected power of the President to use trade tools that may disrupt your wine and other beverage alcohol product clients.

3. SECTION 201[51]—THE "ESCAPE CLAUSE" TO PROTECT U.S. BUSINESSES

The contemporary international trade community of nations has long recognized that free trade may hamper development of a local or domestic industry. Prior to the rules-based trade system adopted after World War II, nations could impose their own protections in whatever manner their economic power and military strength allowed. But under a rules-based system, parameters are agreed upon to address the need to facilitate domestic development of industries.

A limited period of relief from concessions given to other countries for the importation of goods to the affected country is the remedy used. Long recognized

---

Presidential Action and Notification. If Commerce finds in the negative, Commerce informs the President and no further action is required. If Commerce determines in the affirmative, the President, upon receipt of the report, has 90 days to (1) determine whether he/she concurs with its findings; and (2) if so, determine the nature and duration of the action to be taken to adjust the subject imports. The President may decide to impose tariffs or quotas to offset the adverse effect, without any limits on their duration, or take other action. The President may exclude specific products or countries. After a determination, the President must implement the action within 15 days, and submit a written statement to Congress explaining the action or inaction within 30 days. The President must also publish his determination in the Federal Register. https://sgp.fas.org/crs/misc/IF10667.pdf.

49. U.S. Department of Commerce, *Section 232 Investigation on the Effect of Imports of Steel on U.S. National Security*, https://www.commerce.gov/issues/trade-enforcement/section-232-steel (last visited Aug. 31, 2022).

50. 50 U.S.C. §1701.

51. USTR has two Section 201 proceedings going on at present, neither of which relate to beverage alcohol. United States Trade Representative, Section 201 Investigations, https://ustr.gov/issue-areas/enforcement/section-201-investigations (last visited Aug. 31, 2022).

under the General Agreement on Tariffs and Trade (GATT),[52] section 201[53] provides this type of relief. Presidents have used this tool differently.[54]

More formally titled "Action to facilitate positive adjustment to import competition," section 201[55] directs the International Trade Commission (ITC) to undertake an investigation, upon petition by the domestic industry, and determines whether the good is being imported into the United States in such increased quantities as to be a substantial cause of serious injury, or the threat thereof, to the domestic industry producing an article like or directly competitive with the imported goods. The ITC upon an affirmative determination makes a recommendation to the President. The President then may impose an overall quota, a tariff rate quota, or tariffs on the imported goods.

The standards and criteria applied by the ITC in conducting its investigation and preparing its recommendation to the President are transparent, codified in detail[56] and, if the President imposes limitations on trade concessions[57], the ITC is

---

52. General Agreement on Tariffs and Trade, Oct. 30, 1947, A. XIX.

53. 19 U.S.C. §2251-2254.

54. *See* Adam F. Holmer & Judith Hippler Bello, *Section 201 of the Trade Act of 1974: The Reagan Record*, 13:2 N.C. J. Intl. L. 185-223 (1988).

55. 19 U.S.C. §2251.

(a) Presidential action If the United States International Trade Commission (hereinafter referred to in this part as the "Commission") determines under section 2252(b) of this title that an article is being imported into the United States in such increased quantities as to be a substantial cause of serious injury, or the threat thereof, to the domestic industry producing an article like or directly competitive with the imported article, the President, in accordance with this part, shall take all appropriate and feasible action within his power which the President determines will facilitate efforts by the domestic industry to make a positive adjustment to import competition and provide greater economic and social benefits than costs.

(b) Positive adjustment to import competition

(1) For purposes of this part, a positive adjustment to import competition occurs when—

(A) the domestic industry—

(i) is able to compete successfully with imports after actions taken under section 2254 of this title terminate, or

(ii) the domestic industry experiences an orderly transfer of resources to other productive pursuits; and

(B) dislocated workers in the industry experience an orderly transition to productive pursuits.

(2) The domestic industry may be considered to have made a positive adjustment to import competition even though the industry is not of the same size and composition as the industry at the time the investigation was initiated under section 2252(b) of this title.

56. 19 U.S.C. § 2252.

57. 19 U.S.C §2253.

Subsection (a)(3) authorizes a wide range of actions that the President may take:

(3) The President may, for purposes of taking action under paragraph (1)—

(A) proclaim an increase in, or the imposition of, any duty on the imported article;

(B) proclaim a tariff-rate quota on the article;

(C) proclaim a modification or imposition of any quantitative restriction on the importation of the article into the United States;

(D) implement one or more appropriate adjustment measures, including the provision of trade adjustment assistance under part 2 of this subchapter;

mandated to monitor developments with respect to the domestic industry, including the progress and specific efforts made by workers and firms in the domestic industry to make a positive adjustment to import competition.[58] After three years, the ITC must report to the President on the progress made by the domestic industry, and the President may modify or terminate the limitations on trade concessions.[59] The President is required to report to Congress on his/her actions at designated periods.[60]

4. SECTION 301[61]—ACTIONS BY THE UNITED STATES TRADE REPRESENTATIVE—RANGING FROM PEACE NEGOTIATIONS TO "THE NUCLEAR OPTION"

Section 301[62] is a powerful trade enforcement tool used both for combatting unilaterally an unfair trade practice against the U.S. or enforcing a WTO dispute settlement decision in favor of the U.S. It includes investigations by USTR and the implementation of remedies in the form of the withdrawal of trade concessions from a country found by the Appellate Body of the WTO as acting inconsistent with that country's trade obligations to the complaining country.[63] That is, the "withdrawal of trade concessions" is a *de facto* "monetary penalty" and "acting inconsistent with a country's trade obligations" is a *de facto* "violation."

(E) negotiate, conclude, and carry out agreements with foreign countries limiting the export from foreign countries and the import into the United States of such article;

(F) proclaim procedures necessary to allocate among importers by the auction of import licenses quantities of the article that are permitted to be imported into the United States;

(G) initiate international negotiations to address the underlying cause of the increase in imports of the article or otherwise to alleviate the injury or threat thereof;

(H) submit to Congress legislative proposals to facilitate the efforts of the domestic industry to make a positive adjustment to import competition;

(I) take any other action which may be taken by the President under the authority of law and which the President considers appropriate and feasible for purposes of paragraph (1); and

(J) take any combination of actions listed in subparagraphs (A) through (I).

58. 19 U.S.C. §2254(a).

59. 19 U.S.C. §2254(b).

60. 19 U.S.C. §2253(b).

61. *See* Section 301 Investigations, *supra* note 22.

62. 19 U.S.C §2411. While commonly referred to as a Section 301 investigation, in reality the entire set of provisions cover 19 U.S.C. §§2411-2420. There are very detailed steps designed to provide due process and keep Congress and the public advised on USTR actions.

63. The nomenclature of international trade disputes is its own style. The offensive term "violation" is not used but, rather, a party, that is a country, is said to have acted inconsistently with its international trade obligations, a much more diplomatic accusation...though still an accusation. Likewise, the terms "penalties" and "sanctions" are avoided. Instead, in the case of a finding by the Appellate Panel of the WTO that a country has acted inconsistent with its trade obligations, the remedy is the withdrawal of trade concessions made to the noncompliant country by the complaining country. For example, in the Airbus proceeding at the WTO, the U.S. was authorized to withdraw trade concessions to the European Union up to $7.5 billion in volume of trade from the EU to the U.S. The remedy was not that the U.S. could impose retaliatory tariffs ("additional duties") in terms of a certain number of dollars.

Section 301 is the most common trade enforcement tool used by USTR.[64] The current massive tariffs ("additional duties") on goods imported from the People's Republic of China is the result of a Section 301 investigation and 11 investigations of the Digital Services Taxes (DST).[65] The Section 301 investigation of the French DST had the potential to impose tariffs on Champagne and sparkling wines from France. Section 301 investigations are self-initiated by the Executive Branch[66] or are the result of a petition from an interested party.[67] In representing clients in the

---

64. *See* Section 301 Investigations, *supra* note 22.

65. Office of the United States Trade Representative, Section 301-Digital Services Taxes, https://ustr.gov/issue-areas/enforcement/section-301-investigations/section-301-digital-services-taxes (last visited Aug. 31, 2022).

66. 19 U.S.C. §2414.

67. 19 U.S.C. §2412.

(a) Petitions

(1) Any interested person may file a petition with the Trade Representative requesting that action be taken under section 2411 of this title and setting forth the allegations in support of the request.

(2) The Trade Representative shall review the allegations in any petition filed under paragraph (1) and, not later than 45 days after the date on which the Trade Representative received the petition, shall determine whether to initiate an investigation.

(3) If the Trade Representative determines not to initiate an investigation with respect to a petition, the Trade Representative shall inform the petitioner of the reasons therefor and shall publish notice of the determination, together with a summary of such reasons, in the Federal Register.

(4) If the Trade Representative makes an affirmative determination under paragraph (2) with respect to a petition, the Trade Representative shall initiate an investigation regarding the issues raised in the petition. The Trade Representative shall publish a summary of the petition in the Federal Register and shall, as soon as possible, provide opportunity for the presentation of views concerning the issues, including a public hearing—

(A) within the 30-day period beginning on the date of the affirmative determination (or on a date after such period if agreed to by the petitioner) if a public hearing within such period is requested in the petition, or

(B) at such other time if a timely request therefor is made by the petitioner or by any interested person.

(b) Initiation of investigation by means other than petition

(1) (A) If the Trade Representative determines that an investigation should be initiated under this subchapter with respect to any matter in order to determine whether the matter is actionable under section 2411 of this title, the Trade Representative shall publish such determination in the Federal Register and shall initiate such investigation.

(B) The Trade Representative shall, before making any determination under subparagraph (A), consult with appropriate committees established pursuant to section 2155 of this title.

(2) (A) By no later than the date that is 30 days after the date on which a country is identified under section 2242(a)(2) of this title, the Trade Representative shall initiate an investigation under this subchapter with respect to any act, policy, or practice of that country that—

(i) was the basis for such identification, and

(ii) is not at that time the subject of any other investigation or action under this subchapter.

(B) The Trade Representative is not required under subparagraph (A) to initiate an investigation under this subchapter with respect to any act, policy, or practice of a

domestic wine industry, you may want to utilize the petition process to address any discriminatory actions by a foreign country that hurt your client's sales in the U.S. or its ability to export the product. After the initiation of the investigation, USTR "shall request consultations with the foreign country concerned regarding the issues involved in such investigation."[68]

Section 301 is used to implement a favorable decision from the WTO Appellate Body in a dispute settlement proceeding. After the U.S. received a favorable decision in the Airbus subsidy matter, USTR used Section 301 to impose retaliatory tariffs on $7.5 billion of goods or services exported from the EU to the U.S. The important point here is that it does not mean that the U.S. may collect $7.5 billion in additional duties annually. For example, suppose the volume of wine trade with France exporting wines to the U.S. is $1.0 billion annually. This means USTR has $6.5 billion remaining in volume of trade with the EU on which it may impose retaliatory tariffs. In other words, the U.S. may withdraw trade concessions previously made to France not to impose duties on French wines imports. USTR would apply a retaliatory tariff against the French wine imports. Another important point is the WTO decision does not control the percentage of the retaliatory tariffs applied on the value of the imported goods. While USTR imposed a 25 percent tariff on wines from France and several other EU countries, it could have imposed a 10 percent or a 100 percent retaliatory tariff.[69]

In any Section 301 investigation that concludes that retaliatory action by the U.S. is appropriate, USTR must propose a retaliation list of goods and/or services for publication in the Federal Register and for public comment that in most instances includes public hearings. For an attorney with a client importing a good appearing on the proposed list, this stage of the procedure is the most important. USTR always proposes more goods on the list than it could actually impose

---

foreign country if the Trade Representative determines that the initiation of the investigation would be detrimental to United States economic interests.

(C) If the Trade Representative makes a determination under subparagraph (B) not to initiate an investigation, the Trade Representative shall submit to the Congress a written report setting forth, in detail—

(i) the reasons for the determination, and

(ii) the United States economic interests that would be adversely affected by the investigation.

(D) The Trade Representative shall, from time to time, consult with the Register of Copyrights, the Under Secretary of Commerce for Intellectual Property and Director of the United States Patent and Trademark Office, and other appropriate officers of the Federal Government, during any investigation initiated under this subchapter by reason of subparagraph (A).

(c) Discretion

In determining whether to initiate an investigation under subsection (a) or (b) of any act, policy, or practice that is enumerated in any provision of section 2411(d) of this title, the Trade Representative shall have discretion to determine whether action under section 2411 of this title would be effective in addressing such act, policy, or practice.

68. 19 U.S.C. §2413.

69. The total dollar amount of these collections is available. U.S. Customs and Border Protection, Department of Homeland Security, Trade Statistics, https://www.cbp.gov/newsroom/stats/trade (last visited Sept. 7, 2022).

retaliatory tariffs on at the time of entry. Accordingly, the aim of your representation at the public hearing in testimony and in written comments is to convince the panel why your client's good should not be on the final list. Justifications include that there are no domestic sources or sources in other countries to provide this type of good. As you can imagine, wine interests present arguments that are aimed at convincing USTR to select another good, and this results in controversies between purveyors of the various goods.[70]

Under the Section 301 framework, USTR is required to review and revise, if appropriate, the retaliatory tariffs after the first 120 days, and then every 180 days thereafter.[71] During the course of the retaliatory tariffs, USTR may remove the retaliatory tariff on one good and substitute another good from the list. Note that USTR can only impose a retaliatory tariff on a good or service that was on the proposed list for public comment. A new comment period would be required if USTR wanted to impose a retaliatory tariff on a good or service not on the original proposed list. USTR may terminate the Section 301 action when the President decides the unfair or discriminatory practice of the foreign country no longer exists or that it is inappropriate to continue the Section 301 action.[72]

One cautionary note about Section 301 investigations and enforcement actions that are self-initiated by the Executive Branch or pursuant to a petition by an interested party: The foreign country that is the target of the USTR investigation may challenge the grounds for any enforcement action that is imposed by the U.S. by filing a consultation and dispute settlement proceeding at the WTO against the U.S., provided the foreign country is a Member State of the WTO.

D. Trade Negotiations Framework Procedural Steps

Negotiations impacting trade occur in two venues. International organizations like the World Trade Organization, World Intellectual Property Organization, World Health Organization, Food and Agricultural Organization, CODEX Alimentarius, and Asian Pacific Economic Cooperation, among others, negotiate agreements at general assemblies and in standing committees or councils made up of Member States of the international organization. These negotiations themselves are not covered in this chapter, but their outcomes, as relevant to wine trade, are covered. Attorneys can represent their client's positions in these types of international organizations through advisory committees and informal meetings with USTR and

---

70. In a Section 301 investigation and enforcement action other than one based on a decision by the WTO Appellate Body, there is a discretionary "exclusion" process where the importer of a special good can seek to be excluded from the retaliatory tariff. For example, imagine USTR were to impose a tariff on all glass bottles from China. However, if a certain bottle from China is necessary for an applicant's business, and the bottle was not available elsewhere and not in demand from other businesses, USTR would likely grant the exclusion.

71. 19 U.S.C. §2416.

72. 19 U.S.C. §2417.

Departments of Agricultural and Treasury officials on the U.S. delegations to these organizations.

The second venue for trade negotiations are individual negotiations by the U.S. with other countries or regional economic blocks such as the European Union through the European Commission. For major trade negotiations that will require approval by the Senate or new legislation by both Houses of Congress, prior to start of the negotiations the President and the congressional leadership must agree on the goals of the U.S. at the negotiations and a framework for ongoing consultations with Congress during the negotiations. This arrangement is enacted into a law called Trade Promotion Authority (TPA). The TPA negotiations are when Congress has the greatest input (and leverage) on goals and outcomes. As such, this is the early stage where attorneys can brief Members of Congress on their client's concerns with the aim of getting those concerns addressed in the final TPA bill.

1. "FAST TRACK" NEGOTIATIONS AUTHORITY

The Trade Agreements Act of 1974[73] created the concept of "fast track" authority for the President to negotiate trade agreements. The trade agreements eligible for "fast track" negotiations are multilateral and plurilateral, as well as free trade agreements with individual countries or occasionally with regional blocks, such as the CAFTA-DR FTA (Central America-Dominican Republic Free Trade Agreement). There are three steps in this process of Trade Promotion Authority. TPA must be approved by Congress for a period of time, and frequently it is linked to a specific trade negotiation. For example, it was enacted for the period 1975 to 1980 for the Toyoko Round of multilateral negotiations and for the period 1988 to 1993 for the Uruguay Round negotiations and then extended into 1994 for the conclusion of those negotiations.

The three steps for TPA are:

1. Joint development by the White House and Congress on goals of negotiations.
2. Ongoing consultations with Congress during the period of negotiations.
3. A "fast track vote" by Congress of approval or non-approval without an opportunity for amendments to the text or filibuster of the bill. (This is why the White House will agree to the TPA approach to a trade negotiation.)

2. CONSTITUTIONAL POWERS OF THE PRESIDENT AND THE CONGRESS INTERPLAY IN TRADE

Trade Promotion Authority reflects the debate on the constitutional powers of the President and those of the Congress over trade relations with other countries.

73. 19 U.S.C. §2101.

It is a narrow path to walk because many of these positions are implied powers from general provisions of the Constitution. Under Article II, Section 3, of the Constitution, the President "shall receive ambassadors and other public ministers" from other countries. From this text springs many powers of the Executive to make foreign policy and global trade decisions exclusively.[74] For example, this text implies the right to recognize or not recognize a nation.[75] But the Constitution also gives certain powers to the Legislative Branch over foreign policy and global trade. The Senate has the constitutional power to give advice and consent to the President in approving a resolution of ratification for treaties.[76] The Senate has the power to give consent to the appointment of a U.S. ambassador to another country or international institution. Under the foreign commerce clause, the House of Representatives and the Senate have a degree of authority over foreign trade as a commercial matter.[77] The vesting of the foreign policy power exclusively in the Executive Branch reflects a similar decision for making the Executive Branch the Commander in Chief of the military services—both situations frequently require immediate actions or responses such that the delays inherent in the congressional decision-making processes would not fit. Like several other topics covered in this chapter, this lesson on the Constitution could cover an entire chapter itself; rather, the summary here is to ensure that you are aware of this arrangement as you advise your clients on formulating strategies to resolve wine trade matters.

3. TRADE ADJUSTMENT ASSISTANCE

Congress and the president understand that trade agreements will result in some job losses in the U.S. Trade Adjustment Assistance (TAA)[78] funds are appropriated by Congress to help U.S. workers displaced by a trade agreement to train for new jobs and offers assistance to firms, farmers, and communities.[79] Again, this is an early time in a trade negotiation to represent a client's interests where that client may be a business or community that is projected to lose jobs if the trade negotiations are successful.

---

74. Congressional Research Service, U.S. Constitution Annotated, *Right to Receive Ambassadors and Other Public Ministers: Overview*, https://www.law.cornell.edu/constitution-conan/article-2/section-3/right-to-receive-ambassadors-and-other-public-ministers-overview (last viewed Aug. 31, 2022). This excellent commentary explains the breadth of the Executive's powers under this simple seven-word phrase in the Constitution.

75. President Harry Truman was able to recognize the State of Israel within 11 minutes of its creation in 1948. See Harry S. Truman Library, *Recognition of Israel*, https://www.trumanlibrary.gov/education/presidential-inquiries/recognition-israel (last visited Aug. 31, 2022).

76. U.S. Const. Art. II, §2. The power of the Senate with respect to treaties is not even referenced in Article I in the listing of the powers of Congress. *See* U.S Senate, *About Treaties,* https://www.senate.gov/about/powers-procedures/treaties.htm (last visited Aug. 31, 2022).

77. U.S. Const. Art. I, §8.

78. For examples of trade adjustment assistance, see U.S. International Trade Commission, *The Year in Trade 2021, Operation of the Trade Agreements Program*, 73rd Report,89-93 (Aug. 2022) https://www.usitc.gov/publications/332/pub5349.pdf .

79. 19 U.S.C. §§2251, 2401(g).

E. FUNDAMENTAL TOOLS OF INTERNATIONAL TRADE

There are "tools of the trade" in all professions, and international trade is no less the case. The federal government has negotiated many types of agreements with other countries or trading blocks to set rules of trade in wine.[80]

1. TREATIES

For wine and other beverage alcohols, the two most well-known treaties of relevance are the accession by the United States to the World Trade Organization and the USMCA that subsided the North American Free Trade Agreement.[81] Within the framework of the Uruguay Round Agreements, the Agreement on Trade-related Aspects of Intellectual Property (TRIPS) addresses geographical indications and trademarks relating to wines. The TRIPS Agreement is discussed in Chapter 6, Wine Brands and Appellations of Origin.

2. FREE TRADE AGREEMENTS

Free trade agreements (FTAs) are bilateral negotiations between the United States and another country.[82] They are comprehensive in nature with chapters covering rules of origin, financial services, telecommunications, intellectual property, customs administration, government procurement, and market-access, among others.[83] For international wine trade purposes, the important feature about FTAs is that the United States will only include distinctive designations for beverage alcohol products in the market access chapter and not in the intellectual property chapter.[84] This is consistent with the U.S. position that trademarks are an appropriate method to comply with its international obligations under the WTO TRIPS Agreement on geographical indications.

3. EXECUTIVE AGREEMENTS

The president has inherent powers to enter into trade agreements with other countries. When the topic or subject matter of the agreement does not require

---

80. There are other tools such as anti-dumping and countervailing duties and quotas and Tariff Rate Quotas (TRQ) used by USTR, International Trade Commission, and Department of Commerce that are not covered in the chapter.

81. This treaty has Market Access provisions on Bourbon, Tennessee Whiskey, Tequila, Mezcal, and Canadian Whisky.

82. Free Trade Agreements *supra* note 10.

83. By way of example, the US-Chile FTA: Office of the United States Trade Representative, Final Text, Chile Free Trade Agreement, https://ustr.gov/trade-agreements/free-trade-agreements/chile-fta/final-text, (last visited Aug. 31, 2022).

84. *See e.g., id.,* at 3, National Treatment and Market Access for Goods, §E – Other Measures, Art. 3.15, Distinctive Products.

congressional action to implement, these are referred to as Executive Agreements. Subject matter experts from Executive Branch departments, bureaus, and offices provide technical support to USTR in trade negotiations and serve on the USTR delegations. For the government lawyers on these delegations, the question frequently is whether the Executive Branch can implement the position agreed on in the negotiations under existing law or regulations. This approach allows USTR to agree to positions without having to justify directly those positions to Congress.

The Wine Accord (2006)[85] with the European Union and the World Wine Trade Group (WWTG) agreements on mutual recognition of oenological practices[86] and the wine labeling agreement[87] are all Executive Agreements on wine trade. The U.S.-EC Distilled Spirits Agreement (1994)[88] and the U.S.-Mexico Tequila Agreement (2006)[89] are also Executive Agreements but are not discussed in this chapter.

4. WINE ACCORD (2006)

As mentioned earlier, TTB's predecessor agency, ATF, started becoming more involved with wine and spirits global trade in the 1980s. The international trading place meant more wines were being exported and imported from and by many countries around the world.

Between the U.S. and the EU, there were two fundamental areas of concern: wine making practices for the U.S. and geographical indications and traditional expressions for wine made in Europe. The termination or repeal of semi-generic wine names in the U.S. for wines that were not from the named European appellation was the goal of the European Commission. In turn, for many years, the U.S. faced non-tariff trade barriers when exporting its wines to the EU because of the New World wine making practices, such as ion exchange, that were not acceptable to the European winemakers. Starting in 1983, USTR and the European Commission held "talks" to assess whether formal negotiations should be held to negotiate a wine accord or agreement to resolve all of these issues. At the same time, based on an exchange of letters, ATF commenced a decision-making

---

85. TTB, *U.S./EC Wine Agreement* (Mar. 10, 2006), https://www.ttb.gov/agreements/us-ec-wine-trade-agreement (last visited Aug. 31, 2022).

86. World Wine Trade Group, *Agreement on Mutual Acceptance of Oenological Practices* (May 31, 2019), https://legacy.trade.gov/td/ocg/oenological.htm (last visited Sep. 1, 2022).

87. World Wine Trade Group, *Agreement on Requirements for Wine Labeling* (Jan 23, 2007), https://legacy.trade.gov/td/ocg/labeling%20agreement.htm (last visited Sep. 1, 2022).

88. TTB, *European Union Distilled Spirits and Spirit Drinks Agreement* (Mar. 15, 1994), https://www.ttb.gov/images/pdfs/us-ec-spirits-agreement.pdf (last visited Sep. 1, 2022). Between 1986 and 1994, USTR and the European Commission held talks on wine trade with the aim of starting negotiations on a wine accord. To show some progress in the overall talks, the U.S. and European Commission decided on a quick and straightforward agreement on distilled spirits.

89. TTB, *Trade in Tequila Agreement* (Nov. 11, 2016), https://www.ttb.gov/itd/ttbgov-trade-in-tequila-agreement, (last visited Sep. 1, 2022).

process[90] to determine whether the domestic wine labeling regulations on foreign non-generic names of geographical significance used in the designations of wine should be expanded from a single regulation to a new stand-alone Part of the regulations with many more names listed.

During these talks or consultations and subsequently in the negotiations, the European Commission would give "derogations" (exceptions) to the U.S. that would allow entry into the EU of U.S. wines produced with wine making practices not authorized in the EU. The derogations would last for various periods of times from six months to two years depending on the sentiments of the European Commission about the status of the talks or negotiations. These talks or consultations occurred when ATF was promulgating a new Part 12 on Foreign Nongeneric Names of Geographic Significance Used in the Designation of Wines to the regulations.[91] The names under consideration had been submitted by the Member States to ATF and were listed in a notice of proposed rulemaking. After reviewing the public comments and researching the wine names, ATF published a final rule that listed far fewer names than expected by the EU. This result added some tensions to the talks or consultations with the European Commission.

Additionally, significant paperwork, called the VI-1 form, was required with laboratory tests for the U.S. wines. At the time, U.S. law allowed the importation of wines from another country that were produced using good commercial practices, a somewhat vague standard. The negotiating goals were asymmetric for several reasons that made the negotiations more difficult than usual. Trading wine names for wine making practices was difficult to measure in value. Likewise, the standard of good commercial practices in wine making generally allowed EU wines to enter the U.S. unimpeded, whereas U.S. wines were impeded in entering the EU marketplace.

In 2006, the parties reached an "Agreement Between the United States and the European Community for Trade in Wine" or the "Wine Accords."[92] This is an Executive Agreement. The key provisions of the Wine Accord are:

1. Recognition of each other's existing current winemaking practices.
2. A consultative process for accepting new winemaking practices.
3. The United States limiting the use of semi-generic EU wine names in the U.S. market. "Angelica"[93] is the only semi-generic name not covered by the Wine Accord. A grandfather clause allows the continued use on domestic wines of the EU semi-generic names provided the label bears the same brand and fanciful name AND appeared on an approved certificate

90. Non-generic Designations of Distinctive Types of Grape Wine Having Geographical Significance, ATF Notice No. 492, 48 Federal Register 51333 (November 8, 1983) (codified at 27 C.F.R. pt. 4).

91. Foreign Nongeneric Names of Geographic Significance Used in the Designation of Wines, 55 Fed. Reg. at 17960.

92. TTB, *Agreement Between the United States of America and the European Community on Trade in Wine* (Mar. 10, 2006), https://www.ttb.gov/images/pdfs/us-eu-wine-agreement.pdf (last visited Sep. 1, 2022).

93. The name is derived from Los Angeles.

of label approval issued by TTB before March 6, 2006. Nothing in the Wine Accord restricts a winery from selling or transferring the approved label to another winery.

4. The EC allowing under specified conditions for the use of certain regulated terms on U.S. wine exported to the EC.
5. Recognizing certain names of origin in each other's market.
6. Simplifying certification requirements for U.S. wine exported to the EC.
7. Defining parameters for optional labeling elements of U.S. wine sold in the EC market.
8. Exemption of EC natural grape wines containing 0.5 to 22 percent alcohol by volume from U.S. wine certification requirements.

The objectives of this Agreement are forward looking: (a) to facilitate trade in wine between the Parties and to improve cooperation in the development and enhance the transparency of regulations affecting such trade; (b) to lay the foundation, as the first phase, for broad agreement on trade in wine between the Parties; and (c) to provide a framework for continued negotiations in the wine sector. However, since 2006, there have been few follow up wine trade meetings with the European Commission and there are no commitments, at present, for an additional wine agreement.

5. WORLD WINE TRADE GROUP AGREEMENTS

In June 1998, a group of New World wine producing (and consuming) countries met in Zurich, Switzerland to explore forming the New World Wine Trade Group (the name World Wine Trade Group (WWTG)) was adopted later). Representatives from Australia, Argentina, Brazil, Canada, Chile, New Zealand, South Africa, and the United States attended the meeting.[94] On the basis of the mission and objectives established in Zurich and later in Mendoza, Argentina, the WWTG moved rapidly into putting these into practice by concluding two international trade-liberalizing agreements, discussed below, sharing a great deal of useful information, and establishing principles on wine regulatory policies and practices by governments.[95]

During this same time period, the International Office[96] of Vine and Wine (OIV) was developing a new charter to update the original one from 1924. All of the WWTG countries were OIV members, except for Canada, which had an application for membership pending with the OIV. One reason for establishing the WWTG was to provide a counter-voice to the Old-World dominance of the OIV.

94. World Wine Trade Group, *Mission Vision & Objectives of the WWTG*, https://www.wwtg-gmcv.org/mission (last visited Sep. 1, 2022).

95. World Wine Trade Group, *Wine Regulatory Principles*, https://www.wwtg-gmcv.org/principles (last visited Sep. 1, 2022).

96. The final charter revised the name to the International Organization of Vine and Wine.

In 2000, when the U.S. ended its OIV membership and Canada withdrew its application, the other WWTG countries remained in the OIV.[97]

a. Agreement on Mutual Acceptance of Oenological Practices (MAA)

Adopted in 2001, the MAA recognizes that each WWTG member has established acceptable mechanisms for regulating wine-making practices and in turn agrees to accept the wine-making practices of all other parties. Its goal is to facilitate trade in wine and to avoid the imposition of obstacles to such trade, through parties permitting the importation of wine produced in another party that is produced in accordance with that other party's laws, regulations, and requirements related to oenological practices and the mechanism to regulate them.

The MAA provides for mutual recognition of oenological practices approved by each party. This also enhances the international acceptability of wine produced in WWTG countries. Adoption of the principles of the MAA by additional countries would facilitate trade in wine, both within the region and internationally.

Under U.S. law[98], a foreign winery producing natural wine for export must produce that wine in accordance with U.S. wine-making practices, materials, and processes unless the exporting country has an MAA with the United States.

b. Agreement on Wine Labeling Requirements (2007) and Protocol (2013)

Under the Labelling Agreement, the WWTG participants have agreed to a "single field of vision" approach to wine labeling commonalities. Four key common elements of information (country of origin, product name, net contents, and alcohol content) are deemed to comply with domestic labelling requirements if they are presented together in any single field of vision on a label on the container. In early 2013, phase two of the Labelling Agreement was concluded through the Protocol to the Agreement on Requirements for Wine Labelling. This extends the earlier Agreement on Labelling by providing for a degree of harmonization of rules regarding alcohol tolerance, variety, wine region, and vintage and added the names of countries that acceded to the Labeling Agreement since 2007.

Finally, while not an Agreement, the WWTG has a Memorandum of Understanding on Certification Requirements. The Certification MOU provides that routine certification of wine composition should not be required other than on

---

97. The U.S. was disappointed that Argentina, Australia, Chile, New Zealand, and South Africa did not end their membership with the OIV at this time. Such departures would have undercut the ability of the OIV to assert world-wine community status with four of the continents having major wine production no longer having member representation at the OIV. In this writer's view, Australia, New Zealand, and South Africa gained greater roles in the OIV following the departure of the U.S. As a final note, the UK and Denmark did leave the OIV when the U.S. departed. The UK has since rejoined.

98. 26 U.S.C. §5382.

health and safety grounds consistent with WTO rules, as well as requiring that any certification must be in line with CODEX Alimentarius standards.[99]

F. INTERNATIONAL ORGANIZATIONS AND TRADE ASSOCIATIONS ON WINE TRADE

Various international organizations have mandates that cover, in some respect, international wine trade. While countries through their governments are the official members of these entities, frequently private sector input is sought and, in some cases, the representatives of the private wine sector are included on government delegations. The key organizations are listed below.

1. INTERNATIONAL AND INTER-GOVERNMENTAL ORGANIZATIONS

a. World Trade Organization (WTO) (Geneva)

The WTO[100] is the pinnacle of trade bodies and the ultimate setter and arbitrator of the rules of the international trading system. It represents the economies of 164 member countries and there are an additional 25 countries whose governments hold observer status at the WTO.[101] The WTO agreements set the benchmark rules of trade that other trade agreements between countries and regions must adhere to and prevents provisions in these other agreements that are inconsistent with the WTO rules. However, those other agreements may be "WTO-plus" because they provide trade obligations that exceed those set by the WTO agreements.[102]

The WTO trade agreements are multilateral and plurilateral agreements. The TRIPS Agreement[103] is a multilateral agreement whereas the Agreement on Government Procurement is a plurilateral agreement. In recent years, the WTO has stalled by sharp policy divisions between its members and allegations that some members are failing to abide by their WTO commitments and accession agreements. The inability of the "Doha Development Round," which started in November 2001, to reach significant agreements and conclusions exemplifies the

99. World Wine Trade Group, *Memorandum of Understanding on Certification Requirements* (Oct. 20, 2011), https://legacy.trade.gov/td/ocg/2011%20WWTG%20MOU.pdf (last visited Sep. 1, 2022).

100. World Trade Organization, www.wto.org (last visited Sep. 1, 2022).

101. World Trade Organization, *Members and Observers* (Jul. 29, 2016), https://www.wto.org/english/thewto_e/whatis_e/tif_e/org6_e.htm#observer (last visited Sep. 1, 2016).

102. The U.S. frequently describes the market access provisions of a Free Trade Agreement as "TRIPS plus."

103. The TRIPS agreement is discussed in Chapter 6. The Agreement on Technical Barriers to Trade (TBT) and the Agreement on the Application of Sanitary and Phytosanitary Measures (SPS) are the two Agreements that also impact wine trade. *See* Robert M. Tobiassen, *On Common Ground*, 13 Transnat'l Law 75 (2000).

stalled nature of the WTO.[104] Many members are calling for major reforms of the WTO, including the U.S. and EU. Until then, it is likely that plurilateral agreements are more likely to be negotiated.

b. World Customs Organization (WCO) (Brussels)

The WCO has 184 Members (three-quarters of which are developing countries) that are responsible for managing more than 98 percent of world trade. For wine trade purposes, the importance of the WCO is that it manages the master Harmonized Tariff Schedule (HTS) framework that is uniformly adopted by countries around the world. This role impacts HTS subheadings in Chapter 22, which include wines. In the U.S., the Harmonized Tariff Schedule of the United States (HTSUS) is managed by the International Trade Commission.[105]

c. International Organization of Wine and Vine (OIV) (Lyon)

Founded in 1924, the OIV today operates under a charter adopted in 2001.[106] Its membership represents 48 countries and 17 observers. Working groups and commissions at the OIV cover a wide range of topics relating to wine and spirits from grapes such as brandy. It covers technical standards on oenological and viticultural practices, labeling and economics of the wine marketplace world-wide, assembles annual data on annual wine production, and has been delegated the standards authority by the European Commission for new wine-making practices. The OIV holds observer status at the CODEX Alimentarius Commission but does not hold observer status at the WTO.[107]

The U.S. was an observer and then a member of the OIV between 1986 and 2000. The U.S. fully participated and in good faith on the Groups of Experts, Commissions, and Executive Committee and sent delegates from the Departments of Agriculture, Commerce, Health and Human Services through the Food and Drug Administration, and Treasury, with ATF being the lead agency. The U.S. wine and brandy industries also sent technical experts to assist and serve on the U.S. delegation. Nevertheless, the larger context of trade challenges concurring at that time made it a difficult for the U.S. at the OIV. The Wine Accord negotiations with the European Commission would spill over into OIV positions and resolutions in support of the EU. Similarly, the negotiations leading to the WTO agreements occurred between 1986 to 1994. The OIV viewed itself as the international expert on all issues related to wine and expended its efforts to influence the TRIPS negotiations in favor of EU positions, which were ones not supported by the U.S.

---

104. World Trade Organization, *The Doha Round*, https://www.wto.org/english/tratop_e/dda_e/dda_e.htm (last visited Sep. 1, 2022).

105. World Trade Organization, *Harmonized Tariff Information*, https://www.usitc.gov/harmonized_tariff_information (last visited Sep. 1, 2022).

106. The International Organisation of Vine and Wine, *About*, https://www.oiv.int/en/the-international-organisation-of-vine-and-wine (last visited Sep. 1, 2022).

107. WTO, International intergovernmental organizations granted observer status to WTO bodies, https://www.wto.org/english/thewto_e/igo_obs_e.htm (last visited Sep. 4, 2022).

As a result, the U.S. frequently found itself at odds with the OIV working groups and resolutions. The U.S. fully supported and participated in the negotiations that developed the new charter adopted in 2001. But the U.S. stakeholders concluded that the new charter failed to address adequately U.S. concerns, and the Secretary of State gave formal notice of withdrawal from the OIV in six months.

d. CODEX *Alimentarius* Commission

The CODEX is the world's standard settling body on food safety that includes wine and is under the jurisdiction of the Food and Agriculture Organization (FAO) of the United Nations and the World Health Organization (WHO). It has 189 members representing 188 countries and the European Union.[108] Currently, the Codex Alimentarius Commission has 243 Codex Observers consisting of 60 intergovernmental organizations (IGOs), 167 nongovernmental organizations (NGOs), and 16 United Nations agencies and offices. CODEX is one of the few standards bodies recognized by the WTO as authoritative.

As noted, the OIV holds observer status at the CODEX but it has been unsuccessful in its efforts to gain recognition by CODEX as the standards body delegated to handle wines.

Finally, the WWTG advocates that the labeling principles approved by the WWTG set a benchmark in wine labeling, giving clarity and consistency in information shown across different world-wide markets. WWTG advocates that these principles provide the basis for a global standard if adopted by sufficient international bodies and countries. The Codex Alimentarius Commission does not, at present, have an international standard for wine labeling. The WWTG is not an observer at the CODEX.

e. World Health Organization (WHO) (Geneva)

One of the myriad health mandates of the WHO focuses on alcohol consumption.[109] Launched in 2010, the "WHO Global strategy to reduce the harmful use of alcohol"[110] is a major action plan. The SAFER Initiative, launched in 2018, is directed at "a world free from alcohol related harm."[111] Countries supporting the WHO initiative may enact domestic laws that limit the sale of wine or increase the price through taxes, among other approaches.[112] These laws will

---

108. Food and Agriculture Organization of the United Nations, *CODEX Alimentarius International Food Standards*, https://www.fao.org/fao-who-codexalimentarius/about-codex/members/en/ (last visited Sep. 1, 2022).

109. World Health Organization, *Alcohol*, https://www.who.int/health-topics/alcohol#tab=tab_3 (last visited Sep. 1, 2022).

110. World Health Organization, *Global strategy to reduce the harmful use of alcohol*, https://www.who.int/publications/i/item/9789241599931 (May 31, 2010) (last visited Sep. 1, 2022).

111. World Health Organization, *The SAFER initiative*, https://www.who.int/initiatives/SAFER (last visited Sep. 1, 2022).

112. Further discussion of approaches to reducing alcohol-related harm are discussed in Chapter 9.

impact the wine you export to these countries in international trade. Recall that the WHO lead the world-wide health campaign initiative against tobacco products[113] that resulted in the Framework Convention on Tobacco Control (FCTC).[114] The World Health Assembly (WHA) is the decision-making body for the WHO, and the U.S. representative is positioned to voice concerns raised by the wine industry that are consistent with U.S. government interagency views.[115]

f. Organization for Economic Cooperation and Development (OEOC) (Paris)

The OECD[116] mandate covers social, economic, environmental, and revenue topics, and the organization has issued papers on health and alcohol consumption including wine in the context of financial[117] and health[118] costs to society in various countries.[119] OECD has 38 member countries representing the major economically developed nations and five key partner countries representing a significant portion of the world's population.[120] Decisions are made by the Council on a consensus basis and each member country and the European Commission has an ambassador on the Council.[121] This means the U.S. wine industry has an opportunity to share its views with the U.S. Ambassador attending the Council sessions.

g. Asian Pacific Economic Cooperation (APEC) (Singapore)

APEC[122] was formed in 1990 and currently has 21 member countries on both sides of the Pacific Ocean, which forms the commonality of the APEC model.[123] APEC is the premier Asia-Pacific economic forum, and has the primary goal of supporting sustainable economic growth and prosperity in the Asia-Pacific region.[124]

---

113. World Health Organization, *Tobacco*, https://www.who.int/health-topics/tobacco#tab=tab_1 (last visited Sep. 1, 2022).

114. World Health Organization, *WHO Framework Convention on Tobacco Control*, https://fctc.who.int/ (last visited Sep. 1, 2022).

115. World Health Organization, *World Health Assembly*, https://www.who.int/about/governance/world-health-assembly (last visited Sep. 1, 2022).

116. Organization for Economic Co-operation and Development, https://www.oecd.org/ (last visited Sep. 1, 2022).

117. OECD, *Tackling Harmful Alcohol Use* (May 12, 2015), https://www.oecd.org/health/tackling-harmful-alcohol-use-9789264181069-en.htm (last visited Sep. 1, 2022).

118. OECD, *Alcohol Consumption*, (2021) https://data.oecd.org/healthrisk/alcohol-consumption.htm (last visited Sep. 1, 2022).

119. OECD, *Preventing Harmful Alcohol Use United States* (2021), https://www.oecd.org/unitedstates/Preventing-Harmful-Alcohol-Use-Key-Findings-USA.pdf (last visited Sep. 1, 2022).

120. OECD, *About*, https://www.oecd.org/about/ (last visited Sep. 1, 2022).

121. OECD, *Organisational Structure*, https://www.oecd.org/about/structure/ (last visited Sep. 1, 2022).

122. Asia-Pacific Economic Cooperation, https://www.apec.org/ (last visited Sep. 1, 2022).

123. APEC, *History*, (Mar. 2022) https://www.apec.org/about-us/about-apec/history.

124. APEC, *Mission Statement*, (Sep. 2021), https://www.apec.org/about-us/about-apec/mission-statement The full APEC Mission Statement is:

APEC has a Wine Regulatory Forum (ARF) that supports initiatives to improve trade in wine and wine regulations in the APEC member countries.[125] The ARF is a public-private venture with both government officials and industry representatives and is a forum where you may have input as a lawyer for your client. In 2016, the ARF approved an APEC Model Wine Export Certificate.[126] APEC has published two reports on the efforts and outcomes of the ARF.[127] Future work of the ARF is contingent on funding.

2. TRADE ASSOCIATIONS FOCUSED ON WINE

Domestic and foreign trade associations are strong influencers of trade policies and positions.[128] The U.S. associations frequently reach out to the Executive Branch and Capitol Hill to give input on trade problems and challenges. They also provide input to USTR on its annual estimate report on foreign trade barriers harming U.S. businesses.[129] Representatives of U.S. trade associations sit on advisory committees, as discussed earlier. Finally, U.S. trade associations frequently brief ambassadors and trade, commercial, or agricultural attachés at embassies in Washington, DC.[130]

"APEC is the premier Asia-Pacific economic forum. Our primary goal is to support sustainable economic growth and prosperity in the Asia-Pacific region.

"We are united in our drive to build a dynamic and harmonious Asia-Pacific community by championing free and open trade and investment, promoting and accelerating regional economic integration, encouraging economic and technical cooperation, enhancing human security, and facilitating a favorable and sustainable business environment. Our initiatives turn policy goals into concrete results and agreements into tangible benefits.

125. APEC Sub-Committee on Standards and Conformance, *Regulatory alignment helps manage risk in APEC wine trade* (Nov. 7, 2012), https://www.apec.org/press/news-releases/2012/1107_wine (last visited Sep. 1, 2022).

126. *Id.*

127. APEC Sub-Committee on Standards and Conformance, *APEC Wine Regulatory Forum Report* (Sep. 2011), https://www.apec.org/publications/2011/09/apec-wine-regulatory-forum-report (last visited Sep. 1, 2022); APEC Sub-Committee on Standards and Conformance, *APEC Wine Regulatory Forum Report 2012* (May 2013), https://www.apec.org/publications/2013/05/apec-wine-regulatory-forum-2012 (last visited Sep. 1, 2022).

128. Wine Institute (U.S.); WineAmerica (U.S.); International Federation of Wines and Spirits (FIVS); Comité Européen des Entreprises Vins (CEEV) (EU); Fédération du Commerce d'Exportation des Vins et Spiritueux de France (FEVS) (France); and similar wine associations are present in South Africa, Chile, Argentina, New Zealand, Australia, Italy, Germany, Spain, UK, Portugal, Austria, Georgia, and Moldova, among others.

129. Office of the United States Trade Representative, *Reports and Publications,* https://ustr.gov/about-us/policy-offices/press-office/reports-and-publications (last visited Sep. 1, 2022).

130. The National Association of Beverage Importers (NABI), Washington, D.C., maintains ongoing relationships with many Embassies of countries who export wine, distilled spirits, and beer/malt beverages to the U.S. This enables NABI to have up-to-date information on the laws and regulations in other countries and provides a point of contact to raise concerns or questions from U.S. importers over legal or practical activities in the exporting country.

Wine trade associations on every continent (except Antarctica) undertake similar actions in their home countries, and in other countries through their embassies and consulates, as well as official industry delegations visiting another country or informal visits by a group of industry members.

G. CONCLUSION—THE CHALLENGE OF THE FUTURE

Intertribal, regional, and world trade have been around for many millennia and will continue into the future millennia.[131] Wine trade dates back at least to 1200 BC/BCE,[132] and today represents billions of dollars in global trade. Trade does not operate in a vacuum, but changes to fit in every time and place. Is it evolving to something better each time? Is it simply morphing? Is it dying and transforming into a new creature? Or is it just a game like virtual reality or metaverse?

"There is nothing permanent except change."[133] The global business landscape is ever changing; domestic politics are unpredictable; and global alliances shift. We see mergers and acquisitions resulting in large market concentration in the U.S. and globally with multinational companies; at the same time, the White House is looking to promote competition and restore a balance that was the norm over 40 years ago.[134] We face constant and core supply chain disruptions where fixes are really a global game of Whack-A-Mole. Routinely, we have Presidential elections with trade policy positions changing, sometimes dramatically, with every new Administration, and globally we see shifting country alliances. And, of course, there always will be future trade wars.

---

131. For a collection of eclectic and original writings covering trade for more than 500 years, *see Trade*, Lapham's Quarterly 13:3 (Spring 2019). The articles show first-hand the intertribal, regional, and world trade scenarios of the past 500 years.

132. Vine Pair, *How Wine Colonized the World*, https://vinepair.com/wine-colonized-world-wine-history/ (last visited Sep. 1, 2022).

133. Heraclitus (Greek philosopher, c. 535 BCE-c. 475 BCE), a quote reformulated any number of times over the centuries, although the sentiment always remains the same (and true, for that matter).

134. Joseph R. Biden Jr., The White House, *Executive Order on Promoting Competition in the American Economy* (Jul. 9, 2021), https://www.whitehouse.gov/briefing-room/presidential-actions/2021/07/09/executive-order-on-promoting-competition-in-the-american-economy/; The White House, *Remarks by President Biden At Signing of An Executive Order Promoting Competition in the American Economy* (Jul. 9, 2021), https://www.whitehouse.gov/briefing-room/speeches-remarks/2021/07/09/remarks-by-president-biden-at-signing-of-an-executive-order-promoting-competition-in-the-american-economy/.

Knowing the fundamental tools of international trade and their origins, understanding that trade decisions are based in both public policy and political reality, and being fully cognizant of the context and culture of the times will enable lawyers (and others) to find creative, innovative, and correct solutions to the future challenges of trade in wine for the millennia to follow. Knowledge is the keystone here.[135]

135. For those readers who desire more knowledge about international law principles and practices beyond the wine sector, Brownlie's Principles of Public International Law (Oxford University Press) is highly recommended as a single volume resource. First published in 1966, it is now in its Ninth Edition and is regularly updated with new editions. James Crawford, Brownlie's Principles of International Public Law (9th ed., Oxford University Press 2019). It is considered one of the classic treatises in this field.

CHAPTER 11

SHOULD WE REGULATE CANNABIS LIKE ALCOHOL?

Jason Barker, Emily Gant, and Richard Mendelson

INTRODUCTION

Richard Mendelson

We wine lawyers are constantly imagining what Prohibition must have been like in the United States. Terence Winter's Boardwalk Empire and Ken Burns' Prohibition, among other productions and publications, give us a clue. But the full extent of the violence and lawlessness during those fated 13 years from 1920 to 1933 seems unimaginable 100 years after the fact.

Understanding this period of American history and what Ann-Marie Szymanski has called the "pathway to Prohibition" is essential for wine lawyers, because many of our current laws and regulations governing "intoxicating liquors" were devised during that time. They are part of the legacy of Prohibition. Perhaps that is why so many of them are counter-intuitive and arcane, designed, as I wrote in *From Demon to Darling: A Legal History of Wine in America*, to "solve problems past," problems that either don't exist today or that persist in a vastly different cultural, social, and economic setting.

Often neither the legislators nor the regulators know why these laws were adopted in the first place, yet they are loathe to change them, fearful of a return to the excesses of the Prohibition era. Their reticence is misplaced. The temporary reforms of federal and state alcoholic beverage laws and regulations occasioned by the pandemic, when shelter-at-home and safer-at-home orders were issued and many on-sale premises were shuttered, included 19 separate items of regulatory relief adopted by the California Department of Alcoholic Beverage Control ("ABC"). At the time of their adoption, ABC stated that it had "carefully considered the public's health, safety, and welfare in providing this relief, and the Department has concluded that the decision to defer enforcement of these measures, exercised on a temporary basis, will not jeopardize the public's health, safety, or welfare." There have not been any significant abuses of the relaxed or, in some cases eliminated, rules, no endangerment of public health. In fact, these measures have changed consumer preferences and buying habits (e.g., eating outdoors, free deliveries, virtual tastings, sales through pass-out windows), yet it is unlikely that many of these reforms will become permanent.

This underscores the importance of carefully considering the main policy objectives and the key legal approaches for regulating a product coming out of Prohibition, whether it is intoxicating liquors, cannabis, or some other banned substance. That framework will shape the public attitudes and customs surrounding the newly legalized product for years to come. John D. Rockefeller, Jr. was prescient when he commissioned Raymond Fosdick and Albert Scott after Repeal to study the alcohol regulatory systems around the world and make recommendations on what legal framework would work best in the United States. Fosdick's and Scott's *Toward Liquor Control*, published in 1933, is still a classic text for any wine lawyer.

Alcohol entered and exited from Prohibition by amendments to the U.S. Constitution. Cannabis entered Prohibition by a law of Congress, the 1980 Controlled Substances Act, which lists cannabis as a Schedule I substance with a high potential for abuse and no currently accepted medical use.[1] Notwithstanding this federal law, cannabis is now being legalized in numerous states for medical and/or recreational use through various voter initiatives and state laws, which vary significantly from state to state.[2] The federal government has either turned a blind eye or openly accepted these state measures so long as they meet specific criteria.[3]

---

1. Under the Controlled Substances Act ("CSA"), substances are categorized into five schedules, depending on their therapeutic benefit and their potential to result in abuse, diversion, dependency, and addiction. Brian T. Yeh, *The Controlled Substances Act: Regulatory Requirements*, Congressional Research Service (Dec. 13, 2012), available at https://sgp.fas.org/crs/misc/RL34635.pdf. Schedule I is the most restrictive. Marijuana and tetrahydrocannabinols ("THCs") are classified as hallucinogens on Schedule I, along with mescaline, peyote, psilocybin, MDMA, and LSD. 21 C.F.R. 1308.11(d). Hemp is excluded from Schedule 1. The 2018 Farm Bill, formally entitled The Agriculture Improvement Act of 2018 (Pub. L. 115-334, amending 21 U.S.C. §802(16), 812(c)), defines hemp as the cannabis plant, or any part thereof, including its extracts and cannabinoids, having a THC concentration of not more than 0.3percent on a dry weight basis. Hemp, as so defined, is not marijuana for purposes of the CSA.

2. Decriminalization and/or legalization of cannabis for medical use in states has typically preceded legalization for recreational use. In California, for example, the voters approved Proposition 215, the Compassionate Use Act of 1996, that allowed a qualifying patient and her caregiver to cultivate and possess cannabis for medical purposes. Cal. Health & Safety §11362.5(2). Oregon and Washington followed suit shortly thereafter. In 2012, Colorado became the first state to approve, by initiative, the recreational use of cannabis. Colo. Const. Am. 64 (Use and Regulation of Marijuana); Colo. Const. Art. 18, §16. Today, 37 states and the District of Columbia have enacted laws allowing the use of cannabis for therapeutic purposes, and 19 states and the District of Columbia permit the adult use of cannabis. National Conference of State Legislatures, *State Medical Cannabis Laws* (Jul. 17, 2022) https://www.ncsl.org/research/health/state-medical-marijuana-laws.aspx.

3. In 2013, the U.S. Department of Justice ("DOJ") issued a memorandum intended to guide U.S. attorneys in the exercise of enforcement discretion, known as the "Cole Memo." The Cole memo essentially stated that it was not a DOJ priority to take enforcement action against persons or entities

I did not focus on the cannabis legalization movement until I observed that many state initiative campaigns adopted as a rallying cry, "We'll regulate cannabis like alcohol." This is meant to reassure voters that there is already a tried-and-true method to regulate the cannabis industry; we'll regulate it like alcohol. This slogan worked in Alaska, California, Colorado, Maine, and Massachusetts. As stated in Colorado's Amendment 64, which was adopted by the voters in 2012: "In the interest of the health and public safety of our citizenry, the people of the State of Colorado further find and declare that marijuana should be regulated in a manner similar to alcohol." Today, there is a Coalition to Regulate Cannabis Like Alcohol, a bill in Congress entitled The Regulate Marijuana Like Alcohol Act, and a ballot initiative in Ohio called The Regulate Cannabis Like Alcohol initiative.

As practitioners and students of wine law know well, there is no such thing as a single body of alcoholic beverage law. There are different local, state, and federal laws for wine, spirits, and beer. There is a federal tied-house law and numerous state variations on that theme. There are license states and control states. Some states have alcohol franchise laws; others do not. Some states allow local option; others prohibit it. There are one-tier, two-tier, and three-tier systems of distribution, depending on the state. There are state and federal excise taxes.

There have been efforts over time to adopt uniform alcoholic beverage laws. Perhaps the most comprehensive effort was the Columbia University and Coca-Cola Company joint project to fashion a model Alcohol Beverage Act in 1979. In the end, that model law, although well-reasoned, was not adopted by a single state. Currently, the Uniform Law Commission, also known as the National Conference of Commissioners on Uniform State Laws, is considering a uniform law on direct-to-consumer ("DTC") shipping. Initially conceived of as a direct-to-consumer distilled spirits shipping law, it morphed into a wine DTC shipping law. When the Commission realized that numerous state DTC shipping laws already exist, with numerous variations, the effort changed again to one focused on compliance. That

---

involved in cannabis activities if those activities were lawful under state cannabis laws, whether medical or recreational. However, DOJ would consider enforcement action if those activities negatively impacted eight specific federal interests. Those enforcement priorities include preventing the distribution of marijuana to minors; preventing revenue from the sale of marijuana from going to criminal enterprises, gangs, and cartels; preventing the diversion of marijuana from states where it is legal under state law in some form to other states; preventing state-authorized marijuana activity from being used as a cover or protection for the trafficking of other illegal drugs or other illegal activity; preventing violence and the use of firearms in the cultivation and distribution of marijuana; preventing drugged driving and the exacerbation of other adverse public health consequences associated with marijuana use; preventing the growing of marijuana on public lands and the attendant public safety and environmental dangers posed by marijuana production on public lands; and preventing marijuana possession of or use on federal property. U.S. Dept. of Justice, Guidance Regarding Marijuana Enforcement (Aug. 29, 2013), available at https://www.justice.gov/iso/opa/resources/3052013829132756857467.pdf.

Former Attorney General Jeff Sessions rescinded this memo. However, no notable enforcement action has been taken to date. U.S. Dept. of Justice, Office of the Attorney General, Marijuana Enforcement (Jan. 4, 2018), available at https://www.justice.gov/opa/press-release/file/1022196/download.

law is now known as the Alcohol Direct Shipping Compliance Act and, as of fall 2022, is still under consideration.

Although uniformity may be unattainable, there are several common policy concerns that governments regulating recreational cannabis or wine use must address.[4] Depending on the outcome of those deliberations, specific legal approaches will form the foundation of the government's laws and regulations. In this chapter, I first identify five key policy concerns facing both cannabis and alcoholic beverages: consumer access, product safety, market organization, trade practices, and labeling and advertising. In each policy area, I list a series of questions that cannabis and alcoholic beverage lawyers should ask.

KEY POLICY ISSUES

Consumer access and social consumption: Who has the right to possess, cultivate, and sell cannabis? At what age? In what amounts? In what locations, with what notice, if any, and on what days and at what times? What about cultivation, consumption, or sale in proximity to schools, churches, child-care centers, parks, residences, and establishments with liquor licenses like bars, restaurants, and hotels? Are these same activities allowed on federal lands? Must the area of consumption be designated and even blessed by the regulatory authority, typical of designated areas for smoking tobacco? Can local jurisdictions ban the possession, cultivation, or sale of cannabis, otherwise known as local option? Should producers, wholesalers, and retailers of alcoholic beverages be able to sell cannabis at their licensed premises? Should cannabis be able to be transported or sold across state lines, e.g., to other states that authorize adult use, which is not allowed today?

Do the answers to these questions depend on a comparative risk assessment of cannabis and alcoholic beverages?

Product safety: There are numerous cannabis product types, including flower, pre-rolls, concentrates (hash, wax, etc.), vape oils, tinctures, capsules, edibles (gummies, cookies, beverages, etc.), and other cannabis-infused or cannabis-derived preparations. They differ in potency. Should the cannabis laws differ for the different product types? Should all the products be able to be sold in the same locations to the same people? Should states require childproof containers for some of these products, and how would those requirements compare with the closures for alcoholic beverages?

How should the state ensure that the cannabis products are safe? Some states like California require quite elaborate laboratory testing of cannabis products to ensure that they meet quality and safety standards; other states do not have

---

4. This policy discussion relates specifically to the recreational use of cannabis, not medicinal use. Although some of the policy and legal issues are identical, medical use involves issues of therapeutic applications, physician prescriptions, standard of care, and qualifying medical conditions.

mandatory testing. Should a person or entity with a license for testing cannabis be able to hold other cannabis licenses, e.g., as a cultivator, distributor, or dispensary?

Market organization: The most obvious ways in which lawmakers regulate cannabis and alcohol are through a tiered system of license holders with licenses granted by the state, consisting of manufacturers, wholesalers/distributors, and retailers. These tiered licenses may be supplemented by "tied-house" laws that prohibit cross-ownership and give "things of value" between the tiers. This keeps the tiers operating independently without undue influence exerted by one tier over the other; prevents vertical integration of manufacturers, wholesalers, and retailers; promotes fair competition; and may protect the small operator who otherwise couldn't compete with the large players.

Trade practices: Tied-house and free goods laws prohibit advances, discounts, gifts, loans, product displays, and other "things of value" from a supplier to a retailer. Contracts for the sale of cannabis that are contingent upon the sale of something else may be prohibited, as they are with alcohol. Also suspect is the practice of "gifting," where a business sells a product or service and provides cannabis as a "gift" in return. What cannabis-related promotional activities are allowed?

Labeling and advertising: What information is required, optional, and prohibited? Is the use of cultivar names regulated? Are ingredient lists required in a manufactured cannabis product? How about nutritional information and allergen disclosure? Are therapeutic health claims allowed? Is THC, CBD, and other cannabinoid content required to be stated on the label like alcohol content on a wine label? Are track-and-trace identification numbers shown on the label? Is there a Government Warning? What advertising is or should be allowed? Can cannabis pricing information be included in the ad? What about ads that target young persons? Can third-party marketers who hold no cannabis license publish cannabis ads?

We now turn to actual examples of state regulatory enactments for cannabis in select states that have authorized adult-use cannabis in the United States. The sections are written by two leading cannabis lawyers, Emily Gant and Jason Barker, who will offer their perspectives based on the cannabis laws of Washington, Oregon, California, and New York. These sections are not intended to be summaries of the cannabis laws of those states, because those laws may be outdated in short order. Instead, I have asked the authors to select one or two policies or laws that help us to understand whether cannabis has been and should be regulated like alcohol in their states.

It is important to note that the states under review are in varying stages of defining how their markets will be regulated and, in fact, are very different markets from the perspective of broader economic impact. We first turn to Washington and Oregon. These neighboring Pacific Northwest States were among the first adopters of adult-use cannabis: Washington in 2012 and Oregon in 2014. As discussed more fully below, the regulatory models implemented in these states are probably more aptly described as pragmatic rather than innovative; however, there are some important variations from the traditional alcoholic beverage regulatory model. And while regulators in Oregon and Washington did not have the luxury of regulating a market for cannabis products with any maturity at all, the states of California and New York, as later adopters of adult-use cannabis measures in 2016 and 2021, respectively, have at least been able to contemplate regulatory models with some marketplace innovation in mind.

For Oregon and Washington, the focus will be on the nuts and bolts of the cannabis laws in those jurisdictions with an analysis as to how they differ from the alcoholic beverage laws of those States. For California and New York, the focus will be less on the literal application of the evolving laws in those states and more on the theoretical considerations for the regulation of intoxicating products in those markets, with a nod towards the progression of social custom and consumerism.

WASHINGTON AND OREGON

Emily Gant

Should we regulate cannabis like alcohol? As early adopters in the adult-use cannabis space, voters in Washington and Oregon took divergent paths on this question.

Passed by Washington voters in November 2012, Initiative 502 ("I-502") explicitly utilized an alcoholic beverage model, calling for a "tightly regulated, state-licensed system similar to that for controlling hard alcohol."[5] While an exaggeration, one could argue that the drafters of I-502 took the Washington State alcoholic beverage statutes, stripped out every exception to the tied-house laws, swapped out the term "alcohol" for "marijuana," and dusted off their hands.

Washington State alcoholic beverage and adult-use cannabis licensees are governed by similar, if nearly identical, core tenets: (1) the Washington State Liquor and Cannabis Board ("WSLCB") has jurisdiction over both industries; (2) there is an extensive disclosure and vetting process; (3) the statutes call for a three-tier model; (4) there are tied-house restrictions limiting (or precluding) cross-tier ownership between the retail and non-retail tiers; (4) there are trade practice rules focused upon avoiding exclusion and undue influence; (5) purchase and consumption of the product are limited to those aged 21 and over; (6) the WSLCB notifies local jurisdictions before issuance of the relevant license and allows the

5. Initiative 502 (Washington State 2012), https://apps.leg.wa.gov/documents/billdocs/2011-12/Pdf/Initiatives/Initiatives/INITIATIVE%20502.pdf. I-502 utilized the term "marijuana." In 2022, the Washington Legislature replaced the term "marijuana" with "cannabis" throughout the statute, finding that "the use of the term 'marijuana' in the United States has discriminatory origins and should be replaced with the more scientifically accurate term 'cannabis.'" H.B. 1210, 2021 Sess. (Wash. 2022), https://app.leg.wa.gov/billsummary?year=2022&billnumber=1210&initiative=false.

municipality an opportunity to object; and (7) the State collects taxes from these operations.

Faced with the same question, Oregon voters went the other way. Passing with approximately 56 percent of the vote in 2014, Ballot Measure 91 expressly rejected a tied-house model.[6] Because there are "no 'tied house' prohibitions," Oregon cannabis licensees may vertically integrate. In the same vein, Oregon cannabis licensees may extend or buy cannabis on credit, and may, in some instances, engage in trade practice activities that would trip over alcohol's undue influence rules. That said, there are still some similarities in the regulation of alcohol and cannabis in the State: (1) both are governed by the Oregon Liquor and Cannabis Commission (the "OLCC"); (2) those with ownership, control or a financial interest undergo a disclosure and/or vetting process; (3) the OLCC seeks input from the local governing body before license issuance; (4) purchase and consumption of the product are limited to those aged 21 and over; and (5) taxes generated from the licensed operations benefit state and local governments.

One could write an entire book on Washington and Oregon cannabis laws, addressing the various nuances in each jurisdiction's rules. For purposes of this section, though, we focus on a comparison of the states' alcoholic beverage and cannabis laws. With that goal in mind, the following passages provide a deeper dive into marketplace organization and tied-house laws to demonstrate how Washington and Oregon treat cannabis similarly to, and differently from, alcoholic beverages.

A. WASHINGTON

With I-502, Washington leaned heavily on its alcohol roots, as seen by its use of the three-tier system.

Washington organizes its alcoholic beverage licensees into three tiers:

- **Suppliers**, which produce alcoholic beverages. Wineries, breweries, and distilleries fall into the supplier category.
- **The middle tier**, which buy alcoholic beverages from suppliers and other non-retail licensees and sell to retailers. Wholesalers and importers are both members of the middle tier.
- **Retailers**, which sell alcoholic beverages to consumers. There are *off-premises retailers*, like grocery and liquor stores. There are also *on-premises retailers*, like bars, restaurants, hotels, golf courses, bowling alleys, and other locations where a consumer drinks the alcoholic beverage at the licensed premises.

6. Ballot Measure 91 (Or. 2014), https://www.oregon.gov/olcc/marijuana/documents/measure91.pdf.

Unlike "quota" jurisdictions, Washington does not limit the number of liquor licenses a person or an entity may hold within a particular tier, or the number of liquor licenses within a set radius. So, Mendelson LLC could hold any number of Washington winery licenses in the state, and Barker Inc. and others could operate any number of restaurants within the same city.

Washington cannabis licensees also fall into three tiers:[7]

- **Producers**, which grow cannabis plants.
- **Processors**, which typically process cannabis flower and trim into other forms of cannabis products, like distillate, concentrates, wax, pre-rolls, and edibles.
- **Retailers**, which sell final cannabis products to consumers. All cannabis retailers are *off-premises retailers*, as Washington does not allow for consumption at a cannabis-licensed premise.[8]

As of August 2022, Washington cannabis licensees are limited to no more than three producer and/or processor licenses, or no more than five retail licenses.[9] This limitation applies both to the entity holding the license and to all persons with ownership of or control over the licensed entity. So, let's say that NewCo is owned by Richard Mendelson, Jason Barker, and Emily Gant. As an entity, NewCo can hold no more than three (3) producer and/or processor licenses, or no more than five (5) retail licenses. As owners of NewCo, Mendelson, Barker, and Gant are subject to the same limitations, even if different entities hold the other licenses.

For both industries, Washington groups licensees into "non-retail" and "retail" categories. "Non-retail" consists of the supplier and middle tiers for alcohol licensees, and of producers and processors for cannabis licensees. "Retailers" are those selling directly to consumers. While still utilizing a three-tier model, Washington allows cross-tier ownership between non-retail licensees for both industries, subject to certain restrictions. As an example, Jason Barker could hold interests in both a Washington winery license and a Washington wholesaler license, so long as he did so through different entities and met other requirements. Similarly, Mendelson LLC could hold a producer license, a processor license, or a producer/processor license at one or more Washington locations.

Turning to notable differences between Washington's regulation of alcoholic beverage and cannabis, Washington permits certain cross-tier ownership between retail and non-retail liquor licensees. Like many states, Washington disallowed cross-tier ownership between retail and non-retail liquor licensees for years, citing

7. There are other types of Washington cannabis licensees, like laboratories and transportation licensees. This chapter focuses on the most common license types, namely, producers, processors, and retailers.

8. Although many liquor-licensed entities are eager to promote "weed tourism," a Washington liquor licensee cannot allow for cannabis consumption at the liquor-licensed premises.

9. Wash. Admin. Code §314-55-075 (2022) (producer licenses); Wash. Admin. Code §314-55-077 (2022) (processor licenses); Wash. Admin. Code §314-55-079 (2022) (retailer licenses). There are also restrictions on the number of retail licenses issued, per municipality.

tied-house considerations. Per local lore, many years ago, an owner of a Walla Walla winery became engaged to an owner of a Walla Walla restaurant. Before their marriage, they needed to determine who would divest of their ownership, making for some sticky engagement conversations. Since that time, Washington changed its strict prohibition on cross-tier ownership for alcoholic beverage licensees.[10] Under current Washington law, a person or entity with an ownership in a certain supplier or middle-tier alcohol license types can have a direct or indirect financial interest in certain retail licenses via different entities, unless the interest results or is more likely than not to result in undue influence over the retailer, or has resulted or is more likely than not to result in an adverse impact on public health and safety. The same is not true for Washington cannabis licensees, as the rigorous cross-tier ownership provisions remain firmly in place.

As another distinction, Washington requires all persons or entities with ownership in or control over a cannabis licensee to meet residency restrictions.[11] All applicants must have resided in Washington for at least six (6) months prior to applying for the license. This requirement applies to all persons and all entities found in an entity's organizational chart, even if multi-tiered. This includes owners, directors, officers, and managers of manager-managed limited liability companies. In contrast, there are no residency requirements for Washington liquor licensees. As an example, a French citizen could apply for a Washington winery license, even though she resides in Bordeaux and not Washington State. The residency requirements can present challenges for those in the Washington cannabis industry, inhibiting their ability to procure new investors or to sell the entity or its assets.

B. OREGON

Like Washington, Oregon utilizes a three-tier licensing model for both alcoholic beverage and cannabis licensees. On the alcohol side, the OLCC issues supplier (winery, brewery, distillery, etc.) licenses, middle-tier (wholesaler and importer) licenses, and retailer (on- and off-premises) licenses. Similarly, it issues producer, processor, and retailer cannabis licenses.[12]

As discussed above, Oregon applies a tied-house model to alcoholic beverages, but not cannabis. So, Gant LLC could not, say, produce and distribute Gant Wine, own the Gant Hotel, and exclusively sell Gant Wine at the Gant Hotel in Oregon. This would violate Oregon's tied-house laws on cross-tier ownership, undue influence, and exclusionary practices. Conversely, Barker Inc. could vertically integrate its Oregon cannabis operations. Holding producer, processor, and retail licenses, Barker Inc. could grow and process cannabis under the Barker brand, own

10. Wash. Rev. Code §66.28.290 (2022).

11. Wash. Admin. Code §314-55-020 (2022).

12. Oregon has other available license types, including wholesaler, laboratory, and researcher licenses. Again, this chapter focuses on producer, processor, and retailer licenses.

the Barker Retail Shop, and exclusively sell the Barker brand at the Barker Retail Shop. Due to the express disavowal of tied-house restrictions, this vertical integration and exclusion is permissible under Oregon laws.

Oregon does not limit the number of licenses held by any given person or entity, whether for alcoholic beverages or cannabis. During the infancy of the legal Oregon cannabis market, production substantially outpaced demand. This dramatically lowered the price and arguably increased the temptation for diversion into the illicit market. Since that time, the OLCC has periodically closed (and reopened) the window for new cannabis applications to address these issues.

While an Oregon cannabis licensee may hold any number of licenses, Oregon limits the number of producers per tax parcel. There cannot be two (2) or more producers with common ownership on the same tax parcel. This is an apparent effort to avoid "mega" cannabis farms held by "big agriculture" or comparable businesses. There are no comparable "tax parcel" rules applying to Oregon alcoholic beverage licensees, however.

Finally, Oregon does not have residency restrictions for either alcoholic beverages or cannabis. For many, this makes the Oregon cannabis market more attractive than that of its neighbor to the north, as there is a bigger pool of qualifying investors and buyers.

C. SO, WHICH MODEL IS BEST?

Many early adopters, like Washington and Oregon, were arguably "going rogue." These states legalized adult-use cannabis in the face of federal illegality, little state-level precedent, and significant other unknowns.

At the outset, states like Washington did not know whether the federal government would seize adult-use cannabis and its proceeds, arrest licensees, initiate forfeiture proceedings, or take other adverse enforcement action.[13] After issuance of the Cole Memo, however, many states took comfort that the federal government was unlikely to knock down the doors of its state cannabis licensees (or, for that matter, those of state cannabis regulators for aiding and abetting liability), so long as they had a solid, robustly enforced regulatory scheme. The Cole Memo reads, in part:

> The Department's guidance in this memorandum rests on its expectation that states and local governments that have enacted law authorizing marijuana-related conduct will implement strong and effective regulatory and enforcement systems that will address the threat those state laws could pose to public safety, public health, and other law enforcement interests. A system adequate to that task must not only contain robust controls and procedures on paper; it must also be effective in practice. Jurisdictions that have implemented systems that provide for regulation of marijuana activity must provide the necessary resources and

---

13. Granted, certain states had legalized medical marijuana long before, without significant federal enforcement action.

> demonstrate the willingness to enforce their laws and regulations in a manner that ensures they do not undermine federal enforcement priorities. [14]

In the alcoholic beverage regulations, these states already had "strong and effective regulatory and enforcement systems" that addressed threats to "public safety, public health, and other law enforcement interests." It appears that these states did not want to push the envelope too far by both legalizing adult-use cannabis and creating a regulatory model out of whole cloth. So, they mirrored the alcoholic beverage rules, which were a known quantity.

Respectfully, however, those drafting I-502 (and to some extent Ballot Measure 91) missed a golden opportunity to evolve. This was a chance to build upon best practices (and jettison outdated laws) from the alcoholic beverage world, and not merely cut-and-paste from its rules.

There are aspects of the alcoholic beverage rules that can, and arguably should, apply in the cannabis context. As examples, no one wants drug cartels or other illicit elements in the legal cannabis industry, such that there is value in a disclosure and vetting process comparable to that for alcoholic beverages. Just like a Certificate of Label Approval ("COLA") tells a consumer about the alcohol content of his chosen bourbon, that same consumer should be able to review the label for a cannabis edible to evaluate potency and other product safety information. From a public safety perspective, it is important to keep adult-use cannabis out of the hands of minors and to curtail drugged driving.

And, despite the comments above, there are benefits of standing on the shoulders of those coming before you. Even if they experienced a learning curve on the mechanics of cannabis cultivation, processing, and sale, regulators had a framework upon which to build in the form of the alcoholic beverage regulations. Further, there are significant cross-market opportunities between these two industries. Many alcoholic beverage companies are eager to join the U.S. cannabis industry, and have the knowledge, equipment, and infrastructure to seamlessly enter this market. Assuming that federal legalization will, at some point, occur, alcoholic beverage companies are uniquely situated to capitalize upon the similarities in the production, wholesale, storage, and retail sale of these two products.

That said, this is a rare time in history, akin to the early post-Prohibition era. States have an opportunity to evaluate which aspects of the alcoholic beverage rules are worth continuing into the cannabis space and which are ready for retirement. As more states look to legalize adult-use cannabis, here are some questions for consideration:

- Should the state allow vertical integration, extensions of credit, exclusive outlets and comparable trade practices, or are such restrictions necessary to avoid marketplace domination and other "evils" of the tied house?

---

14. Guidance Regarding Marijuana Enforcement, *supra* note 3.

- Does the state want to encourage the "craft" equivalent in the cannabis industry? If so, what is the best means to accomplish this goal? Reduced licensing fees? Different privileges?
- Given that persons of color experienced disparate enforcement of cannabis-related crimes, should the state have a social equity component to its licensing regulations?
- Which state agency is best suited to regulate cannabis? Should jurisdiction lay with the state's alcoholic beverage agency, thus increasingly the likelihood that the state will borrow some (or most) elements from the alcoholic beverage regulations? A state Department of Health, suggesting a focus on the prescriber and qualifying patent? A state Department of Agriculture, like those regulating hemp? A new agency altogether? If state law borrows from alcoholic beverage concepts, but grants cannabis-related jurisdiction to someone other than the state's liquor agency, does the state run the risk of inconsistent interpretation and implementation of similar laws?
- Assuming that federal legalization occurs, is TTB the appropriate federal agency to govern the industry? As cannabis companies look to interstate commerce, many want to utilize the same or a markedly similar label throughout the country to sell their product. Should there be a COLA- or formula-equivalent for cannabis products?
- How do states ensure that products are safe for human consumption, and that consumers understand the potency and substance of what they are ingesting?
- With so many alcoholic beverage companies eager to expand into the cannabis industry, how should the state and the federal government address the intersection of alcohol and cannabis? Upon (presumed) federal legalization, can an alcoholic beverage licensee hold a cannabis license at the same premises? Will regulators allow alternating proprietorships between alcohol and cannabis licensees? Can, say, a distiller share equipment with a cannabis processor making distillate? May an on-premises retailer allow for consumption of both alcohol and cannabis? If so, how can the licensee best train its staff to assess for over-consumption, if a customer has consumed both products?

With approximately a decade of adult-use cannabis under our belts, we are seeing states use models nearly identical to alcohol; models with the reverse of alcohol; and models somewhere in between. As a practitioner regularly advising those in both industries, I believe that a model that learns from, but does not directly mirror, the alcoholic beverage regulatory scheme is most likely to find long-term success.

California and New York

Jason Barker

Cannabis and wine are each agricultural commodities with distinctive terroir and distinguished genetics, but do the historical policy considerations for the regulation of wine merit similar regulatory treatment of cannabis in California and New York? In this section, I explore the regulatory enactments of California and New York where, remarkably, adult-use cannabis is now legal and consumable for nearly one-fifth of the U.S. population.[15]

Perhaps one of the most intriguing facets of alcoholic beverage regulation is the nearly uniform acceptance of "tied house" laws across the U.S.—a market organization structure that is unique to, if not somewhat a hallmark of, traditional alcoholic beverage regulation. We understand that the policy rationale for preventing tied houses in California once centered on temperance, with the underlying notion that vertical ownership structures enabled aggressive sales practices and, consequently, overconsumption at the point of sale. However, the Ninth Circuit's 2017 *Retail Digital Network* decision concluded, under First Amendment commercial speech scrutiny, that a temperance rationale could no longer justify California's tied-house rules for alcoholic beverages and instead reasoned that such restrictions upon inter-tier relationships could only be justified as a means to limit or prohibit marketplace dominance.[16]

Now that temperance is dead and—perhaps even more pertinent—the majority of retail cannabis dispensaries do not offer on-premises consumption, what policies should dictate behavior at the point of sale for consumers or suppliers promoting their brands? In California, now the largest adult-use cannabis jurisdiction in the country, the proliferation of on-site consumption locations has been minimal, and the vast majority of retail sales outlets are for off-sale only.

As a burgeoning local cannabis market with an eye towards more expansive cannabis use, the City of West Hollywood, California, allows for on-site consumption areas pursuant to a licensing plan which must include, among other requirements, detailed descriptions of how the visibility of consumption will be

---

15. 2020 Census Results, U.S. Census Bureau, https://www.census.gov/programs-surveys/decennial-census/decade/2020/2020-census-results.html (last visited Aug. 28, 2022).

16. *Retail Digital Network v. Prieto*, 861 F.3d 839, 851 (9th Cir. 2017) (en banc). *Retail Digital Network* involved a challenge by the purveyor of liquid crystal advertising displays for use within liquor stores against the operation of a California tied-house law designed to prohibit concealed advertising payments to retailers through cooperative advertising arrangements with alcoholic beverage suppliers. The advertiser argued that the law impermissibly burdened commercial speech under the First Amendment. After rejecting temperance as compelling rationale in support of the law in question, the Ninth Circuit ultimately upheld that law by concluding that "it directly and materially advances the State's interest in maintaining a triple-tiered market system, and because there is a sufficient fit between that interest and the legislative scheme." Interestingly and in perhaps a signal of even more cynical views regarding the constitutionality of tied-house laws to come, the Eighth Circuit rejected similar advancement and tailoring arguments in broadly invalidating Missouri's tied-house scheme under the First Amendment. *Missouri Broadcasters Ass'n v. Schmitt*, 946 F. 3d 453, 462 (8th Cir. 2020).

limited from any public place and how access will be limited to persons 21 years of age or older.[17] At first blush, these types of requirements are more akin to an adult bookstore than a saloon. There appears to be a tension for cannabis that does not exist with alcoholic beverages regarding the broader marketplace acceptance of cannabis as a legitimate public commodity. What is society saying about the merits of cannabis consumption if a sports bar on the corner has large glass windows with LCD screens glowing between giant alcoholic beverage brand signs while the cannabis shop next door has opaque windows and security cameras? One of the offshoots of the cannabis prohibition and the attendant transition to a legal market is an overall lack of widely accepted social traditions with respect to the public consumption of cannabis. Putting aside secondhand smoking concerns, can a cannabis café eventually replace or coexist with a coffee shop or the local watering hole?

New York's marketplace, with final regulations still pending, is very much in formation; however, there is a provision in the authorizing statute for on-premises consumption licenses.[18] This will be a very interesting license to observe in operation, especially when you consider the prevalence of urbanization in certain parts of New York.

What do the states say with respect to marketplace ideology and tied house? Neither California nor New York's statutory enactments include any explicit reference to management of commerce, marketplace dominance, or temperance.[19] California and New York have taken very different approaches. Other than a testing laboratory license, which must be completely independent and unaffiliated with other licenses,[20] California does not restrict a singular owner or its affiliates from simultaneously owning licenses in multiple tiers of the cannabis distribution chain.

In contrast, New York has very specific tied-house requirements, although in certain circumstances vertical integration is permitted. New York includes *classic* tied-house language prohibiting those in the supplier tier (*i.e.*, those authorized to cultivate, process, or distribute cannabis) from being interested, directly or

---

17. *West Hollywood Municipal Code, §5.70.20(13)*. California's cannabis law defers to local governments to determine whether on-site consumption is permissible. Cal. Bus. & Prof. §26200(g) (2021).

18. N.Y. Cannabis Law §77 (2022).

19. New York's cannabis law reads in salient part: "The intent of this act is to regulate, control, and tax marihuana, heretofore known as cannabis, generate significant new revenue, make substantial investments in communities and people most impacted by cannabis criminalization to address the collateral consequences of such criminalization, prevent access to cannabis by those under the age of twenty-one years, reduce the illegal drug market and reduce violent crime, reduce participation of otherwise law-abiding citizens in the illicit market, end the racially disparate impact of existing cannabis laws, create new industries, protect the environment, improve the state's resiliency to climate change, protect the public health, safety and welfare of the people of the state, increase employment and strengthen New York's agriculture sector." N.Y. Cannabis Law §2 (2022). As of August 2022, New York has yet to publish permanent regulations with respect to various substantive matters, including for tied-house and trade practices.

20. Cal. Bus. & Prof. §26053(b) (2022).

indirectly, in any premises where any cannabis product is sold at retail.[21] The supplier tier is also prohibited from making gifts to or entering into any exclusive dealing arrangements with any retailers.[22] There is a notable exception, however, for the holder of the so-called registered organization adult-use cultivator processor retail dispensary license (an "RO License") in New York. An RO License allows the holder to own and operate a vertically integrated cannabis business and to exercise privileges in the supplier and retailer tier. In taking a page out of federal tied-house law for alcoholic beverages, New York's law concludes that a vertically integrated operator cannot improperly influence itself as a retailer, and accordingly the holder of an RO License is excluded from the tied-house prohibitions for its own simultaneous operations in the supplier and retailer tiers.[23]

It is interesting to note that the now revoked 2013 Cole Memorandum (the "Cole Memo"), which is the closest thing we have to federal regulatory policy for adult-use cannabis (and serves as the policy pillar for state tracking requirements),[24] makes no mention of point of sale or marketplace organization as core enforcement concerns of the U.S. Department of Justice.[25] So, unlike state tracing and tracking of plant material and cannabis products where substantial uniformity exists across the adult-use states as a result of the Cole Memo, other policies such as market organization and potency are likely to vary significantly.

Given the patchwork legality of cannabis, should multi-state market dominance be a concern or even an objective? The Pacific Ocean states of California, Oregon, and Washington have been on the front foot of progressive legislation since the 1970s. Interestingly, these locavore states led the national charge on medical marijuana, craft beer (via vertically integrated brew pubs), and now adult-use cannabis. But, in the absence of federal legislation regarding market organization and commerce, could the legislative enactments within this region forever alter the landscape of legal adult-use cannabis in the U.S.? Or could they be essential for the survival of legal adult-use cannabis within these states? As has been widely documented, various market inefficiencies have plagued the adult-use market on the West Coast, including excise tax rates, product contamination, and illegal market infiltration.

In an ironic parallel to other governmental policy issues of today (such as inflation, for example), it is not entirely clear what is more threatening to the success of a legal adult-use cannabis market, the federal government's decision to

---

21. *Supra* note 18 at §80(1)(a).

22. *Supra* note 18 at §80(1)(c), (d).

23. *Supra* note 18 at §80(2). *See also* 27 C.F.R. 6.33(a) (2021) ("Outright ownership of a retail business by any industry member is not an interest that may result in a violation of" the federal tied-house ownership restriction).

24. Each of California and New York impose plant and cannabis product tracking requirements throughout the distribution chain. Cal. Bus. & Prof. Code §26067(a) (2021); N.Y. Cannabis Law §78(1) (2022).

25. Guidance Regarding Marijuana Enforcement, *supra* note 3.

act or to do nothing at all.[26] While the popular drumbeat of cannabis advocates tends to favor federal legalization of cannabis—that is, the affirmative enactment of federal law that authorizes the commercialization of cannabis via a taxing and licensing scheme similar to beverage alcohol—it seems as though some other form of federal deregulation of cannabis is a distinct possibility.[27] In this latter scenario, certain states would presumably attempt to operate within trading zones involving other adult-use states in support of alleviating oversupply and to engender further commodification of cannabis through an interstate platform principled by relative state law uniformity.

In perhaps a nod to these possibilities, Senate Bill 1326 was introduced in the California Legislature ("SB-1326") in February 2022. SB-1326 authorizes interstate agreements between California and other states with legal cannabis markets to enable interstate commerce between California and such other states. To participate in an interstate agreement with California, the contracting state must have substantive legal requirements with respect to tracking and tracing, testing standards, packaging and labeling, advertising, and quality assurances that meet or exceed California's requirements.[28] Even more remarkably, an agreement pursuant to this enactment shall require the contracting state to affirmatively impose restrictions upon advertising, marketing, labeling, or sale that meet or exceed those restrictions imposed by California. SB-1326 does not become effective in the absence of certain federal deregulation or legalization events.[29]

On its face, this enactment—or a similar law—would appear to provide various lanes for future state uniformity in various substantive areas with respect to the regulation of cannabis, especially given California's overall stature in the cannabis marketplace. However, the First Circuit's August 2022 decision in *NE Patients Group, et. al. v. United Cannabis Patients and Caregivers for Maine*[30] casts doubt about whether such an interstate model could survive under the Dormant Commerce Clause even if cannabis remains illegal under the laws of

---

26. Currently, the commercialization of adult-use cannabis is prohibited by federal law. Under the Controlled Substances Act, cannabis and related compounds are included in Schedule I, making them illegal under federal law. *See* 21 U.S.C. §812(c) Schedule I (c) (2021).

27. Arguably, federal deregulation has already occurred for state-level medical marijuana programs. Beginning with fiscal year 2015 and the so-called Rohrabacher-Farr amendment, Congress has continually included a mandate in its annual appropriations bill that none of the funds allocated to the Department of Justice be used to prevent the states from implementing their own laws with respect to medical marijuana. *NE Patients Group, et. al.* v. *United Cannabis Patients and Caregivers for Maine*, 2022 WL 3442203 *4 (1st Cir. 2022). Another possibility for deregulation in lieu of full-blown federal legalization could involve "descheduling" of cannabis under the Controlled Substances Act. Descheduling of cannabis would effectively remove state-level commercialization of cannabis from the operation of the Controlled Substances Act.

28. Cannabis: interstate agreements, S.B. 1326, Cal. Leg. (2022), as amended through Aug. 18, 2022.

29. Effectiveness of SB-1326 can occur in scenarios other than federal legalization of cannabis. SB-1326 will also become effective if Congress "defunds" Department of Justice interference with the implementation of adult-use state cannabis laws or if the Department of Justice or the Attorney General issues an opinion or memorandum authorizing interstate transfer of cannabis or indicating that such practices will be tolerated under the Controlled Substances Act. *Supra* note 28 at §26308.

30. *NE Patients Group*, WL 3442203 (1st Cir. 2022).

certain states or federal law. In concluding that Maine's residency requirements for officers and directors of medical marijuana licensees violated the Dormant Commerce Clause, the First Circuit rejected the commonly held belief that the Dormant Commerce Clause was inapplicable to commodities made illegal under federal law.[31]

While SB-1326's imposition of California law requirements with respect to the laws of other states may have been dubious from the get-go in the case of federal legalization,[32] does the First Circuit's view of the Dormant Commerce Clause and cannabis, should it become the majority view, foreclose the possibility that one state can impose affirmative legal requirements on another state in the case of multi-state agreements? Put differently, if an adult-use state is unwilling to agree to California's heightened standards, could it allege that such a requirement violates the Dormant Commerce Clause under the logic of *NE Patients Group*?[33]

Beyond market organization, brand development and consumer use experiences will undoubtedly shape the long-term success of adult-use cannabis. Similar to alcoholic beverage products, cannabis products exist along a spectrum of choices and intoxicating effect. Will cannabis eventually be regulated according to product potency or perceived intoxicating effect? Generally speaking, under the federal-state regime for alcoholic beverages, the excise tax operates progressively by product category in accordance with the relative alcoholic content as a percentage of volume or weight for such product category. With this in mind, it is not hard to imagine a scenario whereby cannabis is taxed progressively based upon the amount of THC.[34] New York has adopted this approach.

New York's adult-use cannabis tax is complex and is imposed at two stages of the distribution process: first, at the time of sale from distributor to retailer; and, second, at the time of sale from retailer to consumer.[35] The former tax is dynamic and based upon the amount of THC in the product and is further variable depending

31. *Supra* note 30 at *8-9. In rejecting this argument, the First Circuit stated: "We are thus reluctant, given such Founding-era worries, to construe the negative aspect of the dormant Commerce Clause in a way that would essentially require us to ignore the potential for a trade war to be destructive whenever its genesis could be traced to a single state's effort to attain predominance in a market that federal law deems unlawful."

32. "California Might Legalize Interstate Cannabis Sales" *Canna Law Blog*, https://harrisbricken.com/cannalawblog/california-might-legalize-interstate-cannabis-sales (last visited Mar 17, 2022).

33. Notably, the First Circuit reasoned: "[T]he negative implication of the commerce power may pose an independent bar to a state regulation of an interstate commercial market even when Congress chooses to exercise its affirmative commerce power with respect to that same market without also preempting that state regulation." *Supra* note 30 at *5. From this premise it seems to follow that if Congress acts affirmatively to defund enforcement of cannabis violations under federal law and does not preempt state law, the Dormant Commerce Clause will continue to invalidate any state law that burdens any other state law with respect to the sale of cannabis in interstate commerce and regardless of whether cannabis remains illegal under state or federal law.

34. THC or tetrahydrocannabinol "most often refers to delta-9 THC, a specific type of THC that is the main psychoactive component of the Cannabis Sativa L. plant." *THC, Practical Law Glossary Item w-021-7925* (last visited Aug. 29, 2022).

35. N.Y. Tax Law §493 (2022).

upon the product type.[36] The retail-level tax is equal to 13 percent of the total amount charged to the consumer.[37]

In contrast to New York, California's 15 percent cannabis excise tax, initially collected by distributors from retailers, is based upon the average market price of products to be sold at retail without variability based upon the potency of the products sold.[38]

The imposition of excise tax as a possible pricing deterrent begs the age-old question for "vice taxes" on intoxicating products generally. Does the overall price of an intoxicating product, like wine, materially impact a consumer's product preference or the consumer's decision to make a purchase at all? In the earliest stages of the adult-use markets in the U.S., one could credibly argue that the cannabis industry did itself few favors in terms of affirmative promotion of consumer understanding with respect to product dosing or advisable consumption practices.[39] And, while packaging and labeling may require listing of total amounts of THC per package, does this really mean anything to new consumers in a novel market?[40] Unlike the rich tradition in alcoholic beverages in the U.S. that existed both before and after Prohibition, cannabis lacks the meaningful social traditions and experience of its intoxicating bedfellows. This lack of product consumption experience results in a regulatory crossroads of sorts. How do we regulate a potentially dangerous intoxicating commodity while also trying to promote a nascent marketplace for a product that may lack social acceptance?

Cleverly, California has introduced appellations of origin for cannabis as a possible bridge towards the expansive popularity of wine in that State.[41] Similar to American Viticultural Areas ("AVAs") for wine, California's cannabis law now allows for a group of licensed cultivators within certain geographical areas to petition the California Department of Food and Agriculture for recognition as a distinctive region for cannabis cultivation based upon documented standards, practices, and cultivation requirements unique to such region.[42] Arguably, it is this type of fusion between brand awareness and product standardization that is needed

---

36. The different products are taxed as follows: Cannabis flower is taxed at a rate of five-tenths of one cent per milligram of the total THC; concentrated cannabis is taxed at the rate of eight-tenths of one cent per milligram of the total THC; and cannabis edible products are taxed at the rate of three cents per milligram of the total THC. *Supra* note 35 at §493(a).

37. *Supra* note 35 at §493(b), (c).

38. Cal. Rev. & Tax §3401(a)(1) (2022).

39. In regard to possible effects or characteristics of a product, California law provides that a cannabis good *may*, but it is not required to include information regarding "characteristic anticipated effects" if such information can be substantiated as truthful and not misleading. Cal. Code Regs. tit. 4, §17409(a) (2021). The term "characteristic anticipated effects" is defined to include "any physiological effect (a temporary effect on the body related to the consumption of cannabis goods) that is common to or expected from the particular cannabis strain, but excludes any claim of health benefits (i.e., claims of therapeutic action as a result of the consumption of cannabis goods)." *Id.*

40. Cal. Code Regs. tit. 4, §17409(b) (2022) (requiring total THC label disclosures for various cannabis product types); N.Y. Cannabis Law §81 (2022) (mandating that New York's cannabis regulations require disclosure of total THC for each product).

41. *See generally* Cal. Code Regs. tit. 3, §§9000 et. seq.

42. *Supra* note 41.

to lead cannabis out of the doldrums of patchwork regulation and lack of product uniformity towards the brighter future enjoyed by the various product categories of alcoholic beverages. The creation of a meaningful brand hierarchy for cannabis will further serve to break through public reservations of cannabis as a legitimate commodity. Only time and thoughtful legislation and industry involvement will show us whether the future will bring a robust cannabis marketplace where a pre-roll is enjoyed with friends in place of, or as a compliment to, a glass of wine.

* * *

In conclusion, the question of whether cannabis will be regulated like alcohol largely remains an open one. Thus far, beyond licensing, product tracking, taxation, and threshold pedigree determinations, there is no clear consensus across the adult-use states for the regulation of cannabis, especially in terms of market organization and tied house. In Washington and New York, concepts of tied house have been incorporated, while in California and Oregon a strict separation of tiers has been avoided. As the ambitions of economic growth and general marketplace acceptance continue to spur regulatory policy for a new commodity, the debate continues as to whether it makes sense to legislate against marketplace dominance or even temperance as a threshold matter for an intoxicating product. At this point in the regulatory history of alcoholic beverages, compelling arguments can be made against the traditional "tied house" model as a desirable regime. What if, for example, other federal circuits further determine that intrastate "tied house" policies are incompatible with federal law? Certainly, at that point, it will be short on charm as a regulatory underpinning for cannabis.

Only time and continued marketplace acceptance of cannabis will tell us if adult-use cannabis can survive and even thrive in spite of a patchwork of regulatory models both borrowing and departing from the traditional regulatory model for alcoholic beverages. As the federal prohibition of cannabis continues, perhaps it is worth remembering a lesson from the days of Prohibition: It is not those who are well regulated that pose the greatest risk to a lawful marketplace for an intoxicating product; it is those who are not regulated at all.

FOR FURTHER EXPLORATION

Richard Mendelson

Because wine law covers so many fields of law, it is impossible to provide a comprehensive list of books for the wine lawyer's library. In fact, many wine lawyers may never be involved in a case involving land use, intellectual property, or international trade. Some may be litigators and others transactional lawyers. Some may devote their entire careers to federal practice involving TTB, FDA, and the FTC, while others may handle only local or state alcoholic beverage licensing and compliance matters. The nature of a wine lawyer's practice will depend on his or her clients (wineries, wholesalers, retailers, marketing companies, glass manufacturers, barrel makers, etc.), the clients' activities (wine production, wine distribution, wine marketing, direct shipping, auctioneering, import/export), geographic location (urban versus rural and, of course, the particular state in which the lawyer practices), and the lawyer's specific interests and experience.

Notwithstanding the diversity of the field, there are several essentials for any wine lawyer's library. First and foremost, a winery lawyer must keep close at hand copies of the U.S. Constitution, the Federal Alcohol Administration Act (U.S. Code, Title 27), the Internal Revenue Code (U.S. Code, Title 26), and the various regulations, rulings, procedures, industry circulars, and rulemaking activities of the Treasury Department's Alcohol and Tobacco Tax and Trade Bureau (TTB), along with a bookmark to the TTB's excellent website, www.ttb.gov. Each state has its own alcoholic beverage regulatory authority, laws, regulations, policies, and procedures, and these also should be part of the wine lawyer's library, along with any related health and safety, revenue, or penal provisions concerning alcoholic beverages. Commerce Clearing House publishes a worthwhile compendium of state and federal alcoholic beverage laws known as the *CCH Liquor Control Law Reporter*, available on a subscription basis, which includes regular updates. A similar resource is *The Digest of Wine and Spirits Law*, which is also subscription based. While these two resources are excellent, nothing substitutes for personal contacts with the regulators. Knowledge of the organization and the personnel of each of the various alcoholic beverage regulatory authorities is essential.

A wine lawyer's library should include texts on wine law history generally and Prohibition specifically. There are many excellent books on these subjects by competent academicians, sociologists, historians, economists, and lawyers. I recommend the following: a copy of the National Prohibition Act, known as the Volstead Act (1919); *Report on the Enforcement of the Prohibition Laws of the United States* (1931), by the National Commission on Law Observance and Enforcement; *Legislative History of the FAA Act*, published by the Federal Alcohol Control Administration's Office of General Counsel (September 15, 1935); Raymond Fosdick and Albert Scott's *Toward Liquor Control* (1933); Randolph Childs's *Making Repeal Work* (1947); Thomas Pinney's two-volume set, *A History of Wine in America* (1989 and 2005); my own *From Demon to Darling: A Legal History of Wine in America* (2009); W.J. Rorabaugh's *The Alcohol Republic* (1979); Jack Blocker's *American Temperance Movements: Cycles of Reform* (1989); Richard Hamm's *Shaping the Eighteenth Amendment: Temperance Reform, Legal Culture, and the Polity, 1880-1920* (1995); Norman Clark's *Deliver Us from Evil: An Interpretation of American Prohibition* (1976); and Anne-Marie Szymanski's *Pathways to Prohibition: Radicals, Moderates, and Social Movement Outcomes* (2003).

There are several invaluable websites in addition to that of the TTB. On the domestic front, the National Institute on Alcohol Abuse and Alcoholism (NIAAA) maintains the Alcohol Policy Information System (APIS) at http://alcoholpolicy.niaaa.nih.gov. APIS addresses a variety of alcohol policy issues, including underage drinking, drinking and driving, drinking and pregnancy, alcohol taxation, and retail sales laws. I also recommend the websites maintained by the following associations: Wine Institute, the trade association of California wineries, at www.wineinstitute.org; Wine and Spirits Wholesalers of America (WSWA), the national trade organization representing the wholesale tier of the wine and spirits industry, at www.wswa.org; the National Conference of State Liquor Administrators, at www.ncsla.org; and the National Alcohol Beverage Control Association, representing the control states, at www.nabca.org. These organizations publish useful statistics and also track wine law topics of current interest.

In the area of public health, the current edition of the *Dietary Guidelines for Americans* published by the U.S. Department of Agriculture and the U.S. Department of Health and Human Services, particularly the section on Alcoholic Beverages, is a must read. So is *Alcohol: No Ordinary Commodity*, by Thomas Babor et al. (2d ed. 2010). I also recommend *Alcohol and Public Policy: Beyond the Shadow of Prohibition*, edited by Marc Moore and Dean Gerstein (1981), and Philip Cook's *Paying the Tab: The Costs and Benefits of Alcohol Control* (2007). For the perspective of two health prevention advocacy groups, visit the website of the self-styled alcohol industry watchdog Alcohol Justice, at www.alcoholjustice.org, and read *The Booze Merchants: The Inebriating of America*, by the Center for Science in the Public Interest (1983).

In the area of marketing, I recommend *Wine Marketing and Sales: Success Strategies for a Concentrated Market* (2019) by Janeen Olson, Liz Thach, and Paul Wagner.

On international wine law topics, there are two excellent websites in English. The first is a public site maintained by the Organisation Internationale de la Vigne et du Vin (International Organization of Vine and Wine, or OIV), an intergovernmental body headquartered in France, at www.oiv.int. The *Bulletin de l'OIV*, its quarterly journal, is available online and includes English translations. OIV also publishes many texts on a wide range of topics involving wine law, history, economics, viticulture, enology, and public health. Second, the Fédération Internationale des Vins and Spiritueux (International Federation of Wines and Spirits, or FIVS), a worldwide organization open to all sectors of the alcoholic beverage industry, maintains an international regulatory database known as FIVS-Abridge that is available on a subscription basis.

I highly recommend the conferences hosted each year by the CLE (Continuing Legal Education) on Wine, Beer and Spirits Law and by the International Wine Law Association (known by the abbreviation of its French title, AIDV, for Association Internationale des Juristes du Droit de la Vigne et du Vin, www.aidv.org). The papers presented at these conferences are generally excellent, and the conferences provide a wonderful opportunity to meet other wine law professionals from private law practice, the government, and academia. The American Bar Association also has a Beverage Alcohol Practice Committee within its Section on Administrative Law and Regulatory Practice.

There are several excellent educational programs that include a wine law component. The program that I direct on Wine Law and Policy at the University of California, Berkeley Law, was the first of its kind in the United States, but since its inception in 2007, wine law has been taught at many other law schools and is often included as a topic in wine business courses taught at universities offering a Master of Business Administration (MBA) degree. The University of California at Davis (UC Davis) hosts two annual programs that cursorily address wine law topics: the Wine Marketing Program, jointly sponsored by OIV, UC Davis Extension, and the UC Davis Department of Viticulture and Enology; and the UC Davis Wine Executive Program, sponsored by the Graduate School of Management and the Department of Viticulture and Enology.

Abroad, the University of Montesquieu–Bordeaux IV and the University Paul Cézanne (Aix-Marseille) each offer a master's degree in Vineyard and Wine Law, and the University of Reims Law School has a Wine and Law program that offers a master's degree in Wine and Spirits Law and a summer program in English on Wine Law. OIV also offers a 16-month post-graduate degree through the University of Paris West in Management of the Wine and Vine Sector, portions of which are taught in various countries.

Of course, knowledge about wine itself, separate and apart from the law, is invaluable. If you cannot work in the industry or make your own wines, I recommend that you keep Jancis Robinson's *The Oxford Companion to Wine* (fourth edition, 2015, with a fifth edition in process) close at hand and that you get to know the product and the wine market by becoming an avid wine consumer and a serious wine taster.

INDEX

Figures, notes, and tables are indicated by f, n, and t following the page numbers.

C

G